ANDREAS VESALIUS OF BRUSSELS
1514–1564

Andreas Vesalius at the age of twenty-eight. The only known authentic portrait, from the *Fabrica*.

ANDREAS
VESALIUS
OF
BRUSSELS
1514-1564

C. D. O'MALLEY, *Charles Donald*

UNIVERSITY OF CALIFORNIA PRESS
Berkeley and Los Angeles
1965

UNIVERSITY OF CALIFORNIA PRESS
BERKELEY AND LOS ANGELES, CALIFORNIA
CAMBRIDGE UNIVERSITY PRESS
LONDON, ENGLAND
© 1964 BY THE REGENTS OF THE UNIVERSITY OF CALIFORNIA
SECOND PRINTING, 1965
LIBRARY OF CONGRESS CATALOG CARD NUMBER: 64-15917
DESIGNED BY WARD RITCHIE
PRINTED IN THE UNITED STATES OF AMERICA

FOR

F. K. O'M.

22258

*Until now there has been only one full-scale biography of Vesalius—
that of Moritz Roth, published just over seventy years ago. For a long
time there was no need for further extensive consideration of Vesalius's
life since Roth's biography could claim the distinction of being definitive.
In recent times, however, and with no little debt to Harvey Cushing,
Charles Singer, and the anniversary year of 1943, there has been a considerable increase in the Vesalian literature. Such studies, together with
newly discovered documents, have finally assumed sufficient importance
to warrant a second biography to supplement that of Roth. Even so, there
remain extensive periods in Vesalius's life about which very little is
known. For example, there is little direct information on the three years
he spent in Paris, and, whether for good or bad, the solution to that problem in the present work has been to give an account of the normal life
of a medical student at that time and to assume that Vesalius's Parisian
years were spent in much the same way. There are also later periods in
his life, even after he had gained a position of prominence, which are
similarly obscure and can be only hazily reconstructed through consideration of his associates and of the events in which he likely participated.
It is hoped that such matters as have been introduced for this reason can
be read with interest even though Vesalius is not always on stage.*

*The major weakness of Roth's biography lies in its too enthusiastic
appreciation of Vesalius's achievement without sufficient credit to his
predecessors and contemporaries. A natural reaction to this has led some
later writers to belittle Vesalius unjustly, and in the present biography an
effort is made to restore a proper balance. In regard to Vesalius's achievement it has been possible to refer to the judgments of his contemporaries,
but his influence upon his successors is too vast a subject for consideration
here, nor does it properly belong in a biography. The reader may gain
some idea of its importance by referring to Harvey Cushing's Bio-
bibliography of Andreas Vesalius.*

*The decision to undertake the present study was fortified by a Guggen-
heim Fellowship in 1952, for which at this long distant time I wish to
express my sincere appreciation. It permitted the beginning of a search
for materials, continued in successive years with visits to almost every
spot known to have had a Vesalian association. A grant from the National Science Foundation (G-18558) has been of the greatest help in
bringing the work to a conclusion, and again my warmest thanks.*

The search for information has been as exhaustive as possible, and it is a pleasure to say that, whether carried on in person or by correspondence, it was always assisted with the greatest courtesy. Although the search did not always turn up information, it did frequently lead to the welcome compensation of lasting friendships. From the beginning two friends in particular were unwearying in their help, but both, alas, are no longer with us. John Fulton, whose generosity is known to so many, was ever ready to make available the Vesalian treasures of the Historical Library, Yale University School of Medicine, and the Librarian, Miss Madeline Stanton, aided, abetted, and continued this generous policy. Until his death three years ago, Charles Singer provided me with an invaluable correspondence course, climaxed each year by a kind of Vesalian seminar in his home in Cornwall. In addition, I am greatly indebted to Professor Luigi Belloni, Director, Institute for the History of Medicine, University of Milan, Italy; Dr. Maria Luisa Bonelli, Director, Science Museum, Florence, Italy; Mr. G. S. T. Cavanagh, Librarian, Duke University School of Medicine; the late Dr. Ruben Eriksson, formerly Librarian, Karolinska Institute, Stockholm, Sweden; Professor Max H. Fisch, Department of Philosophy, University of Illinois, who has kindly allowed me to make full use of one of his excellent papers dealing with Vesalius; Dr. C. E. Kellett, Shotley Bridge, County of Durham, England; Dr. Joshua O. Leibowitz, Jerusalem, Israel; Dr. Sten Lindberg, Keeper of Rare Books, Royal Library, Stockholm, Sweden; Dr. Robert J. Moes, Los Angeles, California, ever ready to share the Vesalian treasures of his personal library; Dr. F. N. L. Poynter, Librarian, Wellcome Historical Medical Library, London; Dr. Dorothy M. Schullian, formerly of the National Library of Medicine and now Curator of the History of Science Collection, Cornell University Library; Dr. Reinhard Timken-Zinkann, Bonn, Germany; and Dr. Gerhard Wolf-Heidegger, Director of the Anatomical Institute, Basel, Switzerland. My thanks, too, to the library authorities of the University of Uppsala, Sweden, for permission to reproduce photographs of certain items from the collection of the late Erik Waller; to the Bulletin of the Medical Library Association for permission to quote from an article published therein; to the William Rockhill Nelson Gallery of Art, Kansas City, Missouri; to the Cincinnati Art Museum; to the Bibliothèque Royale de Belgique; to the Direktion der Bayerischen Staatsgemäldesammlungen for permission to reproduce maps and portraits from those collections; and to The John Crerar Library, Chicago, for permission to employ a manuscript reference to Vesalius.

The manuscript was read by Professor William C. Gibson, Department of the History of Medicine, University of British Columbia, and by Dr. Edwin Clarke, formerly of the Department of History of Science and Medicine, Yale University, and now associated with the Wellcome Historical Medical Library. I have profited greatly from their criticisms.

CONTENTS

PLATES

NOTE: The initial letters are from the *Fabrica* of 1543 with the exception of
those of Chapters VI, IX, X, and XI, which are from the revised edition
of 1555.

Chapter I

PRE-VESALIAN ANATOMY

✥

NDREAS VESALIUS is now recognized by most scholars as the founder of modern anatomy. In the past there has been mention of a very few others deserving this honor: Fallopio, for instance, declared that Berengario da Carpi restored anatomy and that Vesalius perfected it, and it is true that Berengario had occasional flights of freedom from the stultifying Galenic tradition of his day. But the question is not of the first importance, for, whoever may be designated as the founder, it was Vesalius who made the foundation secure by his factual contributions and, more important, by his method of presentation and by the scientific principle he enunciated as fundamental to research. His constant reiteration of this principle obliged anatomy to remain modern, and thereafter the Vesalian method became firmly established and was required of all investigators if only for the sake of retaining professional respect. The meaning of the terms modern anatomy and the Vesalian method will be dealt with later, but to realize the importance of these contributions we must give consideration to those aspects of earlier anatomical investigation that reveal the traditions upon which Vesalius built or that he opposed.

The earliest known genuine student of anatomy appears to have been Alcmaeon of Crotona, who lived in southern Italy, *c.* 500 B.C. Only the slightest fragments of his writing remain, but from these it does appear that he was the first to make dissections of animals, probably goats, and although almost nothing is known of the results, he did make the very important declaration that the brain is the central organ of intelligence. It is of course possible that Alcmaeon had predecessors who conducted similar researches of which all written record has vanished, and it is even more likely that he had contemporaries and certainly successors in this work; however, the results of such observations made upon animals, and probable subsequent conjectures regarding humans, were, no matter how worthy the motivation, restricted in value by the nature of the material employed.

The dissection of the human body, from which alone could arise a true understanding of human anatomy, became possible only when it was no longer believed that such dissection would call down the wrath of the dead upon the "desecrater." In other words, human anatomy could not precede the establishment of a fairly sophisticated religion and philosophy. Although the idea that the body lost all significance after death found expression as early as the time of Heraclitus of Ephesus, in the fifth century B.C., it first gained real importance from Socrates, 470–399 B.C., as his ideas were expounded by his pupil Plato, notably in the *Phaedo*.

The so-called genuine writings of Hippocrates were temporally too close to the establishment of this new attitude toward the body to show any human anatomical first-fruits of such planting. However, it appears that members of the Hippocratic school did conduct anatomical investigation within the permitted limits. In the treatise *On wounds of the head* there is a description of the various sutural patterns of the human skull—made by using the human specimens available from time to time for observation—which was referred to by Vesalius and other anatomists of the sixteenth century.

The first treatise of the Hippocratic school—as distinguished from the so-called genuine writings of Hippocrates—to suggest any human dissection is entitled *On fractures and dislocations*. This work, possibly written in the fourth century B.C. and reflecting the culmination of the Athenian school of anatomy or the beginnings of the Alexandrian, describes the structure of the shoulder joint in a way that indicates human dissection, or at least close observation of the internal structure of that region. It should be noted that the contrast of this particular section of the book with other more elementary parts may indicate later interpolation. Of course such anatomical knowledge did not as yet mean a systematic investigation of human anatomy but, rather, sporadic observation of the parts of the body, perhaps through surreptitious dissection or observation of parts accidentally laid bare in the course of warfare or some other armed engagement.

From the fourth century B.C. onward, then, a new attitude toward the dead, in particular freedom from fear of retribution for the "desecration" of the cadaver, began slowly to become evident. It is especially clear in the writings of Plato, who emphasized the ephemeral character of the body, which was merely the temporary shelter of the immortal soul. Plato's concern was thus more for the soul than the body, and it was his pupil Aristotle, 384–322 B.C., who, although accepting his teacher's view, gave more attention to the soul's mortal dwelling. Aristotle, however, appears not to have undertaken any human dissection, possibly because the force of common opinion was not yet sufficiently influenced by the new philosophy to permit him to do so. Nevertheless, he must be recognized as the first significant figure in the history of anatomy, not only because of his own ideas, but also because in his writings he developed and made influential many tentative views of earlier times. Despite the fact that he was primarily a biologist and so gave only part of his attention to the study of human anatomy, his pronouncements upon this subject were of considerable importance both as fact and influence. They are to be found chiefly in his *Account of animals, Parts of animals, Movement of animals, Locomotion of animals, Generation of animals,* and *The soul.*

According to Aristotle the body is composed of several kinds of substances—blood, fat, marrow, brain, flesh, and bone. These are combined in various simple and compound forms, and the final form that we know as the body is the work of the soul; the departure of the soul leads to formlessness or decomposition. Life is defined as the existence in matter of the power of self-nourishment and of independent growth and decay. Furthermore, since nature makes nothing in vain, there is a purpose or final cause underlying the form of the body, and this purpose is indicated by the activities of the being. Such philosophical ideas, upon which Aristotelian anatomy was based, were influential at least down to the sixteenth century, and, since Aristotelian teleology was adaptable to Christian thought, it was influential in the production of such ridiculous situations as that of students of anatomy showing great concern for the ultimate purpose of an organ and no particular interest in its correct structure.

It is unlikely that Aristotle ever undertook any human dissection, yet there can be no question of his dissection of lower animal forms; and although such investigations produced creditable results, Aristotle's attempted projection of his findings to the human body were naturally not always crowned with success. One of the most influential details of Aristotelian anatomy was one that was incorrect: according to him, and contrary to the earlier pronouncement of Alcmaeon, the brain was of relative insignificance, its function merely to cool the heart by the secretion of phlegm, which possessed the elemental qualities of coldness and moisture. It was the heart that was the seat of sensation and intelligence, the first organ to live, the last to die, and primary to existence. Aristotle also declared that the blood vessels, two in number, arose from the heart, and although he made no general distinction between vein and artery he did call the larger vessel the aorta. His description of the course of the latter is fairly accurate although that of the vena cava is badly confused. It is readily understandable that, since Aristotle considered the nerves to arise from the heart, his description of them, too, suffers.

Of particular structures it may be said very briefly that he distinguished the trachea from the oesophagus, located and understood the use of the epiglottis, had some notion of the larynx, and of the structure of the lungs. His description of the site, shape, and structure of the heart is relatively accurate and was constantly borrowed by later writers. On the other hand, one of his most influential misconceptions was his belief that the number of ventricles of the heart varied with the size of the being and that the human heart possessed three. This view influenced students as late as the sixteenth century, with proponents seeking to explain what the third chamber was and opponents strenuously denying its existence. Finally it may be added that Aristotle understood in very general terms both the alimentary system and the process of alimentation. His statements represent the first considerable body of anatomical knowledge to be preserved, and they were influential for two thousand years.

Succeeding Aristotle, a new school, partly under Sicilian influence, arose in Athens, the so-called Dogmatic school of medicine under the direction of Diocles of Carystos, 384–322 B.C. Although Diocles may have undertaken some human dissection, we know only of his animal dissections, and it was presumably on the basis of such investigations that he wrote a textbook now lost but said to have been the first to employ the word anatomy in its title. Diocles was succeeded by Praxagoras of Cos, whose importance rests upon the fact that he was the first to distinguish between vein and artery, a contribution he promptly lessened by maintaining that the arteries were filled with air and that as they diminished in size until too slender to contain a channel they were transformed into nerve. He may also have recognized the connection of the brain with the spinal cord.

The culmination of this first period of anatomical investigation insofar as concerns the study and description of human material came in Alexandria in the third century B.C. This center of Hellenistic science, founded in 332 B.C., and, after the death of Alexander ten years later, under the control of the Ptolemaic dynasty, developed a scientific and religious sophistication that permitted the intensive studies of human anatomy carried on by Herophilus and Erasistratus. For the first time in history, relatively frequent and consistent human dissection was undertaken. Possibly it was the novelty of this activity, distorted by the passage of time and viewed with hostility by a later and unsympathetic culture, that led to the charge of human vivisection made against the Alexandrian anatomists by Celsus (*fl.* A.D. 14–37), Tertullian (*c.* A.D. 155–222), and St. Augustine (A.D. 354–430).

Herophilus of Chalcedon, born in the last third of the fourth century B.C. and active in Alexandria under Ptolemy I, can be considered the founder of human anatomy as a scientific study. His anatomical writings have been lost, however, and what we know of him is derived from later writers, much of it from Galen.

According to these later accounts, Herophilus not only corrected errors of Aristotle and Praxagoras but, more important, made a number of advances unrelated to any knowledge of the past. He discarded the Aristotelian belief in the primacy of the heart and declared the brain the central organ of the nervous system and the seat of intelligence. He distinguished between motor and sensory nerves, described the cerebrum and cerebellum, of which we have a reminder in the term torcular Herophili, noted the fourth ventricle and the calamus scriptorii, and provided the name for the last. He traced the optic nerves and may have noted the optic chiasma. He described the *rete mirabile* at the base of the brain, probably in sheep, but there is nothing to indicate or to justify the belief that he considered it to exist in the human. That long-held, erroneous belief was finally destroyed nearly two thousand years later by Vesalius. Herophilus, like Praxagoras, distinguished between artery and vein, declaring the former to be six times as thick as the latter, but also corrected Praxagoras's error concerning air in the arteries by maintaining that the arteries contained blood. Much concerned with the pulse, he declared that "pulsation occurs in consequence of the filling and emptying of the arteries," and he realized, although vaguely, a relationship between the heart and the pulse. It was Herophilus who was responsible for the terms "venous artery" (pulmonary vein) and "arterial vein" (pulmonary artery) which were employed by later anatomists, including Vesalius, as late as the seventeenth century. Herophilus seems to have considered the liver as the starting point of the venous system; he also gave the name to the duodenum and may have described the Fallopian tubes. These astonishing accomplishments, the result of unrestrained investigation of the human body, were known to Vesalius, who referred to them on a number of occasions in support of his own activities.

Erasistratus of Iulis, born *c.* 304 B.C. and hence slightly later than Herophilus, was second to him as an anatomist but greater as a physiologist. Indeed, Erasistratus has sometimes been called the founder of physiology. His description of the brain was more extended than that of his colleague, and his studies led him to infer that the greater complexity of man's brain was related to his superior intelligence. Like Herophilus, Erasistratus recognized the division of nerves into motor and sensory. His greatest work, however, was related to the cardiovascular system. He recognized the cardiac valves, although there is also mention of them in the so-called Hippocratic treatise *On the heart,* which may have been slightly earlier. He considered the heart the origin of both veins and arteries, although, unlike Herophilus, he declared the latter to contain no blood. According to his belief, every organ contained three kinds of tubes: veins, arteries, and hollow nerves. In diastole the heart expanded like a bellows and blood was drawn into the right ventricle whence it passed to the lung to nourish it. At the same time, air, or that part of it called pneuma, was breathed into the lung and drawn into the left ventricle, where it was transformed into vital spirit, and was then drawn onward into the arteries, by which it was distributed throughout the body to provide vitality. This vital spirit was the source of the pulse and the body's innate heat, and was consequently the active force causing digestion, nutrition, and assimilation. Some of the vital spirit was carried to the brain, whence it entered the hollow nerves and was in this form responsible for consciousness, sensation, and muscular action. Later, Galen, borrowing the *rete mirabile* from Herophilus and the nervous spirit from Erasistratus, elaborated the whole system and produced what he called animal spirit, which plagued physiologists until well into the eighteenth century. Erasistratus also declared that blood could pass from pulmonary artery to vein, but only in a morbid condition when too much blood had led to rupture and a forced passage, usually indicated by fever and inflammation. This idea, too, was developed by Galen into his idea of anastomosis.

For various reasons the practice of human dissection in Alexandria seems not to have long outlasted Herophilus and Erasistratus but to have ceased, at least openly, about 150 B.C.; presumably it had lost its full vigor even earlier. Nevertheless, results achieved during this brief period were indicative of the significance of direct reference to the human body, and this fact, no matter how dimly recognized from time to time, was not wholly forgotten.

With the ever-spreading Roman influence and, finally, the incorporation of Alexandria into the Roman Empire in 30 B.C., the further decline and ultimate extinction of the medical school was inevitable. Once again respect for the bodies of the dead, by statute as well as because of the general religious sentiment of Rome, made human dissection impossible, although, as mentioned, some interest in past accomplishment remained for a time. Cicero echoed Aristotelian anatomy in his *De natura deorum,* although a more significant résumé of earlier achievements is found in *De re medicina* of Celsus (*fl.* A.D. 14–37), who had a generally competent grasp of anatomical knowledge so far as it had been developed in the Hellenic world. Nevertheless, any further dissection and genuine investigation into anatomy, human or animal, was to be the work of the descendants and direct heirs of Greek and Hellenic civilization.

The first such noteworthy figure was Marinus of Alexandria, who lived about the beginning of the second century and who participated in a brief revival of anatomical activity at Alexandria, producing a treatise now lost and known only through Galen's references to it. Marinus, as well as his shadowy disciples and successors Quintus, Satyrus, Numisianus, Lycus, and Pelops, although known to us only from Galen's statements, deserve passing mention since Vesalius was to refer to them, knowing nothing of their work but considering them as belonging to the pre-Galenic period of actual human dissection. The final pre-Galenic anatomist worthy of remark was Rufus of Ephesus (*fl.* A.D. 98–117), some of whose works have been preserved and who, because his research was limited to animals, was responsible for the long-standing belief that the human liver was four- or five-lobed—an error frequently attributed to Galen and a major target of Vesalian attack.

Although there was no place for human anatomy under Roman civilization, the value of such study had been established, and it was inevitable that an alternative would be sought. Consequently, physicians turned to animals. Efforts were made to carry on research not only in animals generally, but specifically in those most closely resembling the human animal. Of all investigators the most famous and certainly the most influential on later times was the Hellenic physician Galen, A.D. 129(?)–199.

Because of the loss of his predecessors' works and the fact that most remaining fragments of them are found in Galen's writings, where their favorable or unfavorable presentation depends upon his attitude toward them, it is impossible to determine the precise degree of his indebtedness. Nevertheless, we can recognize some debt to Hippocrates, Aristotle, Herophilus, and Erasistratus. Galen's own researches had to be restricted to animals, especially monkeys, which he considered structurally closest to man, and he sought to project the results of these studies upon the human structure. On only two occasions, according to his own words, did he have an opportunity to study the human, and then only skeletons, one cleansed of its flesh by birds and the other by the waters of a river. It is clear he would have preferred to examine human material since he speaks with envy of the earlier period of human dissection at Alexandria and notes as a sight worth seeing the human skeleton that still existed in the then-decayed medical school.

It is a curious fact that, although it is quite clear from Galen's statements that his "human" anatomy was based upon that of animals, in later times, especially in the fifteenth and sixteenth centuries when much of his writing was available, physicians generally assumed his anatomy to have been based upon the dissection of man. Indeed, Vesalius's major problem in proving both Galen's errors and the cause of them was to convince the medical world of this fact, an effort that gained him the hostility of many and especially of those best qualified by their knowledge of Greek to read Galen. This was a matter of great importance since Galen's writings, whether known directly or indirectly, were of supreme authority to anatomy until finally overthrown by Vesalius.

Despite errors that arose from the kind of anatomical material available to him, Galen was a highly skilled investigator, but unfortunately his findings were always tempered by his doctrine of final cause. Borrowed partly from Hippocrates and Plato but especially from Aristotle, and further magnified by Galen himself, this required him always to look for the final cause of any structure as the important element of his research. Such is the theme and defect of his extensive work on anatomy and physiology, *The use of parts,* and it was Galenic teleology that long hindered the proper development of anatomy by requiring that it be philosophical and, in a sense, religious before it could be considered scientific. Even Vesalius, who contributed to the overthrow of Galen's authority, was influenced to present long paraphrases from Galen to justify such an outlook.

Since Galen was limited to the dissection of animals, he chose as his favorite subject the Barbary ape. The one exception to such reliance on the anatomy of lower animals is found in his little treatise *On the bones,* based partly upon the study of human bones; as physician to the gladiators of Pergamon and maybe of Rome, it is quite possible that Galen would have had brief glimpses of internal structures owing to wounds resulting from the brutal and frequently mortal combat of the games.

Galen's major anatomical text is the *Anatomical procedures,* and from it and *On the bones* we can obtain a fair idea of his strictly anatomical knowledge, which included a relatively good understanding of the cranial bones and of a spinal column of twenty-four vertebrae terminated by sacrum and coccyx. His descriptions of these and of the sternum, clavicle, and bones of the arms and legs are roughly correct, although in certain instances—such as the relative lengths of bones, the segmentation of the sternum, and the processes of the vertebrae—Vesalius was later able to demonstrate discrepancies from the human forms indicative of simian osteology. Galen's description of muscles has been termed a genuinely pioneering achievement; it is certainly true that he made many elaborate dissections of muscles, which he described in detail, and if his descriptions are sometimes difficult to criticize from the point of view of human anatomy, this is the result of fortuitously close resemblance between the particular human and animal structure. Vesalius also criticized at length Galen's projection of animal myology upon the human. Despite a rough idea of the venous distribution, Galen's angiology was heavily dependent upon his simian source. However, he fully demonstrated the existence of blood in the arteries and opposed Aristotle's doctrine that the human heart contained three ventricles. His description of the brain is not especially noteworthy, but his classification of the cranial nerves as he knew them into seven pairs was influential for fifteen hundred years and was accepted with some reservations by Vesalius. His description of the abdominal organs contains a number of errors, some of which Vesalius was later to expose.

Although Galen's carefully detailed dissections and descriptions were in many ways an extraordinary achievement, his physiological experiments were perhaps even more remarkable. His studies of the loss of sensation and motion related to severance of the spinal cord at different levels, the effect upon the voice of ligation of the recurrent laryngeal nerve, and his experiments upon the intercostal muscles and nerves, pericardium, and heart were wholly original and were repeated by Vesalius about fourteen hundred years later to usher in the revival of experimental physiology.

Unfortunately, however, Galen was not content with such experiments but also developed a physiological system for which he had no experimental proofs and to which he adapted his anatomical system, also without proof. Parts of Galen's theoretical physiology remained influential as late as the latter part of the eighteenth century and influenced the anatomical thinking of even such a distinguished seventeenth-century scientist as René Descartes.

Briefly, and with emphasis upon those aspects of the system with which Vesalius was compelled to grapple, Galen contended that when food was ingested it was moved along to the stomach and thence to the alimentary canal by the action of fibres in the coats of these organs, straight or lengthwise, transverse and diagonal, which had the power of drawing or attracting substances or grasping and retaining them. The fibres were also in the coats of the blood vessels, where they were responsible for any movement of the blood. Almost to the end of his life Vesalius gave allegiance to this doctrine although, naturally, neither Galen nor Vesalius had ever seen the fibres.

When the nourishment had been attracted into the alimentary canal it was withdrawn or attracted as "chyle" by the mesenteric vessels, thence into the portal vein, and finally into the liver, where it was elaborated into venous blood and imbued with natural spirit. The natural spirit, a substance that appears to have been Galen's invention, was considered necessary for the functioning of the "natural" or abdominal organs.

The blood so prepared was then attracted by the fibres of the veins and, as it moved through them, irrigated and nourished the tissues. When the blood arrived, by way of the vena cava, at the right ventricle of the heart, the impurities that had been picked up were carried off by the pulmonary artery to the lung, whence they were exhaled, and most of the venous blood was attracted back into the general venous system. A small part, however, moved by minute—and of course imaginary—pores through the heart's septum from the right into the left ventricle. Here, through the agency of the innate heat of the heart in the left ventricle, the blood was imbued with vital spirit, essentially a refined part of the air breathed in by the lung and passed on by the pulmonary vein to the left ventricle. This blood, now imbued with vital spirit—for which concept Galen was indebted to Erasistratus—was attracted through the arterial system to maintain the body's vitality, although it seems likely that the movement of the blood itself was only sufficient to make up any deficiency and that it was primarily vital spirit that was attracted. Thereafter impurities and excess heat were withdrawn for discharge through the pulmonary vein to the lung and so out of the body, to be replaced in the blood by a fresh supply of vital spirit. The indrawn air, incidentally, cooled the heart; failure of the system produced overheating or fever.

Part of the blood and vital spirit passed or was drawn through the internal carotid arteries to the base of the brain where it was further refined in the network of arteries called the *rete mirabile* to produce animal spirit, the substance responsible for sensation and motion. Here again Galen had borrowed from his Alexandrian predecessors, although his acceptance of the *rete mirabile* as a structure in the human brain was clearly his own error. It was, however, from Erasistratus that Galen accepted the belief that the nerves were hollow and that sensation and motion were produced by the passage of animal spirit through these hollow nerves. The manufacture of the ultrarefined animal spirit left a residue in the form of phlegm or pituita, which was ultimately excreted from the brain through minute openings in the cribriform plate of the ethmoid bone and thence into the mouth and nostrils.

Such in its simplest form was the Galenic physiological pattern as it relates to the present context; as with his anatomy, so too was the medical world saddled with Galen's physiology for many centuries to come. The survival of such a large proportion of his writings, his recognized ability, and his manifest confidence, coupled with the intellectual decline supervening upon his death, prevented the development of any competing system. With no alternative, it became necessary to recognize pores in the septum of the heart, motive fibres in the vessels, hollow nerves, and a *rete mirabile*. It would later require a bold medical heretic to challenge both Galen's anatomy and his physiology.

The death of Galen in A.D. 199 marked the end of any anatomical investigation in the West, although in the Byzantine and Moslem civilizations traditions of both Alexandrine anatomy and Galenism retained a degree of vigor for some centuries. As late as the ninth century, Theophanes reported, in his *Chronologia* (810–814), the earlier (756) seizure of a Christian renegade who was turned over to surgeons who "opened the still living person from the pubis to the chest to study the human structure." Whether the account is true or not, the fact that it was written indicates the tenacity of the earlier Alexandrine tradition of scientific inquiry. A related report from the Islamic world is that of the ninth-century Jewish surgeon Johannes Mesaweigh, who remarked of his retarded son that were it not for the specific prohibition he "would find nothing objectionable to vivisection of my son in order to discover the cause of his stupidity." He further asserted with regret that human dissection was prohibited on religious grounds and in consequence he was compelled to dissect monkeys. Such spirit of inquiry, ruthless as it may appear, had died out in the West for reasons of cultural alteration and decline, theological as opposed to ecclesiastical prohibition, and the belief that antiquity, no matter how dimly comprehended, had already amassed all knowledge.

From about the eighth to the thirteenth century intellectual leadership of the civilized world passed to the Moslems as trustees of the classical heritage, and it was during this period that many of the most important Greek medical writings were translated into Arabic, to become in turn the guide for Moslem medicine, the source of Moslem commentaries, or the influence that compelled Moslem physicians to write within the tradition of Greek medicine. No original investigation of anatomy was permitted in the Moslem world, which would seem to mean that the anatomical knowledge of Islam was merely that of Galen in Moslem dress. However, the discovery a generation ago of the remarkable description of the pulmonary circulation of the blood written by Ibn-Nafis in the thirteenth century suggests that there may have been some independent activity, although any certainty of this must await investigation of the many Arabic medical writings hitherto unstudied. For the moment it can only be said that, based upon what is known, the Moslem world became a trustee for the preservation of Greek medicine and a reservoir, albeit a muddy one, from which the West would ultimately recover the long-lost tradition. This fact was all the more important since western Europe no longer had any comprehension of the Greek language and the recovery had to be made from Arabic to Latin.

This recovery by translation began with Constantine the African, born in Carthage but eventually established as a monk of Monte Cassino in the latter part of the eleventh century. Translation became more active in the twelfth century, and in 1127 Stephen of Antioch produced a version of a work of Haly Abbas containing an anatomical section. Most important of all the translators from the Arabic, however, was Gerard of Cremona, 1115–1185, who had established himself in Toledo. Of his many translations none was of greater significance than his rendering of Avicenna's *Canon,* and it was to Avicenna, Haly Abbas, and Rhazes, also translated by Gerard, that most Western medical knowledge gave its allegiance before the sixteenth century. Since these three Arabic authors depended upon Galen for their anatomy, European anatomy received a Galenic character with Moslem overtones.

That Moslem medicine was not wholly under the authority of Galen, however, and that some spirit of inquiry remained, even if of necessity discreet, is perhaps reflected in the Emperor Frederick II, who was educated and lived much of his life in Sicily in a culture still under strong Moslem influence. In the latter part of the thirteenth century, Fra Salimbene related in his chronicle that on one occasion Frederick "provided an excellent dinner for two men after which he ordered one to go to sleep and the other to go hunting. The following evening he ordered their stomachs to be emptied in his presence in order to see who had better digested the meal, and the surgeons decided that he who had slept had had the better digestion." Salimbene's story, indicative of the somewhat puzzling personality of Frederick, *Stupor mundi,* for his Western contemporaries, was, perhaps partly because of clerical hostility toward him and partly because of developments soon to occur, recast by others as an experiment decided through examination of the stomach content by post-mortem dissection.

In the same way another story, never documented, recounts that in 1238 Frederick ordered a public dissection to be performed every five years at the medical school of Salerno. There is, however, documentary evidence that Frederick, who controlled Salerno and the medical profession in southern Italy, decreed that no surgeon could practise unless he had studied anatomy for one year. Whether or not serious efforts were made to enforce the decree, anatomy at this time was still performed upon animals.

As yet prohibition of human dissection seems to have been based upon social opposition, although it is impossible to determine whether it was chiefly lay or ecclesiastical. At the height of Salerno's fame in the twelfth century, its physicians clearly declared the dissection of the human body to be a "horrible" action "especially among us Catholics" and since Salerno declined in the thirteenth century it was to have no share in the development of the study of human anatomy. Curiously enough, although the dissection of the human body was termed horrible, the practice of its dismemberment, boiling, and removal of the bones for easier transport to the native land had long been carried on among the northern nations of Europe, especially for the bodies of crusaders who had died in the distant East. This practice was later frowned upon by the church, even when the former "horrible" practice of human dissection had gained some sanction. A second procedure that can be traced back to Egypt, that of embalming, gained no opprobrium and presumably was an influential forerunner of the post-mortem dissection of the late thirteenth and the fourteenth centuries. As early as the ninth century such embalming included placing preservatives within the body, which naturally required a prior opening and the removal of at least some of the viscera. We do not know who performed these functions in earlier times, but by the fourteenth century the practice was in the hands of the surgeons. Furthermore, attention has been directed to the use during this period of the term "anatomize" in conjunction with the performance of Caesarean section.

It appears therefore that the human body had for a considerable time been subject to at least partial dissection, although the action had been directed by motives other than inquiry into the nature of the human structure. This sort of utilitarian dissection was henceforth pursued much more boldly, although, with some exceptions, more time would pass before it would be performed specifically to gain human anatomical knowledge. No doubt Galen's authority, as it was then known, was hindering, and the few early "scientific" dissections were performed with the hand of Galen and observed through his eyes. Nevertheless by the fourteenth century there was faintly perceptible, even if not yet truly effective, a spirit of detached inquiry.

The first instances of what may be called human dissection were performed not primarily for study of normal human structure but rather with the hope of discovering some abnormality of structure that would explain a medical or legal problem. The fact that the examiners were not acquainted with the normal human structure and hence would have had great difficulty in determining abnormality apparently bothered no one.

The first such examination known is mentioned in the chronicle of Fra Salimbene for the year 1286. It was a year of great sickness:

In Cremona, Piacenza, Parma, Reggio, and many other cities and bishoprics of Italy there were many deaths among both men and hens; in the city of Cremona one woman in a short period of time lost forty-eight hens. A certain doctor of medicine caused some of them to be opened and found a vesicular aposteme at the tip of each hen's heart; he also caused a dead man to be opened and found the same.

The casual manner in which Salimbene mentions the autopsy, virtually an incidental remark since he then returns to discussion of the mortality among and the scarcity of the hen population, suggests that this was by no means the first such examination of a human cadaver. Thereafter fairly frequent autopsy examinations were made in an attempt to solve medical problems and to seek proper treatment of various epidemic diseases, especially the bubonic plague which appeared in Europe with such sudden and devastating effect in 1348.

Post-mortem dissection for legal purposes began slightly later. The first known instance of medical examination of this nature seems to have been that mentioned by the surgeon William of Saliceto, *c*. 1210–*c*. 1280. It concerned a cadaver examined about 1275 to determine whether or not certain wounds inflicted had been sufficient to cause death. However, the body was not dissected. Similarly, in 1295 the body of a Bencivenne was exhumed to allow surgeons to determine whether or not wounds on it had been of mortal nature. A third case of this sort is recorded for the year 1300.

In 1302 there occurred the first recorded case of medico-judicial dissection. In February of that year a certain Azzolino died under conditions that led to suspicion of poisoning, but at an autopsy examination by two physicians and three surgeons it was concluded, as a result of "the evidence of our senses and of our anatomization of the parts," that no foul play had been involved.

In view of the dissections already mentioned and the complete lack of indication of novelty or of distaste, it would have been curious indeed if Italian physicians, or more likely surgeons, had not undertaken occasional dissections of more academic nature. At the close of the thirteenth century the Bolognese surgeon Taddeo Alderotti, *c.* 1223–1295, in commenting on a Hippocratic aphorism, stated that he must remain uncertain about the comparison between the breast of a pregnant woman and of one aborted, because "I have not seen the dissection of a pregnant woman." One assumes from his words that he had been present at or participated in the dissection of a man or a nonpregnant woman earlier than this particular incident.

So far as we know, writings about human anatomy had hitherto been based upon the dissection of animals and upon earlier authorities such as Galen—or whatever portions of his writings were available—and Avicenna. Furthermore, anatomical treatises had been merely parts of works on surgery. The *Anothomia* of Mondino da Luzzi, probably written in 1316, may be termed the first modern work on anatomy in that it is wholly devoted to its subject, so recognizing anatomy as a distinct discipline. It is also at least partly the result of Mondino's own dissections of human bodies. It is arranged according to the needs of a time that had few cadavers to work with, and no way of preserving those, so that the most perishable parts had to be dissected first. Thus the work is first concerned with the contents of the abdominal cavity, next with the thorax, then with the head and the extremities. Such dissection usually took four days and much of the nights. It is frequently stated that Mondino set this pattern, but it was the conditions of the time that required it.

Although the *Anothomia* is nominally based upon human dissection, in actuality Mondino relied largely upon such of Galen's writings as were known to him, and those of Avicenna. He dissected merely to experience for himself what they had written and certainly with no thought of putting his authorities to the test. Nevertheless the fact that he did perform his own dissection occasionally led him to discoveries, even if for the most part he observed the cadaver through the eyes of his authorities and consequently found nothing contradictory. Thus he found the stomach to be spherical, the liver to have five lobes, the spleen to secrete black bile through imaginary channels into the upper or cardiac mouth of the stomach, and a duct to run from the gall bladder to the stomach. He also described a uterus divided into seven cells, yet he did note the different origins of the spermatic vessels on the two sides. His description of the heart, derived from Avicenna, stated that he had found it to possess three ventricles, and the cavity of the brain was described as divided into three ventricles, the anterior one double. He accepted Galen's idea of seven pairs of cranial nerves and the brain as the source of intelligence and sensation, but he was sufficiently torn between his authorities to accept also the Aristotelian idea that the brain cooled the heart's vital spirit. The *Anothomia* was very popular and went through many editions, even as late as the sixteenth century. In fact it was the only work wholly devoted to anatomy until the sixteenth century and marked a distinct step forward, acting also, no doubt, as an inducement to others to perform similar dissections.

A point of special interest in his work is Mondino's remark, in reference to the bones of the skull, that "you will see them better if you boil them," which suggests that the prohibitory bull (1299) of Boniface VIII was not always observed, although apparently Mondino himself did observe it since he adds that "owing to the sin involved in this I am accustomed to pass them [bones of the skull] by." This papal bull was directed not against human dissection but against the practice, already mentioned, of boiling the dead bodies of those far from home, such as crusaders, so that at least their bones might be shipped home for burial. The papacy, it may be added, never issued any statement specifically opposing dissection although there seem to have been instances in which overzealous local ecclesiastical authorities, by interpretation or misinterpretation, did oppose the practice.

Mondino's successor at Bologna, Nicolo Bertucci (d. 1347), continued the new practice of human dissection and was the teacher of Guy de Chauliac, a French surgeon of great influence whose advocacy and practice of dissection gave that activity wide, extra-Italian support. By this time the practice had been so fully established at Bologna that when Pope Alexander V suddenly died there, on 4 May 1410, Pietro d'Argellata (d. 1423) described his post-mortem examination in a manner suggesting that such occurrences were by then rather commonplace.

There seems, then, little doubt that the University of Bologna was the first home of the revived practice of dissection and study of the human body that was more and more encouraged by the medical faculty throughout the fourteenth century. As similar activities developed elsewhere in Europe, in addition to whatever indigenous factors may have promoted them, the influence of Bologna can frequently be shown. The subjects for dissection in Bologna were then, no doubt, as later, executed criminals. The supply of such bodies seems always to have been limited, however, and it appears that at least early in the century students occasionally obtained cadavers through extralegal means, sometimes probably on the urgings of their teachers. There is record of the prosecution of four medical students for grave-robbing as early as 1319. It was partly as a result of this situation that a document of 1405 provided that thereafter, to avoid such improper activity, no one might acquire a body without the permission of the rector.

In view of the popularity of human dissection and because too large a crowd of spectators would detract from the educational value, no more than twenty students were allowed at the dissection of a man and no more than thirty at that of a woman, the larger number permitted at the latter event presumably because of its lesser frequency. The attendant students, moreover, had to be in the third year of their medical studies and, if previously spectators at a male dissection, had to wait a year before seeing another. If a student had seen two such dissections, his further attendance was permitted only when the body was female. A revised version of the statute was issued in 1442, declaring that two bodies were to be made available annually by the civic authorities for dissection, one male and one female, or, if necessary two male. Such bodies were to be of executed foreign—that is, non-Bolognese—criminals. In Bologna as elsewhere the statutes or ordinances regarding dissection were assisting and regulatory rather than primarily permissive since nowhere does there appear to have been legal prohibition of human dissection.

The earliest recorded human dissection at the University of Padua seems to have been performed in 1341 by Gentile da Foligna (d. 1348), who is declared to have discovered a gallstone in the cadaver. Gentile was probably a product of Bologna and hence a disseminator of Bolognese influence, but also, since Padua had been established as a kind of offshoot of Bologna, this latter influence was reflected in the similar references to anatomy in the statutes of the younger school.

Elsewhere in Italy such records as exist suggest the beginning of human dissection at Venice in 1368, Florence in 1388, Siena in 1427, Perugia in 1457, Genoa in 1482, Ferrara at an undetermined but slightly later date, and Pisa in 1501.

The Bolognese influence on the practice of anatomy outside Italy is indicated by the activities of the Norman surgeon Henri de Mondeville, *c.* 1270–1320. At Montpellier in 1304 he lectured on anatomy, using large diagrams showing stages in the course of dissection—possibly a product of his earlier studies in Bologna where he was a contemporary of Mondino. These illustrations, described by him in the anatomical section of his treatise on surgery, have disappeared, but not before copies, still in existence, were made of them on a reduced scale (1314). There is some question whether the illustrations supplemented human dissections that he performed or whether, because human dissection was not yet practised at Montpellier, they were used as a substitute. There is an equivocal statement by Mondeville in which, referring to the head, he remarks, "If you cannot procure a true human head . . ." In any event, he was the first link between Bologna and Montpellier.

As at Bologna, actual human dissection at Montpellier probably preceded regulation; it was not until 1340 that it received official recognition by a statute of the university that provided for a biennial anatomy. It has been suggested that here, too, the influence of Bologna was felt, since the physician to a series of popes at Avignon from 1342 to 1362, and possibly earlier, was the surgeon Guy de Chauliac, who had studied at Bologna under Bertucci, and who has been proposed as having had influence upon the statutes. However, it is more likely that, as elsewhere, the regulatory ordinance needed no advocacy from without but was the normal consequence of the practice already in operation. In 1391 human dissection was recognized at the University of Lerida which, like Montpellier in 1340, was part of the kingdom of Aragon.

In Paris the situation may have been somewhat different, at least around 1340 when Guido da Vigevano, actually from Pavia, published a brief illustrated anatomical work introduced by the statement, "Because the Church prohibits dissection of the human body." So far as is known this statement was not true unless it represented some ultraconservative position of the ecclesiastical authorities in Paris or of the theological faculty of the University of Paris. Certainly Guido must have known his statement was not true, since he was probably a product of Bologna, and there is evidence that he had practised human dissection. Nevertheless, the theory of some local prohibition is given support by the fact that the earliest dissection recorded in Paris, the post-mortem examination in 1407 of the body of Jean Canard, Bishop of Arras, was followed by no further recorded human dissections for over half a century.

Despite the growing number of universities in which human anatomies were performed, the true worth of this discipline to the students is subject to serious doubts. The dissections were annual or sometimes biennial and the number of students privileged to attend such demonstrations, which lasted for only a few days, was limited strictly. Furthermore, to finish the dissection in such a brief time, it had to be carried on almost nonstop with little opportunity for the student to digest and comprehend even such inadequate fare as was offered to him. The demonstration also came to be controlled by the physician who, however, did not deign to approach the cadaver but left that menial work to two men, an unlearned barber or a surgeon, who did the actual dissecting, and a second assistant, the ostensor, whose task was to point out structures as they were dissected or described or read about by the distant physician. Whereas Mondino was deferential to the authorities but still did his own dissection and so was occasionally in a position to note something new or unusual, this was not true of the physician or professor who was no longer able even to visualize what was described in the text from which he read.

In Italy the commonly used text came to be that of Mondino who, with very few exceptions, had sought to follow Galenic procedure as it was known through the medieval filterings and who, therefore, observed through the dimmed eyes of a medieval Galen. Elsewhere, as in France, the anatomical section of Guy de Chauliac or Henri de Mondeville was popular, but everywhere the result was the same. The infrequent dissection was performed for the small group of spectators not as a means of investigation but merely for illustration of the authority, which was always, in essence, a diluted Galenism. Toward the end of the fifteenth century, as Galen's writings came to be available directly from the original Greek texts, the belief developed that the true answers to all medical questions were to be found in these recovered texts. In consequence medieval authorities gradually fell into disrepute while bondage to Greek authorities became a stronger obstacle than ever before to independent research.

To this obstacle of authority may be added that of terminology. Examining Mondino's very influential Latin text, one is immediately confronted by a number of terms that are completely meaningless today, such as *mirach* for the anterior abdominal wall, *zirbus* for the greater omentum, and *venae guidem* for the jugular veins. These veins were also called *venae apopleticae, venae somni,* and *venae profundae,* or occasionally *venae guidem* referred specifically to the external jugulars but *venae apopleticae* to the internal. This nomenclature represented the efforts of translators, some of them inexpert and many with little or no medical knowledge, to render Arabic terms into Latin. As a result, the reader without understanding of Arabic was unable to determine the derivation of such terms even if, as was unlikely, the translator could, and hence false derivations from Latin and Greek were frequently developed. Since, moreover, Arabic treatises had been turned into Latin at different times and by a variety of translators, like terms were sometimes rendered from Arabic into Latin for completely different structures, or sometimes there were duplicate words for a single structure—or even triplicate or quadruplicate words because of vestiges of Latin and Greek terminology. Obviously, therefore, a great need existed for clarification of anatomical terminology.

Some correction of this situation occurred at the opening of the sixteenth century, first through the publication in 1502 of the *Onomasticon* of Julius Pollux (*c.* A.D. 134–192) which contained a classical anatomical vocabulary with brief explanations of the meaning of the terms. The first anatomical treatise to rely to any degree upon the recovered classical usages was a posthumous work of Giorgio Valla, *De humani corporis partibus* (1501), a slim treatise otherwise of no significance. A second but longer and more popular work that gave further currency to revived Greek terminology was the *Anatomice sive de historia corporis humani* (1502) of Alessandro Benedetti. Nevertheless the new, more precise vocabulary did not become immediately effective, and several decades later Vesalius still felt compelled to list all known forms of anatomical terms for the sake of clarity.

Related to the problem of terminology was that of illustration, not only because illustrations might clarify matters otherwise obscured by confused nomenclature, but also because when new body structures were found there were at first no terms by which they might be described. There is evidence that diagrams were employed for explanation of anatomical problems as early as classical times and that the "five-figure series" of illustrations of bones, veins, arteries, nerves, and muscles of the twelfth century are copies of earlier figures that go back as far as the sixth. These, however, as well as those fourteenth- and fifteenth-century illustrations that were products of the revived practice of human dissection, have only the most minor significance for depiction of anatomical detail, since they were usually drawn to present not what was seen in dissection but what tradition required.

The impulse to naturalistic anatomical depiction seems to have come from the art world rather than the medical. Artists began to make their own observations and sometimes even their own dissections in order to study the superficial appearance of the body at rest and in movement. Such study was of course directed toward an artistic goal, and usually the artist neither dissected nor illustrated anything deeper than the superficial muscles; the one great exception was Leonardo da Vinci who had become ever more interested in anatomy and physiology and so finally ceased to be primarily an artist. However, since his work was not published it had no effect on the general course of the development of anatomical studies and hence falls outside present consideration.

Obviously the proper procedure was to employ an artist to make any necessary illustrations under the direction of the anatomist, although for some time such direction remained influenced by tradition rather than by genuine observation. An instance of this curious situation may be seen in the illustration of a female figure, in the *Fasciculo di medicina* (Venice, 1493), which displays a uterus obviously drawn from observation but surrounded by organs that are wholly fanciful. Similarly, in the *Spiegel der artzney* (Strasburg, 1518), there is an illustration displaying a series of dissections of the brain clearly made from direct observation, yet a further illustration on the same page depicts abdominal viscera that have no relation to reality. Furthermore it had not as yet been realized that illustrations, even those few that might faithfully portray anatomical structures, were meaningful only if related to the text. The additional fact that an accurate illustration could be reproduced in multiple accurate copies by means of the printing press had been realized by botanists some years before the value of this new technological advance occurred to the anatomists.

As yet no one had realized the total significance of the several factors that would be brought together by Vesalius to make the *Fabrica* the remarkable work it is, although in the first two decades of the sixteenth century several Italian anatomists did make some use of one or more of them. It has been indicated that contributions to a somewhat more precise and classical terminology had been offered by Giorgio Valla and Alessandro Benedetti, the latter also publicizing and popularizing anatomical studies. It is doubtful, however, that he performed more frequent dissections than the two required annually by statute of the University of Padua. His contribution to the body of anatomical knowledge was nil. On the other hand, the posthumous *Anatomiae annotationes* (1520) of Alessandro Achillini, 1463–1512, while using a wholly medieval vocabulary and presentation, occasionally reveals a considerable degree of independent judgment, so that to Achillini belongs credit for the first descriptions of the trochlear nerve, the seven-boned tarsus,

and some reservation about the existence of the Galenic *rete mirabile.*
Yet none of these works was illustrated.

Of much greater importance and deserving of more extended consideration was Giacomo Berengario da Carpi (*c.* 1460–1530). In 1502 he was appointed to the chair of surgery and anatomy at Bologna where he remained until 1527, enjoying great popularity as a teacher despite, or perhaps because of, a somewhat fiery and even quarrelsome nature. Berengario wrote two works, a *Commentaria* on the text of Mondino (1521), and a compendium of it entitled *Isagoge brevis* (1522 and 1523). It was on the basis of these books, especially the former, that Fallopio remarked some forty years later that Berengario was the restorer of anatomy.

The *Commentaria* is an extensive work of almost a thousand pages in which the author gives first a chapter of Mondino's medieval text, superficially treated with the reverence due a classic, and then in his commentary upon the chapter proceeds to criticize and emendate. According to his own words he had performed several hundred dissections, a number that ought perhaps to be received with some reservation. Still, he did far more dissecting than his predecessors and, more to the point, he recorded what he had observed in the course of dissection and criticized the statements of earlier writers, including Mondino, because they had not relied upon the testimony of their own senses. Although Berengario did not always employ this scientific attitude, it was inevitable that, as the first man to put considerable trust in his own vision unclouded by Galenist or Moslem views, he would make a number of contributions. Hence we find that he expressed disbelief in the existence of the *rete mirabile* for the simple reason that he had never been able to find it. He likewise refused to give credence to the medieval belief in the multicelled uterus. Berengario was the first to describe the anastomosis between the portal vein and the inferior vena cava, a single umbilical vein, the thymus gland, the seminal vesicles, the arytenoid cartilages of the larynx, the tympanic membrane, and two ossicles of the ear (malleus and incus). He also was the first to note the vermiform appendix, and the fact of the larger proportional size of the chest of the male and the pelvis of the female. He denied the existence of a separate third ventricle of the heart as posited by Aristotle, but he sought a compromise by declaring that this was a reference to the pores in the interventricular septum, that figment propounded by Galen for passage of the blood from right to left ventricle.

Berengario was the first man not constantly overwhelmed by earlier authorities, either Galenic or Moslem. This does not mean he did not occasionally—even frequently—accept the errors of these authorities, nor that he ever asserted as a policy that their words must be accepted only with verification, as Vesalius later did about Galen. Rather, from time to time Berengario saw things as they truly were and was sufficiently pugnacious to say so.

Unlike Achillini, Berengario was no philosopher, and unlike Benedetti —as is obvious from his text written without polish or use of the new classico-humanistic vocabulary—he was not a literary humanist. Nevertheless, though he made no particular contributions to anatomical nomenclature, he was aware of the desirability of replacing the medieval anatomical vocabulary, in one instance remarking of an illustration of the veins: "In these figures can be seen the course of the *salvatella* of Mondino and Rhazes, the *sceylen* of Avicenna, the *salubris* of Haly, and that branch of the *basilica* that ends between the little and the ring finger which Rhazes also calls the *salvatella*." It was partly in an effort to provide a descriptive clarity not then verbally possible that he made a serious effort to give a new meaning to anatomical illustration.

Berengario had a sincere interest in art; no less a person than Benvenuto Cellini, the celebrated Florentine goldsmith and sculptor, verified this fact, and from other sources we are aware that Berengario's interest led him to build up a considerable art collection that included Raphael's painting of John the Baptist. As a result of these factors he was the first anatomist to have a fairly good idea of the true significance of anatomical illustration and of what its relationship to the text ought to be. This means not that he succeeded in his purpose but rather that he was groping in the proper direction. If one observes earlier anatomical illustrations it becomes immediately apparent that they are not proper representations of the human structure or its parts, that they are not used with system or true purpose, and so serve no end except perhaps as traditional symbols. Berengario's contribution, crude as was its result, was to integrate text and illustration. The text described, and the illustration was intended to assist that description, especially where phrases or the confused anatomical vocabulary were unable to convey the proper meaning. It was a contribution of very great significance, although, again, for the direction it took rather than the immediate achievement.

It remained for Vesalius to develop all these factors to a degree far beyond that of his predecessors, to correlate them with remarkable skill, and for the first time to propose a consistent and genuinely scientific principle as a guide to anatomical investigation and study.

Chapter II

THE ANCESTORS
OF ANDREAS VESALIUS

HE earliest known published account of the ancestors of Andreas Vesalius was written by the anatomist himself, in 1546, for his *Letter on the china root.* Apparently Vesalius's words represent a family tradition, and it is therefore not astonishing to discover what we may confirm from other sources, that they convey a mixture of fact and legend:

> I frequently heard my father, of pious memory, say that although [grandfather] Everard died before he was thirty-six years old he had held my great-grandfather John's post as physician to Mary, the wife of the Emperor Maximilian. John lived on for many years, teaching medicine at Louvain in his old age when he was no longer fit for court service. His father Peter had been a physician as is known from his treatise on the fourth *Fen* of Avicenna as well as from certain books transcribed for him, which are still in the possession of my mother and which are such as were common to physicians of that time, manuscript copies made at great but now unnecessary expense.[1]

A second general source of information is the charter by which Vesalius was created a Count Palatine in 1556, for which it is assumed he supplied the biographical information.[2] The discrepancies between the two accounts may be explained by the fact that Vesalius was away from home while writing the earlier statement; in the later charter, because of its official nature, it seems likely he made greater effort to discover and provide a correct genealogy, possibly after consultation with other members of his family and investigation of any existing family archives.

In discussing his ancestors in the *Letter on the china root*, Vesalius remarked that during an enforced residence of several months in Nimwegen in 1546 he had found an opportunity to make a side trip by which, as he writes, "I was able to observe the tombs of the Witing family in the very ancient and famous [town of] Wesel in Cleves whence they originated, and I found the recollection of these ancestors of mine to be a very pleasant and sacred memory."

This ancestral family, called variously Wijtinck, Witinch, Witincx, and Witing, was originally native to the flourishing commercial town of Wesel at the confluence of the Rhine and the Lippe. Vesalius referred to it as "Wesel in Cleves," but the town, incorporated in 1241, had been a member of the Hanseatic League and, as late as 1521, an imperial free city. Nevertheless, Wesel was subject to the Duke of Cleves in 1546 when Vesalius made his pilgrimage to the original seat of the Witing family, where no doubt he gazed with proper reverence upon the tombs of his forebears. Perhaps he saw the tomb of Peter Witing, although the most recent student of Vesalius's family genealogy has declared that there is no record of any such person and that the earliest direct ancestor known was an Everard Witing (d. 1470), father of the John whom Vesalius mentions.[3]

Despite the somewhat shadowy figure of Peter Witing, we do find clear record of other members of the Witing family who were prominent in the local affairs of Wesel, although their exact relationship to the branch from which Vesalius ultimately derived is not known. An Eberhard Witing was burgomaster of Wesel in 1414 and 1428, and somewhat later a Hermann Witing was repeatedly burgomaster: 1452–1455, 1461–1462, 1466–1468, 1472, 1475, and 1477–1478.[4] According to Vesalius, his great-great-grandfather Peter was a physician of some scholarly attainment and repute who had written a treatise on the fourth *Fen* of Avicenna and, as we learn from Vesalius's charter of ennoblement, had attended upon the Emperor Frederick III.[5] However, Vesalius provides us with no information regarding the period of this Peter's imperial service during Frederick's long but ineffectual reign, which extended from 1440 to 1493, nor with any indication of the physician's life span—which would, however, have begun toward the close of the fourteenth century. Now we learn that this pretty story is most likely family legend and that Peter's medical manuscripts in the possession of Vesalius's mother must have descended to her from some other family source.

There is no question about the existence of John, the son of Peter Witing according to Vesalius, or of an Everard, according to the most recent inquiry [6] a man of some distinction who left many records and so provided strong documentary evidence regarding not only himself but his descendants as well. Whether John, born shortly after the opening of the fifteenth century, was a native of Wesel or Brussels, he was first mentioned in 1429 in a matriculation list of the newly founded University of Louvain. There he was recorded as *Johannes de Wesalia, doctor in medicinis*,[7] suggesting that he was already a mature man who had attended and obtained his degree from some other university—which was the only possibility for any Netherlander or, as with John, perhaps any native of the region of the lower Rhine valley, until the opening of the University of Louvain. Thus John Witing from Wesel, or, in the Latinized form he employed, Johannes de Wesalia, by distinguishing his or his family's place of origin provided a new name for his branch of the family; and, as that family came to identify itself with Brabant, so any significance of Wesalia as indicating a place of origin was lost, and the name Witing was replaced by Van Wesele, Vésale, and Vesalius.

At the opening of the University of Louvain in 1426 the professor of medicine was Jan van der Neel of Breda. In 1428 an assistant, Henri de Coster, or d'Oisterwyk, was added to the medical faculty, and thereafter when Neel took leave of absence, in 1430–1431, d'Oisterwyk was temporarily in charge of medical teaching with, in turn, the assistance of Johannes de Wesalia.[8] However, d'Oisterwyk appears to have been an unsuccessful teacher, and with the return of Neel he was apparently dropped from the faculty of medicine in favor of Johannes de Wesalia, whose success over the years can be gauged from the gradual increase of his stipend and his eventual achievement of what might be termed the chairmanship of the medical faculty.[9] His title was *medicinae doctor et professor*. At the request of the magistracy of Louvain, which wished to have a course in "mathematics," Johannes de Wesalia, who was recognized as having some skill in that discipline, was offered the "mathematical" lecture by the faculty of arts in 1431. During this time he held a secondary position in the faculty of medicine, receiving a relatively small quarterly salary of fifteen Rhenish florins,[10] but apparently he decided that his future lay in this field and therefore he declined the alternate position.[11] Previously, at the close of August 1430, he had been elected *rector trimestriel*, that is, rector for a period of three months, in accordance with the early practice at Louvain.[12] He was elected for a second time in 1433,[13] and for a third time on 29 November 1438.[14]

Throughout the *Acta*, which contain the discussions and official decisions of the University's faculty, there are frequent mentions of Johannes de Wesalia as a representative of the medical faculty on various committees for the election of the rector, as a judge in cases requiring disciplinary action within the university, and as a deputy of the university in various negotiations between it and the civic government of Louvain. In the full session of the faculty, on 25 February 1437, Johannes de Wesalia and Jan van der Neel are recorded as having appealed to the university for warnings and citations against students for nonpayments of fees,[15] and in 1446 there began a long-drawn-out contest between Johannes de Wesalia and Ludovicus de Dienst for the chair of medicine.

In 1443, sometime after 31 May, the date of the last reference to him in the *Acta* of that year,[16] Johannes de Wesalia took leave of absence from the university and allowed Ludovicus de Dienst[17] to act as his substitute. Why or for exactly how long Johannes de Wesalia was absent from the university is unknown. The first mention of him after his return is on 25 February 1446.[18] Thereafter, in the general session of the faculty, on 31 May 1446, this statement was made:

Johannes de Wesalia, doctor in medicine, explained in what way Master Ludovicus had been appointed in the year 1443 to maintain and to administer the lectureship in ordinary in medicine . . . in the name of and in the place of Master Johannes until the return of the same Master Johannes, and how the same Ludovicus had promised . . . to yield and hand over immediately the said lectureship in ordinary . . . as soon as the same Master Johannes should return to make the request; and how he had already requested many times that

[Ludovicus] should yield, but he had not yet done so to the grave prejudice of the honor and prestige of the said Master Johannes.[19]

As a result, Johannes requested the faculty to use its disciplinary power to remove Ludovicus as the usurper of his lectureship. In his defense Ludovicus replied that although he had been appointed temporarily to the chair, he had been appointed by the then-burgomaster Jocobus Utenlyemingen with the promise that, upon the return of Johannes, he, Ludovicus, would be rewarded with a prebend; that he recognized the position of Johannes de Wesalia and was obligated to him for many things, yet he could not relinquish the chair until he had received the promised compensation.

In the usual manner in such cases, the rector of the university appointed a committee to investigate the problem, and on 2 June 1446 it rendered its decision that the chair must be vacated on behalf of Johannes, but, in recognition of the claims of Ludovicus, Johannes must pay him "twenty to twenty-six" florins within a week.[20] The case continued with appeals from both sides [21] until, in the general session of the faculty, on 7 March 1447, with Johannes condemned finally to pay, the rector, in accordance with a perquisite of his office, laid claim to one-third the sum.[22]

It has been demonstrated from the archival records of Brussels that Johnnes de Wesalia became city physician; and although no evidence for the year of his appointment has been discovered, yet the fact that the last record of him in the university *Acta* is dated 1447 suggests that his appointment was no earlier than that year. A further document of 1471 concerned with a decrease in the city expenses and a reduction in the stipend of the city physician indicates his employment at least until that date,[23] although the reduction in stipend may have caused him to shift his services to the House of Burgundy. Yet if Vesalius's charter of ennoblement, in which Johannes is mentioned as physician to Duke Charles "for a long time," is correct, "for a long time" could mean at most only from 1467—when Charles inherited the ducal title—to 1476 —when Johannes died.

Johannes de Wesalia was twice married, the first time to Mathilde van Ellick, a union which produced five children: Everard, Jeanne, Henry, Paul, and Adolph. Two other children, Agnes and Barbe, were the result of a second marriage to Agnes Swarts or Sweerts, who survived her husband and thereafter married John, son of Nicolas de Costere, on 21 May 1477. Johannes died on 28 May 1476.[24] Doubt must therefore be expressed about Vesalius's recollection that Johannes was physician to "Mary [of Burgundy] wife of the Emperor Maximilian." Actually, Mary's father, Charles the Bold, did not die until the year after the death of Johannes and before Mary's marriage to Maximilian, but it is quite possible that Johannes as physician to the duke also rendered some service to the duke's daughter, who would later be the "wife of the Emperor Maximilian." It was also to Johannes that the heraldic device of the three weasels was officially granted by Frederick III, but for what cause or service is unknown.[25] Thus Johannes was responsible for both the later family name and the family device. The three weasels were also, incidentally, the insignia of the town of Wesel.

In the course of his life Johannes succeeded in acquiring a considerable fortune, possibly the source of the financial well-being of the later generations of the family, which seem never to have suffered any financial exigencies. Johannes eventually acquired the manor of Ter-Holst near Overyssche as a fief held from the duchy of Brabant, gained by purchase on 31 October 1464 from Jean Van den Bossche, also called Van der Holst. Several years later Johannes acquired a seigneury at Vieil-Héverlé and a water mill near Vaelbeke with its banal rights. Still later these properties, as well as those of the Witing family in Cleves, went to the sons of the first marriage of Johannes, to Mathilde Van Ellick.[26]

Of the several children of Johannes, the eldest was Everard. It is difficult, because of problems of chronology, to reconcile the Everard de Wesalia who matriculated at the University of Louvain in 1449 with the son of Johannes de Wesalia. Since we know that Everard died *c.* 1485 and that matriculating students were frequently about fifteen years old, he would then have lived to be far older than our knowledge of him indicates. In any event, Everard was mentioned as a doctor of medicine and a soldier by Molanus, an early historian of Brussels who, without citing the year, states that Everard died *quarte kal. Augusti* and lay buried near the altar of the Trinity in the collegiate church of St. Peter in Louvain.[27] Since we have record that after his death his brothers and sisters fell heir to his property in Cleves, which they sold, his death must have been before the date of the document of that sale, 19 July 1485.[28] We may, incidentally, consider this sale as marking a break with the old homeland and therefore now substitute the name Van Wesele or Vésale for Witing as the family name. There is evidence that Everard had already received his medical degree by 1461, since in that year he was paid a sum of money for medical services rendered,[29] and we must deny Vesalius's statement that Everard died when scarcely thirty-six years old and prior to his own father.

Everard was physician to the Archduke Maximilian, who had become regent of the Netherlands by reason of his marriage to Mary of Burgundy, and received from him an annual pension previously mentioned. According to Vesalius's charter of ennoblement Everard was also physician to Mary, who died in 1482, and to their children Philip, future father of Charles V, and Margaret. It may well have been, as Vesalius wrote, that Everard "took my great-grandfather's post as physician to Mary, the wife of the Emperor [but then Archduke] Maximilian." If the charter of ennoblement is correct in calling Everard physician to Margaret of Austria, it could only have been during the first several years of her life, since she was born in 1480 and he was dead by July 1485. However, there seems no reason not to accept Vesalius's further statement in the *Letter on the china root:* "I have his learned commentary on the books of Rhazes as well as his commentaries on the first

25

four sections of the *Aphorisms* of Hippocrates and some mathematical works, which indicate that he was a man of singular ability." [30] Everard was eventually advanced to the rank of knight,[31] but did not live to enjoy his honor for long.

One of Everard's brothers, Paul, is on the matriculation list of the University of Louvain for 29 August 1469 as "Paulus Wijtinc de Wesalia, diocese of Cambrai," undertaking the arts course in the Pedagogy of the Lily. Eventually he became M.A.[32] Little more is known of him except that he became affianced to Barbe Mast in the church of Sainte-Gulde in Brussels, 30 October 1488.[33] More is known of Henry, who matriculated at Louvain, 20 August 1465, identified as of the diocese of Liège, and who also entered the Lily.[34] Henry was apparently the man of business. It was he who, on behalf of all the children of the deceased Johannes, sold the manor of Ter-Holst to a Frederick Baers on 26 July 1487, and, as secretary of the town of Vilvorde, his name is even now to be found signed to a number of documents from the close of the fifteenth century. He died on 12 October 1525 after having been married twice, first to Ode Simoens, still alive in 1478, then to Marguerite de Ritar, who lived until 25 August 1537 and was then buried near her husband in the church of Vilvorde. Adolph, who was affianced to a Marguerite Serclaes in the church of Sainte-Gulde, 30 August 1497, became lieutenant-governor of the fortress of Vilvorde.[35]

Little is known of the sisters. Jeanne, the eldest, married Roland t'Seraerts or t'Serants and, with him, took possession of a seigneurie at Corbeek-Dyle near Louvain, 9 August 1456.[36] Her husband was one of the seven *échevins* of Brussels in 1460, 1487, 1488 during the civil war which was then ravaging the country, and 1502.[37] During the course of the civil war the cities of Brabant in general opposed Maximilian, who was then governing the territory in the name of his son Philip the Handsome, but Henry van Wesele remained faithful. As a result of his loyalty, the archduke handed over to Henry the goods of the t'Seraerts, which had been declared confiscated, but which Henry returned to their owners after the declaration of peace in 1489. The other daughters of Johannes de Wesalia were Agnes and Barbe. Barbe Wytincx became the wife of Jean Maubeert, and is mentioned in a document of 23 October 1530, and again in 1542 as a widow. Agnes, after being twice married, was still alive as a widow in 1517.[38]

In the next generation we find Andries Van Wesele, the illegitimate son of Everard Van Wesele and Marguerite s'Winters. There has been no mention of him hitherto in any of the family documents, which is possibly explained by his illegitimate birth (*c.* 1479). Moreover, and again possibly related to this situation, his imperial service was of a more humble sort than that of his illustrious predecessors. Andries had been trained as an apothecary, although we do not know where, and took imperial service. It has been said that he first served Margaret of Austria before entering the service of Charles V. At some date now unknown he married Isabel, born *c.* 1493, daughter of one Jacob Crabbe—whose family, contrary to occasional assertions, was Brabantine rather than English in origin—and Catherine Sweerts. Virtually nothing appears to be known of Jacob Crabbe, but he must have been of some local importance if he was the person of that name who served the city of Brussels as a *receveur*, or tax-collector, in 1487, 1489, 1491, and 1495, and as a plebeian councillor in 1494, 1498, 1500, and 1504. He died in 1527.[39]

As a dowry for his daughter, Jacob Crabbe provided a property situated on Helle Straetken, or Hell's Lane, more recently called the Rue du Manège. Thus the new home of Andries and Isabel Van Wesele was located in the southern part of Brussels not far from the city wall lying to the east. At that time the city was divided into ten *quartiers,* each in turn divided into ten sections, an arrangement originally established to promote an equable distribution of the burden of military service. The location of the Van Wesele home placed it in the *quartier de la Haute-Rue,* so named from a major thoroughfare, the Rue Haute, which led from the center of the city to the southern gate of Porte d'Obbrussel. Within the *quartier* the house was more precisely located within the *section du Sablon,*[40] so called from the Église du Sablon. Hence the Van Wesele family lived in an area fairly near the Banendael, or Bovendael, a large undeveloped section of Brussels, later called the *quartier des Minimes,* extending from the Hôpital St. Pierre-aux-Lepreux, near the southern gate of the city, northward to the Galgenberg. The Bovendael was the refuge of indigents and prostitutes, who had long constituted a problem since they tended to wander forth into the more respectable region of the Rue Haute.[41] Between the Bovendael and the Van Wesele home rose the Montagne de la Potence, or Galgenberg, partly open field and partly wooded, at the top of which were the instruments of torture and execution used upon condemned criminals, and where the remains of these unfortunates were left hanging indefinitely at the mercy of birds and the passage of time. This area is today covered by the Palais de Justice.[42]

In this home, in its far-from-cheerful setting, the children of Andries and Isabel Van Wesele were born. The first child was christened Nicolas; of him little is known except that he is mentioned in a list of citizens of Brussels in 1526,[43] and it may be that his Christian name was reflective of a family friend, Nicolas Florenas, or Herco, to whom consideration will be given later. The second child was André or Andreas, who was in time to become the most famous member of the family; then François, destined for a legal career but influenced by his brother's activities to study medicine.[44] The fourth child was Anne, later the wife of Nicolas Bonnaert, *barbier de corps* of Charles V who, toward the end of his life, gave Bonnaert the functions of *bailli* of Zeerikzee in Zeeland.[45] Nicolas Bonnaert and his wife also became the owners in Brussels of the celebrated house called the Cantersteen, which they left to their children, and which was later occupied by the Société de la Grande Harmonie.[46]

Chapter III

THE YOUTH OF VESALIUS
IN BRUSSELS AND LOUVAIN,
1514–1533

ESPITE lack of absolute certainty as to the date of birth of André, or Andreas Vesalius as we shall call him, it seems most probable that he was born on 31 December 1514. This presumption is based upon a horoscope of Vesalius cast by Girolamo Cardano,[1] who was well acquainted with his subject, at least by correspondence, and who, in his various writings, appears to have possessed considerable information about details of Vesalius's life.[2] Indeed, Vesalius himself provides some information by remarking in the dedicatory preface to the *Fabrica*, dated 1 August 1542, that at that time he had not yet reached his twenty-eighth year.[3] Had the horoscope been cast at the time of his birth it would have been cause for much rejoicing in the Van Wesele household. "Zeal and skill of hands," an "admirable mind and eloquence," "glory," "celebrity after death"—all would suggest remarkable if not uncanny prognostication had not the subject already been famous when the horoscope was cast.

On the more mundane level we have almost no information about his early life in Brussels. Owing to the frequent and lengthy absences of his father, Andreas and his brothers and sister must have been raised by their mother, a woman of great competence although not devoid of all the superstitions of that age. In future years, in the *Fabrica*, when discussing foetal coverings, Vesalius was to remark:

> Sometimes during childbirth, with the outermost covering still adhering very strongly to the uterus, the foetus first makes its appearance with the innermost covering wrapped around its head, legs, or arms. In such cases women carefully and superstitiously preserve it, and also it is greatly sought after by occult philosophers. As mothers always preserve both the innermost and second [covering] for the sake of their sons—as I saw my very dear mother do—so the outer covering is scraped from the second, after which these membranes are carefully washed, lightly stuffed with straw, and dried like bladders.[4]

Vesalius does not make clear to which of the Van Wesele children his mother's action referred, but it must have been to his younger brother

Franciscus or to some other unmentioned later child, perhaps dead at birth or during infancy.

The absences from home of Andries the father, an imperial pharmacist, were because of his position, which compelled him to travel with the emperor's train. Thus, for example, as early as 1517 the children were deprived of the presence of their father, then absent in Spain,[5] and there is record of another absence in 1521.[6] It may be assumed that there were many other but unrecorded such instances, although the father was presumably in Brussels in 1525 when both he and his neighbor and relative Jean Martin Stern had their homes reconstructed, with the result that they extended several feet out into the public thoroughfare, for which the two men were compelled to pay an annual tax of two *deniers*. Jean Martin, it may be added, was not only a relative but also a pharmacist, and years later, when referring in the *Fabrica* to student days in Louvain, Vesalius was to acknowledge his own relationship to the family Martin Stern, or Stella, of whom the most notable members were the jurists Guillaume and Jean, and their brother Michael, a printer who became a citizen of Basel in 1555.[7]

For lack of any evidence to the contrary, we can only assume that young Andreas Vesalius began his formal education in Brussels somewhere around 1520. By that time there were satisfactory elementary schools in the city—notably that of the Brothers of the Common Life, whose schools throughout the Netherlands had played no little part in the improvement of the educational methods and curriculum of elementary schools. On 29 July 1515, the city government of Brussels granted the Brothers of the Common Life permission to teach grammar, logic, and music to sixty children of the city and to receive from each of them a tuition of six *sous*. The school was a success from the start and came to include among its students youthful members of the best families of Brussels.[8] If young Andreas received the best available preparatory education, as later he appears to have had the means of gaining the best medical education, it is likely he attended this school. It was located in the west central section of Brussels in the Place de Saint-Géry at some distance from Helle Straetken, but could be reached by following the Rue Haute into the center of the city and then continuing along the Rue de la Violette, Rue de l'Ami, Rue des Pierres, and so into the Place de Saint-Géry.

With the completion of these elementary or "trivial" studies—grammar, dialectic, and rhetoric—presumably toward the close of 1529, and so prepared for the university course, young Andreas, now about fifteen years old, left Brussels for Louvain. Although boys of that time developed self-reliance at an early age, it was still desirable to make the trip to Louvain in company with either a group of students leaving for the same destination or possibly with some merchant's company. The dangers of the road could not lightly be dismissed. However, whatever party Vesalius traveled with, it most likely left Brussels by the gate called Porte de Louvain, which opened onto the Chemin de Louvain leading directly toward the famous university town no great distance away. This was probably during the month of February 1530, since the young student matriculated under the name of "Andreas van Wesel de Bruxella" on 25 February 1530 [9] and took up residence in the Pedagogium Castrense, or Castle School, which we may liken to a college of the university.

In the years immediately after the opening of the university in 1426 it had been found that the lack of a generally available and adequate elementary education had frequently resulted in students being insufficiently prepared, especially in the all-important command of Latin, to carry on university studies. Because of this, a number of pedagogia or preparatory schools had developed in Louvain and ultimately become associated with the university. Their primary function had originally been to give the students sufficient training in the Latin needed in all activities of the university, and the schools were numerous at first, but consisted of little more than a master and a group of students. Gradually university supervision had reduced their number, improved their quality, and widened the scope of their teaching. [10]

In 1446 the faculty of arts of the university had given official recognition to four of these pedagogia, which had names reflecting commonplace associations such as the Lily, so-called because of its proximity to an inn called the Lily Flower, the Porc, the Falcon, and the Castle. Gradually these four schools took over the teaching of the seven liberal arts—the trivium and the quadrivium—and their faculties came to constitute the faculty of arts.

The Castle School, with which young Andreas Vesalius was associated, was near the gate of the first wall of the city and took its name from the Rue du Château, later renamed Rue de Malines, which led to a hill on which the fortress, or Château de César, as it was called, was situated. In accordance with the organization of the pedagogia, the school was directed by a regent, assisted by a subregent, two primary and two secondary professors. During the period in which Vesalius was a student in the Castle, the regent was Cornelius Brouwers, called Scultetus, of Weert, who held the position until his death in 1539. However, as a canon of St. Donation in Bruges and as governor of the College of Saint Jérôme at Leyden, he was frequently absent and consequently turned the direction of the school over to the subregent Joannes van den Bossche, who was succeeded in this secondary position in 1529 by Joannes Scarleye of 's Hertogenbosch. [11] In addition to the subregent, there may have been the following professors teaching during this period: Joannes Herck of Rethy, Antonius Corvilanus, and Joannes Reinerus of Weert. [12]

After having established his residence in the Castle, Vesalius matriculated by registering his name with the rector of the university and paying his tuition, the minimum amount since he was neither of noble family nor as yet twenty-five years old. He then swore to observe the laws and statutes of the university, to maintain a peaceful and proper existence, and to shun heresy and remain true to the Roman faith. [13] In its efforts to protect the young students, the university, through its statutes, provided many specific prohibitions, the breach of which could result in fine or imprisonment. Thus the student must not bear arms, dice in public taverns, or be found walking the streets of Louvain at night [14]—and an ordinance of Charles the Bold stipulated that "night" be interpreted as beginning at nine o'clock in the summer and at eight in the winter.[15]

We can identify several of the other young students at the Castle who were contemporary with Vesalius. Most notable was Anthony Perrenot de Granvelle, 1517–1586, who entered the Castle in 1528, and who was later chancellor of Charles V and of Philip II, as well as successively bishop, archbishop, primate of the Netherlands, and cardinal.[16] The friendship that developed between Vesalius and Perrenot was a lasting one, and the future anatomist later referred several times to his boyhood friend who upon occasion used his high position to be of service. A second contemporary was Gerard van Veltwyck, c. 1505–1555, who entered the Castle in 1528 to begin an education that led eventually to high diplomatic posts in the imperial service, membership in the privy council, and the reward of the Golden Fleece.[17] He, too, was mentioned later by Vesalius. Georg Casant, or Cassander, 1513–1566, entered the Castle in 1531, and although Vesalius never mentioned this later-distinguished patristic scholar, Cassander was eventually the recipient of one of the several accounts of the final days and death of his former schoolmate.[18] Still other contemporaries in the Castle were Louis Gennes, or Gensius, ultimately headmaster of Bergues-St. Winoc,[19] who, although never mentioned by Vesalius, maintained correspondence with Andreas Masius, 1514–1573,[20] a friend of Vesalius in Louvain days and later his patient.

The curriculum of the Castle was directed toward the student's attainment of the degree of master of arts, roughly the equivalent of the present-day bachelor's degree. Thus the master of arts was the requirement for entrance into a graduate or professional school. Latin and Greek, both language and literature, philosophy, and rhetoric comprised a major portion of the necessary studies, usually imparted by the lecture system, although the student's participation was occasionally required in the form of argumentation in support of set theses. Later, in the *Fabrica*, Vesalius gave a brief glimpse of his academic life in the Castle when he wrote:

I recall clearly that when I was at the Castle School of the University of Louvain —certainly its leading and most distinguished school—I devoted myself to philosophy. In such commentaries on Aristotle's *De anima* as were read to us by our teacher, a theologian by profession and therefore, like the other instructors at that school, ready to introduce his own pious views into those of the philosophers, the brain was said to have three ventricles.[21]

The teacher mentioned may well have been the subregent Joannes Scarleye, professor of philosophy in the Castle as well as successively baccalaureate and then licentiate in sacred theology. Presumably Vesalius was embarked on the arts course, a necessity for his later matriculation into a professional school, but a course of study that quite obviously had a strong medieval flavor. There is no way of ascertaining which of the many medieval commentaries of Aristotle was employed at the time of the aforesaid incident, although actually the concern in this instance was with pseudo-Aristotelian matter since the *De anima* contains nothing on the three ventricles of which Vesalius speaks. His recollection continues to explain that the students were being introduced to the medieval notion of the location of the five senses in the brain, apparently a kind of primitive study of psychology, and that they not only took notes on this matter, but "we were shown a figure from a certain *Margarita philosophica* . . . which we depicted, each student according to his skill as a draughtsman, and added it to our notes." One can easily identify the figure Vesalius copied from Gregory Reisch's *Margarita philosophica,* a late medieval encyclopedia first published in 1502.

We are provided a second glimpse of the curriculum when, in later years, concerned with the formation of the foetus, Vesalius recalled two medieval texts that were apparently intended as part of the arts course, although the first introduced him to medieval errors on the subject of embryology. "I recall that while I was still a boy learning the rudiments of dialectics I read [on the subject of embryology] in that very unlearned book of Albertus Magnus, *De virorum mulierumque secretis,* as well as what Michael Scot presents barbarously and ignorantly on that subject and on physiognomy." [22] The *Secreta mulierum et virorum,* of which Albertus may or may not have been the author, was a very popular work and available in a large number of editions. Michael Scot's thirteenth-century treatise *Liber physiognomiae,* printed at least as early as 1477, was also popular and readily available. Vesalius was presumably concerned with the section dealing with procreation, possibly the origin of the belief that the uterus was divided into seven cells. [23]

Such recollections make it appear that even well before he had entered upon his medical studies Vesalius may have had some interest in that direction, and this view is somewhat strengthened by what may be termed his extracurricular research. For instance, these remarks, containing incidentally a reference to his cousin, are found in the *Fabrica:*

Matters of this sort are also described by lawyers, and in addition to what I learned [from their writings], also I learned from my relative Guillaume Martin Stern, a learned man, well-read in both kinds of law and a remarkable student of the works of nature, when the foetus ought to be called complete, as well as the opinion of our divine Hippocrates who asserted that one of seven months' birth is complete. This was on an occasion when we had a lengthy discussion on the formation of the foetus. [24]

In addition to the studies Vesalius pursued in the Castle, possibly he attended lectures in the Pedagogium Trilingue, which were free and open to all students regardless of their school affiliation. This college had been founded by the beneficence of Jerome Busleyden, as its alternate name of Busleyden's College indicates, primarily for the study of the three classical tongues: Greek, Latin, and Hebrew. The professor of Latin was Conrad Wackers Gockelen, called Goclenius, who began his teaching in 1519 with a mastery of his subject that won the warm praise of Erasmus and that, in 1539, led Gemma Phrysius, a friend of Vesalius, to call Goclenius one of the *lumina* of the University of Louvain. It was perhaps in the Pedagogium Trilingue that Vesalius acquired his considerable fluency—as well as unfortunate verbosity—in Latin. How well Vesalius knew Greek has remained a question, but whatever the extent of his knowledge, possibly greater than sometimes credited to him, he may have acquired some of it from Rutger Ressen, or Rescius, of Maeseyck, who obtained the chair in Greek in 1518 when insufficient funds made it impossible for the College to attract a more distinguished scholar.[25] The lectures of Rescius appear to have been well received at first, although later his inadequacy by comparison with Goclenius, his colleague in Latin, became apparent—so much so that at one time Rescius despondently thought of resigning, only to be dissuaded from it by Erasmus in 1522.[26] About 1525 Rescius married and accepted a boarder into his wife's house—one Jean Sturm, who studied in Louvain from 1524 to 1528 and who, as we shall see, was either already, or was later in Paris, a friend of Vesalius.

Although Vesalius's knowledge of Hebrew was slight, and years afterward he studied that language with a Jewish physician, Lazarus de Frigeis, he may possibly have attended some of the lectures on Hebrew in the Pedagogium Trilingue. For most of the time during which he was resident in Louvain, the professor of Hebrew was Joannes van Campen, or Campenis, who, however, in 1529–30 entrusted the rudiments of the language to Nicolas Beken, called Clenardus, later a scholar and humanist of some fame.[27] In February 1532 Campensis was succeeded by Andreas van Gennep, or Balenus, of Basel.

It is not known whether Vesalius had already determined upon a medical career when first he matriculated at Louvain or whether this decision was made only after he had been studying there for some time. In any event, his first published writing, the *Paraphrasis in nonum librum Almansoris* (1537), is dedicated to Nicolas Florenas in terms that acknowledge the advice that physician had given him: "When you became aware several years ago that I was going to study medicine you desired to prescribe for me an excellent and useful system for studying the Hippocratic art, which I have followed with the greatest possible diligence." That these words contain more sincerity than the usual flattery of such dedications is suggested by the dedication of the *Venesection letter* of 1539, also to Florenas, in which the latter is termed "patron of my early studies" and one to whom "I owe whatever erudition or suggestion of such attainments I possess"; and "anyone observing the mutual understanding between us . . . might regard you as my parent rather than my friend." We may interpret Vesalius's reference to his decision of "several years ago" to study medicine as referring to some period during his residence in Louvain. It may have been originally intended that he follow his father into the profession of pharmacy, or possibly it had been planned, as with his brother Franciscus, that he undertake a legal career. It is tempting to consider that all such plans, whatever they may have been, were altered by the legitimization of his father in October 1531, and that perhaps the boy might now have aspired to follow the family tradition of imperial service on a more exalted level than that of pharmacy.

It must have been a time of rejoicing for the Van Wesele family when the emperor acknowledged the petition:

. . . [of] our well-loved *valet de chambre* and apothecary, Andries de Wesele, natural and illegitimate son of the late Everard, in his lifetime doctor, council-lor, and noted physician of our cherished lord and grandfather the Emperor Maximilian . . . and by this Everard conceived of the body of Marguerite 's-Winters . . . supplicating very humbly his desire for legitimization and re-moval of the blemish upon his birth by our favor.

The fact that the legitimization, which was granted, was also per-formed without payment was in itself an honor, ". . . in considera-tion of the continual service which [Andries] has performed for us in his capacity of *valet de chambre* and apothecary and which we hope he will continue to perform.[28]

Whatever the motive, once determined upon a medical career young Andreas Vesalius would need advice that perhaps his father could not give him; or perhaps his father was too frequently away from home. In either event, the physician Florenas, a friend of the family and for one reason or another serving *in loco parentis,* could well fit the need. Florenas had himself studied at Louvain, where he had received the master of arts degree in 1509, which suggests that he was a little younger than the boy's father. After having studied medicine he entered practice in Bruges but interrupted it for a period of study in Bologna, whence he returned to Bruges, then went to Arras in 1529, to Mechlin, and finally took im-perial service. In his capacity of imperial physician he followed the em-peror to Spain, where a possibly hyperbolic statement of Vesalius in the dedication to the *Venesection letter* terms him "archiater." Florenas was knighted in 1540.[29] If Florenas advised Andreas on the course of study to be followed, he may also have suggested pursuing his studies in Paris rather than in Louvain, despite the fact that the young man's dis-tinguished ancestor Johannes de Wesalia had held a chair of medicine in the latter university. Certainly at this time the quality of medical educa-tion in Louvain was not high, and anyone able to do so was well advised to seek his training elsewhere. Let us assume, therefore, that with this decision made, the young student remained in the family home until about the close of August 1533, when he set forth for Paris to continue his studies.

Chapter IV

MEDICAL STUDIES IN PARIS, 1533–1536

ESALIUS must have been settled in his quarters in Paris by September 1533,[1] and possibly he took lodgings with Jean Sturm. Sturm had recently come from Louvain where Vesalius may have met him, or possibly Rutger Rescius, with whom Sturm had boarded in Louvain, had suggested such lodgings.[2] The fact of Sturm's renting quarters to students is clearly indicated in a letter of Pierre Schriesheimer, latinized as Siderander, of Strasburg. In that letter, dated 28 May 1533, and addressed to Jacques Bédrot, professor of Greek and Latin at Strasburg, Siderander had much to say about student life and affairs in Paris. In the course of his remarks he stated that he had wished to lodge with Jean Sturm in company with Swiss and German students, but Sturm had demanded thirty crowns, which he was unable to pay. "I plan to change my lodgings at the end of the month and take my meals at the home of a certain printer who asks only twenty crowns. Up till now I have always paid twenty-four although occasionally more."[3] If Vesalius did lodge with Sturm, it is merely further indication that his family, in comfortable financial condition, provided him with ample funds.

The medical school reopened on 14 September, the Feast of the Exaltation of the Cross, although the official and ceremonious reopening did not occur until 18 October. At some time around the middle of September Vesalius must have presented himself to the proper authorities in the school's offices in the Rue de la Bûcherie and produced his baptismal record certifying that he was of the Catholic faith and giving his name, place of birth, and nationality. When Vesalius left Louvain for Paris in 1533 he was too young to be admitted to the degree of master of arts, but we may assume that he had completed the requirements for it, in which event the student usually was promoted when he came of age. Therefore, since the degree was required for entrance into the medical school of Paris, it is likely that he had with him documentary evidence indicating that he held the degree potentially, or else that he had a special license, sometimes granted by the University of Louvain, which would mention him in the list of promotions as *extra ordinem*. This is another point on which we have no information.

We do have some information concerning isolated incidents in Vesalius's years in Paris, but these far from cover the approximately three years he spent there. For the most part we can do little more than describe the usual academic life of the medical student in Paris, and for this we must turn to the statutes of the faculty of medicine. These statutes were first brought together in 1350 and, although subject to some modifications in succeeding years, they remained basically the same until 1602. Unhappily the original volume of statutes has disappeared, but prior to their loss a French translation of them was published.[4] A second source of information is the Commentaries of the faculty of medicine. Each dean had the responsibility of keeping a record of all significant activities and decisions of the faculty during his term of office, and these records or Commentaries run from 1395 to 1786. Those through 1516 have been published;[5] the later ones, including those for 1533–1536 when Vesalius was in Paris, remain unpublished.[6]

According to the statutes of the faculty of medicine no one could obtain the baccalaureate in medicine unless he had already received the degree of master of arts and then pursued a course of study in medicine for thirty-six months, or four academic years. Under certain conditions, however, if the student lacked the degree of master of arts he might acquire the baccalaureate after forty-eight months of residence, although if the candidate came from a foreign university the length of his course was doubled.[7] This was the letter of the law, but it was frequently softened in practice, and there were instances of candidates petitioning successfully for the right to take their examinations well before completion of the prescribed course.[8] Nevertheless, the three years Vesalius spent in Paris would not under any circumstances have met the requirement of length of study, and there is no evidence that he had reached the point of petitioning for his examination at the time he left in 1536. There is no mention at all of Vesalius in the Commentaries—but students prior to their baccalaureate were not as a rule mentioned individually. Nor do we know whether entrance into the medical school was governed by age,[9] although Vesalius, in his nineteenth year, was somewhat younger than most entering candidates.

At any rate, with the details of registration attended to and his fees paid, Vesalius matriculated in the medical school of the University of Paris and became a candidate for the baccalaureate in medicine. He was now termed a *philiater*, one devoted to medicine.

By present standards the medical school was modest in the extreme. The faculty of medicine was far from wealthy and the growth of its property had been slow and beset by difficulties. In 1470 it rented from the Carthusians a building in the Rue de la Bûcherie [10] which it proceeded to alter to suit its purposes and then purchased outright in 1486.[11] The ground floor appears to have been used for lecture halls [12] and the first floor served in part for an assembly hall.[13] In 1513–1514 the faculty began the acquisition of a neighboring residence with its garden, the Trois-Rois, and gained complete possession in 1533.[14] In 1529 a new chapel had been constructed in the location formerly held by the faculty's library,[15] although the records do not indicate where the library was moved. In the course of rebuilding the chapel the floor was raised some three feet and glass windows were installed, representing the Virgin and St. Luke surrounded by kneeling students.

The faculty of medicine was composed of doctors of medicine who taught regularly in the school and who were known as regent doctors. A regent doctor gained his position only after he had taught at least two years without interruption and had presided over the disputation of a thesis.[16] Those doctors of medicine who did not teach were called nonregent and usually had no part in the administration of the school's affairs, although occasionally they might be summoned to special and extraordinary assemblies. An exception was made for certain doctors who held positions of importance elsewhere that did not permit them to participate in the affairs of the school. Thus a royal doctor would be considered—if he desired—as an honorary member of the faculty, an honorary regent doctor.[17] Subject to the faculty, but not members of it, were the students of all grades, candidates for the baccalaureate, the licentiate, and the doctorate.

The faculty was a democratic body and elected its own officers for stated periods of time. At the head of the faculty were two regent doctors, the "ancient" or oldest doctor, and the dean, the actual director of affairs. The ancient, however, had mainly an honorary and venerable status which led all to arise upon his entry into the school,[18] and it was customary for the banquet of St. Luke and the examination of candidates for what was called the *probatio temporis* to be held in his house.[19] He did, however, have two perquisites of some importance. On the occasion of examinations when money gifts were presented to the faculty, the ancient received a gift double the amount received by the others; and, if need be, in the absence of the dean he was empowered to convoke the regent doctors.[20]

Vesalius probably first became acquainted with the dean when that official stamped the new student's certificate and pocketed a fee of six *sous*.[21] The dean who performed this function for Vesalius in 1533 was Jean Vasses of Meaux.[22] As the chief administrative officer, the dean, who spoke and acted for the entire faculty, had little time for teaching and was seldom a professor; indeed, he frequently had to call upon one of his predecessors for administrative assistance. It was the dean's task to discipline, to preside at examinations, and to approve theses. The Commentaries, statutes, and seals [23] of the faculty were in his charge, and he was required to make a further redaction of the Commentaries for the period of his tenure of office. He was also trustee of the goods and funds of the faculty, for which he had to render an account within two weeks of the end of his term of office. It was only the dean who had the authority to convoke the faculty—unless he were absent, when, as has been said, it might be convoked by the ancient.

The dean's powers spread beyond the faculty of medicine, since he, at least in theory, presided over the examination of surgeons and apothecaries, and was empowered to visit the shops of the apothecaries to observe the quality of their drugs. It was also the dean, at least in theory once again, who dispensed the cadavers for anatomy, not only in the medical school but also to the surgeons of the College of St. Côme and to the students.[24]

The dean's position was one of great prestige as well as power. With the ancient he assisted at the autopsy of a deceased king and signed the death certificate, and then, dressed in ceremonial costume of scarlet hose, robe, and cap, he followed the royal funeral cortege. If the dean were to die in office, he had the consolation of a splendid funeral with twelve torches, whereas a dean who had completed his term, or a professor, was allowed only six torches, and an ordinary regent doctor a mere four.[25]

The dean was elected on the Saturday following the Feast of All Saints, and although the method of electing him had from time to time been subject to controversy and was later changed, as yet he was chosen by four electors. These electors were regent doctors chosen one each from the four nations of the university—French, Picard, Norman, and German, the somewhat artificial categories of university members according to place of origin. In actual practice there were many Englishmen in the German nation, which, prior to the long and bitter struggle of the Hundred Years' War, had even been called the English nation.[26] Vesalius was associated with the medical school during the election of Jean Tagault as dean in 1534; Tagault continued in that office during the remainder of Vesalius's student days in Paris.[27]

The faculty had one other type of official, the beadle, who was the servant of the faculty rather than an officer in it, and Vesalius may first have come to know of the beadles when he attended the mass celebrated at the official reopening of the school on 18 October. There were two beadles, a principal and an underbeadle, nonacademic assistants to the dean and faculty. It was the task of the beadles to convoke the regent doctors orally or, on occasion, by signed announcement from the dean, and they assisted in various capacities at examinations, at mass, and generally at all assemblies of the faculty. They announced the courses to be given, and three times a year read the statutes of the medical faculty to the students.[28] Each beadle had a silver mace as his insignia of office.[29]

At nine o'clock on the morning of 18 October, the day of St. Luke, patron saint of physicians, the official reopening of the school of medicine took place with the celebration of a solemn mass in the school's chapel. The curate of Saint-Étienne-du-Mont, officially invited by the bachelors of medicine on the preceding Saturday, presided. This spectacle was both the first opportunity that Vesalius had to see the whole school—faculty and students—assembled, and his first participation in any function of the school. A procession led by the beadles carrying their silver maces opened this solemn affair. Next came the dean, resplendent in purple cassock, scarlet robe bordered with ermine, and square bonnet; on either side of the dean walked the two professors, and thereafter, in order of age, the older group of regent doctors, followed by the younger. In the rear of the faculty came the licentiates, the baccalaureates, and the unqualified students. Vesalius, possibly somewhat hesitant on this first occasion, was in the final group; absence would have caused him to be fined the sum of two *sous*.[30]

After the celebration of the mass there was appropriate music followed by a sermon. Then the dean advanced to the altar to present a gift to the officiating priest, and when this had been done the principal beadle announced the set phrase, "Gentlemen, my masters, to your assembly," whereupon the regent doctors gathered in the upper hall of their school to consider affairs of the faculty.

Vesalius was then at liberty until nine o'clock the following morning when a mass was celebrated for the deceased regent doctors,[31] after which everyone moved on to the school's assembly hall where the principal beadle read the statutes aloud for the benefit of the students.[32] This was necessary since infringements of the statutes were subject to the penalty of a fine. For example, it was necessary for Vesalius to know that once he had entered the medical school he must not frequent the Rue du Fouarre, the location of the faculty of arts,[33] and that he must attend mass every Saturday.[34] To ensure that the students were properly acquainted with these statutes, they were read to them on two other occasions, after the Christmas holiday and at the end of the school year in June.[35]

Except for those courses conducted by the bachelors, which might begin earlier, the courses given by members of the faculty of medicine, that is, the regent doctors, commenced the second week of November and were continued daily until the 28 June, with the exception of certain feast days ordained by the church, as well as the faculty's own holidays: Friday and Saturday before Easter, Pentecost, Christmas, Thursday of each week, days of processions of the rector of the university, feast days of St. Nicholas in May, St. Luke in October, St. Catherine in November, and St. Nicholas in December. The lectures were delivered in Latin except for one course in surgery, given in French.[36]

The teaching in the medical school was carried on in two forms, the lectures given by the regent doctors called ordinary lectures, and the exposition made by the bachelors called *cursus*. Although any regent doctor could and was supposed to teach, usually in the afternoon, in 1506 it had been determined that thenceforth two regent doctors would be chosen each year, subject to reëlection, one to give a daily lecture in the morning and the other in the afternoon. Those so chosen were called professors-in-ordinary, and each was granted a salary of twelve *livres*,[37] later raised to fifteen. Their number remained fixed at two during the period of Vesalius's studies in Paris. The professors-in-ordinary chosen for the academic year 1533–34 were Jacques Froment, or Fourment, and Jean Fernel; those for 1534–35 were Jean Fernal and Jean Guinter, for whom the salary was raised from fifteen to twenty-five *livres;* and those for 1535–36, Vesalius's final year in Paris, were Guinter and Froment.[38] The teaching of the professors-in-ordinary and the regent doctors was carried on from eight to eleven o'clock in the morning and from two to four in the afternoon, and so long as the class of one of the professors-in-ordinary was in session all other instruction, public or private, was prohibited.[39]

Generally, but not always, the first year's courses dealt with those subjects we would call materia medica, pharmacy, and physiology; the second, with pharmacy, pathology, and surgery; the third, with physiology, materia medica, and pathology; and the fourth, with physiology, surgery, and pathology.[40] A more specific teaching program was assigned to the two professors, which guaranteed that the curriculum would be covered. One year they were required to teach the "natural subjects"—anatomy, physiology, and botany—and the "non-natural"—hygiene and regimen. The following year instruction was given in subjects "contrary to nature"—pathology and therapeutics.[41]

The regent doctor, discoursing from his high chair, leaned heavily on exposition of ancient and medieval writers such as Hippocrates, Galen, Theophilus—*On urines* and *On the pulse*—Isaac—*De viatico*—Avicenna, Averroes, Avenzoar, Rhazes, and the precepts of the Salernitan school. Although these medical texts remained in use during the period that Vesalius was in Paris, gradually greater emphasis was placed upon the recovered Greek classics of medicine.

The *cursus* was given by the bachelors at five o'clock in the morning during the summer months and at six o'clock in the winter, and for this reason they were sometimes known as *Legentes de mane* or early morning lecturers. The bachelors, although not part of the faculty, were nevertheless closely attached to it by an oath of obedience and loyalty, and by a promise to assist at all ceremonies and to remain celibate during the remainder of their studies for the licentiate or doctorate. They were required, furthermore, to hold four courses,[42] but unlike the regent doctors they discoursed from a small chair, and their courses were strictly regulated and in some degree represented a version of what they as students had had professed to them previously by the regent doctors. Thus, according to the outlines given them by the dean, they were required to devote fifty lectures to the *Aphorisms* of Hippocrates, thirty to the *Regimen,* thirty-eight to the *Acute diseases,* and thirty-six to the *Prognostics.* In similar fashion and in accordance with the requirements they proceeded to specific allotments of lectures on Galen, Avicenna, and so on.[43]

There is a catalogue of the faculty's library in 1516 that indicates a great preponderance of medieval and Moslem works. Of Galen at that time there was little and of Hippocrates less,[44] but until the end of the fifteenth century the library had grown mainly on the strength of legacies so that it did not necessarily represent the most recent medical opinion. The opening of the sixteenth century had ushered in the revived classical school of medicine and witnessed great activity in the publication of the Greek texts of Galen and Hippocrates and the even more-frequent publication of Latin translations of them by such men as Linacre and, in the faculty itself, Jean Vasses and Guinter of Andernach. Some reflection of the conquest made by the classical physicians is seen in the decision of the faculty in 1526 to purchase the Greek text of Galen published by Aldus in the previous year and a similar decision in the following year to purchase the works of Hippocrates.[45]

Vesalius did not remain in Paris long enough to take the examinations for the baccalaureate in medicine, but it is of interest to note what those examinations comprised and therefore what sort of preparation he must have been making. The examinations for the baccalaureate were usually held every two years, in the even-numbered years, although exceptions were sometimes made to this regulation. By order of the dean and the regent doctors the examinations commenced at the beginning of March, having been previously announced toward the middle of February by proclamations signed by the principal beadle and posted on the doors of the school and in the squares of the city. They consisted of oral examinations on anatomy, physiology, hygiene, pathology, and botany; two theses, one on pathology or physiology, the other on hygiene; and finally an examination in anatomy and surgery.[46]

After mass on the Saturday preceding the fourth Sunday before Easter, the candidates for the baccalaureate, in their academic dress, gathered in the upper hall of the school where they were met by the dean and regent doctors. One of the candidates spoke on behalf of all of them and requested admission to the examination, a formal action called the supplication, and in response the oldest of the doctors present interrogated each candidate on his name, place of birth, religion, and, as a formality, asked him a question on a medical subject. In addition, the candidates were required to supply a certificate of good moral character signed by three doctors of the faculty. These testimonial letters had to bear the seal of the faculty, for which the candidates were required to pay the fairly large sum of six *livres* to the faculty and one *livre* ten *sous* to the principal beadle, and were then presented to the dean of the faculty.

On the following Saturday, after mass, the regent doctors assembled in their hall to hear the report on the testimonial letters, and, if all was in order, the following week was given over to examinations: Monday for physiology and anatomy, Tuesday for hygiene, Wednesday for pathology—all, of course, in Latin.[47] The examination was extensive, with each examiner usually questioning the candidate for about half an hour, so that each day the candidate might be questioned for a total of two or three hours. Thursday was a holiday, and the questioning was taken up again on Friday when, with the dean and the oldest of the regent doctors present to begin the interrogation, each candidate was given an aphorism of Hippocrates about which several questions were asked and several contradictory syllogisms were presented in order to promote discussion and so determine the student's dialectical ability. With this, the first part of the examination was completed.[48]

The following day, Saturday, after mass, all the doctors assembled in their hall to hear the report on each candidate, whereupon by a voice vote they determined the admission or refusal of the candidates. Thereafter the new bachelors were introduced into the hall where the dean presented them with the results of the examinations together with an oath of loyalty and submission to the faculty. Although the successful candidates were now termed bachelors, the examination was still incomplete.[49] The candidate had next to undergo an examination on botany which took place in May or June, although in Vesalius's time this examination was more an exercise than a regular examination since the student was required merely to take note of the plants in the botanical garden and present a catalogue of them to the dean.[50]

The rest of the academic year and the summer vacation were used to prepare for sustaining the theses, which began in November. The first of these was the "quodlibet thesis"; as its name implies it was a thesis chosen on any subject of physiology or pathology, and mention of it can be found as far back as one can read in the Commentaries. The subjects of the theses were usually of little intrinsic importance but were chosen more to given indication of the dialectical skill of the student. The sustaining of the theses began on the first Thursday after the feast day of St. Martin, 11 November, and one candidate was presented each successive Thursday in sessions lasting from six in the morning until noon, until all had finished. The dean presided and directed the discussion, granting or refusing the right of speech, and when the examination was over the question of success or failure was put to the assembled doctors for decision.[51]

During the winter, after the quodlibet thesis, the examination in anatomy took place. In the new statutes of the faculty of medicine, drawn up toward the end of the sixteenth century, a week was given to this examination. On the first and second days the students dissected the abdomen and viscera; on the third, the chest; the fourth, the head; the fifth, the muscles; the sixth, the vessels and nerves; and on the seventh they took an examination in osteology. This sort of examination, however, was more likely an ideal seldom achieved because of the scarcity of cadavers. The students were also held to answer questions on the position, relationships, construction, and uses of the parts, and this part of the examination must frequently have been preponderant.[52]

Finally, from Ash Wednesday to St. Peter's feast, on 29 June, the new bachelors were required to defend a thesis on a subject of hygiene. This was called the Cardinal thesis, in memory of Cardinal d'Estouteville, who had been given charge of the University of Paris in 1452 and who, in the course of his reforms, had provided greater freedom and autonomy for the faculty of medicine.[53] With this thesis successfully defended, the new bachelor finally was fully entitled to his degree.

Such then was the program of examinations for which Vesalius was preparing up to the summer of 1536, when he was compelled to return to the Netherlands.

The faculty of medicine, like the entire University of Paris, was exceedingly conservative. From the latter part of the fifteenth century a knowledge of anatomy was required of candidates for the baccalaureate in medicine, yet dissections were infrequent, and although this situation was somewhat improved after an appeal of the faculty to the Parlement of Paris in 1526, anatomical dissection remained fairly uncommon until after the period of Vesalius's residence in Paris. A brief digression on the history of anatomical instruction in Paris in the fifteenth and early sixteenth century will help to illustrate the situation.

After the autopsy examination of 1407, previously mentioned, there is no further record of human anatomy performed by the faculty of medicine until 1478 when the Commentaries note that the sum of 18 *onzaines* was paid to the executioner "for bringing the body of one who had been hanged to the place of anatomy." [54] This record gives no indication of the incident being a novelty, and it seems a fair presumption that similar but unrecorded anatomies had been performed earlier. However, anatomical study was not yet generally attractive to physicians; although anatomy of some sort was part of the medical curriculum, it was not considered as an entity but as an aid to surgery—which was performed, if major, by members of the guild of surgeons and, if minor, by the barbers.

The guild of surgeons had long sought the respectability, prestige, and exemptions of membership in the university, but the faculty of medicine was opposed to this and sought control over the surgeons, so that what had been friendly relations between the two groups gradually turned into hostility in the latter part of the fifteenth century. Naturally the barbers, too, aspired to a better position and recognized better training as a requirement for it. Since surgical training properly needed some knowledge of anatomy, the barbers appear to have turned to the physicians for this latter discipline, but whether at first to the faculty in general or to individuals within the faculty is not certain. At any rate, such anatomies as were conducted by the faculty in the later fifteenth and early sixteenth centuries were at least partly for the instruction and control of barbers, partly for fees received, and partly, no doubt, as a result of the friction between physicians and surgeons.

Owing to the casual manner in which the Commentaries were written, perhaps in some degree a deliberate effort at concealment, the purposes of the anatomies are not always clear. Thus in the academic year 1481-82 an anatomy is mentioned as performed for the students of the faculty.[55] In 1483-84 payment was made to one "Philip Rogier, surgeon," [56] presumably for performing a dissection for the faculty—so indicating not only the ignorance of anatomy prevailing among the physicians, but also that long-standing attitude in which the physicians refrained from actual contact with the cadaver and contented themselves with parroting remarks from a surgical text, frequently with little bearing on the observable aspects of the dissection. The medieval character of anatomical instruction is indicated by the fact that the text usually employed was that of Guy de Chauliac. So in 1493–94 "it pleased the faculty to allow one of the masters of the faculty to lecture to the barbers in Latin, and from time to time to explain in French, from Guy [de Chauliac] or other authors." [57] In 1498–99 the surgeons protested against the faculty's lectures to the barbers from "Guy de Chauliac or other books of surgery." [58] Nine students of the faculty are recorded as having paid the fee for attendance at the anatomy of 1483–84. [59] An anatomy was held in the year 1485–86, attended by seventeen students, and on this occasion it was performed by Jean Lucas, one of the regent doctors, [60] suggesting that possibly the surgeons were now loathe to participate in dissections that might benefit the barbers.

The resentment of the surgeons was expressed in a complaint to the faculty, in 1491–92, in which it was asserted that the barbers had independently obtained the body of an executed criminal and that certain members of the faculty had not only demonstrated its anatomy but furthermore in French rather than in Latin. [61] The employment of Latin seems to have been in the ancient tradition of power and control by a kind of priestly class through its possession of the keys to the esoteric mysteries, in this instance the Latin language. This surreptitious dissection presumably was in addition to that recorded for the same year and attended by twelve candidates for medical degrees. [62] The anatomy of 1492–93 appears to have been a kind of defiant answer to the surgeons since it is recorded that in addition to medical students those present included not only a "theologian who wished to be present at this kind of anatomy," and "another person whose name was not asked because of the confusion," but also two barbers. [63] The list of expenses for this occasion helps to explain the "confusion." Payments had to be made to the executioner and his two assistants as well as to the boatman who had brought the cadaver across the Seine from the convent of the Celestines. Breakfast for those involved in the dissection created further expense, as did payment to the two men who removed the head of the cadaver and buried it at night to avoid "the outcry of the people"; furthermore, after the anatomy, which obviously could have been no more than a hurried examination of the internal organs, the body was buried in the cemetery of St. Severinus, which entailed the cost of vinegar to wash the body, wax candles for the burial service, and a fee for the priest who celebrated a mass for the soul lately of this particular body. There was also expense for a dissection table and for washing and cleaning the building, since this anatomy had been held in the medical school in the Rue de la Bûcherie. [64]

Although the account suggests fairly obviously that there was some irregularity attendant upon this particular dissection, its greater importance lies in the fact that it locates the place where the dissection was held. A place for dissection had been and was to remain a problem by the very nature of the activity. It was at about this time, on 26 October 1493, that a proposal was offered in the faculty for the purchase of a garden and vineyard to serve as an outdoor anatomical theatre.[65] However, this came to nothing, and on 28 June 1494 a second proposal was made for buying the property of a Jacques Yvain, near the abbey of Saint-Victor, with the thought that the garden would serve for anatomical demonstrations.[66] This, too, came to nothing. The problem of location became an embarrassment. The experience in the faculty's building had not been a happy one and presumably was, if possible, not to be repeated. In January 1498 the question of location was reason for convoking the faculty,[67] as it was again in October 1499 when it was announced that "no place had as yet been obtained for the anatomy." [68] In February 1505 the Hôtel de Nesle was employed for an anatomy that "lasted for three full days, but was only of the natural members," [69] that is, the parts of the abdomen. An anatomy was performed in Ave Maria College near Saint-Étienne-du-Mont in 1508–09 [70] and again in 1510–11.[71] In 1512–13 resort was once again made to the school of the faculty in the Rue de la Bûcherie,[72] although on this second occasion no mention was made of the cost of cleaning the school afterward, and perhaps by this time some more or less permanent arrangement had been contrived. This appears to be borne out by an entry in the Commentaries for the year 1518 referring to the receipts "from the anatomy performed publicly in the school." [73]

Although the struggle between the faculty of medicine and the guild of surgeons was not brought to an end until 1516, at which time, for the sake of certain advantages, the latter, like the barbers, accepted a subservient position to the physicians,[74] surgeons appear to have been participating in the anatomies for some years. As indicated, on at least one occasion a surgeon seems to have performed the actual dissection while, it may be assumed, the physician lectured from his *cathedra* or high chair. This situation was no doubt frequently repeated, and especially after 1516 it must have been the general practice of which Vesalius was to complain reminiscently in the *Fabrica*. The participation of the surgeons is further indicated by the fact that from the year 1495–96 they paid one-third of the expenses of the anatomies.[75]

Parisian anatomy, it appears, remained medieval through the first several decades of the sixteenth century, and was in some respects below the level achieved by Mondino in the fourteenth century in Bologna, since he at least made his own dissections. This situation was partly due to a provincialism that had caused insufficient communication with the great Italian universities and a consequent failure to appreciate the work being done in them. There was no mention of Mondino, Achillini, or Berengario in Paris before the third decade of the sixteenth century, although it is difficult to subscribe to the view occasionally expressed that they were wholly unknown there, especially since an edition of Alessandro Benedetti's anatomical treatise was published in Paris in 1514. Even so, Benedetti's work seems not to have been particularly influential, and the Paris of Vesalius's time was only just developing to the point where it could appreciate the advances being made in Italy. Publishers, ever quick to recognize a changing intellectual climate and to meet a new need, are a pretty reliable gauge of such situations, hence it is interesting to note that at this late date two editions of Mondino were published in Lyons, in 1528 and 1531. But there was no anatomical text originating from Paris before 1535. Parisian anatomists of the early sixteenth century depended solely upon such instruction as could be found in the anatomical portions of medieval surgical works such as that of Guy de Chauliac.

It was not until the second decade of the sixteenth century, in part owing to the interest of Francis I, that any considerable interest in the classics was aroused among Parisian scholars. It was the patronage of Francis I that enticed Italian humanistic scholarship to Paris, some of it concerned with medicine; but classical scholarship in medicine specifically, which referred especially to Greek medicine, was introduced to the faculty of medicine by one of its members, Jean Ruel, or Ruellius, 1479–1537. Yet Ruel, despite his knowledge of Greek medical texts and his influential position in the faculty, did not himself have an interest in Galen. This was the interest of Jean Vasses of Meaux, dean of the faculty when Vesalius enrolled in the school. As already indicated, the faculty by that time had become sufficiently imbued with the new interest in classical medicine to purchase in 1526—perhaps on the urging of Vasses—the Aldine edition of the Greek text of Galen. For most the purchase meant little more than the recognition of an obligation to have a set of "classics" on the library's shelves. Far more important were the accurate Latin versions of particular works, and Galen in Latin dress first asserted himself in Paris, if not in the faculty of medicine, in 1514, when Henri Estienne published a small collection of texts of Galen originally translated into Latin by Nicolo Leoniceno of Ferrara, 1428–1524. Thereafter, Latin editions of Galen's writings became more frequent.

Because the medical faculty of Paris tended to regard medicine as an entity and anatomy had not yet achieved the dignity of a separate discipline—nor did it loom very large within the general subject of medicine —dissection was retarded and surgery, which probably contained a larger amount of anatomy than did medicine, occupied a subservient position. Nevertheless, a change was at hand: although the medical humanists had been dealing with the task of translating and commenting upon the medical, as contrasted to the anatomical, texts of Galen, by 1528, just prior to Vesalius's arrival in Paris, there had begun to be concern with the books of anatomical content.[76] In that year, Simon de Colines, who had married the widow of Henri Estienne and so was the logical publisher to continue the work, published Latin translations of several texts of Galen that provided a basis for a new and Galenic anatomical teaching: the *Use of parts*, in the fourteenth-century translation of Nicolas of Reggio, the *Movement of muscles*, translated by Leoniceno, and the *Introduction to medicine*, a pseudo-Galenic treatise in the version of Guinter of Andernach. Finally, in 1531 Guinter translated the first nine books of the *Anatomical procedures* and thereby made available Galen's full teaching on anatomy, including a detailed study of dissection.[77]

Because of the suddenness with which Galen became known in Paris, along with the lack of knowledge of the Italian studies that in part revised or corrected his doctrines, there occurred the dramatically rapid establishment of an enslavement to Galenism which produced in turn a new Galenic conservatism. This, however, did not mean the immediate ousting of all medieval works from the curriculum—certain of them were still required—but it did tend to prevent any original work that might overthrow the authority of Galen; or at least such discoveries as occurred were made to fit into the Galenic anatomical or physiological scheme. There was no spirit of free inquiry.

By the time Vesalius arrived in Paris Galenism was in the ascendancy, and there is no indication that at that time he sought to rebel against it, influenced as he was by the general spirit of Galenism then pervading the faculty of medicine and by the personal influence of two of his teachers in particular, Jacobus Sylvius and Guinter of Andernach.

In one statement in Vesalius's subsequent *Letter on the china root* three of his teachers in Paris are mentioned by name: Vasses, Fernel, Oliverius —and "certain others." [78] Vasses we know as the dean of the faculty of medicine when Vesalius arrived in Paris in 1533; Jean Fernel was the distinguished physician who has been so ably studied by Sherrington; [79] but of Oliverius nothing is known, and it is rather astonishing that his name should be recalled by Vesalius ten years after he had left Paris. Since the name Oliverius is not included among the regent doctors listed in the Commentaries, and there is no mention of any bachelor or licentiate of such name, it seems possible that Vesalius's memory had played him false. [80] At any rate, among the "certain others" mentioned by him as his teachers in Paris two in particular were to be frequently referred to: Jacobus Sylvius and Jean Guinter of Andernach. Both men were leaders of Parisian academic medicine, particularly of anatomy, and both had considerable influence upon Vesalius during his studies in Paris and afterward. It seems desirable, therefore, to devote some consideration to them, and especially to Sylvius, who was to have a relationship with Vesalius, although mostly one of hostility, through the remainder of his life.

Jacobus Sylvius, 1478–1555, of Amiens, came to Paris originally at the invitation of his brother Franciscus, professor of letters and principal of the Collège de Tournai. Under this fraternal direction Jacobus acquired considerable command of Latin and Greek and in particular an elegance of Latin style which distinguished his later writings. After the acquisition of this fundamental humanistic training, as well as further study of Hebrew with François Vatable and of mathematics with Jacques Lefèvre d'Étaples, he devoted himself to reading and studying the Greek texts of Hippocrates and Galen. Recognizing the significance of anatomy, despite the finality of the Galenic canon, he sought association with those members of the faculty of medicine who performed dissections for the course in surgery, notably Jean Tagault. Sylvius later described Tagault as *mihi in re medica praeceptor undequoque absolutus*,[81] and there is a story to the effect that Sylvius later advised Tagault on stylistic changes to improve the presentation of his *De institutione chirurgica* (1543).

Following these studies, and presumably on the example of Galen, Sylvius set forth to travel throughout France and thereby to complete his studies in botany and pharmacy. Upon his return he proceeded to give private lessons and consultations but, since he lacked any degree from the faculty of medicine, he was compelled to desist, and determined to take his degree at Montpellier.

Sylvius matriculated in 1527, but, presumably because of his age and the reputation he already possessed, the faculty of medicine disregarded the statutory requirements and granted him the baccalaureate in 1529, and the following year he received the degree of doctor of medicine. Next he went to Lyons where he published a small treatise, *Quaestio de vini exhibitione in febribus,* and thereafter he returned to Paris.

A relationship with the medical faculty through degree was still necessary for him to teach in Paris, and Sylvius petitioned the faculty of medicine to take the necessary requirements for the baccalaureate and licentiate. The Commentaries inform us that:

[On] 28 June 1531 the faculty was convoked to hear the request of the learned Doctor Jacobus Sylvius who supplicated for approval of the requisite time for the baccalaureate examination; he furthermore sought that several months after the adoption of the rank of baccalaureate he be admitted for response to the Cardinal question, and if necessary in regard to the matter of a thesis for disputation, and that he thereupon be admitted to the licentiate. His supplication and elegant discourse having been heard, it pleased the faculty to admit the aforesaid Sylvius to examination and rank of baccalaureate, subject to examination and payment of fees. The faculty will consider the other matters later, although favorably because of his publications.[82]

Thereafter, with his degree, Sylvius was permitted to teach at the Collège de Tréguier. Still later the faculty of medicine granted full recognition to his course, as well as to that of Jean Fernel who, although a regent doctor, also taught outside the faculty of medicine:

On 27 January [1536], the dean of the faculty being Doctor Tagault, it was decided in a convocation of the doctors that those who lecture outside the school of medicine may henceforth lecture in the school and receive the same fees from the scholars. This was decided for the sake of Jean Fernel, who lectures in the Collège de Cornuaille, and Jacobus Sylvius, baccalaureate of the school of Paris, who professes medicine in the Collège de Tréguier.[83]

After the faculty's decision, Vesalius might have been able to study under Sylvius for about six months at most, unless he had previously attended the class in the Collège de Tréguier without credit. However, Sylvius had not yet acquired the considerable reputation he was later to have. Unfortunately, it has not always been appreciated that the famous Sylvius belongs to the period after 1536, the year in which Vesalius left Paris, but it is a fact which should be kept in mind as one reads the account given below which provides us with some idea of Sylvius's strong personality, a factor in his relations with students even before the years of his greater fame.

Some indication of that greater fame is given by Moreau, a seventeenth-century biographer, who asserts that Sylvius was a far more popular lecturer than Fernel and notes that he had an edition of 900 copies of Gattinaria's *Practica,* printed for his general lecture course, all of which were sold to the students within several days and another issue required. This must be a reference to Sylvius's *Morborum internorum curatio ex Galeno praecipuè & Marco Gattinaria* (Paris, 1545), and so refers to a period almost a decade after Vesalius had left Paris. However, it was his course in anatomy that was best remembered. Noël du Fail, the celebrated writer and jurisconsult, had the following recollection of it, although once again in the post-Vesalian period:

> I recall having heard the eloquent Jacobus Sylvius lecture on Galen's *Use of parts* to a remarkable audience of scholars of all nations; but when he exposed those parts which we call shameful, there was no bit or portion he did not identify in good French by name and surname, adding the appearances and likenesses for the greater amplification of his remarks, which would have been delusive and unpleasant or uninteresting if he had not done so. I have seen him bring in his sleeve, because he lived all his life without a servant, sometimes a thigh or sometimes the arm of some one hanged, in order to dissect and anatomize it. They stank so strongly and offensively that some of his auditors would readily have thrown up if they had dared; but the cantankerous fellow with his Picard head would have been so violently incensed, threatening not to return for a week, that everyone kept silent.[84]

Although Sylvius published nothing in the 1530's that gives us an idea of his anatomical knowledge or the general attitude toward the subject at that time, yet there is no question of the strength of Galen's influence upon him. He was, moreover, a forceful and influential personality equipped with a strong but misguided zeal, and it is possible that he recognized a fellow-zealot in young Andreas Vesalius and singled him out for special attention and encouragement. Sylvius's activities, whatever their purpose at the time, were of the sort that Vesalius was to extol in the *Fabrica.* Sylvius did not allow others to dissect while he, content, lectured in superior isolation from his chair; like the later Paduan Vesalius, and as the author of the *Fabrica* was to recommend, Sylvius the lecturer on anatomy was also the dissector.

In the preface to his *Fabrica* Vesalius was to state that he would not have succeeded in his anatomical studies "if when I was studying medicine in Paris I had not put my hand to the matter but had accepted without question the several casual and superficial demonstrations of a few organs presented to me and to my fellow-students . . . by unskilled barbers."[85] This could not be a critical reference to the teaching of Sylvius, since with him Vesalius would not have dared uninvited to put his hand to the matter, and, as will be indicated shortly, he did not study any genuinely human anatomy with Sylvius. It is much more likely that the reference was to the course in anatomy taught in the faculty of medicine. Nor, in view of the words of Noël du Fail, given above, can the following description of the professor of anatomy refer to that fierce figure; rather it refers to the more conservative, traditional teaching methods found in the university, that is, technically inept because the work of "unskilled barbers," and if it is a reference to any single individual it is far more likely a caricature of Guinter of Andernach:

> . . . that detestable procedure by which usually some conduct the dissection of the human body and others present the account of its parts, the latter like jackdaws aloft in their high chair, with egregious arrogance croaking things they have never investigated but merely committed to memory from the books of others, or read what has already been described. The former are so ignorant of languages that they are unable to explain their dissections to the spectators and muddle what ought to be displayed according to the instructions of the physician who haughtily governs the ship from a manual since he has never applied his hand to the dissection of the body. Thus everything is wrongly taught in the schools, and days are wasted in ridiculous questions so that in such confusion less is presented to the spectators than a butcher in his stall could teach a physician.[86]

These remarks present a proper criticism, and the question is one of determining the target—as has been suggested, possibly Guinter. Rather than voicing any criticism of Sylvius, however, Vesalius consistently gave him praise. In his first work, the *Paraphrasis,* he referred in the preface to "my erudite teacher Jacobus Sylvius," and as late as the preface (August 1542) to the *Fabrica,* Sylvius was called "the never-to-be-sufficiently-praised Jacobus Sylvius." [87]

It is not until the *Letter on the china root* of 1546 that we find Vesalius making any adverse statements about Sylvius, and these were in the form of a defense against an attack already mounted and initiated by the latter. Furthermore, having presented his defense, Vesalius was content to say no more about the matter, and in the revised edition of the *Fabrica* in 1555 he dropped out any reference to Sylvius. It appears that Vesalius may have been wrongfully charged with ingratitude to Sylvius, and that his attitude as expressed verbally was first appreciation, then in 1546 shock and anger at what he considered quite properly an unjustified attack, and finally a dignified silence.

Vesalius was, it seems, appreciative of the teaching of Sylvius, who had aroused his enthusiasm for dissection and introduced him to the subject, as he wrote, on "brute animals," but whether or not Sylvius taught him any human anatomy is unknown and seems unlikely. In the *Fabrica* Vesalius spoke of Sylvius only in reference to the dissection of lower animals, and it is doubtful whether Sylvius had many cadavers available before 1536—the year in which the faculty of medicine permitted its students to take his medical course for credit, and the year in which Vesalius was compelled to leave France. Writing in 1546, Vesalius declared that he had learned very little human anatomy from Sylvius, and that merely out of a book:

> I don't know if Sylvius paid any attention to the remark in my books . . . that is, that I have worked without the help of a teacher, since perhaps he believes

that I learned anatomy from him, he who still maintains that Galen is always right. Sylvius, whom I shall respect as long as I live, always started the course by reading the books *On the use of parts* to us, but when he reached the middle of the first book, the anatomical part, he announced that this was too difficult for us, just beginning our studies, to follow, and that it would be troublesome for him and for us. Therefore he omitted the subsequent books as far as the fourteenth and then read the following. As a result he completed a book in five or six days without ever calling our attention to the fact that Galen contradicts himself elsewhere, as he frequently does, and without indicating that Galen said things which are false. He brought nothing to the school except occasionally bits of dogs. We were so sedulous in following the dissections of our teacher that after his lectures he often tested our ability. It happened one day that we showed him the valves of the orifice of the pulmonary artery and of the aorta, although he had informed us the day before that he could not find them. Since Sylvius omitted the chapter dealing with the vertebrae, as well as many others, during his so-called course—which he was then giving for the thirty-fifth time—and read nothing else anatomical except the books *On the movement of muscles,* in which he everywhere agreed with Galen, it is not astonishing that I write that I have studied without the aid of a teacher.[88]

If we can accept Vesalius's statement, and the more we can test his assertions from other sources the greater becomes our respect for his veracity, it would appear that he enjoyed no human anatomical instruction under Sylvius. What he acquired was skill in the technique of dissection and a comprehension of Galenic anatomy by comparison of Galen's text with the anatomy of animals such as the dog. In Louvain, after Paris, he acquired some celebrity because of his more highly developed technique in dissection, not for his anti-Galenism which was to manifest itself only later in Padua.

There is a tendency to judge Sylvius from the position he acquired after Vesalius left Paris, notably from his book *In Hippocratis et Galeni physiologiae partem anatomicam isagoge*, published in 1555—although said to have been written in 1542, the same year Vesalius completed the composition of the *Fabrica*. Because of the later relationship between the two men, some attention ought to be given to this book.

Sylvius's *Isagoge*, a brief work compared to the *Fabrica*, indicates that although its author was certainly a Galenist he was not such a blind partisan as he has been frequently described, nor was he the fanatical Galenist he later appeared in the *Vaesanus* of 1551. The *Isagoge* is a systematic account of anatomy based on Galen plus a certain amount of dissection; it was also influenced by the anatomical treatise of Nicolo Massa published in Venice in 1536, and to be considered later. In fact, the references to Massa's book permit us to say that Sylvius's book could not have been written before the publication of Massa's work. In the later *Vaesanus*, immediately after a reference to Nicolo Massa, Sylvius mentioned an Antonio Massa, surgeon of Paris, "very learned and highly skilled in the dissection of bodies," who "died a few days ago." [89] Quite possibly this was a relative of the Venetian physician and may first have brought Massa's treatise on anatomy to the attention of Sylvius and of Parisian anatomists.

It may have been Massa's book that caused Sylvius, at least for a time, to bring his ardent Galenism under some control, although later that control was completely sacrificed as a result of rancor toward what he considered the ingratitude and misguided independence of his former student. Although Vesalius called attention directly to Galen's errors in the *Fabrica*, in the *Isagoge* Sylvius tended to avoid such erroneous passages and thereby any discussion of Galen's fallibility, which in this way he nevertheless acknowledged tacitly. The *Isagoge* therefore represents what Sylvius considered the best of Galen, although his loyalty and the limits of his dissection led him to retain numerous Galenic errors.

In his description of the heart, for example, Sylvius described the ventricles and the septum between them, but said nothing of any passage leading through the septum. Indeed, he stated that blood from the right ventricle is carried to the lungs through the pulmonary artery, and blood mixed with spirit from the left ventricle into the aorta,[90] but curiously he made no mention of a passage of blood through the septum. Since this was a matter of vital importance in Galenic physiology, the absence of any mention of it is striking and suggests that Sylvius had reached his conclusion as to Galen's error through independent dissection or otherwise. He may have been influenced here by Massa, who suggested that the interventricular septum is hard and impervious, and it seems possible—although, in view of our knowledge of Sylvius, somewhat astonishing—that after reading Massa's account he dissected the heart and came, perhaps unwillingly, to the same decision. His failure to mention any route for the blood except from the ventricle to the lung overthrew by implication the whole Galenic cardiovascular physiology, although it is unlikely that he, or Massa before him, saw the consequences of his remarks.

Nor did Sylvius accept the *rete mirabile* as a structure in the human: "This plexus, seen by Galen under the gland, still appears today in brutes."[91] Thus Sylvius implied not Galen's error, but an alteration in the human structure with the passage of time. However, he must himself have recognized Galen's error since here once again was a factor essential to Galenic physiology. According to Galen it was in the *rete mirabile* that the vital spirit carried thither in the blood was changed into animal spirit, necessary ultimately for thought and muscular movement. In this matter Sylvius had advanced beyond Massa, who still accepted the existence of the *rete mirabile* in the human brain.

It is possible that Sylvius, through years of defending Galen, had reached a point from which he could not withdraw without humiliation and loss of prestige and that he was therefore silent on certain points where the results of his dissection differed from the teaching of Galen. He was aware that Galen's descriptions were largely based upon animal dissection,[92] and that this must be taken into account when a discrepancy occurred between Galenic anatomy and observation from human dissection. However, according to Sylvius, mankind differed according to period and region of existence, and the man of his day differed from that of Galen's.[93] In sum, Sylvius may be termed as usually an industrious and capable anatomist, willing to recognize Galenic error provided the fact of Galen's error was not publicized. If it was publicized, so steeped and learned was he in the classical writings and so long their champion that he was compelled to spring to even a puerile and ludicrous defense or an emotional attack such as that in the *Vaesanus*. Yet the number of correct anatomical descriptions, or at least modifications of Galen, to be found in the *Isagoge* suggests considerable independent human dissection by Sylvius.

Italian dissectors had already reached or were reaching numerous anti-Galenic conclusions, but Sylvius appears to have remained unfamiliar with much of their literature. He had become acquainted with Mondino, and after 1536 he referred frequently to Massa. However, he seems to have been still ignorant of Berengario da Carpi, and in his reference to the auditory ossicles referred only to Massa's description. It may therefore be assumed that his more-correct anatomical knowledge was the result of his own research, although the possibility of correspondence with Vesalius until 1543 cannot be overlooked. Finally, it must be stressed that he considered himself as gaining knowledge of the anatomy of a new or altered man different from the man known to Galen: "The azygos vein [was] always observed under the heart by Galen in those in whom the sternum formed of seven bones made a longer thorax, but in our bodies, because of the shortness of the sternum and thorax, it arises more or less above the heart and pericardium." [94]

Sylvius may be said to have developed into a good and even a dramatic teacher, and the *Isagoge* is a systematic textbook of modified Galenic anatomy, notably superior in its classification of muscles. It is certainly clearer in this respect, although not in terms of full anatomical description, than the *Fabrica*, and has been called the foundation of modern muscle nomenclature. Sylvius also popularized a number of anatomical terms such as gastric, intercostal, popliteal, axillary, mesenteric, and subclavian.[95] These matters, however, belong to the period after Vesalius left Paris.

Turning from anatomy as taught by Sylvius in the Collège de Tréguier to the anatomy course taught in the faculty of medicine as part of the curriculum leading to the baccalaureate in medicine, it may be said first that it was, for obvious reasons, taught during the winter. Cadavers, difficult to obtain, at least officially, were generally those of condemned criminals, and their distribution was regulated and controlled by the dean of the faculty of medicine. Anatomy was therefore not a commonplace event; but what might have been a compelling spectacle, as it was later in Padua and Pisa when conducted by Vesalius, was deadened and stultified by the manner of presentation.

The professor of anatomy did not need to be a skilled dissector since he spoke from the height of his chair and allowed another to handle the scalpel. He was further assisted in his teaching by a student chosen by the other students, although preference was usually given to one of the bachelors of medicine. This student was charged with the recapitulation in Latin of the professor's lesson, and when Vesalius enrolled in the medical school this student assistant, known as the *archidiaconus studentium*, was one Thomas de Nobescourt,[96] not yet a bachelor. Although we have no record of the name of the later "archdeacon of students," it is possible that Vesalius held this position under Guinter.

This was the kind of anatomical instruction Vesalius criticized in the cited passage from the *Fabrica*, and it is highly probable that he was thinking of Guinter of Andernach when he made his remark. Speaking directly of Guinter's anatomical demonstrations, he declared them of little value. They lasted only three days and, despite Guinter's Galenism, were rather medieval in character.[97] So far as the abdomen was concerned, according to Vesalius, the dissections consisted of little beyond the conventional separation of the muscular coverings and a general display of the viscera. "For, except for eight abdominal muscles shamefully mangled and in the wrong order, no other muscle or any bone, and much less an accurate series of the nerves, veins or arteries was ever demonstrated to me by anyone." [98] The stress on the muscles of the abdominal wall was a legacy of medieval anatomy. Yet in all fairness to Guinter one ought to note, if not necessarily accept, his own later statement in his *De medicina veteri et nova:* [99]

[The ancients before Galen, especially in Alexandria] . . . taught how to dissect and observe whole and freshly dead [human] bodies; first they demonstrated and explained the lower venter, then the thorax, head, and the parts of each. Afterward they explained the muscles and nerves in other bodies and in still others the veins and arteries, both superficial and deep. Thirty years ago I also employed this method of teaching and performing anatomy. Later, Andreas Vesalius, who formerly assisted me when I was lecturing publicly on medicine, and after him Realdo Colombo, distinguished professor of medicine, followed the same practice in their large works on anatomy.

Despite his words, Guinter was certainly not skilled in dissection, but he was a kindly man, friendly to his students, and generous enough to praise Vesalius in print on several occasions. Although Vesalius's criticism of Guinter, by implication and also by name, was probably justified, yet it would have been the decent thing for him to have restrained his pen.

Jean Guinter of Andernach, near Coblentz, 1505–1574, after a youth spent in quest of learning in Utrecht, Deventer, Marburg, Goslar, Louvain, and Liège, reached Paris in 1527. He became baccalaureate in medicine on 18 April 1528 after two witnesses had sworn to the statement that he had already studied medicine at Leipzig for sufficient time to compensate for his deficiency of residence at Paris.[100] On 4 June 1530 he and Jean Fernel became licentiates,[101] and on 29 October 1532 he received the doctor's bonnet.[102] He was listed among the regent doctors on 6 February 1533,[103] and on 7 November 1534, the same day Tagault was chosen dean, Guinter and Jean Fernel were named professors at a salary increased from fifteen to twenty-five *livres,* although Fernel's appointment was thereafter postponed. By this time Guinter had already been recognized for his translations of Galen and of Paul of Aegina and, as the Commentaries state, he had translated the larger part of Galen's and all of Paul's writings.[104] He was, of course, a Galenist and far more a philologist than a physician or anatomist.

In 1536 Guinter published his *Institutiones anatomicae*. Vesalius was undoubtedly aware of the work whether or not he was still in Paris when it appeared.[105] In the dedication to Nicolaus Quelain, Guinter calls attention to the number of physicians in Paris who, he wrote, were little short of being imposters. They had developed a meaningless jargon and were never loathe to prescribe, although their ignorance of the human body made such prescriptions venturesome if not lethal.

How many Rabbins of physicians there are today, who widely declaim themselves as Hippocratics or Galenists or greater than those, and do not even understand the books of the anatomists, who have not attended dissections or demonstrated them to others. If you withdraw the title [of physician] from them, you will find only dispensers of syrups and purges, delighting their patients' palates rather than curing their diseases. Nor are those lacking who have several cures they have received from I don't know whom, like some hidden treasure but for the deception of mankind. They are unskilled in every art, not to speak of medicine, using deaths, as is said, for experiments. These impostors have become so shameless that at Paris before that world-famous and noble gathering of physicians they dare falsify the art of medicine for which they have substituted deception and self-advertisement.

Possibly these remarks were partly the result of the active prosecution of certain medical astrologers by the faculty of medicine at this time. In particular, the faculty spent no little effort and, as the Commentaries indicate, money in its legal action against Jean Thibault, court astrologer and archfoe among these "empirics" and astrologers—"an empiric Jean Thibault, truly a man without any learning and meriting the very worst in respect to medicine." [106] Therapy, continued Guinter, required a knowledge of the body, and he proposed to present in concise form what he had hitherto learned from Galen's writings, which he hoped would be easily understood by the students.

His treatise was therefore completely Galenic, but his purpose somewhat foreshadowed Vesalius's later demands, in the preface to the *Fabrica*, that the true physician be thoroughly versed in anatomy. Guinter's treatise is in four books arranged for practical use, dealing first with the more corruptible internal organs, and then with those that are less susceptible to immediate putrefaction; hence it follows that form first made popular by Mondino. It is apparent that Guinter had discussed his work with Vesalius, and in one instance he gives Vesalius credit for discoveries regarding the spermatic vessels:

The spermatic vessels are composed of two veins and two arteries, one of each on either side, branches of the vena cava and the aorta, carrying down blood through the iliac region into the testes. They differ from one another in their origin. The vein on the right takes origin not from the side of the vena cava itself but from almost the middle, below that [vein] that goes to the kidneys. The

[vein] that extends to the testicle on the left side issues from that [vein] that goes to the kidneys; sometimes a little branch from the vena cava is added and united to it.

These spermatic vessels, which are attached to the back by slender fibres, are extended downward, and as they approach the iliac region arteries are joined to them which arise [from the aorta] very differently than the veins from the vena cava. I believe that no anatomist hitherto has mentioned this, let alone noticed it. Recently we discovered them after long investigation of the parts and through the skill of Andreas Vesalius, son of the Emperor's apothecary—a young man, by Hercules, of great promise, possessing an extraordinary knowledge of medicine, learned in both languages, and very skilled in dissection of bodies. However, they are found with difficulty because, like the adjoining parts, they are bloodless and whitish, and anatomists, content with the assertion that few or no veins go to the lower parts unaccompanied, have neglected to follow them to their origin.[107]

This is a passage of some importance relative to Guinter, Vesalius, and the general state of anatomical studies in Paris at the time, and has been given detailed consideration by the late Charles Singer.[108] The passage is not so clear as might be desired, but it must be kept in mind, as Singer pointed out, that Guinter was thinking in terms of Galen's physiology, and to follow his description it is necessary to realize that his use of the terms origin and termination as applied to the veins ought to be reversed. Even so, since the spermatic veins are not usually so whitish or bloodless as described, it seems more likely that his reference is to arteries, which tends to confirm Guinter's lack of ability as a dissector. Nevertheless, the discovery, as Guinter wrote, was not his but that of Vesalius who, although already more capable than his teacher, was, according to this description, still far from the clear-eyed systematic anatomist we associate with the *Fabrica*.

The discovery, which is not very clearly presented, appears to include the facts that the "origins" or terminations of the spermatic veins differ on the two sides; that in the early part of their course the spermatic artery and vein do not run together; that the spermatic vein has a different origin from that of the artery. Although both Cushing [109] and Singer [110] believed that the first of these possibilities represents the discovery, yet the latter historian noted that all three are depicted in Vesalius's first plate of the *Tabulae anatomicae*. Of even more significance than this discovery made by Vesalius is its reflection upon the conservative and local position of the Paris medical faculty. Actually the spermatic veins had been described by Galen in Book XIII of his *Anatomical procedures* which, although early lost to the West from the Greek corpus, had survived in an Arabic translation. In this latter form it had been known to and used by Avicenna,[111] who had described the veins, a fact curiously overlooked by or unknown to Guinter and Vesalius. Furthermore, Mondino had not only described them, but indicated that Avicenna was the source of his knowledge.[112] Here is an example of the superiority of medieval anatomical knowledge over that of the renaissance as reflected in Paris. In

Italy, however, this particular bit of anatomical information was known to Mondino and thereafter to Berengario da Carpi [113] and Nicolo Massa,[114] the last devoting some four pages to his description. The whole matter emphasizes the fact that, with the exception of Benedetti's work, the Italian anatomical writings were still unknown or at best little known in Paris.

Although Guinter mentioned Vesalius only in connection with his description of the spermatic vessels, years later he remarked that "when I presided at a public dissection at Paris . . . Andreas Vesalius assisted me." [115] Why, then, this single, or indeed any, allusion to the student? Singer considered it somewhat forced and unusual, "perhaps an attempt of a great teacher to press the claims of a favorite pupil for some appointment—a 'testimonial' in fact." [116] But Vesalius was hardly prepared as yet for any sort of appointment. It might have been that Guinter felt obliged to mention at least once the name of the student whose skill in dissection had assisted him in the composition of the *Institutiones,* and he chose an instance at random. It appears likely that Vesalius had done other dissections related to the descriptions in the book, and it may be hazarded that the description of the azygos vein was based upon his efforts.

A further point of some significance is Guinter's brief mention of Vesalius as "learned in both languages," that is, Greek and Latin. From time to time there has been question of the extent of Vesalius's knowledge of and facility in Greek, of whether the Greek phrases he introduced into his writings were merely an effort to express an erudition he did not possess, and whether he was really capable of collating the Greek texts and revising the Latin versions directly from the Greek when later he edited several of Galen's works for the Giunta edition. With regular study under Rescius, at Louvain, he ought certainly to have gained some competence in the language, but more important here is the praise from Guinter, one of the leading Greek scholars of the time, and a major translator of Galen. His remark leaves little doubt of his student's accomplishment in the language.

Returning to the question of what modern as opposed to classical anatomical texts were known in Paris, it may be said that Benedetti's appears to have been the only one until the appearance in 1535 of Andres de Laguna's brief anatomical treatise, and, in the following year, about the time Vesalius left Paris, Guinter's *Institutiones anatomicae*. Guinter's book will be considered further in another context, but attention must now be directed to Laguna's somewhat revealing treatise which has hitherto been overlooked.

Andres de Laguna, 1511?–1560, from the region of Segovia in Spain, first pursued his studies at Salamanca, whence he went to Paris, and in the Commentaries of the medical faculty of Paris he is listed as a bachelor of medicine in 1532–33.[117] He probably remained in Paris until 1536, when he returned to Spain to continue his studies at the universities of Alcalá and Toledo, finally obtaining the degree of doctor of medicine from the latter institution. He and Vesalius must have been acquainted in Paris, and were to renew that acquaintance a few years later when they were both serving as military surgeons with the imperial forces.

Before leaving Paris, Laguna published a small and now very rare anatomical treatise, *Anatomica methodus, seu de sectione humani corporis* (Paris, Iacobus Kerver, 1535), which further indicates the state of anatomical studies during the period of Vesalius's residence in that city, noting that unofficially there was more activity and possibly less conservatism in procedure than official university presentation would indicate. The content of the book made little contribution of an anatomical nature, being almost completely under the influence of the revived classical medicine, with many references to Galen and Hippocrates and a considerable flourish of Greek. Laguna did, however, mention Benedetti to take issue with him [118] and declared Mondino "not so unlearned as barbarous." [119] Of his contemporaries in Paris he referred to Tagault as of admirable doctrine [120] and mentioned "the very careful and faithful translator of the Greeks, Jean Guinter." [121] There is no mention of Sylvius, but this is easily explained by the fact that Sylvius was not a member of the faculty of medicine and had not yet acquired the fame of his later years.

Although such remarks do indicate the influence of classical medicine in Paris at the time and the apparent ignorance of most of the work being done in Italy, Laguna also made several remarks in regard to human dissection that suggest something of the initiative Vesalius was to demonstrate in the dissection room—possibly even following in the pathway marked out by the Spanish student. Indeed, they may have instigated a more or less simultaneous rebellion against the staid practices of Parisian anatomy. Thus Laguna wrote:

> When an anatomy of the human body was performed at Paris, I, with my fellow-students of the art of medicine, and even the barbers to whom the task of dissecting had been entrusted, were repelled and fled from the cadaver by reason of the foetor of the intestines. Thus it was acknowledged by all that the caecum intestine, to which they had never directed their eyes, had only one orifice, until I seized a scalpel and dissected the caecum intestine and clearly demonstrated to all that there were two openings of the same sort, one through which it received and a second through which it expelled, for I had read in Mondino, not so unlearned as barbarous, that the matter was such as I observed it. [122]

Still further evidence of human dissection in which the student participated is found in the case of "a certain noble dissected by me this year [1535] after his funeral." [123] And "also in the same month a noble hero was dissected by the very learned Doctor Tagault at Étampes," [124] presumably assisted by Laguna. Moreover, in his description of the kidneys another reference is made to human dissection at Paris in which he participated, sufficiently detailed to suggest that the task was not wholly conducted by barbers. [125] Of the abdominal muscles Laguna wrote, "It is necessary that you learn from this illustration the arrangement and composition of these [abdominal] muscles, you who are little experienced in anatomy," but the illustration of the muscles presented in his book is crude, diagrammatic, and utterly worthless—the same figure used in the 1496 edition of Pietro d'Abano's *Conciliator*.[126]

In short, some of the students and faculty were willing personally to investigate the human body even though their purpose was to verify Galen. Hence, possibly before, certainly at least contemporaneously with Vesalius's studies in Paris, dissatisfaction with the usual method of academic dissection was voiced by others, and some of the professors appeared willing to allow the more energetic and precocious students to replace the barber at the dissection table. However, this was by no means a criticism of Galen's anatomy.

If now we attempt to evaluate the anatomical training Vesalius received in Paris, we may first give our attention to the available texts. As has been indicated, he had at his disposal some Western medieval surgical writings and the major Moslem treatises such as those of Avicenna, Rhazes, and Abulcasis, as well as the anatomical writings of Galen, which had not only been translated into Latin but had immediately gained a predominating influence. In addition, toward the end of his Parisian period two contemporary works became available, those of Laguna and of Guinter of Andernach.

As far as instructors in anatomy were concerned, we know definitely of only two, Sylvius and Guinter—the former probably making important contributions to his student's training in dissection, but only upon animals, and the latter appearing at least to have provided Vesalius with the opportunity for dissection of the human cadaver. Probably, however, we ought also to include the name of Jean Tagault.

Dissection materials were admittedly scarce, although osteological specimens were not a very great problem, since the student might resort to cemeteries where human remains were apparently given the most superficial interment. On several occasions Vesalius referred to the visits he made to the Cemetery of the Innocents. "In Paris in the Cemetery of the Innocents I saw a large collection of mandibles as well as of other bones." [127] Later, in 1546, he recalled that he had spent "long hours in the Cemetery of the Innocents in Paris turning over bones," and that, on one occasion, because of his enthusiasm, at Montfaucon "I was gravely imperiled by the many savage dogs." [128] These forays in search of bones were not mentioned as something unusual, but merely as an accompaniment to some other reference such as that to a particular osteological description, and it seems likely that Vesalius was doing no more than any other student genuinely interested and ambitious. On several expeditions he mentioned a companion. It may even have been that the student at Paris was prompted by his teacher to such activity, as Vesalius was later to urge his own students in Padua. Osteology was required and obtaining materials for its study was apparently something left to the resources of the student. Referring to still another expedition to the Cemetery of the Innocents, Vesalius wrote of the many piles of bones which had been disinterred, and continued:

When I first studied the bones with Matthaeus Terminus, distinguished physician in all branches of medicine and lifelong friend and companion of my studies, our supply was very abundant. After we had studied them long and tirelessly we dared at times to wager with our companions that even blindfolded we could for the space of a half-hour identify by touch any bone offered to us. Those of us who wished to learn had to study all the more zealously since there was virtually no help to be had from our teachers in this part of medicine.[129]

Turning to dissection itself, we find that the student was faced with a greater problem. Reference has already been made to Vesalius's criticism of anatomical instruction, and he continued this criticism by adding that he had been introduced to anatomical dissection, which was merely "the casual and superficial demonstration of a few organs presented to me and to my fellow students in one or two public dissections by unskilled barbers." [130] However, during the same period he was studying the dissection of "brute animals," the true Galenic dissection material, under the direction of Sylvius,[131] and the experience gained in this Galenic dissection gave him sufficient audacity, if not knowledge, so that "at the third dissection at which I was ever present and at the urging of my fellow students and the teachers, [I] conducted it publicly and more completely than was usually the case." [132]

Vesalius was to acknowledge his debt to Sylvius, but it should also be noted that Guinter, lecturing, we may assume, from his high chair and therefore distant from the cadaver, was willing to wave aside the barbers usually performing the actual dissection and allow it to be conducted by his students.[133] Considering the times and the conservatism of Paris, Vesalius had unusual opportunities, so it is regrettable that he made the further remark that he would not have succeeded in his anatomical studies "if I had not put my hand to the matter." It may be true, but it is ungenerous, at least in the usual interpretation, since he was allowed to do that very thing. Presumably, too, he was allowed considerably more activity in dissection, and the mention he makes of it may be looked upon as merely a sampling. There is, for example, the case of the "prostitute of fine figure and in the prime of life, who had been hanged" and whom "I first dissected in a public anatomy." [134] This must have been the incident to which Guinter referred many years later in his *De medicina veteri et nova*: "Once in Paris when I presided over the public dissection of a female cadaver, Andreas Vesalius assisted me." [135] No doubt Vesalius did a good deal of dissection for Guinter's *Institutiones* in addition to the single instance referred to by Guinter in that work, and in the *Venesection letter* of 1539 Vesalius recalled further dissection in an effort to trace the course of the haemorrhoidal veins.[136]

So far as we know, this constituted the anatomical training received by Vesalius in Paris,[137] although it is possible that Guinter initiated him into vivisection. As Guinter said: "If you desire to do so, it is certainly of value to investigate everything accurately in live dogs. Formerly in Paris I frequently did this in these animals, sometimes privately, sometimes with a few auditors and students"; [138] and it is quite possible that Vesalius was among those students. It would be incorrect to liken the Vesalius of Paris to the later author of the *Fabrica,* and it is important to remember that although Vesalius in Paris may have been extraordinarily inquisitive, and he had acquired unusual skill in the technique of dissection, his vision was still considerably clouded by Galenism if, indeed, he was not a completely devoted Galenist.

The last of our scanty records of Vesalius's years in Paris is a collection of Galen's writings published in 1536 that bears the young student's signature; the collection also contains the signature of Michael Securis (Hatchet), an English physician who studied in Paris a few years later, suggesting that Vesalius had sold or given away some of his books before his departure.[139] It is tempting to think that this symbolized Vesalius's liberation from Galen's authority, but that event was still a few years away.

Chapter V

MEDICAL STUDIES IN LOUVAIN, 1536–1537
Paraphrasis in Nonum Librum Almansoris

OR the date of 2 August 1536, the Commentaries of the medical faculty of Paris contain the following statement:

A great fear possessed everyone as the forces of Flanders, Hainault, and Burgundy and their followers advanced into Picardy where those most criminal of men ravished nuns, despoiled churches, seized several fortresses, and perpetrated many other horrors. They had determined to destroy or at least to sack the city of Paris, impelled to this by the emperor Charles who too rashly had sworn—O impious and inhuman man—that if it were possible he would not desist until he had destroyed the kingdom of our most Christian king, Francis I, had left him only enough land in which to bury his body, and had overthrown the kingdom of France forever. What could be said that was more inhuman, cruel, and unworthy of a Christian prince? But through God's providence matters turned out far otherwise than the emperor had desired, and he fled shamefully, taking his army and departing from our soil.

In fact France was the aggressor in this war, and it was a result of the aggressive advance of a French army into Savoy, with the ultimate aim of seizing Milan, that the emperor Charles V, on 25 July 1536, directed one imperial force into Provence and ordered a second to advance along the Flemish frontier with France.[1] With some bloody exceptions the war was waged on both sides without energy or enthusiasm and was brought to an end by the truce of Aigues-Mortes on 18 June 1538,[2] yet it had forced Vesalius to break off his studies in Paris. As the Commentaries indicate, the Flemings were singled out as a specific enemy, and accordingly Vesalius's status in France was that of an enemy-alien. His origin was of course attested by the baptismal certificate that he had presented to the dean of the faculty of medicine when he had matriculated in 1533. As he wrote later, "due to the outbreak of war I returned from Paris to Louvain."[3]

Probably the young student paid a visit to his parental home in Brussels during the remainder of the summer and then proceeded to Louvain for the opening of the new term in the autumn, for it was most likely in Brussels, shortly after his return from Paris, that he participated in an autopsy performed upon a young girl in the train of the Countess of Egmont:

When I had returned from my visit to France I was invited by the physician of the Countess of Egmont to attend the autopsy of an eighteen-year-old girl of noble birth who, because of an enduring paleness of complexion and difficulty in breathing—although otherwise of agreeable appearance—was thought by her uncle to have been poisoned. Since the dissection had been undertaken by a thoroughly unskilled barber I could not keep my hand from the work, although except for two crude dissections lasting three days, which I had seen at school in Paris, I had never been present at one. From constriction of the thorax by a corset [4] the girl had been accustomed to wear so that her waist might appear long and willowy, I judged that the complaint lay in a compression of the torso around the hypochondria and lungs. Although she had suffered from an ailment of the lungs, yet the astonishing compression of the organs in the hypochondria appeared to us to be the cause of her ailment, even though we found nothing that would indicate strangulation of the uterus except some swelling of the ovaries. After the attendant women had left to shed their corsets as quickly as possible and the rest of the spectators had departed, in company with the physician I dissected the girl's uterus for the sake of the hymen. The hymen, however, was not entirely whole but had not quite disappeared, as I have found is usually the case in female cadavers in which one can barely find the place where it had been. It looked as if the girl had ripped the hymen with her fingers either for some frivolous reason or according to Rhazes's prescription against strangulation of the uterus without the intervention of a man. [5]

As this autopsy was one of his first, it made a considerable impression upon Vesalius. In the second edition of the *Fabrica* he referred to it again, adding details that suggest a death from pneumonia—"a great whiteness and softness of the lungs" and a generalized anemia—but which he says was caused by "strangulation of the uterus." In the simplest terms, strangulation of the uterus, caused by such things as "gross vapors" or the humors, was considered to distend the uterus upward to the diaphragm and make breathing difficult. It was believed that the complaint could produce faintness, hysteria, and even death.

It was in this same case that for the first time Vesalius observed a corpus luteum:

In addition to the vessels, the ovaries of women have internally certain sinuses filled with a thin watery humor. In the course of dissection when an uninjured ovary is first compressed, like an inflated bladder it usually squirts forth this humor with a crackling noise and to an astonishing height, not unlike a fountain. In women that humor is white, like very thick whey, but I have also found it yellowish like somewhat thickened egg yolk in two girls of high nobility who before death suffered from strangulation of the uterus. In their cases merely one of the sinuses of one ovary protruded like a rather large pea, stuffed with a yellowish humor which tinted the adjoining parts as we observe man's colon to be rendered yellowish by the gall bladder, where it is carried under the liver. As this humor or liquor rarely occurs with such color, so also it had a very pronounced and offensive odor, undoubtedly the poisonous cause of those symptoms of strangulation of the uterus that frequently arise in the brain.[6]

A second dramatic incident was Vesalius's theft of the remains of a malefactor from the gibbet outside Louvain. From the context of the account it appears that this must have occurred shortly after his arrival in Louvain, probably in the autumn of 1536, and it is also in this anecdote that we are introduced to another of his friends in Louvain, the later-celebrated mathematician Gemma Frisius: [7]

> Because of the outbreak of war I returned from Paris to Louvain where, while out walking with that celebrated physician and mathematician Gemma Frisius and looking for bones where the executed criminals are usually placed along the country roads—to the advantage of the students—I came upon a dried cadaver similar to that of the robber Galen mentions having seen. As I suspect the birds had freed that one of flesh, so they had cleansed this one, which had been partially burned and roasted over a fire of straw and then bound to a stake. Consequently the bones were entirely bare and held together only by the ligaments so that merely the origins and insertions of the muscles had been preserved. . . . Observing the body to be dry and nowhere moist or rotten, I took advantage of this unexpected but welcome opportunity and, with the help of Gemma, I climbed the stake and pulled the femur away from the hipbone. Upon my tugging, the scapulae with the arms and hands also came away, although the fingers of one hand and both patellae as well as one foot were missing. After I had surreptitiously brought the legs and arms home in successive trips—leaving the head and trunk behind—I allowed myself to be shut out of the city in the evening so that I might obtain the thorax, which was held securely by a chain. So great was my desire to possess those bones that in the middle of the night, alone and in the midst of all those corpses, I climbed the stake with considerable effort and did not hesitate to snatch away that which I so desired. When I had pulled down the bones I carried them some distance away and concealed them until the following day when I was able to fetch them home bit by bit through another gate of the city.
>
> At first, however, I was unable to cut the ligaments because of their extraordinary hardness, and so I attempted to soften them in boiling water; finally and secretly I cooked all the bones to render them more suitable for my purpose. When they had been cleansed I constructed the skeleton that is preserved at Louvain in the home of my very dear old friend Gisbertus Carbo, companion in my boyhood studies and later distinguished as a student of medicine as well as of other branches of learning. With considerable effort I obtained the missing hand, foot, and two patellae from elsewhere and prepared this skeleton with such speed that I was able to convince everyone that I had brought it from Paris. Thus any suspicion of having made off with the bones was destroyed, although later the burgomaster was so favorably disposed toward the studies of the candidates in medicine that he was willing to grant whatever body was sought from him. He attained no little knowledge of anatomy and was in regular attendance whenever I conducted an anatomy there.[8]

The burgomaster was Adrian of Blehen, or Blehenius, who had assumed office in 1530.[9]

That the burgomaster of Louvain was a staunch supporter of medical studies, especially of anatomy, by no means reflected the attitude of the faculty of medicine, and no doubt Vesalius met the necessity of continuing his studies at conservative Louvain with reluctance, especially since it meant transferring from a faculty of great lustre to one that had hardly and grudgingly begun to acknowledge the new medicine of the renaissance. Even after the opening of the sixteenth century, which witnessed the publication of the Hippocratic and Galenic corpora, as well as precise Latin translations of their contents, the medical faculty of Louvain remained content to pursue a somnolent and medieval course. There had been a few slight exceptions, such as Joannes Spierinck (d. 1499), who asserted that his countrymen ought to be treated with their own herbs and decoctions of them rather than with the exotic prescriptions of Avicenna. However, there is the suggestion that this view indicated not so much a revolt against the medieval and an urge to improve the quality of medicine as an intolerance of things Moslem. More sensible, perhaps, was the view of Jacques van den Eetvelde, who became professor of medicine at Louvain in 1507 after somewhat enlightening studies in Italy, and who opposed uroscopy as belonging to an old and obsolete tradition.[10]

Of greater moment were the oral and printed utterances of Hubertus Barlandus, a relative of the distinguished humanist Adrian Barlandus, who had attended the Lily of Louvain. Upon gaining the licentiate of medicine he studied in Paris and Montpellier, and while returning to the Netherlands stopped in Strasburg long enough in 1529 to publish a new edition of the *Epistolae medicinales* of Manardus—an indication that he had become a supporter of the new Greek medicine. Upon his return to Louvain, Barlandus sought to dissuade his former professor, Arnold Noots, from his attachment to the Moslem and medieval school, but found his efforts unavailing since Noots declared he would rather be wrong with Avicenna than right with any Greek physician, certainly an unequivocal statement of position. Then, taken into the service of Anthony of Berghes, governor of Namur, Barlandus issued an attack on the conservative position of Noots: *Velitatio cum Arnoldo Nootz medicinae apud Lovanienses doctore . . . Avicennae locis aliquot aliis adhuc dormitatio ostenditur, simul Galenus ab hominis morsibus aliquot defenditur* (Antwerp, 1532). The work is of interest not only because of the controversy it aroused between the medieval or Moslem school of medicine and the new Galenism, but also because Vesalius was to refer to the matter in 1539 in his *Venesection letter*.

Although Barlandus had no official or academic association with Louvain, except as a former student, he may, through his writings, have contributed to the ultimate modernization of medical teaching in that university. At least he lived long enough to witness the ousting in 1542 of the two conservative members of the medical faculty whose position he had criticized a decade earlier.

These two ordinary professors of medicine were Arnold Noots of Halle, already mentioned as the target of criticism, who had been appointed in 1526 to give the afternoon lecture, and Leonard Willemaers of Louvain, who had been appointed for the morning lecture.[11] Their ability may be judged from the charges eventually brought against them, which were such as Barlandus might have made. It was declared to the town authorities that both professors were living in the wrong century and that they had no idea of modern medical method and content—in short, that they were ignorant of the new Galenic medicine. Especially did the students object to Noots, declaring that he gave them nothing but unintelligible and unexplained medical terms drawn from Avicenna.[12]

Because of the slight attendance in the medical school there were only two other professors, beneficiaries of canonries of the second foundation —that is, supported from the revenues of the canonries of St. Peter's in Louvain in accordance with an approbation granted by Pope Eugenius IV in 1447. At this time the first of these was Johannes Heems of Armentière, called Armenterianus. Originally a priest, Armenterianus became a doctor of medicine and, on 23 November 1525, professor of medicine, a position he retained until 1559. He was also regent of the Lily and on four occasions (1529, 1532, 1535, 1550) was rector of the university. He died 1 July 1560.[13] The second professor, chosen at the same time and holding his position until 1532, was Cornelius Stephanus;[14] he was succeeded in 1536 by Charles Goossins, or Goswinus (1507–1574), M.D., 1539.[15] Although not a target of the students' displeasure, at any rate during the period of Vesalius's residence in Louvain, neither do these men appear to have been any inducement for Vesalius to remain, and he went elsewhere to obtain his final degree in medicine. Nevertheless, at Padua in 1538 he dedicated a book to Armenterianus, and in the dedication sent his greetings to Willemaers. This latter instance must, however, have been the result of a personal rather than a professional regard since elsewhere he also mentions favorably the *Velitatio* of Barlandus, although it was strongly condemnatory of the Louvain faculty of medicine.

From the later *Venesection letter* we receive a brief glimpse of the situation in Louvain and an indication that Vesalius had not only contempt but a strong dislike for at least one further member of the faculty, Jeremiah Drivère of Brakel, called Brachelius (c. 1504–1554). Drivère was a student of the Falcon and gained his undergraduate degree from there in 1522. He probably stayed on as a teacher or tutor since he was admitted to the academic senate in 1531 as a member of the faculty of arts. Thereafter he took up medical studies and in conjunction with them attended the Greek lectures of Rescius in the Pedagogium Trilingue in order to read the original texts of the classical physicians. Drivère's first publication was his *Disceptatio de securissimo victu a neotericis perperam praescripto* (Louvain, 1531), an attack on the diet that physicians prescribed in cases of arthritis. An immediate reply to this treatise brought forth an answer from Drivère entitled *Commentarius de victu ab arthriticis morbis vindicante*, in 1532. In that same year he also joined in the venesection controversy.[16]

The venesection controversy represented one aspect of the wider struggle taking place between the defenders of medieval medicine and the proponents of the revived and purified classical school. Venesection as a method of therapy based on recognition of the humoral doctrine was acknowledged by all, but the crux of the controversy was over the manner of employing it. In general two conditions of the body were considered to require venesection. In the first, the humors were judged to have surpassed their normal proportion in the body and produced what was called plethora or plenitude; this led to a feeling of heaviness and difficulty in movement, or tension, soreness, and pain. In the second, there was an imbalance in the normal proportion of the humors, with some one of them in the ascendancy, and this was called cacochymia. The excess of humors or of a single humor might be reduced by one of two kinds of venesection, the withdrawal of blood by revulsive or by derivative bleeding. The former drew the blood, and hence the excess of humors in the blood, away from the area affected by the complaint, whereas the latter drew them to the area. The medieval practice, based on Moslem medical opinion, was chiefly the employment of revulsive bleeding with venesection performed at a site as far as possible from the location of the ailment.

With the revival of Greek, and the publication and study of Hippocrates and Galen in Greek as well as in new, literal Latin translations, it became apparent that the medieval method of revulsive bleeding represented only one aspect of the classical teaching on the subject, while the exaggerated medieval form of revulsive bleeding—which required venesection on the side of the body opposite the ailment, and even such strange procedure as bleeding from the great toe—had no sanction at all.

The attack on the medievalists appears to have been opened by Pierre Brissot, 1478–1522, a physician of Paris who, during an epidemic of "pleurisy" in 1514, announced that he had employed venesection based upon his interpretation of classical teaching with excellent results. His method of revulsive bleeding was to open a vein of the arm on the side of the body affected, and, since "pleurisy" existed in a region drained by the vena cava, he denied that bleeding from the other side of the body according to the medieval view was necessary. Brissot's original activities in Paris gained him small support, although objection to his procedure was as yet local. It was not until he had moved to Portugal where, in 1518, he again employed his new method of venesection in a second epidemic of "pleurisy" in the city of Evora that the controversy became widespread. Here he was attacked by Denis, the royal physician, to whom Brissot replied; but owing to his death his reply was not published until 1525.[17] By this time European physicians had become divided in their defense of the old medieval practice or their support of the new classical school, and the contest over venesection as a facet of the wider dispute of medieval versus classical medicine became violent.[18]

Among the earliest supporters of Brissot's stand, because they were early supporters of the revived Hippocratic and Galenic medicine, were Giovanni Manardi, or Manardus, 1462–1536;[19] Leonhart Fuchs, 1501–

1556; [20] and Matteo Corti, or Curtius, 1475–1542.[21] Drivère entered the controversy in 1532 with his *De missione sanguinis*, in which he said that, according to his reading of Hippocrates and Galen, instead of one single method of bloodletting both the old and the new methods should be employed—which led him to be looked upon as giving some tacit support to the older Moslem opinion that advocated solely revulsive bleeding. Fuchs replied to Drivère in his *Apologiae tres* (1532), to which Drivère made answer in 1535 in *De temporibus morborum & opportunitate auxiliorum*.

Vesalius did not write anything on this controversy until his *Venesection letter* of 1539, but in that work he hearked back to discussions on the subject at Louvain and indicated that he was a Galenist, an ardent supporter of the new views, and thereby an opponent of his teacher Drivère whom at that time he had opposed vocally as he was to do later in print:

> I am sure that you recall what I wrote some time ago of the physicians of Louvain.[22] Among them there was one, in his own opinion very learned and for some unknown reason extraordinarily self-satisfied, who in a large assembly of very erudite men had the impudence to call Manardi, Fuchs, Corti, and Brissot the Lutherans of physicians after I, accepting their judgment, had perhaps too sharply attacked his opinions about venesection in a public discussion. . . . This worthy fellow believed that like Lutherans they ought to be ridiculed with every sort of injustice and on every pretext. Indeed, inflated with self-assurance and arrogance, he was prone to despise everyone else and to advance all sorts of heresies, being incapable of anything else. He asserted shamelessly that he was accordingly forced to employ such strong words drawn from vulgar speech lest we, as yet candidates, be infected by their pestiferous error.[23]

A second reference to his Louvain teacher, in which he is named, also indicated Vesalius's allegiance to the revived classical school in contrast to the lingering medieval element in the faculty of medicine:

> I recall having read some time ago Barlandus's worthy book criticizing the physicians of Louvain,[24] sent by its author to that very learned and well-read man Jean Guinter.[25] I believe that this work—at which Brachelius jeers in his later *Apologia* against Fuchs because the printers had formerly refused it—was by no means unknown in Paris, especially since I have learned that the Parisian printers have been searching diligently for the manuscript.[26]

Drivère did not receive his degree of doctor of medicine until 1537, and therefore his teaching during Vesalius's year in Louvain must have been in a subordinate capacity such as that of the baccalaureates in the medical school in Paris. Hence, as what we may call an instructor rather than a professor, his prestige was not sufficient to overawe the students, and it was presumably for this reason that Vesalius, as he wrote, dared to attack "perhaps too sharply" his opinions about venesection [27]—and Vesalius, then a young, devoted, and overimpetuous Galenist fresh from Paris, was perhaps too harsh in his judgment. Although Leonhart Fuchs, one of the "Lutherans of physicians" whom Vesalius was defending, referred to Drivère as a "patron of Arabic madness," nevertheless he closed his *Apologia adversus Brachelium* with the remark, "would that all employed the same moderation of spirit as Jeremiah [Drivère] in controversies over medical questions." [28] Somewhat more indulgence is also shown to Drivère by a fellow student of Vesalius, Guillaume Pantin, or Pantinus, of Thielt, an admirer of the later-famous anatomist and one who sought to maintain communication with him.[29]

Two other possible acquaintances of Vesalius at this time were Livinus Lemmen, or Lemnius, 1505–1568—although any acquaintance would have been established at Mechlin, the home of a mutual friend Joachim Roelants, since Lemnius had left Louvain by 1534 [30]—and Rembert Dodoens, 1517–1585, the physician and botanist, who was, however, still in Louvain.[31]

We do not know the precise sequence of Vesalius's activities in Louvain. We do know, of course, that he was completing his studies in the faculty of medicine, and it is quite possible that when he took up those studies something was known of his exploits in Paris. Certainly he would have brought back, if possible, a copy of Guinter's *Institutiones* to demonstrate both what he had already accomplished and the high opinion in which he was held for these accomplishments by the famous Parisian professor. It may have been for some such reason that he was given the rather unusual permission to conduct the anatomical demonstrations to which he later referred in the *Fabrica,* a performance that seems to have attracted spectators from other parts of the university as well as from the medical school. Although we do not know how many dissections Vesalius performed in Louvain, it seems likely that the indulgent professor who permitted them was that Armenterianus to whom Vesalius later dedicated his revision of Guinter's *Institutiones,* possibly because of an esteem growing out of this situation. Nor ought we to forget Vesalius's expression of gratitude to the burgomaster Adrian of Blehen, who generously made cadavers available upon request. It was certainly an unusual privilege for a student not yet a baccalaureate.

At Louvain . . . where for eighteen years the physicians had not even dreamed of anatomy, in order to assist the students of that university and to acquire greater skill in a subject still obscure but of the greatest importance for medicine, I dissected with somewhat greater accuracy than at Paris and lectured on the entire structure of the human body. As a result, the younger professors of that university now seem to be seriously engaged in gaining a knowledge of the parts of man, fully appreciating what valuable philosophical material is to be acquired from this knowledge.[32]

The final episode of which we have record in Vesalius's academic career in Louvain was the preparation and publication of his *Paraphrasis in nonum librum Rhazae medici arabis clariss. ad Regem Almansorem.*[33] This may have been the substance of a thesis he defended for his degree of bachelor of medicine, and such assumption is supported by his designation of himself on the title page as *auctore Andrea Wesalio Bruxellensi medicinae candidato.* The date of publication was February 1537 and,

69

since the academic year did not close until the Vigil of the Assumption of Mary,[34] there would have been ample time for the presentation and defense of the thesis if it had not already been defended before publication.

The book is a sorry bit of typography, but perhaps it is all that could be expected from Rutger Rescius, its printer-publisher, who, as has been mentioned, was also professor of Greek in the Pedagogium Trilingue. Rescius was able to devote only part of his time to printing and publication, which he had undertaken more for gain than for any genuine interest in the matter.[35]

The *Paraphrasis* was dedicated to Vesalius's mentor, Nicolas Florenas, whose advice the young student had followed so that "I have finally reached that part of medicine called curative, of greater excellence than the other [parts] studied for its sake, and also far better suited for application." In short, Vesalius was on the point of completing his medical studies for the degree of bachelor of medicine. However, as a Galenist and filled with knowledge of Galenic therapy, he was amazed at the medieval therapy he observed about him and that was taught at Louvain, presumably by Noots and Willemaers. "And then I began to marvel greatly at the methods normally employed by many physicians today for treating ailments, so much at variance with the methods of the learned Greeks . . . and fixed in the traditions of the barbarians and Arabs." Hence, filled with enthusiasm and confidence, "I decided that it would not be inappropriate . . . very carefully to compare the therapy of the Arabs with that of the Greeks."

Moreover, as a former student of the Parisian faculty of medicine, Vesalius was able to relate that "the eminent physicians of Paris also strongly recommend this method to their students, hoping that in consequence, increasing little by little through the efforts of those practising the art, it will come to flourish everywhere."

In accordance with the advice of Florenas, "I first chose Rhazes and zealously compared his writings to those of the Greeks as a touchstone, for I had heard my very erudite teacher Jacobus Sylvius declare him to be first among those of his race in the art of treatment." In the translation of Rhazes hitherto available, "you will find very few remedies that have not been written incorrectly and obscurely or even identified by Arabic names." Hence the fault was not entirely that of Rhazes but at least in part the result of incompetent translations, and what was therefore needed was emendation.

As a result "I undertook to emendate the translation of Rhazes so that I might free other candidates of medicine from such immense labor, and so that thereafter the author himself might reach men's hands purged not only of barbarous medicaments and words unknown to Latin ears, but also with his whole discourse improved." Thus "I did not always attempt to translate literally—which is perhaps desirable in a translation —but rather I made a paraphrase, adding freely what I judged to be necessary, and explaining in greater detail what seemed too obscure."

Vesalius might also have added that he did not translate Rhazes because he was incapable of doing so. Florenas may have been aware of this and perhaps smiled indulgently at this piece of youthful bombast which, however, created for those unacquainted with Vesalius the idea of greater linguistic skill than he truly possessed. What he had done was to improve the existing translation stylistically, to identify drugs from context or perhaps occasionally from discussion with some orientalist, and to add marginalia calling attention to classical views or casting doubt upon some of Rhazes's remarks.

Whether or not the *Paraphrasis* was a thesis, it bears the characteristics of one, both merits and defects, and we need not spend much time on its contents, which had no share in the author's later fame. It is true that its Latin is less barbarous than that of the earlier translation, and occasionally Greek terms are introduced, in a sense symbols of the school to which Vesalius gave allegiance. Marginalia present the classical treatment where it differed from that of Rhazes. For example, in cases of profound lethargy for which Rhazes proposed the use of clysters, Vesalius noted that "in lethargy Paul and Alexander employ venesection." [36] Vesalius gave contemporary names of drugs, as with *liquor Cyrenaicus praestantissimus* which "pharmacists today call assa foetida"; [37] on another occasion he was forced to write that something called *terra sigillata* was not to be found in the modern pharmacopeias, [38] and he risked a guess as to the meaning of *xylocaracta*, writing, "I believe [it is] the shreddings of certain astringent woods." [39]

In his dedication, Vesalius wrote that Rhazes "deserves to be freed of barbarisms . . . Especially since in that slender work he has given consideration to almost all the local diseases and seldom differs from the decisions of the Greeks"; therefore the problem was to make Rhazes respectable by means of reconciliation of terms. This became difficult in the chapter *"De laterali dolore qui PLEURITI Graecis dicitur,"* [40] where the introduction of Greek terms suggests the struggle that had arisen between the medieval and revived classical schools over the question of therapeutic venesection in cases of "pleurisy." Here there could be no compromise, since Rhazes announced the removal of blood from a part neighboring the site of the ailment to be dangerous, and in an extensive marginal note Vesalius presented the new procedure and termed the Arabs HAIMOPHOBOI, that is, fearful of blood. On the whole, the *Paraphrasis* has no more than antiquarian interest today. The therapy of Rhazes was based upon the use of drugs, many of them fantastic, and upon Hippocratic and Galenic doctrines that had been reinterpreted and altered with the passing centuries, but always within a vaguely defined Galenic structure. Vesalius's annotations also are confined, by a more exact Galenic physiology and medicine, and as a result one must not expect, nor does one find, any free inquiry in this treatise.

It is of interest that Vesalius, so staunch a partisan of the revived Hippocratic and Galenic medicine and therefore a critic of the medieval practices based upon Moslem opinion, should have chosen Rhazes as a subject. However, as he admitted, he was following the suggestion of his mentor Florenas, and no doubt he was also influenced by Sylvius who, despite his strong Galenism, recognized that although most Moslem writings might be condemned, a few contained contributions worth consideration.

In March of that same year (1537) a second edition, somewhat superior in typography to the first, was published in Basel under the imprint of Robert Winter.[41] In this edition Vesalius's name was not accompanied by the words "candidate in medicine," and it may be assumed that either he had successfully completed the requirements for his degree or he confidently anticipated their completion. We do not know whether he made the trip to Basel himself or whether he sent his manuscript there by carrier. At any rate, by this time the work ought rightfully to have been forgotten and probably would have been had not Vesalius later acquired fame. In 1544 the *Paraphrasis*, without the dedication, was inserted into an edition of the *Opera omnia* of Rhazes published in Basel, and in 1551 and 1586 separate editions of the *Paraphrasis* were published, one in Lyons and the other in Wittenberg.[42]

Chapter VI

PADUA,
1537–1542

FTER republication of the *Paraphrasis* in Basel in March 1537 all trace of Vesalius is lost until 1 December of that year in Padua. It seems likely that once he had the baccalaureate in medicine he returned to Brussels where a family council discussed the next step in the young man's education. Advice may have been sought from Nicolas Florenas, that friend of the family who had studied at Bologna; since the war with France was still in progress, precluding a return to Paris, it was possibly Florenas who advised Vesalius to go to Italy to continue his studies, although the latter might already have learned something about Padua during his years in Paris. According to the Commentaries of the Paris medical faculty, at the beginning of the year 1535–36 one of the students, Guido Bougier, "doctor of Padua and bachelor of Montpellier," petitioned the faculty of medicine to be received into the ranks of its bachelors.[1] Hence this former Paduan student may have provided information about Padua which was influential in Vesalius's later decision to pursue his studies in that Italian university. Despite any such personal influence, however, the young bachelor was probably aware that, of all the Italian medical faculties, that of Padua was then the most renowned. Before discussing Vesalius's career in Italy it will be best to consider the special position that Padua held in the world of learning.

The University of Padua originated about 1220 when difficulty between the town and the University of Bologna led to an exodus of legal students, some of them going to Padua where it appears that Roman law was already being taught. In Padua, too, trouble later arose between towns and gowns, although the school managed to survive, partly because of new difficulties in Bologna. In 1260 a code of statutes was drawn up and in 1346 Pope Clement VI confirmed the school's right to the title of *studium generale*.

Formerly under the control of the Dukes of Carrara, Padua became subject to Venice in 1440, but both reigning powers supported the development of the university. In 1399 Francesco of Carrara had provided the university with its first building and assigned a tax on oxen and wagons for the salaries of the professors. Under Venetian rule salaries were increased, and no doubt this assisted in attracting and keeping the university's distinguished faculty. It was during Venetian domination that Padua gained its greatest glory and became the university-town of the Venetian republic. Venetian subjects were forbidden to study elsewhere without special dispensation, and in time a course of study in Padua became required of those wishing to enter Venetian governmental service.

At first the university had been dominated by the faculty of law, but by the end of the fourteenth century the faculty of medicine had gained sufficient separate status and independence to begin acquiring the fame that was to make it the most distinguished school of medicine in Europe in the sixteenth century. Even before the close of the fourteenth century its celebrity was such that patients from far away had begun to seek out Padua in hope of cure for ailments elsewhere looked upon as incurable.[2]

There was one brief period of decline, beginning in 1509, when a combined attack upon Venice by the major powers allied in the League of Cambrai required the republic to give all her energies and resources to the problem of survival. However, a new formation of the states known as the Holy League, and now including Venice, directed European aggression against France and so removed the danger from the Venetian republic as well as the heavy drain upon her resources. When in 1517 a committee of Paduan citizens requested renewed support of the university, Venice agreed but at the same time took over its immediate direction by replacing the former Paduan magistrates with three Venetian overseers known as *Riformatori dello Studio di Padova.* From the viewpoint of Venice, the university had become more important than the town in which it was located, or as Bernardo Navagero, one of the later *Riformatori* and a friend of Vesalius, expressed it, "without the university Padua would not be Padua."

Such was the new order of administration when Vesalius arrived to complete his studies. Both students and professors were subject to the *Riformatori,* and under their direction new regulations were put into effect. Members of the faculty were elected for regular terms of up to four years with a possible extension of two years, and only after a longer period of service might an exceptional professor be elected for life. Furthermore, to prevent pressures from being applied unduly by families of great social or financial prestige and so possibly endangering the high academic quality of instruction, except for individual cases based solely upon merit no patrician of Venice or any citizen of upper class Paduan society was permitted to hold a chair in the university.

When a scholar was added to the faculty he was allowed full freedom to teach as he desired, the only restriction being that he must not precisely repeat his course of lectures annually but only after the passage of several years, during which time he must have offered a varied intellectual diet. Later, in accordance with this philosophy, Vesalius was permitted to reorganize the presentation of the anatomical demonstration in a manner contrary to that prescribed in the university's statutes. Professors were not allowed to leave, even during vacation time, except with permission of the authorities. They were required to teach a prescribed number of hours or be fined in proportion to the lectures they had not given. They were further subject to fine if they did not succeed in drawing a certain number of auditors to their lectures, and they had to give a required number of public lectures in addition to what were called private lectures, that is, those exclusively for the students enrolled in the professor's course.[3]

Although it may be assumed that Vesalius had matriculated at Padua at the opening of the new term in the autumn of 1537, we catch no glimpse of him until December. Nevertheless, we know that, in accordance with the statutes of the university, "within a month after his arrival" he must have presented himself before the rector, in that year Lodovico Muzio,[4] and sworn that "he would obey him and his successors and abide by all our statutes." At that time Vesalius presented his name and nationality, paid thirty pence into the treasury of the university, and another four to the university's notary for his services.[5]

The academic year began on 18 October, St. Luke's day, "or at least the day following," with a convocation of faculty, students, the local bishop, and certain civic officials. The University of Padua did not indulge in so much pageantry as Vesalius had experienced in Paris, since lectures began on the day following the convocation and continued, except for certain holidays, until the Feast of the Assumption of the Virgin on 15 August.[6] This may appear to have been an excessively long school year, but holidays were more frequent than at Paris, since besides a weekly holiday on Thursday there were forty-three special holidays.[7] According to the statutes the degree of bachelor of medicine required a minimum of three years, attendance at all the regular lecture series, "practice with some famous physician for at least a year," and proof that the candidate had "visited the sick." [8] Vesalius's three years at Paris and one year at Louvain apparently satisfied the residence requirement not only for the bachelor's degree but for the degree of doctor of medicine as well. He had not served a year with a "famous physician," but no doubt at Padua as at Paris some of the requirements were occasionally honored in the breach. The fact that Vesalius was invited to join the faculty upon completion of his examination suggests that he had made an unusually favorable impression upon his teachers, and something of this sort may have accounted for the waiving of a requirement.

The additional requirement of visiting the sick was apparently fulfilled by Vesalius, who later referred to that period "when I was treating the sick in Venice under the direction of the most famous professors there." [9] This refers to the method of clinical teaching carried on by the professors, most notably by Giambattista da Monte. As the *Fabrica* represented a movement in anatomical studies away from the authority of man directly toward nature, so in the field of medicine some of the

Paduan faculty had recognized that the medical student could frequently gain more knowledge at the bedside of a patient than from medical treatises. It was this return to Hippocratic principles that permitted Padua to establish the first clinical teaching in Europe, partly under the influence of Girolamo Fracastoro and thereafter greatly developed by Giambattista da Monte, 1489–1551, of Verona. Da Monte held successively the chairs of practical and theoretical medicine, organized clinical teaching at the hospital of San Francesco in Padua, and took the students directly to the homes of the sick.[10] However, Vesalius's words suggest that he fulfilled the requirement of visiting the sick in Venice rather than in Padua, perhaps because of a greater supply of teaching material there and perhaps as the result of some arrangement between the medical faculty of Padua and the Collegio dei Fisici of Venice. If it is true that his words refer specifically to the city of Venice rather than to the Venetian state, which included Padua, it may have been at this time that he first became acquainted with Joannes Stephanus of Calcar, a fellow Netherlander and student artist in Titian's studio, who will be discussed later, as well as the Venetian physician Nicolo Massa, who has already been mentioned.

The procedures required for the examinations of a candidate for a degree were carefully laid down in the statutes. First there was the requirement of a "private examination" of the candidate, which determined whether he was sufficiently prepared for the ordeal of the "true" or official examination. If the candidate was judged to have done sufficiently well in the private examination, his sponsors or *promotores*, two or more in number, presented him to the rector of the university and to the bishop or his vicar, and a time was then set for the true examination, which was divided into two parts. In the first the candidate was liable for solution or judgment of a number of points or questions which the examiners had agreed upon beforehand. If he was successful, he was then required to discuss or argue a thesis. The examination took place in the presence of the medical faculty, the rector or his representative— who had the right of silencing any examiner who appeared to be influenced by personal dislike of the candidate—and the bishop or his vicar.[11]

There are university documents still in existence that indicate Vesalius's successful completion of the several examinations. The first document carries the date of Saturday, 1 December, and records that the first examination, directed by Hieronymus Maripetrus, the dean, was held "in the church of Sant' Urbano, in the morning." Afterward, it was decided that "for merit in medicine, with the largest diminution of seventeen and one-half ducats [from the normal fee] for Andreas Vesalius, son of another Andreas," the examination had been passed, as we might say, with great distinction.[12] The second document, of 3 December, records "the trial of the aforementioned Andreas in medicine, who was approved unanimously."[13] A third and final document, of 5 December, carries the rubric "Examination in medicine of the aforementioned

Andreas Vesalius" and informs us that this final examination was conducted in the bishop's palace and that:

> . . . the aforesaid Andreas Vesalius was examined separately and thoroughly in medicine on the matters assigned to him yesterday, and because he conducted himself very well in this, his rigorous examination . . . he was approved unanimously and judged sufficient in medicine. . . . Immediately the distinguished doctor of medicine Francesco Frigimelica, in his own name and in that of the other doctors and cosponsors, granted him the insignia of the faculty.[14]

The following day Vesalius took over the chair of surgery and anatomy, although there appears to be no official document that records his appointment unless it can be read into the one mentioned immediately above. Otherwise, the fact is found only in the document that records his reappointment in October 1539, which also indicates that his annual salary had been increased from an original forty florins to seventy.[15] Some study has been made of the annual salaries of the Paduan medical faculty from which it seems that the chair of surgery and anatomy was considered of little importance at the time. It is true that when Vesalius left Padua in 1542 his salary had risen to an annual 200 florins, but, although the prestige of his chair had gained enormously, the salary was still small compared to the 1,000 florins received by Giambattista da Monte in 1546 for the chair of medical practice, and to the equal or even higher salaries received by other holders of chairs of medicine.[16]

Although this appointment so soon after Vesalius had received his degree appears unusual, it was not wholly exceptional. Joseph Struś (Struthius) of Posen received his M.D. at Padua in October 1535 and immediately afterwards was chosen *explicator extraordinarius medicinae theoreticae*, a post he held until 1545.[17] As for Vesalius, it will be recalled that he had been mentioned previously in print with some praise by Guinter of Andernach, although the *Institutiones anatomicae* was not such that its author's recommendation would carry any great weight in Padua, and Vesalius himself had published his *Paraphrasis*, but that certainly was not, or ought not to have been, important as a recommendation for the position he received. The only other possible explanations for his appointment are the impression he may have made during the few months in which he was a candidate for the degree, and the quality of his examination, plus the fact that the chair to which he was appointed was not at that time of great significance, as the list of his predecessors indicates. Whatever the reason, Vesalius was appointed professor of surgery to succeed Paolo Colombo of Cremona.

Turning once more to the statutes, we read that all those assigned to lecture had individually to take an oath of obedience to the rector and promise to observe the statutes. Furthermore, the lecturer had to promise that he would not be absent on the days of lectures except with the consent of the rector,[18] that even though it might not affect his lectures he would not be absent from Padua for more than three days without the rector's consent, and, if this were gained for a time during which he was supposed to lecture, that he would provide a substitute at his own expense.[19] When Vesalius consulted the time assigned him for his lectures he must have read, "Let those lecturing on surgery begin either at the nineteenth hour or the twenty-second according to the desire of the auditors, and let the lecture be for one hour." [20] Since the hours were counted from midday, this meant either seven o'clock or ten o'clock in the morning. There could be no question about the determination of the time since a bell in the tower of the bishop's palace tolled the hours daily during the term,[21] and, further, there was therefore no excuse for any lecturer to exceed the time allotted him and thereby prevent the use of the lecture hall by his successor. Were this to happen, the lecturer at fault was penalized one day's salary.[22] A further requirement was that of the public disputation. "Every teacher lecturing in the arts or in medicine must at least twice a year undertake a public disputation in the faculty in which he lectures, once before Easter and once after." [23] Failure to comply resulted in a financial penalty.

In his appointment to the faculty, Vesalius was described as *Explicator Chirurgiae*, and since the already distinguished Giambattista da Monte was similarly designated, there appears to have been no differentiation or distinction in academic titles. We are therefore at liberty to call Vesalius a lecturer or professor in the literal sense of the term rather than according to our modern usage. As has been stated, Vesalius's position was not a particularly important one relative to the chairs of medicine, and his predecessors had been far from distinguished. Riccoboni's list of previous *Explicatores Chirurgiae* begins in 1520 with Pietro Mainardi of Verona, followed in 1523 by Giambattista Pigafeta of Vicenzo, in 1525 by Jeronimo Vails of Spain, in 1526 by Nicolo Musico of Padua, in 1530 by Giambattista Lombardi of Padua, in 1535 by Francesco Litigato of Lendinara and Marcantonio Montagnana of Padua, and in 1536 by Paolo Colombo of Cremona.[24] There had for a time been a second chair of surgery, now joined to the first, and both held by Vesalius.

Physically the university had originally been comprised of a variety of houses scattered throughout the city. Eventually it collected around a large inn, once the Palazzo Maltraversi, called the *Hospitium Bovis Magnificum*, or, to the students, *il Bò*, the ox.[25] According to a document quoted by Facciolati,[26] on one occasion in the year 1477 the medical faculty attempted to convene as usual in the church of San Martino, but "when the doctors were unable to enter because the doors were shut against them from within, they went to the *Hospitium Bovis* . . . which they chose as their place of meeting." In 1493 the Venetian government took over the inn and began its conversion into a large university building, which still remains, called the Palazzo della Sapienza, but popularly still *il Bò*. The jurists were the first to enjoy these new quarters, and only as construction permitted did the medical faculty follow, in 1542.[27] Hence we do not know where Vesalius held his lectures until that year. However, John Caius, who obtained his M.D. at Padua in 1541, has some information bearing upon this matter:

> When I first went to Italy the lectures on the arts in Padua were given in the somewhat humble and obscure dwelling of a certain Paduan citizen at San Biagio. Before my departure [in 1543], however, other more magnificent schools had been built at the expense of the Venetian senate which controlled the city. These are in the Piazza del Bò near the school of jurisprudence and were the only buildings the university possessed. The quarters of the students were as yet in the homes of the townspeople.[28]

Apparently Caius anticipated that, as at Cambridge, so at Padua there would eventually be colleges for the students.

Returning to Vesalius's academic appointment, it may be said that it was he who made the chair of surgery important—or rather its anatomical duties, originally of secondary nature, which he performed in conjunction with surgery. It is also worthy of note that despite the suddenness with which he was appointed to the medical faculty he was apparently willing and ready to take up his duties immediately. Our information on this matter comes from a collection of manuscript lecture notes now in the National Library in Vienna, written by a student named Vitus Tritonius *Athesinus*, that is, from the district of the Adige. Very little is known of Vitus Tritonius. From his notes it appears that he was already studying at Padua in 1535, that he attended lectures on Hippocrates given by Leonardo Faventino in 1536, and other lectures by Giunio Paolo Crasso, Oddo degli Oddi, and Francesco Frigimelica. From 24 December 1536 until its completion on 24 January 1537 he attended a dissection carried out by Giovanni Antonio Lonigo, a Venetian surgeon, on behalf of Paolo Colombo, Vesalius's predecessor in the chair of surgery.[29] Vitus Tritonius appears to have struck up a close friendship with Vesalius so that he was able to note of the new teacher, on 24 December 1537, ". . . Andreas Vesalius of Brussels, my dear friend and companion." Vesalius was to reciprocate later in the *Fabrica* by declaring ". . . Vitus Tritonius *Athesinus*, a very dear companion of my studies." [30] Vitus is no longer mentioned in the second edition of 1555, suggesting, in accordance with Vesalius's practice, that he was dead by that time.

In Vitus Tritonius's notebook, we find, beginning on fol. 118r, ". . . Vesalius. Treatment of a phlegmon," and on fol. 184r, "Anatomy performed at Padua 6 December 1537 by Andreas Vesalius of Brussels, the most skilled and diligent of all anatomists." Thus Vesalius had begun two courses, the first as professor or lecturer on surgery, since the treatment of a phlegmon was a surgical procedure, and the second on the complementary anatomical demonstration. It should also be noted, even if we discount praise arising from friendship, that Vesalius had already acquired some distinction as an anatomist, which possibly helps to explain his appointment to the Paduan medical faculty.

Although Vitus Tritonius began his notes on the surgical lecture on fol. 118r and those on the anatomical demonstration on fol. 184r, the surgical lecture fills only eight leaves while the anatomical takes up twenty. It is apparent that the professor of surgery was more interested in his subsidiary duty, and the notes on the "Treatment of a phlegmon" bear this out, since they indicate that Vesalius borrowed his remarks from Avicenna's *Canon* (Book IV, fen 3, chap. iv, sec. 3),[31] possibly a by-product of his reading for the *Paraphrasis* or his preparation for his examination at Padua. He may already have concluded that lectures on surgery were merely time wasted without sound anatomical knowledge and hence have given little more than formal recognition to the required lectures.

The course in anatomy was an entirely different thing, but before we consider Vesalius's first anatomy at Padua we must observe the statute regarding this subject, the instrument he employed to develop the famous Paduan chair of anatomy:

> Adhering not only to our ancient statutes, but as well according to the praise-worthy custom of all Italian universities, and not only for the use of our scholars but also for the health of the whole human race, we have decided that, after the beginning of the term and before the end of February, the rector, otherwise subject to a fine of fifty pounds, and the councillors, otherwise subject to a fine of twenty pounds, shall seek to obtain and have available the cadaver of some legally executed criminal. That is, of one male and one female, or at least one of them . . . unless such criminals were from Paduan territory or citizens of Venice. If no [executed] criminal is immediately available, then let him be sought in an outlying area.
>
> When the anatomy is to be performed, let the rector and the councillors choose two students who have studied medicine for at least two years, and if possible those who have seen other anatomies. Let it be their duty to see that the instruments and all other necessary things are provided and to collect the fees from those wishing to watch the anatomy [the amount of the fee being based upon the expenses of the anatomy]. And let them see to it that only matriculated scholars and those who have studied medicine for at least a year are admitted. The rector, with one companion, all teachers giving lectures, and all doctors of the medical school, as well as two poor scholars, are to be admitted free.

Furthermore—although the practice was later altered by Vesalius—the rector and the councillors were to depute one physician of the faculty to read the text of Mondino, a second to demonstrate and verify the text upon the cadaver, and a surgeon to perform the actual dissection.[32]

Vesalius's first anatomy was carried out between the 6 and 24 December upon a male body, eighteen years old. Although we must depend upon the notes of Vitus Tritonius, and we cannot be sure how well he understood, it appears that Vesalius was still heavily indebted to Galen and Galenic authorities. Thus in the notes, presumably dictated by the lecturer, we find the statement: "To understand and to enumerate the muscles of the face exactly, you will refer either to Guinter or to Galen," and "[Vesalius] intended to describe the distribution of the third pair of cerebral nerves at greater length, but because it is so elegantly de-

Medieval dissection scene from an edition of
Mondino's *Anathomia* (1495). The dissection
is performed outdoors by a surgeon while the
physician sits on his high chair or *cathedra*.

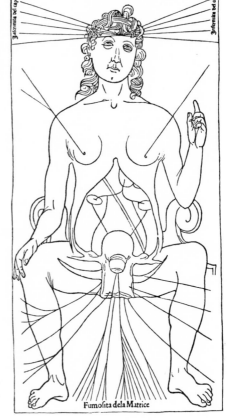

The first printed delineation (1493) of an internal organ—the uterus—made from direct observation. The drawing is otherwise traditional.

PLATE I

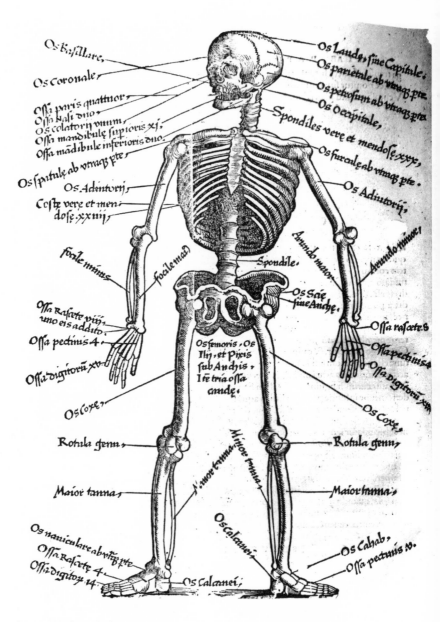

A pre-Vesalian skeleton clearly indicating traditional, nonhuman, and even imaginary osteology. The terminology is medieval.

PLATE 2

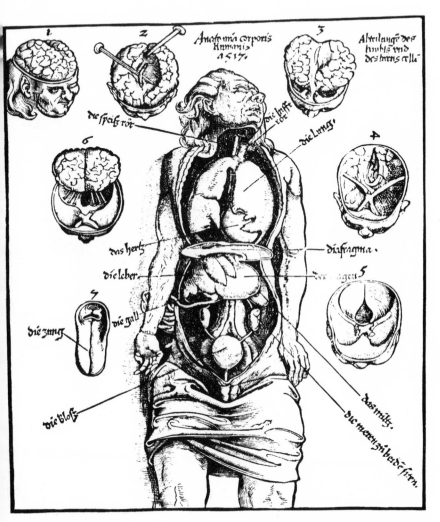

Illustration of brain dissection from direct observation (1517). The novelty is emphasized by the wholly traditional central figure.

PLATE 3

Vesalius's horoscope drawn up by Girolamo Cardano (1547). Historical Library, Yale Medical Library.

1514.die 30 Decembris, hora 17. mi. 45. post meridiem.

Cor cœli, 18 ♎.

Andreæ Vesalij.

Hæ in dissectione corporũ admirabilis,antiquisq̃ merito c̃parandus, opus prima inuenta scripsit, sanè adeò egregiũ,ut negotium penè totũ absoluerit,celebris in uita,iam nunc Cæsaris medicus, & post fata etiam ce, lebris futurus. Si genitura hæc sua est,ad amussim omnia conueniunt,nam Mars in quadrato Lunæ potentis in octaua, studiũ & agilitatẽ manuũ præ, sar. Mercurius in trino Iouis, & Venus in quadrato, ingeniũ mirabile, & fœcundiam pro artis conditione, imo supra eam,decernunt. est enim medi, cus insignis. Luna in opposito Solis,memoriã & scientiã, & multos dat ho, stra,clarũ etiam facit:quia nocturna est genitura. Saturnus cũ corde Scorpij, in sextili Mercurij,ingeniũ profundũ.memoriã,studiũ.Spica Virginis in cor, de cœli, gloriã ex arte, quantã quilq̃ alius. decet etiã animaduertere Martẽ aspicere Solẽ in sua exaltatione existentẽ, tũ Lunã in suo esse domicilio, hæc gratiã apud Principes decernũt.illud solum deest,quod nullus Planeta ho, ruscopi locũ possidet,iuxta decreta nostra.   yy   ij

Plan of the region of Brussels in which Vesalius was born and where, years later, he built his home. After Alphonse Wauters (1897).

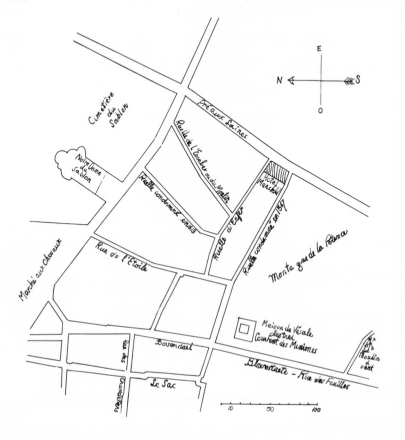

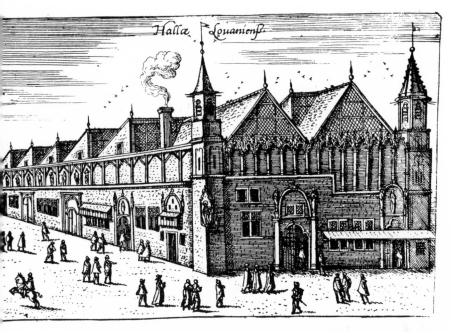

Les Halles, Louvain. The university as it appeared in 1606.

LIBER.X. TRAC.II. DE POTENTIIS

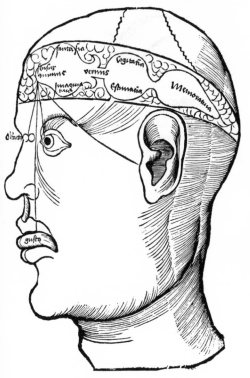

Figure displaying the location of the senses in the brain and alluded to by Vesalius as part of the curriculum in the Castle School of the University of Louvain. From Gregory Reisch, *Margarita philsosphica* (1503).

PLATE 5

Title page of Guinter of Andernach's Latin translation of Galen's *Anatomical procedures* (1531). The dissection scene displays the physician standing at the head of the cadaver, but allowing a barber or surgeon to perform the dissection. Wellcome Historical Medical Library, London.

PLATE 6

Jacobus Sylvius. Historical Library, Yale Medical Library.

JACOBVS SYLVIVS.
D. der Arzneykunde geb. 1478 gest. 1555.

ANDERNACVS.* 34.

Gallia te iuuenem audiuit, Germania seruat,
Vtile constanter dum profiteris onus.
Interpres artis Veteris, πολλῶν τ'ἀνὸς ἀνδρῶν
Sanas, quos alij deseruére diu.

G 4

Guinter of Andernach.

PLATE 7

IN HIPPOCRATIS

ET GALENI PHYSIO-
LOGIÆ PARTEM ANATOMICAM
Iſagoge, à Iacobo Syluio rei medicæ apud
Parrhiſios interprete Regio conſcri-
pta, & in libros tres
diſtributa.

PARISIIS,

Apud Ioannem Hulpeau ad ſcholas
Marchianas.

1 5 5 5.

Cum Priuilegio Regis.

Title page of Sylvius's *Isagoge* (1555).

NICOLAI MASSA VENETI
ARTIVM ET MEDICINÆ DOCTO
ris Liber Introductorius Anatomiæ, ſiue diſſe-
ctionis corporis humani, nunc primum ab
ipſo auctore in lucé editus, in quo quã
plurima mébra, operationes, & utili-
tates tã ab antiquis, quã a moder-
nis prætermiſſa manifeſtantur,
Opus ſane tam medicis, quam philoſophis
perutile, ut ſtudioſis lectoribus patebit.

Cautum eſt Priuilegiis ſanctiſſimi Domini Papæ noſtri,
& Senatus Venetorũ, ne quis impune hunc libel
lum imprimere audeat, aut alibi impreſſum
uenundare, pœnis in eis contentis.

Title page of Massa's *Liber introductorius anatomiae* (1536). Historical Library, Yale Medical Library.

M D XXXVI.

PLATE 8

Inſtitutionum

Anatomicarum ſecundū Galeni ſen
tentiam, ad candidatos Medicinæ,
libri quatuor, per Ioănem Guinte-
rium Andernacum Medicum.

TEMPVS.

PARISIIS
Apud Simonem Colinæum.
1 5 3 6

Title page of Guinter of Andernach's
Institutiones anatomicae. Paris, 1536.
Duke University Medical Center Li-
brary, Trent Collection.

INSTITV
TIONVM ANATO
MICARVM SECVNDVM GALE
ni ſententiam ad candidatos Medicinæ Libri Quatuor, per Ioannem
Guinterium Anderna-
cum Medicum.

B A S I L E AE,
M. D. XXXVI.

Title page of the slightly later edition, Basel, 1536. Historical Library,
Yale Medical Library.

PLATE 9

Title page of a collection of Galen's writings owned by Vesalius while a student in Paris and bearing his signature. Wellcome Historical Medical Library, London.

HIPPOCRATIS
COI, MEDICORVM OMNIVM
longè principis, opera quæ ad nos extãt
omnia: per ~~————~~ Medicum
Physicum latina lingua conscripta, &
denuò ex toto recognita.

Addito Indice fœcundissimo.

FRO BEN.

BASILEAE, ANNO
M. D. LIIII.

Cum gratia & priuilegio Imp. Ma/
iestatis ad annos quinq.

Title page of a collection of Hippocrates's works owned by Vesalius in 1554 or later and bearing his signature. From the original in the Uppsala University Library, Waller Collection.

PLATE 10

Nineteenth century depiction of the theft of a body from the gibbet outside Louvain.

GEMMA· PHRISIVS· DOCKVMENSIS
Esme de Boulonois· fe

GEMMA FRISIUS.

Gemma Frisius, the later-celebrated mathematician, who assisted in the theft.

PLATE II

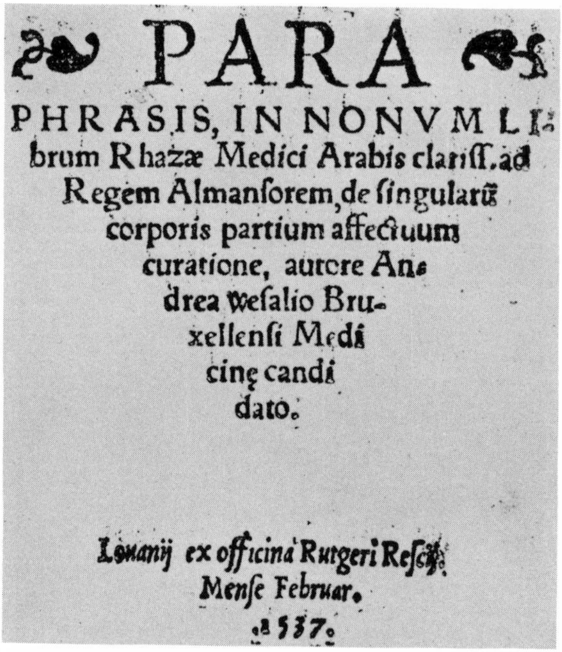

PARA
PHRASIS, IN NONVM LI-
brum Rhazæ Medici Arabis clariſſ.ad
Regem Almanſorem,de ſingularũ
corporis partium affectuum
curatione, autore An-
drea Weſalio Bru-
xellenſi Medi
cinę candi
dato.

Louanij ex officina Rutgeri Reſch.
Menſe Februar.
1537.

Title page of Vesalius's first published writing. From the original in the Uppsala University Library, Waller Collection.

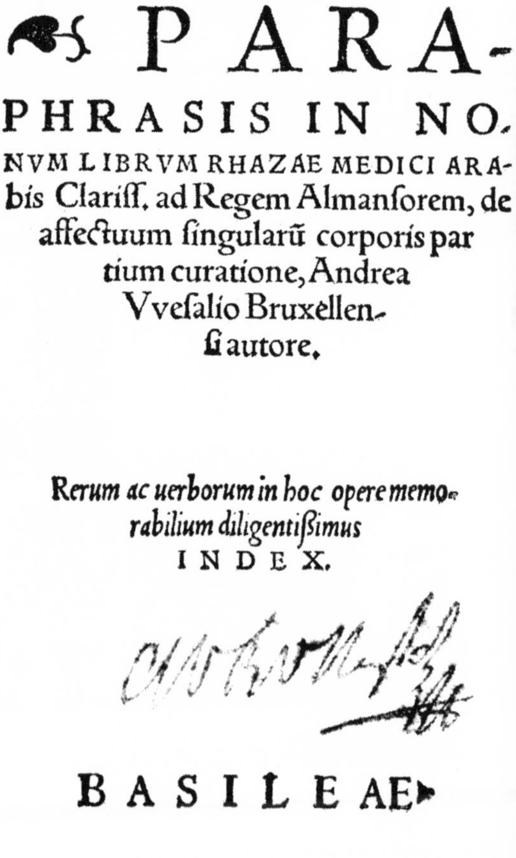

PARA-
PHRASIS IN NO.
NVM LIBRVM RHAZAE MEDICI ARA-
bis Clariſſ. ad Regem Almanſorem, de
affectuum ſingularũ corporis par
tium curatione, Andrea
Vveſalio Bruxellen-
ſi autore.

Rerum ac uerborum in hoc opere memo-
rabilium diligentiſſimus
I N D E X.

B A S I L E AE

Title page of the later edition, Basel, 1537. Historical Library, Yale Medical Library.

PLATE 12

GYMNASIVM   PATAVINVM

The University of Padua as it appeared in 1600. The building was not completed until about the final year of Vesalius's residence in Padua.

PLATE 13

FRANCISCVS FRIGIMELICA PATAVIN.
PHILOSOPHIÆ. PROFESSOR

Francesco Frigimelica, one of Vesalius's sponsors for his degree.

ODDVS DE ODDIS PATAVINVS
PHIL. ET MED. PROFESSOR

Oddo degli Oddi, another sponsor.

PLATE 14

Marcantonio Genua.

MARCVS ANTONIVS DE PASSERIBVS
à Genua Patauinus Philosophiæ Dottor

Giõ: Batta Da Monte
Medico Filosofo di Verona
nato ad 1489 morì ad 1551

Giambattista da Monte.

PLATE 15

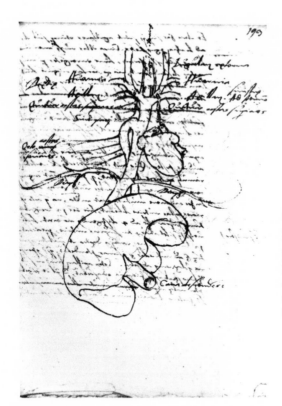

Copy by Vitus Tritonius of one of the diagrams drawn by Vesalius for the students at his first Paduan dissection, December 1537. This may be compared to the first *tabula* of Vesalius's *Tabulae anatomicae* (1538), plate 17.

Vitus Tritonius's sketch of Vesalius's drawing of the nerves which was stolen and published by Macrolius (1539); compare plate 20, and also Vesalius's revision that appeared in the *Fabrica*, plate 35. Austrian National Library, Vienna.

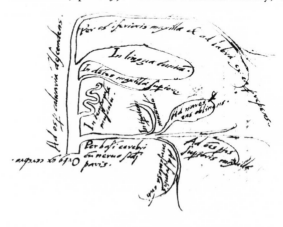

PLATE 16

scribed in Guinter's *Institutiones anatomicae,* he decided that it would be sufficient to refer the reader thither rather than to transcribe it here."

The dissection was carried out according to the medieval pattern established by Mondino: abdominal cavity, thorax, head and neck, brain and extremities; and for at least part of the demonstration a dissected dog was used for comparative purposes,[33] a procedure later greatly developed by Vesalius. Contrary to the provisions of the statutes, Vesalius was already lecturer, demonstrator, and dissector all in one, and he employed the texts of Guinter of Andernach and Galen rather than that of Mondino.

The abdominal organs appear to have been passed over very quickly; greater emphasis was placed on the venous system, which is understandable in view of the then-current controversy on venesection and the fact that Vesalius in his surgical lectures had already been dealing with the treatment of a phlegmon by bloodletting:

Then the distribution of the portal vein, of the arteries that go to the mesentery, stomach, etc., as well as some of their nerves, were considered; but since recollection of this demonstration may be confirmed by the chart that the surgeon [Vesalius] has displayed and that he will have printed, I have decided not to record these things.[34]

Of special importance is Vitus Tritonius's note on the haemorrhoidal veins:

Whether they are led from the portal vein or the vena cava is still in dispute . . . It ought to be noted that through the middle of the spine at the cavity in which the bladder exists, three branches descend in the same order, filled with darkish blood, which seem to originate with the vena cava before the bifurcation, and by some are considered and demonstrated as the haemorrhoidals . . . but my good friend Andreas Vesalius, upon inspection, considered them to be arteries crossing under the vena cava and originating from the aorta, all three of them not far from one another.[35]

It was to this passage that Vesalius was to refer in 1539 in his *Venesection letter,* and it appears likely that the ailing friend whom he mentions below was Vitus Tritonius:

Last year I investigated the haemorrhoidal veins very carefully for a friend who was with me and who was troubled by them from time to time. First I dissected out three arteries that we found clearly arisen from the aorta where it lies on the sacrum. The students who were standing about declared that these had formerly been demonstrated to them as the haemorrhoidals, and indeed they looked like veins because of the congestion of the spirituous blood in them. . . . However, they are arteries and terminate in the foramina of the sacrum, not in the end of the rectum intestine.

Vesalius's earlier researches had led him to doubt that these were the haemorrhoidal veins as others declared, and in consequence he began to consider the possibility that the haemorrhoidals might be given off from branches of the portal vein:

I traced a branch of the portal vein, which had been left in the body with the rectum intestine, and I observed that it extended to the end of that region, although not in a straight line but following the remaining twistings of the intestines as far as the anus comprising the end of the rectum intestine.[36]

Thus in this reference to his first anatomy in Padua, Vesalius not only gives us further information on the cadaver, which "had not yet reached its nineteenth year and seemed to be of excellent constitution without any abnormalities," but also indicates that, although he was still forced to rely in considerable measure on Galen and the Galenists, insofar as his skill and experience permitted he was attempting to form his judgments on the basis of his anatomical findings. His next words indicate this clearly and may mark one of the turning points in his career. As a result of his decision based on his observation during dissection, "I gave careful consideration to the possibility that anatomical dissection might be used to check speculation." [37] In the intellectual climate of Padua, faced with the responsibility of demonstrating and lecturing on human anatomy, Vesalius was perhaps finding it difficult to justify certain Galenic doctrines with the visible evidence of his dissection. It is important, moreover, to note that, unlike Sylvius, he did not hesitate to call attention to those instances where Galen could be demonstrated as fallible.

Another matter referred to later in the *Venesection letter* was the investigation of the azygos vein, a term apparently coined by Guinter in Paris and possibly introduced to Padua by Vesalius. The azygos vein, as Vitus Tritonius recorded, goes about the heart from the right side of the vena cava, but in this particular cadaver it constituted an anomaly, supplying twelve ribs on the right side and none on the left.[38] Whether Vesalius did indeed make this statement or not, there is no reference to it in the *Venesection letter* where, recalling his first Paduan dissection, he declared that "when the duty of publicly demonstrating and dissecting was first requested of me at Padua, I indicated to a large and learned group of spectators that this vein nourishes all the ribs of the body of each sex." [39]

The dissection was not carried out completely since, as Vitus Tritonius recorded, putrefaction of certain parts prevented their demonstration:

The muscles of the shoulder giving motion to the forearm remained, but these as well as the muscles of the loins, dorsum, etc., were not demonstrated because of putrefaction . . . Of the eleven muscles that, according to Galen, are in the lower leg, I can say nothing with assurance since with the [anatomy] coming to a conclusion, they were discussed too quickly to allow me to give them careful thought and to learn them.[40]

Upon completion of this first dissection Vesalius articulated the skeleton, his first in Padua, to which attention will be given in another context.

Vitus Tritonius remarked that "the chart that the surgeon has displayed and that he will have printed" as an aid for the students made it unnecessary to record certain parts of the demonstration. Later he added: "It is to be hoped that we shall be aided by those illustrations which may perhaps be published, containing depictions of the nerves, veins, and arteries of the whole body." [41] In the manuscript of this student there are four drawings, his copies of Vesalius's diagrams, crudely and probably hastily sketched but bearing some resemblance to the drawings by Vesalius that were published in the *Tabulae anatomicae* of 1538: a diagram of the hepatic and cystic ducts with the gall bladder and common duct, of which a more finished descendant is to be found in the *Fabrica;* [42] a drawing of the liver, the superior vena cava with branches, and the heart, recognizable as a forerunner of the second *tabula;* a drawing of the heart and part of the anterior aorta, a source of the third *tabula;* and a very crude diagram of the branches of the trigeminal nerve. This last has no parallel in the *Tabulae anatomicae,* although in the preface to that work Vesalius mentioned that he had prepared such a figure. The diagram in the notebook of Vitus Tritonius is certainly no fair indication of what the Vesalian original was, but it does faintly suggest that figure, now lost but once published in Cologne as a plagiarized version—which will be mentioned later [43]—as well as the illustration of the brain and cranial nerves to be found in the *Fabrica.*[44]

The existence of these four diagrams or drawings requires that we consider the preface to the *Tabulae anatomicae* of 1538. In that preface Vesalius stated that in the course of his surgical lectures he had been called upon to consider the treatment of inflammation by bloodletting. During the discussion of bleeding by derivation or revulsion, a central matter of the venesection controversy, he "had incidentally made a drawing of the veins." This "so pleased the professors and students of medicine that they urged me strongly to provide a similar delineation of the arteries and nerves. Since the conduct of dissections was part of my duty, and since I knew that this kind of drawing possessed no little value for those attending the dissections, I acceded to this request."

Here, then, is the origin of the illustrations Vesalius used for his first dissection in Padua—one of them previously prepared for his surgical lectures. They showed a distinct advance in the pedagogy of anatomy, since the drawings were nontraditional and the result of an effort, unsuccessful as it may have been, to depict exactly what the anatomist had observed. That he still, to considerable degree, saw through the eyes of Galen in no way destroys the novelty of this new teaching device, and there is some indication that the drawings were prepared prior to the dissection and so depict a greater degree of Galenism than that which controlled his thinking during the actual course of the dissection. It is also important to note, as Vesalius clearly indicated, that although his drawings had mnemonic value they were not to be used in lieu of actual dissection and observation of the human body, but in the absence of a plentiful supply of cadavers many members of a large class of students must have been thankful for this alternate source of information.

Despite Vesalius's explanation of the origin of his drawings, it seems likely that there were previous sketches. Certainly the information in them could not have been based entirely on the single anatomy of December 1537, particularly since there is considerable representation of simian anatomy. The drawings are a composite of tradition, animal anatomy, and some human anatomy. Vesalius's draughtsmanship, as exhibited in the *Tabulae anatomicae*, was the result of previous practice in sketching, and the drawings for his first Paduan anatomy were based partly on these previous efforts. The factor of time alone would require it.

The dissection of December 1537 was a kind of common denominator for three brief works published in 1538 and 1539, the *Tabulae anatomicae*, a revised edition of Guinter's *Institutiones anatomicae*, and the *Venesection letter*. These three works also have another factor in common, since they reveal Vesalius as still considerably a Galenist, although the new influences of Padua were resulting in increasing instances of independent thought.

The earliest of the three works is the *Tabulae anatomicae*, dedicated to Narcissus Parthenopeus, the emperor's protomedicus. Although the dedication, a part of which has already been mentioned, is fulsome, it is also of some biographical importance. Among other things it demonstrates Vesalius as still somewhat naïve and unacquainted with the true arrangement of the imperial medical hierarchy. The young writer probably hoped that his dedication, as others of that period, would yield some return in the form of favor or substance, indicating that Vesalius assumed the imperial protomedicus to be a person of importance. The fact is, however, that this official had little except his title of premier physician, rarely came into contact with the emperor, and from this period did not participate in the emperor's medical care. The dedication, wasted as far as any benefits from it were concerned,[45] begins with an explanation of the genesis of the *Tabulae*:

> Not long ago, most learned Narcissus, after I had been appointed to the chair of surgical medicine at Padua, I was discussing the treatment of inflammation. I had come to explain the view of the divine Hippocrates and of Galen on revulsion and derivation and had, incidentally, made a drawing of the veins in order to demonstrate more easily what Hippocrates meant by *kat' ixin*. . . . This figure of the veins so pleased the professors and students of medicine that they urged me strongly to provide a similar delineation of the arteries and nerves.

The Vesalian *Tabulae* have been described as "without artistic merit" but as revealing Vesalius to be a "very competent biological draughtsman." There had already been traditional and pseudoanatomical drawings, but Vesalius's effort was the first significant one to make detailed anatomical and physiological drawings for men trained in medicine, and, because of the content, it was "the first pictorial exposition of the Galenic physiological system." As Vesalius's first important pedagogical device, it was a genuine novelty for both students and professors, who demanded more, and although Vesalius acceded to these requests he added the very proper caution that "I believe it is difficult if not hopelessly impossible to obtain genuine knowledge of the parts of the body . . . solely from illustrations . . . although no one denies that they are excellent aids to memory." His caution, however, went unheeded, and his drawings, looked upon primarily as a source of anatomical knowledge, were immediately and unskillfully copied. In consequence, "since many have vainly attempted to copy what I have done, I have entrusted these illustrations to the press with the addition of my skeleton, recently articulated for the benefit of the students, and depicted from three aspects by the distinguished contemporary artist Joannes Stephanus [of Calcar]."

As mentioned by Vitus Tritonius, Vesalius, as early as December 1537, had spoken of the publication of the drawings, which must have been subjected to crude plagiarism almost as soon as they were presented to the students, but whether they were revised for publication is unknown. The three figures of the skeleton were, of course, drawn between the end of the year, when the anatomy was completed and the skeleton mounted, and sometime in March 1538, when it would have been necessary to turn the drawings over to the block cutter. These *Tabulae anatomicae*, or *Tabulae sex* as they are sometimes called, were therefore one of the several novelties Vesalius introduced into medical and anatomical pedagogy, and if any proof is required of the impression created by them it is readily available in the fact of the plagiarisms which quickly followed.

The *Tabulae anatomicae* are six large woodcut illustrations of anatomy and physiology, measuring 19 by 13½ inches. The first three, drawn by Vesalius, are physiological diagrams of the portal, caval, and arterial systems on which are printed brief texts describing the structures illustrated. There seems every likelihood that they differ little if at all from those diagrams for the dissection of 1537. If we accept Vesalius's words literally, there was no difference at all, although as published there is no drawing of the nerves but in its place is an unmentioned one of the liver and its vessels as well as the organs of generation.

Several factors of importance are represented, chiefly by the illustrations and to a lesser degree by the brief text identifying the various structures. The illustrations were drawn from observation of human and animal anatomy with Vesalius as the draughtsman observing, sometimes clearly, sometimes with vision clouded from reading Galen's texts—but since the *Tabulae anatomicae* have been so thoroughly studied by the late Charles Singer [46] it would be a matter of supererogation to dwell on them at length, and a few examples will suffice to indicate Vesalius's position as an anatomist in 1538.

The portrayal of the liver in the first and second *tabulae* suggests that he had relied upon dissection of the ape, and consequently his representation of the organ as human is incorrect, a transference of animal anatomy to the human—a type of error later to be one of the chief targets in his critical attack upon Galen in the *Fabrica*. Although the liver in question has the five lobes of medieval tradition, Vesalius did depict the prostate [47] for the first time, and possibly as a result of his dissection of December 1537. In the second *tabula*, referring to the caval system, the superior and inferior venae cavae are of the ungulate type, again indicating Galenic influence and most likely drawn with the assistance of Galen's *Dissection of the veins and arteries*. In his depiction of the upper intercostal veins Vesalius admits his reference to the ape, and possibly his reference to the azygos vein is based upon Galen's description. The illustration of and reference to the position of the kidneys is also Galenic. In the third *tabula* Vesalius has drawn the *rete mirabile*, the "marvelous network" of vessels at the base of the brain in which vital spirit was supposedly altered to become animal spirit. Although the network does exist in ungulates, its nonexistence in man indicates Galen's guidance of the pencil once more, and later in the *Fabrica* Vesalius admitted his error and confessed himself greatly astonished at his "stupidity." [48] In this same *tabula* the heart portrayed is an ape's, as is the aorta, which resembles that described by Galen in his *Dissection of the veins and arteries*. On the other hand, certain arteries suggest the human.

These three *tabulae* are followed by the three views of the skeleton, which appear to have been included as an afterthought to give greater completeness to the printed collection of illustrations. Drawn by Joannes Stephanus of Calcar, they are the work of a fairly good draughtsman, possibly chosen for the task because he was a fellow Netherlander; but whatever the reason for the choice of Joannes Stephanus—usually conveniently but incorrectly known as Calcar—it set in motion an argument that is still alive as to whether or not he was the major draughtsman of the later *Fabrica*.

As we might expect from the greater accessibility of osteological material and Vesalius's longer experience with it, the skeletal drawings display superior anatomical knowledge, although even here Galen's influence creeps in occasionally as in the depiction of a sternum of seven segments. On the other hand, Vesalius asserts his doubts concerning Galen's statement that the lower jaw is divisible into two parts, a matter later stressed in the *Fabrica* as a major part of the attack on Galenic anatomy. The skeleton, that of the youth of eighteen, the subject of Vesalius's first Paduan anatomy, was obviously not articulated entirely correctly. The artist faithfully recorded the errors, which indicate that Vesalius's knowledge of the skeletal structure was as yet imperfect; and the poor delineation of certain aspects of the skeleton, such as the pelvic bones, sacrum, and lumbar vertebrae, also makes it readily apparent that this artist was not responsible for the far superior skeletal figures of the later *Fabrica*.

Despite such criticisms, the drawings were a genuine novelty. They were the first published anatomical figures of sufficient size and detail to permit the very examination that has revealed their errors. In 1538, however, the errors were not realized and the detail suggested a value that, from our point of view, was not present—except possibly in the delineation of those aspects of Galenic anatomy that were not at fault, and the few correct reflections of Vesalius's human dissection of December 1537.

Granting a considerable following of older anatomical tradition, nevertheless the *Tabulae* do show an advancement, and certainly they represent a break with the past in the very conscious effort to integrate text with illustration. Also, even then Vesalius had a larger venture in mind, and had he not been compelled to deal with the problem of plagiarists these *Tabulae* might never have been published. They might have remained merely sketches exhibited to the students and possibly worked over and revised later as a preliminary to the *Fabrica*, as was done with the diagram of nerves. However, since Vesalius felt that inferior plagiarism required publication of the *Tabulae*, he closed his dedication with a hint of things to come: "Should I find them acceptable to the learned, I hope to add something more considerable."

As Singer and Rabin point out,[49] the *Tabulae anatomicae* are also important in the history of the development of anatomical nomenclature. The problem of proper terminology had long been a vexing one, and Vesalius's attempted solution was the most elaborate to date. What he did was present not only the Greek and Latin terms drawn from several sources, including some contributions of Guinter of Andernach,[50] but also the Hebrew words and some Arabic or arabicized words in Hebrew letters, although he did not possess the knowledge of Arabic or Hebrew that his work might suggest. Rather, these terms indicate collaboration with some now-unknown Jewish physician. The *Tabulae* contain the most extensively multilingual anatomical vocabulary produced up to that time.

If we try to sum up the significance of the *Tabulae anatomicae*, we may say that they represent a period of transition in Vesalius's career. He was no longer a complete Galenist and had come to realize through his own research and observation that Galen was not infallible. For instance, of the coccyx he wrote: "The descriptions of Galen . . . are not always consistent; I have observed that they do not suit these two bones [coccyx and sacrum]." It was natural that the easier access to bones would lead Vesalius first to observe discrepancies in Galenic osteology; after only three or four months in Padua his experience in human dissection was not great, so that for the time being he continued to rely on animal dissection or on the word of Galen, and since Galen had based much of his anatomy on the ape, Vesalius's dissection of that animal often confirmed Galen's authenticity.

Nevertheless, advances were being made. Galen's word was subject to doubt in respect to osteology. Such doubt, however, was not a consistent policy and there would have to be further dissection before Vesalius would develop the principle of refusing to accept past authority until his own researches had proved it true. But the beginnings are found here. Although Galen admitted in his writings that he was restricted to non-human materials—a fact frequently overlooked in the sixteenth century —the important thing was to free anatomy from its dependence upon the idea of authority or, to put it another way, to make the study of human anatomy dependent solely upon dissection and observation of human specimens. In the *Tabulae anatomicae* Vesalius made the first steps in that direction, following thoughts he had had upon this subject in the course of tracing the haemorrhoidal veins in December 1537.

In the *Tabulae* the illustrations are more significant than the scanty text, but together they represent one aspect of the later *Fabrica*—that is, illustrations with explanatory indices. If we add to these elements of the *Tabulae* the text of Vesalius's revised edition of Guinter's *Institutiones anatomicae*, soon to be considered, we have in crude form the three components of the *Fabrica*. For the moment, however, Vesalius had neither time nor necessary research experience for anything so elaborate as that later work, although when in the preface to the *Tabulae* he speaks of his hope of adding "something more considerable," presumably he already had in mind some future conjunction of these three elements.

The *Tabulae* were printed in Venice "at the expense of Joannes Stephanus of Calcar," [51] and the presumption is that the artist received the profits of the sale as compensation for his drawing of the skeletal figures. It was apparently a profitable venture since the work was immediately popular, and the known existence of only two complete copies today suggests that it was literally read to pieces. Vesalius considered the work one of which he could be proud, and he sent a copy to his father for presentation to the emperor, who appears to have been gracious in his reception of the gift despite the fact that it had been dedicated to another.[52]

Booksellers and printers, too, appreciated the work, at least its salable nature, and despite the clearly displayed papal, imperial, and Venetian privileges,[53] the copyrights of that age which forbade unauthorized reprinting, the possibility of profits and the knowledge that the prohibitory privileges could not be enforced led to immediate and widespread plagiarism.

In the summer of 1542, as the wood blocks for the illustrations to the completed text of the *Fabrica* were being packed for dispatch to the printer in Basel, Vesalius wrote a letter to accompany them and to explain the arrangement of the illustrations which he desired.[54] Continuing with a reference to the privileges being obtained for the protection of his new work, he was led to recall his earlier trials at the hands of plagiarists, but with reference to the places of plagiarism rather than to the names of plagiarists who had produced editions of his *Tabulae anatomicae*.

After some uncomplimentary remarks about such booksellers and printers "who have now become ubiquitous," he referred to the plagiarism of Augsburg as "wretched imitations of those woodcuts prepared in Venice." However, the "engraver at Cologne who put his hand to those same *Tabulae* was far more inept and unskilled" even though some had declared that "the printer had made my elegant illustrations even more pleasing." Furthermore, he "added a delineation of the nerves poorly copied from a rough sketch I had drawn . . . for one or two friends during the course of my work." This presumably was that drawing we know Vesalius to have made but which was not included in the published *Tabulae anatomicae*, although it was crudely copied by Vitus Tritonius. Although "at Paris the first three *tabulae* were produced expertly," the plagiarist of Strasburg "whom Fuchs has denounced so strongly because of his plagiarisms . . . ought to be cursed by the students since he has shamelessly reduced the size of the *Tabulae*, which could never be large enough." And as if this were not bad enough, there was still another plagiarist publishing equally inferior works in Marburg and Frankfurt.[55]

It has not been particularly difficult to identify some of the persons responsible for the plagiarisms and they have been discussed at some length by Choulant and Cushing. More recently Sten Lindberg, curator of rare books in the Royal Library, Stockholm, discovered a collection of such plagiarisms bound into a copy of Thomas Geminus's further plagiarism, *Compendiosa totius anatomiae delineatio* (London, 1545), and Lindberg's consequent study has thrown additional light on the problem.[56] The plagiarist of Augsburg was Jobst de Necker, a printer and engraver, who in June 1539 issued his unauthorized edition of the *Tabulae* with better copies of the illustrations than Vesalius's letter indicates.[57] The plagiarist of Strasburg, who is described with special and deserved harshness, was Walther Ryff, who was responsible for a long series of plagiarisms between 1541 and 1545 and even later, in which he was not above altering Vesalius's figures and placing illustrations borrowed from other works with them;[58] and the guilty party in Marburg and Frankfurt was Johannes Dryander, a physician and mathematician of Marburg, who published his plagiarisms between 1541 and 1557.[59] It appears that it was not until some years later that Vesalius finally associated Dryander with these publications.[60]

Vesalius was especially irritated, and rightly so, by the crude plagiarisms of reduced size published by Ryff and Dryander, but it is doubtful that he ever saw Necker's plagiarisms, since, in fact, his copies are creditable and the dimensions of the illustrations not much reduced. Vesalius must have seen the work of the unnamed plagiarist of Paris, since he gives him some measure of credit, noting further that only the first three *tabulae* had been reproduced, those that had been drawn by Vesalius himself. The identity of this plagiarist has long been in doubt,[61] but Lindberg's find has now definitely revealed his identity.

Among the broadsides discovered is a set of the Paris plagiarism of the Vesalian *Tabulae*, excellent, full-sized copies with the Vesalian text verbatim except for an effort to correct such typographical errors as appeared in the Venetian originals, and carrying the imprint *Parisiis apud Christian Wechelum sub scuto Basiliensi in vico Jacobaeo.*[62] Although these plagiarisms are undated, Lindberg presents a theory that appears fully acceptable for a dating of 1538, and an explanation as to why, according to Vesalius, at first only three of the six *tabulae* were published. In 1536 Wechel, as mentioned earlier, had published his *Osteotome*, those two illustrations of the skeleton once referred to by Choulant[63] and

Roth [64] but now disappeared. In 1538 Wechel published a second edition of his *Osteotome*, of which a copy is included among the broadsides discovered by Lindberg.[65] Lindberg proposes that Wechel, upon becoming acquainted with the Vesalian *Tabulae* of the same year, decided to copy and publish only the first three and substituted his own *Osteotome* for the three skeletal figures of Calcar.[66] Later, this combination proving unsatisfactory, he added the three *tabulae* containing the Calcar figures to the three *tabulae* already published and issued the complete series in 1538–1539 as it exists in the Royal Library in Stockholm.[67] The plagiarism in this latter form was unknown to Vesalius, or at least he never mentions it.

Through the revelation of the plagiarism of Paris it becomes possible to identify that of Cologne. A set of the first three *tabulae* without imprint was discovered in the grand-ducal library at Darmstadt and ascribed incorrectly, as we now know, to Paris by several bibliographers,[68] although Roth, without actual proof, hazarded the guess that they were properly the first three sheets of the Cologne plagiarism.[69] Their differences from Wechel's plagiarism, and the fact that the introduction to them contains the assertion that "from the very elegant original delineations we have reproduced the body even more elegantly," an echo of Vesalius's words about the Cologne plagiarism, leave little doubt that this is a fragment of that particular work.[70]

There is additionally Vesalius's reference to the theft of his sketch of the nerves. Whether or not this sketch was appended to the edition of the *Tabulae* produced in Cologne cannot be determined from the incompleteness of the sole known copy of that work. However, at one time there existed a single sheet illustrating part of the brain and the cranial nerves, published in 1539,[71] the work of an Aegidius Macrolius who identified himself as a lecturer on anatomy at Cologne and referred to Vesalius in highly flattering terms as "Andreas Vesalius, than whom none since Galen has been a more conscientious and genuine student of anatomy . . . [and who] has conferred an inestimable benefit upon scholars." [72] Macrolius does not refer to the *Tabulae anatomicae* in his brief text, and his plagiarism has no relationship to that particular work but, as he stated, "We came possessed of this some time ago, merely in sketch form, but so neatly done that I believe the author desired it to be in the hands of all, and we have accordingly turned it over to the printer." In short, someone had purloined the sketch of the nerves to which Vesalius makes reference in the preface to the *Tabulae*.[73]

In May 1538, one month after the publication of the *Tabulae anatomicae*, Vesalius completed a revised edition of Guinter's *Institutiones anatomicae*, which was soon thereafter published in Venice.[74] As we have seen, this work had originally appeared in 1536 in two editions, the first in Paris and the other in Basel.

It seems astonishing to find Vesalius issuing an edition of his teacher's book less than two years after its first publication, especially since it was done without authorization from Guinter, and it may be presumed that profits, if any, went into the pocket of the younger man. The critic of plagiarists was therefore unfortunately a plagiarist himself. On the other hand, his share in the composition of the original edition may have been sufficient to give Vesalius some sense of proprietorship, at least enough to justify his action to himself if not to Guinter. Moreover, the students needed a text to accompany the lectures and demonstrations in anatomy, and Galen's texts, notably *On the bones* and the *Anatomical procedures*, although still treated with great respect, would no longer do, except in part, since the young anatomist was beginning to diverge from some of the Galenic doctrines. Guinter's own edition of his *Institutiones*, although conveniently brief, was yet too strong a reflection of Galen and was not sufficiently full in its description of anatomical techniques. A new, revised, and somewhat extended edition seemed indicated, containing certain corrections of Guinter, and thereby of Galen, as well as an extension of certain passages to suit what Vesalius considered the needs of the students.

The new edition was dedicated to Joannes Armenterianus, one of Vesalius's teachers at Louvain, not a physician of great distinction but apparently one of his favorites in that university. In later years Vesalius was to write a somewhat cynical letter to Jean Sturm on the art of dedication, but either he had not yet perfected that art or he had not had time fully to evaluate potential patrons. The two dedications to Nicolas Florenas, 1537 and 1539, can be readily explained as the result of genuine regard. The dedication of the *Tabulae anatomicae* to Narcissus Parthenopeus was due to failure to understand the meaningless position of that archiater and bore no fruit. Hence, considering the practices of that age, it is difficult to comprehend the waste of this present dedication on Armenterianus. Possibly Vesalius, still somewhat immature, wished to impress his former teacher with his accomplishments, or he may have been undecided about his future and retained some thought of a return to the Netherlands and a teaching career at the university where his great-grandfather had previously professed with distinction; but we ought not to overlook the pleasant possibility that Vesalius had a genuine personal regard for Armenterianus; personal regard seems to be the only reason for sending greetings in the same dedication to Willemaers, that professor of medicine who was ousted from Louvain four years later as the result of students' criticism of his ineffectual and medieval teaching.

Turning to the content of the dedication we find first that Vesalius expressed himself in favor of compendia such as that made by Guinter, and, although the reduction of prolix matter into a concise form had use in other branches of medicine, "in anatomy, I believe, it is not only useful but necessary." Here, surely, he must have been thinking only of a dissection manual or perhaps he had not yet fully envisioned the proportions of the *Fabrica* to come. As yet a Galenist, Vesalius was concerned with that anatomy "perfected by Galen in almost forty books," and it appeared to him that Guinter had done an excellent job in digesting this mass of Galenic learning into his brief treatise—which, however, was badly disfigured by typographical errors:

I therefore thought that I should be undertaking a work greatly desired by students if by care and effort I were to present the result of his meritorious studies in a revised and corrected edition. I was frequently asked to do this, and I trust to the generosity of the author who, I believe, will not be offended by it, since I did considerable study under his direction, a teacher both generous and learned.

The numerous typographical errors are declared the justification for the new edition of the *Institutiones*—and certainly the typography is in need of emendation—but a comparison of the two editions, Guinter's of 1536 and Vesalius's of 1538, also shows the student to have taken great liberties with his teacher's text. Sentences have been deleted or added, usually the latter, and in some instances wholly new paragraphs have been introduced. Although it is easy to say that the younger man was anxious to display his learning and to demonstrate his grasp of the technicalities of dissection, yet in fairness to Vesalius it must be said, too, that Guinter had been deficient in the technique of dissection. It was Vesalius's proficiency in this that had led to his employment by Guinter, and it was the same ability that had distinguished Vesalius on his return to Louvain; finally, it was a *sine qua non* of his overthrow of Galen's supremacy. Guinter, for example, wrote: "First with your scalpel draw a line in the skin from the mucronate cartilage through the umbilicus to the pubic bone." [75] Vesalius preceded this with the statement, "With the cadaver lying supine and cleansed of its hair," and then modified Guinter's words to read, ". . . a line from the mucronate cartilage, or a little above." [76] Shortly thereafter Guinter wrote, "For the two tendons of both muscles are seen to join into one," [77] and Vesalius, retaining this statement, aded, "wherefore they cannot easily be separated." [78] There are many such additional details, worthy of applause on the score of precision and the infinite capacity for detail that was to make the *Fabrica* a work of such immensity and a classic of pedagogy. Finally, were one to assume that the ambitious young Paduan professor would allow modesty to overcome his sense of the necessity for publicity and would therefore delete the praise given him by Guinter,[79] a reference to Vesalius's edition [80] would undeceive him.

On a less personal level, there are some additions of considerable importance that reflect the researches of an independent investigator, one of the most significant being that which deals with the "Motions of the heart." According to Guinter:

By these fibres [of the heart] a double motion occurs. When the long fibres come together and the others are relaxed and separated, the heart is distended and dilated, which is called diastole. On the other hand, when the long fibres have been relaxed and the broad ones come together, the heart is constricted, and this is called systole. However, a brief period of rest occurs between these motions, when the heart is contracted upon itself, but with all the fibres and especially the oblique acting.

When [the heart] is dilated it draws spirit from the lung for refrigeration, and enjoys it during the period of rest; when it is contracted it expels the sooty vapors, the source and origin of native heat, the motions of the pulse, and of the animal faculty.[81]

Vesalius's presentation of the first part of this account was verbatim, but he expanded the second paragraph considerably and also cleared up the meaning of the latter part of it:

When [the heart] is dilated it draws spirit from the lung by way of the pulmonary vein for the sake of refrigeration, and blood from the vena cava; when it is contracted it expels the sooty vapors through the pulmonary vein, blood into the lungs through the pulmonary artery, and spirit through the aorta into the whole body. For the heart is the source and origin of native heat, pulsation, and the animal faculty. Therefore it is proper to inquire whether the pulse is the same in the heart and in the arteries; that is, whether the transmission of material from the heart occurs on its contraction, and the introduction of material on its distention.[82]

In the 1539 edition of his *Institutiones* Guinter incorporated some of this extended passage,[83] as he likewise incorporated other Vesalian additions. Nevertheless, it appears that he did not realize the full importance of Vesalius's somewhat tentative observation that cardiac systole is synchronous with arterial expansion, a matter to which Vesalius was to return in the following year in the *Venesection letter*.

A second passage to which Vesalius was also to refer in the *Venesection letter* concerns the haemorrhoidal veins. In the *Institutiones anatomicae* of 1536 Guinter remarked:

Now it is desirable to approach the bladder and its neck, which resembles the Greek letter Σ—if first you have inspected the veins, which are branches of that great divarication in each leg where the aorta ascends to the vena cava. Those veins called the haemorrhoidals go forth from there, and by them the melancholic humor is drained.[84]

Vesalius altered this slightly, both to give a more precise description of the shape of the bladder's neck and to display less affirmation regarding the haemorrhoidal veins:

Now it is desirable to approach the bladder and its neck, which resembles the Roman letter S—unless injured by an instrument—if first you have inspected the veins, which are branches of the great divarication in each leg where the aorta ascends to the vena cava. Those veins called by many the haemorrhoidals go forth from there, and by them it is believed the melancholic humor is drained.[85]

In his edition of 1539 Guinter altered this passage under the influence of Vesalius's emendation but, playing safe, he described the neck of the bladder as resembling the Greek Σ, as he had previously stated, or the Roman S, as Vesalius had described it. Furthermore, he, like Vesalius, now declared the so-called haemorrhoidal veins to be given that name not by all, as his original edition implied, but "by many."

Still another matter of interest concerns the conclusion of Book III of the *Institutiones*. In the edition of 1536 Guinter concluded with a description of the anatomy of the ear.[86] Vesalius retained this description but added a brief statement: "Here I shall pass over the muscles of the neck and spine, reserving them for another place, since they cannot be included in this brief treatise." [87] Naturally, one immediately wonders if Vesalius was thinking of that larger work to take shape as the *Fabrica*, but in any event Guinter took the hint since the *lacuna* is filled in his edition of 1539.[88] In that edition Guinter also altered his remarks on the *rete mirabile* [89] to a verbatim copy of what Vesalius had written in the previous year,[90] and included [91] as well what his former student had remarked on the lobes of the liver.[92] The most extensive borrowing from Vesalius was the long description of the spleen [93] which Guinter took over in its entirety.[94]

Vesalius's edition of the *Institutiones anatomicae* may be said to have fulfilled several purposes. Probably he saw in his revision a fairly simple method of calling attention to himself and, within the framework of Guinter's treatise, of indicating his anatomical discoveries or revisions which were as yet insufficient to justify a separate work; additionally, his revised version was superior as a dissection manual to Guinter's original edition or, indeed, to anything else that was available.

The *Institutiones* of 1538 gives a truer and more flattering idea of Vesalius's anatomical development than does the *Tabulae* published a month earlier. The *Tabulae* refers back to the dissection of December 1537, or even earlier, and its relatively inclusive nature required that Vesalius depend upon animal anatomy and Galenic description once he had exhausted his still-limited knowledge of human anatomy. In the *Institutiones* he was free to emendate those parts of Guinter's text for which he felt competent and otherwise to remain silent. Although his emendations were not significant enough for his name to be recalled later on the basis of this work alone, they do indicate distinct advancement over the *Paraphrasis* and a bit more independence of authority than the *Tabulae*.

At some time in 1538, having obtained permission from the rector, Vesalius made a trip to Bologna. In the *Venesection letter*, of which the completed composition is dated 1 January 1539, he remarked that "some months ago I visited Bologna," [95] and we may take this to refer to the vacation period at Padua, from the latter part of August until the middle of October. Otherwise it would have been a costly trip, since he would have had to find and pay a substitute to take over his lectures. The trip was partly also, no doubt, to visit the medical faculty which had a long and distinguished tradition—and Vesalius's old mentor, Nicolas Florenas, had studied in Bologna and might still have had friends there. Among the physicians in Bologna at that time none was better known or more respected than Matteo Corti, or Curtius, and Vesalius informs us that he had gone to Bologna "partly for vacation and partly to visit him." The visit was taken up with discussion of problems relating to venesection, and Corti "showed me three printed editions of his treatise" on that subject.[96]

In the course of their discussion the two men came at loggerheads over the "fibres" of the veins. This doctrine, derived from Aristotle and later developed by Galen, was a belief that the organs of the body had three coatings of fibres—straight, oblique, and transverse—which controlled the "natural," or, roughly, the involuntary actions, such as the motions of the heart and of the digestive tract. The straight fibres were presumed to attract substances, the oblique to retain, and the transverse to expel. At that time Vesalius considered that the walls of the veins were composed of three such sorts of fibres "by which these vessels perform their natural action and motion" and that their structure "corresponds to the structure of the stomach and intestines, uterus, heart, and bladders." [97] Eventually the controversy over the existence or nonexistence of the fibres became heated and then bitter, although it is not clear whether hostility arose during the visit or as a result of Vesalius's assertion in the *Venesection letter* of his belief, accompanied by criticism of Corti's disbelief, in the fibres. Vesalius refrained from mentioning his opponent by name, but Corti, a somewhat irascible man, could easily recognize that the criticism was aimed at his opinion, and reference to "a certain self-declared famous professor of medicine at Bologna" did nothing to mitigate the situation.[98] A further meeting and dispute early in 1540 merely increased the hostility. Cardano, who knew Corti personally and Vesalius indirectly, later wrote that Vesalius had shown a remarkable restraint despite the very manifest hostility of his opponent during this dispute.[99]

Vesalius continued to hold to the Galenic doctrine of the fibres in the veins, even illustrating these nonexistent structures schematically in the *Fabrica* [100] and maintaining this view as late as 1555 in the revised edition.[101] However, in the *Examen* published in 1564 he finally relinquished it and was able to look back somewhat humorously if not ruefully on his youthful quarrel with Corti almost a quarter century earlier:

> I recall how sharp the controversy once was over these matters with Matteo Corti in Bologna, when I declared that fibres of the veins were perceptible in dissection of bodies, and so provided Corti and his followers, who had some time previously published their conclusions, no little opportunity for attacking the fibres. For when I had separated the substance of the veins in search of the fibres, I dissected it raw and boiled, and, by Hercules, to tell the truth, the fibres had come from the imagination of our authors [i.e., Galen]. Finally, when I had come to have serious doubts and rejected the whole matter as a vulgar opinion . . . our dispute over what vein ought to be opened in venesection was so much "goat's wool." [102]

The *Venesection letter* [103] was in part the fruit of Vesalius's trip to Bologna in 1538 and his discussions with Corti who, as Vesalius remarked in his letter, had just published the third edition of his own treatment of the subject.[104] Furthermore, as Vesalius noted, venesection was a topic of wide interest which aroused such strong feeling that the supporters of the medieval concept of bloodletting had succeeded for a time in having the newer practice of Brissot prohibited by edict in Spain.[105] It may also be recalled that the subject had been considered by Vesalius in his first lectures as professor of surgery at Padua, and, indeed, the *Tabulae anatomicae* owed their inception to the general interest in the subject. Thereafter the dispute with Corti "some months ago" [106] had acted like a trigger, releasing Vesalius's pen, and the little book was written between the end of summer and the opening of the new year in 1539.

Intrinsically the *Venesection letter* is of little significance, since it was based upon a belief in humoral pathology and its complementary therapeutics. On the other hand, the work had the distinct merit of illustrating the anatomist's further movement away from traditional and authoritarian anatomy in the direction of independent investigation and judgment. The opposing schools of venesection, the medieval or Moslem, and the new classical one based on the Greek revival, have been previously mentioned.[107] Vesalius's allegiance was to the latter, and it was on this basis that he asserted that "in all inflammations of the sides of the thorax or of the thoracic vertebrae" that required bloodletting, "the right axillary [basilic] vein must be opened." [108]

Like other and previous writers on the subject, Vesalius sought to demonstrate that his view had the support of Hippocrates and Galen. This was standard procedure, and Vesalius assured his readers that he would be afraid to contradict "the authority of Galen which I hesitate to dispute . . . almost as if I were secretly to doubt the immortality of the soul." [109] This statement, however, was *pro forma*, and in fact Vesalius had little hesitation in expressing his doubts if his anatomical investigations warranted such heresy. Here, then, is the significance of the *Venesection letter*. The basis of Vesalius's theory of bleeding rested not on the authority of the classical physicians but rather upon his knowledge of the anatomy of the venous system—which he presumed to be correct, although in fact it was somewhat faulty. Faulty or not, Vesalius's presentation of the anatomy and continuity of the vessels carried far more weight than a mere array of authorities, especially when it could be demonstrated, or at least asserted, that the statements of the authorities were in conflict with the true anatomy of the venous system. Henceforth the debate on venesection could be carried on properly only by resort and reference to the dissection table, and it was in line with this idea that Vesalius pondered that question already mentioned, "the possibility that anatomical dissection might be used to check speculation."

Two other matters of some importance, although unrelated to the thesis of the *Venesection letter,* deserve attention. First, the observation that cardiac systole is synchronous with arterial expansion. Vesalius had given this some consideration the year before in his edition of Guinter's *Institutiones anatomicae,* or, as he stated in his current work, "I quietly expressed my doubts regarding that theory about which all physicians are very positive, whether the arteries and heart beat in the same way as the pulse." Now he presented his opinion more boldly:

96

When the heart is contracted it diffuses [vital] spirit into the aorta and blood into the pulmonary artery; this motion of the heart is systole. When, however, the ventricles of the heart are dilated, the heart receives air from the pulmonary vein and blood from the vena cava; this motion is properly the diastole of the heart. When the arteries are dilated, I believe that they are filled with vital spirit from the heart which they distribute throughout the body. However, when they are contracted I consider it obvious that the sooty vapors are expelled. Hence the motions of the heart and arteries are contradictory and contrary.

Such observation was apparently the result of vivisection, such as Vesalius may have first observed under Guinter in Paris, or similar studies which, as will be mentioned later, Vesalius asserted he had originated in Padua: "To some degree this can be proved during vivisection if one hand is placed upon the artery lying on the sacrum and the other grasps the whole of the intact heart." [110]

As in his previous writings at Padua, so here Vesalius gives general as well as more specific promise of things to come:

I shall omit for the present the movements of the head [111] as well as the muscles and nerves which at my modest suggestion students do well to study. Indeed, with the favor of the gods, I shall discuss this subject more fully at another time . . . With regard to the rest of my studies there is little to say at present. I have now almost completed two illustrations of the nerves; in the first, the seven pairs of cranial nerves have been drawn, and in the other all the small branches of the dorsal marrow. I feel that these must be held back until I have produced illustrations of the muscles and of all the internal parts. This year I tried a plan by which these things might be accomplished during the dissections, but it was unsuccessful with so large a group of spectators. If bodies were available here as they sometimes are elsewhere, not for long would the students lack such a useful work, especially since many distinguished men are constantly urging me to it . . . besides others, Marcantonio Genua, our distinguished professor of philosophy . . . has strongly urged me to the task. . . . If bodies become available and Joannes Stephanus, the distinguished contemporary artist, does not refuse his services, I shall certainly undertake that task.[112]

The closing part of this statement, referring to the artist Joannes Stephanus, has led to considerable controversy in attempts to identify the artists of the *Fabrica*, but this matter will be considered later.

The *Venesection letter* concludes with the words: "Padua, from the house of the sons of the most illustrious Count Gabriel of Ortemburg, 1 January 1539." It is likely that these sons of the Count of Ortemburg, of lower Austria, with whom Vesalius seems to have been living, were students in the university, although probably not of medicine. The efforts of Roth,[113] like the later ones of Cushing,[114] to identify the house were unsuccessful, and how long Vesalius lived with these young men is unknown, but probably it was until the end of the academic year 1538–39.

In addition to whatever contributions to the knowledge of anatomy had been made by the new professor of surgery, we must note also the advances in pedagogy instituted by him in that brief period from December 1537 through 1539. We know that Vesalius was dissector, demonstrator, and lecturer in the course of his first public anatomy, and it may be assumed that he filled the same position in any other dissection undertaken. Vitus Tritonius, who left the record of the anatomy of December 1537, was also present at the public anatomy of the previous year, and his account of it permits us to compare Vesalius with his predecessor in the chair of surgery and anatomy. The dissection of 1536 is recounted very briefly in contrast to the full account of the Vesalian dissection of the following year, so suggesting that the former contained no novelty worthy of more extended treatment. The earlier demonstration had not been carried out personally by Paolo Colombo, the *Explicator chirurgiae,* but by Giovanni Antonio Lonigo, a surgeon summoned from Venice.[115] The situation was therefore somewhat akin to that at Paris so strongly criticized by Vesalius later in the *Fabrica;* that is, the professor entrusted the dissection to another while he himself retained his academic *cathedra,* presumably discoursing from the text of Mondino. This was in accordance with the university's statutes, but it was a practice discarded by Vesalius as one of his major contributions to the improvement of anatomical teaching.

The success of the new Vesalian methods was attested by both students and authorities of the university, and a document of October 1539 indicates the esteem in which the new teacher was held by both: "The excellent Master Andreas Vesalius . . . has aroused such admiration in all these students, [that in his reappointment] let there be added another thirty florins to the annual salary of forty florins he has at present." [116] This appreciation was also reflected in an invitation to give a series of extramural anatomical demonstrations in Bologna.

In consequence of this invitation, in January 1540 Vesalius made a second trip to Bologna where he remained throughout the month, for at least some of this time as the guest of one of the members of the Bolognese medical faculty, Giovanni Andrea Bianchi, or Andreas Albius in the latinized form.[117] It was also at this time that Vesalius made the acquaintance of the Aristotelian philosopher, Lodovico Boccadiferro.[118] Vesalius's invitation had come from the Bolognese medical students who, although they had lost control of the university to the civic authorities, appear still to have retained the right of inviting prominent scholars for special series of lectures. Vesalius had been invited to present a series of anatomical demonstrations jointly with lectures given by Matteo Corti [119] whom he had previously visited in 1538—that briefly amiable acquaintance which had, however, seriously deteriorated.

Corti's lectures, which began on 13 January, were concerned with the medieval anatomical treatise of Mondino, supported or rectified by reference to Galen. This was the very sort of thing to which Vesalius was so strongly opposed, anatomical lectures without resort to the body and derived solely from the word of past authorities. It had apparently been the plan that the demonstrations would illuminate the lectures, but such a plan was doomed from the start, since in addition to whatever personal dislike existed between the two men, Corti was a Galenist while Vesalius was rapidly freeing himself from that camp. Corti considered dissection of little value since he believed it merely confirmed Galen's words already available in printed texts, and Vesalius firmly believed that all knowledge of the human structure must be acquired only through dissection and observation of the human body. The tension was certainly not lessened by Corti's tendency to suggest that Vesalius was a mere dissector, perhaps superior to a surgeon, but, since he was willing to step down from the *cathedra* and employ a scalpel, hardly a respectable physician.

The Vesalian demonstrations, for which "three human bodies and six dogs and other animals" had been provided, began on the morning of the 15 January following Corti's fifth lecture and were held in the church of San Francesco, in which the dissection table was encircled by four tiers of benches "so that nearly two hundred persons could see the anatomy." It was during this demonstration, when Corti opposed Galen's opinion to that of Vesalius regarding the insertion of the rectus abdominis muscle, that the latter indicated the direction in which he was moving by declaring that if his statement did not agree with Galen's, he would nonetheless demonstrate that he was right and Galen wrong. Vesalius's declaration in later years that he had lectured three times on Galen's book *On the bones* before he dared oppose that entrenched authority [120] would place his open opposition at Padua in the winter of 1539–1540. He had then just asserted his scientific independence in Padua and this further assertion in answer to Corti was an echo of it. It was sufficiently novel and sufficiently irritating to the conservative members of the audience so that they felt called upon to demonstrate their displeasure by marching out of the hall.

Of course Vesalius's scientific principle did not lead him immediately to see and observe correctly all the structures of the body, and in those instances where he believed Galen correct, although he had not yet tested all of them, he was content to refer the students to the appropriate Galenic passage. On the other hand, he now denied that the liver had five lobes. "There is no truth," he said, "in what others say about the five lobes of the liver," and referring to Galen by name he declared that his explanation of the movements of the head was false. Nevertheless, dissection of the sheep's head together with the human caused Vesalius to fall into one of the errors he criticized in Galen—that is, to project animal anatomy upon the human. In this specific instance he retained belief, which he was later to deny in the *Fabrica,* in the existence of the *rete mirabile* at the base of the human brain.

The anatomist of 1540 was merely a dim suggestion of the author of the later *Fabrica,* yet it was at Bologna that he enunciated the principle that was to guide his research and that would, in so few years, produce the founder of modern anatomy. Bologna was a kind of testing ground for that new principle and, despite some hostility, on the whole it was received with favor, especially, as one might expect, by the young students. These Bolognese demonstrations also indicate that Vesalius had already worked out the pedagogical techniques to which he was to refer later in the *Fabrica* as the methods he used for teaching his students in Padua. Thus we find that he usually followed the dissection of a human cadaver with that of a dog as an exercise in comparative anatomy, as a means of repeating dissections otherwise impossible with a limited supply of cadavers, and as an explanation of the falsity of Galen's animal anatomy as it had been projected upon the human. The skeleton was constantly present, its bones used as a means of orientation for other structures of the body; frequently, too, the positions of the bones were sketched upon the surface of the body with charcoal to supplement this orientation, while sketches and diagrams of all sorts were also employed, as well as occasional references to the *Tabulae anatomicae.*[121]

The favor with which these demonstrations were received by the students was extended to still further demonstrations—but carried on elsewhere, it appears, than in the church of San Francesco—during which the body of a French priest, removed illegally from a burial vault by the students, was anatomized.[122] It was also at Bologna that Vesalius confirmed the fact, if confirmation were needed, that the "bones of the aged differ from those of youth, and those of youth from those of children."

I truly learned so in my last anatomy at Bologna when countless bones of the newly born, of old men of ninety, and of the middle-aged were enthusiastically brought to the [medical] school by the students, since prior to the dissection of the muscles, I had lectured on Galen's book *On the bones.* Many of them broke into tombs and collected the unclaimed bodies from the mortuary in order to obtain bones for study. Naturally some had acquired the bones of old men, some those of children, and still others those of various ages.[123]

As a gesture of appreciation to his host, Andrea Bianchi, Vesalius mounted two skeletons, an ape and a human, the latter "articulated from the bones of the French priest." [124] This deliberate preparation of such a spectacular display of comparative anatomy—the first recorded—not only contrasted Galenic to human, or Vesalian, anatomy, but also was a special exercise in comparative osteology that provided Vesalius with proof that Galen's description of the processes of the lumbar vertebrae was derived not from human but from animal sources. Declaring later in the *Fabrica* that he had hitherto confirmed Galen's description of the spinal processes in dogs and other animals, but had never observed them in the simian vertebrae, Vesalius added: "This process was hidden from me until in Bologna I undertook the complete dissection of an ape; then I articulated its bones, as well as those of a human. I did this for Giovanni Andrea Bianchi, the famous professor of Hippocratic medicine at Bologna."

The demonstrations in Bologna had the further significance of being a kind of guide *in parvo* for the more extensive anatomical demonstrations of the *Fabrica.* "All the things I consider in this work [i.e., *Fabrica*] I undertook in one and the same winter in . . . Bologna amidst a crowd of spectators and in the same order in which I have arranged them in these present seven books." [125]

Possibly it was also during this visit to Bologna that Vesalius observed the beggar "whose head was squarish but a little wider than long," [126] as well as what appears to have been an accident resulting in the exposure of the heart of the victim, which could be "observed while he was still alive." [127] Most likely Vesalius returned directly from Bologna to Padua to resume his duties at the university in February, and in October he was rewarded by an increase in his annual salary.

Nothing further is known of his activities until we find him sharing quarters with the English student John Caius, 1510–1573, who, after preliminary studies at the University of Cambridge, had come to Padua in 1539 and received his degree of doctor of medicine in May 1541. Since he began his studies with the opening of the term in the autumn of 1539, it is most likely that he was referring to his first academic year, 1539–40, when he mentioned "Andreas Vesalius, who lived with me for eight months in a house in Padua, the Casa degli Valli, or, as the Paduans call it, Ca Valle, near the Ponte delle Paglia—during which time he wrote and illustrated his books *De humani corporis fabrica*." [128] Caius also remarked that it was during this time that both he and Vesalius were occupied with a review of Galenic texts—Vesalius for his contribution to the Giunta edition of Galen's *Opera omnia*, 1541–1542. Since, according to Caius, Vesalius was already at work on the *Fabrica*, he was certainly at this task as early as 1540 and possibly a little earlier. From Caius's other words we learn that at the same time Vesalius was revising the Latin translations of certain of Galen's works for the newly planned and elaborate Giunta edition. Ultimately a rift developed between Caius and Vesalius, the result of their differing views on the significance of Galen's writings, but more important was the bearing that Vesalius's intense study of Galen, tested by concurrent human dissection, was to have upon the composition of the *Fabrica*. Here a brief digression on the Giunta Press and its new edition of Galen is desirable.

The Giunta family, originally native to Florence, had in the person of Lucantonio Giunta removed to Venice about 1480 and established a publishing and bookselling business. Later, in 1503, Lucantonio undertook to print as well as to publish, and the most important of all the Giunta publications were the successive editions of Galen's *Opera omnia*. The first two editions, of 1522 and 1528, appear to have been little more than careful reprints of the fourth edition of Galen, published in Pavia, 1515–1516, although the second Giunta edition of 1528 was slightly augmented.[129] These Latin translations of Galen, a necessity for the physicians of that time, seem to have been a financial success, and Lucantonio determined not only to continue the venture but to improve the next edition so that it would at once become the standard collection of Galen's writings and prevent competition from other publishers. This new edition required either revision of older, faulty translations or completely new renderings by competent scholars, mostly what we may describe as the scholar-physicians, and some effort was made to collate more manuscripts of Greek texts in order to improve the Latin versions and even to add hitherto unprinted works. There is indication of this in a reference by Caius to Vesalius's revision of the *Anatomical procedures:*

A few notes in Greek turned up in an old Greek manuscript in the possession of the Giunta family. They were transcribed by Agostino Gadaldino, an affable and learned man who at that time was superintendent of the printing house of the Giuntas, and were sent to Andreas Vesalius . . . so that he might use them in his emendations of the Latin anatomical writings of Galen.[130]

The "affable and learned" Agostino Gadaldino [131] was editor-in-chief, and the celebrated Paduan physician Giambattista da Monte, Vesalius's colleague, worked out the organization of the individual writings according to subjects and possible authenticity. Together the two men chose the editors and translators of the individual works. Lucantonio Giunta, the instigator of this ambitious project, died in 1537 or 1538, before its completion, and the task continued mainly under the direction of his son Tommaso, with publication in 1541–1542.[132]

The financial success of the new venture may be estimated from the Basel reprint of Froben in 1542, possibly undertaken to ease the problem of distribution of the heavy folio volumes, and from the numerous later Venetian editions. Only the original Giunta edition of 1541–1542, however, contains the important and revealing letter of Agostino Gadaldino, given here in part:

Agostino Gadaldino of Modena to Students of Medicine:

It is possible from many examples to appreciate the ever-great efforts of Lucantonio Giunta and his sons to promote the advantage of studious mankind. There is nothing whence we may perceive this better and more clearly than to-day when they have demonstrated the greatest magnanimity by seeking to bring to light and to publish in Latin all the works of Galen . . . Giambattista da Monte of Verona, who at present professes medicine in the University of Padua to everyone's great admiration and applause . . . has very clearly indicated what order ought to be observed in the reading as well as in the publication of the [complete] works of Galen, since it is realized that the works of Galen are a necessity and that without them it is hardly possible to care for the sick. [The Giuntas] resolved that they would seek this great advantage for mankind and publish these works without regard to effort or expense.

Since they knew that a large number of them had never been published in Latin and that those that had been published in translation were full of corruptions and mistakes—perhaps more the fault of the existing corrupt Greek manuscripts the translators used than of those who rendered them into Latin—they determined to make every effort to discover the most ancient manuscripts from the various libraries of Italy so that those works that had been printed might be collated and restored to their pristine splendor. This was done with almost complete success, since many very fine and noteworthy things were discovered in those manuscripts which were lacking to the printed editions; and also by referring to these manuscripts further errors were prevented from creeping into this work of theirs.

Then men learned in languages as well as in medicine were employed to translate into Latin all the works of Galen that had not yet been put into that language; and of those works that had been translated into Latin but, as I have said, poorly, because of the corruptions in the manuscripts, they recast some, corrected some, and retranslated others. By a combination of zeal, diligence, and the help of those more ancient manuscripts, these learned men have given us more nearly correct and clearer translations of the works than the Greek texts of the printed editions offer. Those who are willing to employ their leisure for a comparison of these translations with the Greek will easily observe this. In regard to those works that were considered to require only correction, better translations of portions were made through careful revision, but it was not done in such a way that some books were accepted, some rejected, some partly revised, and others retranslated to the injury of anyone or the destruction of anyone's reputation, because it is readily apparent that errors of this sort had crept into these books through the corruptions of the manuscripts rather than through the negligence or inability of the individual translator.

Since good Greek manuscripts were available so emendated that the [old] Latin translations were no longer considered suitable unless they could be restored by new translations, [the Giuntas] believed that the venture should not be undertaken in such a way that mankind be defrauded of such great value through superficiality. This should be understood by all good men, especially when they realize that the Giuntas not only put forth effort and undertook responsibility for this common usefulness, but also went to very great expense. They spared nothing that would advance the work. There is almost no one who, having understood the great significance of the undertaking, did not aid it, for not only did many offer their translations and emendations to assist so distinguished a work, but those themselves to whom the translation and revision of the books had been committed were influenced not by any reward but rather by the desire to aid so worthy a project. For what reward, even from some great emperor, would compensate their efforts?

It was the intention of the Giuntas to have new translations made of many of those books that have been merely revised, but because it seemed to them and to those who daily demanded this new work that too long a time would elapse if new translations had to be awaited, they saw to it that those who had translated them in the first place should hardly recognize them any longer as their own. Understand that not only those works have been corrected that have the word "revised" at their beginning or display marginal corrections, but those marginal annotations cannot properly be called more than the smallest part of all the corrections that have been inserted into the whole work, and as the term "revision" indicates that those [particular] books have required the greatest correction, so it may not be denied that there were other emendations elsewhere. However, the table of contents placed at the beginning of the volume will explain clearly and exactly what books have been emendated and the sort of correction.

In order that nothing might prevent these works of Galen issuing from the Giunta press fully revised, it devolved upon me, who had been put in charge, to compare them with the Greek manuscripts and to oversee the printing. I was careful that everything be printed as accurately as possible, but the burden was so great as to be almost beyond my strength. Every day I was compelled to read through so much that often there was not enough time for me to consider and weigh things one by one as was required. Nevertheless, I do not hesitate to assert that I did everything with the greatest care and diligence, never evading labor or vigilance, and because of my assiduous concern and too-great solicitude I fell into a long and grave illness and for many days and months it was necessary that this task be carried on by another. As a result of my diligence you have all except the introductory matter, spurious works, and a large part of the fifth section of the work, of which the corrections and emendations were overseen by that learned man who substituted in my place. If you should find anything in these works that may seem to have slipped by with too little consideration and that does not fully satisfy your very sharp judgment, I beseech you to ascribe it to lack of time rather than to any lack of diligence on my part, and —such is your kindness—that you will pardon me who, with whatever knowledge and capability I possess, and I freely confess that it is slight, was responsible for all this. The Giuntas promise you that if hereafter any other translations of books of Galen come to light, extant but not printed—which they hope will happen—as well as those that have already been printed but in some part may be judged better than these of theirs, they will also publish them—not, however, in this large format but in smaller type so that everyone may obtain them more cheaply.

Gadaldino completed his letter by calling attention to some, although not all, of the contributors to the enterprise. Among these was:

Andreas Vesalius of Brussels, celebrated and distinguished contemporary professor of dissection, who has presented us with the *Dissection of veins, arteries, and nerves*,[133] corrected in many places; and, finally overcome by our entreaties and arguments as well as by those of his friends, since we pointed out to him that too great a wrong would be committed if, through fear of offending his preceptor Andernach—for he feared this—he were to deprive mankind of so great usefulness, he emendated the books *On anatomical procedures* with such effort that he almost remade them.

Recalling that Vesalius appeared to have had no qualms about revising Guinter of Andernach's *Institutiones anatomicae* in 1538, one may reasonably be astonished at his hesitation to revise his preceptor's version of the *Anatomical procedures*, unless he had received a strong protest from Guinter following the appearance of the *Institutiones*. In any event, judging by the number of minor alterations introduced by Vesalius, the statement of Gadaldino that "he almost remade" the work may be acceptable, although the earlier version remained basically untouched since most of the alterations had little to do with the fundamental translation into Latin but represented an attempt at a clearer, more literary, presentation. For example, a passage from Book I in Guinter's version reads: *Pectus omnium quadrupedum latissimum habet humerorum claviculas humanis similes, faciem rotundam, collum exile;* Vesalius's revised version is: *Et pectoris os omnium quadrupedum latissimum habet, claviculas humanis similes, faciem rotundam, collum breve.*

In a few instances Vesalius employed marginal annotations to call attention to his revisions, although why some of these passages were singled out is difficult to comprehend. Of a passage in Book II, accepted verbatim from the earlier version, Vesalius remarked: "I, Vesalius, have retained the version of the [former] translator although it is not faithful to the Greek text, which appears to have been mutilated, since here it ought to be said that those two tendons are occasionally attached to the same ligament and sometimes, separated from each other, to different ligaments." In one instance in Book VIII he noted the possibility of using the term *sinibus ossium* in place of *capitibus ossium*, although, presumably on the basis of the text, he retained the latter phrase despite its appearing dubious to him on anatomical grounds. In only these two instances do the marginal annotations suggest that Vesalius made any particular use of his anatomical knowledge in the course of his revision; otherwise his guide appears to have been a literary one. In Book VI he placed one short passage in brackets and noted that "this is not to be found in any of the manuscripts," but he does not explain why he retained the passage nor on what authority he altered its Latinity from the earlier version of Guinter of Andernach.

In most respects, then, the revisions appear to be much like those of the medicophilologists, and one may wonder to what extent Vesalius employed Greek texts for his revision and to what extent he relied upon John Caius. It has been said that the two men were sharing quarters. Indeed, Caius, as will be noted below, called attention to some differences of opinion over interpretation of terms. Despite Gadaldino's slightly exaggerated description of the effort made by the Giuntas to procure manuscripts for collation, some effort was made to improve the texts and translations and, according to Caius on one occasion Gadaldino sent Vesalius some Greek notes he had transcribed from a manuscript in the Giunta family:

These notes, although of little value to Vesalius and me, since they were basically unsound, nevertheless spurred us on to seek out other manuscripts. Upon searching, I discovered another Greek manuscript among [Cardinal] Bessarion's books in the library of San Marco in Venice. It was helpful in several places.[134]

At the same time Caius was preparing the Greek text of the *Anatomical procedures* for his own publication of 1544. A difference of opinion over the correctness of the Greek text seems to have contributed to the rift between the two men—Caius and Vesalius—and it is also likely that Vesalius occasionally indicated that however verbally correct the text of Galen, anatomically it was incorrect. When Caius recalled the incident in his *De libris propriis* in 1570, the vividness of his recollection of what had occurred thirty years before suggests the strength of the argument.

Inevitably Vesalius was a follower and admirer of Galen, but his admiration was more and more limited by a comparison of the Galenic canon with his own anatomical findings in the human cadaver, so that he recognized the possibility of error in Galen. On the other hand, Caius considered Galen faultless and believed that if demonstrable error appeared in a Galenic text it represented a faulty Greek manuscript or faulty translation into Latin, a view that is at least more plausible than the conservative stand of Jacobus Sylvius who declared that any human variation from the Galenic description indicated degradation of the human species. Despite the fact that Caius belonged physically to the generation of Vesalius in which the dissection of human specimens was under way and the scientific treatment of anatomy had begun, he belonged spiritually to that previous generation in which the medical humanists had believed that Galen held the key to all medical problems and that accurate Latin translations from sound Greek texts were the greatest boon they could offer to the medical world. Obviously such a staunch defender of Galen could not possibly remain on terms of amity with a critic such as Vesalius, and at the end of eight months they parted company. The difference of opinion that led to the split remained and is reflected in several of Caius's later statements against Vesalius.

To return briefly to the Giunta edition of Galen's works, it should be noted to the publishers' credit that they did live up to their promise to improve upon the Latin texts in future editions and to introduce whatever new works might be discovered. Considerable change was introduced into the later editions of Vesalius's contributions. Some indication of this is given in their titles: "The book on the dissection of the veins and arteries, presented in Latin by Antonius Fortolus *Ioseriensis*, thereafter corrected by Andreas Vesalius of Brussels, and [now] in many places revised according to the Greek manuscripts by Agostino Gadaldino," and "The nine books on the anatomical procedures, once presented in Latin by Jean Andernach, and after the very careful revisions of Andreas Vesalius of Brussels, and also of others, revised in several places according to the Greek manuscripts." In the first work the revision, mostly philological and based upon the collation of Greek manuscripts, is considerable, but more addition than correction, and only once does Gadaldino expressly call attention to what he considers an error in the Vesalian version.

The title of the revised—much longer and far more important—version of the *Anatomical procedures*, as given above, makes no mention of the identity of those who made the revision, and the marginal emendations are, in relation to the size of the work, far fewer than in the *Dissection of the veins and arteries*. Vesalius's version of the *Anatomical procedures* is seldom criticized as inaccurate, although the implication of inaccuracy is possibly there in such phrases as, "Others consider that this should be read . . ." In one instance, Book II, chapter 8, a critic is mentioned by name: "Bartolomeo Eustachi, distinguished physician and noted professor of anatomy, advised that this reading is incorrect." In addition, a careful comparison of the Vesalian version of the text with the later, revised version indicates that, for the sake of better expression and clarity, a great many unindicated, minor changes were made in such things as punctuation, shortened sentences, the substitution of nouns for pronouns, and the choice of more precise descriptive terminology. Such changes usually amount to little more than the deletion or substitution of a single word, but on occasion an entire clause has been altered.

Although the editors of the successive Giunta editions of Galen were temperate in their treatment of the Vesalian versions, Caius, as we might expect, was forthright in his criticism. It was inevitable that, as the complete Galenist, he would be displeased with the Vesalian version of the *Anatomical procedures*, the more so since he had at the same time prepared an annotated Greek text of the treatise, published in Basel in 1544. Hence, in later years he wrote:

> I extended my commentaries on that work, and among other things I discussed the ginglymus, because recent anatomists have illustrated it by an incorrect figure, and the septum [lucidum] of the brain as separating, not supporting, because that place in Book IX of Galen's anatomy is incorrectly emendated by Vesalius.[135]

If we turn to Caius's edition of the Greek text of the *Anatomical procedures* we find that his remarks are almost wholly philological, interesting chiefly for the information about his relations with Vesalius. Caius's first concern is with the question of the authenticity of a Galenic phrase he feels that Vesalius was wrong in deleting:

> When Andreas Vesalius and I once shared the same dwelling and used to compare our anatomical studies, he, on the strength of certain manuscripts with interpolations from an ancient codex, considered that these things ought to be deleted. However, I do not know whether what was written there was actually from that codex or was the interpretation of the transcriber.[136]

He makes further reference to the dispute, this time over the proper sequence of four Greek words: "In the manuscripts I said Vesalius had shown me, this [phrase] was written in a reverse order. . . . But I was suspicious of the reliability of the texts since they smacked more of the interpretation of the scribe than of the trustworthiness of age." [137]

Another reference, although similarly philological, is especially interesting since it is the sole instance in Caius's writings of any commendation of Vesalius:

> I would have undertaken to portray this remarkable matter with the pencil, as a thing worthy to be understood by a well-informed man, except that it has already been considered in the books of Andreas Vesalius of Brussels and Giambattista Canano of Ferrara, experienced anatomists in whose books this and other things have been so graphically and excellently depicted that nothing more can be desired.[138]

A final critical reference to Vesalius is found in Caius's autobiographical *De libris propriis* in reference to his own Greek edition of the *Anatomical procedures* of 1544: "I warned the reader in those commentaries or annotations [to the text] of certain places in the anatomical books of Galen that Vesalius corrupted when Antonio Giunta the Venetian printer gave him the task of revising them." [139]

The choice of Vesalius to revise the text of the *Anatomical procedures* is indicative of the stature he had attained in Padua. It was appropriate for Galen's major work on anatomy to be emendated by a professor of anatomy, yet the revision required a skilled philologist perhaps even more than a skilled anatomist who was also revealing himself as a critic of Galen. Thus the choice of Vesalius suggests he had a greater ability in Greek than he is sometimes credited with as well as a distinguished position in anatomical studies well before his reputation was so greatly enhanced by the publication of the *Fabrica*. The success of his teaching in the university and of his public anatomies, the acclaim gained by the *Tabulae anatomicae* and to a lesser degree by the *Venesection letter*, and no doubt the invitation to lecture in Bologna, indicating a more-than-local appreciation, all contributed to the development of this renown. His was one of the few names singled out for special mention by Gadaldino, and this distinction is supported by the words of Simon Arborsellus, doctor of medicine, vice-rector (1540) and rector (1541) of the faculty of arts and medicine, who published a small tract around 1545 in which he chose to recount as noteworthy a conversation he had had with "Andreas, the learned anatomist and surgeon of Padua," [140] at some time during the years prior to the appearance of the *Fabrica*.

Aside from the question of the choice of Vesalius to participate in the revision of the Galenic texts for the Giunta edition, there is the question of why he was willing to undertake such a task when, as Caius informs us, he was already launched upon the overwhelming one of composing the *Fabrica*. The answer most likely is that the composition of the *Fabrica* required close perusal of Galen's writings, especially the *Anatomical procedures,* and the additional burden was not so great as it may seem at first thought. Any collation of manuscripts was invaluable to Vesalius, since otherwise there would always have been doubt as to whether the disparity between his findings in dissection and the words of Galen was because of fault in Galen or in an erroneous text.[141] If any further assurance of Galen's dependence upon the dissection of animals, and so his unreliability as a guide to human anatomy, was required before mounting the attack, this work of revision must have supplied it.

Although Vesalius's friendship with John Caius was short-lived, that established with two other men during this Paduan period was lifelong. The first of these friends, referred to in the *Venesection letter,* was the philosopher Marcantonio Genua,[142] mentioned again in the *Fabrica* as one who urged Vesalius to undertake the task and encouraged him during it.

Vesalius's second lasting friendship made during his Paduan days was with a young Augsburg patrician, Wolfgang Peter Herwart.[143] This young man, approximately the same age as Vesalius, in later years brought Vesalius into close touch with the leading physicians of Augsburg. This friendship was also acknowledged in the *Fabrica* where its author suggests that the work could not have been completed without the assistance—possibly financial—given by Herwart. Earlier, however, on 29 April 1542, Vesalius wrote his first known consilium, or medical opinion, regarding a young man "about twenty-seven years old" who had totally lost the vision of one eye and appeared to be in danger of losing that of the other.[144] The consilium—addressed to Herwart—is a lengthy one, possibly because it was a maiden effort and possibly because Vesalius was seeking to demonstrate both his friendship and gratitude for assistance toward the completion of the *Fabrica*. Such advice as he offered is clear illustration of the ignorance of ophthalmology that then prevailed, and it is apparent that Vesalius, as a young physician, was still strongly influenced by the terrifyingly complicated Galenic pharmacopoeia. In later years, and after much experience as imperial physician, he was to become somewhat cynical toward such elaborate mysteries.

A second consilium, undated but probably belonging to this same period, has recently been discovered, "Consilium Dominj Andreae Vesalij ad praeservandum et curandum calculum pro D. Lienharto Haug." It is handwritten and bound with the consilia of several other physicians in a book in the library of Georg Palma, 1543–1591, city-physician of Nuremberg.[145] Still a third consilium, regarding epilepsy and tinnitus,[146] appears to have been a product of these years at Padua or, if later, still prior to 1546.

Nothing further is known with certainty about Vesalius's life in Padua until the summer of 1542 when he had completed the *Fabrica* and prepared for his departure. No doubt he was more and more concerned with the composition of that work through 1541 and 1542, but despite this preoccupation he appears to have carried on his teaching duties satisfactorily since in 1542 his annual salary was further increased to 200 florins, almost three times the amount granted him in 1539. Furthermore, in 1541 he appeared briefly to be about to receive what might be termed a teaching assistant, whether because his growing reputation was attracting more students or whether his burdens were to be lightened until the completion of the *Fabrica*, is unknown.

There were actually two chairs of surgery, both of which had been held as a single post by Vesalius since his appointment in December 1537, but in a document dated 10 August 1541 it is declared that through the solicitations of a certain Joannes Antonius Schilinus—probably the holder of some sort of administrative position in the university—Realdo Colombo had been chosen for the second chair, "although with the stipulation that the excellent Master Andreas Vesalius holds a letter of confirmation for both chairs of surgery." [147] However, a later document of 17 October declares, "we confirm and approve in all except that part where mention is made of the second chair of surgery for which Master Realdo Colombo was chosen; for the present we desire only Master Andreas Vesalius to give the surgical lecture for which he was appointed by the Senate." A further document of 30 December reinforces this decision.[148] There is no indication whether this latter decision was made solely by the local authorities, who had decided that they dare not override a decision of the Senate, or whether Vesalius did not wish Colombo to participate in his program. Possibly, had the second chair been relinquished, Vesalius's moderate income might have been affected.

Realdo Colombo's relationship to Vesalius and the significance of his single publication, *De re anatomica,* are of sufficient importance to justify some consideration of his life. He was born in Cremona (Milanese), about 1515, the son of an apothecary and presumably a relative of that Paolo Colombo of Cremona who had preceded Vesalius in the chair of surgery and anatomy at Padua during the academic year 1536–37. It may have been that relationship that determined Realdo's presence in Venice and Padua. First venturing upon a career in surgery, Realdo apprenticed himself to Giovanni Antonio Lonigo, the Venetian surgeon who had performed the public anatomy at Padua in December 1536 for Paolo Colombo. In 1540, after seven years' tutelage in surgery, possibly dissatisfied with the limited career of the surgeon, which at that time was subordinated to the profession of medicine, Colombo began the study of medicine at Padua.[149] Especially attracted to anatomy, he studied with Vesalius—who at first looked upon his student with favor and mentioned him with friendliness in the *Fabrica* [150]—and after Vesalius's departure in 1542 Colombo was appointed to his chair, first on a temporary basis and later for a term of years.[151] However, he was not hesitant to criticize his predecessor, and, as we shall see, the unexpected and brief return of Vesalius to Padua in December 1543, just in time to hear himself being criticized by his former student, led to the sudden development of hostility that was to be lifelong, so that a generation later Vesalius was still referring to Colombo in the bitterest terms.[152]

Chapter VII

PREPARATION OF
THE *FABRICA* AND *EPITOME*

T WAS stated earlier that from 1538 onward Vesalius appears to have had in mind generally an anatomical study of fairly elaborate form. There was a hint of this in the *Tabulae anatomicae*, repeated with more confidence in the *Venesection letter*. However, it is uncertain when he finally formulated his plans for the *Fabrica* and set to work on that large task, although it must have been in 1539 or 1540. Possibly the favorable reception of his anatomical demonstrations in Bologna in January 1540 was the final factor to put the project into operation. Some years later in the *Letter on the china root* Vesalius remarked that he had lectured at Padua three times on Galen's book *On the bones* "before I dared call attention to his mistakes." [1] Since this Galenic text was usually employed during the winter anatomical course, which Vesalius first gave in 1537, courage to oppose Galen would seemingly have been gathered during the academic year 1539–40, and we are aware that he did oppose Galen during the anatomical demonstrations at Bologna. [2]

At first thought it may seem surprising that once the plan had been determined upon so much was accomplished in so short a time, especially since the purely mechanical task of writing the extensive text was far from slight. One may wonder, too, where in the midst of his teaching duties Vesalius found time for both anatomical investigation and composition. Some clue to this may exist in a further statement in the *Letter on the china root* in which he remarked that when he was at Padua he could concentrate on his work, since he then had no domestic responsibilities and his time was pretty much his own to carry on his researches, adding, in reference to one of those later attacks upon his criticisms of Galen:

I could have defended myself against this attack with a much larger number of arguments than at present if I still had as much time as was formerly available to me when I was at the university, devoting myself to study rather than to the practice of medicine. Then I could stay home whenever I desired. [3]

To understand how the *Fabrica* was composed between perhaps the winter of 1539–1540 and the summer of 1542 it is necessary to consider what Vesalius was attempting to do. The *Fabrica* is a monograph describing human anatomy, seeking to provide the reader with the fullest possible description of the human body, and therefore the presentation is far more detailed than that of any of its predecessors or its successors for a considerable time to come. This called for the correction of erroneous views, many of them inherited from Galen and from medieval sources, and the extension of earlier and frequently brief descriptions. Occasionally the author called attention to some hitherto wholly neglected anatomical structure, but more often he was required to correct some details and to add others for the elaboration of descriptions that were originally so brief as to be no more than passing references to curiosities. Thus Vesalius's burden was somewhat lightened by these pre-existent descriptions, although it was his plan—not fully realized, however—that all of them must be verified by reference to the human cadaver. A study of the *Fabrica* indicates that this method was followed with commendable care for more than half the entire work, mainly the sections dealing with bones, muscles, heart, and brain. The remainder of the *Fabrica* is, with some exceptions, more traditional, although no book of it is without some indication of this Vesalian method of investigation. Perhaps the original standards set by the author were too high to be maintained consistently by one pioneer investigator through such an extensive study, and undoubtedly the time he allotted himself for his task was limiting.

The actual composition appears to have been the result of extensive reading plus investigation, and it seems likely that much of the investigation was undertaken during the so-called private dissections, those conducted and explained by Vesalius solely for his students. He looked upon these students as colleagues and assistants, and it seems likely that class sessions were to some degree what might today be termed research seminars. The arrangement of the chapters of the *Fabrica* gives some support to such a view. Some of the dissections were apparently carried on by Vesalius alone, or possibly with certain chosen students, in his own dwelling, upon cadavers from rifled tombs or from executions, and, as he wrote in the *Letter on the china root,* sometimes kept in his bedroom for several weeks.[4] Unquestionably he was an enthusiast, and just as unquestionably it was best that he had no domestic responsibilities at that time.

Although the extensive text of the *Fabrica* has long and properly been recognized as the monographic foundation of modern anatomy, little or no recognition has been given to it as a classic in the field of pedagogy, and it will not be amiss at this point to consider Vesalius's practice and views on the teaching of anatomy as they are offered in the *Fabrica.* Between the end of 1537 and the beginning of 1539 he had presented three important methods of instruction: personal dissection, superior illustrative material, and a dissection manual—that is, his edition of Guinter's *Institutiones* tailored to his purpose. Beyond this he could not go, at least for formal instruction, without a greater supply of dissection material. This supply seems to have become available during 1539, thanks to appreciation of his work by the authorities and the appointment of a sympathetic judge of the criminal court, Marcantonio Contarini, who provided the bodies of executed criminals,[5] and even made the time of execution dependent upon the anatomist's needs. In 1546, after Vesalius had entered imperial service, but hearking back to his Paduan days, he remarked reminiscently, "I shall no longer bother to petition the judges to delay an execution to a time suitable for dissection."[6] Nor should we overlook Vesalius's own initiative in the procurement of cadavers—of course illegally—as he became more confident of his position. Yet even with such assistance as he received, he must always have suffered from a shortage of dissection material, especially when we recall that there were no satisfactory preservatives. The very fact that Vesalius mentions keeping bodies in his home for several weeks—certainly an extremity that must have been exceedingly unpleasant—is a fair indication of the paucity of material. How many cadavers were available to him cannot be ascertained; it is clear, however, that most of them were male and that his experience with the female cadaver was relatively limited.[7] This was no doubt owing in part to the fact that much of his material was supplied by the executioner and that the greater number of criminals were male.

With increased opportunity for human dissection from 1539 onward, Vesalius was in a position to verify his suspicion, which had grown almost to certainty, that Galenic anatomy was based on nonhuman sources. As a result he propounded two doctrines which were thenceforth fundamental to his teaching: first, because of its source, much of Galenic anatomy was fallacious; and second, knowledge of human anatomy was to be acquired only from human sources. These doctrines were personally presented to his students, and the *Fabrica* was composed to present them outside the University of Padua.

Considered in this light, the *Fabrica* was the gospel of a new method of anatomical investigation. In Padua, both gospel and its proof were presented directly by Vesalius; for those elsewhere it was presented in the *Fabrica* with its painfully complete descriptions, its advice on how to repeat the Vesalian dissections, its indirect encouragement to body snatching if necessary, and its illustrative and diagrammatic guides to aid recognition of details, and to supplement the reader's shortage of dissection material. The *Fabrica* reflects fully Vesalius's method of instruction from about 1539 to 1543.

Like any true scholar, Vesalius advised recourse to the sources, in this instance human bodies, and if bodies were not readily available the student was encouraged by word of mouth, or, in the *Fabrica,* by anecdotal precept, to seek them out for himself. It is significant that wherever Vesalius traveled to give extramural lectures a wave of body snatching ensued;[8] the various anecdotes in the *Fabrica* give no indication of repentance, and the following incident even suggests amused recollection:

The handsome mistress of a certain monk of San Antonio here [in Padua] died suddenly as though from strangulation of the uterus or some quickly devastating ailment and was snatched from her tomb by the Paduan students and carried off for public dissection. By their remarkable industry they flayed the whole skin from the cadaver lest it be recognized by the monk who, with the relatives of his mistress, had complained to the municipal judge that the body had been stolen from its tomb.[9]

Presumably the judge was Marcantonio Contarini, who must have had suspicions regarding the incident, and it was this cadaver that was the source of the illustration of the uterus in Book V of the *Fabrica*. The Vesalian incentive to grave robbing and body snatching may have contributed to the decision of the Venetian senate (1550) to threaten further such violations of the law with severe penalties.[10] Later on, in the *Letter on the china root* (1546), Vesalius expressed what may have been remorse when he declared: "I shall not advise students to observe where someone has been buried or urge them to make note of the diseases of their teachers' patients so they may [ultimately] secure their bodies."[11]

Once the material was available, dispensing with the barber who had formerly done the dissecting while the professor lectured from a book, Vesalius himself performed the dissection, "so that often here [in Padua] and in Bologna I conducted the anatomy; and having dispensed with the ridiculous fashion of the universities, I myself [both] demonstrated and lectured." At least in public dissections, and presumably as a preparatory step in private ones, he also encouraged the participation of his students. "I strive [to see] that public dissections be carried on as much as possible by the students."[12]

However, there was much investigation that could be carried out on the living, and just as he described such research on himself, his associates, and students, so Vesalius advised the reader of the *Fabrica* to undertake similar investigations. The eruption of the author's molar teeth, painful as the event was, provided a lesson in anatomy:

> The hindmost teeth . . . erupt for the first time after puberty and sexual maturity and thereupon afflict man with the greatest torture . . . Physicians pay little attention to this fact. They either extract other teeth or, having convinced themselves that the teeth have been attacked by a vitiated humor, burden the sick with pills and suchlike remedies, although no more-effective cure can be offered to the sufferer than light scarification of the gums over the last tooth or sometimes drilling of the bone. I myself recently experienced this; as I write, my thirty-second tooth is erupting in my twenty-sixth year. Many of the skulls met with in cemeteries also prove this fact, for in them the aforesaid posterior teeth are still resting or are hidden in a sort of cavity, one or the other of their cusps perforating the thin bone. My very dear friend Joannes Paulus Guiducius of Urbino recently showed me just such a skull.[13]

One could also place his hands over the rib cartilages and gain some notion of the movement of the thorax in breathing:

> So that you may more clearly understand what I say, first place each hand at the cartilages of the false ribs and experience the fact that here they draw the ends of the cartilages inward and upward by the force of the inhaled air; then, leaving one hand in place, put the other extended at the posterior region of the ribs, and again when you have taken a breath note how the ribs are separated near the back and how the cartilages are compressed.[14]

Pressure applied to the nerves of the thumb or elbow produced a numbness which could give some understanding of the course and action of the nerves:

> You will be amused to observe the series of the nerves in your own hand; if you compress the nerves in the thumb of one hand completely to the bone or apply pressure to the elbow so that by that compression you prevent transmission of the animal spirit, the part in which the nerves are inserted will become numb. Do it near the joint of the elbow which is not covered with flesh . . . and if you compress the fourth nerve of the thumb for some time, you will feel the external region of the thumb and index finger . . . become numb.[15]

Observation of those able to move their ears, such as a distinguished doctor of laws at Padua, could help the student to comprehend the muscles involved:

> The posterior origin of this muscle is wholly in the region of the spine [of the vertebrae] of the neck; thence it is carried along the base of the occipital bone and under the ear, so creeping forward until it reaches the root. Indeed, it sometimes ascends here so that by its aid some men—not just brutes such as asses—can move their ears as may be seen here in Padua, in, among others, a doctor of laws of great charm as well as notable erudition, in the pleasant-mannered Claudius Symionius of Forlì, and the bold, brave, and active Petrus Ravascherius of Genoa.[16]

Vesalius was constantly on the watch for anomalies, especially because of their disparity from the Galenic description. Not only was he ever inquisitive about the curious, but he sought wherever possible to discover the why and how of these things, even though it meant extra time and effort. His students were admonished to watch for and report all such cases. So in the case of a papal oarsman, Vesalius was not content with the findings at autopsy but interrogated the members of the crew:

> I never saw the smallest part of the passage of the gall bladder extended into the stomach except in one of the oarsmen of a papal trireme. Just as certain other of his organs, especially about the ribs and thoracic muscles, differed from the structure of other men, so this passage was divided into two branches; the lesser or more slender was inserted into the fundus of the stomach where the vein that goes about the right side of its lower region first joins to the stomach. The man seems to have been of a hot and dry temperament. In order to learn whether he had been accustomed to the complaint of bilious vomiting, as Galen asserts is frequent in men of this type, I carefully inquired of his friends if they had observed anything of this sort. They replied that they had never seen him vomit or be sick even in the roughest weather, and they all agreed that he was very robust, that he could blow a horn with one very long breath, and could by far surpass all his comrades in the depth of his voice and in counting numbers with one breath.[17]

In this particular instance Vesalius was concerned with disproving Galen's statement, repeated by medieval writers, that in man one of the biliary ducts ended in the stomach. As late as the opening of the sixteenth century Gabriele Zerbi maintained that two ducts always issued from the gall bladder, one emptying into the duodenum and the other into the fundus of the stomach. It was in consideration of this theory, as well as his own contention that the bile duct "is separated farther from the stomach's orifice than other anatomists generally realize," that Vesalius described this case of anomaly. Although examination of the oarsman's body seemed to support Galen's teaching, Vesalius properly declared the condition, which he had never seen before, to be anomalous and hence in no way evidence supporting Galenic anatomy.[18] It should be emphasized that Vesalius constantly recognized the possibility of anomaly and sought to base what he considered the correct description of any structure only upon multiple observation. "I am not accustomed to say anything with certainty after only one or two observations." [19]

Attention was also drawn to the curious "double-jointed" condition of the Genoese youth Johannes Centurius:

We see that certain persons can bend outward to a considerable degree not just the first joint of the fingers, but all the rest, and particularly the third. An instance of this is well illustrated in the case of Johannes Centurius of Genoa, a youth of the brightest hope and the most accurate judgment . . . who bends his fingers—which are unusually round, long, and well-suited for all artifices and elegance—so remarkably to the rear that he is able to hold water in them just as we in the palm.[20]

Nor did Vesalius overlook those children with deformed heads, used by mendicants to attract attention and to extract alms. In these observations he provided what may have been the first recorded description of hydrocephalus:

The fourth type of nonnatural shape, also enumerated by Hippocrates, is one in which the head projects more noticeably to the sides at each ear than in the anterior and posterior regions . . . Galen . . . contends that this shape . . . in the nature of things cannot exist, although a boy with multiple deformities and somewhat mentally deficient may be seen today in Venice with a head of this shape. Indeed, at Bologna a beggar wanders about whose head is squarish but a little wider than long. Furthermore, at Genoa a small boy is carried from door to door by a beggarwoman and was displayed by actors in Brabant; his head is without exaggeration larger than the heads of two men and bulges on either side. We sometimes see other nonnatural head forms even in the eminently learned. Such skulls are not infrequently found in cemeteries, as may be ascertained if one searches in the cemeteries of that region of the Alps which looks toward Styria.[21]

Even theatrical performers could be made to serve for instruction, because "as often as . . . we observe performers raising huge weights [grasped in the teeth] we learn the strength of the temporal muscles and how, in relation to their mass, the most powerful service of all the muscles have been entrusted to them." And:

To mention only one instance of men biting, I recently saw an actor in Padua who raised from the ground in his teeth an iron pole weighing twenty-five pounds; then, erect and holding it in his mouth, he bent backward and hurled it, point first, into a wall, a distance from the actor, as I measured it, of thirty-nine feet. Furthermore, I recently heard that in Venice a Turk had held a far greater weight in his teeth; to the astonishment of all, with his teeth he handled in various ways—as if it had been a rod—a beam carried to him by five men.[22]

Nor was time spent at the table free from its moments of anatomical investigation, for, "although it is possible to observe [the tendons] while dining on any animal, you may best do this when some cut of beef has been placed upon the table."[23]

It was dissatisfaction with the formal and traditional method of instruction that led Vesalius to write that "as things are now taught in the schools, with days wasted on ridiculous questions, there is very little offered to the spectators that could not better be taught by a butcher in his shop,"[24] and throughout the *Fabrica* there are frequent admonitions to consult the various techniques developed by butchers. Thus, "the division of the vena cava under the higher region of the sternum near the root of the neck, which [division] butchers seek when they are about to bleed oxen and swine";[25] and "I would consider this [matter] at greater length and detail except that anyone may go to a butcher's shop and observe the site, form, and size of the cow's uterus and other things in the structure of the parts which ought to be considered carefully."[26] To strip the skin from the whole abdomen and thorax, "you will skin the whole area in the manner of a butcher, incising in one line from chest to pubic bone . . . and cutting away."[27] So, too, one should consult the midwives and, if possible, as Vesalius had succeeded in doing, be present with them at childbirth. However, "not without my strongest entreaties did the midwives admit me into their midst at childbirth."[28]

Vesalius was the dedicated scientist who thought of every human phenomenon in terms of its relationship to the structure and function of the body. His interest in the question of fluid in the pericardium, and perhaps also the question of pores in the cardiac septum, spurred him on in his enthusiasm to overcome what must have been at least some revulsion, even in that insensitive age, and carry off for examination "the still-pulsating heart with the lung and the rest of the viscera" of a wretch just quartered alive.[29] All these activities are recorded in the *Fabrica* as a guide for the reader, and we may assume that such practices were also urged upon Vesalius's students in Padua.

The always insufficient supply of human cadavers compelled Vesalius also to use lower animals, which he declared desirable under any circumstances, not only for corroboration or disproof of Galen's animal anatomy, but also for the independent study of comparative anatomy of which Padua was the first great center. "As I teach the part [in the human] I attempt to demonstrate it separately in some animal,"[30] wrote Vesalius; moreover, "physicians ought to make use not only of the bones of man, but, for the sake of Galen, of those of the ape and dog; and, for Aristotle, birds, fishes, and reptiles articulated, or at least disarticulated."[31] The dog was most commonly used. "I was accustomed to observe all these things in brute animals, and especially in dogs, since the supply of them was never failing," [32] but "most of my supply [of apes] was of the tailless kind." [33] Hence the rhesus monkey depicted on the title page of the *Fabrica* was not the usual specimen.

Although Vesalius may have been introduced to vivisection by Guinter of Andernach in Paris, he claims that he tried it as a result of reading Galen. "I first employed it for myself alone and then publicly in Padua and Bologna," [34] but the vivisection "proved rather contrary to Galen's teachings than a support for them." Vesalius used vivisection as an instructional method for the study of thoracic movement in breathing, since "the vivisection of the dog, or whatever other animal may be at hand, teaches the function of the diaphragm." The fullest discussion of this is in the last chapter of the *Fabrica* in which he recognized that, although the dissection of dead bodies provided information of an anatomical nature, the proper understanding of physiology could only be gained from dissection of living specimens.

As might be expected from an anatomist so concerned with anatomical illustration—although it must be remembered that illustrations in the *Fabrica* were not intended for his own students—Vesalius had an extraordinarily well-developed visual sense, and it is apparent in his verbal descriptions of anatomical structures. Since nomenclature had not yet been fixed and many structures had been described only vaguely, a good visual sense was not only a desirable quality for the anatomist but one to be developed in the student as well. As a teaching and mnemonic device Vesalius used it to make the student recall some ordinary object to which the anatomical structure might be compared. Thus there were "bones that are shaped like a wedge, as that bone of the head called SPHĒNOEIDĒS because it is wedge-shaped; those that resemble a yoke and so are called ZYGŌMATA in Greek but *iugalia* by us . . . that shaped like the shuttle used for weaving ribbons, as the bone of the forearm called the radius." [35] The trapezius muscle resembled the cowl of the Benedictines as it falls over the shoulders:

If you will consider the [trapezius] muscle of each side, which will be considered the second among the movers of the scapula, you may contend that the Franciscans, Jacobites, and especially the Benedictines, have borrowed the form of their cowl not from Satan, who tempted Jesus in the desert, but from the shape of those muscles; that is, insofar as [the cowl] covers the scapula. [36]

Some of Vesalius's terms have been accepted into modern anatomical terminology so that in some degree this aspect of his pedagogy plays the same role today as in the sixteenth century. Thus of the auditory ossicles, "that somewhat resembling the shape of an anvil or molar tooth, as the smaller ossicle [incus] . . . and that resembling a hammer, as the larger ossicle [malleus]." [37] The valve of the left atrioventricular orifice "you may aptly compare to a bishop's mitre." [38] Of our present cricoid cartilage, he wrote:

No name has been given to this cartilage, and therefore it will be called by the special name of innominate. However, if anyone carefully inspects its appearance, and compares it to the shape of anything, and thence wishes to give it a name, he will discover that it resembles most closely that ring which Turkish bowmen put on the right thumb so that by its assistance they can draw the bowstring more fully.[39]

Later, Fallopio was to supply the term "cricoid" by accepting Vesalius's description and substituting the Greek form of the word "ring." [40] The intestinal tract, "although the same continuous body, yet since it extends in many different twists and turns, varying in shape," and is not every-where the same in respect to site, substance, and form, recalled to Vesalius that Parisian thoroughfare running from the gate of Saint Jacques and changing its name and dimensions as it proceeded, a thoroughfare that, because of the proximity of part of it to the medical school, was very familiar to him:

So in Paris the thoroughfare from the gate of Saint Jacques to that called Saint Martin, even though it is straight and without twists and turns, nonetheless, if my recollection is correct, changes its name six times. First it borrows its name from Saint Jacques, then from a little bridge, thereafter from the church of Notre Dame, not much later from its bridge, then from a tavern, and finally from Saint Martin's church.[41]

Although such descriptions were required by the fact that so many anatomical structures had multiple names that the same name was some-times used for several structures, or, as in the case of the innominate cartilage, now the cricoid, there was no name at all, Vesalius also sought in the *Fabrica* to introduce a purified, more standardized terminology by a return wherever possible to the Greek or to a Latinized version of it. As a result, the *Fabrica* is studded with Greek terminology, not the long quotations that earlier seem to have been almost a requirement to indi-cate one's classical and Hellenistic attainment, but merely the Greek names of anatomical structures. It was a process of clarification not only to aid the anatomist but also to instruct the student.

These, then, are some of the aids to better instruction employed by Vesalius, and underlying everything was his insistence that the student dissect and study the cadaver at first hand. The *Fabrica* was for those who did not have either direct access to the Paduan professor or to a ready supply of dissection material. The very bulk of the work suggests that no important detail of instruction had been left out, and, as illustrations of anatomical structures were included to clarify particular anatomical problems, so the title page, which will be considered separately, indicates in an entirely realistic manner the over-all procedure to be followed.

In the *Tabulae anatomicae* Vesalius presented his readers with ana-tomical terms in Arabic and Hebrew as well as in Latin and Greek, and this effort was continued in the *Fabrica*. It was, of course, partly the result of continuing uncertainty of verbal usage, partly no doubt the author's desire to display a wider linguistic knowledge than he may ac-tually have possessed, but partly also it was a reflection of his constantly inquiring mind. Something has already been said of his anonymous Hebrew adviser for the *Tabulae,* and those competent to judge have declared that that assistant could not have been the same one employed during the composition of the *Fabrica.* We know the name, if little more, of the latter, since Vesalius mentioned it in the course of explaining his method of listing anatomical terms:

> I have decided to give in the index principally a simple list of the names of the bones, first presenting those I use in the text; then the Greek; then, any others in Latin taken from authoritative writers, and all that in such way that it may have value. After these will follow the Hebrew, but also some Arabic, almost all taken from the Hebrew translation of Avicenna through the efforts of Lazarus de Frigeis, a distinguished Jewish physician and close friend with whom I have been accustomed to translate Avicenna.[42]

Considerable effort has been spent in attempts to identify this Lazarus de Frigeis, but thus far without success. The most recent and extensive effort was that of the late Shelomo Franco of Jerusalem.[43] Although his research produced no conclusive identification, he felt it most likely that Lazarus was of a family originally from Hungary, and he called attention to the fact that the name Frigyies exists in Hungary and Rumania with variants such as Frjgyes and Frigies, while one of the heroes of the Risorgimento was a Hungarian Jew, Gustavo de Frigyesi, d. 1878. Today there also exists in Italy a family called Frigessi di Rattalma, originally the Hungarian Frigyes. Furthermore, the transliteration of Hebrew terms from the first book of the *Canon* of Avicenna was made by Lazarus according to the pronunciation used by the Jews of Italy, thus suggesting either that he had been born in Italy or that he had been taken there while still very young. As the origin of Lazarus de Frigeis is an unsolved puzzle, so too is it puzzling that mention of him in the later *Fabrica* of 1555 omits the phrase "distinguished Jewish physician." [44] There is also uncertainty as to whether he lived in Venice or Padua, and in which of those two cities, or if possibly in both, he studied Avicenna with Vesalius. As will be mentioned later, Lazarus is most likely represented as one of the spectators in the dissection scene on the title page of the *Fabrica.*

It must be added that the text of the *Fabrica* contains no great amount of superficially spectacular discovery. This is not astonishing since Vesalius's purpose was a correct description *in extenso,* and he deliberately sought to avoid the presentation of isolated bits of factual information, however novel, unless he could place such information within its proper context.[45] Yet in Vesalius's day his correction of Galenic error must have been a tremendous novelty now difficult to appreciate.

In addition to such correction, at least one of the greatest Vesalian contributions was the extended description elaborating previous brief statements or descriptions, sometimes little more than curiosities, into comprehensible statements of anatomical significance—such as that of the two ossicles of the ear, the malleus and incus. These ossicles, seemingly first mentioned by Berengario da Carpi, were described very briefly: "Two small ossicles . . . which are moved by the moving of the air and strike one against the other. According to some they are those things that, because of this motion, cause sound in the ear, and that is a thing truly worthy of note and seen by few." [46] Nicolo Massa likewise described them briefly: "Inwardly . . . are two ossicles like little hammers. They are both movable and attached and are moved at the motion of the said membrane, which in imitation of the Greeks is called meninx. When you observe that motion in its place you will understand that hearing occurs when sound or harmony is caused by the motion of the little hammers." [47] Although this account is slightly longer than that of Berengario, Massa had described the ossicles as resembling little hammers and failed to recognize their much more fitting resemblance, as Vesalius saw, to a hammer and anvil (malleus and incus), which suggests that Massa had not fully appreciated their appearance. Vesalius, possibly aware of these two brief accounts and decidedly not the discoverer of the ossicles, nevertheless described them so graphically that his names for them have been retained, and he produced a description so complete that it comprises an entire chapter, sufficient for comprehension for practical purposes. [48]

Illustrations were added to the text partly to compensate for scarcity of dissection material and partly because the anatomical vocabulary had not been developed to the point where it was equal to the full task of exposition. Moreover, the charge of verbosity frequently made against Vesalius, correct as it may be on occasion, must be understood in the light of this need for comprehension; the *Fabrica* was planned with teaching constantly in the author's mind. Whatever other purposes the work served, it was to be read by physicians who had wrongfully divorced themselves from this branch of medicine, and their study of the text and its illustrations—since many of the readers would have neither the time nor the opportunity for study in the dissection room—would help them to a better comprehension of anatomy and thereby lead to a general improvement in medicine.

We may therefore visualize Vesalius between the years 1539–1540 and 1542 reading the works of earlier writers on anatomy, [49] pondering, carrying on his investigations and teaching, noting discrepancies from his own observations and additions to the body of anatomical knowledge, even perhaps writing chapters of his book and essaying them as lectures to his students. Nor should it be overlooked that at the outset of this period he had already revised three of Galen's works, especially the *Anatomical procedures*, for the new Giunta edition of Galen's works. Such close study of Galen's text must have helped assure him that he was on the right track and that Galen had followed the wrong one.

In addition to his studies of the classical physicians Vesalius must, for the first time upon his arrival in Italy, have learned of the writings of the major Italian anatomists, who, with the exception of Mondino and Benedetti, had been unknown to him in Paris and Louvain. It is possible that as early as the autumn of 1537 he read the studies of Alessandro Achillini and Berengario da Carpi, perhaps profiting from the latter, and possibly it was then that he studied the contributions of Julius Pollux and Giorgio Valla to a revised anatomical terminology.[50]

He may even have come into direct contact with the Venetian physician Nicolo Massa whose anatomical treatise he had certainly read, although it is doubtful that that somewhat overrated work was as important to Vesalius's achievements as has sometimes been said. Massa's book does contain contributions and some correction of Galenic errors, but it remains under the shadow of Galen and does not consistently enunciate the new scientific principle basic to the *Fabrica*. Nevertheless, because of the importance placed upon Massa's treatise in the past, and because he was alive throughout Vesalius's years in nearby Padua and was possibly an acquaintance, some attention must be given to this Venetian physician.

Nicolo Massa of Venice, 1485–1569, after receiving his degree at Padua became a member of the College of Physicians of Venice in 1521. He was a successful physician, especially because of his treatment of syphilis, about which he wrote a book, and Alvise Luisini dedicated his *De morbo gallico*, 1566–1567, to him. At eighty Massa became blind but continued his practice and his studies, and to console him in his affliction Luisini wrote a dialogue, *La cecità,* in which Massa as one of the speakers is made to refer often to his own personal life and works. He suffered from a morbid fear—or perhaps a lack of faith in his fellow practitioners—that he might be buried alive, and consequently he left instructions in his testament that, after he had been pronounced dead, several days must pass before his actual interment.

Throughout his career Massa gave considerable attention to anatomical research of which the result was a book entitled *Liber introductorius anatomiae* (Venice, 1536), republished without alteration in 1559. Dedicated to Pope Paul III with a plea for greater anatomical study among physicians, it remained the best brief textbook of anatomy until Colombo's treatise in 1559. Indeed, the reissue of Massa's book in that year suggests an attempt to compete with the new work.

The *Liber introductorius* follows the arrangement of Mondino, who is called "a man much celebrated in anatomy," and only that is presented that can be seen in the dissection of a single body and is most urgently required for a comprehension of medicine. There is a promise of a more extended work dealing with other matters, but this work was never published. Although Massa did not hesitate to recognize the value of Galen, stating that despite criticisms of him and of other ancients they were still the true founders of anatomy, and that information could even be gained from the Arabs, yet he also emphasized the need for human dissection. Some criticism of the animal basis of Galen's anatomy seems to be expressed in the remark that "we shall see whether or not the parts of apes are completely like those of man as some believe," and although Massa admitted his indebtedness to Mondino and to his own near-contemporaries, Zerbi and Berengario, yet he felt that current anatomists wrote at too great length about nonessentials, some wasting effort in philosophical argument and others knowing only the names of things they had never observed. These statements are in part to Massa's credit, yet he never considered anatomy as a separate subject for research, but solely as an adjunct to medicine. Nor did he consistently proclaim a scientific principle as the guide to investigation. Frequently, after having displayed a wholly praiseworthy scientific detachment, he would again fall completely under Galenic authority or naïvely accept some bit of medieval tradition.

Thus the *Liber introductorius* is based partly upon the writings of earlier men and partly upon the author's own experience. Massa performed a number of autopsy examinations, notably in the hospitals of SS John and Paul and SS Peter and Paul in Venice, frequently in the presence of other physicians. Permission for these examinations appears to have been readily granted him by the relatives of the deceased, and in one instance the suggestion for such examination was actually initiated by the son of a deceased parent. Massa refers to such dissections in the years 1526, 1527, 1532, and 1534 as well as to others on the bodies of stillborn infants.[51]

Within its limits, and despite a fairly large residue of Galenic anatomy, the *Liber introductorius* represents the experiences of a shrewd practitioner. It is not, however, of such significance as some have asserted and attempted to prove by grouping together those observations worthy of merit but failing to heed the more traditional content. Massa's best descriptions are extremely brief and often little more than curiosities which require expansion for intelligent comprehension and utility. Vesalius never mentions the work, although a remark in the *Fabrica* may be an oblique reference to Massa, but the purpose and spirit of the *Liber introductorius* were vastly different from like aspects of the *Fabrica*. On the other hand, the work did influence Jacobus Sylvius who referred to it frequently in his *Isagogae,* a clear indication of Massa's Galenic compromise.

To return directly to Vesalius, it seems most likely that he composed the books of the *Fabrica* in the order in which they appear in the published work. Nevertheless, in a reference to an acquaintance named Christopher Pfluegel and an incident occurring at Louvain in July 1542,[52] there is evidence that interpolations were made, at least in the first book of the *Fabrica*, at about the time when, according to the preface, the entire manuscript had been completed. This fact, incidentally, suggests that Vesalius did not send parts of the manuscript to the printer as they were completed, but instead sent it in its entirety sometime during the summer of 1542. A statement of Vesalius in Book I also informs us that he was at work on that book in 1540. Writing of the teeth in Chapter VI of Book I he remarked: "As I write, my thirty-second tooth is erupting in my twenty-sixth year." [53] There is a suggestion of the time of composition of Book II, as well as an indication that the books were written in their published numerical sequence, in a remark made by Fallopio in his *Observationes anatomicae.* There he stated that Vesalius did not have access to Galen's *Dissection of muscles* during the composition of Book II,[54] and a study of that book corroborates this statement. Since the *Dissection of muscles* did not become available in the Giunta edition until sometime during 1541, we seem therefore to have a *terminus ad quem* for the completion of Book II. Such is the paucity of our information on the time and chronological sequence of the composition of the *Fabrica*.

As we have so little data on the composition of the text, so also our knowledge regarding the drawing of the illustrations is negligible. Nevertheless, possibly because the illustrations have been studied vigorously whereas the text is seldom read today, opinions on the subject of their draughtsman or draughtsmen have on occasion been accompanied by strong and even heated convictions.

The first reference to the illustrations is in the *Venesection letter* in which Vesalius wrote: "With regard to the rest of my studies there is little to say at present. I have now almost completed two illustrations of the nerves; in the first, the seven pairs of cranial nerves have been drawn, and in the other all the small branches of the dorsal marrow." [55] It does not appear, however, that Vesalius was thinking of the *Fabrica* as it was to be, but rather of another work, or perhaps an enlarged version of the *Tabulae anatomicae,* since he continued: "I feel that these [illustrations] must be held back until I have produced illustrations of the muscles and of all the internal parts." Thus it seems that whatever the publication was to be, it was held up for want of illustrations rather than text. Slightly later in the same work he added that "if bodies become available and Joannes Stephanus [of Calcar], the distinguished contemporary artist, does not refuse his services, I shall certainly undertake that task [of publication]." [56] That remark, despite the fact that Calcar may or may not have been available, has frequently led to the conclusion, untenable in the judgment of the present writer, that the superb title page, skeletons, and "muscle-men" of the *Fabrica* must be attributed to his draughtsmanship. A brief history of the artistic attribution of the illustrations will reveal some of the difficulties.

There appears to be nothing in the *Fabrica* to identify any artist or artists, nor immediately after publication was there anything stated about them in the writings of others. The first direct reference to the production of the illustrations is a remark by Vesalius himself in the *Letter on the china root.* It is, however, illuminating on only one point. After referring to his trials with artistic temperament, he speaks of a plurality of artists or draughtsmen and possibly wood-block cutters. "[No longer] shall I have to put up with the bad temper of artists and sculptors [engravers? i.e., wood-block cutters] who made me more miserable than did the bodies I was dissecting." [57] Another but somewhat indirect reference is made by Annibale Caro in his *Dicerie.*[58] In one part of that work, ascribed to the period 1540–1543, Caro makes mention of the "anatomy of Vecelli [i.e., Titian]," a reference that seems to concern the illustrations of the *Fabrica* and suggests that they were made by artists in Titian's studio. During the year 1540 Caro passed some time with Titian, which lends authority to his statement. It has been pointed out that attribution to Titian or his studio does not represent a later tradition that, on the basis of quality, substitutes a greater name for a lesser, since up to this time Calcar had not been mentioned. Rather it represents contemporary information presumably from Titian or his associates.

The first mention of Calcar as draughtsman is found in the writings of Vasari, although not in the first edition of his *Vite de piu eccellenti pittori* (1550), but in the second edition that appeared in 1568 [59] when Vasari was an old man, Calcar long since dead, and the *Fabrica* in print for a quarter century. Aside from the question of why the account was not included in the first edition, the suspicion that its inclusion in 1568 represents the rambling reminiscences of an old man is somewhat supported by the vagueness of the statements. Referring to Calcar, Vasari wrote: "The designs that the excellent Andreas Vesalius caused to be engraved and issued with his work were by his hand, and they do him lasting honor." [60] Charles Singer pointed out that the word "work" is written by Vasari in the Italian singular form *opera;* thus, since Vesalius produced three illustrated works (in 1538 and 1543), we are privileged to decide that the statement refers to the *Tabulae anatomicae* of 1538, since there is no question about Calcar's delineation of the three skeletons in it. A second statement by Vasari is chiefly indicative of a faulty memory since, referring back some twenty-three years to 1545, he mentioned his friendship with Calcar and added that he "died young at Naples when great things were hoped of him; it was he who designed the anatomy for Vesalius." [61] Since Calcar probably died in 1547 at the age of forty-eight, it is difficult to consider him either "young" or at an age "when great things were hoped of him," especially in that very mortal age. The third reference mentioned "the eleven large illustrations planned by Andreas Vesalius and designed by [Calcar]." [62] Here very obviously is confusion compounded, since "eleven large illustrations" does not fit the six *Tabulae anatomicae* nor is it the correct number for the illustrations of the skeletons and "muscle-men" of the *Fabrica*, which Calcar's proponents declare to have been made from his drawings. Nor can we justly accept one statement on behalf of Calcar and deny another because it injures his case.

What appears to be the next reference to Calcar as the draughtsman of the *Fabrica* is found in a letter written by Dominicus Lampsonius to Ludovicus Demontiosus in 1589. Here the attribution to Calcar, since it is based upon Vasari, has as its only significance that it is apparently the first literary reference to Vasari's account. [63] Similarly drawn from Vasari is the account of Karel van Mander, 1548–1600, published in 1604. [64]

Thereafter, Vasari's attribution of the illustrations to Calcar appears to have been ignored or forgotten, and an edition of anatomical illustrations, including the skeletons and "muscle-men" of the *Fabrica*, was published about 1670 and attributed to Titian, either from a tradition stemming from Annibale Caro or another source, or by guess only from observation of the illustrations. [65]

From this time on until after the middle of the nineteenth century Calcar's relationship to the *Fabrica* appears to have been neglected. In 1852 Ludwig Choulant, although not expressing himself with certainty, leaned toward ascription of the drawings to Calcar. He made no mention of Vasari but seems to have based his conclusions upon the fact of Calcar's three drawings for the *Tabulae anatomicae* and Vesalius's mention of the artist in the *Venesection letter*. In 1877 Edouard Turner credited Calcar not only with the three skeletons of the *Tabulae anatomicae* but also with the five muscle-figures and the two nude figures of the *Epitome*, suggesting but not stating categorically that the remaining illustrations of the *Epitome* and those of the *Fabrica* were by another.

As judgment had once gone to the extreme of declaring Titian himself the source of the illustrations, so from the end of the nineteenth century a contrary and likewise extreme attribution gave all credit to Calcar. Some have even gone to great lengths to belittle Vesalius's textual contribution. Thus E. Jackschath of Tilsit published a paper in 1902 in which he sought to prove that the *Fabrica* was an elaborate plagiarism from Leonardo da Vinci.[66] More recently an effort was made to prove Calcar the major figure in the composition of the *Fabrica* and Vesalius little more than a hired hack writer who supplied a text to accompany the illustrations.[67] Such efforts, however, have been the product of a kind of Latin illiteracy, a study merely of the illustrations and a theory developed without recourse to the evidence of the text. The disproof of such curious ideas is easily available, but it requires reading the Vesalian texts and the comments of Vesalius's contemporaries.

If we now attempt a positive statement regarding the illustrations, based on such slight factual evidence as exists, we know that Vesalius employed more than one artist and we know that in 1539 he already had two drawings almost completed. There is no certain evidence that they were the work of Calcar, although it is quite possible that he did make them from Vesalius's rougher indications or outlines. There is no proof either that these were the drawings finally used for the *Fabrica*, but it is probable that they were. We also know that the artists were not given a free hand but were, at least in the composition of the "muscle-men," under Vesalius's direct supervision. On this matter we have his words:

When I am about to undertake the dissection of a man I pass a strong cord under the lower jaw through each jugal bone to the vertex of the head, tied like a noose, and either more toward the forehead or the occiput, depending upon my desire to suspend the cadaver either with the head erect or depressed. I place the longer end of the noose across a pulley fixed to a beam of the room, and by it I draw the suspended corpse now higher now lower, and take care that it may be turned in every direction in accordance with the requirements of the task; and again, when desired, I am able to rest it on a table, for the table can easily be accommodated to the position of the pulley. It was in this way that the cadaver was suspended for the delineation of all the illustrations of muscles, just as the seventh illustration displays, although when that was delineated the rope was twisted back to the occiput for the sake of the muscles conspicuous there in the neck. If perhaps the lower jaw has been removed in the course of dissection or the jugal bones have been broken, nevertheless the sinuses carved for the temporal muscles will hold the noose sufficiently securely. One must beware, however, lest the noose be placed around the neck, unless the several muscles connected to the occipital bone have already been dissected. The suspension of the body in this way is very helpful since the human body lying on the table can be turned now on its chest and now on its back.[68]

Concerning the identity of the artists there is almost no information. If we consider the statement of Vasari as a reference to the *Tabulae anatomicae*—the most sensible interpretation—and give a measure of credence to the words of Annibale Caro, then the artists or draughtsmen were from Titian's studio. As a member of that group there is no reason why Calcar should not have participated in the work, although a comparison of the great skeletons of the *Fabrica* with those of lesser quality in the *Tabualae anatomicae*, acknowledged as the work of Calcar, suggests that the former were drawn by a superior but today unknown artist. The high quality of draughtsmanship in the "muscle-men" suggests the same source, perhaps a youthful genius who died early and so left only this record of his ability. He may, too, although not conclusively, be identified with the title page scene.

One has only to examine the illustrations to recognize the diversity of artistic quality, from the peak reached by the artist of the skeletons and "muscle-men" downward several degrees, although it would be a bold person who sought on this basis to determine the actual number of artists employed. Furthermore, we must not overlook Vesalius himself. He had previously demonstrated competence as a biological draughtsman, and there is some indication that a few of the lesser figures in the *Fabrica* were the work of his own pencil. In this regard the legends to the illustrations deserve some examination. Usually in the legend we find some such statement as, "We have depicted," or, "We represent," phrases suggesting the collaboration of dissecting anatomist and artist. The use of the plural, too, is usually for some fairly complicated structure of which the drawing would seem to require trained draughtsmanship. However, in a few of the more-primitive illustrations, such as that of the uterus, the expressions used are, "I have attempted to represent"[69] and "I have delineated."[70] If we recall the manner in which Vesalius's students had stolen this particular body of the mistress of a monk, and the hue and cry that resulted, we can realize that there may have been other instances, like this, in which drawings had to be made with dispatch and could not await the arrival of an artist. Nor should we forget the statement of John Caius referring to that period of shared dwelling with Vesalius in Padua "during which time [Vesalius] wrote and illustrated his books *De humani corporis fabrica*";[71] this must, of course, refer mainly to Vesalius's planning of the illustrations and direction of the artists, but does not entirely deny him some share in the actual draughtsmanship.

In 1546, in his *Letter on the china root,* Vesalius wrote in some irritation against Thomas Geminus's plagiarism of the *Fabrica's* illustrations, declaring that Geminus had plagiarized, among other things, "the courses of the vessels, which my friends know that I myself depicted in my books."[72] If, then, we turn to Geminus's plagiarism we find that for the "courses of the vessels" he borrowed the large illustration of the portal vein, the "venous man," the "arterial man," the cerebrovascular system, the pulmonary vein and artery, and the large folding plate of veins and arteries.[73] The intricacies of draughtsmanship displayed in these illustrations seem at first glance probably beyond the ability of Vesalius, yet, just as his knowledge of Greek has long and improperly been discounted, so too perhaps his ability as a draughtsman. Nor can we ignore his words on Geminus's plagiarism that seem to imply that no matter who may have done the other drawings—and possibly because they were by others he did not feel he could complain so loudly—in those on "the courses of the vessels" he was the draughtsman and therefore entitled to complain vociferously. Furthermore, as he wrote, his friends could vouch for his efforts. Although these remarks were generally known through the publication of his book in 1546, and again in 1547, no voice of artist, anatomist, or enemy was ever raised against Vesalius's assertion. His words, therefore, must be given serious consideration.

As we have so little information on the artists of the anatomical figures themselves, so the quaint landscapes placed behind the "muscle-men" must also remain anonymous, even though they have occasionally been ascribed to Campagnolo. It was first pointed out by Jackschath[74] that when these backgrounds are placed together in proper sequence a hilly landscape results which seems to be that of the Euganean Hills some six miles southwest of Padua, and more recently Dr. Willy Wiegand has presented conclusive evidence for this identification.[75] However, the draughtsmanship of the landscape is inferior to the best of that in the *Fabrica,* and its inclusion must have been determined by the streak of Vesalian fantasy that led him to place a spear or shovel in the hands of the skeletons and determined the activities of the *putti* in the initial letters of the text. Vesalius's concern seems to have been to have a landscape behind each "muscle-man" rather than to show it as a whole. Presumably, therefore, the drawing of the entire landscape was cut into sections to fit and the wood-block cutter or designer ordered to include a portion with each "muscle-man." This would account for the sequence of landscape views not agreeing with the sequence of the "muscle-men."

The landscape scenes have no significance except for an indirect identification of Padua and can only be justified on the grounds of fantasy and decoration, yet for this very reason we gain some understanding of the importance Vesalius attached to his book. It is apparent in the dedicatory preface that he considered the *Fabrica* of epochal significance, representing a point of division between long centuries of authoritarian domination and the new age of observational science and scientific method, and accordingly it seems likely that he wanted to embellish his great work in every possible way.

The further use of decorative or historiated initial letters will be considered later. It is sufficient for now to note that although the scenes represented are related to the text, showing such matters as body snatching, dissection, and vivisection, or scenes of medical and surgical practice, yet the minute size and lack of precise detail, as well as the use of *putti* as actors in them, suggest once again Vesalian whimsy or fantasy, carried here to boisterous lengths.

Whether the drawings for the illustrations of the individual books of the *Fabrica* preceded the text or whether, indeed, there was any definite system is impossible to say. In a few instances we know that Vesalius worked with the original drawings before him, since, apparently forgetting that the figure printed from the block would be reversed, he confused right with left in his description.[76] At other times he may have had proofs available from the blocks, such as those he eventually sent to the printer. This may have been true of the illustration of the whole scheme of the nerves,[77] since a small illustration was added to it to correct an error of the engraver of the original block who had omitted certain lettering.[78]

There must have been times of depression and discouragement. The plan of appealing only to observation of the human structure could not always be maintained for so vast a work concluded in so short a time, and occasionally Vesalius was obliged to compromise and to accept the ancient authority of Galen. On the other hand, where, as in the first two books, he resorted extensively to his own investigations and inevitably opposed many Galenic teachings, he must have had some realization of the possibility that he would be bringing old friendships to an end, and that the publication of the *Fabrica* would be met in some quarters with hostile criticism rather than friendly welcome. Then, too, there must never have been sufficient material for research, with the result that certain lines of investigation would have had to be postponed until cadavers became available, either through regular channels or by extraordinary means; the hiatus that must have occurred in his studies from time to time would have been frustrating, to say the least. Furthermore, constant comparison was required between the word of Galen and the results of investigation, since, although it was true that Galenic error had to be pointed out and corrected, yet the truths of Galen were to be cherished and preserved.

The texts of Galen were for the most part available in accurate Latin translations—and, as we have seen, Vesalius had made important contributions to the Giunta edition which rapidly became the standard Latin version of Galen—yet the serious scholar would consult the original Greek text, as well as any new manuscripts that might turn up. On one occasion Vesalius referred with considerable irritation to an episode in which he was refused permission to examine such a manuscript of Galen's *On the bones*, a work of fundamental importance for him. While considering the crucial matter of the bones of the jaw and Galen's reference to them, available in Latin translation,[79] Vesalius became concerned about certain ambiguous statements and wondered whether he had "understood Galen from a knowledge of the facts or from the translator's rendering." Obviously the thing to do was to consult the original Greek manuscript, but:

Preparation of the Fabrica *and* Epitome

Certain individuals unconcerned about the benefit of mankind, or even jealous [of the efforts of others], conceal the Greek original so that under no circumstances, or at any time, would they allow me to consult it. Balamio and Cardinal Rodolfo [of Carpi] admitted their possession [of the Greek text] but said it was in such condition that it could not be lent to me. However, I shall strive to get along without this book, as well as certain other works of Galen they have concealed to prevent their use, or more correctly—since they themselves can't use them—to provide food for worms.[80]

Here we have not only evidence of strong irritation but also some indication of the thoroughness with which Vesalius sought to pursue his task.

It appears that all these problems, to which must be added that of the artistic temperament of the draughtsmen already alluded to, at times led Vesalius to thoughts of giving up his project or perhaps settling for something on a lesser scale. There may be some suggestion of this in his remark that two friends in particular encouraged him:

Marcantonio Genua . . . foremost professor of philosophy, unsurpassed among the Paduans for the diversity of his learning, to whom students owe such fruit as may be plucked from these results of my labors, [was] in fact primarily the instigator of this slight initial effort. Then, too, there could be no more interested adviser than Wolfgang Herwart, patrician of Augsburg and a man of rare abilities, whose unparalleled love of letters and of those who cultivate them, deserves immortality. My devotion to him is lifelong because he did everything possible to aid the completion of this work.[81]

There remains one further matter related to the illustrations for the *Fabrica,* that of the preparation of the wood blocks. It appears beyond doubt that the blocks were cut in Venice, but the identity of the cutter is unknown, and we can only observe his skill and note the very few instances of error, such as the omission of some lettering to which Vesalius, as noted above, directed attention. Furthermore, the amazing fact of the preservation of the blocks down into the twentieth century has permitted a study of the technique of the cutter by Dr. Wiegand.

The blocks were of pear wood, sawed with the grain. The resultant surface was one that would ordinarily have been brittle and difficult to cut without damage to the finer lines, but this problem was solved by first rubbing hot linseed oil into the surface of the block to give it greater equality of texture and elasticity. For this reason, and because of the superior workmanship of the Venetian block cutters of that period, an unusual degree of delicacy was gained in the shading lines. In particular the finer shading lines did not end abruptly but rather by a curve cut downward on the face of the block, and it was this technique that gave a softened effect instead of an abrupt termination to the lines in the printed illustration.[82]

The dedication of the *Fabrica* is dated 1 August 1542, presumably but not necessarily indicating the completion of the text by that date, and Vesalius's letter to Oporinus, printer of the *Fabrica,* announcing that the wood blocks were about to be shipped to him from Venice, is

dated 24 August 1542. In that letter there is no mention of the manuscript, and, in view of its presumed earlier completion, it had possibly
already been sent to the printer with an explanation for the delay of
the rest of the material. Whatever the reason, perhaps a defective block,
a last-minute drawing that needed to be cut, or a final set of proofs, it
was not until this later date that the great task was completed by its
author and could be relinquished to the care of the printer in Basel.

When we recall the time, energy, and money Vesalius had invested
in the composition of the *Fabrica,* as well as his sense of the destiny his
book was to have, it is obvious that he would not have been content to
entrust his manuscript to any printer at random. Certainly there were
excellent printers in Venice, and he had already had dealings with the
Giunta firm which could probably have done a competent job. Nevertheless, Vesalius chose a printer in Basel, although this necessitated the trans-
fer of the precious wood blocks to that city and so their exposure to the
dangers of a trans-Alpine journey. As it turned out, the choice of Joannes
Oporinus was an excellent one, partly explicable by some consideration
of the man himself.

Joannes Oporinus, or Herbst,[83] to give the vernacular form of his name,
was born in Basel on 25 January 1507. His father, originally from
Strasburg, had settled in Basel sometime prior to 1492, where he followed the profession of painting. As a result the boy grew up in a milieu
of artists and printers and must have gained an early familiarity with
that combination of art and typography that later would contribute to
the excellence of his books in general and of the *Fabrica* in particular.
Nevertheless, because of early indications of intellectual ability he was
sent to Strasburg where he studied Latin and Greek for four years under Beatus Rhenanus and Hieronymus Gebwyler, whence he returned
to Basel to continue his studies in the university of that city. When his
father could no longer contribute to his education, young Joannes for
a time held a subordinate teaching position elsewhere and, on his return
to Basel, took employment with the celebrated Froben press as a copyist
of manuscripts. By this time he was well on his way to becoming not
only a skillful and artistic printer but a scholar-printer and humanist
as well. It was in conjunction with the humanistic conceit of the time that
he now chose a classical name for himself, based on the fact that his family name was also the German equivalent of autumn. His choice was
determined by Martial's epigram beginning *Si daret autumnus mihi
nomen, Oporinos essem:* "Were Autumn to give me my name, I should
be Oporinus."

In succession Oporinus held several teaching posts, studied Hebrew
under Thomas Plater and law under Boniface Amerbach, and in 1526
married the widow of a friend named Zimmerman, or, classically, Xylo-
tectus. It was a poor choice, since she was an ill-tempered shrew whom
the young classicist frequently compared to Socrates's Xantippe. In the
same year that charlatan of genius, Paracelsus, had accepted the post of
town-physician to Basel, where he also lectured on medicine, and Oporinus

became both his student and secretary, eventually following his stormy master from Basel, which he had made too hot for himself, to Colmar. Life with Paracelsus was both exciting and unpleasant, and Oporinus finally returned to Basel with little knowledge of medicine other than the peculiarities of his somewhat erratic teacher's practice.

In 1533 a kindly death relieved Oporinus of his Xantippe, but his marital experience did not prevent him from marrying a second widow shortly thereafter, pleasant but with three sons, all with little sense of the value of money.[84] In that year he also became professor of Latin in the University of Basel, and in 1537 professor of Greek in the newly founded Pedagogium, or college of liberal arts. Two years later, however, lacking a doctor's degree and unwilling at the time to acquire one, he was compelled to relinquish his position and for the remainder of his life was associated with printing and publishing. As early as 1536, and possibly to supplement his income for the needs of his improvident family, Oporinus had become one of four partners—with Thomas Plater, Balthasar Ruch, known as Lazius, and Robert Winter—in a printing firm.

Johann Herwagen the elder, one of the more distinguished printers of Basel, had persuaded Thomas Plater, then teaching Greek in the Pedagogium, to assume the additional task of corrector to his press with the result explained in Plater's own words:

As I saw that Herwagen and the other printers had a good thing, winning big returns for little work, I thought I might do well to become a printer too. Oporinus, who had also done a good deal of correcting for the presses, was of the same mind. And there was a good typesetter, Balthasar Ruch, a man of high spirits and a good friend of ours, who was all for joining us. We had the will, but we had no money. But there was Oporinus's brother-in-law, Robert Winter, whose wife took a fancy to being a printer's lady when she saw what a fine figure the printers' wives cut, putting her in the shade. She had enough as it was, but she wanted more. So she persuaded her man Robert to become a printer along with his brother-in-law Oporinus. The four of us accordingly became partners: Oporinus, Robert, Balthasar, and I. We bought up the equipment of Andreas Cratander. He and his son Polycarp had become printers, but his wife wanted them to give up the dirty business, as she called it. He sold us the equipment for 800 gulden, to be paid within a certain time.

Some of the early books of the new firm carried the imprint of Plater and Lazius, others of Winter, but none of Oporinus. Although the *Institutiones anatomicae* of Guinter of Andernach in 1536 and the *Paraphrasis* of Vesalius in 1537 were published under the single imprint of Winter, yet Oporinus, who had more knowledge of medicine than the other partners, may well have corrected proof for the two books—despite the sorry results in Guinter's book, which gave Vesalius an excuse for his revised edition of 1538. Vesalius, who very possibly had been in Basel to arrange for the publication of his *Paraphrasis*, must have formed a good impression of at least some of the partners, since his *Venesection letter* was published by the firm in 1539, although once again under the single imprint of Winter.

The partnership was not a financial success nor was there constant amity among the partners. Lazius, as typesetter, resented the proof corrections made by Plater to the extent of a bloody fight between the two men one evening, which marked the end of the common enterprise. Incidentally, Lazius's resentment of criticism may help to explain the erroneous text of Guinter's *Institutiones anatomicae*. At any rate, Oporinus and Winter attempted to carry on the firm for a time but finally separated, and Oporinus became sole proprietor in time to assume full responsibility for the printing of the *Fabrica* and *Epitome*.

With the passing years the house of Oporinus came to surpass all other printing firms in Basel, both in quantity and quality of production, and ultimately gained international renown. The work of Oporinus appealed especially to scholars because of its relative freedom from errors, owing to the fact that the learned proprietor read much of the proof himself, and in addition to any esteem Vesalius may already have had for the publisher, this must have been further inducement to entrust the *Fabrica* to him. Furthermore, Oporinus was not averse to taking risks in what he considered a worthy venture.

From those early days of service to Paracelsus, he had frequently been involved in unorthodox affairs. It was Oporinus, for example, who gave shelter to Sébastien Castellio in 1543 when the heretical religious views of the latter led to his being driven from Geneva by Calvin. Later Oporinus was to publish a number of Castellio's writings, including his bitter denunciation of Calvin's destruction of Servetus. It was also Oporinus who published Theodor Bibliander's Latin translation of the *Koran* which aroused much excitement and even led to a short jail term for the publisher. If Oporinus was attracted to the unusual and unorthodox, certainly the novelty of presentation and content of the *Fabrica*, which represented scientific and pedagogical heterodoxy, must have appealed to him. The results were to prove the wisdom of this particular combination of author and printer, since for both men the completed book was a masterpiece. It is said to have been Vesalius who suggested to Oporinus the printer's mark—Arion on the dolphin—first used by Oporinus for the *Fabrica;* up to that time he had had no mark distinctly his own. With some variation in design and size he used the mark throughout the remainder of his publishing career, which ended with his death in 1568.

Although Oporinus presumably had the main text of the *Fabrica* in advance of the wood blocks, the complex relationship of text to illustrations was such that he could not even begin to design the book before the arrival of the blocks, and it was probably not until the latter half of September that he was in a position to take the first steps. At any rate, it was not until after the middle of September that the precious cargo arrived in Basel, accompanied by the letter written by Vesalius in

Venice on the 24 August. This letter, "To my very dear friend Joannes Oporinus, Professor of Greek at Basel," which Oporinus decided to include in the *Fabrica* [85]—although the content of the letter suggests that this may also have been the wish of Vesalius—gives us certain valuable information.

Vesalius, with the help of the anonymous block cutter and Nicolaus Stopius, manager of the Venetian branch of the merchant house of Bomberg, had carefully packed the blocks. The actual cartage to Basel was undertaken by a firm of Milanese merchants, the Danoni. Unfortunately the letter does not state the route that was followed, and this has led to some dispute. However, it seems most likely that it was over the St. Gotthard Pass, the route most frequently used for transit from upper Italy to Basel.[86]

With the cargo arrived, Oporinus was able not only to take receipt of the contents but to study the accompanying letter, already mentioned. From it he learned, even before unpacking the shipment, that each wood block was accompanied by a proof—the pulling of which may have contributed to the tardy dispatch of the blocks—as well as by the descriptive text for each illustration and full directions for the arrangement of the illustrative material. Furthermore, Vesalius stated that he intended to come to Basel as soon as possible and to stay "if not for the whole period of printing, at least for some time." He would bring with him a privilege granted him by the Venetian Senate against unauthorized reprinting of the *Fabrica*. A second and imperial privilege obtained somewhat earlier would be sent from Brussels by his mother—presumably Vesalius's father was then with Charles V in Spain. Finally, a privilege was promised from the King of France. However, all such privileges were of little value against booksellers and publishers, wrote Vesalius, and then proceeded to take account of the plagiarisms published at the expense of his *Tabulae anatomicae*. Finally, wrote Vesalius, and these words would have been meaningless unless it had been his intention from the start that this letter be published:

I shall gladly send the wood blocks to any careful printer and give whatever literary help I can. Likewise, I shall attempt in every way in my power to hinder any inept person from reproducing the illustrations which were made with so much labor for the general use of the students, so that regardless of whatever inflated title may be prefixed to them they will not come into human hands as if they had been published carelessly by me. This is the particular reason why I prepared the wood blocks at my own expense, and now once again I urge that they be employed by you as correctly and elegantly as possible.

Oporinus must have begun work on the great task by 1 October, and although the colophon to the *Fabrica* bears the date of June 1543, presumably marking the completion of the work, as we shall see later it was not actually completed until the end of July. A master printer has attempted, within the framework of our scanty knowledge of Oporinus's establishment and from the physical appearance of the book, to provide some knowledge of the technical aspects of the production.[87] It has been assumed that a good compositor would require five hours to set an average page of the work and make it ready for the press, so that for about seven hundred pages several compositors would be necessary to complete the task in the allotted time. Moreover, the curious error in pagination in the *Fabrica,* which begins after page 312 and continues for about a hundred and eighty pages, in which the pagination is a hundred less than it should be, suggests two crews of compositors working more or less independently of each other. The type is a "creditable roman letter, by no means as handsome as the earlier Jenson, nor as comely as the later Garamond, and of no especial significance." The italic is that known as "Basel italic," and was "highly esteemed at the time abroad as well as at home, having succeeded in popularity the Aldine italic." The text type is of a size known as *Grobe Texte,* equivalent to our sixteen point, and "there are about 5,000 characters to a page not counting spaces, but throwing in the smaller type in the margins for good measure." The question of the speed with which the compositors could work depended upon the supply of type available, and nothing is known of Oporinus's resources. By the hand method of casting type then employed, a good workman could have cast the type for one page in a couple of days, "and for the successful, uninterrupted operation of one press, allowing two compositors and two men at press, some three hundred pounds of type would have been required as a minimum, and an equal amount for each press employed."

The *Fabrica* was printed as a folio on demy-size paper, and generally three folios were put together to make a gathering of twelve pages. "The paper used is rather thin and soft . . . Oporinus' paper was probably made at Basel, for there had been paper mills there for more than a century." The press work could just possibly have been done on two presses in the time we know to have been devoted to the work.

If we now leave the manuscript and wood blocks in the capable hands of Oporinus and turn our gaze back to Venice, we find that after the dispatch of those materials to Basel, Vesalius vanishes from sight. The only direct source we have to explain his absence from Padua after the summer of 1542 is a statement in Colombo's *De re anatomica,* in which, referring to that period, Colombo recalls that Vesalius "was detained for a long time in Germany [i.e., Switzerland] to look after the publication of his work *De humani corporis fabrica.*" [88] From a university document dated 10 December 1543 it appears that because of his absence his salary had been withheld, and the university authorities requested the *Riformatori* "to grant that Master Andreas Vesalius be restored his salary that was wrongly withheld from him during the last year when permission had been given him to leave without being penalized." [89] Thus we are aware that Vesalius did not fully intend to sever his connections with the university upon leaving Padua. It is true that in the summer of 1543 he sought appointment to the imperial medical staff, but until that had been accomplished it would have been unwise of him to resign from his Paduan chair. This view that his absence in 1542 was only temporary is further supported by a document dated 19 January 1543 which confirmed the appointment of Realdo Colombo as a substitute at a salary of twenty florins.[90] However, it is nowhere clear exactly when Vesalius left Padua, although according to the matriculation register of the University of Basel he arrived in that Swiss city sometime in January 1543.[91]

It has been proposed with considerable plausibility that, during this period from the end of August until the opening of the new year, Vesalius traveled to and spent some time in Ferrara where he would have had the opportunity for a reunion with his brother Franciscus, then studying medicine in the local university, and no doubt he was invited to join the circle of physicians, including Franciscus Vesalius, that met regularly in the house of Giambattista Canano.[92] It appears, therefore, that it must be to this period that Levin Lemnius referred when he wrote that he "heard Master [Andreas] Vesalius, the highly distinguished and very learned man, tell of a certain Moorish swimmer brought to Ferrara who, without taking further breath, could sustain one unbroken note longer than four very strong pugilists." [93] It was also during this trip, as suggested by Roth,[94] that Vesalius, having become acquainted with Giambattista Canano, was privileged to see the first fasciculus of Canano's *Musculorum humani corporis picturata dissectio,* to which he referred years later in his *Examen* when speaking of Canano: "Before the publication of my books *De humani corporis fabrica* . . . I saw the depiction of those muscles [of the hand]." [95] This remark gives further evidence of a visit in the summer or autumn of 1542. It has also been suggested [96] that Vesalius, having with him proofs of some of the illustrations for the *Fabrica,* showed them to Canano and thereby determined the latter not to continue the series of his own publication. It is a plausible if not conclusive theory as to why the five additional projected fasciculi of Canano's work never appeared.[97]

Little is known of Vesalius's life during his sojourn in Basel. Presumably he was occupied with proofreading the text of his book and making minor alterations. However, the typographical correctness of the text was most likely due to Oporinus, who had gained a reputation for such meticulousness. Vesalius's efforts were more likely expended upon the factual content. There are two clear instances of alterations that must have been made in Basel. In the notes to the illustration of the vena cava he wrote: "In the illustration, that obscure little branch that faces '8' [in the diagram] ought to have been carried more downward, but I do not know by whose negligence [it was not], mine or the engraver's." [98] In the book on the nerves, a small illustration was added with the notation: "Through some carelessness I omitted 'l' and 'm' in the first figure," that is, the root of the phrenic nerve, from the illustration, "Thirty pairs of nerves." [99] On the other hand, both Oporinus and Vesalius overlooked the very obvious error by which the illustration of the fourth "muscle-man" is presented as "Prima musculorum tabula," [100] an error corrected by Geminus in the plagiarism he published in London in 1545. Nor did either of them note the two small circular figures, referring to the aorta and pulmonary artery, printed upside down.[101]

During Vesalius's residence in Basel and several months before the publication of the *Fabrica* there occurred a crime of violence of sufficient —although sordidly dramatic—interest to be recorded by several contemporary chroniclers. It was an incident that had a relationship to Vesalius, since ultimately he was to dissect the body of the executed criminal and construct from its bones a skeleton still to be seen almost intact in the museum of the Anatomical Institute of the University of Basel. The crime for which the malefactor was to pay with his life was attempted murder, the result of a triangle composed of a Jacob Karrer from Gebweiler in Alsace, a ne'er-do-well previously exiled from Basel for lesser offenses, his wife, righteously but indiscreetly indignant and reproachful, and a second and bigamous wife acquired by Karrer after his banishment from Basel. The incident was first and most accurately described by Johannes Gast, deacon of St. Martin's in Basel and a friend of Vesalius: [102]

On 12 May [1543] a worthless fellow, who had several times been apprehended in crimes for which he ought to have been executed but had instead been set free through the clemency of the Senate, was seized and proscribed. He had an honest wife who preferred not to follow such a husband lest she be implicated in his evil deeds; she lived virtuously among us, supporting herself by hard work as a laundress. It happened in this year that meat was very expensive, and she went into the next district to buy meat, not for herself but at the request of her neighbors. By chance she met her husband who had another wife with him whom he had openly married. The unfortunate [first] wife was astonished that her husband dared to do this while she was still living, for she had not divorced him since she had hoped for his rehabilitation. Recovering from her astonishment she addressed her husband in these words: "Good husband, is that woman whom you have with you your wife? Tell me, have you married her? Why are you silent, why have you turned pale? Why have you dared to add another to your crimes?" At last he began to deny everything. "This is not my wife," he said; "I wished her to remain home but she followed me." When the other woman whom he had married heard this, she spoke out: "Certainly you are my husband, you married me in the regular way in church two years ago."

However, as is usual in wine taverns, many drew near, desirous of hearing the conversation, and the husband took himself off, resolving upon a great crime. Unknown to anyone, weapons in hand, he went into an empty field where, hidden in the bushes, he awaited his first and legitimate wife who, all unsuspecting, had bought the meat and then set out for home in company with her neighbor. When she stopped to rest for a little while in a convenient place in the field, her husband leapt forth from the bushes, seeking her with drawn sword and lance in hand, and when this savage husband had inflicted many wounds and almost cut off her left arm, he fled, leaving her half dead.

This matter was made known to our Senate by another neighbor, and it then undertook to have the husband apprehended. The Senate gathered in the third hour of the afternoon and ordered the citizens to search for the scoundrel in the adjacent districts and to bring him into the city. Almost thirty stalwart citizens were soon collected, who set forth fully armed, and the wretched man was seized, brought back, and thrown into jail. His wife was cured by the surgeons, but her husband was beheaded, and Master Andreas Vesalius, the very famous physician, dissected him and erected his skeleton. The skeleton is still preserved in the university in his constant memory.

Chapter VIII

THE PUBLISHED *FABRICA*
AND *EPITOME*

RINTING of the *Fabrica* was completed, or completion was hoped for as the colophon indicates, in June 1543, but Vesalius, who was on hand for the publication of the book into which he had put such effort, was not able to obtain a bound copy for presentation to the emperor until the beginning of August—although the sheets may have been available for purchase earlier. The author's satisfaction must have been great as he examined the completed work, the masterpiece of Oporinus, the foundation work of modern anatomy, and an unprecedented blending of scientific exposition, art, and typography.

If we look first, as no doubt Vesalius did, at the title page (see plates), we note that the title is preceded by the author's name, the common practice of that age, especially with Latin titles, and is in much larger, blacker type than the actual title. This may have been the result of the printer's typographical design rather than the author's desire to ensure his fame. However, throughout the *Fabrica* any names of contemporaries were printed in obvious, black letters, and it was Vesalius's usual practice when he developed a dislike for anyone not to indulge in the vituperation common to the age but merely to delete the name from his writings. Hence it appears as if Vesalius felt the inclusion of a name in his great book would give that person a degree of immortality, and that none deserved this prominence more than the author himself, who also indicated that he was a "professor of the Paduan school of physicians," or, as we would put it, of the medical school of the University of Padua.

After the author's name comes the title of the book: *De humani corporis fabrica libri septem* (Seven books on the structure of the human body). There has been some discussion about the meaning of the word *fabrica,* whether "structure," "fabric," or "workings." Since there is no unanimity on the correct translation, the present writer has determined upon "structure" as best representing Vesalius's concern with the underlying bony structure of the body.

As one reads the title of this work it is difficult to keep the eyes from wandering to the dynamic scene that surrounds it and that has also been the subject of considerable discussion.[1]

There has been little disagreement as to the artistic merit of the design or the skill of the block cutter. The perspective, the clarity, the varied emotions skillfully indicated by the posture of the figures, and, finally, the general conception of the composition all contributed to the production of one of the finest and certainly most striking woodcut illustrations of the sixteenth century.

As Vesalius posed his anatomical specimens and hired draughtsmen to draw them, so here he designed the scene and then hired some draughtsman, unknown today except as the probable artist of the skeletons and "muscle-men," to make the final drawing. Except possibly for the decorative framework, the scene is far too closely related to the text to have been the conception of the artist.

Attempts have sometimes been made to demonstrate this scene as symbolic of the victory of Vesalius over Galenism. But it must be remembered that what criticisms Vesalius made of Galen were solely factual and based upon comparison of specific anatomical findings with the Galenic text. Because of his great veneration for the classical physician he would never have resorted to self-congratulatory or vaunting criticism, especially since, although demonstrating a more correct view of anatomy based upon human dissection, he still sought as much as possible to salvage Galen's reputation.

The present scene, therefore, will be regarded as having at most an unwitting symbolism. As Vesalius was always concerned with facts rather than symbols, so here he has presented two factual scenes in one. The first, a public anatomy, is obvious. The second is not so obvious unless one has closely related text and illustration. Vesalius's new and advanced pedagogical methods were one of his most important contributions, and in the title-page scene we have therefore not only a great anatomical representation, but a great pedagogical one as well.

Here we find depicted a public anatomy such as was required by statute of the University of Padua. The stones or pebbles in the foreground, to the left of the scroll enclosing the privilege and the vegetation growing out from the masonry of the arches, suggest an outdoor scene, possibly in the court of the university, its quadrangular form and less-elaborate architecture altered to suit the artistic conception. There are some grounds for believing that the rounded architectural background, the figures looking down from above, and those clinging to the columns, as well as the semicircular arrangement of the spectators, are an adaptation from a woodcut of a theatre scene to be found in editions of Terence (1497) and Platus (1511), both published in Venice.[2]

Within the architectural framework and on either side of the Vesalian arms, the lion of St. Mark—of which a whole sculptured figure was originally to be found over the entrance to the university—is represented on the entablature, as well as the ox's head, symbolic of the student's name for the University of Padua, *il Bò,* recalling that the school had once been situated in a tavern called the Ox or Hospitium Bovis. Thus a relationship to the university is indicated. Below, within the open space, has been placed a three-tiered platform on which the spectators are standing, and before each tier is a railing—in short, this is an anatomical theatre, the first known illustration of one. "With the help of a carpenter," wrote Vesalius, "a fine theatre can be erected, which may on occasion hold more than five hundred spectators." [3] Hence this theatre is relatively small.

As to the particular details within the architectural framework, we may first note the contrast between right and left. At the top are two figures, on the right an older, bearded man and on the left a younger man looking down through openings or windows on the scene below. The presentation is far more imaginative and artistic than the somewhat similar illustration from the Plautus, but attempts to identify these figures are meaningless.

In the panel beside the window at the left are the letters I and O, the former drawn through the latter and so suggesting the Greek letter *phi*. According to Dr. Wiegand the initials were cut at the same time as the rest of the drawing and not inserted later. [4] Hence, as part of the original design cut on the wood block in Venice, they certainly are not the initials of Ioannes Oporinus, as has been suggested, nor does it seem likely that they are the initials of Ioannes Stephanus of Calcar who can in no way be identified with this title page. Although these initials therefore remain a puzzle, it is possible that they represent a pious but classically expressed *Iovis Optimus*. [5]

Returning to consideration of the right and left sides of the scene, at the left is a naked figure grasping the column, possibly representing surface anatomy, and in obvious contrast to both the female body being dissected and its exposed internal anatomy. If its expression indicates the artist's intention, the male figure may be expressing horror or loathing of the fate before it as it observes the dissection in progress. On the right, and balancing this naked figure, is a fully clothed youth. He has arrived late, like so many students, but so intense is his interest that, by standing on the end railing of the second tier of the theater, he risks a fall. [6]

The contrast of left to right continues to the bottom of the scene. On the left below the naked man is a youthful spectator impetuously leaning out over the rail and over the shoulder of the spectator standing before him in the lowest tier who braces himself with his right arm but does not show the indignation he manifests in the similar scene in the second edition of the *Fabrica*. On the right is a cowled, bearded figure standing quietly and displaying intense but restrained interest. It may be that the profile view of this person was arranged to recall Vesalius's words regarding the trapezius muscle, since he declared its shape to resemble the cowl of the Benedictines. [7]

Below, on the left, is a young man more interested in the antics of a monkey than in the dissection. His youthful appearance and wandering interest suggest immaturity and a poor scholastic record. This may

The published Fabrica and Epitome

be one of those students of whom Vesalius wrote: "They complain of the difficulty of the subject and blame me for undertaking too much in a single demonstration." [8] In contrast, an older man on the right is concerned with someone kneeling or sitting at the end of the lowest tier of the theatre, but only to quiet him so the discourse will not be interrupted. Finally, on the left is a young man, seated, in possession of a rhesus monkey (*Macaca mulatta*), a species sometimes but not most frequently employed by Vesalius,[9] and so representing an exceptional instance. On the right a stooping man controls a dog. The monkey, like the dog, was an accessory to human dissection for, says Vesalius, "as I teach the part I attempt to show it distinct in some animal." [10]

Returning to the massed spectators at the top of the theater we first note several furtive figures in the background. One may be a woman, possibly one of the few emancipated ones of that age, but more likely it is either one of the midwives who had been concerned with the fate of the woman whose body is being dissected, or a recollection of those women—the "three savage Venetian prostitutes," whose crime Vesalius recounts in the *Fabrica* [11]—who were interested in the presumed magical properties of parts of the body. On the highest tier of the theatre we note a variety of persons, actions, and costumes. Some of the figures are students, some of the older, bearded figures may be teachers, Paduan officials, or merely interested townsmen, since this is a public anatomy. Prominently to the fore is a member of the clergy "whom," says Vesalius, "we have in great numbers as spectators." [12] To the right of this cleric a student consults a text.[13] Although, as the second edition of the *Fabrica* indicates more clearly, the covers of the book are marked not with C. G., that is, Claudius Galen, but merely with decorative ellipses, most likely it is a Galenic text. "Galen never inspected a human uterus," wrote Vesalius, and calls attention to errors on the subject in three of Galen's treatises, the *Use of parts, On semen,* and *On dissection of the uterus.*[14] Because of the nature of the dissection it seems probable that it is one of these three works the student holds, observing Galenic errors by contrast of text and dissection—or possibly he is as yet an unrepentant Galenist. At the far right another spectator holds a closed book while he points toward the dissection, thus, in contrast to the student with the open book, indicating the greater knowledge to be gained from such research. More centrally placed is a bearded figure in Jewish garb, probably Lazarus de Frigeis whom Vesalius described as a "distinguished Jewish physician and close friend with whom I was accustomed to translate Avicenna." [15]

Moving down a tier we find only one unusual thing. These spectators are giving rapt attention, but the one on the right has the added advantage of an eyeglass, an advantage also enjoyed by another with spectacles in the group immediatly around the cadaver.

We come now to the central part of the scene. At the top are the Vesalian arms, originally presented to Johannes de Wesalia in the fifteenth century by the Emperor Frederick III,[16] and consisting of three weasels which, however, look more like coursing greyhounds, the whole supported by two *putti* standing on the elaborate frame enclosing the title. Below is the articulated skeleton demonstrating the importance of osteology to anatomy, because reference must constantly be made to it during the course of dissection. "Anatomists," said Vesalius, "retard the inexperienced student if they do not first explain the bones," [17] and, "as it becomes necessary you may readily illustrate on the skeleton, which should be handy . . . [and] which is always profitably employed during dissection for various things that are valuable and useful to know about the structure of the human body." [18] The skeleton, behind the dissection table, appears to be seated upon a railing with its legs dangling, contrary to Vesalius's instruction that it be supported by an iron rod.[19] It does, according to his instruction, grasp a pole for a more picturesque appearance,[20] although unfortunately the pole extends upward so far that its proximity to the decorative cartouche enclosing the title makes it appear to be a trident. The skeleton seems rather large, but whether it was that of an unusually large person, or whether the size is the fault of the artist or a means of drawing attention to the importance of osteology, is unknown. Possibly the size has some relation to that of the gigantic female figure accompanying the Vesalian portrait to be considered hereafter.

On the dissection table, which Vesalius described as "carefully planned by me to be as convenient as possible for the task," [21] rests a somewhat large and stout female cadaver, opened to display the abdominal cavity with some of the organs removed. It is the same dissection seen in the twenty-fourth figure of Book V, and is explained as follows:

The peritoneum and the abdominal muscles have been opened and pulled to the sides. . . . Then we have resected all the intestines from the mesentery, but we have left the rectum in the body as well as the whole of the mesentery of which we have to some extent separated the membranes so that its nature is exposed to view. However, the present figure has been drawn for the special purpose of indicating the position of the uterus and bladder exactly as they occurred in this woman; we have not disturbed the uterus in any way, and none of the uterine membranes has been destroyed. Everything is seen intact just as it appears to the dissector immediately upon moving the intestines to one side in a moderately fat woman.[22]

It is the body of a woman, said Vesalius, who, "in fear of being hanged had falsely declared herself pregnant. However, by order of the judge she was interrogated by midwives who declared her not at all pregnant," [23] and presumably after her execution the body was handed over for anatomical purposes on order of the judge of the criminal court, at that time Marcantonio Contarini.[24]

On the table are also a few bits of equipment, a pen and inkwell, sponge, scalpel, razor, and lighted candle. The lighted candle serves no immediate purpose since, according to Vesalius, "you will employ this for the skin, for by burning the skin you will force the epidermis to separate from it like a blister." [25] There is also an oddly shaped object that, in the title page to the second edition, is somewhat unconvincingly transformed into a piece of paper with writing on it. On the shelf under the table are a few bones, but hardly enough to be in keeping with Vesalius's instruction that several boxes of them should be available.[26]

Vesalius is demonstrating and lecturing on the female organs. He is dressed in the same costume he wears in his portrait, except that here it lacks the shoulder buttons. Although it cannot be stated with certainty, it does appear that he has purposely been portrayed as somewhat smaller or shorter than the average-sized spectator. There is, moreover, a resemblance between his appearance on the title page and in his portrait, although the oddly disparate size of head to body, so noticeable in the portrait, is not present in the title page representation, indicating that the artist portrayed him from life—or, if he used the portrait, was aware that the disproportion was incorrect. One oddity is what appears to be a series of rings around the right index finger, and it seems likely that these are tracheal cartilages and that they recall Vesalius's method of teaching the anatomy of the trachea.

Standing about the dissection table with Vesalius are his students who are participating in the dissection. Although for the moment in which this public anatomy is recorded pictorially it is right that Vesalius should be the central figure, otherwise, as he wrote, "I strive that in public dissection the students do as much as possible so that if even the least trained of them must dissect a cadaver before a group of spectators, he will be able to perform it accurately with his own hands; and by comparing their studies one with another they will properly understand this part of medicine." [27]

It is quite possible that, because of the particular dissection problem represented, Vesalius thought of the student group as including the "very dear companion of my studies," Vitus Tritonius, whose notes on Vesalius's first Paduan dissection have already been mentioned.[28] He, with Vesalius, was, as Vesalius wrote, concerned over the unsolved problem of the "evacuation of menstrual blood from veins running to the uterus; but how this occurs and through what veins in particular . . . perhaps you are in doubt like me and . . . Vitus Tritonius." [29]

In addition to the students, two men, one standing on either side of the table, are given special prominence. The figure to the left is unusually large, and it is proposed that this is the Augsburg patrician Wolfgang Herwart, while the one on the right, who appears to be admonishing the dog for barking and so disturbing the demonstration, is the Paduan philosopher Marcantonio Genua. It seems only proper that these two men, who had so much to do with the composition of the *Fabrica*, according to Vesalius,[30] should be given this recognition.

Finally, at the foot of the table are two assistants, once the actual dissectors and still employed, but now reduced to lesser importance: Their function was to sharpen razors for the anatomist's use.

The three leaves following the title page contain the preface dedicated to the emperor.[31] According to the theme of the preface, medicine

✤ PRAESTANTISSIMO CLARISSIMOQVE VIRO DOMINO
D. NARCISSO PARTHENOPEO, CAESARIAE MAIESTATIS MEDICO PRIMARIO.
Domino suo & patrono, Andreas VVesalius Bruxellensis S.D.

ONſta pridem, Narciſſe doctiſſime, quum Patauii ad medicinæ chirurgicæ lectionem delectus, inflammationis curationem pertractarem, diui Hippocratis & Galeni de reuulſione ac deriuatione ſententiam explicaturus, uenas obiter in charta delineaui, ita ratus quid per ᵗᵘ Hippocrates intellexiſſent facile poſſe de, monſtrari. Noſti namque quantum hac tempeſtate, ea dictio diſſentionum atque contentionum, etiam inter eruditos, de uena ſecanda concitauerit, dum alii fibra, rum conſenſum ac rectitudinem, alii aliud neſcio quid, indicatæ Hippocratem affirmant. Verum illa uenarum delineatio tantoperè medicinę proſeſſoribus ſtudio, ſisque omnibus arriſit, ut arteriarum quoque & neruorum deſcriptionem, à me obnixè contenderent. Quis uerò ad meam pertinebat profeſſionem Anatomes ad, miniſtratio, ipſis deſtt è non debui, potiſſimum quum ſcirem eiuſmodi lineamenta, his qui ſecanti adſuiſſent, non mediocre commodum allatura. Aliàs ſiquidem ſuæ partium corporis, aut ſimplicium pharmacorum cognitionem ex ſolis picturis, ſeu formulis uelle aſſequi, ut arduum, ſic quoque uanum ac impoſſibile omnino ar, bitror, ſed ad memoriam rerum confirmandam apprimè conducere, nemo negauerit. Cæterum cum plurimi hęc fruſtra imitari conarentur, rem prælo cõmiſi, atque illis tabellis, alias adiunximus, quibus mecum ᵗᵘⁿ nuper in ſtudioſorum gratiam conſtructum, Ioannes Stephanus, inſignis noſtri ſeculi pictor, tribus partibus appoſitiſſimè expreſſit, magno ſanè uſu eorum, qui non modo honeſtum, ſed pulchrum, ſed etiam utile ac neceſſarium iudicant ſummi opificis ſolertiam artificiumque contemplari, & domicilium illud animę (ut Plato ait) inſpicere. Præterea ſingulis partibus, quàquam id in præſenti negocio non admodum ex ſententia confici potuit, ſua nomina aſſcripſimus, barbaris, quæ etiam peritiores in pluri, morum libris ſubinde remorari ſolent, minimè prætermiſſis. Quòd autem ad rei ueritatem attinet, nullum hic uenarum ductum puta, quem Patauini ſtudioſi in huius anni confectione, à me demonſtratum non atteſtabuntur : ut interim ſileam de Pariſiis præceptoribus meis longe doctiſſimis & Louanienſibus medicis, apud quos non ſemel Anatomen publicè adminiſtraui. Porrò ut nouus hic noſter conatus, alicuius patrocinio commendatior in lucem auſpicato prodeat, & ancipitem iudiciorum aleam ſecurius experiatur, celebritati illum nominis tui nuncupa, re uiſum eſt partim quòd præter incomparabilem uariarum linguarum cognitionem, eximiam quandam ſingularémque Anatomes, ſicut etiam medicinę & philoſophię, ſcientiam adeptus ſis : adeò ut meritò apud nationes omnes, tanquam præcipuum peritiſſimorum medicorum & literatorum hominum, decus ac ornamentum ab eruditiſſimis quibuſque prædiceris : deinde quòd inter clariſſimos uiros ut polleas animi prudentia, integritate, mira erga omnes naturę manſuetudine & gratia, ut CAROLVS QVINTVS Inuictiſſimus Romanorum Imperator ſemper Auguſtus, acerrimus ingeniorum æſtimator, non ſuæ dumtaxat ſanitatis tuendę, aut amiſſę recuperandæ præcipuum ubi locum concrediderit, uerum etiam te uniuerſis Regni Hiſpaniæ ac Neopolitani medicis pharmacopolarúmque officinis, in florente etiàm ætate tua, certa fidiſſimum cenſorem præfecerit, complaribúſque honoribus & muneribus, inter tot præclaros alioquin uiros, ampliſſimè illuſtrauerit. Suſcipe itaque Vir ornatiſſime, hoc chartaceum munuſculum, ea humanitate, qua me quondam exceptiſti, dum non exiguis beneuolen tię ſignis, animum erga me tuum peculiariter declaraſti, aliquod ſi gratum tibi ac ſtudioſis fore intellexero, aliquando maiora adiiciam. Vale Patauii Calẽ. Apri. An. ſalutis. M.D.XXXVIII.

✤ IECVR SANGVIFICATIONIS
OFFICINA, PER VENAM PORTAM, QVAE GRAECIS
πλεχ ϊⁿⁱˢ, Arabibus verò ᵘ ͣⁿᵛᵗ vaidhescoer appellatur, ex ventriculo & inteſtinis chylum trans
ſumit, ac in lienem melancholicum ſuccum expurgat.

GENERATIONIS ORGA,
NA, SVPERIVS VIRI, INFERIVS MVLIERIS.
Tertia figura ſemen deferentium vaſorum implantationem refert.

A Cauum, ſeu ſimum iecoris.
B Vena portæ, iecoris manus.
C Ramuli in ſinum bilis veſiculæ.
D Ad pancreas & cephyſim, ſeu duodenum inteſtinum.
E Ad dextrum gibbi ventriculi.
F Ad dextrum fundi ventriculi & ſuperiorem omenti membra nam.
G Portę bifurcatio maxima.
H Per omenti inferiorem mem, branam & puerres delata, va, riè diſfunditur.
I In omenti membranam inferiorem, parte dextra.
K Per ventriculi cauum, eius ac teniẽm nu, meroſis propaginibus amplectens.
L In membranam omenti inferiorem parte media, quę primum in duas, deinde in plu, rimas exiguas venulas diuaricatur.
M Multiplicem duplẽx, per rectum lineam lienis porro implantatur : hæc ſiculentus ſanguis in lienem transmittitur.
N Vtraque ad ventriculi gibbi ſiniſtram, & ſecunda ſatis obſcurè ad ventriculi os procedit.
O In ſiniſtrum fundi ventriculi, & ſuperi, orem omenti membranam : hæc non madi, ocrem excrementi lienis portionem in vẽ, triculum excerni putauerim.
P Numeroſę inter meſaręi membranas dì, ſtributæ hac excurrit : ob hac ne, at 'a caua, hæmorrhoides ſunt? non enſim certo affirmaro. Nam ex vtraſ, vena ra, mi in eam partẽ ptinent, & etiã maiores à portæ : per portam melancholicum ſen guinem expurgari, forti alunum animal uertenti, apparebit. ✤

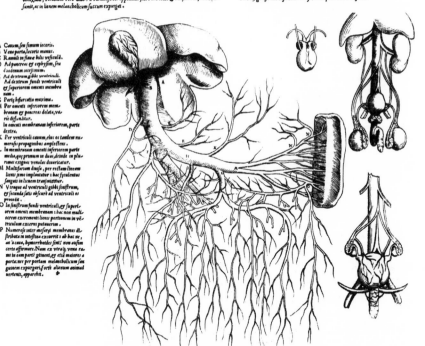

GALENVS VENAE PORTAE RAMOS PRAECIPVOS SEPTEM ENVMERAT.

First *tabula* of the *Tabulae anatomicae* (1538) displaying both the traditional representation of the five-lobed liver and the first depiction of the prostate gland.

PLATE 17

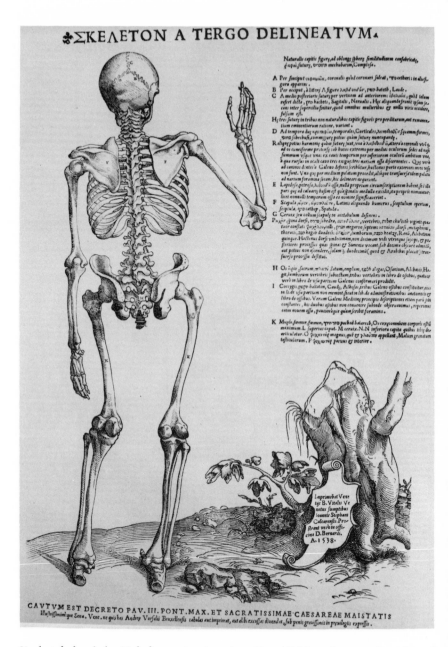

Sixth *tabula* of the *Tabulae anatomicae* (1538) exhibiting the posterior view of the skeleton by Calcar and the colophon.

PLATE 18

TABVLAE TRES DE ANATOMIA VENARVM ET ARTERIARVM QVA:
RVM DVAE VENAS IECORIS CONTINENT. IN PRIMA EST, IN IECVR EX MESARAICIS POR:
recta porta vena dicta.In altera, vena concaua nuiuⱥ appellata cum ſuis ramis ex hepatis gibbo prodiens. Tertia, proceſſus arteriæ sorti ex corde natæ complectitur.

PRAESTANTISSIMO CLARISSIMOQVE VIRO DOMINO D. NARCISSO PARTHENOPEO, CAESAREAE MAIESTATIS
Medico primario,Domino ſuo & patrono,Andreas Weſalius Bruxellenſis S. D.

ON ita pridem,Narciſſe doctiſſime,qualm Patauij ad medicinæ chirurgicæ lectionem delectus inflammationis curationem pertractarem,diui Hippocratis & Galeni de reuulſione ac deriuatione ſenten tiam explicaturus,venas obiter in charta delineaui,ita rarus quid per xar' ην Hippocrates intellexiſſet,facilè poſſe demonſtrari.Noſti namque quantum hac tempeſtate,ex dicto diſſentioum atq; conten tionum etiam inter eruditos,de vena ſecunda concitauerit,dum alij ſibraru contenſum ac rectitudineᵈ , alij aliud neſcio-quid,indicaſſe Hippocratem affirmant. Verùm illa uenarum delineatio tantoperè medicinæ profeſſoribus ſtudioſiſque omnibus arriſit, vt arteriarum quoqꝫ & neruorum deſcriptionem , à me obniſè contenderent.Quia verò ad meam pertinebat profeſſionem Anatomes adminiſtrare, ipſis deeſſe non debui,potiſſimum quàm ſcirem exiſimodi lineamenta,his qui ſecarei diſtuiſſent,nõ mediocre commodum allatura.Aliis ſiquidem aut partium corporis,aut ſimplicium pharmacorum co gnitionem ex ſolis picturis,ſeu formalis velle aſſequi,vt ardum,ſic quoque vanum ac impoſſibile omnino arbitrorſed ad memoriã rerum confirmandã apprimè conducere, nemo negauerit.Cæterùm cũ plurimi hæc fruſtra imitari conarentur,tè præi-cõmiſ,atq; illis tabellis,alias adiunximus,quibus meti ex Oxvᴠᴠ nuper in ſtudioſorum gratiam conſtrudi,Ioannes Stephanus,inſignis noſtri ſeculi pictor, trebus partibus appoſitiſſimi expreſſa, magnoſanè vſa eorum,qui nos modo honeſtum,aut pulchrá, ſed etiam vule ac neceſſarium iudicant ſummi opificis ſolertiã artificiiſmque contemplari, & dumici laũ illud anima(vt Plato ait)introſpicere.Præterea ſingulis partibus,quanqua id in præſinti negocio non admodum ex ſententia confici potuit,ſua nomina aſſcripſimus,barbaris,quæ etiam perltiores in plurimorũ libris ſubin dè remorari ſolent,minimè retermiſſis.Quⱥ ſid alii ad rei veritateᵐ attinet, nulli hic apicem ductũ pura, quæ Patauini ſtudioſi in huius anni confectione,à me demonſtratum non atteſtabuntur: vt interim ſileã de Parſiis varè exproribus meis longè doctiſſimis & Louanienſibus medicis,apud quos non ſemel Anatomen publicè adminiſtraui.Poterã vt nouus hic noſter conatus alicuius patrocinio obmendatior in haceʃ auſpicatò prodiret, & am iudiciorũ aleã ſecurius experiantur,celebritati illi nominis mi nuncupare viſum eſt:partim quod præter iacõparabilē em variarū linguarum cognitioni,extmiam quandã ſingularemque Anatomes , ſicuti etiã medicinæ & c ſophiæ,ſcientiã adeptus ſis,adeò vt meritò apud nationes oẽs,tanquã præcipuum peritiſſimorũ medicorum & literatorũ hominum decus ac ornamentũ ab eruditiſſimis quibuſq, prædicteris:deindè quòd inter clariſſimos viros ea polleas animi prudentia,integritate,mira erga oẽs naturæ mandſuetudine & gratia,vt Carolus quintus Inuictiſſimus Romanorũ Imperator ſemper Auguſtus,acerrimus ingeniorũ ⱥſtimator,non fi diũturat ſanitatis memor, aut arctiſſ recuperandæ præcipuã tibi loci concrediderit,verũ etiam te vnkierſa Regni Hiſpaniæ ac Neopolitani medicis,pharmacopolariũ, officinis,in ſorente erãnum quæe tua,cru ſidiſſimi cenſorẽ præfecerit, cõpuriⱥaⱥ, honorubus & munerbus,inter xox præclaros alioⱥui viros,amplſiſimi illuſtrauerit.Suſcipe itaq; vir ornatiſſime,hoc chaticeli munuſculum,ea humanitate,qua me quondã excepiſti , di non exiguis benevolentiã ſigniſ , amauit erga me tuum peculiarter-declarauiquod ſi gratum tibi ac ſtudioſis fore intellexero,aliquando maiora adduciam.Vale Patauij Calend.April.Anno ſalutis.M.D.XXXVIII.

IECVR SANGVIFICATIONIS OFFICINA,
PER VENAM PORTAM,Q VAE GRAECIS πλκγκτις,
Arabibus verò ﺍﻟﺒﺎﺏ Huariſdhaſcoer appellatur,ex ventriculo & inteſtinis chy lilitraníumit,ac in lienem melancholicum ſuccum expurgat.

GENERATIONIS ORGANA,SVPERIVS
VIRI, INFERIVS MVLIERIS. TERTIA FIGVRA
ſemen deferentium vaſorum implantationem refert.

A Concau,ſeu ſimum iecoris.
B Vena porta,ſeorſis manas.
C Ramuli in fluxæ bilis ueſaiⱥ.
D Ad pácreæ et oeſophⱥm, ſeu duodenum incriſinum.
E Ad dextrum gibbi ventriculi.
F Ad ſinumfundi ventriculi et ſuperiorem omenti mem branæm.
G Porta biſurcatio diuiſæ.
H Per omenti inferiorem nᴂbra nem et pancreas delata,nᴂ vìì diffunditur.
I In omenti membranæm inferio orem,parte dextra.
K Per ventriculi auum, eiuſ et tandem numeroſis propagines hoc emplectitus.
L In membranæm omenti inferio rem parte media, quæ primum in ſinæ, deinde in plurimas exiguas wᴂ uulas diuaritur.
M multiplrium diuiſ,per rectum lineᴂ ve niſ ſinæ implantatur:hac ſoculentus ſen guii in lienem tranſmittitur.
N Vtroqꝫ ad ventriculi gibbi ſiniſtrũ, et ſecundⱥ ſatis obſcurè ad uentriculi os prodiit.
O In ſiniſtrumfundi ventriculi,et ſuperio rem omenti membranæm: hæc uᴂ medio crem excremanã lienis portionem in ub triculum extrui panxeriū.
P Numeroſè inter meſⱥ et membranæ diſ ſtribuũ in inteſtina excurrit: ab hac nᴂ, in à duas,hæmorrhoides ſinⱥ, non auſin ario affirmare. Nam ex utroq; uena ra mi in eam partem pertinent, er etiã ma liorei à portⱥnæc per portam melancho lium ſanguinem expurgari,ſorti alienum animaduertentiꝫ,apparebit.

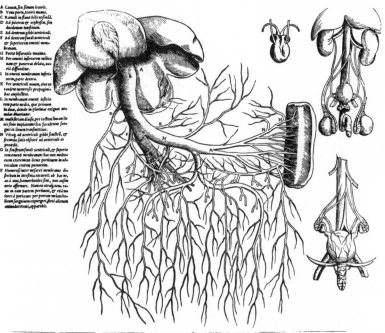

GALENVS VENAE PORTAE RAMOS PRAECIPVOS SEPTEM ENVMERAT.

PARISIIS APVD CHRISTIANVM ₩ECHELVM SVB SCVTO BASILIENSI IN VICO IACOBAEO.

First *tabula* of the Paris plagiarism of Vesalius's *Tabulae anatomicae*.
Courtesy of Dr. Sten Lindberg, Royal Library, Stockholm.

PLATE 19

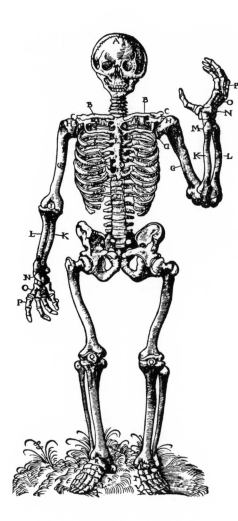

Skeletal figure, presumably derived from the *Osteotome* (1536) and added to the Paris plagiarism in 1539. Courtesy of Dr. Sten Lindberg, Royal Library, Stockholm.

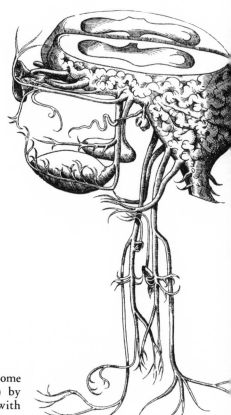

Vesalius's nerve drawing, stolen by some unknown person and published (1539) by Macrolius. This should be compared with plates 16 and 35.

PLATE 20

Title page of Vesalius's revised edition of Guinter of Andernach's *Institutiones anatomicae* (1538). Historical Library, Yale Medical Library.

INSTITVTIONVM
ANATOMICARVM SE.
CVNDVM GALENI SEN/
tentiam ad candidatos Medicinæ
Libri Quatuor,per Ioannem
Guinterium Anderna/
cum Medicum.
AB ANDREA VVESALIO BRV/
xellensi,auctiores & emendatiores redditi.

Venetijs in Officina D. Bernardini
M D XXXVIII.

ANDREAE
VVESALII BRVXELLENSIS,
SCHOLAE MEDICORVM PATAVINAE
professoris publici, Epistola, docens uenam
axillarem dextri cubiti in dolore laterali secandam: & melancholicum succum ex uenæ
portæ ramis ad sedem pertinentibus,purgari.

BASILEAE.

Title page of the *Venesection letter* (1539).

PLATE 21

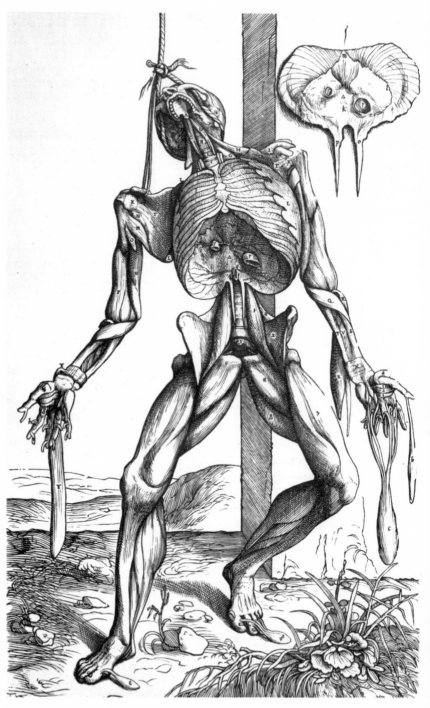

The seventh "muscle-man" from the *Fabrica*. Vesalius used this method of supporting the cadaver during the preparation of the dissection and illustrations of the "muscle-men."

PLATE 22

X.V

JOHANNES CAIUS. *Med.*   *Gonnevill* & *Cay* Coll:
Fund. *Alter*   *A.* MDLVII.
Hanc effigiem a Tabula,   *in istius Coll. factam*
J. Faber A. 1714

John Caius.

PLATE 23

Si famam æternam Typicæ do fedulus arti:
Aeternum cur non reddat & ipfa decus?

M.   D.   LXIIX.   T   iij

Joannes Oporinus.

Remains of the skeleton articulated by Vesalius
in Basel in 1543. Courtesy of Professor Gerhard
Wolf-Heidegger, Anatomical Institute, University of Basel.

PLATE 24

ANDREAE VESALII
BRVXELLENSIS, SCHOLAE
medicorum Patauinæ professoris, de
Humani corporis fabrica
Libri septem.

CVM CAESAREAE
Maiest. Galliarum Regis, ac Senatus Veneti gratia & priuilegio, ut in diplomatis eorundem continetur.

Title page of the *Fabrica* (1543).

PLATE 25

COLISEVS SI   VE THEATRVM

Title page of the writings
of Plautus, Venice, 1511.

Donatello's "Heart of the miser," San Antonio, Padua.

PLATE 26

CORPORIS   HVMANI OSSA
POSTERIORI   FACIE PROPOSITA.

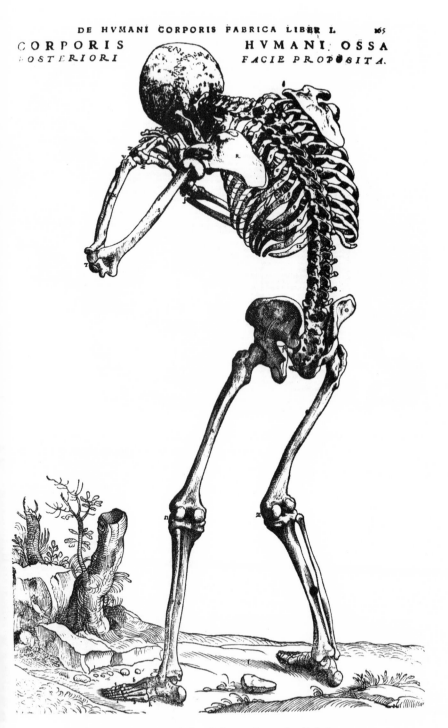

Posterior view of the skeleton from the *Fabrica*.

PLATE 27

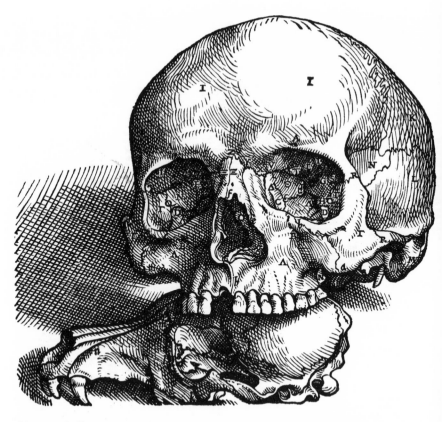

Human skull resting on that of the dog to display aspects of human osteology in contrast to those of the animal, as well as errors of Galen's pseudohuman anatomy.

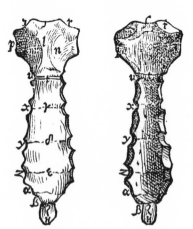

Anterior and posterior views of the pectoral bone or sternum.

PLATE 28

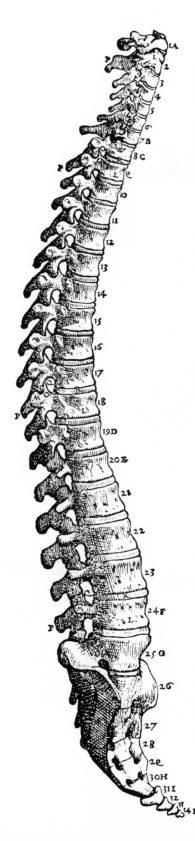

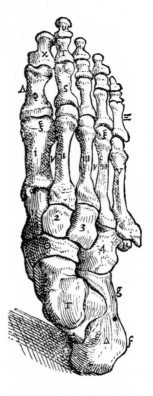

Bones of the foot with the Os Vesalianum represented at *u*.

The vertebral column, of which the curvature is incorrectly presented, probably due to Vesalius's method of mounting the vertebrae on an iron rod, and a sacrum of six pieces.

PLATE 29

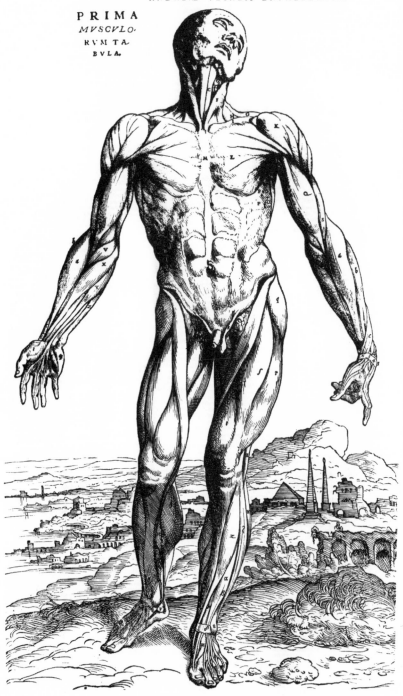

PRIMA
MVSCVLO·
RVM TA·
BVLA.

The first "muscle-man."

PLATE 30

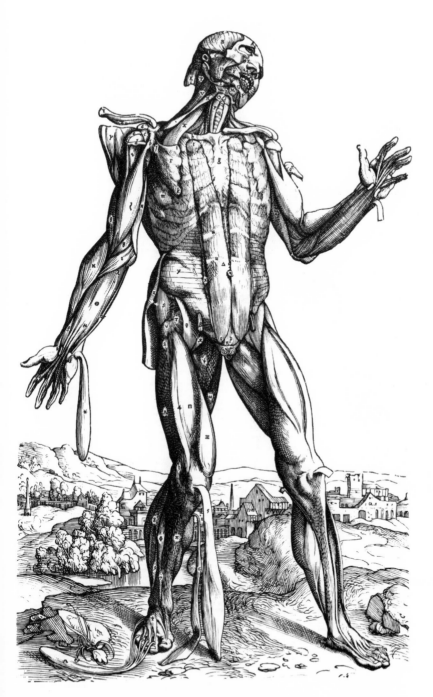

The fifth "muscle-man" displaying the extension of the rectus abdominis
muscle, for which Vesalius has been unjustly criticized. At X a nonhuman
muscle is included to demonstrate an error of Galen's animal anatomy. From
the *Fabrica* (1555), to reveal, by contrast with the preceding illustration,
how the lettering on the figures was made more legible in the revised edition.

PLATE 31

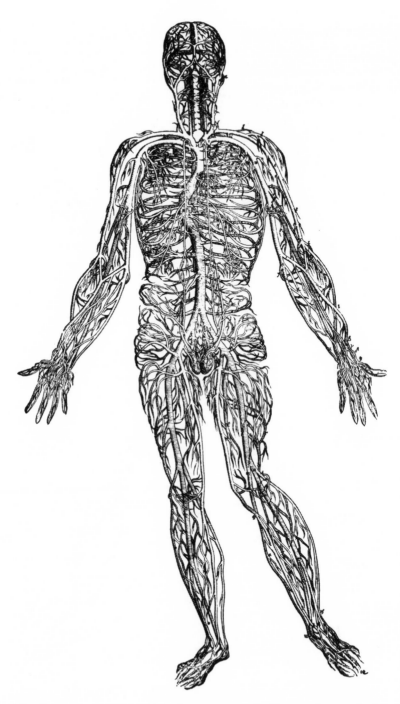

The "venous man" in which the vena cava is illustrated as a single, continuous structure.

PLATE 32

is properly composed of three parts: drugs, diet, and what Vesalius terms the use of the hands, by which he refers to surgical practice and its necessary preliminary, a knowledge of human anatomy which can only be acquired by dissecting human bodies with one's own hands. Although the importance of the study of human anatomy looms larger as the preface proceeds, at first Vesalius's complaint concerns the failure of physicians to employ what he terms the "triple method of treatment," a calamity that set in "after the Gothic invasions and the reign of Mansor, King of Persia."

Physicians, he said, had become diagnosticians without the requisite training, and were therefore dubious prescribers of drugs, of which the actual administration had fallen under the control of apothecaries; and the surgical art had been relegated to rude and untrained barbers. It was no wonder that "so many jibes are frequently cast at physicians and this holy art is mocked." Indeed, the situation had become so bad that, were a physician to attempt to perform surgery, he would have been slandered by the "rabbins of medicine"—a term Vesalius apparently adopted from Guinter of Andernach—to the detriment of his practice and prestige. The worst loss of all, since it was basic to everything else, was the knowledge of human anatomy, and little improvement could be expected if no consideration was given to a more satisfactory method of teaching it. Vesalius knew whereof he spoke since he had had the experience of poor teaching of this sort in Paris. However, he gives no names of lecturers against whom he was inveighing; and although he certainly was not critical of Sylvius at this time, quite possibly he had Guinter of Andernach in mind as well as various other members of the faculty, since there was then no special professor of anatomy in the Paris faculty. Under such conditions as Vesalius described, his anatomical training would have been meaningless if he had not taken some initiative.

It is true that from our twentieth-century point of view there is a lack of reticence about his statements of his own achievements, but even so these remarks have sometimes been subject to unfair criticism. His boast, as it is called, represents no greater assertion of his own achievements than is found in the books of his contemporaries, many of whom accomplished far less. It is important that we do not judge Vesalius by the standards of our day, as many have done, but by those of his own, a time in which individual fame and glory were quite obviously sought after. Moreover, his criticism was hardly that of an ungrateful student, since he condemned a method rather than any individual—the only Parisian teacher he mentioned by name was Sylvius, and the remarks about him were commendatory. Finally, his criticism was valid, and we have the evidence of his contemporary, Andreas de Laguna, who made equally strong but less publicized assertions about the poor quality of official Parisian anatomical instruction in those very years.

However, having presented his doleful picture of the state of anatomical pedagogy, Vesalius was able to express some hope, presumably based

The published Fabrica and Epitome

upon observations during his Italian years. The teaching was changing in a few schools, not the least of them being of course Padua, where, he said:

> I have already conducted anatomy very often . . . and in Bologna, and discarding the ridiculous fashion of the schools, I demonstrated and taught in such a way that there was nothing in my procedure that varied from the tradition of the ancients, and the construction of no part met with remained unstudied.

By ancients Vesalius meant the pre-Galenic writers on medicine, "Eudemus, Herophilus, Marinus, Andreas, Lycus, and other distinguished anatomists," known only through excerpts in the later works of Galen. Despite the greatness of this last-named writer, "he never dissected a human body; but deceived by his monkeys—although he did have access to two dried human cadavers—he frequently and improperly opposed the ancient physicians trained in human dissection." Those pre-Galenic anatomists had dissected human bodies and passed on their knowledge by training boys in dissection at home. However, even the writings of the ancient anatomists had perished and the only remaining hope was that the medical faculties of the universities might take charge of anatomical training. There was some prospect that this would transpire, "and there is hope that [anatomy] will soon be cultivated in all our schools as it once was conducted in Alexandria in the age of Herophilus, Andreas, Marinus, and other distinguished anatomists." It was in this cause that the *Fabrica* was written, and it was to be a record of demonstrations for those who attended Vesalius's dissections and would offer a detailed and illustrated description for those denied the opportunity for dissection and observation.

Despite his good intentions, Vesalius was aware that his books would be subject to criticism on several grounds. The illustrations, despite their value as aids to understanding, would be criticized as an effort to replace actual dissection, although no one had sought more than he to encourage dissection. Furthermore, his frequent indication of Galen's errors would not endear him to the Galenists—especially since he was only twenty-eight years old. Hence he would need the support of some mighty person to ensure the success of his book, and none, of course, could be more helpful than the emperor himself. No doubt, too, the work would be pleasing to the emperor, just as the anatomy of Alessandro Benedetti, dedicated to the emperor's grandfather Maximilian, had so pleased that earlier monarch.

Even so, it was not Vesalius's purpose to write a flattering preface such as had become customary in which greatness impossible of fulfillment was attributed to the patron, but, despite his determination to avoid any such ridiculous dedicatory formula, he was compelled to admit, although briefly, the near divinity of the emperor and his superiority to all other mortals. Relative to the usual adulatory character of sixteenth-century dedicatory prefaces, Vesalius's remarks are somewhat restrained, and his account of the decline of medicine in general and of anatomy in particular contains much more solid substance than was usually found in such prefaces.

As the preface contains some interesting biographical information, so too does Vesalius's letter to Oporinus, previously referred to, which follows on the next leaf.[32] It is especially interesting for the account it gives of the plagiarists of the *Tabulae anatomicae,* and for its indications of Vesalius's ideas on anatomical exposition and pedagogy, as well as of his diligence in directions to the printer to ensure the quality of what he realized was to be a work of the greatest importance.

Finally we come to the portrait of Vesalius, which faces the first page of the text of the *Fabrica.* It is the only known authentic portrait of the author, and that it pleased him and therefore is very likely a good representation is indicated by the fact that it was employed not only in the *Fabrica* but also in the Latin and German editions of the *Epitome,* published in the same year, in the *Letter on the china root* of 1546, and in the second edition of the *Fabrica* in 1555.[33] However, as with so many things related to Vesalius, this portrait provides some problems for the investigator. First is the relationship of the head to the body, the former appearing disproportionately large. Second is the obviously good draughtsmanship of the head and the inferior quality of that of the body. These two problems appear related, and, in the absence of any better thesis, that presented by Charles Singer [34] is the most plausible. The head is "obviously a 'speaking' likeness of a real man." Energy, quick wit, and ready humor are apparent. "It is the facies of a man of action, and it is easy to feel that this is one who could construct the great book." Apart from the head, however, there are many faults of draughtsmanship in the body: perspective, the relative proportion of hand, forearm, upper arm, body, and, of course, the strange proportion of body to head. "The right hand is without a wrist." The body being dissected is almost impossibly large compared to Vesalius, and its hand is several times the size of his. On the basis of this contrast of the head to the other aspects of the scene, Singer proposed that some capable artist was responsible for the head either as a painting or a drawing; pleased with the result, Vesalius placed it in the hands of a block cutter with directions as to the setting for the remainder of the scene. This craftsman reproduced the portrait itself competently, but competence in one skill did not ensure success in another. The block cutter was not a trained artist, as his clumsy effort indicates. The worst blunder was the size he gave the cadaver, possibly copied from a sketch by Vesalius, a necessity insofar as anatomical detail was concerned. Nevertheless, Vesalius must have been pleased with the result since he used the illustration so frequently, but he certainly cannot have been pleased with the general draughtsmanship; hence it must have been the likeness of the head that gave him pleasure.

Although Singer's thesis regarding the disparate qualities of draughtsmanship may possibly be the answer to that particular puzzle, other problems remain, but first a few more words about the proportion of Vesalius's head to his body. If we turn back to the scene on the title page, it is barely possible to decide that Vesalius is depicted with a large head but not extraordinarily so, certainly nothing like the disproportion in the portrait. If then we turn to the newly drawn and engraved title page of the *Fabrica* of 1555 we find Vesalius with an enormous head relative to his body. This has been taken by some as proof of the extraordinary proportions of the portrait. The fact is, however, that the artist of the later title page never saw Vesalius and took his dimensions from the portrait. He was, in short, deceived like many of later times and did not consider that greater reliance ought to be placed on the superior quality of draughtsmanship of the title page.[35]

Vesalius's elaborate costume in the portrait, certainly not suited to the dissection room, need not bother us. It is the same costume he wears in the dissection scene on the title page and represents that element of fantasy he so frequently exhibits and that is further manifested by the background of column and drapery. More puzzling is the size of the female body which, incidentally, is the same body used for the dissection scene on the title page. In the 1555 edition of the *Fabrica* we are told that the body was that of an unusually large woman,[36] but certainly Vesalius does not describe the body as that of a giant. One student has suggested that the body was intentionally magnified to express "the grandeur of anatomy." [37] It may be further added that had the body not been drawn in such large proportion the all-important dissection of the arm would not have appeared so clearly. However, in view of the paucity of information, a wholly satisfactory explanation seems impossible.

If we now turn our attention to the table, or perhaps it is the surface of a column, we note two statements on its edge. The upper indicates Vesalius's age as twenty-eight and the year as 1542.[38] He was obviously proud—as well he might be—of what he had accomplished in his youth, a fact to which he had already called attention in the preface. Below these indications of chronology is the phrase OCYUS IUCUNDE ET TUTO, most likely a paraphrase from Celsus who quotes Asclepiades to the effect that treatment ought to be *tuto, celeriter, jucunde*,[39] "safe, swiftly and pleasantly performed." On the surface of the table or column are a razor, scalpel, and a very poorly drawn inkpot and pen. Leaning against the inkpot is a scroll with writing on it which relates to the dissection of the arm then in progress. The text may be translated as follows: "Of the muscles moving the fingers. Chapter 30. Since in the former book I investigated the construction of the five bones of the fingers . . . other than . . ." [40] Here another puzzle arises from the fact that this text is a faulty transcription, or certainly a variant, of part of the first sentence of Chapter XLIII, Book II, of the *Fabrica*,[41] but it is certainly not to be found in Chapter XXX. Why, then, both a variant text and an incorrect citation of the chapter? Moreover, as perhaps a minor point, the chapters of the *Fabrica* are numbered in Roman numerals rather than Arabic. The suggestion has been made tentatively that this particular puzzle may be explained as the fault of an illiterate block cutter,[42] but although a single slip might be explained in this way, or even two, three points of difference seem too much. No definite answer to the problem appears forthcoming, but a further hypothesis may be advanced. Since the text on the scroll bears no relation to a "Chapter 30" of the *Fabrica* or to Galen's *Anatomical procedures* or the *Dissection of muscles*, it is possible that it refers to a chapter 30 of Vesalius's volume of "Annotations on Galen" which he possessed in 1542 and intended to publish but which, he declared, he destroyed in a moment of vexation induced by his unfavorable reception at the emperor's court.

The dissection of the gigantic figure's forearm is complementary to the text of the scroll, whether for the purpose of demonstrating Galenic error or otherwise. Spielmann speaks of the portrayal of "one of Galen's anatomical errors," [43] but Cushing calls attention to the fact that, if the purpose were to flaunt some error of Galen, "what particular error it might have been remains obscure." [44] In this instance, if criticism was aimed at anyone it seems more likely to have been Aristotle than Galen, and possibly over the question of whether there were four or five metacarpal bones. Aristotle recognized five, but Vesalius accepted Galen's enumeration of four, and so for the moment was a supporter rather than a critic of Galen.[45]

It is too frequently overlooked that Vesalius criticized Galen only when he felt that the facts warranted such action. He never went out of his way to do so, and certainly he would not unnecessarily have made a public example of the "prince of physicians." It is quite possible that, in composing the scene to accompany his portrait, Vesalius was reminded of his experiences in Paris when "I attempted to display the muscles of the arm," a reference to the true beginning of his anatomical studies which led up to the publication of the great work. The reference is therefore quite possibly autobiographical in intent and recalls the modest beginning of the career that was to reach its spectacular climax with the publication of the *Fabrica*.

One final matter to consider before going on to the anatomical content of the work is that of the initial letters. Since these have already received much attention elsewhere,[46] there is no need to give more than brief notice to them here. Historiated initial letters had long been used in both manuscripts and printed books and were certainly no novelty, although the relation of the scenes within the initials to the content of the *Fabrica* is more realistically presented than was usual, and there is, furthermore, an uncommon, fantastic, and bizarre quality in the depiction of *putti* and dwarfed men performing the more grisly actions associated with anatomy of that day. The scenes provided an opportunity to illustrate certain minor matters mentioned by Vesalius, and might almost be considered pictorial footnotes.

If attention is now directed to the general content of the *Fabrica*, it is immediately apparent that it is not arranged according to the medieval order of dissection established by Mondino. As mentioned earlier, its arrangement is much closer to that of Galen in his *Anatomical procedures*, first made available in Guinter's translation in 1531 and then revised by

Vesalius for inclusion in the Giunta edition of Galen's writings. This became the classic textbook of anatomy, one to which Vesalius made frequent reference in the *Fabrica*.[47] The similar arrangement of the *Fabrica* made for easier demonstration of Galenic error. At the same time, it must be emphasized that Vesalius's purpose was not fundamentally to make adverse criticism of Galen but rather to correct, expand, and add.

Book I on the bones, although slightly shorter than Book II on the muscles, is one of the several major contributions in which particularly telling blows are struck against Galen's animal anatomy, and in consequence will be given extended consideration as representative of what Vesalius achieved or sought to achieve. Generally speaking, of all dissection material bones were the most readily available, and furthermore the bony structure of the body assumed a much greater importance in the eyes of Vesalius than it had in those of his predecessors. It was the foundation, the structure to which everything else must be related. The femur, for instance, did not always mean merely a bone of the leg but, through a process of orientation from the underlying and fundamental bony structure, could also mean the leg with all its parts; the muscles were related to the bones they moved as the first, second, third, and so forth, muscle of the leg, arm, or whatever the bony structure might be. This significant role of the bones was immediately declared in the opening words of the first chapter:

Of all the parts of man, bone is the hardest and driest, the most earthy and cold, and, finally, with the sole exception of the teeth, devoid of sensation.

God, the Supreme Architect, in his wisdom formed material of this temperament, placing it beneath the surface as a foundation for the whole body, for the substance of the bones serves in the structure of man the purpose fulfilled by the walls and beams of houses, the stakes of tents, and the keels and ribs of ships.

Because of their strength some of the bones, such as those of the legs and thighs, the vertebrae of the back and virtually all the bones connected to them, were formed as props of the body. Others, like ramparts, protective palisades, and walls, such as the skull, the spines of vertebrae and their transverse processes, the breastbone and the ribs, were constructed by nature for the protection of other parts. Certain others were placed before the joints to prevent them from being moved too freely or bent to an excessive angle. Indeed, special ossicles, compared by professors of anatomy to sesame seeds because of their size, were formed for this purpose, and some of them were articulated to the second joint of the thumb, to the first joints of the remaining four fingers, and to the first joints of the five toes. By not first explaining the bones, anatomists delay the inexperienced student and, because of the difficulty of the subject, deter him from a very worthy examination of the works of God.[48]

In this first statement, with its Galenic echo, we have also been introduced to the teleological argument that pervades the *Fabrica*. The structure of man had been thus fashioned for an ultimate purpose. It was by no means a new proposal since it is to be found in Aristotle, Galen, and the medieval anatomists, but where Vesalius's predecessors might have been content with the final cause, illustrative of God's purpose, and from that deduced—or frequently failed to deduce—the structure, Vesalius, on the other hand, began by studying the anatomical structure as the key to purpose.

Furthermore, according to Vesalian osteology the bones not only prop and support, as also asserted by Galen, but—a newer, dynamic quality —they control movement and by their structure may assist movement.

Additionally the bones differ in accordance with the function given them. There is obvious difference of size and shape, and some bones are compact in structure, others cancellous. "There are some bones that are completely solid . . . such as the two nasal bones." "Some bones are externally covered with an almost continuous crust or layer and appear solid, but when broken apart are seen to be full of minute holes and cavities." "Some bones have a large and deep hollow. . . . The individual bones usually contain such a concealed cavity . . . [such as] the digital bones . . . especially the terminal bones of the first and second digits, although Galen thought otherwise." This was a criticism of Galen's anatomy to which Sylvius was to refer with bitterness in later years.[49] The hollow spaces in the bones are filled with marrow, the nourishment of the bones, sufficient to fill the need for greater or lesser lightness, strength, and durability. Some bones are solid, others pierced by foramina for the transmission of such things as spinal marrow through the vertebrae; the pubic bones have a foramen larger than any other, for the sake of lightness.

I believe the teeth to be endowed with sensation lacking to the rest of the bones, although it ought not to be stated too confidently that the bones lack all sensation since distinguished physicians assert that bones sometimes experience pain. . . . However, they are unaware that almost all bones are covered by a membrane—in Greek called PERIOSTEON—of which the purpose appears to be to provide some bones with sensation.[50]

Vesalius continues: "Cartilage is softer than bone, but earthy and, next to bone, the hardest of the parts of the body. Unlike bone it is solid and contains neither foramina nor little cavities. It is without sensation or marrow." Like bone, cartilage is used as a prop or support, and because of its smoothness and resilience is found at joints and articulations. The appearance, quality, and use of articular and costal cartilage, fibrocartilage, and the cartilages of the larynx, trachea, nose, and ears are described in Chapter II of the *Fabrica.* "In younger bodies the cartilages are soft but in the older they become hardened so that they may then be classified as of the nature of fragile and friable bone."[51]

The following two chapters, III and IV, deal with terminology relative to bones and cartilage and the various kinds of commissures and articulations, "since man must not lack motion that, if anything, may be considered the most notable characteristic of an animal; and since motion could scarcely be achieved without divisions and bony commissures, it was most fitting that man be ingeniously constructed of many bones." With some modification Vesalius adopted the Galenic scheme.

The *published* Fabrica *and* Epitome

After this introductory material, presented in detail, the description of the skeleton begins, literally from top to bottom, and within the limits of sixteenth-century opportunities for research not much was overlooked. The three great skeletal figures [52] are truly representative of Vesalius's grasp of human osteology. There are errors, of course, but they are few when one considers the scope of the study, the anatomical heritage, and the paucity of cadavers. Galen's errors, usually the result of confusion of animal and human anatomy, are indicated as examples of what must be avoided—and indicate again that human antomy can only be learned reliably or scientifically by the dissection and observation of human material. Yet Vesalius continued to maintain that there was much in Galen that was worthwhile and ought to be preserved.

The common teleological outlook of the two men is found in the opening words of Chapter V:

How the human head is formed for the sake of the eyes is clearly demonstrated, as Galen taught, by the eyes of crabs, beetles, and certain animals lacking a head, in which the eyes are placed at the end of extended processes and not below, although the mouth, nose, and ears are located in the chest. That the eyes need an elevated position is evidenced by sentinels against incursions of enemies and bandits, who ascend walls, mountains, or high towers, and by sailors who, for the same reason, climb to the yardarms of ships with the intention of observing land sooner than those on the deck below. Therefore, since the animals mentioned are covered by a testaceous, hard skin, the eyes could be placed advantageously and with safety on long processes because they are more durable and could be covered externally by a tunic, likewise hard and testaceous, derived from the skin.

In man, owing to his body substance and the softness and thinness of the membrane covering the eyes, the entire eye of necessity had to be soft and could not be placed on a long process without danger. Therefore, since it was inappropriate to place the human eyes at a lower level because of their function, and not fitting to attach them by naked necks, because nature did not wish to prevent their use nor endanger their security she created an elevated position and so neatly protected them from danger. Above, she set eyelids, eyelashes, and the frontal bone to protect the eyes, and below, in addition to eyelids she placed cheekbones and cheeks. The nose was erected between as a wall for the parts. Outwardly, very stout bone occupies the outer angle of the orbit so that the eyes are hedged about on all sides by raised and extruding parts and advantageously lie hidden in a depressed valley.[53]

It is also in this chapter that Vesalius considers variations in head shapes, a concern that may be said to mark the beginning of physical anthropology. The natural shape of the head "is prolonged in the form of an elongated sphere, the anterior and posterior parts having greater prominence and projection."

All other shapes varying from this may be considered nonnatural, such as those in which the anterior eminence produced at the synciput, or higher part of the forehead, is lost and the posterior, at the occiput, remains. Likewise what is seen to be obviously the opposite of this in which the posterior eminence at the occiput is lost and the anterior remains. The third type, still further opposed to the natural, is that in which both eminences of the head, that is the fore part which exists in the forehead and the posterior in the occiput, are abolished and the head is observed to be perfectly round, the exact shape of a sphere. . . . The fourth type of nonnatural shape, also enumerated by Hippocrates, is one in which the head projects more noticeably to each side than to the anterior and posterior. This is dissimilar from the natural shape of the head in every way, just as if in the natural shape you were to imagine the face at one ear and the posterior region of the neck at the other. Galen contends that this shape was imagined but cannot exist naturally, although a boy with multiple deformities and somewhat mentally deficient may be seen today in Venice with a head of this shape.[54]

In the course of his discussion of head shapes Vesalius describes what appears to be a case of hydrocephalus.[55]

Chapters IX and X, describing respectively the upper and lower jaw, contain strong criticisms of the Galenic reliance upon animal anatomy, and in the former chapter attention is drawn to Galen's error of ascribing the premaxillary bone and suture of the dog to man:

Since Galen has established special bones [premaxillary] in which the incisor teeth are implanted, it therefore follows that by placing excessive reliance on his apes he has formed man too much in their image. For in dogs, apes, pigs, and other animals that possess strong, projecting canine teeth, two conspicuous sutures or harmoniae—as previously stated—are seen that are absent in man.[56]

In conjunction with his criticism Vesalius presents a bizarre but arresting illustration of a human skull resting upon that of a dog.[57] Although it was meant to call attention to the issue of Galenic animal anatomy in contrast to human, it may also be considered as one of the earliest illustrations of comparative anatomy, and Vesalius himself seems to have been so pleased with the illustration that he used it twice in the *Fabrica*.[58] Yet, as a reminder that one must be exceedingly sure of one's position before calling attention to the faults of others, this very illustration convicted him of an error, since it displays the ethmoidal labyrinth as a separate bone, a mistake corrected some years later by Fallopio.

As in this chapter, so in the following one on the lower jaw Vesalius again struck a blow against Galenic anatomy. On the strength of Galen's pronouncement it had been held that the jaw was formed of two bones, and it was against this view that Vesalius wrote:

The jaw of most animals is formed of two bones joined together at the apex of the chin where the lower jaw ends in a point. In man, however, the lower jaw is formed of a single bone, and the apex of the chin is observed to be blunt and not pointed as in other animals. In fact, no part of the jaw is more difficult to cut. Furthermore, I have never observed a jaw to be separated by boiling or after decaying in the ground, although I have inspected great numbers of jaws —as well as other bones—elsewhere but particularly in the Cemetery of the Innocents in Paris, and never did I find one divided into two parts. On the other hand, the jaws of dogs, cattle, and asses can be easily pulled apart even without the aid of boiling. Nevertheless, Galen and most of the skilled dissectors after the time of Hippocrates asserted that the jaw is not a single bone, and, on the ground that it could be unfastened at the very end of the chin by boiling, they declared it to be fused in that region. However this may be, so far no human jaw has come to my attention . . . constructed of two bones. Furthermore, if, among the multitude of mankind, I should ever happen to observe such a jaw in some doglike human dwarf or child, I should not immediately assert that the human jaw consists of two bones.[59]

The final statement of this quotation is of importance as further indication that Vesalius drew his conclusion not from a single instance, and so a possible anomaly, but from repeated investigations and observations.[60]

Chapter XI on the teeth is one of the weaker chapters of Book I. The teeth are considered as bone, and Vesalius failed to recognize a primary and a secondary dentition, to be described a few years later by Fallopio and Eustachi. Yet he deduced the nourishment of the tooth by the pulp,[61] and on the matter of the number of teeth he was able once again to remind the reader that the best way to learn anatomy is by the study of structure rather than acceptance of the statement of an earlier authority. "Although Aristotle and many others ascribe a greater number of teeth to men than to women," yet, as Vesalius observed, "since no one is prohibited from counting the teeth it is obvious that it is as easy for anyone to test this assertion as it is for me to say it is false." [62]

Despite its general competence, the longish chapter on "The foramina of the head and of the upper jaw" displays ignorance of the lachrymal duct and an erroneous belief, extending back to classical times, regarding excretion from the brain of the so-called pituita or phlegm, considered excrement resulting from the manufacture in the brain of animal spirit. According to Galen, the pituita was excreted into the nose through the cribriform plate of the ethmoid bone, but, much to the ire of Sylvius, Vesalius declares Galen in error. "Galen described this bone incorrectly, writing that it is perforated like a sieve or sponge to transmit the pituita from the brain . . . However, it is not at all perforated by such small foramina, and its surface is wholly unbroken and solid." [63] Since Galen's route was anatomically impossible, Vesalius continues, the true route for the pituita was otherwise, and he describes what he considered the true course of its descent [64]—of course, equally impossible anatomically and bitterly opposed by Sylvius.[65]

This problem represents one of the times when Vesalius was dissatisfied with Galenic anatomy yet, for lack of an alternative, he had in some way to make his own anatomical views square with Galen's physiology. It is to Vesalius's credit that he sought to describe anatomical structures as he saw them even though this meant increased difficulty of reconciliation with the Galenic physiology of his day; in this instance, however, he was led into error as great as that he criticized.

Aside from occasional ignorance, there were also times when Vesalius was guilty of the same general sin he criticized in Galen—the substitution of animal material for human. However, the immensity of the task he had set for himself, the relative scarcity of human dissection material, as well as the speed with which he had composed the *Fabrica,* are perhaps somewhat extenuating circumstances, although it is difficult to excuse his failure to mention the use of animal specimens when ostensibly he is referring to a human structure. Thus in Chapter XIII, which deals with the hyoid bone, despite such a statement as, "In man this bone is constructed far otherwise than in those quadrupeds we have hitherto examined," Vesalius does not present a true description of the human structure. His illustration [66] and description appear to have been drawn from the dog.

Chapter XIV on the bones of the back opens with a further teleological argument:

> Quite properly nature, the parent of everything, fashioned man's back in the form of a keel and foundation. In fact, it is through the support of the back that we are able to walk upright and stand erect. However, nature gave man a back not only for this purpose, but, as she has made various uses of other single members she has constructed, so here too she has demonstrated her industry.
>
> First, she carved out a foramen in all the vertebrae at the posterior part of their bodies, so preparing a passage suitable for the descent of the dorsal marrow [i.e., spinal cord] through them. Second, she did not construct the entire back out of unorganized and simple bone. This might have been preferable for stability and for the safety of the dorsal marrow, since the back could not be dislocated, destroyed, or distorted unless it had a number of joints. Indeed, if the Creator had in mind only the ability to withstand injury and had no other or more worthy goal in the structure of the organs, then the back would have been created as unorganized and simple. If anyone constructs an animal of stone or wood, he makes the back as a single continuous part, but since man must bend his back and stand erect it was better not to make it entirely from a single bone. On the contrary, since man must perform many different motions with the aid of his back it was better that it be constructed from many bones, even though in this way it was rendered more liable to injury.

Moreover, there was good reason for the varying size of the bones of the back:

> The vertebral bones are not of equal size, nor is the foramen carved out for the transmission of the dorsal marrow constant in size. For the sake of harmony it was better that the smaller always be made the superior, in which case the supported should be smaller than the supporting. Thus it is that the sacrum was created by nature as the largest of the bones of the back, placed like a base beneath the twenty-four vertebrae and joined to two very large [innominate] bones that, together with the sacrum, strongly stabilize the body. If one moves upward from the sacrum, the second largest bone of the back is the vertebra articulated to the sacrum. . . . Of the others, each varies in size in proportion to its distance from below. This diminution in size reaches as far as the head itself, where as an exception there is a vertebra a little larger than the one beneath it. The description of the first cervical vertebra will show that there was good reason for this, and it will be taught that the first is wider than the rest of the cervical vertebrae for the sake of a proper insertion for the fifth [superior oblique] and sixth [inferior oblique] muscles moving the head, and the origin of the second [trapezius] muscle elevating the scapula. Therein you will also hear that the second cervical vertebra is stronger and larger than the third because of its articulation.[67]

It is immediately apparent that the accompanying illustration [68] of the spinal column is incorrect in its curvature, possibly as a result of Vesalius's method of mounting the skeleton, that is, supporting the spinal column on a rigid iron bar and hence giving an unnatural posture to the skeletal figure.

The following chapter deals with the cervical vertebrae and is particularly concerned with the first and second vertebrae and their relation to the movement of the head. To accompany the discussion there is an illustration of these two vertebrae, repeated in Book II for the discussion of the muscles associated with the movements.[69] Vesalius investigated the movements at the atlanto-occipital and atlantoaxoid joints in considerable detail and, with like thoroughness, points out Galen's erroneous opinions, giving anatomical proof of their lack of validity. In three works, the *Anatomical procedures, Use of parts,* and *On the bones,* which Vesalius cites at some length, Galen had asserted that lateral flexion and rotation occurred by a lifting and then separation of the surfaces of the atlanto-occipital joint on one side or the other. Vesalius denies this, declaring that separation occurs at no joint since nature "strives always to keep the bones of a joint in contact and never separated from one another," and asserts that this Galenic error once again was the result of reliance upon animal anatomy. In contrast, the Vesalian description, emphasizing the convex nature of the surfaces of the joint and the function of the ligaments and muscles—the latter structures not discussed, however, until Book II—is a reasonably accurate portrayal of these complex movements. Because Vesalius was so critical of Galen in this instance and pointed out his errors in such detail, Sylvius was later to make this the point of a particularly bitter attack on his old student.[70]

Chapters XVI and XVII deal respectively with the thoracic and lumbar vertebrae, the discussion of the latter being of considerable importance in the attack on Galen. Preceding this chapter are four figures of vertebrae, one of which carries the legend, "We have illustrated the right [for left] aspect of a lumbar vertebra from a caudate ape so that you may readily observe the position and shape of the processes to be described." [71] Here the purpose was to indicate that the anticlinal spine and accessory processes illustrated as described by Galen were proof of Galen's use of the ape for his description of the human vertebrae. Whatever other doubts Vesalius may have had of the trustworthiness of Galen's anatomy, and certainly the study of the human lower jaw had already led him to anti-Galenic conclusions, this present discovery made in Bologna in January 1540 appears to have been, as Vesalius writes, a very strong determining factor. It was the outgrowth of the comparative study of those two skeletons he had articulated in Bologna, one human and the other simian.[72]

In the following chapter Vesalius discusses the sacrum and coccyx. In regard to the former he calls attention to Galen's description of it on one occasion as formed of four segments—"In the books on the *Use of parts* Galen makes frequent mention of the sacrum and there he pronounces it to be formed of four bones"—and at another time as constituted of three—"Galen in his book *On the bones,* which he composed after the books on the *Use of parts,* and now more skilled in the dissection of apes, considers the sacrum to be formed of three bones." [73]

In view of the correctness of Vesalius's criticism, once again calling attention to error arisen from dependence upon the dissection of animals, it was unfortunate that he then proceeded to describe and illustrate a sacrum composed of six segments: "Under the lumbar vertebrae in man there are usually ten bones of which six constitute the sacral bone." [74] Despite the qualifying "usually" and the fact that six is the number sometimes found, he was later justly criticized for choosing an unusual rather than the usual example of a five-piece sacrum. Indeed, the illustration of the sacrum in the *Fabrica* indicates that it was that of a middle-aged man, unlike most of the osteological specimens in the illustrations, which were those of several more youthful persons.[75] About twenty years later in his *Examen* of Fallopio's criticism, Vesalius was to explain his choice.[76]

Chapter XIX, describing the bones of the thorax, includes the information that the number of ribs in man is the same as that in woman:

The ribs are twelve in number on each side in man and woman, for rarely are only eleven seen, although sometimes I have observed thirteen. . . . The popular belief that man is lacking a rib on one side and that woman has one more rib than man is clearly ridiculous, even though Moses, in the second chapter of Genesis, said that Eve was created by God from one of Adam's ribs.

It is also in this chapter that Vesalius deals with another matter of importance in the attack on Galen. At the beginning of the chapter is an illustration of the breastbone, or sternum.[77] The sternum of the ape is formed of seven segments and that of the human of six, and these facts were recognized by Vesalius who writes, "In these animals [apes, dogs, calves] the breastbone is formed of seven bones, as is to be seen by anyone feasting [upon an animal]." [78] Coming to the description of the human sternum he writes:

If you were to observe the human sternum—which, if it be compared with the bones of other animals, is generally wider but much shorter—you would see that it is far otherwise [than the Galenic description]. I can affirm with certainty that I have never discovered seven bones in the human sternum, nor indeed are the bones always of the same number in man. In adults usually three are seen.

The first of the three bones, the manubrium, is "notably wide and also somewhat thick, although it is wider than it is thick." The second bone, the body of the sternum, or gladiolus, "is much wider than it is thick, and it is narrower in the upper part where it is joined to the first bone." The third bone, the xiphoid process, "is somewhat wide and thin, and in its lower part degenerates into the mucronate cartilage." Moreover:

If you join the three pectoral bones together, you will observe the resemblance to the handle of a sword, for the upper part of the first bone, which is very wide, resembles that part of the handle which rests under the little finger in one's grasp. The second bone joins that part [of the handle] that the whole hand grasps, in which are the hollows prepared for the cartilages of the ribs in the form of pits that [in the handle of a sword] would provide a firm hold for the fingers, and these pits would serve that use we seek in swords through roughness of the handle. . . . The third bone with its cartilage can be compared to the remaining part of the sword.[79]

Vesalius's criticism of the Galenic description of the sternum was another matter that strongly aroused the Galenists. Sylvius maintained that any difference was due not to error on the part of Galen, but to a decline of the human stock, and that since man no longer possessed the great chest of the Roman it was not astonishing that the parts of the sternum had been reduced in number.

Chapter XX deals with "the substance ascribed to the base of the heart, or the bone of the heart." According to Galen this *os cordis*, which indeed exists in young ruminants as a cartilaginous plate that becomes calcified in older ones, was found by him in the heart of an elephant. According to Vesalius it is certainly not found, as Galen declared, in the human heart:

Those who, following Galen, have undertaken to write the description of the human body have declared that there is a bone, in the base of the heart, comparable to that one in the upper part of the larynx called the hyoid from its resemblance to the letter U. Nor was it enough for those men to form a bone in this way in the base of the human heart, but they must add to their discourse that the base of the heart, indeed the whole heart, is strengthened by this bone as is the root of the tongue by that bone placed before the larynx. . . . Now let us put aside this sort of imagining of men and let us condemn their stupidity that leads them, full of pride, to prepare the bone of the stag's heart mixed with I-don't-know-what gems and gold for affections of the heart, although the bone of the stag is no different from that of the calf, dog, or swine. . . . And that ossicle which apothecaries have assured me was taken from the heart of the stag I consider nothing other than the larger ossicle of the hyoid bone of the lamb.[80]

In the chapter describing the humerus we read that "the humerus, according to Galen, is, with only the exception of the femur, the largest of the bones of the body. Nevertheless, the fibula and tibia are distinctly of greater length than the humerus." The implication is, of course, that Galen's error was once again the result of his concern with the anatomy of the ape.[81] Moreover, the bones of the fingers "are hard and dense, although, contrary to Galen's assertion, not wholly lacking in marrow." [82]

Chapter XXVIII, on "The ossicles resembling sesame seeds," Vesalius's account of the sesamoid bones, has been called the most complete in the literature and the source of most of the traditional information in modern textbooks. In his discussion he had another opportunity to scoff at one of the superstitions still current in the sixteenth century:

Of those ossicles, there is one that devotees of magic and occult philosophy recall at length when they say that there is a human bone resembling a chickpea. They declare that it is incorruptible and lies hidden in the earth after death as a seed from which man will issue forth on the day of final judgment. Indeed, there is a bone, located more externally on either side, that has the appearance of the middle part of a shelled chickpea, and in very large men that ossicle is such that dice may easily be prepared from it. Nevertheless, according to the commentaries of the Arabs, these ossicles differ from the description given by occult philosophers because, although more solid and resistant to destruction than other bones, they can be broken and burned. However, the dogma by which it is contended that man, whose immense structure we are now discussing, arises from an ossicle of this sort I leave for the discussion of the theologians who consider only themselves at liberty to argue and pronounce on the resurrection of souls and immortality. Because of them I shall say nothing of the marvelous and occult powers of the internal ossicle of the right thumb. . . . That ossicle is called Albadaran by the Arabs and by those occult and gloomy philosophers, and it is better known to superstitious man than to students of anatomy.[83]

By a descending progression, in which attention is called to Galen's error of describing the patella as wholly cartilaginous,[84] the bones of the feet are reached in Chapter XXXIII. In the illustration of these bones preceding the text there may be observed, at the base of the fifth metatarsal, the small ossicle known as the "Os Vesalianum," the identity of which has been the source of some confusion. Despite its rarity Vesalius describes it as not uncommon, and it has been suggested that it was the sesamoid that he saw, although the size of the ossicle in the illustration indicates an infrequent accessory ossicle.[85] Chapters XXXIV through XXXVII concern the nails, and cartilages of the eyelids, ears, nose, and trachea, and it is in this last chapter that he describes the ringlike cartilage of the trachea, comparing it to the ring worn by Turkish archers—a hint Fallopio later accepted and used to give the cartilage the name cricoid.[86]

The final two chapters take up, respectively, the preparation and mounting of the skeleton [87]—the dramatic account, given earlier in the present work,[88] of the theft of a body from the gibbet outside Louvain—and the total number of the body's bones.

Book II opens with directions for the observation and use of the illustrations, the famous "muscle-men," indicating the teaching value Vesalius placed upon them—as well, probably, as a certain pride in these remarkable figures he had commissioned:

At the beginning of the present book there has been placed a series of sixteen illustrations which will be common to all the chapters of the second book and which can just as well be gathered here at the beginning as at the end. The first fourteen display complete men, and the first in order of these contains the delineation of the anterior view of man; the second, the side; the third, fourth, fifth, sixth, seventh, and eighth also display the anterior view but posed more to this or that side because of the nature and position of the muscles illustrated. The six [illustrations] following the eighth offer the posterior view of the body, and almost all are so posed that what is seen in the first is shown dissected in the subsequent one and hangs from its insertion. Then all the illustrations so fit one to another that, to the one which expresses the anterior view, another succeeds which displays the posterior. To the third can be added the ninth, then to the fourth the tenth; then follow the fifth, the eleventh, the sixth, the twelfth, the seventh and the thirteenth; then the eighth, and to this succeeds the fourteenth.

It is advisable also that you observe these illustrations of the muscles in each series for the sake of what they show individually, which you may ascertain from those indices of letters placed as near by as the typography permits. You may refer to these from the context of the chapters, not only for the first fourteen illustrations but also for the fifteenth and sixteenth, whenever it may seem advisable to you to examine the delineation of the muscles that are mentioned. I shall prefix special illustrations to very few chapters of the second book, only to those of which the muscles could not be readily depicted in the separate illustrations. Then an illustration will be placed before the first chapter, especially suited to display the differences of the ligaments, and at the beginning of the second chapter will be placed those figures I have considered suitable for understanding the arrangement of the muscles.

It will not be enough to observe some muscle on one plate, even if I shall have noted it by a letter, but, to see where each one originates or terminates, you must investigate throughout and in particular notice where the whole of it is seen, which usually occurs where many letters are used for one muscle, in particular where, beyond the arrangement of the others, it is denoted by a particular Greek capital letter. Therefore, when you inspect that [muscle] in the illustration, do not fail to observe what that muscle you are looking at rests upon and what it lies under.

However, there is no need to explain at greater length the method of using the illustrations, since each one, according to his own ingenuity and skill in anatomy, can set up his own aims and method of use. Because I have so arranged the figures of the muscles in the complete illustrations, the joints with their muscles are not depicted one by one in the individual chapters. This was done especially for this reason: if those joints had been depicted separately, they could be identified by no one except a very highly skilled anatomist. Now, however, when all things have been correlated, it is clear to anyone in what region each muscle may be found; hence it was very necessary that the complete illustrations be delineated in this way, even though the joints might have been expressed separately. Moreover, if I had wished to present the muscles in the individual or make use of them in some other way, they would still have been available to the student and I would have been saved expense and labor. It would not have been greater effort for me to have presented individual parts or joints, separately delineated, than it was to have these complete figures prepared, and to have given to the artist and to the block cutter now the head, now an arm, now a leg or thorax, as appears in the plates that have already been presented [in Book I]. Furthermore, the same task of turning over the leaves always faces the reader since the same page cannot contain the figure of the muscles, the declaration or index of letters, and then the description of the muscles.

These famous figures, some of which have been continuously reproduced down to the present, although displaying virtually all the superficial muscles—and to that degree forming an anatomical treatise by themselves—were also meant in part for the aid of artists. This is notably true of the first, second, third, and ninth figures, and is so declared by Vesalius in the opening paragraph of the text accompanying the first "muscle-man":

The published Fabrica and Epitome

This illustration presents mainly the anterior aspect of the body, from which I have removed the skin with the fat and fleshy membrane and all the nerves, veins, and arteries. It had been my intention to leave this illustration, as well as the following, free of lettering so that it might not appear spotted to the observer, since the third [illustration] is really the first I prepared for teaching purposes, for the present one—but not the following—displays what we do not observe skillful painters and sculptors to emphasize often in muscular and, as it were, ideal representations of men. Those membranous markings seen on the face and neck of the third illustration and also the arrangement of the fibres in the muscles perplex the artist, sculptor, and modeler, whose studies it seems desirable to aid. Moreover, it is not enough for them to understand exactly the superficial muscles, for in addition to an accurate knowledge of the bones they must have a full understanding of the function of each muscle so that they may know when to depict a muscle as shorter, longer, more prominent, or compressed. They must keep constantly in mind the axiom that when a muscle moves a bone it contracts to its belly, as it were, becomes shorter and, as it gathers toward the middle of its belly, much more prominent. Then, on the contrary, when the muscle releases the bone and the bone itself is moved by something other than muscle, the belly of the muscle—as far as concerns those artists—is extended, subsides, and is least prominent.

Turning now from the illustrations to the text of Book II we find ligament considered in the first chapter and defined as "a body taking its origin from bone or cartilage or from some other tough membrane, lacking all sensation, hard but nevertheless softer than cartilage, white, performing various services for man." It has several uses:

Because ligament is so tough it will safely bind a joint, but does not prevent it from being moved as much as is necessary, nor is it easily broken; and this is the particular and primary use of ligament. . . . Ligament is inserted from bone to bone, like the ligament of the joints of the humerus and of the knee, or from cartilage into cartilage, like that attaching the cartilages of the larynx, or from bone into cartilage, like those ligaments that join the cartilages of the ribs to the pectoral bone. Thus a chain of joined bones and cartilages is formed, the sole purpose of the ligament being to bind them together.[89]

As a second use, "ligament contains the tendons in their sinuses lest they slip out or be raised from them." And:

We observe that this skill of nature is imitated in bridles of which the rings are connected to the yokes of horses so that with the reins drawn through a long course, through rings, even without being ridden the horses are readily guided. These ligaments, like that ring of the bridle, are held transversely by tendons or grasped circularly. . . . we call them sometimes transverse, sometimes annular.

This description is accompanied by a small inset figure illustrating the function of the transverse ligaments of the ankle during contraction.[90] Ligaments also envelop and protect the parts, and sometimes form a division or septum such as "that ligament that, extended along the length of the forearm between the ulna and radius, divides the muscles occupying the internal region of the forearm from the external." As a further use, ligament may "enter into the constitution of muscles for which it supplies not the least substance."

161

Chapter II discusses the nature of muscle and opens with a consideration of earlier views, principally that of Galen. In brief, according to
Galenic theory, muscle was a mixture of nerves and ligaments divided
into fibres and forming an extended course of which the interstices were
filled with flesh.[91] A small illustration graphically presents this Galenic
doctrine.[92] According to Vesalius, however:

> Muscle, an instrument of voluntary motion, as the eye of sight and the tongue
> of taste, is divided into many fibres partaking of the nature of ligament and
> fabricated of flesh containing and strengthening them, taking into itself mean-
> while branches of veins, arteries, and nerves, and by the aid of the nerves never
> lacking animal spirit so long as the individual is healthy.

Of these components, "I consider this flesh to be the particular organ of
motion and not merely the stuffing and support of the fibres." [93]

There is great variation in the origin of muscles. Some arise from bone,
some from cartilage, "as all the muscles of the larynx"; some arise from
membrane, as "the muscles of the eye," some from ligament, "of which
sort are the two flexing the first joint of the thumb"; some arise from
another muscle, "as those which by the circular muscle of the anus, just
as two fingers, are wrapped around the urinary passage where it begins
to be carried under the bodies of the penis"; some arise from no special
part, "but membranous parts in some regions become fleshy and muscle-
like" as "the muscles formed from fleshy membrane in the neck and face
of man." Moreover, "not all the muscles take origin merely from one
part, because many arise from several bones." [94] In like manner there
is great variation in the insertion of muscles: [95]

> The shape of all muscles is by no means the same. There are certain ones you
> may appositely compare to a mouse or lizard, if you will think of it with the feet
> cut away, or a fish . . . you may liken the head of the muscle to the head of
> a lizard, fish, or mouse, the belly to the trunk of the body, the tendon to the tail.
> There is a muscle of this order arisen from the internal tubercle of the humerus
> and inserted at the root of the metacarpal bone by which the index finger is
> supported and which serves for flexion of the wrist.[96]

In fact, however, muscles have many shapes which can be used to
distinguish them: triangular, quadrangular, and pyramidal. The trapezius muscle resembles the cowl of the Benedictines, other muscles are
long and narrow, some are broad. Other distinctions are those of size,
color, and position—that is, whether superficial or deep—and although
most muscles have a simple and single arrangement of fibres, there are
some variations of these. Still further distinction may be based upon the
composition of the muscle's head and origin, belly, and the nature of its
tendinous insertion and usage.[97]

Vesalius's arrangement is based upon the use of the muscles according to
regions of the body. Thus he refers to them as the first mover of the arm,
the third mover of the back, and so forth, an unfortunate choice making
for needless confusion and inferior to the arrangement and nomenclature
later established by Sylvius. This is followed by a consideration of the

number of muscles, which Vesalius concluded to be impossible of absolute count.[98]

Chapters V and VI deal with the skin, fat, and underlying *membrana
carnosa* or fleshy membrane. The subject is introduced at this time because "I am going to consider the movers of the skin as often as mention
occurs of the fleshy membrane." [99] In regard to this last substance, "many
falsely believe that it extends universally under the skin," and also, as
Vesalius demonstrates, "it is frequently separated by as much as three
fingers' breadth of fat."

> Men of the kind born solely for the ostentation of the lecture chair ought to
> consider more carefully that Galen spoke not about men but about his apes in
> whom no fat intervenes between the membrane and skin, and the membrane itself
> is attached to the skin not merely by fibres but everywhere. . . . Therefore it is
> not so difficult to separate the skin of man from the uninjured membrane as of
> apes, dogs, and those animals from which Galen describes anatomy.[100]

Chapter VII describes and illustrates the instruments of dissection,[101]
from which only forceps appear to be lacking. This brief chapter is followed by the description of the individual muscles "in that order in
which they can all be dissected in one body," commencing with that
"moving the skin of the forehead"; [102] the somewhat incomplete description of the frontalis muscle was emendated by Fallopio about a generation later. Vesalius was even more unfortunate in Chapter X, in which he
erroneously attributes the function of raising the eyelid to the orbicularis oculi muscle,[103] for which he was likewise criticized by Fallopio.
The muscles of the eye, four recti and two oblique,[104] are described in
Chapter XI, but Vesalius was so injudicious as to add a seventh, the retractor bulbi illustrated at the beginning of the chapter; [105] as Fallopio
was later to point out, it is not found in the human. Vesalius writes:

> In addition to the six muscles of the eye mentioned, there is another large
> muscle [retractor bulbi] completely surrounded by the others and by that fat
> we have mentioned; this large muscle alone constitutes a figure similar to that
> the first six together form. That muscle also takes origin from the dural mem-
> brane surrounding the optic nerve, but a little more anteriorly than the first
> six, for their origin is more remote from the body of the eye than this one that
> we now mention. Its origin is similarly fleshy, as is also the rest of the body of
> the whole muscle, which, going around the optic nerve and extending forward
> from its origin, becomes dilated just a little in the form of a cone and, touching
> the posterior seat of the eye, is implanted in it in the manner of a circle. . . . I
> am amazed that this has not been counted as a muscle by other anatomists.[106]

In these several chapters Vesalius is not always at his best, although it
ought in justice to be remarked that Fallopio's later, friendly, but proper
criticisms would not have been possible had he not had the *Fabrica* upon
which to build his further investigations over a period of nearly twenty
years. Unlike many critics, Fallopio recognized this debt.

A detailed description of the muscles "moving the cheeks, lips, and
alae of the nose" is provided in Chapter XIIII, in the course of which

Vesalius discusses the platysma, buccinator, zygomaticus, quadratus labii inferioris and superioris, dilator naris, and orbicularis oris muscles.[107] He failed to describe the caninus and nasalis muscles and appears to have looked upon the extrinsic muscles of the ears as appendages of the platysma, and it is in the account of this last-named muscle that he recalls, as mentioned earlier, certain of his friends who were able to move their ears.[108]

The chapter on the muscles moving the lower jaw is opened by a reiteration of the legend that, unlike man and other animals, the crocodile "alone has an upper jaw that is mobile." [109] As for the motions of the human lower jaw, they are performed by the masseter or masticatory muscle assisted by the temporal, and attention is called to Galen's error of describing the two muscles as one; in addition, there is mention of the internal and external pterygoids and the digastric. The full description of these muscles is concluded with some remarks illustrating the strength of the temporal muscle, to which reference was made earlier.[110]

The succeeding chapters on the muscles of the arm and of the scapula are far superior to anything written previously in both general and detailed correctness and are strongly critical of the simian character of Galen's references to these structures. In Chapter XXVIII Vesalius returns to a previous attack by a discussion of the muscles moving the head, of which the introductory words lend themselves to quotation:

In the former book, when I considered at some length the construction of the first and second vertebrae, I mentioned that the head is moved by special and by secondary motions, for as the arm is raised so the forearm is likewise raised, and just as the horseman moves with the horse, so also the head necessarily follows the motion of the neck. Thus as often as the neck is moved by special motions, so likewise the head is moved by secondary motions, as when the neck is extended, is drawn to the rear, is bent forward or to one side, that is, inclined to the shoulder, or in whatever way it is nodded or extended or raised upward. Moreover, the head can be moved by a special motion so that with the neck quiescent it is flexed or extended or carried posteriorly or anteriorly, but it cannot be moved to the sides except with the aid of the neck, since with the neck rigid and immobile no one will concede that the head inclines to the shoulders, although Galen seems incorrectly to hold this view in the fourth book, *On anatomical procedures.* Furthermore, in addition to the flexion and extension that, in my opinion and contrary to the conclusion of Galen, the head has upon the first cervical vertebra, I proposed in the former book that another motion was given to the head, and that is another special motion of the head by the aid of which it is circumducted on its axis like a kind of wheel, whether it is flexed or extended with or without the neck, and contrary to the dogmata of Galen this was said to be related to the second vertebra.

Therefore it will be of value to review all the muscles that serve the individual motions of the head and then those which control the movements of the neck. Thus it will be necessary to review the cervical muscles in the account of the muscles moving the back, which I wish you to learn from his books exactly as Galen described them. I am not constantly going to follow in his footsteps, even though I must describe them clearly and truly, but I shall bind myself to his arrangement for what it is worth so that the coryphy of anatomists may be understood.[111]

As he had done with the bones, so Vesalius endeavored to identify and give the fullest possible description of every muscle and its function, and an examination of the "muscle-men" indicates the thoroughness with which that task was performed. Book II together with Book I represents the major Vesalian achievement in terms of accuracy of description and the most telling blows against Galen. Vesalius was, of course, sometimes confused, as in his attempt to distinguish the deeper muscles of the back, and there were other sorts of errors, some of which have been indicated. Occasionally Vesalius has been wrongfully accused of error, as in the instance of the exaggerated upward extension of the rectus abdominis muscle in the fifth "muscle-man." [112] Upon reading the verbal account accompanying this illustration it becomes clear, however, that he did this to indicate the appearance the muscle would have had according to Galen's animal anatomy and that he demonstrated the real limit of the muscle in man by a line drawn across it at the level of its insertion.[113] His description of this muscle in the main body of the text,[114] where its insertion is correctly described, is not like the abnormality frequently interpreted from the illustration, which was the work of the pedagogue seeking by the comparative method to impress a lesson upon the students.[115] The same procedure is used a second time in this same illustration where at X a nonhuman muscle is displayed, both, as Vesalius writes, to fill up an empty space and to demonstrate a muscle described by Galen as human but in fact canine.

As Vesalius sometimes deliberately placed incorrect structures in his illustrations for teaching purposes, so he occasionally noted such erroneous, usually Galenic, descriptions in his text when they did not readily lend themselves to graphic delineation. Thus, for example, in Chapter XXVI, dealing with the muscles moving the scapula, he has the equivalent of four paragraphs for this purpose, describing in detail the muscles that Galen projected from the ape to the human.[116] Still another teaching device was a combination of comparative anatomy and indication of the nonhuman anatomical description of Galen, as found in Chapter XXXVI, where, in consideration of the muscles moving the thorax, the student is advised to undertake parallel dissection of man and dog.[117]

It is also in Book II that Vesalius resorts frequently to chapters dealing with the dissection procedure he had employed to arrive at his description of particular groups of muscles. These directions were included for those readers who were far from Padua and who might best learn by repeating the Vesalian dissections, and thus by a comparison of animal and human anatomy could prove to themselves the fallacies of Galen's doctrines and the necessity of basing one's knowledge solely upon investigation of the human cadaver.[118] Criticism of Galen's anatomy naturally continues throughout the remainder of Book II since, as the correct description is given, the erroneous or Galenic one had to be indicated, as well as the reason for the error.[119]

Book III on the vascular system opens with the statement that although the books on the bones and muscles must properly come first, thereafter the reader may determine for himself the sequence of the remaining books and not necessarily follow the Vesalian arrangement of them.[120] The vein, continues Vesalius, has a coat or covering in which are woven three kinds of fibres, which amount to three coats.[121] Here Vesalius retained the Galenic doctrine that in certain organs of the body there were three kinds of fibres, straight to attract, transverse to propel, and oblique to retain—a subject, it may be recalled, about which he disputed with Corti in Bologna. So strong was his belief in these fibres that he presents an illustration of a part of the vena cava marked with them,[122] and it was not until almost twenty years later, answering Fallopio's criticisms of the *Fabrica*, that he finally admitted that the fibres had been the product of his imagination.[123] The veins had also another covering wherever they were in contact with some potentially injurious, hard body.

The creator formed all the veins that they might, as their primary purpose, carry blood to the individual parts of the body, although certain branches of them, as the branches of the portal vein, are used for the attraction of nourishment . . . to the portal of the liver, and others for the repurgation of excrement, as those that carry blood separately into the kidneys.[124]

After explaining the historical distinction between the rough artery or trachea and the smooth artery for blood and vital spirit, the coats of the latter are described:

The arteries, like the veins, are formed of a membranous body suitable for compression, collapse, and then distention, but they are very solid, tough, and formed of several coats. The artery has two special coverings of which the external compares in strength and thickness to the special covering of the vein, but the internal, in the opinion of many of the leading anatomists, is considered to be five times as thick as the former and so the whole body of the artery to be six times as thick as the vein. . . . The coverings of the artery like those of the vein are formed of fibres, and the internal is woven merely of transverse, the external of straight and some slightly oblique, but of no transverse. The internal coat of the artery contains a kind of skin like the surface of the intestines and stomach, clearly very similar to a wide and continuous spider's web, conspicuous in the larger arteries and described by some as a third coat of the artery.[125]

And, in accordance with the prevailing Galenic doctrine: "The arteries were formed so that they might carry vital spirit and blood, forcefully diffused, through the whole body to the individual parts and restore the innate heat. . . . constantly dilating and constricting while the being lives." [126]

Of the veins there are four principal trunks: two in the abdomen, the portal vein and the umbilical vein in the foetus; and two in the thorax, the vena cava and the pulmonary artery (arterial vein).[127] Two arterial trunks, the aorta and the pulmonary vein (veinlike artery), formed the basis for the entire arterial system.[128] Both veins and arteries are here and there supported or cushioned in long transits by glands such as the pancreas and thymus.[129]

The description of the venous distribution begins with the portal vein since, although Galenic anatomy was in the course of being overthrown, Galenic physiology remained as yet virtually untouched. Accordingly it was believed that nourishment was drawn from the intestines as chyle by the mesenteric veins and conducted by way of the portal vein to the liver for the production of blood. Consequently the portal system received elaborate consideration, although its intricacies sometimes led Vesalius astray. Curiously he declares that the portal vein terminates in the liver in "five branches," a holdover from the earlier belief that the liver was divided into five lobes, a belief that, elsewhere in the *Fabrica*, he strongly denounces.[130] On the other hand, it is to Vesalius's credit that he gives a generally accurate description of the pancreaticoduodenal veins and the right and left gastroepiploic veins,[131] and as well the correct arrangement of the inferior mesenteric veins. He was especially proud of his correction of the old, erroneous belief that the haemorrhoidal veins were related to the caval system, and referred back to that discovery in his dissection at Padua in December 1537.[132]

The vena cava is described and depicted as a single, continuous vessel, the traditional view based partly upon animal anatomy and partly upon the belief that the heart had only two chambers. This presumed continuity was the result of including the right atrium as a passageway for this vessel, and hence the inferior and superior venae cavae of today were considered a single vessel extended, as Vesalius wrote elsewhere, "like a straight stick into the right side of the base of the heart and emerging from the left side of the ventricle." [133]

The real point of contention with Galenic anatomy was over the origin of the vena cava, which Galen had declared to be the liver, a view opposed by Vesalius who replied that it was the heart since the caliber of the vena cava was greatest at that point:

> Contrary to the conclusion of Galen, and no matter how strong the opposition, we must recognize . . . that the orifice that extends to the right ventricle of the heart is greater than the dimension of the body of the vena cava wherever else you may wish to measure it. The following chapter will teach the falsity of Galen's statement in which he asserts that the capacity of the vena cava is very large where it is joined to the liver.[134]

Yet Vesalius recognized the Galenic doctrine that blood was manufactured in the liver and therefore that the vena cava must acquire blood from that source. Nevertheless, the relative size of the vessel indicated its origin, although there were many who would fail to appreciate that the anatomy of the vein was the decisive factor in determination of the dispute, and there were many traditionalists who would seek to defend the Galenic doctrine by nonanatomical arguments. The very thought of such inconsequential dispute, perhaps the memory of past disputes, was infuriating to Vesalius:

> I do not agree that the origin of the vena cava is [in the liver], but I do not wish any chance remark about its origin, oral or written, to give occasion for certain calumniating, goatish physicians to concern themselves merely with trifles while they reject information about the bones and muscles and the rest of the arrangement of the vessels as if they were of no importance. Were they able to raise some accusation against me here, they would traduce me by their astonishingly pestilential hatred, conniving tacitly at innumerable places where I have already shown the anatomical lapses of Galen.[135]

Yet if his opponents fell into error, so did Vesalius, although in extenuation of his confusion it must be remembered that no one hitherto had attempted to trace the vessels in such detail in the human cadaver. Galen was the sole detailed guide, and it was not difficult to follow his descriptions in the relatively common animal specimens. It was quite another matter, however, to trace the vessels in detail in rapidly putrefying, more uncommon human material, a difficulty compounded by years of training in Galenic anatomy and consequent confusion of recollection and observation as well as uncertainty as to whether variation from Galenic description was Galenic error or anomaly. For whatever reason, Vesalius's text on the course of the vena cava contains several blunders. He illustrates the right renal vein higher than the left,[136] although he states that the reverse is also found. He describes and delineates an azygos vein of somewhat exaggerated size,[137] and declares that "the internal [jugular vein] is more slender than the external, even more so than many believe." [138]

The presentation of the arterial system, less important than the venous system so long as Galenic physiology held sway, displays a like combination of Galenic animal and human anatomy. This is very notably apparent in the illustration of the "arterial man" where the arrangement of the branchings of the aortic arch illustrate simian anatomy.[139] In regard to the distribution of the cerebral vessels Vesalius was especially puzzled, and his descriptions are almost wholly based on traditional views, particularly his assertion that the carotid artery and jugular vein empty into the cerebral sinuses.[140]

Book IV opens with an explanation of what is meant by nerve, an explanation that limits that term and distinguishes it from the several other uses to which it had previously and confusingly been applied:

> Leading anatomists declare that there are three kinds of nerves . . . since they commonly give the name nerve to the ligaments binding the bones together and forming not the smallest part of muscles. They usually include tendons and all enervations [aponeuroses] of muscles under the name nerve. They also number a third kind of nerve, that which I am about to consider, that is, long, rounded organs without any apparent internal cavity . . . slipping from the skull or dorsal vertebrae and carrying down animal spirit from the brain to produce the animal faculty for the parts of the body.

Furthermore:

Because the brain and the dorsal marrow are the source of the nerves, and because the nerves arise partly from the brain and partly from the dorsal marrow,
they have not been investigated by all. Some consider the heart as the origin of
the nerves, others the dural membrane which surrounds the brain, but none the
liver or other organs of that sort. . . . From dissection of the body it is clear
that no nerve arises from the heart as it seemed to Aristotle in particular and
to no few others.[141]

In regard to origin:

There are those who affirm that the origin of the nerves is from the hard or
thick membrane of the brain—among whom the most ancient was Erasistratus.
However, they saw merely the exterior part of the nerve arisen from the dural
membrane of the brain. Each nerve is formed of three substances, a middle substance very much like the inner substance of the tree which undoubtedly takes
origin from the brain and resembles the coagulated and hardened substance of
the brain, and two exterior substances, one very much like the innermost substance which I have discovered to take origin from the thin membrane of the
brain, and the other from the dural membrane.

As to substance:

The substance of the brain and of the dorsal marrow extending from it do
not everywhere preserve the same hardness or shape, and also the nerves taking
origin from them do not correspond to one another in substance but differ very
much in hardness and softness. This results from the origin of the substance from
which the nerves issue. For this reason the optic nerves . . . are especially soft;
those that take origin from the dorsal marrow where it ends in the sacrum are
very hard. Then, because of the length of their course, the nerves are found to
be either hard or soft, and those of sight, taste, and hearing are soft nerves because they extend only a short distance.[142]

Nature had three purposes in the distribution of the nerves: "First,
for the sake of sensation in the organs of sensation; second, for movement
in the parts that must be moved; third, for indication of pain in all the
other parts." The organ of sensation requires a softer nerve than that
serving movement.[143]

"The number of pairs of nerves taking origin from the brain . . . is
seven"; [144] this was the same number recognized by Galen, and with
some modification Vesalius sought consciously to adapt his classification
to that of his classical predecessor; although realizing that the number
might be increased, "I shall not depart from the enumeration of the
cranial nerves that was established by the ancients." [145] Vesalius did not
look upon the olfactory nerve as a nerve, although he declared the olfactory bulbs to be the site of olfaction. "I shall not call the organs of
olfaction nerves, because they do not come from the aforementioned amplitude of the calvarium," even though "some anatomists have considered
them as such and counted them as the first pair." [146] He considered the
optic nerve as the first, for which he provided an extensive description:

Each nerve of the first pair is carried somewhat obliquely forward under the base of the brain where the sinus terminates, through which the gland receives the cerebral pituita; the right nerve is extended to the left and the left to the right. Then in their progress from origin they unite and are so mixed that in no way can you distinguish right from left, so that it is a vain question whether the right nerve in this conjunction is on the right side or whether it is carried in a continuous course on the left. Although that coalition of the nerves is nothing other than a common body from which both nerves are said to arise, yet the origin of that body from the substance of the brain has not been investigated and to that degree the origins of the nerves appear remote.

The nerves continuing from their conjunction out from the calvarium are then separated from one another and advance through foramina carved out for them into the site of the eyes and outside the cavity of the calvarium. They are taken as a whole into the eyes, not implanted accurately in the center of the rear of the eye, but the right nerve seeking the eye is implanted more at the right side of the rear; that that goes to the left eye enters at the left side of the center of the rear of the eye and, like the nerve of the right eye, degenerates or is expanded into a broad tunic.[147]

Vesalius then recounts some of his unusual findings at dissection:

At Padua the body of a youth executed by hanging was used for public dissection—his right eye had been plucked out by the executioner a year before; then a woman, executed in the same way whose right eye had withered away from an early age, the left, however, remaining completely healthy. The woman's right optic nerve in its whole course was seen to be much more slender than the left, not only where it was inserted into the eye, but also in its origin and in the right side of the conjunction of the nerves; furthermore, as the right was more slender, so it was also seen to be harder and redder, as was also the case of the youth; but his right optic nerve was almost as thick and soft as the left.[148]

It was also in his discussion of the optic nerves that Vesalius denies the crossing of the nerves in the optic chiasma. Related to these investigations is the curious case of:

. . . that one whose optic nerves I saw to be neither united nor to touch one another, but the right was reflected to the left in that region where it issued a little way from the calvarium, as if the nerves did not meet for the sake of union but that they might advance more readily through their foramen from the calvarium.

He was so interested in this anomaly that he introduced a figure of it into the *Fabrica* and sought to discover what effect the condition had had upon vision. "I took great pains to find out from that man's acquaintances whether or not everything had appeared double to his eyes, but I learned nothing except that he never complained of his vision which was always excellent and his acquaintances were unaware of any double vision." [149]

Vesalius denied the common belief that the nerves were hollow to permit the passage of animal spirit through them, the cause, so it was believed, of sensation and motion:

I can assert that I never found any passage of that sort even though I dissected the optic nerves of live dogs and other large animals for this purpose, and the head of a man as yet warm and scarcely a quarter hour after his decapitation. I inspected the nerves carefully, treating them with warm water, but I was unable to discover a passage of that sort in the whole course of the nerves. Nor was it at all apparent in the juncture of the nerves, even though it ought to have been apparent there if, according to Galen's opinion, this is the reason the nerves are united.[150]

This is a declaration of importance since it indicates that even though Vesalius accepted the belief in passage of animal spirits by way of the nerves he did not allow it to affect his observation.

Despite several instances of commendable observation, Vesalius was not wholly successful in his efforts to trace the cranial nerves to their origins, and his idea of the general scheme of their peripheral distribution shows a certain amount of confusion and error.[151] Nevertheless, the level of knowledge in the text and illustrations of the *Fabrica* was well above that of contemporary works and was not surpassed for a generation. He was more successful in tracing the spinal nerves,[152] although compared to some of the other books of the *Fabrica* that on the nerves is of lesser quality.

In Book V the description of the gastrointestinal system begins with an account of the oesophagus which Vesalius declares to be constructed of two coats, asserting that there were two kinds of fibres, "longitudinal, to attract nourishment, and transverse, to push it toward the stomach." [153] Tracing the oesophagus to the stomach, Vesalius describes the position of the latter organ and notes that contrary to Galen's belief it is not constant in position but varies according to the amount of its content. He also describes the three coats of the stomach and records a local incident to demonstrate that its pyloric opening can expand to a larger dimension than that granted to it by Galen:

A cunning Spaniard indicated that he was not unaware of the amplitude of this orifice when last year he stole a noble matron's necklace of forty pearls as well as its gem-mounted golden cross and clasp—all for the favor of a Cretan prostitute who had refused him her favor until he first paid her fifty gold pieces. When he had agreed to her terms, she [in turn, had in the meantime] prevailed upon her noble Venetian protector to let her wear for greater adornment his wife's very elegant necklace—which here is frequently not the smallest part of the dowry— and kept it hung around her neck, even in bed, lest it be stolen. The Spaniard, gazing greedily upon the necklace that would repay him the price of the prostitute's services, employed himself as lustily as possible so that she might fall into a pleasant sleep; thereafter he unclasped the necklace and swallowed the pearls one by one, then the cross and the clasp, lest any trace of his theft remain. Hence it is clear that the lower orifice of the stomach, even if it is more constricted than the upper, nevertheless is sufficiently ample so that it sometimes transmits even very large objects.[154]

Vesalius next describes the omentum, by which term he meant the greater omentum and transverse mesocolon, and he was reminded of a query put to him by Joannes Dryander, of whose share in the plagiarisms of the *Tabulae anatomicae* he was not yet aware:

That diligent man Joannes Dryander, professor of medicine and mathematics . . . in a long and erudite letter asked me my opinion of the Hippocratic aphorism in which it is denied that abnormally obese women conceive, because the mouth of the uterus is compressed by omentum.

The chapter concludes with some consideration of the pancreas, described, however, solely as a prop and cushion for some of the vessels and the stomach.[155] The intestines receive a full and reasonably accurate description.[156] The vermiform appendix, correctly and anti-Galenically located, appears to have derived its modern name from Vesalius's declaration of its resemblance to a "thick, coiled worm rather than to an intestine," although for the most part he seems to have preferred the term "blind (*caecum*) intestine." The appendix is clearly depicted in three illustrations.[157]

After a description of the mesentery, including the peritoneal attachments to the colon and small intestines but not those to the transverse colon,[158] the liver comes under consideration. Vesalius subscribed to that aspect of Galen's physiology that placed the manufacture of the blood in the liver, since there was as yet no alternative; nevertheless, he not only denied that the vena cava takes origin from the liver but also that the liver is composed of concreted blood.[159] His strongest blow against Galen was the denial of the belief in the liver's multiple, usually five, lobes, a criticism based upon both observation of the human liver and comparative anatomy. According to Vesalius the number of lobes increases with the descent in the chain of animal life. In man the liver has a single mass, and as one examines the livers of monkeys, dogs, sheep, and so on these multiple lobes not only become clearly aparent but once again prove Galen's dependence upon nonhuman materials.[160] Discussion of the liver is followed by a separate chapter on the gall bladder, in which Vesalius was able to correct Galen's erroneous belief that there was a bile duct opening into the stomach as well as one into the duodenum.[161] Some of his researches into this problem have already been mentioned.[162]

The substance of the spleen is "thick and very darkish in color, like a very solid sponge or light pumice, filled with rare and concreted blood, interwoven of numerous delicate fibres and filaments. . . . These involved branchings or fibres are everywhere covered with a very thick and feculent blood."[163] The spleen was subject to certain interesting pathological conditions. So, for example, in one case of hypertrophy and hardening "in one suffering from leprosy that had not yet driven its roots very deep, I found the spleen to be much enlarged and turgid."[164] Another case, possibly involving carcinoma of the tail of the pancreas, was that of "a Paduan citizen who had been detained three years in prison; he finally died of jaundice and was publicly dissected, and we found his spleen to be very slight . . . with fat attached to its gibbous part, concreted in the form of very white and hard stones. The substance of the organ was dry and very hard."[165] The purpose of the spleen had long been a puzzle and a great many theories had been put forward about its function, the commonest being, as Vesalius writes, that it is "a receptacle for the dregs and feculent part of the blood made in the liver, and just as the gall bladder is provided for the thinner and lighter excrement, so the spleen for the thicker and heavier." He himself had no answer and did not hesitate to express his ignorance. "I dare affirm nothing regarding that eructation of the excrement of the spleen into the stomach, nor, indeed, does dissection clearly reveal to me that which professors of anatomy assert boldly and categorically." [166]

In regard to the position of the kidneys, Vesalius had begun to move away from the erroneous view expressed in the *Tabulae anatomicae*, and although his illustration locates the right kidney higher than the left, he states in his text that, although this does occur, the reverse is also true; [167] this of course explains the similar possibilities of location of the renal vessels mentioned above.[168] Despite his partial error of traditionalism he was by no means satisfied with the further traditional belief that the pelvis of the kidney was divided into two parts by a filter and that, after blood had entered the upper half or cavity, the urine passed separately through the filter into the lower chamber and thence into the ureter.[169] In conjunction with his own different opinion, he presents three accurate illustrations of the details of the pelvis of the ureter and the calyces as they are in the dog since, as he declares, the human kidney is too fatty for clear presentation of details.[170] Dissatisfied not only with the anatomy but with the physiology of the kidney as previously presented by the followers of Galen and "self-satisfied Protheans sitting in their high chairs and disdainful of dissection," [171] Vesalius proposes, on the basis of his new anatomy of the kidney, that the "serous blood" was deliberately selected or drawn into the kidney's membranous body and its "branchings" and there freed of its "serous humor" in the same way that the vena cava was able to select and acquire blood from the portal vein.[172] This excrement was then carried by the ureters to the bladder, which is satisfactorily described as to location and structure, and when the bladder had been sufficiently filled to cause relaxation of the sphincter urethrae, the urine passed out by way of the urethra.[173]

The Vesalian account of human generation and of the generative organs is, with some exceptions, below the level of achievement reached elsewhere in much of the *Fabrica*. This lower quality is perhaps characterized by the assertion that both male and female secrete semen,[174] a statement that can be traced back as far as Aristotle. The discussion of the male organs of generation is somewhat better than that of the female. At least part of Vesalius's investigation, such as that of the seminal vesicles, appears of necessity to have rested upon animal anatomy.[175] In contrast, the prostate, first noticed briefly by Massa in 1536, is described as the "attendant (*assistens*) gland" and is clearly distinguished from the seminal vesicles,[176] while the asymmetry of the spermatic veins, with which Vesalius had been acquainted as early as 1536, is noted and delineated.[177] In the course of his description of the penis [178] Vesalius introduced the curious instance of a Paduan student who had two openings in the glans, one for semen and the other for urine,[179] but this statement could only have been based on hearsay information rather than on any direct observation.

In his description of the uterus Vesalius denies the medieval doctrine of the division of that organ into seven cells [180] and states that the traditional representation of the horned uterus was the result of animal anatomy, to which Galen had contributed.[181] To emphasize this point he illustrates the uterus of the cow and the dog [182] as well as of the human,[183] that of the monk's mistress whose body was acquired by dubious means.[184] How the menstrual flow occurs and by what veins he confesses he did not know,[185] and he failed to mention the uterine tubes described by Fallopio in 1561.[186] In conjunction with these investigations Vesalius undertook to clear up the meaning of the term cotyledon, or, in his terminology, acetabulum, the subject of considerable confused argument for which Galen was held in some measure responsible.[187] An entire short chapter is devoted to the discussion in which, especially in the later *Fabrica* of 1555, Vesalius demonstrates that the true cotyledons are found only in the uterus of the ruminant.

The discussion of the foetal coverings is very poor owing to inability to obtain sufficient pregnant human specimens and foetal material for dissection. Vesalius himself recognized the inadequacy of his discussion which was revised and considerably emendated in the *Letter on the china root* of 1546 and in the *Fabrica* of 1555, after he had succeeded in increasing his experience with the proper types of material. In the first edition of the *Fabrica* he stated that, since he had been compelled to study foetuses and uteri in nonhuman materials,[188] of necessity he had had to rely upon past authorities and dissection of animals, the very thing he preached against—and his results proved an object lesson. The best he could offer was a description of the foetal coverings in the dog, which might at least be compared with Galen's account and so test the latter's reliability in the case of this animal.[189] Vesalius, it appears, was puzzled. He likened the annular or zonary placenta of the dog to what he described as the outermost of three membranes and called it the chorion; his second membrane, the true chorion, he called the allantois; and the third he declared the amnion.[190] His errors were further enlarged by his illustration of the human foetus equiped with the annular placenta of the dog,[191] although he was fully aware of the incongruity of such presentation. These errors were probably the worst, or certainly the most spectacular, in the *Fabrica*, but corrections and genuine contributions were made in the later edition.

The penultimate chapter of Book V discusses the breast.[192] This chapter supported the then-current view that during pregnancy the suppression of the menses was the result of diversion of this blood, by way of the inferior to the superior epigastric and internal mammary veins, to the breast, which then enlarged and converted the menstrual blood into milk.[193] Finally there is a long chapter on the dissection procedure to be followed to observe for oneself what was discussed in the book.[194]

Book VI opens with successive and capable chapters dealing with the pleural membranes, diaphragm, trachea, and glands of the throat, among which Vesalius appears to include the thyroid in an illustration of the trachea, tonsils, and cervical lymph nodes.[195] His descriptions of these glands are superior to anything earlier:

> There are three kinds of [glands], one attached to either side of the trachea at the root of the larynx. . . . The second is placed higher on the larynx in a space that, when we gape, appears midway between the nasal foramina and the larynx. . . . Its substance is similar to that of other glands, but much more fungous, especially that saliva may be created and moisten the trachea, oesophagus and whole cavity of the mouth. . . . The third kind resembles the glands of the inguinal region and axillae, and is contained in numbers under the roots of the ears and in the whole space circumscribed by the lower jaw.[196]

After a brief and uninspired chapter on the uvula, he undertakes a series of chapters on the heart and lungs. His text is based upon his observations in the human cadaver, although the accompanying illustrations of the heart appear possibly to be of animals,[197] perhaps because of inability to preserve the human organ long enough for artistic purposes. Giving attention, then, to his text rather than to the illustrations we must note that once again he expressed many objections to the classical teachings about these organs. He declared that the lung, which he, like others of that time, considered a single, divided organ, possessed only four lobes, and erroneously denied to it that fifth lobe that Galen had declared was for support of the trunk of the vena cava.[198] He furthermore denied Aristotle's assertion that the exterior surface of the pericardium was fatty,[199] and Galen's statement that it was not attached to the diaphragm.[200] As an anatomist he appears to have been impatient with one aspect of the story of the crucifixion as recorded in the gospel of St. John:

> It is our custom, as it is also that of the French, to leave those who have been hanged on the gallows—as on a kind of cross—at the public highways outside the cities. If the weather is warm, within a few days after the hanging the bodies swell up into an astonishing mass as if they were bladders distended by water. I recollect that once in the warm season I skinned some dogs it order to examine the movement of some muscle; through carelessness I had not disposed of the bodies and, since they had been left by chance in the sun, a great quantity of serous water collected in the peritoneal and thoracic cavities. But let me hasten on to consideration of the heart, lest I find myself involved in the theologians' sacred question of the mysterious abundance of water of our Saviour Jesus Christ, for I must not in the slightest degree upset the complete veracity of the authentic gospel of St. John by my considerations of the effect of a hot sun on those who have been hanged or otherwise executed.[201]

This impatience with irrelevant dispute, at least as concerned anatomy, was, as we have seen, nothing new—in this case a reference to the question of whether water issued from the wound in Christ's side or water and blood mixed. Originating in the gospel of St. John, the story had been considered through the passing centuries by both theologians and anatomists, with Berengario da Carpi treating it *in extenso.*[202] Obviously Vesalius was not sympathetic to miraculous aspects of his science.

The substance of the heart, he considered, was made up of fibres "contained and compressed by flesh." There were three kinds of fibres, as in other organs, straight, transverse, and oblique, but where in other organs the different kinds of fibres were distinguished by layers, in the heart they were mixed together. Indeed, "in proportion to the mass of the heart, its chief substance is constituted of fibres, and if you compare that substance to muscle, the fibres contained and compressed by flesh are very numerous." The substance of the heart, however, although approaching the nature of muscle, could not really be such:

> As the fibres of the heart in their arrangement have something in common with the fibres of the muscles, so also they serve motion, but wholly differently. The motion of the muscles is voluntary, whereas that of the heart is natural [i.e., involuntary] and without weariness, wholly untiring through the inscrutable industry of the Creator, and by no means controlled by our judgment, nor dependent in any way, like muscular motion, on the nerves from the brain.

The straight fibres were responsible for dilatation of the heart and the transverse for contraction, and, because of the difficulties of comprehending their actions, Vesalius described the construction of a model that might somewhat clarify the problem:

> The straight fibres effect the dilatation of the heart, which is the attraction of its tip to the center of the base and the distention of the heart on all sides. This can be duplicated if you place a bundle of rushes on a circular wickerwork surface in that same arrangement. With the head of the rushes gathered together to form a pyramid, drop a cord from the middle of their point through the center of the circle; when this is pulled downward the pyramid is rendered shorter and much more capacious. If you wish to understand as well as possible the dilatation of the heart, let the wickerwork surface correspond to the base of the heart and the collected heads of the rushes to the point. Then the rushes and the cord will correspond to the straight fibres, the rushes corresponding to those fibres that are in the sides of the heart both anteriorly and posteriorly, and the cord to those very compact fibres in the fleshy septum of the heart between the two ventricles —although I have been unable to devise anything that is similar in every way to the motion of the straight fibres.
>
> It is easier to compare the action of the transverse or circular fibres to something and this is easily done, for these particularly control the contraction of the heart, which is the withdrawal of the point from the base and therefore a lengthening of the heart. This is achieved by those fibres as often as the straight ones, upon being relaxed, are compressed and gathered—rather as if the cord were first drawn up into that pyramid and then relaxed. You can do this with your hands or with a noose by compressing the rushes inwardly at the middle of the pyramid, so lessening their hollow and at the same time rendering them longer.[203]

Like all his contemporaries, Vesalius regarded the heart as formed of two chambers. The right atrium was not a chamber but provided for the continuity of the inferior and superior venae cavae, considered as a single, extended vessel, and the left atrium was part of the pulmonary vein. After speaking of the two ventricles, he turned his attention to their walls, and especially to the wall or septum dividing the right from the left. It was in the course of these remarks that he cast doubt upon the accepted view that there were passages or pores extending through the septum from the right ventricle into the left:

The surface of each ventricle is very uneven and possesses many pits impressed very deeply into the fleshy substance. They do not exist only at the sides where the right ventricle looks to the left but—even though stated otherwise by all other anatomists—appear throughout the entire surface of the ventricles, not only in freshly killed things but continuously and so long as you may desire to preserve the heart, still observable in a dried heart. Furthermore, in addition to the unevenness that the pits produce on the surface of the ventricles, which is somewhat more noticeable in the left ventricle, both [ventricles] have within themselves certain fleshy "explantations" or processes that are smooth and slender and terminate in membranous fibres continuous with the lower part of their membranes [valves]. These fleshy processes are particularly observed at the apex of the ventricles and in their lower part, and I consider that they give strength to the [valves] of the orifices of the heart. The septum of the ventricles having been formed, as I said, of the very thick substance of the heart . . . none of its pits—at least insofar as can be ascertained by the senses—penetrates from the right ventricle into the left. Thus we are compelled to astonishment at the industry of the Creator who causes the blood to sweat through from the right ventricle into the left through passages which escape our sight.[204]

Next turning his attention to the vessels of the heart, Vesalius denied Galen's statement that the vena cava originated in the liver:

From the lowest part of the right side of the base of the right ventricle, the vena cava arises from an ample and widely open orifice, and immediately from its origin—that in extent greatly surpasses the capacity of the whole vein while its bulging circle is apparent as far as the termination of the substance of the heart—it travels upward to the root of the neck and downward toward the diaphragm; nor, as perhaps some may believe, does the vena cava, arisen in this way from a single origin, separate into two trunks like the aorta, but it is extended like a straight stick into the right side of the base of the heart and emerges from the left side of the ventricle, extending without any division through the pericardium.[205]

Moreover:

[Galen] did not notice that the orifice of the vena cava has been observed to be three times the size of the orifice of the aorta, as it truly is, nor, just as we have said, that the orifice of the pulmonary vein is larger than the orifice of the aorta . . . but I find no pleasure in pursuing these and many other matters at greater length.[206]

The excellent chapter on the cardiac valves contains the suggestion that the valve of the left atrioventricular orifice resembles a bishop's mitre,[207] so providing the name of the mitral valve. This is followed by a brief chapter describing the auricles, and by the final two chapters that discuss respectively the functions of the heart according to the Galenic pattern—retained by Vesalius with some disquiet and for lack of an alternative—and the procedure required for dissection of the heart. In the second of these chapters he gives strong expression to his opinion of ecclesiastical censorship over the problem of the heart as the site of the soul. After reference to the opinions of the major ancient philosophers on the location of the soul Vesalius continues:

> Lest I come into collision here with some scandalmonger or some sort of censor of heresy, I shall wholly abstain from consideration of the divisions of the soul and their locations, since today, and especially among our people, you will find a great many censors of our very holy and true religion. If they hear someone murmur anything about the opinions of Plato, Aristotle or his interpreters, or of Galen regarding the soul, even in the conduct of anatomy where these matters especially ought to be examined, immediately they judge him to be suspect in his faith and somewhat doubtful regarding the immortality of the soul.
>
> They do not understand that this is a necessity for physicians if they desire to engage properly in their art, to apply remedies correctly to an ailing member, to give consideration to those faculties that guide us, their number, what each is individually, and in what member of the being it is located. . . . As if one were unable to propose any error in the decisions of those grave authors, or to corroborate their reasons by something new, or to oppose the superficial arguments of others; as if the most holy faith by which we gain salvation through pious works, and by which the souls of men achieve eternal felicity, must be questioned and discussed only according to the teachings of those authors and according to opinions supplied by weak human reason.[208]

Book VII provides a description of the anatomy of the brain accompanied by a series of detailed illustrations revealing the successive steps in its dissection. Until at least the end of the fifteenth century knowledge of the brain had remained medieval, based not so much upon Galen's doctrines as upon a debased tradition, a situation that permitted Vesalius to introduce his discussion with a notably severe criticism:

> Who, immortal God, will not be amazed at that crowd of philosophers and, let me add, theologians of today who, detracting so foolishly from the divine and wholly admirable contrivance of the human brain, frivolously, like Prometheans, and with the greatest impiety toward the Creator, fabricate some sort of brain from their dreams and refuse to observe that which the Creator with incredible providence shaped for the uses of the body. They parade their monstrosity, shamelessly deluding those tender minds that they instruct.

In the previous book Vesalius had acknowledged the soul, but here his concern was with the anatomy of the brain, which he felt should not be determined by philosophers or, more particularly, theologians, and he recalled his years at Louvain when he had first been introduced to the subject by a theologian.[209] In consequence of the ignorance of such persons, and at best their dependence upon animal anatomy, he was able to give an ironic twist to that criticism usually directed against Galen. The student, he writes, on the basis "especially of the teachings of theologians" and the superficial resemblance of the brain of the quadruped to that of the human, might consider animals to possess not only reasoning power but even a soul.[210]

Vesalius's account, unlike that of the targets of his criticism, was based upon the dissection and study of the human brain divorced from any theological implications, and it was a more complete and more nearly correct exposition than anything produced earlier and for some time to follow. Since, however, most of Book VII has been translated into English [211] and reference may readily be made to that translation for anatomical details, attention here will be directed only to one matter of especial interest: Vesalius's revision of Galenic and medieval ideas of brain function.

Until the time of Vesalius, illustrations of the brain and any accompanying text stressed the localization of intellectual activities in the ventricles, three or four in number and usually spherical, since it was assumed that, in the living being, animal spirit exerted a pressure that produced such form. The anterior ventricle or ventricles had been considered the region of perception and imagination, the middle ventricle of cogitation and judgment, and the posterior of memory. Gradually during the sixteenth century this theory of localization was destroyed and with it the significance of the ventricles.

According to the then-prevalent theory, sensation and motion were the work of an ultrarefined substance called animal spirit which was developed in the brain. This was produced from the vital spirit of the heart that passed to the brain by way of the internal carotid arteries, and there in a fine network of vessels called the *rete mirabile*—in fact nonexistent in the human brain although present in that of the ungulate—the vital spirit was subjected to further refinement and became animal spirit. For lack of any alternative theory, animal spirit retained its presumed importance as late as the second half of the eighteenth century, and investigators up to that time, unhappy as they might be, were compelled to attempt explanations of brain functions more or less within the framework of this ancient theory.

The existence of the *rete mirabile* in the human brain had been first tentatively denied by Berengario da Carpi,[212] thereafter accepted by Nicolo Massa, who declared that he had frequently seen it,[213] and now firmly denied by Vesalius, who also explained how dependence on animal anatomy had caused otherwise capable anatomists to accept the *rete mirabile* that he himself had delineated in his *Tabulae anatomicae* and even discussed as late as his lectures in Bologna in January 1540:

How many things have been accepted on the word of Galen . . . and often contrary to reason. Among them is that blessed and wonderful reticular plexus which he constantly affirms in his books. There is nothing of which physicians speak more often, and even though they have never seen it . . . yet they speak of it on Galen's authority. Indeed, I myself am wholly astonished at my [former] stupidity and too great trust in the writings of Galen and of other anatomists. In my devotion to Galen I never undertook the public dissection of a human head without having available that of a lamb or ox to supply whatever I could not find in the human, and to insure that the spectators not charge me with failure to find that plexus so very familiar to all of them by name. The internal carotid arteries wholly fail to produce such a reticular plexus as that described by Galen.[214]

Nevertheless, Vesalius could not deny the existence of animal spirit and therefore proposed that vital spirit was gradually altered and refined in its passage through the cerebral arteries, receiving a final perfection through the addition of air entering, as he believed, through the cribriform plate.[215] Caution, however, suggested that he not precisely localize the manufacture, so that he adds: "I believe that this power [of elaborating animal spirit] depends on a suitable balance of the elements of the brain substance." [216] Curiously enough, he continued to subscribe to an older belief that the brain moved or pulsated in the course of this production of spirit.

Although not expressing himself with complete clarity on the matter, Vesalius seemed embarrassed if not wholly dubious about the actual existence of animal spirit. He doubted that it had any role in mental activities and sought without success to find perceptible passages for it in the nerves,[217] finally declaring that he was in a position neither to accept nor deny its function in respect to the nerves—that is, to produce sensation and motion: "I hesitate to dispute whether that very tenuous spirit is directed through passages of the nerves, like the vital spirit through the arteries, whether along the sides of the body of the nerve like light along a column, or whether the nerve force is extended to the parts merely by the continuity of the nerves." [218]

As Vesalius expressed doubts regarding the manufacture and function, if not the very existence of the nervous force recognized at the time, so too he was strongly critical of the accepted role of the ventricles in mental activities. The belief that mental activities were located in the ventricles and activated by the flow of animal spirit into them had already been subjected to some criticism by Berengario da Carpi, who placed such activities entirely in the lateral ventricles.[219] Now Vesalius went a step further by denying any functions to the ventricles except the collection of fluid, the residue of the manufacture of animal spirit.[220] He even denied that the mind could be split up into the separate mental faculties hitherto attributed to it: "I do not understand how the brain can perform the [separate] functions of imagination, judgment, cogitation, and memory, or subdivide the powers of the primary sensorium in whatever other manner you may desire according to your beliefs." [221] As a corollary, he intimated that animal spirit affected sensation and motion but had nothing at all to do with mental activity—in short, Vesalius suggested a divorce between the physical and mental animal.[222]

The discussion of the brain concludes with a chapter on the procedure to be followed for its dissection,[223] but this final book of the *Fabrica* was slightly extended to include also chapters on the organs of sensation, partly repetition of matters dealt with earlier, and a section on experiments in vivisection, mostly derived and developed from experiments described by Galen, although Vesalius does return to a brief consideration of the relationship of the pulse to the beat of the heart. The separation of this material, however, indicates a recognition of physiology as a discipline distinct from anatomy.

The significance of the *Fabrica* has been assessed in a variety of ways. Moritz Roth, who made the fullest study of it, was unfortunately influenced by a kind of hero worship that led him to praise Vesalius's anatomical knowledge beyond its true merit. Some have gone to the other extreme of undeserved derogation. Even Charles Singer, who admittedly recognized the great importance of Vesalius's work but sought to avoid Roth's exaggerated position, occasionally gave more praise to predecessors of Vesalius, such as Nicolo Massa, than was deserved and thereby was less than fair to Vesalius's achievement.

The examples from the *Fabrica* given above have been chosen with the purpose of allowing its author to speak for himself. It is clear that he made many immediate contributions to the body of anatomical knowledge, both by the addition of detailed descriptions of structures already known in the most elementary terms and by the correction of erroneous descriptions. It cannot be denied that he made many errors, yet his contribution, despite those errors, was far greater than that made by any previous book, and for a considerable time all anatomists, even those unsympathetic to his efforts, were compelled to refer to the *Fabrica*. Its success and influence are indicated by the shrillness of the critics, by the plentiful but unacknowledged borrowings of many, and by the declared indebtedness of the generous few, such as Fallopio. It has been pointed out that Colombo, Fallopio, and Eustachi corrected a number of Vesalius's errors and in some respects had advanced beyond him in their anatomical knowledge, which is true, but it must also be noted that Colombo published his anatomical studies sixteen years after the appearance of the *Fabrica*, Fallopio eighteen, and Eustachi twenty. Furthermore, they relied heavily upon Vesalius's work, the detailed nature of which made it relatively easy for others, providing of course they also followed the Vesalian principle of scientific investigation, to correct or to make further contributions. Although such investigators deserve recognition for what they accomplished, yet their accomplishments were built upon Vesalian foundations; indeed, such contributions would have been still further delayed had it not been for the *Fabrica*. Furthermore, Vesalius's declaration that human structure must be compared to animal structure as proof of Galenic fallacy, and his advice that the dissection of animals ought in any event to accompany that of the human, made him the first noteworthy comparative anatomist and the *Fabrica* a considerable influence toward the establishment of comparative anatomy as a basic science.

From a long-range point of view, however, more important than the anatomical information contained in the *Fabrica* were the pedagogical methods and scientific principle Vesalius enunciated. These were beyond criticism and immediately fundamental to medical research and its demonstration, and remain so.

The character of the *Fabrica*, both all-inclusive and restrictive, the effort to provide every anatomical detail but to disregard all extraneous matter such as those aspects of theology and philosophy that had previously and detrimentally been associated with any consideration of the human structure—indeed, the demand that anatomists disregard them and consider their subject as a basic, scientific entity—was something distinctly new.

Determined to present this account *in extenso,* and recognizing the complexities with which he would have to deal, Vesalius was at once faced with the problem of terminology. This he sought to solve in a variety of ways: by explanation of multiple usages, by definition, and by homely examples. The most spectacular solution was the use of large illustrations presented in meaningful detail, the procedure first adopted in the *Tabulae anatomicae,* with an index or explanatory text to accompany them. Curiously enough, the illustrations have been criticized because the structures shown in them are identified by letters or numbers rather than by names, a criticism wholly without validity since names were not yet standardized and their use would not have permitted the necessary identification of all the details discussed in the accompanying indices. To carry this pursuit of detail even farther, diagrams were employed wherever the illustrations could not provide the necessary clarity.

There had been illustrations in earlier books, although never in such number or executed with such minute precision, and they had usually been introduced rather haphazardly with little or no relationship to the text. There was, furthermore, no precedent for the exact marginal references of the *Fabrica* which brought about direct relationship of text to text or to illustrations or even to details within illustrations.

Finally, and once again a distinct pedagogical novelty, were the special chapters explaining the dissections so that the reader might make the same investigations as the author. Thus Vesalius proposed that even his own word be subjected to test. Here there was not only further effort at clarity but also emphasis upon the need for a dissection technique, for which the exposition even includes descriptions of required instruments. Knowledge of dissection procedure was a necessity if the physician were to follow the Vesalian principle of scientific observation, which meant dismissing the barber, disregarding the ancient and hitherto accepted authorities, undertaking one's own dissection, and making one's own observations. Moreover, it was not sufficient to make a judgment on the basis of a single observation of what might turn out to be an anomaly. As Vesalius declared more than once, he drew his conclusions only after multiple observations.

This principle, which required a return to the true source of anatomical knowledge, the human cadaver, did not indicate genuine hostility toward Galen, who remained the prince of physicians if decidedly not the prince of anatomists. It was not difficult to demonstrate Galen's errors of anatomy, but such demonstration was only a means to an end. The matter of importance was the reason for those errors—Galen's attempt to project the anatomy of animals upon humans. From time to time others had pointed to Galenic errors, but hitherto no one had proposed a consistent policy of doubting the authority of Galen or of any other recognized authority until the only true source of anatomical knowledge had been tested—dissection and observation of the human structure. It is true that Vesalius himself did not always follow his own principle, but the important fact is that he consistently enunciated it and indicated a sufficient number of errors where it had not been followed to prove his case and so make a fundamental contribution to science.

Despite critics of Vesalius, with the publication of the *Fabrica* all investigators of anatomy and physiology were compelled to recognize the new principle even though at first some paid no more than lip service to it. It is not difficult to demonstrate that advances in knowledge had been made by some of Vesalius's predecessors, that there are flaws in his own anatomical knowledge, and that his successors pointed out these errors, but his new pedagogical methods and consistently declared principle were uniquely his. These are the basic components of what may be called Vesalian anatomy, the foundation upon which modern anatomy as well as physiology were erected.

The *Fabrica* was not a book for the student still in medical school, however. True, those students at Padua between perhaps 1539 and 1542 had had the gist of it presented to them orally by the author, but the published work, because of its bulk and price, was hardly the sort to be taken into the dissection room. Rather it was meant for the established physician who might be attracted to a study of anatomy as one of the neglected aspects of a true medicine and, more important, for those members of medical faculties who were concerned with teaching anatomy and who might be influenced to direct that discipline along Vesalian lines.

For medical students and those with limited or no anatomical knowledge Vesalius composed a briefer work, the so-called although misnamed *Epitome* of the *Fabrica*,[224] a work that, as we know, was less bulky and expensive, and, because of its greater rarity than the *Fabrica* today, apparently subjected to much greater use.

The *Epitome*, according to its colophon, was published by Oporinus in June 1543. Exactly when it did appear, however, we do not know. As Vesalius was unable to obtain a copy of the *Fabrica* before the opening of August, so the publication of the *Epitome* may have been later than the colophon declares, although as the smaller work it is possible that it was the first actually available.

In the *Epitome* Vesalius returned to the tradition of the *Tabulae anatomicae* in that the illustrations in this brief work seem to have been considered more important than the text. In consequence the format is larger than that of the *Fabrica*, of which the dimensions may have been restricted by the difficulties of binding so bulky a text. Vesalius had once remarked in a reference to the size of his *Tabulae* that they "could never be large enough," and in line with such thinking the pages of illustrations of the *Epitome* are about six centimeters taller than those of the *Fabrica.*

The title page of the *Fabrica* was used again but, because of the larger format, there was room beneath it for an explanatory text in which the reader is advised that he may, according to his own desires and purpose, consult first the six brief chapters or turn immediately to the nine illustrations [225] that follow, each with its index or explanatory text.

The text is arranged somewhat differently from that of the *Fabrica,* since, although the first two chapters deal respectively with bones and muscles, these are followed by chapters on the digestive system, cardiovascular system, nervous system—here including the brain—and finally the reproductive system. This is the arrangement Vesalius advocated "for one wholly unskilled in dissection." [226] Although the work is called an epitome and Vesalius declared it a pathway to the *Fabrica,* such is not the case because the vast text of the greater work could not be compressed into such slight dimensions, and it is certainly not, as he also wrote, a summary. At best it is a compression of selections from the *Fabrica.*

Because of its elementary nature and brevity, however, the *Epitome* was a popular work, and it was this text that Geminus plagiarized, after some mutilation, to accompany the Vesalian illustrations he published in London in 1545.[227]

A second reason for the popularity of the *Epitome* was its nine illustrations. Two of these, delineating the distributions of the blood vessels and the nerves, were borrowed for the *Fabrica,* in which, because of their size, they appear as folded sheets; [228] and one, a skeletal figure, by reason of its smaller size was obviously designed originally for the *Fabrica* and borrowed from that work for the *Epitome.*[229]

As mentioned earlier, in the note to the reader at the foot of the title page, Vesalius proposed that the tyro begin with a study of the six descriptive chapters of text, although, as he added, one might if he so desired first study the illustrations.[230] If this latter method were employed, the reader was to turn to the seventh illustration, that of the "Adam and Eve" figures, the male and female nudes representing surface anatomy [231] and accompanied by a text describing the external aspects of the body, "Names of the external regions or parts of the human body apparent without dissection." Here, to avoid confusion for the beginner, all references to medieval and Arabic terminology such as those in the *Fabrica* were omitted and only the newer Latin terminology given, keyed to Greek forms presented as marginalia.

From these figures the student was supposed to move backward through the illustrations, coming next to that skeleton borrowed from the *Fabrica* and representing the foundation of the body, just as, in the dissection room, it was Vesalius's practice to draw the bones on the intact cadaver for the purpose of orientation. Thence to the next or fifth illustration, exposing the first layer of muscles, and so on until the first illustration, in which only a few of the deepest muscles remain, almost a skeleton. Economy was achieved by having the different figures hold a skull showing various aspects of the dissection of the brain or by placing various smaller structures at the feet of the figures. It is noteworthy that the third illustration displays the rectus abdominis muscle but without that extension observed in the *Fabrica*.[232] In this latter work, meant for more sophisticated students, comparative anatomy and indications of Galenic error were permissible, but in the simplified *Epitome* such things were omitted as being merely confusing to the beginner.

Having followed the figures backward through the dissection and the uncovering of the successive layers of the body, the student might then turn forward to the three illustrations following the "Adam and Eve" figures, those displaying the blood vessels, nerves, and viscera, two of which, as mentioned above, were borrowed for inclusion in the *Fabrica* as folding plates. Each illustration is accompanied by its explanatory text, differing somewhat, notably in its more elementary character, from similar texts in the *Fabrica*.

The ninth illustration, which includes separate delineations of a large number of viscera, is repeated with some minor differences in the viscera displayed, the purpose being that the organs might be cut out and pasted in place on the body. In this way, according to the instructions Vesalius provides, two figures might be built up with the structures of the body shown in relative position on superimposed flaps. Hence the tyro might acquire some useful orientation to the body before he approached a cadaver. It was a procedure that had already been employed in somewhat cruder form, but once again in his capacity of pedagogue Vesalius introduced elaborate refinements into this teaching method. In addition to those other factors that made the *Epitome* a popular book and so have rendered it today much scarcer than the *Fabrica,* the literal cutting up of copies no doubt also played its share.

The *Epitome* is dedicated to the emperor's son Philip in a preface that echoes the remarks on the decline of anatomy in the dedicatory preface to the *Fabrica*. It is dated from Padua, 13 August 1542, and, since the preface to the *Fabrica* bears the date of 1 August, it may be that this intervening period of nearly two weeks was the time of composition or "epitomization."

Most likely a copy of the *Epitome* accompanied Vesalius's presentation of the *Fabrica* to the emperor Charles in August 1543, and it is usually considered that it was this copy, printed on vellum, that was in the library of the University of Louvain until the destruction of that institution in 1914.[233] Recently it has been pointed out that there is likewise a copy on vellum in the library of the Escorial in Spain,[234] and it therefore seems possible that Vesalius also sent a copy of the work directly to Charles's son Philip who was in that country at the time of publication.

Although the *Epitome* was a popular work and today is treasured for its illustrations, it is of little significance by contrast to the *Fabrica* and by itself contributes little or nothing in support of the historical position achieved by Vesalius.

Immediately after the published *Fabrica* and *Epitome* became available to him, Vesalius left Basel to seek audience with the emperor and to present his new works.[235] It was only several days after his departure, on 9 August, that a German translation of the *Epitome* was published, *Von des menschen cörpers anatomey, ein kurtzer, aber vast nützer ausszug, auss D. Andree Vesalii von Brussel bücheren, von ihm selbs in Latein beschriben, und durch D. Albanum Torinum verdolmetscht.*[236] This was the work of Albanus Torinus, 1489–1550, physician, professor, and then rector of the University of Basel.[237] There seems no reason to doubt that Vesalius was aware of, and probably even assisted, the preparation of this translation, which does not fall into the category of those plagiarisms of which he complains so bitterly. As he was to write in 1546, in his *Letter on the china root,* that he would gladly lend his wood blocks to any responsible printer,[238] so now he allowed Oporinus to use them for this publication. Indeed, the fact that Oporinus was the publisher virtually guarantees that the translation had been authorized.[239]

Torinus retained the dedication to Philip but added to it a second dedication to the Duke of Württemberg, to whom he was the physician, a revision Vesalius would understand and regard with sympathy. The dedication is dated 5 August 1543, the day after Vesalius's departure from Basel.

Little need be said about this German edition except, as Sigerist has pointed out, that there were peculiar difficulties in the translation from Latin into a German that at that time had few of the necessary technical terms. Extensive circumlocutions were required, and for this reason, and, as Cushing has pointed out, because of the greater space required for the Gothic type used, the printed German text is longer than the Latin and must have presented a severe challenge to the compositor for its arrangement relative to the illustrations.

As the elementary quality of the *Epitome* contributed to its popularity, so the German translation must have been even more popular than the Latin *Epitome,* probably because the vernacular could be read by barbers and surgeons as well as medical students, and it has become even rarer than the original Latin edition.

Chapter IX

IMPERIAL SERVICE,
1543–1546
Letter on the china root

❧

INCE the *Fabrica* and *Epitome* were available by 1 August 1543, Vesalius prepared to leave Basel. On 2 August, Johannes Gast, theologian and friend of Vesalius, wrote to Heinrich Bullinger, leader of the new religious movement in Zürich, "I am sending you by Quirinus the anatomical works of Vesalius, who is now preparing for his journey. He is going down to Speyer to the emperor, if he has remained there, to whom [Vesalius] dedicated his work." On the following day Vesalius served as godfather at the christening of Hans Rudolph Winter, son of Robert Winter, publisher of the second edition of the *Paraphrasis* and of the *Venesection letter*.[1] This was his last commitment in the city and he was free to leave, presumably on the following day.

When Vesalius left Basel he directed his course to the imperial court, first to present his new publications to the emperor and then to seek employment in the imperial medical service, but exactly where he had the audience is unknown. He was planning to make for Speyer, but on 5 August Charles traveled from Speyer to Worms, on the 6th to Oppenheim, and on the 7th to Mainz, where he remained until the 12th.[2]

Since it had some bearing upon the activities Vesalius was about to undertake, the situation in the empire at this time requires explanation. One of the greatest problems facing the emperor was the matter of rebellion in the duchies of Gelderland and Cleves. By the Treaty of Grave (1536) certain territories of the Netherlands had been renounced to Charles by the Duke of Gelderland, but with the patronage of the King of France the duke sought in 1537 to disregard the renunciation. A short time later the Estates of Gelderland announced that they had adopted the son of the Duke of Cleves as heir, and with the deaths of the Duke of Gelderland in 1538 and the Duke of Cleves in 1539, William, son of the latter, not only inherited his father's title but also became the pretender to Gelderland with the strong support of the French.[3] There seemed some possibility of success for such rebellious action since during this period the emperor was making an unsuccessful attack on Algiers, after which he proceeded to Spain in December 1542 where he was to be embroiled for a considerable time.

With Charles out of the way the King of France prepared to take advantage of his opportunity, and at the close of 1541 completed an alliance with Denmark, Sweden, Scotland, and Cleves.[4] The first fruits of these machinations were the seizure of Stenay, north of Verdun, and open French assistance to Martin van Rossem, Marshal of Gelderland, who attempted to seize and ravage the Netherlands since it seemed only feebly protected by the emperor's sister Mary. Rossem's mixed force of Germans, Danes, and Swedes marched across Brabant toward Antwerp with the plan of ultimately joining with the Duke of Vendôme in Flanders and so cutting the Netherlands in two. Antwerp resisted so strongly, however, that it became necessary to seek some weaker target and Rossem advanced upon Louvain.[5]

In July 1542 the army appeared before the walls of Louvain. Many families and students had precipitately fled at the first approach of the enemy, and the Town Council timidly discussed the question of coming to terms, although it had undertaken some defensive measures such as repair of the walls and moat and a more systematic manning of the watches, and it was at this time that Vesalius's friend Gemma Frisius stood a watch for four days on the walls. The final determination to defend the city appears to have come from the university and its students, and Damiao de Goes, a Portuguese noble who, after a commercial career, had returned to Louvain as a student, had been placed in charge of a student company in which one of the most determined defenders was Christopher Pfluegel of Salzburg, who had matriculated in 1536.[6] Meanwhile the enemy was at the base of the walls for a parley and a demand for ransom of the city. A party of representatives, including Goes and the mayor, Adrian of Blehen—the same who, according to Vesalius, had previously encouraged dissection at Louvain—went forth from the city to meet the enemy. Some stray shots from the wall were considered an act of bad faith by Rossem and led to the imprisonment of Goes and Blehen for a time, although with the stiffening of the defenses of the city the siege was soon lifted.[7] It was to this incident that Vesalius referred in the *Fabrica* when he wrote: "When Christopher Pfluegel of Salzburg . . . was prefect of the students of the University of Louvain, he swiftly and suddenly set free that city for the second time from a great siege."[8]

This Christopher Pfluegel must have become known to Vesalius during the year 1536–37, which the latter spent at Louvain completing his baccalaureate in medicine. The reference to Pfluegel of Salzburg is found in the fifth chapter of the first book of the *Fabrica*, of which the dedication to the emperor is dated 1 August 1542. The reference therefore must have been inserted at some date after the completion of the manuscript since the information upon which it was based could not have reached Vesalius's attention in Padua much before the opening of August 1542. Presumably it was information sent by some friend in Louvain, perhaps

Gemma Frisius, perhaps Pfluegel himself, and we may assume that the safety of Louvain, as well as of Brussels and Mechlin, was welcome news to this Netherlander so far away in northern Italy and apprehensive about the fate of his family and friends.

It was as a result of such incidents that Charles was advancing as rapidly as possible with the plan of chastising the Duke of Cleves and thereafter taking much stronger action against the King of France, and it may not have been possible for Vesalius to have had an audience with the emperor until the latter had established himself at Mainz. At the end of 1542 Charles had departed from Spain for Genoa and so on to Germany. Military preparations were under way for a blow at France, but first attention had to be paid to Cleves. The duke of that state had relied on French support, but at least for the moment France had become a weak reed; the duke then applied for admission to the Schmalkalden League of the Protestant states only to be denied protection by that organization, and so was left exposed to the imperial blow. Düren was attacked and taken by assault on 25 August 1543, followed by the seizure of Jülich, and on 2 September the imperial forces were in Gelderland and marched on Venloo. The Duke of Cleves, helpless and deserted by his allies, appeared before the emperor, kneeled, and asked pardon—which was granted upon surrender of Zutphen and Gelderland and a return of the duke to Catholicism.[9]

From Vesalius's later charter of ennoblement we learn that it was as Charles was preparing to set out on this campaign that the young physician was granted an audience, and presumably it was at this time that he presented the emperor with copies of the *Fabrica* and *Epitome*. The major presentation was of course that of the *Fabrica,* dedicated to the emperor and mentioned by him in Vesalius's charter as "your volume *De humani corporis fabrica* . . . which you presented . . . to us when we were setting out for the campaign in Gelders." The emperor's next words indicate that Vesalius's second purpose had also been achieved: "When . . . you won us easily by your abilities so that we enrolled you as our *medicus familiaris ordinarius.*"[10] Henceforth until the emperor's abdication Vesalius was to retain this official rank, which may be translated as "regular physician to the household" of the emperor. The campaign against the Duke of Cleves, of which Vesalius was to speak later in the *Letter on the china root* as "the war in Gelders from which I returned into Italy,"[11] represented his first imperial service as a military surgeon. It was also service against the prince who then ruled over the home of his Witing ancestors.

What sort of person was this young physician who had just presented his great work to the emperor and entered the imperial service? Some years ago the late Gregory Zilboorg attempted to answer this question,[12] but the paucity of information at his command, as well as his acceptance of legends, produced a rather unfortunate result. Thus to write that Vesalius was "cautious and almost hesitant" and that he "was no fighter" is surely indicative of lack of knowledge of the *Fabrica* and its author. So, too, to accept the legend of youthful dissections of "mice, moles, rats, dogs, and cats" and to use it to support the description of a sadistic element in Vesalius's personality bespeaks some ignorance of the subject of the study. Equally one must hesitate to accept the reference of another writer to Vesalius as "the man of wrath," or the deduction therefrom that he must have had red hair.

It is true that Vesalius's friend and contemporary Reiner Solenander described him as "taciturn and melancholy by nature," and this is likely true, at least to the degree that it reflects something of a reserved and introspective nature. From our own knowledge of his years in Padua and the text of the *Fabrica* there seems little doubt, however, that Vesalius was determinedly enthusiastic within the limits of his interest and, contrary to Zilboorg, quite willing to fight for that interest, even at the expense of friendships. Yet he was not quarrelsome in the unpleasant manner of that age, and his writings, judged by those of his contemporaries, were models of sedate argument, although the intensity of his beliefs, which may be characterized as representing the liberal wing of the medical profession, can be judged from his first reaction to his obscurantist colleagues in the imperial medical service. It must also be remembered that at the time he was only twenty-nine years old. In later years Vesalius adjusted to his situation by developing discretion and a protective coating of cynicism—perhaps it should be termed sophistication. That he had friends and retained them is readily apparent, although it seems likely that he always maintained a degree of reserve, a quality not to his discredit. However, our information regarding Vesalius's personality is much too slight to permit any fair assessment. Suffice it to say that despite his youth he impressed the emperor.

Of Charles's character a great deal more is known, and even before entering the imperial service Vesalius must have heard medical gossip that forewarned him of the nature of the patient with whom he was to be in close association for so many years; nevertheless, the full sense of the frustrations and irritations that would result for the physician could only be gained from actual experience. The decision to enter the imperial service and so continue the tradition of his family was a fateful one since the service, once entered, could not be abandoned; the fundamental result was the disappearance of Vesalius the scientist, to be replaced by Vesalius the practising physician and surgeon. He had convinced himself and announced to the world in the preface to his *Fabrica* that his medical philosophy required such action, yet in years to come, indeed very few years later, he was to regret his decision that, once made, was irrevocable. It was apparently at this time that certain court physicians, no doubt jealous of the position achieved by this young man of less than thirty, in the presence of the emperor and the court criticized the *Fabrica* in such strong terms that the youthfully impulsive Vesalius vowed never again to undertake medical research, and, despite the admonitions of friends, burned the manuscripts of several unpublished works. These included a volume of annotations on the text of Galen, presumably the anatomical part, a commentary on the whole of Rhazes's work *ad Almansorem*, of which he had previously published a commentary on the ninth book, and the outline of a book on materia medica. In later years Vesalius expressed regret over this impetuous and ill-advised action.[13] A further reference to this occasion, or generally to the court physicians whose obscurantism had produced it, is found in his words: "All too well do I know how some . . . have been calumniated before princes by the unlearned who disregard all study and think only of making money. You yourself know how my interest and publications in anatomy were opposed to me when I first arrived at court." [14]

If now we give some attention to the emperor as a man and patient with whom Vesalius was to be intimately associated for the next thirteen years, we should first note that, through inheritance from his mother and by election to the imperial throne, Charles of Hapsburg, or, as he was known after 1519, the Emperor Charles V, became the ruler, actual or nominal, of territories far greater even than those controlled by his famous namesake of Carolingian times. However, such vast possessions in Europe and the New World entailed responsibilities made all the more onerous by the theory of divine and absolute monarchy. Full responsibility for decision and action rested with the ruler so that the state of his health, physical and mental, had ultimately an influence upon the fate of his territories, which in some degree is obvious, in some degree must be left to individual judgment. Nevertheless, it should be apparent that the effect of physcial well- or ill-being upon the emperor's mind must at times have produced varying degrees of elevation or depression of spirit which could not have failed to play some part in his decisions.

As the emperor's far-flung empire was the result of inheritance from many sources, so likewise his physical and mental inheritances were the result of many and various dynastic marriages, of which some might better have been left unconsummated. From his birth in 1500 and through a youth occasionally visited by convulsive fits, which appear finally to have been outgrown, Charles has been described as of delicate physique and constitution which ill accorded with his love for the more vigorous forms of knightly exercise. In time both his spirit and his appetites, over which he frequently had less control than he had over his subjects, tended to break down his already poor constitution.

In appearance Charles was of middle height and, in his youth, was thin if not frail. Most noticeable of all was the "Hapsburg jaw," prognathous and endowed with a thick underlip, which produced not only malocclusion but also a strong tendency to mumble. This prominent disfigurement, appearing clearly in the portrait of the youthful prince by Barend van Orley, was later partly concealed by a beard, although all the skill of Titian was unable to hide it entirely in any of his several portraits of the emperor.

More sombre was the emperor's inheritance from his mother Joanna of Spain whose mind, delicately balanced if not always somewhat unbalanced, was finally toppled completely by the combination of her husband's long absences and infidelities and then his early death in 1506. Presumably Joanna was the unlucky heir of her grandmother, a Portuguese princess who died quite mad. Charles's mother, who lived a long if not lucid life, dying only three years before her son, may well have had an unwitting influence upon his character.

It must be confessed with regret that gluttony was one of the factors that contributed to the emperor's bouts of poor health and so produced both an imperial problem and the problem of an emperor who did not heed the advice of his physicians. Not only the imperial medical staff, but also the emperor's confessor took up the matter, which constituted a sin as well as a dietary abuse. In a letter of 1530 that good ecclesiastic admonished the emperor "not to eat of those dishes which are injurious to you; and every one is aware that fish disagrees with your chest. Remember that your life is not your own, but should be preserved for the sake of others, and if your Majesty chooses to destroy your own property, you should not endanger what belongs to us." The letter continues with a reference to Charles's asthmatic condition and fits of coughing: ". . . I write in much distress for I am informed that your chest is sometimes heard farther off than your tongue. I once wished your Majesty to do some penance for old sins, but if you will change this injunction into a firm resistance against gluttony, it will be to you as meritorious as flint and scourge." A second letter from the confessor to Covos, the Grand Commendador, adds: "It is desirable that you advise him to abstain from everything hurtful. Entreat him to be careful in his diet and to eat wholesome instead of highly spiced food, and especially to avoid fish which is so bad for him." [15]

From an inordinate love of highly seasoned food in large quantity, Charles's palate had apparently lost all sensitivity of taste, and as a result the quantity of spices in his food had constantly to be increased. Then, too, although it appears that he was allergic to sea food, yet he could not overcome his desire in that direction, especially for oysters, eel pies, and anchovies. Gradually the emperor found himself paying for these excesses. He began to put on weight, far too much for his slender frame, and at the same time preoccupations of state compelled a sedentary life broken only occasionally by sudden and violent exercise for which he was by then wholly unprepared.

Charles became a poor sleeper, and, after the age of forty, roughly about the time Vesalius entered his service, he is said never to have had more than four consecutive hours of sleep, which tended to produce a vicious circle since in wakefulness he was prey to his appetite. Gradually a schedule was developed for bed and table. At five in the morning he usually had a fowl prepared with milk, sugar, and spices, after which he retired for a time. Rising once again later in the morning he attended a private mass, held several audiences, attended a second and this time public mass, whence immediately he repaired to the table for the noon meal. So constant did this practice become that the emperor's progress was proverbially termed *dalla messa alla mensa*, "from the mass to the mess." This meal usually consisted of twenty courses, mostly meat and fish. About eight in the evening a dish of anchovies was served him, and a supper followed at midnight.[16] Yet, for his time, despite his heavy feeding, Charles was temperate in his drinking, although nauseously enough he did start the day off with a draught of warm beer. In the latter part of his life he reversed this practice, drinking ice-cold beer before dawn with deleterious results.

In June of 1550 Charles was traveling by boat from Cologne to Mainz and, during the five days consumed by this journey, he began the dictation of his memoirs to one of his gentleman secretaries. Upon reading these memoirs it is interesting to note that the emperor recalled the time and place of each of his attacks of gout, that queen of ailments that apparently had made an incisive and lasting impression upon his memory. It was a heritage the emperor fostered by his dietary abnormalities and eventually passed on to his son, the later Philip II of Spain. As Charles stated in his memoirs, it was "in 1528 that the emperor then en route for Valladolid, was for the first time attacked by gout." [17] These attacks, recalled by the emperor as to time, place, and sequence, gradually became more frequent, crippling, and incapacitating. So, in 1538 when in Genoa with Pope Paul III, the emperor found it impossible to go on to Rome according to plan.[18] In 1542 while in Valladolid he was obliged to forego talks, which he had particularly requested, with the English ambassador.[19] In 1543, after successfully overcoming the rebellious Duke of Gelders and en route for Brussels for a meeting of the Estates-General which he had convoked, Charles was forced to suspend his trip at Diest where the members of the Estates had to find him.[20] Thereafter the attacks became ever more frequent, as Vesalius could then testify from his own observation and experience. It is difficult to say just how much these bouts of illness and the resultant incapacity of the emperor affected imperial affairs, although unquestionably they were influential not only as they prevented prompt decisions and left much business unfinished for long periods of time, but as illness became almost the predominating factor in the emperor's life it tended to emphasize a preëxistent melancholia and ultimately produced a depression of spirit that was a factor of no little importance in leading him to his almost unprecedented abdication of the imperial throne.

The greatest danger, however, as already mentioned, was the emperor's appetite and complete indiscretion in diet. Allusion has been made to Charles's voracity, his early morning meal, the noon menu, the later snack of anchovies, and finally his midnight supper. A contemporary who was often present at this last meal has left us a picture of it which indicates among other things that Charles approached his meals with that singleness of purpose such serious matters deserve:

I have often been present at the emperor's supper. . . . Young princes and counts served the repast. There were invariably four courses, consisting altogether of six dishes. After having placed the dishes on the table, these pages took the covers off. The emperor shook his head when he did not care for the particular dish; he bowed his head when it suited, and then drew it towards him. Enormous pasties, large pieces of game, and the most succulent dishes might be carried away, while his Majesty ate a piece of roast, a slice of calf's head, or something of that sort. He had no one to carve for him; in fact, he made but sparing use of the knife. He began by cutting his bread in large pieces, large enough for one mouthful, then attacked his dish. He stuck his knife anywhere, and often used his fingers while he held the plate under his chin with the other hand. He ate so naturally, and at the same time so cleanly, that it was a pleasure to watch him. When he felt thirsty, he only drank three draughts; he made a sign to the physicians standing by the table; thereupon they went to the sideboard for two silver flagons, and filled a crystal goblet which held about a measure and a half. The emperor drained it to the last drop, practically at one draught, though he took breath two or three times. He did not, however, utter a syllable. . . . He paid not the slightest attention to the crowd that came to watch the monarch.[21]

A second danger, and one particularly irksome to the imperial physicians, was Charles's tendency to give ear to any quack who could promise a quick recovery through the use of a panacea, particularly if the promise also included the suggestion of no dietary restraints—this despite the existence of the imperial medical staff.

Two physicians took at least nominal precedence over the "physician to the household." The physician-in-chief or archiater was Narciso Vertunno who, however, resided in Naples and played little part insofar as the emperor and his court were concerned.[22] Second in rank was Cornelius van Baersdorp, who had become personal physician to the emperor somewhat earlier in 1543 than Vesalius had gained his position.[23] Since Baersdorp was more or less constantly associated with Vesalius until the abdication of the emperor, and then served Charles until his death in Spain, it will not be amiss to introduce certain facts about his life.

Cornelius van Baersdorp, although not the most illustrious physician of his time, was certainly one of the most illustrious persons in the sixteenth century to choose medicine as his career. He was descended from the distinguished family of Borsselen which, according to tradition, had arisen in the ninth century through marriage between the princely families of Swabia and Hungary, and which, as imperial wardens of Zeeland, was invested with the control of the island of Beveland. The first of these feudal lords, Lippold, is said to have founded the town of Borsselen from which the family took its name. However, in time the family grew to such proportions that a division of land became necessary and thereafter the various branches of the family were identified by the particular regions with which they were associated. Cornelius was associated with the branch known as Borsselen van Baersdorp, identified with the village and seigneury of Baersdorp on the island of South Beveland. In 1203, Wolfard IX, baron and seigneur of Borsselen, transmitted to his son the seigneury of Baersdorp and the request that henceforth the son be entitled Baron of Borsselen van Baersdorp.[24]

Cornelius is said to have been born at Baersdorp, the son of Joannes van Baersdorp and Catherine van Maelstede, although the precise year is uncertain.[25] However, it has been stated that he was born sometime during the last years of his father's life, which ended in 1488, and therefore that his birth may have occurred in 1486 or 1487.[26] Very little is known about Baersdorp's early years. In the charter confirming his title of Count Palatine in 1556 it is stated that he had studied in "the most celebrated universities in France and Italy." [27] However, documentary evidence of this period has not been uncovered, and the statement of one writer that he had been a student of Sylvius [28] must be considered doubtful.

Presumably at the conclusion of his medical studies Cornelius returned to practise his profession in Bruges, and it was there that he published his first medical treatise, *Methodus universae artis medici formulis expressa ex Galeni traditionibus, qua scopi omnes curantibus necessarii demonstrantur in quinque partes dissecta* (Hubertus Crocus, 1538). This is a general system of medicine based on Galen. Apparently, too, Baersdorp moved in the humanistic circle in Bruges and was also known to humanists outside the boundaries of that city. This much we may assume from a letter of Adrian Barlandus, which was dispatched from Louvain on 13 February 1535, to Jean de Fevyn of Bruges, concluding with the request that greetings be extended to Baersdorp and Luis Vives.[29]

When Baersdorp was finally appointed as personal physician to the emperor, it must have been more because of his illustrious lineage than because of any particular renown in medicine, despite the statement in his charter of ennoblement that reflects more the years of devoted service after his appointment:

Your great reputation in the art of medicine caused you to be summoned to our imperial court when for the first time we came from Spain into the Province of Lower Germany; then in the midst of our troubles you followed us everywhere, not only in the various wars and campaigns we undertook at that time, notably in our campaign against the French in 1543 near the city of Landrecies.[30]

Although the phrase "great reputation" probably suggests the stature Cornelius acquired in the emperor's eyes in later years, there is no reason why we may not date the beginning of his imperial service in the year of Charles's return from Spain, in 1543. Thus Baersdorp and Vesalius became imperial physicians at approximately the same time, although the former was greater in years and the latter in reputation. It seems likely that the two must have become acquainted, at least professionally, during the campaign against the Duke of Cleves, which for both Baersdorp and Vesalius was the prelude to the more peaceful, if frequently more exasperating, occupation of court physician.

With the subjugation of the Duke of Cleves the emperor was able to turn his attention directly to his major enemy. France had already launched an attack into Luxemburg, and Charles now retaliated with an advance—through Hainault by way of Mons and Le Quesnay—which was, however, brought to a halt before Landrecies, which had been occupied and strongly fortified by Vendôme. Charles, despite the entreaties of his family, had joined the investing imperial army in October. He had been miserably ill and had lost much weight; his harness was "a great deal too wide for him though he had had made a great doublet bombasted with cotton." Nevertheless, all was to no avail. The King of France appeared, only to throw reinforcements into the besieged town, and then withdrew, but the result was successful resistance to the imperialists.[31]

Since the emperor was with the army it is likely that his personal physician Baersdorp was also on hand, especially since Charles had not yet fully recovered from his last bout of ill health. At Landrecies also we meet for the first time a Spanish surgeon named Dionisio Daza Chacon, whose memories of his years of service in the imperial cause contain frequent allusions to Vesalius.[32] Daza Chacon's remarks on this campaign refer to the treatment of gunshot wounds, a relatively new problem since the widespread use of firearms had occurred only recently. At first it had been thought that gunshot wounds were envenomed and that therefore the most drastic treatment was required, such as boiling oil, cautery, and, among other things, a curious plaster composed of ground-up frogs, worms, and vipers; such was the advice of Giovanni da Vigo, 1460–1525, in a work [33] that, regrettably for the soldiers, passed through many editions. Somewhat milder was the advice of Michelangelo Biondo,[34] who recommended avoidance of irritating drugs since he had observed wisely that they had a retarding effect. But it is to Ambroise Paré, 1517–1590, that credit must go for the abolition of the harsh cautery and boiling oil, through publication of his *Methode de traicter les playes faictes par hacquebutes et aultres bastons à feu*, in 1545. Nevertheless, others were also arriving independently at the same conclusion. Bartolomeo Maggi, 1477–1552, whom we shall meet in the company of Vesalius on several later occasions, recommended the simple treatment of gunshot wounds without hindrance to normal secretions,[35] and Leonardo Botallo, b. 1530, denied the poisonous nature of such wounds.[36] It is likely that many military surgeons had empirically acquired similar knowledge of proper treatment although, according to Daza Chacon, in his first campaign Vesalius was still using the older, irritating and less effective method:

> The removal of extraneous things that can be removed without too great effort, but not in the manner in which Vigo and Alfonso Ferri [37] do it since they, believing with great certainty that these wounds are envenomed, commence by cauterizing either with actual or potential cautery, and so they pack the wound with small tents thoroughly soaked in turpentine and oil of sugar which has been well boiled. This is the sort of treatment we employed in the year forty-four [correctly, 1543], during the reign of the Emperor Charles V of glorious memory, at Landrecies, and this is the method that the very learned Vesalius employed so that not only were the wounds festered but very painful and accompanied by poor results.[38]

Thus it appears that Vesalius, using an obsolete treatment, remained with the imperial forces after the close of the campaign against the Duke of Cleves. He may have been with the army when it was preparing to take up winter quarters, but since there is no further mention of him by Daza Chacon it seems unlikely that Vesalius was still with the troops at the beginning of December when the problem of how to prevent frost-bite and its gangrenous consequences among the soldiers arose "in the camp of his Majesty Charles V near Landrecies." [39]

Precisely when Vesalius returned to Padua we do not know. His return, which was only a stop on the way to Pisa whither Duke Cosimo had invited him to present anatomical demonstrations, appears to have been something of a surprise, at least to Realdo Colombo, his former assistant, who was then temporarily holding the vacant chair of anatomy. According to Vesalius, Colombo had for some time been industriously belittling his reputation since, aware of Vesalius's imperial appointment, "little did he think that after the publication of my books I should return to Italy or, as you are aware, control my writings by anatomical observations during the public dissections held in Padua." Previously Vesalius had looked upon Colombo with favor and friendliness and expressed himself in such fashion in the *Fabrica*. Naturally, the current circumstances altered his opinion, and in the *Letter on the china root* (1546), discussing a vein between the stomach and spleen, he referred to Colombo as one:

. . . who learned something of anatomy by assisting me in my work, although he was incompletely educated; several times he had heard in the medical school that I was unable to find a passage or vein—actually a fiction of most anatomists . . . and while I was absent from Padua he dissected a body and boasted that he had found something that was unknown to me. [40]

Caught more or less in the act, Colombo sought to remain as inconspicuous as possible during the remainder of his former professor's visit which, incidentally, seems to have been a very successful one. According to a document from the university archives referring to Vesalius's lectures and demonstrations during those few days, it is stated that "because a year has already passed since he made his last demonstration, everyone has had great desire to hear him. His audience gives testimony of the truth of this, for from the first day to the last he has had an audience of over 500 scholars." We also learn from the *Letter on the china root* of the cadaver used in his last Paduan dissection:

A beautiful prostitute, taken by the students from a tomb in the church of San Antonio of Padua, was employed for the public dissection, the last one held by me in Padua. She had died in three days from an inflammation that, beginning along the azygos vein and its branches, had affected the entire posterior part of the thorax and offered an excellent opportunity for the study of the nature of pleurisy since the rest of her body was slightly emaciated and therefore very well suited for dissection. [41]

At this moment of Vesalius's final departure from Padua, another bit of information gives evidence of the success he had enjoyed there and the immediate success of the *Fabrica* in Germany. This is found in a letter written on 1 January 1544 by Georg Agricola, a physician—although best known for his classic work on mining, *De re metallica*—to his friend and correspondent, Wolfgang Meurer. Agricola refers in his letter to one previously received from Meurer, then a student at Padua, in which Meurer gave praise to two of his teachers, Giambattista da Monte and Andreas Vesalius. In reply Agricola stated that copies of Vesalius's books, the *Fabrica* and *Epitome,* had been available for purchase in Leipzig, but that by the time he had become aware of it the limited number of copies had all been sold so that he had had to place his order in Frankfurt.[42]

Vesalius was in Padua at least until 28 December 1543.[43] At some time thereafter, in company with Petrus Martyr Tronus, a physician of Pavia, he traveled on to Bologna. In that city he stayed with his old acquaintance, Giovanni Andrea Bianchi,[44] who took him on a visit to the medical school where two cadavers were about to be dissected by Bartolomeo Maggi, lecturer in surgery and anatomy at Bologna, 1541–1552, and already mentioned as having written an important book on the new treatment of gunshot wounds.

As a distinguished visitor, Vesalius was requested to present an anatomical demonstration. ". . . my friends Boccadiferro and Bianchi, to whom I owe so much for their great kindnesses to me, and many of the students insisted that I dissect the major parts of a body then available; this dissection continued far into the night." [45] His acquiescence had led to the gathering of a considerable number of spectators, but rather than "the major parts of a body" Vesalius had decided to demonstrate the venous system. His dissection had been so thorough and his discourse so prolonged that the session had gone on "far into the night" until finally terminated, still incomplete, by the discomfort of the cold winter weather. The spectators had refrained from questions and objections, impatient as many of them were, since they had presumed that the demonstration would be continued on the following day. Great was their annoyance, therefore, when on the following morning they learned that Vesalius had set forth at dawn for Pisa.[46] Perhaps he had found he had insufficient time for further delay in Bologna, or perhaps he did not relish the long controversy looming up, especially since the philosophers among the spectators, such as Boccadiferro, would very likely enter the discussion of the veins and inevitably lead it to a consideration of the heart; thereafter the argument of Galenists against Aristotelians would be almost interminable.

Such, indeed, was the case, even with Vesalius departed. Boccadiferro began the discussion by supporting Aristotle against Galen. This was too much for the medical element which displayed its opinion of such anti-Galenic doctrine with hisses. Other philosophers and physicians voiced their opinions for or against Aristotle or Galen, most supporting the latter, and the sole anatomist present, Bartolomeo Maggi, he who had been originally to perform the dissection, gave his support likewise to Galen. Apparently it was a battle of doctrines with no one appealing to the evidence of the two cadavers, despite the fact that an entire day was consumed in this fruitless discussion that Vesalius was lucky enough or wise enough to have avoided.[47] In the preface to the *Fabrica* he indicated that he had already had experience with this sort of situation, declaring, as may be recalled: "Days are wasted in ridiculous questions so that in such confusion less is presented to the spectators than a butcher in his stall could teach a physician."

Thus fortunately escaped, Vesalius continued on his way, reaching Pisa somewhere between the 20 and 22 January 1544, and immediately preparations were made to provide the neccesary dissection materials for his anatomical demonstrations and lectures in that town.

The University of Pisa had its beginnings in the late twelfth century, and in 1343 it obtained the privileges of a *studium generale* through a papal bull of Clement VI. This indication of the growing importance of Pisa appears to have been due at least in part to a great influx of students from Bologna, which had been placed under the interdict of 1338 by Benedict XII. However, this first appearance of importance was short-lived and dealt a severe blow by the Black Death in 1348, so that at times the university appears even to have been suspended. It was not until the following century that any substantial recovery occurred, especially after 1472 when Florence undertook the restoration of the school. At that time the Florentine university was dissolved and Pisa, although a conquest of its great neighbor, was allowed the prestige of being the sole academic center. For a time its university was second only to that of Padua as a scientific school.[48] However, in the sixteenth century, owing to the Franco-Imperial struggle for north Italy, the presence of imperial power and local discord within Tuscany itself, and dissatisfaction and unrest within the university, a disastrous decline set in.[49]

In November 1543 a refurbished University of Pisa was reopened through the efforts of the young Duke Cosimo, 1519–1574, who had gained his ducal throne only six years earlier. Exactly when the invitation had been tendered to Vesalius to give a short course in anatomy at Pisa is unknown, although Cosimo had sent Filippo del Migliore through north Italy in 1542 to recruit teachers,[50] and it seems possible therefore that this emissary may have got in touch with Vesalius in the late spring or summer of 1542 before his departure from Padua and gained his promise to conduct the course that was now about to begin. Probably this was prior to Vesalius's appointment as an imperial physician, since it seems unlikely that, once located in the distant Netherlands, he would agree to the long journey to Italy for such a brief time as he was now to spend in Pisa. Moreover, it also seems unlikely that there was any particular reason for his return to Padua—and certainly it was a surprise to Colombo—except as a stage on the route to Pisa to fulfill an engagement made at some previous time.

According to the statutes of the newly reorganized university, each spring, "when it will be most suitable," there was to be a short period of anatomical demonstration on at least one cadaver, but preferably two, one male and one female.[51] Spring came to be interpreted as the pre-Lenten carnival season, since with classes dismissed for that period it was easier for the students to attend the demonstrations, always a popular attraction.[52] Thus it appears that Vesalius had been engaged not as a regular professor for the academic year, but merely for a brief period commencing about the end of January.[53]

The first document known to refer to Vesalius's engagement in Pisa is a letter written from that city on the 22 January 1544 by Marzio de Marzii, bishop of Marsico, to Pier Francesco Riccio, Cosimo's onetime tutor and current pessonal secretary and trusted adviser, then in Florence. It reads in part as follows:

Vesalius has arrived here to conduct his anatomical demonstrations, and his arrival has greatly pleased his Excellency who has ordered that everything be made ready with all dispatch. A courier has been sent especially to procure two cadavers, and his Excellency has ordered me to write to you to inquire in the Hospital of Santa Maria Nuova for bodies of persons young rather than old, although Campana [54] says it is not necessary that they be very young nor that one of them be a woman. When they have been found, let them be enclosed in two cases and sent as quickly as possible down the Arno by barge or boat. This matter ought to be handled by you secretly, both the procurement of those bodies and their dispatch, and let them be delivered to the convent of San Francesco of the conventual friars where everything will be arranged.[55]

This action was later confirmed by Vesalius in his *Letter on the china root* when he recalled his experiences in Pisa.

The site of Vesalius's lectures and demonstrations in Pisa has been the subject of some controversy. At one time it was proposed that they had been held in the Accademia Cesalpiniana in the Via della Sapienza, and in 1901 an inscription to that effect was engraved in stone and affixed to the building. More recently it has been asserted that, on the basis of new documents, the anatomy was held in the "Palatio Veteri Domini Commissarii Pisani," which corresponds to the present Palazzo del Governo situated in Lung' Arno Galileo Galilei.[56] Thereafter still another student declared that Vesalius taught in that region of Pisa where the Palazzo dell' Ordine de Santo Stefano was built in 1562.[57]

A second letter from Umile Riccobaldi to Riccio, 30 January, indicates that Vesalius had begun his course, although as yet material was scarce, only one cadaver had been sent from Florence, and that one defective:

His Excellency continues to go listen to those learned men. The day before yesterday was Remigio's lecture and that of Brando, and yesterday those of Decano and Lapino. It is amazing how attentively and with what patience he listened and then followed the discussion and arguments.[58] Today there was no anatomy since Vesalius has begun to investigate and lecture on the bones, but he is unable to erect an entire skeleton since the ribs of the cadaver were defective . . . its disease not being, as was thought, pleurisy. He will continue with the preparation of the skeleton later, but there ought to be more bodies— they are available—since he wants to do a good job and make [the skeleton] complete. Therefore, more human bodies, please, as well as those of animals.[59]

After his experiences in Paris, Louvain, and Padua the lack of bones was no particular problem to Vesalius since, as he wrote later in the *Letter on the china root,* "some of the students made keys for the . . . cemetery of San Pisano so that they might investigate the many burial monuments . . . in search of bones." [60] The cadaver sent from Florence, however, was definitely defective although, despite the somewhat confused statement of the correspondents, this defect was in no way related to its indications of pleurisy. In fact, had the ailment been merely pleurisy, there would of course have been no damage to the ribs.

Returning to the *Letter on the china root,* we find that Vesalius had much to say regarding the supply of dissection material available and the uses to which it was put:

When I began to demonstrate anatomy at Pisa there were not enough bones; and since in my anatomical course in this large, newly reconstructed university I intended to follow closely the pattern of my books *De humani corporis fabrica,* I wanted to enable the students to relate the anatomy to my books. By order of the illustrious Cosimo, Duke of Tuscany—granted us by the gods for the benefit of scholarship, and who has done everything that could contribute to the welfare of the students of the university—the cadaver of a nun from some burial vault in Florence was sent on a fast barge for the preparation of a skeleton. Furthermore, some of the students made keys for the beautiful cemetery of San Pisano so that they might investigate the many burial monuments, built like warehouses, in search of bones suitable for study. The tombs most desirable for this purpose were those placed transversely in this cemetery so that rain and wind have access to them, since in the other monuments that are covered all around the bones are less suited for study because of decay and the attachments of the ligaments.

In one of those tombs, on which the epitaph seemed to have been recently placed, there was a hunchback girl of seventeen, who, as I conjectured, had died because of an impediment to respiration caused by her malformation. I could also readily tell that the nun had died of pleurisy since almost the entire left side of the membrane that covers the ribs, but especially the parts near the roots of the ribs, was affected by inflammation. . . .

When the flesh had been removed from the bones of the nun and the girl for preparation of the skeleton, in the presence of a few students I examined the uterus of the girl since I expected her to be a virgin because very likely nobody had ever wanted her. I found a hymen in her as well as in the nun, at least thirty-six years old, whose ovaries, however, were shrunken as happens to organs that are not used. . . . I had never dissected a virgin, except a child of perhaps six years, dead of a wasting disease, which I had obtained in Padua—for the preparation of a skeleton—from a student who had secretly removed it from a tomb. When as usual I had cut everything off the bones very quickly without delaying for the examination of each organ, I dissected the uterus solely for the sake of the hymen; although I found it just as I have seen it recently since the publication of my books, I did not dare make any definite statement about it since I had observed it to be lacking in animals, and furthermore because I am not accustomed to saying anything with certainty after only one or two observations.[61]

A third letter written from Pisa by Riccobaldi on 11 February gave some indication of the success Vesalius was enjoying:

At present the duke is not attending the anatomy, although he would like to do so because he has heard Vesalius's lectures praised for their continual criticism of Galen and Aristotle. In Vesalius's opinion they knew nothing about anatomy. What astonishes everyone is that when he is concerned with the bones he locates them so quickly in the flesh no matter what the part may be.

Indeed, so entranced did the spectators become with Vesalius's demonstrations that one of them, apparently seeking a better view, lost his balance and fell from his bench. "Because of his accidental fall from the benches, the unfortunate Master Carlo is unable to attend and is not very well." [62]

While Vesalius was in Pisa, a distinguished jurist, Marcantonio Belloarmato, suddenly died. Since his family wished the body transported to Siena,[63] Vesalius had an opportunity to perform an autopsy of which his report suggests possibly a liver abscess or a tumor at the head of the pancreas with rupture of the portal vein:

I examined the spleen of the great jurist Belloarmato of Siena, which undoubtedly had long functioned in place of his liver. When he was in a bookshop, whither upon completion of that afternoon's lecture on anatomy I had gone with some of my students, he greeted me and talked for some time about his health, which had not been good for many years. In that conversation I spoke of obstruction of the passages of the liver and of the gall bladder, and also of the spleen, and he announced that the next day he would come to my anatomy and carefully examine those organs—which were to be discussed according to my scheduled sequence. But when he had returned home from the shop and after he had passed several hours in study and then had begun to consider dinner, he was seized by an unusual weakness of body and difficulty of breathing; some remedies his physicians had long considered suited to the flux of bile into the stomach were tried, but he died. Because his body had to be taken to Siena for burial in a family vault, his friends requested a surgeon to remove the organs. He told me about it early in the morning, and I very much wished to know the cause of the sudden and unexpected death of such a distinguished man. I dissected him and found all the blood of the body still very warm and collected in the peritoneal cavity like water, just as it is frequently seen collected in a water bag of skin. An indurated abscess in the trunk of the portal vein had been the cause of the flux of this blood, since it had suppurated and ruptured in one place and provided a passage for the blood. Therefore when I had removed the brain and all the organs and had so arranged the rest of the body as I believed it would be both less harmed and more free from putrefaction, I arranged to have the liver, gall bladder, stomach, and spleen carried to the university, because they provided considerable evidence of his poor health.[64]

Upon the completion of his lectures in Pisa, Vesalius traveled on to Florence where he had an opportunity to perform another post-mortem examination which revealed cholelithiasis, biliary cirrhosis of the liver, and finally rupture of a huge gall bladder into the stomach:

I . . . dissected [the body of] Prospero Martello, a Florentine patrician who had suffered many years from jaundice, and like Belloarmato had died a sudden and unexpected death. I was on the point of leaving Florence and was, in the company of Francesco Campana, private secretary to the duke, riding by the home of Martello when I was prevailed upon by certain gentlemen to investigate the cause of death, along with several surgeons who had already begun to look into the matter. Death was primarily due to the transmission of bile into the stomach, which was swollen with bile; also to the hardening of the liver and its contraction, or thickening, into one mass, although the spleen was softer and larger than normal and seemed to have served for the preparation of blood; the gall bladder was as large as two fists, and somewhat filled with little pebbles which, connected one to another, were very much like grains or seeds of millet, or rather like the rough surface of the common pompholyx of the pharmacists. Wherever I opened veins I found nothing except a very thick bile, and the liquid in the arteries stained my hands no less than the bile itself.[65]

Vesalius had made a very favorable impression in Pisa and, since he had relinquished his ties with Padua, an effort was made to entice him to a similar academic position at Pisa with the large annual salary of 800 crowns.[66] However, because he had already accepted employment in the imperial medical service, the situation was complicated. The emperor had first to assent to relinquish the services of his physician, and a request to this end was transmitted to Charles by the Bishop of Cortona, Tuscan ambassador to the imperial court. Presumably such an effort would not have been made unless Vesalius had given some provisional intimation of acceptance to Pisa, possibly based upon his rude reception into the imperial service, but it all came to nothing. The emperor would not part with his newly acquired physician, no doubt made all the more precious to him by the fact that his services were sought elsewhere, and after vainly seeking Leonhart Fuchs as an alternate choice, the University of Pisa finally settled for Realdo Colombo who took up his position in 1545, although at a considerably smaller salary than that initially offered to Vesalius.[67]

Vesalius's journey to Italy had been possible since, although the Empire and France were officially at war, warfare was hardly feasible during the winter months, and the armies were at rest. However, with spring at hand, preparations got under way for the new campaigns, and in his capacity of military surgeon Vesalius had to travel north to join the forces. It was also upon his return from Italy to take up permanent service with the emperor that Vesalius married Anne van Hamme, a native of Vilvorde and daughter of Jerome van Hamme, councilor and master of the Chamber of Accounts at Brussels, and his wife Anne Asseliers. In July 1545 a daughter was born to the newly married couple, and was also named Anne.[68]

The imperial campaign for the reconquest of Luxemburg was shortly to get under way, directed by Ferrante Gonzaga and Wilhelm von Fürstenberg. On 7 June the city of Luxemburg capitulated without a struggle and the imperial army reformed at Metz preparatory to a traverse of Lorraine to Commercy and Ligny, the key to the Meuse Valley. With little effort these towns were taken on 15 June and 29 June respectively, and the army moved toward Saint Dizier on the Marne, which was reached on 4 July.[69] By this time the emperor had joined his forces, presumably with Baersdorp, although Vesalius may already have been following the engagements.

Saint Dizier was defended by Louis de Bueil, Comte de Sancerre, and by Eustache de Bimont, called Captain Lalande, former commandant of Landrecies, who, upon word of the approach of the imperialists, prepared for the assault by manning the outposts in force and cutting the dykes. The fortifications had been repaired and extended by the celebrated Italian engineer Riolamo Marini. For a time, therefore, the approach to the city was hindered, and in the interim the dauphin, accompanied by the Duke of Orleans and Admiral Annebault, had taken a position at Jallon, between Epernay and Châlons, at the head of about forty thousand troops.[70] The siege of Saint Dizier needed therefore to be carried on without delay, and Charles dispatched orders to Mary of Hungary to send him a corps of pioneers. Meanwhile he established his headquarters at La Justice, and Ferrante Gonzaga, ordered to direct the attack, took up a position in a valley between the Marne and Saint Dizier. Siege trenches were dug and batteries placed and, to control any sorties from the besieged town, René of Nassau, the Prince of Orange, "with a party of Low Germans and six culverins," took a position facing the château.[71] It was here that the Prince of Orange was wounded mortally on 14 July, an incident described in many contemporary dispatches and memoirs, but seemingly most fully by Girolamo Feruffino in a dispatch to the Duke of Ferrara:

> Today at the battery the Prince of Orange was grievously wounded in the right shoulder by cannon fire. It is believed that he will not recover; master Giambattista Cavani, physician of Don Francesco, declares that there is more chance of death than of life. The Marquis of Marignano was at the scene of the disaster, seated on a chair. His Excellency appeared and accepted the chair of the marquis who avoided the shot he would have received if he had remained seated. The prince arrived in turn; his Excellency arose and invited him to sit since he was obliged to go here and there without remaining long in one place. The prince seated himself and so saved the life of his Excellency, for hardly had he seated himself than the enemy fired, suddenly unmasking a culverin or demi-culverin of which the shot struck the good and virtuous prince. . . . The nuncio has informed me that his Majesty in passing by there had stopped for a moment at the battery but had not sat upon that chair.[72]

The wounded prince was carried to the emperor's quarters, "and in the evening [of the following day] about the sixth hour . . . after having been confessed and administered, and in the presence of his Majesty, died." [73]

The loss of the Prince of Orange was a great blow to the emperor, who is reported to have wept at his passing,[74] and Navagero, the Venetian ambassador, remarked:

> This prince had command of eight thousand infantry, the best of those serving his Majesty, and engaged in warfare through love of glory, and affection and devotion for the emperor. He was loved not only by his soldiers but also by the

Spaniards and all the others. His affability, liberality, noble bearing, and valor
caused him to be admired by all. He was only twenty-six years old.[75]

It is curious that Vesalius was not called upon for his services, but it may
be that death from the wound came too suddenly or that his fame was
not yet great enough for him to be summoned as a final hope as he was
later, in 1559, when he was called from Brussels to Paris to attend the
wounded Henry II. Vesalius's only reference to this incident is in the
Letter on the china root where he remarked, "I inspected the viscera of
the Prince of Orange." [76] It was the duty of the military surgeon to prepare for embalming the bodies of those important enough to be taken
home for burial, as in the case of the prince, whose remains were shipped
to Breda.[77] We may assume, however, that Vesalius did not lose the opportunity to observe the internal organs of the dead prince with the eyes
of the anatomist.

Meanwhile, Vesalius was occupied with the wounded of a more humble
station, and he still had much to learn about military surgery, concerning
both the actual treatment of wounds produced by the weapons of warfare and the necessity for swiftness of that treatment. The Spanish surgeon Daza Chacon related that it was at Saint Dizier that he and Vesalius
as well learned the new treatment of gunshot wounds:

> While a little later with the army of his Catholic Majesty before Saint Dizier,
> an Italian surgeon named Micer Bartolomeo, very learned and experienced, came
> to the camp and commenced to treat the wounds in a very different manner
> from that we had used. He had a method of treatment for a contused wound
> by which he had gained much money and credit, without tormenting the
> wounded one as we had done with cautery. As all turned out well and in a very
> short time he cured those who had endured our treatment, when we had ob-
> served and learned the method and its success we determined to follow it, and we
> had much success with it. I hold it for certain that if these cases had been
> treated in the old fashion many would have perished. Also at this time Doctor
> Laguna, he who commented upon Dioscorides, came to the army, and he recom-
> mended the treatment of Micer Bartolomeo to us.[78]

Yet many wounded men were treated "in the old fashion" before the
arrival of Micer Bartolomeo, possibly the Bartolomeo Maggi who had
written on such treatment and whose dissection of two bodies at Bologna
at the end of the year 1543 had been suspended in favor of Vesalius's
demonstration. In his dispatch of 17 July, the Venetian ambassador
Navagero reported a visit from Vesalius, who informed him that the
number wounded in the assault on Saint Dizier was almost a thousand
and that most of the wounds were mortal. The guarantee by Laguna of
the efficacy of the new treatment must have been an influence in determining the imperial surgeons to try it, since Laguna, originally an acquaintance of Vesalius in the medical school in Paris, had gone on to
gain considerable lustre for himself in medicine.

Although Vesalius may now have learned the best mode of treating
gunshot wounds, other aspects of military surgery, according to Daza
Chacon, still found him ill prepared:

Amputation, especially at the elbow joint, is not only very difficult but the most difficult of the whole body. Although Vesalius was highly skilled in dissection and did it better than anyone else of his time, in the year 1544, when the army of his Majesty the Emperor Charles was near Saint Dizier, a certain Captain Solis wished him to amputate his arm. The procedure was indicated and although Vesalius labored at it a long time he was unsuccessful and we had to amputate four finger's-breadths above.[79]

In defense of Vesalius it ought to be added that early surgeons commented upon the difficulties of this particular operation, apparently because of the mistake of regarding the tip of the olecranon as the level of the joint. Reputedly Paré in 1538 was the first to reintroduce the procedure of disarticulation of the elbow, but Daza Chacon's criticism of Vesalius in the above incident seems scarcely credible in view of the latter's great anatomical knowledge. If the criticism is true, it seems possibly due to the sudden removal from academic procedures and the as yet incomplete adjustment to the quite different life of the practising military surgeon.

The siege of Saint Dizier continued, but in the meanwhile there were disquieting reports of increasing French forces at Stenay and Vitry which might well prove an embarrassment to the extended imperial lines. As a result, it was decided in a council on 23 July to undertake the conquest of Vitry under the leadership of Maurice of Saxony, Francesco d'Este, and Wilhelm von Fürstenberg. This was done without great difficulty or loss although, in the attack upon some French and Italian soldiers who had taken refuge in a church, the Seigneur de Hallewyn fell.[80] There appears no question that Vesalius was with the forces at Saint Dizier when René of Nassau received his fatal wound, but it is not possible to say with any certainty whether he remained there or was detached to proceed with the separate force that assaulted Vitry and so attended also the fallen Hallewyn. Yet as Vesalius had prepared the body of the Prince of Orange for embalming, so too must he have taken part in the preparation of the bodies of other notables, since he could remark, "I have inspected the viscera . . . of the Lord of Hallewyn and of several others whose bodies, struck by cannon balls, had to be carried away from our army." [81]

The fall of Saint Dizier appeared to open the way to Paris, but incidents of no immediate concern here intervened to save the capital; a peace was put together, and as usual the heavy costs and burdens of the war remained to plague the common man long after the armies had left the field. In addition, the winter of 1544–1545 was one of a severity almost without precedent. Wine froze in the barrels and was sold by the pound. Despite governmental intervention the failure of the wheat crop led to speculation, inflation of the price of grain, and consequent hunger and starvation. Nevertheless, nothing was allowed to interfere with dynastic pleasure, and erstwhile enemies became comrades in its enjoyment.[82] On 22 October, Queen Eleanor of France entered Brussels, overjoyed to revisit her native town. She was accompanied by her stepson the Duke of Orleans as well as a great entourage including Madame d'Estampes, mistress of the French king. Tournaments, games, and balls followed in rapid succession.[83]

On 7 November the Estates also assembled in Brussels, and it was because of these varied affairs that Charles was detained in or near Brussels for the balance of 1544.[84] Thus it seems likely that Vesalius was also there as imperial physician, and no doubt he made the most of this opportunity for a reunion with his family and old friends. It was not long, however, before the emperor was once again in need of medical attention. On 2 December he had gone to Ghent, but two days after his arrival he suffered an attack of gout which was to last for six weeks.[85] As soon as he was able to travel his physicians advised him to return to Brussels, where the air suited him better, and on 15 January Charles set forth. The Venetian ambassador, who was present, wrote that "the poor prince has aroused the compassion of everyone, he is so pale, feeble, and ill. He is carried in a litter entirely enclosed, and it is with the greatest difficulty, supporting himself on a cane, that he is able to reach the litter." [86]

The emperor's woes at this time were increased by deteriorating commercial relations between England and the Netherlands. On 2 January, Nicholas Wotton, the English ambassador to the imperial court, was informed that a whole fleet of Flemish vessels had been captured by the English, and on 5 January the emperor ordered the officers of Flemish ports to arrest persons, ships, and goods of Englishmen. On 20 January, Wotton wrote to Henry VIII from Brussels that "the Emperor, by his physician's counsel, removed from Ghent towards Brussels the 15th present, carried in a litter, being not yet delivered of the gout," and 4 February added that "the Emperor, as it is spoken now, goeth not hence yet this month, and peradventure not this two months. One told me that he intendeth to use the diet of the wood of India, that which I suppose is not the guaiac, but another fashion, lighter to be observed than that." [87]

This was the first time Charles had subjected himself to the new treatment with the china root, and according to the Venetian ambassador there had been difference of opinion among the physicians of the court concerning the treatment to be used, guaiac wood or china root, with some even preferring cautery on the emperor's leg.[88] On 9 February, Wotton finally obtained audience with the emperor:

Coming to him, I found him sitting on a chair, his feet resting upon another low chair, bearing one of his arms in a towel, looking pale and weakly, worse than I saw him at any time before. After some communication of his disease, and how that the next day he was determined to enter into the diet of the wood of India, I began to declare my matter to him.[89]

Accordingly on 10 February Charles for the first time began to take the decoction of the china root, accompanied, at least in theory, by a slenderer diet than usual. The Venetian ambassador informs us that the emperor drank the decoction of the root twice in the morning for a week. His dinner, which followed, was comprised of meat and some wine, followed later by another draught of the decoction, and finally by a supper of almonds, pine nuts, and some pâté. His natural color returned, wrote the ambassador on 22 March, but he was still very weak. His left shoulder was still painful and he moved it with difficulty, while he could not bend the large toe of his right foot except with the aid of his hand.[90]

However, the Venetian ambassador, usually so exact in the information he gathered, appears to have been somewhat misled in regard to the details of the emperor's new treatment and apparently did not gain his information from Vesalius, who could have told him that the self-willed imperial patient was not one to heed the advice of his physicians. Vesalius later gave precise information on this incident in his *Letter on the china root*.[91]

Whatever the value of the china root, and its value was strongly doubted by Vesalius, Charles recovered, presumably as the result of a brief period of restricted diet and mild exercise as well as because of a native resiliency which, as Vesalius writes, was frequently apparent also in times of military activity.[92]

Sir William Paget, who had come over from England to join Wotton in an attempt to persuade Charles to renew the war with France, was very dubious about the emperor's illness and certainly took no stock in his diet, although, of course, the painfulness of the ailment may in some degree have been concealed from this new emissary. At any rate, on 1 March, and therefore before Navagero's account mentioned above, Paget wrote home that he had seen the emperor and "as for his sickness . . . I think verily he hath been no more sick than I am, but useth it for a policy. And as for the diet, he told me himself that he had left it a good while ago, fearing, I trow, I would have judged the same by his countenance, which is lusty, Mr. Wotton saith, as ever he hath seen it." [93] It was true, as Vesalius also indicated, that the patient had misbehaved in regard to his regimen and diet, a comon practice of the emperor, yet his health was hardly recovered. On 27 March the Venetian ambassador wrote, "As to the emperor, I found him very thin and pale. He had a band of black taffeta around his neck which, I suppose, served to support his left arm. The fingers of his hand were very thin and unlike their previous appearance." [94]

This opinion was more in accord with that of the Bishop of Cortona, the Tuscan ambassador, who called attention also to the emperor's tendency to be influenced by quacks—a matter with which Vesalius and Baersdorp were all too familiar:

One cannot write with truth that his Majesty is in good health since he remains debilitated, of poor color and little energy, although he has full freedom of his arm. What appears to me worthy of admiration and sympathy is the fact that his doctors in five months have given him thirteen medicines—of which the weakest was compounded of a drachm of rhubarb and some mushrooms—interspersing them with cassia and pills without number. Although I am aware that Doctor Zabaglia, who has his [Majesty's] life in his hands, is very ignorant, yet I do not know how the emperor can resist such purges and this regimen without the displeasure of his intimate servitors.[95]

Vesalius was in Brussels in attendance upon the emperor until the beginning of April when, finally, the emperor set out for the Diet of Worms,[96] and by then Vesalius was beginning to adjust to his new life and to demonstrate some originality in surgery. The Spanish surgeon Daza Chacon, also in Brussels at this time, gave the following account of Vesalius's surgical activity, which appears to represent the earliest deliberate operation for the relief of osteomyelitis at the lower end of the femur which, according to Daza Chacon, met with entirely favorable results:

> In the year '45 in Brussels, in company with Doctor Vesalius, in regard to a Flemish knight who was called Busquen and was of the chamber of the Emperor Charles: He [the knight] had a very severe pain in the inner part of the right thigh and three months of very serious illness, and because of the very trying and continuous pain he neither ate nor slept. He had been bled and purged many times, and given the china and sarsaparilla; yet all this did not help. We went to him to open the place where the pain was located, although there was no sign of any obstruction, and drew off a quantity of slightly whitish matter. As it came forth, instantly the sick man commenced to rest, to eat, and to sleep; and the outcome was so successful that where he had been almost consumed, now in a short time—as he was a youth—he was restored to full health.[97]

In 1544 Charles had promised that, at the next Diet, he would settle the religious difficulty of the empire, arisen from the Lutheran movement. The new Diet opened at Worms on 14 December 1544, and, although the emperor had been prevented by illness from attending the opening and had sent his brother Ferdinand and other representatives, with the meetings still in progress he prepared to join them.[98] From Brussels he traveled to Mechlin, thence to Anvers, to Lierre, and to Diest. In this last city, on the 1 and 2 May, following his usual annual practice, he celebrated a religious service for the repose of the soul of the late empress.[99] Then, as he wrote in his memoirs, for the fourth time he left the Queen of Hungary, his sister, as regent of the Netherlands, and for the seventh time he went to Worms by way of the Rhine.[100] Vesalius may have been with the imperial train although we have no evidence on this matter.

The religious question as it was considered at the Diet is of no present concern, but two events that occurred during the course of the Diet do have some relationship to Vesalius. By a clause in the Treaty of Crespy, Francis I was obliged to place a certain number of troops at imperial disposal for use against the Turks. Without wholly refusing this obligation, Francis offered to send an ambassador to the Sultan, accompanied by an imperial representative, to negotiate either peace with or a long truce between the Ottoman and Holy Roman Empires. Agreeing to this, Charles chose Vesalius's school-days' acquaintance, Gerard van Veltwyck, who came to Worms on 22 May to receive his instructions and on the same day set out for Venice to meet his French colleague and travel on to Constantinople.[101] In the *Letter on the china root* in 1546 Vesalius was to refer to this embassy and to information brought back by Veltwyck about certain exotic plants.

On 8 June, the emperor's son Philip, to whom Vesalius had dedicated the *Epitome*, became the father of his first son, the ill-fated Don Carlos with whom Vesalius was to be concerned some seventeen years later. The good news, however, was shortly dampened by word of the death of the infant's mother in childbed.[102]

Charles left Worms on 7 August, took ship down the Rhine from Bingen on the 9th, and continued without stop as far as Cologne, having traveled, according to the Venetian ambassador, farther in one day than the members of his court in two.[103] Charles remained in Cologne until 17 August, apparently accompanied by Vesalius who, in the following year, was to refer to "Cologne . . . when I was recently there" and mention meeting "our mutual friend the distinguished physician [of Cologne] Joannes Eck."[104]

From Cologne the emperor continued to Juliers, Maestricht, Saint-Trond, and finally on 20 August he reached Louvain where he was awaited by his sister Mary, regent of the Netherlands during his absence, and returned with her to Brussels for the obsequies of 25 and 26 August related to the death of Prince Philip's wife.[105] It seems quite likely that Vesalius accompanied the emperor and welcomed this opportunity to return to his native city and visit his family and friends.

During the remainder of the year Charles traveled about the Netherlands, eventually making for Utrecht for a chapter of the Order of the Golden Fleece, but was detained at 's Hertogenbosch by another attack of gout "which obliged him to delay and to postpone the chapter until later when he felt better."[106] There had not been a chapter of the order since 1531, at least partly because of the emperor's attacks of illness. In 1543 he had decreed a chapter for May of the following year, but it had had to be postponed as a result of the Diet of Speyer and the problems consequent upon it. Finally, in October 1545, he declared that the meeting would be held in Utrecht in November, but again insurmountable obstacles arose and it was only with the opening of December that he was able to set out for Utrecht. His train was far from pleased, and it may be that Vesalius was numbered among the disgruntled, since winter had set in and made the roads very bad.[107] It was at this time that the emperor's physicians advised him that in the future his health demanded that he rest in the winter and travel only during the milder seasons.[108] Possibly they gave thought on this occasion to their own health as well as the emperor's. At any rate he recovered, whether or not from the ministrations of the physicians, and on Christmas Day was able to attend mass in the cathedral.[109] He left 's Hertogenbosch on the 28th and entered Utrecht on 30 December.[110]

On 2 January 1546 the belated chapter of the order of the Golden Fleece began to hold its ceremonies and feasts at Utrecht.[111] If one considers that the emperor's gout was aggravated by his unwise diet, then a mere glance at the menu for the dinner served at that Saturday meeting and at the one for the similar dinner the following day, 3 January, suggests that Charles's condition was shortly to be aggravated again.[112] Sure enough, on 6 January, Charles had his first symptoms and was unable to attend services in the church.[113] For several days he was compelled to keep to his bed and the chevaliers had to hold their deliberations in his chamber.[114] Charles's condition continued to become worse so that the election of the new chevaliers to the order was postponed until 17 January,[115] and for a time it was thought that Charles would have to return to Brussels to take treatment as in the previous year—that is, with the decoction of the china root.[116] This does not mean that the emperor had no medical attendants with him at Utrecht, since it was his custom to be well attended, and very likely both Baersdorp and Vesalius were at hand. Rather it was the lack of the decoction of the china root or the necessary ingredients for such a decoction in Utrecht, as well as the greater convenience of spending the period of bed rest in Brussels. This attack Charles counted as his twelfth.[117]

However, with the worst of the attack apparently weathered, Charles remained in Utrecht for the conclusion of the ceremonies. On 3 February he departed by way of Wageningen, reached Arnheim on the 4th, Zutphen on the 7th, and Nymwegen on the 9th.[118] Here, as we read in the *Letter on the china root*, Vesalius was left behind to attend the ailing Venetian ambassador Bernardo Navagero. "By command of the emperor and because of the illness of Master Navagero it was necessary for me to delay so long . . . in Nymwegen." [119] He found the task a tedious one,[120] but at least it gave him the opportunity to attend to certain personal interests, notably a visit to the tombs of his ancestors at Wesel, which has already been mentioned.[121]

Since Navagero, in his own right a person of importance, was also a friend of Vesalius from Paduan days as well as the unwitting cause of the composition of the *Letter on the china root* at this time, he deserves some notice. Bernardo Navagero was born in 1507 to Gian Luigi Navagero, senator and member of a distinguished patrician family of Venice, and to Laura or Lucrezia Agostini. After initial studies in Venice under the direction of the grammarian Stefano Plazonio, Bernardo passed to Padua at the age of twenty. There he studied philosophy under Marcantonio Genua, or Genoa, of Padua, and Vincenzo Maggi of Brescia, the former a close friend of Vesalius. After Navagero had obtained a degree in law in 1529, and upon the death of his father, who had left his family in some financial difficulties, he returned to Venice. In 1532 he was admitted to the Collegio de' Savj, a school for those intending to undertake a career in governmental service, and in 1534 he was sent to Dalmatia to investigate the administration of the Venetian agent there, Marcantonio Mula, who had been accused of malfeasance. In 1540 Navagero was made ambassador to Cardinal Ercole Gonzaga, regent of Mantua, and upon his return to Venice became overseer of the trade with Damascus, and then Savio or consultant on military affairs.[122]

In 1543 Navagero was selected as Venetian ambassador to the imperial court. He received his commission at Bassano, 18 September, and reached the imperial camp at Mons where he presented his credentials on 26 October.[123] Thereafter he had an interview with Mary of Hungary but it was not until 20 November at Valenciennes that the emperor finally gave him an audience.[124]

During these years the life of an ambassador to the imperial court was hardly an easy one. In 1543 it had been necessary for Navagero to follow the emperor in the field in the autumn campaign against the French, where he may have met his old friend Vesalius, and the same situation was repeated in 1544 when he did indeed meet Vesalius. Even when Charles remained for a considerable time in Brussels in 1545, the situation was far from restful. The plague had broken out, "increasing rather than diminishing" during the time Navagero spent there.[125] This life of a peregrinating ambassador did not agree with him and, in his dispatch of 22 January 1545, he reminded the doge that he had already spent seventeen months on his embassy, "always in the midst of war, fatigues, and miserable conditions of all sorts," and requested that he be relieved. He was suffering from an old indisposition and a vertigo that was once again giving him trouble. A year passed, and the following January he again mentioned his poor condition which was more and more aggravated by the unfavorable mode of life to which he was forced to submit.[126] Finally, in a dispatch from Nymwegen, he announced that he had been seized by a fever of such violence as to make further travel impossible. The emperor had continued to Ratisbon but had left one of his best physicians in attendance upon the ailing ambassador, "Doctor Vesalius, a great servant of the Venetian Republic, and a good friend of mine."[127] Navagero, with Vesalius in attendance, was forced to remain in Nymwegen until 11 April, although it appears that Vesalius's activities were not too restricted since he was able to pay the visit to Wesel and to give his thoughts to his dispute with Sylvius, which led to the composition of the *Letter on the china root.*

Meanwhile, the Venetian government had finally hearkened to the appeals of its ambassador and had sent a replacement, Alvise Mocenigo, who had expected to meet Navagero at Ratisbon, but learned from his government that "my distinguished predecessor has remained at Nymwegen because of his indisposition."[128] On 14 April Mocenigo wrote that he had heard from Navagero's secretary, who had written on 5 March that the patient was no better and his fever continued, but he was relieved to discover that the emperor had shown his favor to Navagero by leaving a physician in attendance.[129] On 19 April Mocenigo wrote a further dispatch in which he stated that that morning he had seen a letter from Brussels, dated 6 April, in which it was stated that the physician attendant upon Navagero had written to a relative on 25 March announcing that the ambassador was in better shape and hoped from day to day to continue the trip to Ratisbon.

Finally, on 11 April, Navagero and Vesalius were able to proceed, traveling up the Rhine to Cologne, thence by boat as far as Frankfurt, and by wagon to Nuremberg,[130] reaching Ratisbon on 7 May.[131] Navagero was still ill but he had wanted to push on since he was unaware that another Venetian representative had arrived, but so weak was he that for three days after his arrival he was compelled to remain in bed.[132] "I, Bernardo, find myself yet in bed . . . yesterday the fever returned and gave me a little trouble." [133] On 28 May Navagero was "still suffering from his fever," [134] and on 13 June Mocenigo wrote that on the previous day Navagero, although still indisposed, had set out for Venice in a litter.[135]

The case was not a triumph for Vesalius, yet from our point of view there appears little he could have done in that age of limited therapeutics. A dispatch of 10 May described the complaint as a tertian fever, and if this was so the best treatment was probably a change of location.

It may have been at this time that Vesalius was given one of the emperor's goblets, perhaps as a present for his attention to Navagero, which the physician in turn presented to the poet Caspar Brusch. In return for this gift Brusch, crowned Poet Laureate by Charles in 1541, produced a poem, "The Imperial Crystal Goblet which Andreas Vesalius, Imperial Physician, gave to Brusch." [136]

Upon reaching Venice, Navagero consulted physicians there and finally was cured, as he said, "through the efforts of Giambattista da Monte, the distinguished Veronese physician," as well as the former teacher of Vesalius at Padua. Certainly Navagero was able to hold many important positions in the ensuing years, including those of overseer of the University of Padua and podestà of Padua. Upon the death of his wife, Istriana Lando, he entered the church, becoming Bishop of Verona and Cardinal. He died 25 May 1565, thus outliving his physician Vesalius.

Meanwhile, the emperor and his retinue, after leaving Navagero and Vesalius at Nymwegen, had continued to Maestricht, which was reached on 19 February. From 24 to 29 March the imperial party was in Speyer, and entered Ratisbon on 10 April.[137] The Diet for which the emperor had made his journey was a failure before it opened, due to the already convinced differences on both sides of the paramount religious question, and the representatives were slow to gather. The gout that had attacked the emperor at the opening of the year and impeded his travel to Ratisbon once again flared up. On 22 April Mocenigo reported that "yesterday his imperial Majesty began to take the china water." [138] On 28 April Charles was still in retirement and "did not wish to give audience to anyone." [139] On 3 May the emperor was "completing his course of treatment with the china water and was going to spend a week at a castle six leagues from the city [Straubing]." [140] Of course, during this period Vesalius was not available and we may assume that the emperor was attended by Baersdorp and other imperial physicians. Returned to Ratisbon, Charles, despite gloomy forebodings of the failure of the Diet, seems to have become very cheerful and entered into the gay life of the city—so much so as to take a mistress, Barbara Blomberg, who was in time to give birth to the later-celebrated Don John of Austria.[141] With the representatives finally assembled, the Diet opened on 5 June and dissolved on 24 July.[142]

Sometime during this period there arrived in Ratisbon one Francesco d'Este, brother of Ercole II of Ferrara, who had earlier served the emperor in a military capacity, notably in 1544 in the assaults upon Saint Dizier and Vitry.[143] It is not clear whether he had arrived in Ratisbon with the emperor in April or had come later. At any rate, he had fallen gravely ill in the city and upon news of this Ercole immediately sent his physician Giambattista Canano to supervise Francesco's care.[144] Vesalius, too, was consulted, and the two physicians met over the sickbed of their patient. Since mutual admiration had existed from the time of their first meeting in 1542 in Ferrara, they must have been pleasantly surprised to discover that their previous acquaintance could now be renewed. Many years later, in his *Examen*, Vesalius referred to this meeting at Ratisbon when Canano revealed to him his discovery of the existence of valves in the orifices of certain veins, which opposed the reflux of the blood. It is of this incident that Vesalius spoke in reply to doubts on the existence of the valves in the veins expressed by Fallopio in his *Institutiones anatomicae:*

When I visited the ailing Francesco d'Este with [Canano] at Ratisbon, the latter told me that at the commencement of the azygos vein, as well as in the orifices of the veins entering the kidneys and of the vein found near the upper region of the sacrum, he had observed membranes similar to those occurring at the origins of the pulmonary artery and the aorta, and he asserted that they prevented the reflux of the blood.[145]

Upon his arrival in Ratisbon Vesalius had discovered among the letters awaiting him there one from Joachim Roelants,[146] a physician of Mechlin, requesting information about the preparation, use, and value of the china root, the drug that had recently come into vogue and, in certain cases, threatened to replace the older guaiac wood. As has been seen, it had already been employed by Vesalius in treatment of the emperor. Roelants was an old and close friend, and more recently Vesalius had demonstrated an interest in the career of his son who had gone to Paris to study medicine:

When your son left for study in Paris I gave him letters of recommendation for Vasses, Fernel, Oliverius, and others whose knowledge I admire, but especially, as you know, for Sylvius. In my letter [to Sylvius] I added some remarks about our common study and also requested him to inform me if anything in my anatomical books did not meet with his approval, because I thought that whatever I might publish would be of interest to him who has the reputation of a great anatomist in his country, and because I had studied medicine under him.[147]

Sylvius replied in a long and far-from-complimentary letter, transmitted to Vesalius by young Roelants, and during his enforced leisure at Nymwegen Vesalius answered this with a defense of the *Fabrica*, the younger Roelants again being the means of transmittal. The father was aware that an exchange of some sort had taken place. "You wondered what the papers were I sent to Sylvius, and if they were a letter for him what subject it dealt with, believing that it contained something about our common studies that you also would like to know." [148] Vesalius sought to answer these questions in a long letter that, although called the *Letter on the china root,* deals at much greater length with the defense of the *Fabrica* against Galenist attack, and concludes with some observations on his life before and after the publication of that work. The letter was meant to be a personal communication despite its great length, even though it was actually published very shortly afterward through the agency of Franciscus Vesalius, who was still studying medicine in Ferrara. The reasons behind the publication are explained by Franciscus in a prefatory dedication to Cosimo de' Medici, the young Duke of Tuscany:

> Not long ago a young man named Jacobus Scepperus came here to study . . . He showed me, among other things, a letter written by my brother Andreas. . . . he told me he had copied this letter from the original . . . and he said that copies of it were in the possession of various Netherlanders who, like him, thought that it deserved to be published and made generally available. Since several persons here supported this opinion after they had seen it, I at once asked Scepperus to make me a copy of my brother's letter so that I might send it as soon as possible to Joannes Oporinus, a very careful and learned printer. . . . I hoped thus to prevent an undesirable edition of the letter by some mean and careless printer who might publish it solely for his financial gain, and I am well aware of the affection that exists between Oporinus and my brother and of how carefully Oporinus has always printed his works. . . . I have been unable to consult my brother about the publication of this letter, which I believe ought to be entitled a book because of its length and variety of content—since unexpectedly in the writing it grew to the size of a book—except that it is in the form of a letter. . . . I hope [my brother] will approve my diligent efforts and not be angered because I have undertaken this publication, seeking to forestall others.[149]

Turning from the prefatory words of Franciscus Vesalius to those of Andreas in the letter proper, addressed to "that very learned gentleman and dear friend, Joachim Roelants, leading physician of Mechlin," we find that the writer almost at once took up the question of the china root:

> You asked me to describe the way in which the decoction of the so-called china root was recently given to the emperor and to many others of our court, as well as my opinion about the results obtained and for what diseases it was used. My countryman Antonio Zucca [150] has also urged me to answer these questions . . . and it is astonishing to observe how anxiously the German physicians at the princely courts of this region also inquire about the preparation of the decoction. They are never satisfied until they have obtained that prescription they believe we use for the decoction, and there are those who, in seeking to gain this information, have recommended the decoction to their princes so strongly that they in turn have not hesitated to request the emperor to order me to supply them with its prescription. Such is the popularity the emperor's name has given this medicine in a brief time, although in fact he has taken it more by his own choice than on the advice of Master Cornelius, his favorite physician since the departure of Master Caballus.[151]

Earlier, as Vesalius continued:

> . . . when I was treating the sick in Venice under the direction of the most famous professors there, that root had made its appearance and had been received with great hope and praise, but subsequent unhappy results in two cases in which it had been used led to disappointment.[152]

Still later:

> . . . after the use of the china had been discounted and ridiculed by everyone . . . a physician arrived from Antwerp who proclaimed himself the only one who knew the proper preparation of genuine china and was able to bring relief no matter how serious the patient's illness. This man, who did possess a certain degree of knowledge, gained the confidence of the nobility so that the china was sent to the Bishop of Verona . . . but before that good man had really started to take the medicine he departed for the supernal regions. In consequence the china became wholly neglected, and as long as I was in Italy I had no more confidence in it than did my teachers.[153]

Although the vogue of china root had been a short one at Padua and Venice, its popularity had been revived in Brussels at the imperial court:

> Last year the famous Giovanni Batista Gastaldo was confined to his bed through a considerable part of the winter, suffering a weakness of a nervous type below the loins, as well as a weakness of the stomach. He seemed to be restored to health at the beginning of spring and, after he had already begun to recover his health, at the instigation of certain friends, he used the china decoction with successful results, like those Spanish nobles who, as you know, came from Mechlin to Brussels and who more than anyone else sang the praises of the china. . . . Also at that time four or five sufferers from syphilis urged their physicians to prepare the decoction of china for them, too, with a sufficiently satisfactory result in some of the cases; however, in others, who had been gravely afflicted by the disease, we observed much less success than we might have hoped for had we used the decoction of guaiac wood. As a result . . . the emperor at that time looked upon the china with less favor and employed the decoction of guaiac for his gout and generally poor health. Since some, however, were never ending in their praise of the new drug, and several Spanish bishops considered nothing more admirable for all sicknesses than this china, they with other distinguished men urged the emperor on, asserting that not long since the guaiac wood had come to be looked upon with disfavor in Spain and in certain parts of Italy, as various letters of their friends attested. [As a result] the emperor was seized by a desire to employ the china decoction, influenced the more easily because it had been recommended strongly and because it need be used for such a short period while the regimen of diet was less restricted than with the guaiac decoction. In consequence, as soon as it was learned that the most powerful ruler in the world was using the china, others imagined that it was the most wonderful remedy and were not content until they too had made use of it.[154]

However, as Vesalius continues, the emperor's case was no recommendation for the china root:

> The emperor's case is not a very good recommendation since he used it for only two weeks and without a systematic regimen of diet, changing the rules to suit himself whenever he was not suffering from asthma or one of his periodic attacks of gout. Yet it must be noted that a year ago he could not easily move his left

shoulder with the aid of the deltoid muscle, but he can do it now. Furthermore, he is free of the pain in his left leg . . . which a year ago bothered him in walking.[155]

It is fairly apparent that Vesalius was dubious of the medicinal value of the china root. The history of its usage and the result obtained left much to be desired, yet in all fairness the emperor was enjoying better health after his brief and casual employment of the drug, and one could not entirely discount the possibility that the china root had some merit. Vesalius was properly cautious in view of his somewhat limited personal knowledge of the drug, especially since he had not had the opportunity to observe its correct and systematic use on his patients. Moreover:

Thus far I do not even know the proper name of the root that is variously called chyna, chynna, or cyna, and you spell it even echina and achyna. It seems to have taken its name from some island or some place in India or in the New World. It is imported by those who import pepper, cloves, ginger, and cinnamon, by Portuguese as well as by imperial seafarers. They say that it is gathered near the seashore, and probably it grows in swampy places near the sea.[156]

Vesalius also made inquiries:

. . . [of] our mutual friend Gerard [van Veltwyck], who is much interested in botany, if he had gained any certain information about the china root during his mission in Turkey. However, I learned nothing except that it is also imported into Constantinople and employed there by a certain Jew with less success than his patients hoped for and expected. I obtained no information from the merchants except that the china root is found at the seashore and . . . some pretend that they use it against all kinds of diseases in order to create more demand for it.[157]

Despite this ignorance of the root's pedigree and usage, it was considered best to select the heavier, sappier pieces, avoiding the wormy and decayed, and always, of course, remaining on guard against the frauds of the pharmacists.[158] Finally, it ought to be noted that china root lacked taste and odor. In summation: "I believe it less worthy of praise and commendation than the guaiac wood, and note that many of our domestic medicines are able to produce good results in cases where the china root is supposed to be the final word." [159] Although this was Vesalius's opinion, his friend was at liberty to make his own decision and, if he still desired to use the new medicine, the elaborate method of preparing the decoction and the regimen of diet and rest for the patient were fully described.[160]

As the whole subject seems an unprofitable one from our viewpoint, one senses that Vesalius, too, wrote at some length only to satisfy the duty of friendship. It is clear that he had previously investigated the therapeutic value of the china root with all that spirit of inquiry he had used in previous years to investigate the human structure. Medicine as contrasted to anatomy was a far-from-scientific study, but within the possible limits he had found nothing to convince him that the new drug had values to replace guaiac wood in the pharmacopeia. The older drug, as we now know, was also worthless but tradition was on its side.

It seems to have been with some relief that Vesalius passed to his second subject, the defense of his anatomical method and doctrines, as expressed in the *Fabrica*, against Sylvius and the Galenists. The subject is opened with a general statement in which he describes, with no little bitterness and disillusionment, the old, conservative forces against which the new spirit of scientific inquiry had to contend:

During the war just started by our great and merciful emperor with great vigor but no less desire of ensuring peace and unity in Germany—would that this were clear to all—we shall not be very much occupied with the Gallic disease, obstructions of the bowel, and long lasting weaknesses, which are the usual complaints of my patients, but with fractured bones, dislocations, wounds, and the like. . . . Furthermore, I shall sometimes have to resort to surgery if the empirics will permit that. When I see the necessity of surgery I cannot help putting my hand to the task at once, although I avoid it in those illnesses in which medical treatment is clearly indicated, for the judgment of men is so depraved that they contend that surgery does not suit the physician.

This idea is particularly encouraged by those physicians who know nothing of medicine except the use of a few laxatives and syrups prepared for purging humors. . . . In addition, these pestilential creatures calumniate anyone whom they discover to know something unknown to them, admitting that he is skilled in such things but that he is no physician . . . as if great diligence in some of the disciplines underlying medicine might detract from his knowledge of medicine. All too well do I know how some . . . have been calumniated before princes by the unlearned who disregard all study and think only of making money. You yourself know how my investigations and publications in anatomy were opposed to me when I first arrived at court.

But, my dear Joachim, such is our mortal fate, and each has his own trials to bear. We are constantly faced with burdens which make us wish for escape from this life, as all those know who take pleasure in publishing the results of their researches—men who, because they do not know how to be born and pass away unnoticed, so expose themselves to all sorts of insults. It is their own fault that they constantly hear remarks about their writings that gnaw at the soul, and it is for that reason that I am content to live at court far from the sweet leisure of studies. No longer do I profess medicine at Pisa at a salary of 800 crowns, under the patronage of Cosimo de' Medici, illustrious Duke of Tuscany, and Maecenas of the sciences which are declining in most places. Thus I would not consider publishing anything new even if I wanted to do so very much or if my vanity urged me to it.[161]

They ought to be grateful to me as the first who has dared to attack man's false opinions, to lay bare the extraordinary frauds of the Greeks, and to provide our contemporaries with an unusual opportunity for searching out the truth. Such, however, is not the case, and because of Galen's authority you will find many who, having glanced at my efforts only superficially and without investigation of the cadaver, still maintain that what Galen wrote is wholly correct.[162]

Although it was true that:

The writings of many learned men commend my youthful efforts far more than they deserve and willingly confess that they prefer to put trust in their eyes rather than in Galen's writings, nevertheless I understand that there are many who, although they agree that my work has virtue and credit me with ability beyond my merits, yet are angry with me for Galen's sake. Among them is Jacobus Sylvius, leading physician of our day, who, in a letter transmitted by your son, expressed his opinion very strongly even though he declared that he had not read my books *De humani corporis fabrica*. Consequently you can easily gather what was in the letter I sent to you from Nymwegen so that it might be transmitted to Sylvius by your son. In that letter I replied to Sylvius, adding things here and there that, in my disturbed state of mind, seemed a proper reply, but most of them referring to anatomy, remarks by which the falseness of his assertions was revealed and by which my own position was explained.[163]

Sylvius replied in his usual way, declaring that he did not consider himself of sufficient erudition or authority to desire to judge in such an important matter, but that nevertheless he would express his opinion briefly because I had asked for it. After he stated that I had improperly criticized Galen, he asserted that what had offended him most of all was my bold declaration that Galen had not dissected human bodies, that he had only looked at the veins in the hands of living persons, and that he had copied his *Use of parts* from the writings of others. . . . He declared that he remains firmly convinced that Galen's description of the human body is without error in every instance in which I claim that Galen's description is wholly or partly incorrect or that he has been forgetful or explained the body's functions imperfectly or used faulty reasoning to support his doctrines.

Sylvius is the last one from whom I should have expected such an opinion. . . . Nor can I accept his proposal that, if I withdraw my false statements regarding Galen and attribute them to my youthfulness and to the influence of the Italians who oppose Galen, he will do his best during his lectures to conceal from his audience the fact that he does not approve of my work. He wrote that he made this offer because he likes and respects me and wishes to keep my friendship, and because he feels that we could not remain friends if we were to disagree over Galen. In order to frighten me still more, he added that even if he were to remain silent himself, others might disclose his true opinion of my work, for some of his students, whom he considers as very capable anatomists, are sharpening their pens against me because they are indignant that I should make remarks against Galen, master of all physicians. Hence he asked me what I wanted him to do for me in the matter, and of course he meant that I ought to desire to retract and so escape those sharp pens of his students.[164]

This was the first exchange that closed with Sylvius's ultimatum, and to which Vesalius replied; it is this reply, reproduced for Roelants, that comprises the second part of the *Letter on the china root*:

I shall be very happy to write for you in detail what I wrote to Sylvius to confute his arguments. Although I did not keep a copy of my letter, since I replied hurriedly because a messenger was waiting, nevertheless I kept a record of the contents. . . . I began my letter to Sylvius by saying that I was less upset by his remarks because I had seen many very learned physicians and philosophers who had been just as angry as he because I had said such things about Galen. These men could not believe that the father of medicine had made such mistakes in the anatomical books he felt he had written with so much care and accuracy, the more so since it was a subject in which he had acquired greater authority than anyone else, even during his own lifetime. Gradually, however, they began to change their attitude, and there was not one among them who, with the cadaver before him, could continue to defend Galen. However reluctantly, they came to put more faith in their eyes than in the words of Galen. It is my hope that eventually Sylvius, too, will change his mind as he reads through what I have written and that he will not deny me his good will and friendship. However, as I wrote, whatever the case may be I should consider it as merely one of the misfortunes of mortals that must be borne, as I have not yet learned to speak counter to my own belief.

Furthermore, that which he criticized in me becomes greater every day. That youthfulness with which Sylvius charges me has passed, but my increased years have not made me change my opinion. I shall not mention how much I was hurt by the retreat he offered me—the pretense that the Italians dislike Galen, because nowhere is Galen more respected and honored than in Italy. This is fully proved by their publication of his works, even if they have not entirely discarded the Arabs and removed them from the medical curriculum.[165] I should certainly be guilty of the greatest impertinence if I were to accuse such learned men, my kind friends to whom I am indebted, of being responsible for what he calls my error. Those Italians, like Sylvius, usually opposed me, although I had never seen any of them put a hand to the cadaver before they first attended my dissections, and they are well aware that none of them was ever my instructor or helper in these matters.[166]

The letter to Sylvius continued with a general assertion that traditional authority must bow to the evidence of the senses, particularly in respect to Galen, an authority who had probably never seen a human dissection. "He remarks that he had seen two dried cadavers suitable for observation of the skeletal structure, but he never mentions human dissection except in the instance of a German soldier—at which dissection, however, he was not present." [167]

Moreover, wrote Vesalius, since there are distinct differences between animal and human bones, "it is clear that Galen described the bones of the monkey, not of the human." Proof is found in his description of certain sutures of the upper jaw. His statement that the lower jaw could be separated into two parts by boiling is similar indication of animal anatomy, although "respect for Galen compels us to admit that on one occasion he may have observed the jaw of a recently born child . . . to have been composed of two parts." His descriptions also indicate that he had not seen a human hyoid bone nor had he had opportunity to study the human vertebrae and the articulations of the ribs themselves.[168] The descriptions of the sacrum and coccyx in *On the bones* and the *Anatomical procedures* are good insofar as the monkey is concerned, but they are by no means suited to the human. The sternum of seven bones again points to the monkey or dog.[169] One could provide many other instances, too, "to prove that Galen had never been properly acquainted with [the bones of] the human skeleton." [170]

Galen's denial of the existence of fat between the skin and fleshy membrane also indicates he was describing animals rather than man, as can easily be learned by observing a butcher skinning a cow or a sheep.[171] The attribution to man of certain muscles, which he does not possess but the monkey does, is further proof of Vesalius's proper criticism, as is also Vesalius's differentiation between muscles that exist in both, such as the levator scapulae muscle. Galen's description of the trapezius muscle as it refers to man is faulty and could only have been based upon dissection of the dog,[172] and his description of the semispinalis capitis muscle "clearly demonstrates that he had dissected it in the dog and monkey." [173] Furthermore, Vesalius explains why his own description in the *Fabrica* of the foetal coverings was so defective,[174] and recapitulates his arguments in opposition to Galen's views on the movements of the head.[175]

These examples indicate the character of the anatomical part of the work in which the defense against Sylvius's criticisms of the *Fabrica* was based upon a demonstration of Galen's error resulting from dependence upon the dissection of animals. Vesalius was thus stressing those aspects of the *Fabrica* that had been attacked, enlarging upon certain matters he had dealt with already, but emphasizing the reasons for his statements. He did not expect physicians to be won over readily to his point of view since, according to his continued remarks, by and large they still gave their allegiance to Galen; consequently Vesalius found it difficult even to refer to any he would consider true anatomists:

This is the reason I am so greatly astonished at Dryander's letter, shown me by our mutual friend Johannes Eck, eminent physician of Cologne,[176] in which Dryander complained that I didn't enumerate [in the *Fabrica*] the distinguished professors of anatomy of our day, such as, among several others—who they may be I don't know—Jean Guinter, my teacher of anatomy. I esteem Guinter for many reasons, and in my books I call him a teacher of medicine, but I do not consider him an anatomist, and I should willingly suffer him to inflict as many cuts upon me as I have seen him attempt on man or any other animal—except at the dinner table. I believe that Guinter will not be angry, since it is known to many others, when I say that I owe him nothing in this branch of our art or that he has accomplished anything beyond the books of Galen. I believe, however, that Dryander said this believing that he has been injured because he is not included among the well-known anatomists and is unhappy because I wrote that a certain person in Marburg had published illustrations taken everywhere from the books of others as if they were his own. Not for a moment did the thought enter my head that it was Dryander himself who had published those anatomical works that I thought certain printers, borrowing his name to make them more desirable, had published in Latin and German solely for their sordid profit. But if Dryander was the author, as indeed I am now persuaded he was, he gave no reason for including a catalogue of the celebrated anatomists of our day in the preface to my books and he must be content with my general censure of them.[177]

I must bear it calmly that he, like so many others who have hitherto written against me, resents Vesalius, and that it will please him that Cornarius is soon to emendate Galen and Aristotle in all those places where I have criticized them.[178] He wrote this in that same letter to Eck, and yet he desires to be counted among the anatomists who use their own hands. Dryander ought rather to perform that task, using his hands [i.e., dissecting], which Cornarius is about to undertake, thereby interrupting those labors by which he enriches our common studies; especially since this emendation of Galen can only be achieved by systematic, accurate dissections of man, monkey, and other animals and not through Dryander's books, or rather those of others [which he has plagiarized].

May malice and ridicule of one's efforts not discourage an active person and lessen his opportunities and those of others, especially since there are so few who deserve praise for their studies. One ought to devote all effort to seeking the truth, and those who possess some special ability for medicine ought to search for that truth rather than calumniate others. Holding this opinion, I grieve for Cornarius and Fuchs because they have tarnished their otherwise celebrated names by employing such abusive language against one another, they who have been considered abroad as distinguished ornaments of Germany. Let them stop wasting their strength which ought to be used for the glory of Germany and the Netherlands.[179]

Because of my esteem for you and my wish to gossip and converse with you freely, I have written not a true book but rather a letter, and however extended it is it was no effort to write since I was especially aided by my clear recollection of what I had achieved with great effort and despite unpleasantness. I surely deserved something better than the slander of those who are so furiously aroused against me because their studies have not been so successful, because I don't accept Galen, and because I refuse to disbelieve my own eyes and reason for his sake. I am astonished at Sylvius who, later in his letter, seemed to be a little less angry and added that he very much wished that I had treated this subject more quietly and discreetly, here almost seeming to suspect that all is not correct in Galen. He wrote that he wished I had added to Galen's works those criticisms I felt compelled to make [in a separate book], just as his students are doing with the remarks they are taking from my books and whom he seeks to persuade to sharpen their pens against me. However, it is he, not his pupils, who attacks me.

I could have done nothing more worthwhile than to give a new description of the whole human body, of which nobody understood the anatomy, while Galen, despite his extensive writings, has offered very little on the subject, and I don't see how I could have presented my efforts to the students differently. . . . Sylvius advised me to consider well and at length my Annotations on Galen, which I occasionally mentioned in the chapter [in the *Fabrica*] on the muscles moving the forearm, as if I should have made mistakes in my books because of my youth and precipitate publication, when, in fact, without wife, children, and domestic cares, enjoying the pleasant conversation of colleagues, it was the time best suited for anatomical studies.

At present I shouldn't willingly spend long hours in the Cemetery of the Innocents in Paris turning over bones, nor go to Montfaucon to look at bones—where once with a companion I was gravely imperiled by the many savage dogs. Nor should I care to be locked out of Louvain so that, alone in the middle of night, I might take away bones from the gibbet to prepare a skeleton. I shall no longer bother to petition the judges to delay an execution to a time suitable for dissection, nor shall I advise the students to observe where someone has been buried or urge them to make note of the diseases of their teachers' patients so that they might later secure the bodies. I shall not keep in my bedroom for several weeks bodies taken from graves or given me after public executions, nor shall I put up with the bad temper of sculptors and painters who made me more miserable than did the bodies I was dissecting. However, too young to gain financially from the art, and wishing to learn and to advance our common studies, I readily and cheerfully supported all these things.

I shall not speak of the enthusiasm with which I performed public dissections in three Italian universities during three weeks of one year. If I had postponed my writings until the present, when I am older, my anatomical efforts would not now be in the hands of students—my books that may, in the future, be preferred to a reheated Mesue or Gatinaria or Estienne for distinctions, different causes and symptoms of diseases, and their illustrations, or, finally, to a reheated part of the *Servitor pharmacopolarum.*

As for my Annotations, which grew to a large volume, as well as a complete paraphrase of the ten books of Rhazes, *Ad Regem Almansorem,* written by me much more accurately than that one I produced on the ninth book, and the outline for a book on medical prescriptions—a collection of material I believe to have been of no little value—they were all destroyed by me one day together with all of Galen's books I had used in teaching anatomy and in which, in the usual way, I I had written various annotations. When I left Italy and went to the court and those physicians, whom you know, in the presence of the emperor and other important persons, expressed the worst possible criticisms of my books and all that nowadays is published for the advancement of learning, I burned everything with the idea that in the future I should write nothing more. However, I have regretted it several times, and I am sorry that I did not allow myself to be dissuaded by my friends who were present.

Nevertheless, I have no regrets about the Annotations because even if I still had them I couldn't publish them without producing more enemies. Already the few remarks in my books that contradict Galen have made many people furious, and even before my books were published three years ago those people began to prepare a defense of Galen. . . . I do not regret the loss of my copies of Galen's books since they might have fallen into the hands of those who couldn't distinguish between good and bad marginalia. You know yourself how many times it happens during lectures in school, or after a first reading, that one writes notes in the margins of his books that later seem stupid and ridiculous. I say this because I read Galen's *De ossibus* to the students at least three times before I dared call attention to his mistakes, although now I can't be sufficiently astonished at my own stupidity for being so blinded that I didn't understand what was written. However, I regret very much the loss of the Paraphrase because I had given much effort to a comparison of the Moslems, Galen, and other Greeks on those parts of the art discussed by Rhazes in each book.[180]

Finally, Vesalius turned from criticism of the *Fabrica* and the new scientific method that had produced it to one of the results of approval of his efforts—the vexing problem of plagiarism. This was not a new source of irritation since the success of the earlier *Tabulae anatomicae* and consequent plagiarism of its illustrations had caused him to speak forth on the subject in his letter to Oporinus, prefixed to the *Fabrica.*[181] The problem was one on which he had obviously expressed his feelings to his brother Franciscus at some earlier time, since in the introduction to the *Letter on the china root* Franciscus referred to it, although incorrectly charging John Caius with responsibility for that plagiarism produced by Thomas Geminus in London in 1545.[182] Obviously, too, since the complaints of the two brothers refer to crudity of reproduction by the plagiarist and reduction in size of the illustrations, they must never have seen Geminus's handsome copper-engraved reproductions but have heard of them only at second hand. In the words of Franciscus:

Would that the books of the *Fabrica* with its *Epitome* had not been so shamefully and wholly spoiled by a certain Englishman—who had even, I believe, at one time lived with my brother. He added to the *Epitome* . . . certain parts borrowed from [the *Fabrica*] and so completely spoiled that which had first caused it to be admired. Furthermore, its elegant woodcut illustrations were reproduced with such ridiculous crudity that [those of Geminus] have no resemblance to those of Oporinus's magnificent edition. Hence it seems to me that, not unjustly, [Vesalius] may demand that his name be removed from that very inept English edition lest anyone ever believe that he had brought forth such a poorly represented and almost completely ruined series of illustrations of the nerves and vessels. It is astonishing that that plagiarist of the efforts of others, since he suffers so much from the itch for writing, did not read the letter prefixed to the [*Fabrica*] in which my brother wrote that he would willingly send the blocks, which were prepared at his own expense, to any conscientious printer rather than have them reproduced poorly and in reduced size.[183]

This opinion is echoed somewhat more strenuously by Andreas Vesalius at the close of his *Letter on the china root*:

Just now in England . . . the illustrations of my *Epitome* have been copied so poorly and without artistic skill—although not without expense for whoever must bear it—that I should be ashamed if anyone were to believe me responsible for them. For, not to mention other things, the courses of the vessels, which my friends know that I myself depicted in my books, have been so misrepresented that, in addition to the matter of proportion, everything has been shamefully reduced—although figures of this sort can never be exhibited large enough. I am astonished that these very inept plagiarists did not observe what was written by me when I explained the grants and privileges allowed me, that is, that I should much prefer to provide printers with the illustrations than have them copied unskillfully. And if I wrote that at the time designedly, now I wish even more that it be indicated to all of them, because I should rather wish to undergo a great financial loss and to supply whatever is necessary for the elegance of a book than have those things produced by me with no ordinary effort spoiled. This despite the fact that at present everyone believes that whatever things are published are so much the better in proportion to the pomposity of titles and the number of authors involved. And with the favor of the gods, I shall spare no effort to vanquish those plagiarists who are wont to seize upon the labors of others since they are unable to steal anything original from one another.[184]

Be kind enough to see that my friends receive the enclosed letters. Give my kindest regards to all my friends and if they request it, you may permit them to read this letter.

Ratisbon, 13 June 1546.[185]

Chapter X

IMPERIAL SERVICE,
1546–1555

URING July 1546 there was increasing anxiety in Ratisbon over the effects of the still-unsettled religious problem. More and more it appeared that the future religion or religions of Germany would be decided on the battlefield, and already some of the towns in upper Germany were in rebellion, and the Schmalkalden League of Protestant states was meeting in Ichtershausen near Erfurt, arranging to raise an army and to establish diplomatic relations with the King of France. A Swabian army marched from Augsburg to break up the gathering of imperial troops at Nesselwang and Füssen; in fact, war had broken out, but for some months there were no serious engagements and few skirmishes of any significance. Meanwhile, the emperor was waiting undefended in Ratisbon for the arrival of his troops, and when, on 3 August, the Protestant forces reached the Danube and threatened to cut him off from the Tyrol, Charles decided as a temporary measure to march to the Inn, making a detour by way of Landshut on the Isar. There, on 13 August, he received papal reinforcements, and finally, with the arrival of troops from the Netherlands, the imperial army was of sufficient strength and enthusiasm to face the Protestant forces—especially since the army of the League, when faced with decisive action, displayed no little vacillation.[1]

Although Vesalius was with the emperor and the imperial forces during this period we have almost no information about him for some time.[2] On the other hand, there is information regarding Baersdorp, the emperor's personal physician. According to a dispatch of 22 September, written by Alvise Mocenigo, the Venetian ambassador who had replaced Navagero, the emperor had been filled with grief over the death of some of his troops in a skirmish and declared that when the present war was over he would never wage another. These facts had been learned from "that excellent gentleman Cornelius [van Baersdorp], physician to his Majesty."[3] Baersdorp, and presumably Vesalius as well, were for a time in close attendance upon the emperor since, as Mocenigo wrote on 1 October, for some days he had been troubled with gout and had been carried in a litter.[4] As a result, Baersdorp was in a position to bring his influence to bear and gain favors for others as well as recompense for himself. On 18 October the Venetian ambassador wrote that Cardinal Farnese, the Papal legate, had sought permission from the emperor to return to Italy for reasons of health, but, when Charles was unwilling to grant this request, Farnese "had so arranged with his Majesty's principal physician [Baersdorp], promising him a benefice for his son, that he gave such an account of the cardinal's illness to the emperor that the emperor agreed to give him the desired permission." [5]

During this same time the forces of the Schmalkalden League, which had briefly loomed as so great a danger to the emperor, disintegrated, not the least reason for this being the determination displayed by Charles who, once having command of a respectable army, showed great activity. From the latter part of August he was constantly on the move and was declared to have slept in forty different places, often in the field.[6] We may therefore consider that the imperial physicians had also had a rigorous time, whether accompanying the army or its leader. Presumably Vesalius, with the emperor and the court throughout this period, would in the event of battle have been called upon in the capacity of a military surgeon, but we have no precise record of him until shortly before the end of the year when the emperor took residence at Heilbronn, where he remained until 18 January 1547.[7]

Thomas Thirlby, Bishop of Westminster, who had succeeded Wotton as Henry VIII's ambassador to Charles V, wrote from Heilbronn to Sir William Paget, a secretary of state, on Christmas evening 1546, regarding political developments within the Empire. Ulrich, Duke of Württemberg, hitherto one of the rebel princes, had been compelled by events to visit Heilbronn and sue for pardon. Thirlby apparently gained information on this matter as well as other details of the political scene from conversation with Vesalius, as the latter part of his letter indicates:

> Doctor Vesalius, one of the emperor's physicians, dined with me this day, and said that the Duke of Württemberg should come hither to the emperor, and in that the Count [now Elector] Palatine was a travailer; he said further that the said Duke of Württemberg had written to the Duke of Bavaria long since, to be a means to the emperor for him, and in the same letter (as he said) should write, that rather than he should be an outlaw from his country fourteen years, as he was once [1520–1534], he would give all the preachers that he had to the emperor to make a sacrifice of them; with such other light words.[8]

There is little question of the source of Vesalius's information. The negotiations with the erstwhile rebellious Duke of Württemberg, which shortly resulted in his complete submission, were being conducted by the emperor's chancellor, Nicholas Perrenot, Lord Granvelle, then sixty years old—an advanced age for that time—and exhausted by his long and faithful service. His condition was revealed in a letter written to Ercole II of Ferrara by his ambassador Claudio Ariosti: "I have heard Vesalius the physician remark that Monseigneur Granvelle will become seriously ill if he remains here in Heilbronn." [9] This opinion was echoed by Alvise Mocenigo, the Venetian ambassador, who, in his dispatch of 25 December, stated that Granvelle was in Heilbronn but indisposed. He had asked the emperor for leave to return to his home in Burgundy, recalling the burden of his years and his indisposition. With the thought that a physician's word would possibly carry more weight than his own, he had prevailed upon Cornelius van Baersdorp, "the learned physician, because he had performed some good and valuable services for his Majesty," to repeat the request. However, the emperor was chary of losing his able minister's assistance permanently and so replied with a question: "If Monseigneur Granvelle goes to Burgundy will he ever return?" [10] That Baersdorp's services were available in such instances, for a consideration, is indicated by the fact that he had recently intervened successfully on behalf of Cardinal Farnese and thereafter supported the desires of a malingerer who wished to escape the rigors of camp life. The emperor may well have become suspicious of Baersdorp's recommendations.

Returning to the matter of Granvelle, a further dispatch of the Ferrarese ambassador indicates that the chancellor had talked over his problem with Vesalius, although there is no indication that the latter had been asked to intercede: "This morning Vesalius the physician told me that [Granvelle] desired and thought that he would again request his Majesty for permission to withdraw from his household for a time so that he might regain his health." [11]

At the end of 1546 the emperor was still in Heilbronn, with Vesalius, so far as we know, in attendance. On 18 January 1547 Charles left Heilbronn and, traveling by way of Marbach, Esslingen, Göppingen, and Geisslingen reached Ulm on 25 January.[12] During most of this time he suffered from gout and needed the assistance of his physicians; this very unpleasant episode is recalled in Charles's memoirs in the following words:

> The gout came again to torment the emperor at Heilbronn and lasted so long that when he departed from there for Ulm . . . he was not yet fully recovered. After the attack he had suffered on the day of St. Francis he had had one attack after another . . . it can be counted for his thirteenth seizure, and he decided to undergo the regimen and diet.[13]

According to rumor, as reported by Mocenigo, the emperor, finally established at Ulm, would remain there for at least a month, and would again employ the decoction of the china root.[14] Actually the emperor remained in Ulm through 4 March, and it was during this period that Vesalius found an opportunity for a visit to Basel.

The first indication of this visit is found in a letter of Johannes Ulrich Zasius, an imperial councillor, addressed to Boniface Amerbach of Basel. Written from Ulm and dated 27 February, the letter mentioned that Vesalius would carry it to Amerbach and would be able to answer whatever questions the latter might have relating to affairs at the imperial court. A second letter of Zasius to Amerbach, dated 13 March, declared,

"I believe that you have learned from the letter sent by courtesy of Vesalius on 28 February . . ." [15] It thus appears that Vesalius set out for Basel on 28 or 29 February, but his visit seems to have been unannounced. A letter of Oporinus to Heinrich Bullinger, dated 26 February, made no mention of the impending visit, nor did a letter of 1 March, written by Vesalius's friend Johannes Gast, also to Bullinger. [16]

The visit was recorded in the account book of the rector of the university, then Martin Borrhaus, for the academic year 1546–47. Under the rubric "Expenses of the table" is information that the official breakfast provided for the distinguished visitor had cost "3 *solidi*," suggesting that the entertainment was not exactly lavish. Unfortunately, the entries in the account book are not in chronological order, so it is impossible to give a precise date for this event. [17] Nor can we tell whether the visit was for business reasons or merely to renew friendships in Basel. Certainly after the strenuous activities of 1546, and perhaps a too-close association with a demanding emperor who yet refused to follow medical advice, a few days away from the imperial court must have been much to be desired. On the other hand, the question of a second edition of the *Fabrica* may also have been raised, although the first edition had not yet been sold out—as we learn from an interesting letter written on 6 February 1547 by Oporinus to Franciscus Dryander, a Spanish theologian resident in Basel but at that moment a guest of Vadian in St. Gall: "I send you Vesalius's *Anatomy* and *Epitome*, which are sold together to booksellers [i.e., the wholesale price] for five florins and three *batzen*." [18]

Apparently Vesalius had left Ulm with no definite schedule for the length of his visit in Basel or the time of his return to the court. Zasius's letter of 13 March, mentioned above, contained the further remark that "if our Andreas Vesalius is still with you, give him the enclosed letter and tell him that we are setting out from Nördlingen for Nuremberg and directly into Saxony." However, the emperor fell ill in Nördlingen and was compelled to remain there until 21 March, at which time, still ill, he was able to continue his journey, arriving in Nuremberg on 24 March. [19] Immediately a messenger was sent to intercept Vesalius on his return trip and speed him on to the emperor, who apparently felt the need of his ministrations. On 26 March Zasius wrote from Nördlingen: "Yesterday the emperor learned that Vesalius had left Basel and at once sent a courier to intercept him and bring him back more swiftly; for each time the emperor becomes ill, the more willingly does he follow his advice." A further letter of 8 April indicated that the physician had returned and once again taken up his duties at court: "Our Vesalius has returned to Nuremberg." [20]

The apparently apocryphal story of Vesalius's visit to Tübingen, told by Martin Crusius in his *Annales*, seems to belong to these first several months of 1547. According to this story, Vesalius, upon reaching Tübingen, entered a lecture hall of the university only to hear the professor Leonhart Fuchs voicing criticism of the *Fabrica*, whereupon Vesalius is declared to have asked, "Why have you censured me? Have I offended you?" To this Fuchs is supposed to have replied, "Are you Vesalius?" "I am, indeed," was the response, followed by greetings, friendly conversation, and an invitation to dinner.[21] Although Crusius's story is very likely legend, and Fuchs's demonstrable admiration for the *Fabrica* makes his critical remarks about it seem unlikely, yet a visit to Tübingen at this time is not inconceivable since the emperor was on the soil of Württemberg from 15 December 1546 to 5 March 1547, and it is barely possible that Vesalius may have visited the city briefly, either going to or coming from Basel. It is unlikely, however, that he was present the following month at the battle of Mühlberg, by which the threat of the Schmalkalden League was decisively overthrown and the emperor left, at least for the moment, master of Germany.

With victory achieved, plans had been laid for an imperial diet to convene at Augsburg in the summer of 1547. Meanwhile, Henry VIII of England had died in January and been succeeded by the nine-year-old Edward VI under the protectorate of his uncle Edward Seymour, Duke of Somerset, but Thirlby continued as ambassador to the imperial court and was at Augsburg until June 1548, when he was replaced by Sir Philip Hoby. On 15 April Thirlby wrote to Sir William Petre, secretary of state, regarding the emperor, who was already there, and possibly regarding Vesalius as well:

They say that the emperor will remain here until that the Prince of Spain shall come hither with his sister; and that Ferdinand the Archduke shall be married to her in this town.[22] They say that [Philip] shall bring with him eight or ten thousand Spaniards; and that these princes whose names be written in the schedule here enclosed shall accompany them hither; but they say that before August he cannot be here.

They say also that letters be come hither from Lyons signifying that Pietro Strozzi is passed thereby with four thousand Italians; and that the bruit is there that they shall go into Scotland to aid the Scots against us.

The Emperor's physician said also, that the Emperor had been long in great suspicion of the French; but now the Imperials assure themselves that they shall for this year live in peace. This is what they say, and [the physician] says . . .[23]

On 1 June, Sir Philip Hoby arrived at Augsburg to replace Thirlby. He and Thirlby sought a joint audience with the emperor and on the 5th were able to write to the Lord Protector and Privy Council that it had been appointed for that evening:

. . . but by reason, this night past, the Emperor was diseased by a flux, we be now in doubt whether we shall have audience this night or be deferred till tomorrow, and have thought good thus much to advertise your Lordship.

Herewith your Lordships shall receive a copy of a letter concerning the *Interim*, sent from Melanchthon to Carolowicius, one of Duke Maurice's Councillors. Because it was brought to us undeciphered by one of the Emperor's physicians, I, the Bishop of Westminster, suppose that they be the gladder to show it, for that Melanchthon yieldeth so much to their purpose. . . .[24]

Neither of these letters indicates the name of the physician who had provided the information, but we know from other sources that Vesalius was in Augsburg with the emperor, and, although officially in a secondary role compared to Baersdorp, yet secretly he was held in greater esteem by the emperor. On 9 August the Bishop of Forlì wrote from Augsburg to Cardinal Farnese that the emperor's surroundings in Augsburg were not so restful as they should be and that Baersdorp was not to be relied on, so secretly he had permitted Andreas Vesalius to care for the patient. Vesalius had informed the bishop that the illness of the emperor was not without danger, since it could lead to "consumption" or dropsy. On 12 August, Girolamo Verallo, the papal nuncio, wrote to Cardinal Farnese:

> His Majesty is improving so that he has commenced to eat, although as yet he does not retain [his food] well. This morning he ate a plum and a piece of melon, but because he vomited them it is said that he is still debilitated. Although he has no fever he has not much appetite and is only gradually regaining his health.

On the 14th Verallo announced in a short note that the emperor had discontinued the "water of the china" and begun to take the "water of the [guaiac] wood" and was recovering.[25] The emperor's recovery was confirmed by the Venetian ambassador Mocenigo on 16 August, who also wrote that the French general Brissac[26] was counterfeiting illness as an excuse to remain in Augsburg with the emperor and that Baersdorp "at the request of" the general, and presumably for some reward, pronounced his illness to be grave.[27]

In addition to caring secretly for the emperor, Vesalius's activity as a surgeon is revealed by his reintroduction of the classical operation for drainage of an empyema. This was recorded by his Spanish colleague Daza Chacon:

> In the year 1547 when the Emperor Charles was in Augsburg, I saw the very learned Vesalius open an empyema, he who, although he made anatomical dissections almost miraculously—as I have seen many times—was slow in surgery, and thus he entrusted nearly all such to me. He opened this one between the third and fourth [ribs], always keeping as far out as possible to protect the veins and arteries that go from side to side. The effusion of blood was great; although he penetrated the pleura nothing came forth from that which was extravenate, although great care was used. Therefore [the patient] died.[28]

The treatment of empyema by surgery was referred to as early as the Hippocratic aphorisms,[29] but throughout the classical age chief reliance was placed upon cautery, and at the end of the period there was even disapproval of the surgical procedure. In late medieval times once again there was reference to surgery for this condition, but there is no proof that it was more than verbal acknowledgment of possible treatment, and so far as the records are concerned Vesalius seems to have been the first to revive the actual use of surgery. According to Daza Chacon, however, the reported operation was unsuccessful and Vesalius was "slow in surgery," but Roth, perhaps a biased critic, regards Daza Chacon's report as unreliable and erroneous.[30] Indeed, Daza did make an error of omission since he failed to explain that the incision was made over the third rib as counted from below. In 1562 Vesalius was to discuss his procedure in what was for its time a remarkable bit of surgical writing. By then, however, his experience must have been fairly considerable, since he stated that within a few months he had performed the operation no less than four times—three times for thoracic wounds and once for a spontaneous empyema—and in three of the four cases the outcome had been successful.[31] In 1563 Ingrassia, the Sicilian physician, wrote Vesalius expressly to congratulate him and to declare him the first to operate in such cases.[32]

It should be kept in mind that throughout this period war had been in progress between the imperial forces and those of the Schmalkalden League. Despite inferior numbers at the outbreak of the war in 1546, Charles had been able to take advantage of lack of cohesion and resolution among his adversaries, and with the gradual growth of his own forces, notably from the Netherlands, had been able in the late summer of 1546 to wage an aggressive campaign in southern Germany where, among other towns, he had recovered Augsburg. The great merchants and bankers of Augsburg, zealous Catholics and businessmen who saw their commercial activities thwarted by war, were only too eager for submission to the emperor and peace. There would have been no opposition had not the burgher patricians, normally the ruling class, been pushed aside by a democratic movement among the artisans. With their submission, however, Charles was very lenient. In Augsburg he merely levied a moderate tribute, reconstituted the old ruling aristocracy, and left a body of imperial troops for security.

Although man's activities might be controlled, warfare had, as usual, stirred up things beyond human control—in this case an epidemic. Chronicles of the time record outbreaks throughout Germany in 1546, presumably carried initially by the armies but remaining as a legacy after the armies had departed. The most famous instance of epidemic disease at this time was the outbreak of typhus in the spring of 1547 at Trent, in northern Italy, which led to the temporary removal of the historic Council of Trent to Bologna. The incident is doubly interesting because the physician in charge was Girolamo Fracastoro, who in 1546 had published his celebrated *De contagione* on the general question of epidemic disease and, more particularly, provided the first notable description of typhus.

The outbreak in Augsburg in the summer of 1547 is far less well known. The following account by Daza Chacon, colleague of Vesalius, is of considerable interest since the part played in it by the Spaniard might just as well have been played by Vesalius. We have, moreover, a picture of the general fear of plague, the obvious ignorance of the manner of its transmission, and an aspect of the practice of public health in the mid-sixteenth century:

Being in Germany in the city of Augsburg, which the Emperor Charles . . . had entered the eve of Saint James in the year 1547, bringing with him the

Duke of Saxony as a prisoner, and many troops as a bodyguard; all were lodged within the city, and there were many exalted persons there, [such as] the King of the Romans, Ferdinand . . . with his two sons Maximilian and Ferdinand, and all the princes of the empire, including the Electors. The city [then] began to be pricked by the plague . . . [and] his Majesty ordered that two large houses be sought outside the city, and that in one of them should be gathered the Germans infected by the plague and in the other the Spaniards . . . and that they should be given surgeons of their own nations as well as everything else necessary.

The Spaniards chose a very large house that the Fuggers owned, an eighth of a league from the city, in which there were large rooms and stoves as well as many marvelous water devices, for a stream that carried considerable water passed through the middle of the house. His Majesty charged the Duke of Alba . . . to appoint a surgeon for those who would be in that house, who must not leave or . . . enter the city. Thereupon the duke sent for one of his Majesty's surgeons named Master Vicente Sierras . . . Master Vicente saw not only the great labor but also the great danger involved and sought to excuse himself; the duke urging him . . . he replied that he would not do it, and the duke, who was offended, ordered his name erased from the king's book. Likewise the duke ordered other, older surgeons who were present, but they all had good reasons for excusing themselves. Hence his Excellency sent for me and proposed the matter, the service I should perform for God, his Majesty, and the benefit of the state. I considered that if God could be served by my death, I could not avoid acceptance, although I realized the very grave danger in taking up battle against an invisible hydra that kills without injury to itself . . . the duke thanked me, and informed his Majesty, who said he would accept my services.

I visited the aforesaid house to see to its arrangements . . . [the duke] ordered everything that I requested, servants as well as supplies . . . He also ordered that the servants, once entered to serve, should not leave until I left, and, outside, three men were appointed to do nothing but come and go from the house to provide whatever should be ordered; these were not to enter but would hand in whatever was necessary and receive orders for what I requested through a window made in the front door. Inside the house there were many servants who performed the necessary duties: nurses, cooks, and others to clean the house, three women to wash the clothes, and two practitioners to help me.

When all this was arranged and a hundred beds prepared for the sick . . . I first undertook to have the house cleaned as much as possible and then I ordered many very large fires to be built not only in the rooms but also in the courts . . . the rooms were washed in the ordinary way with water and vinegar, and with these preparations the air became so clean and purified that, when some friends came to see the preparations that had been made for the reception of the sick and saw the cleanliness and the fragrance that was in all the rooms, they considered it better to stay there than to return to the city, because they realized that there they would be more free and safe from the plague than in Augsburg, and they were right.

When all was prepared, I ordered that I and the sick people and the others of the house should be so well prepared that those taken by the plague who might come would not be able to infect us with their disease. For this purpose I had certain perfumed concoctions made . . . composed of one ounce of very fine laudanum, one drachm each of powders of lemon rind and of lemon seed, one drachm each of camphor and saffron with orange water. Every morning

232

before breakfast we all took what Pliny recommends so highly, a composition that the great Pompey found written in Mithridates's own hand . . . and on that day that he took it the same Mithridates was certain that he would be immune to all kinds of pestilence . . . It was made of two walnuts, two dried figs, twenty rue leaves, and a grain of salt, all mixed with wine . . . but . . . we chewed it without mixing it with any liquid, and with these remedies God was served in that we were preserved from the plague and from other illnesses, for of all those who were confined there not one became ill.

When it was understood that everything was ready, the sick were brought in . . . all had those pestilential buboes in the groins . . . the manner of treatment was as follows . . . I would open the lesions obliquely with a lancet and then put a cupping glass so as to draw from the surrounding parts and take out what was infected there. Then I would cauterize them with actual cauteries until it seemed to me that the evil quality that had been introduced was consumed. I performed this cure on tumors that were cardinal color, and those that were black, those that were getting black, and those that were lemon color. In the case of the reddish and pinkish ones, I contented myself with opening them and washing them with lye and hot salt, and after this I put inside a very small bit of *soliman* or a troche of minium and on top I would oil the circumference with theriac, and even put it inside because it not only has the property of expelling poison taken by mouth, but of attracting poison so that it can be expelled, as Galen said.

We did not forget the other necessary remedies. . . . It was arranged that the rooms should be very bright with a great deal of light, and that the patients should talk to each other, for in that way they would sleep less; they were ordered to scrub their legs thoroughly, were given ptisans with sugar and almonds and broths of good fowl; and finally they were given very good things to eat, because as Avicenna says: In general those who free themselves from this sickness are those who are vigorous and eat well. By day they were provided with invigorating conserves, drank barley water and lemon-peel water, bugloss water or merely water mixed with syrup of citron.

Finally the inmates were subjected to the very complicated combinations of drugs so characteristic of the sixteenth century pharmacopeia:

The medicines that combat the plague . . . are tormentil, snakeweed, absinthe, aloes, mastic, myrrh, dittany, bolarmenico, water germander, amber, musk and oil of behen.

With the aforesaid arrangements . . . there was such great success as to be amazing, for of the eighty-two patients that were brought to that house only two died. . . . The remaining eighty were cured; and I dare write this because there are many living witnesses, and it is attested by the books of the same hospital. . . .

After having completed this matter, I was sent out of Augsburg for more than two months . . . and they did not let me into the court until it was thought that I was no longer infectious. And I assure you that for this service —for it can so be called—no favor was done me.[33]

While Daza Chacon was thus concerned with Spanish victims of the epidemic, as well as with the failure of the authorities to give recognition for his services, Vesalius remained in attendance upon the emperor, who continued his residence in Augsburg despite the ravagings of the epidemic there into October.[34] We have one brief glimpse of him in the memoirs of Bartholomew Sastrow, who was in Augsburg at this time:

> The emperor, far from giving even the smallest banquet, kept nobody near him; neither his sister, nor his brother, nor his nieces, nor the Duchess of Bavaria, nor the electors, nor any of the princes. After church, when he reached his apartments, he dismissed his courtiers, giving his hand to everybody. He had his meals by himself without speaking a word to his attendants. One day, returning from church, he noticed the absence of Carlowitz. "Where is our Carlowitz?" he asked of Duke Maurice. "Most gracious emperor," replied the latter, "he feels somewhat feeble." Immediately the emperor turned to his physician "Vesalius, you had better go and seek Carlowitz, he is not well; you may be able to do something for him." [35]

No doubt Vesalius took advantage of this protracted sojourn in Augsburg to renew his acquaintance with his old friend Wolfgang Herwart, and no doubt, too, it was through this Augsburg friend that he was brought into close touch with those members of the Augsburg medical profession—Gasser, Stenglin, and the two Occos—with whom he retained both friendly and professional ties.[36]

Two further incidents related to the year 1547 are known only through Girolamo Cardano. This later-distinguished physician and mathematician was at this period lecturing on medicine, self-confessedly without great success, at Pavia and Milan, when he received an invitation to become physician to Christian III, King of Denmark. There is no indication whether the invitation had first been tendered to Vesalius, who had proposed Cardano as a substitute, or whether Vesalius had merely been asked to suggest someone for the post. As recalled by Cardano:

> The next year [1547] through the instance of Andreas Vesalius, a man of highest standing and my friend, an offer of 800 gold crowns yearly was made me by the King of Denmark. This I was not eager to accept—although he even offered living expenses—not only on account of the severity of the climate in that region, but also because the Danes are given to another way of worship. I felt that perhaps I might not be very welcome there, or else might be forced to abandon the doctrines of my country and my forebears.[37]

The second incident refers to an error of judgment made by Vesalius in surgery performed upon Cristoforo Madruzzo, Cardinal of Trent, and a devoted servant of the emperor. Although the remark is therefore uncomplimentary there is little reason to doubt it since Cardano at all other times spoke of Vesalius with the utmost favor and respect. So we are informed that "after Vesalius had published his [*Fabrica*], he erred in his surgery when he operated upon the foot of the Cardinal of Trent so that a brief period of lameness followed." [38]

In the latter part of 1547 Vesalius was called upon to give his advice regarding the malady, possibly poliomyelitis, of a child of the noble family of Stubenberg.[39] On 10 November, Wolfgang von Stubenberg wrote from Kapfenburg to ask his brother-in-law Adam von Dietrichstein, 1527–1590, the later-distinguished diplomat then at the imperial court in Augsburg, to present the case to Vesalius and seek his advice. According to Stubenberg, the youth, named Balthasar, walked on the outer side rather than on the sole of his foot, which he also tended to swing rather than walk on. Furthermore, the foot, as well as the lower leg, had become withered and was considerably smaller than its mate. The situation appeared to be deteriorating and the boy was using crutches. Vesalius's advice, it was stated, would be appreciated and perhaps he could be persuaded to take charge of the case. A brief case history accompanied the letter.[40]

Adam von Dietrichstein replied from Augsburg on 6 January 1548 that he had taken the matter up with Vesalius and had given him the report of the ailment. The latter, after reading it, replied that he had little advice to offer that could be useful, particularly since the messenger who was to carry the reply was leaving very soon and there was not much time for consideration of the report which, incidentally, suffered from lack of detail. In sum, Vesalius did not promise any help, and in regard especially to the withered leg he could offer nothing except the Galenic remedies already in use.

In addition to this brief report transmitted by Dietrichstein, Vesalius wrote a short consilium, or opinion,[41] remarkable for the fact that he offered no method of treatment since he felt his information was too slight. He did discuss various anatomical defects that might have led to the condition, and in particular he warned of the danger of attempting treatment without full knowledge of the cause of the ailment. The general tone of the consilium, which can be dated either at the end of 1547 or the beginning of 1548, is one of mature common sense based upon a sure grasp of the anatomy of the extremity.

Only one further incident relating to Vesalius can be associated with this Augsburg period, but it is of some interest since it indicates his scientific position as contrasted to the superstitions common to that age. On 16 April 1548, the Bishop of Forlì mentioned in a dispatch that a monster had been born and was yet living despite the fact that its liver was outside the body. "Although Vesalius is not directly acquainted with the case and considers it remarkable, as an anatomist he says that it is a thing that is possible and laughs at the many auguries the common people have made."[42]

Charles left Augsburg 13 August 1548 and, traveling by way of Ulm, Esseling, Stuttgart, Worms, and Oppenheim, he took ship at Mainz and reached Brussels on 22 September.[43] His health would no longer endure a rapid passage, so he remained in Brussels through the balance of the year, briefly attacked again by the gout in November.[44] It was then that a Neapolitan doctor, attracted by the knowledge that the emperor was ready prey to quacks and panaceas, came to Brussels expressly to treat him, promising marvelous results. The Neapolitan succeeded no better than the emperor's own physicians and in time was sent packing.[45]

Meanwhile, a revolt in Guienne against the gabelle, or tax on salt, prompted Charles to negotiate with the English government for a joint reopening of hostilities against France. Maximilian of Egmont, Count of Buren, was the imperial envoy. The count returned in December, from what had proved a fruitless mission, with a severe anginoid inflammation of the throat. According to the numerous contemporary accounts, after examination by Vesalius the count was informed that he had only a few hours to live and was advised therefore to put his affairs in order. The prognosis proved correct. Although the story, or rather its details, must be suspect, yet it is dramatic as told at some length by Brantôme. Moreover, by implication Vesalius emerges as a person of position in the social world as well as in the medical:

The Count of Buren died in Brussels [23 December 1548], and in the manner of his death displayed a noble and unsurpassed courage. This chevalier of the Golden Fleece fell suddenly ill . . . Andreas Vesalius, physician to the emperor Charles went to visit him immediately, and after he had felt his pulse, which seemed to him too rapid, remarked frankly that if the rules of his profession did not deceive him, the count would be dead in five or six hours. Hence as a good friend he advised the count to look to his affairs. Matters turned out as the physician had foretold so that Vesalius was responsible for the most noble death ever heard of since kings have worn crowns. The count calmly ordered his two best friends, the Bishop of Arras, since become Cardinal Granvelle . . . and the Count of Aremberg, called to him, so that he might commend them to God. Within those five or six hours, he made his will, confessed, and received the holy sacrament. Then, wishing to arise, he had brought to him the most rich, handsome, and sumptuous of his clothing, which he donned; he had himself armed from head to foot in his richest and handsomest armor, even to the spurs; he put on the collar and the great cloak of the Order [of the Golden Fleece] and a hat in the Polish style—which he wore because he liked it more than any other sort of hat. Thus with his sword at his side, superbly dressed and armed, he had himself carried in a chair into a chamber of his dwelling where were waiting several colonels and seigneurs, who wished to see him before he died; because the rumor had flown here and there throughout the whole city that in a short time his soul would leave his body.

Carried into the chamber, seated on his chair, and before him his saddle decorated with his feathers and plumes, and with his gauntlets, he asked his two close friends to call all his captains and officers whom he wished to see to commend them all to God, one after the other; this was done . . . recommending now this one, now that one, to M. d'Arras, to recompense them according to their merits, giving a horse to this one, a mule to that, and to another a greyhound or a complete set of clothing.

Having commended all his officers and servitors to God and touched their hands, he asked for a drink . . . so that he might drink to the health of his imperial master. He then gave a noble account of his life and the honors he had received from his master, gave his collar of the Golden Fleece to the Count of Aremberg to return to the emperor . . . and, supported under the arms by two of his gentlemen, he drank the wine . . . expressing his thanks to the emperor and saying many fine things worthy of eternal memory. . . .

Finally, sensing the end, he hastened to commend the Bishop of Arras and the Count of Aremberg to God . . . Then, turning his head and seeing Master Vesalius behind him, he embraced him and thanked him for his timely warning.

Finally he said, "Carry me to the bed," where no sooner was he placed than he died.[46]

Years later Vesalius referred in matter-of-fact tone to the post-mortem findings, saying, "In the lung of the never-to-be-sufficiently praised Count of Buren, after his very severe angina, I saw an extensive suppurating mediastinal abscess." [47] Whatever the precision with which Vesalius had prognosticated the death of Egmont, the story, which appears to have had wide circulation, made a considerable stir and was frequently related by contemporary chroniclers,[48] but among the more superstitious it led not so much to the enhancement of Vesalius's reputation as a diagnostician as to the belief that his powers emanated from witchcraft.[49]

The emperor remained in Brussels through the first six months of 1549 where, partly as a result of the imperial successes against the Lutheran princes, partly in anticipation of the arrival of Prince Philip from Spain, much jousting and feasting took place.[50] It may be assumed that Vesalius was at court, and he may from time to time have been called upon to assist imperial recovery from dietary excesses or to patch up jousters who had played their mock warfare too enthusiastically.

Granvelle, the imperial chancellor, already well on in years, was ill once more. As previously indicated, in 1546 he had sought to retire from the court to regain his health, a request the emperor had refused. Now his condition was much worse, and during late spring the imperial physicians, Vesalius among them, tried without success to restore the chancellor to good health. Indeed, Granvelle's son, the Bishop of Arras, later successor to his father's position, was so disturbed that he sought secretly to gain further advice and opinion from leading French physicians. In a letter of 29 June addressed to the imperial ambassador in Paris, the bishop wrote:

I send you an analysis the physicians here have made of the condition of [Granvelle], presented simply for you to gain the advice of Fernel, Sylvius, and other principal physicians of France, whom I request you to consult without naming the patient. . . . You will place the charges to my account . . . I send you three copies of what the physicians here have put in writing, which you may use as seems best to you.[51]

Granvelle was "confined to his bed, tormented with pains in his legs." [52]

Meanwhile, Charles's chief concern had been the arrival of his son in the latter part of June and a tour of the Netherlands with him, which began in July. Vesalius for the first time now saw the future Spanish monarch whom he was to serve from 1559 to 1564, and it may have been part of his duty to accompany the imperial party as it toured the country, allowing the prince to become known. There was doubtless need for his services since banquets were frequent and jousts vigorous. One of the latter, held in Binche, was fought so furiously that "some were wounded and a number of horses killed." [53] Whatever the state of the imperial health throughout the tour, Charles returned to Brussels in

November once again crippled by gout, which required him to undergo a course of treatment.[54]

There is little precise information on Vesalius throughout the year, and the silence is in contrast to his growing reputation—as a physician as well as anatomist—that was no little enhanced by the accounts of his prognostication in the case of the ill-fated Egmont. An indication of his fame is the flattering dedication to him of a new edition of the works of Alessandro Benedetti published by the Basel professor Marcus Hopper.[55] Tribute is paid to Vesalius's labors on behalf of anatomy and to his abilities as imperial physician. In fact it would appear from the dedication that such good health as the emperor enjoyed was entirely owing to Vesalius.

Whatever pleasure Vesalius may have gained from this flattering dedication must have been at least partly diminished by the appearance of a new book by Sylvius. This was a revised edition of Balamio's translation of Galen's *On the bones* accompanied by a commentary in which Sylvius sought to defend Galen against the attack made upon him in the *Fabrica*.[56]

Hitherto Sylvius's expression of displeasure had been limited to correspondence with Vesalius, which, as has been seen, contributed to the publication of the *Letter on the china root*, and such utterances as the French physician may have offered to his students and auditors. This new edition of *On the bones* was Sylvius's first resort to print in his contest with his former student, and, although the target of his remarks was obvious, Vesalius was not mentioned by name. He was, however, referred to as a madman (*vaesanus*), a term used as the title of Sylvius's continued and much stronger attack of 1551.

This first printed assault was relatively mild, and the defense of Galen to a large degree comprised of an effort to demonstrate that his osteology was based upon the study of human bones—clearly indicating the shattering effect of Vesalius's demonstration of its animal basis. The preface is divided between assertions of Galen's sole concern with human bones and scorn for his unnamed adversary. "I assert that [Galen's] book *On the bones* deals solely with human bones; I say this lest any slanderous person seek an opportunity for transferring some of Galen's statements to the bones of apes, similar but not the same as the human and in part very dissimilar." Furthermore, "Galen declared that he had written this book solely about human bones as [being] the most perfect of all," and, "do not believe that Galen wrote his osteology about the bones of man and ape in common." Moreover, "since all that Galen teaches in this little book *On the bones* applies so neatly to the human, as we have taught from nature's account and many skeletons to about four hundred auditors, what purpose would have been served by using the ape's bones?" If, however, there was anyone of calumnious nature who refused to believe what he had heard, one who refused to accept either Galen's text or Sylvius's commentary, then let him in his scorn come to Sylvius's home

238

where he might see and touch all those things discussed, "since there is greater faith in sight than in hearing and most of all in touch." [57]

At this point Sylvius directed his attention to the source of the misunderstanding: "Honest reader, I urge you to pay no attention to a certain ridiculous madman, one utterly lacking talent who curses and inveighs impiously against his teachers." The attack was then turned indirectly against the illustrations of the *Fabrica* with the remark, "I am unwilling to reproduce here illustrations of the bones with their names" because, he continued, today everyone might easily see and study the actual bones: illustrations are fictive, give a false proportion and, "obscured by much shading," offer "a poor and difficult method of learning." [58]

Compared to the later *Vaesanus* of 1551, Sylvius exercised remarkable restraint. He did, however, fire one shot that hit home, since Vesalius saw to it that the lettering on the illustrations was less obscured by shading in the revised edition of the *Fabrica*. Sylvius's commentaries to the chapters of *On the bones* seek to give authority to his defense of Galen by frequent reference to the human skeleton, although it is obvious that by observing with the eyes of his classical mentor Sylvius very frequently saw what did not exist or failed to find what did. All the skulls available to Sylvius in Paris, "whether fresh or dried," displayed passages "the size of a pinhead" for the discharge of pituita from the brain into the nostrils and throat. Vesalius's denial of this particular Galenic doctrine had apparently been especially resented by Sylvius who—now elderly and possibly somewhat arteriosclerotic—continued, "Let no one give heed to that very ignorant and arrogant man who, through his ignorance, ingratitude, impudence, and impiety denies everything his deranged or feeble vision cannot locate." [59] As "Galen had very frequently observed it in human skulls," so Sylvius had likewise seen the premaxillary bone, "whole and perfect in four skulls" and "imperfect in many." [60] Regarding the movements of the head, which had been strongly attacked in the *Fabrica*, it is true that the account in *On the bones* permitted some range of discussion, but the controversy "is happily composed" in the *Use of parts*. [61]

The sacrum, wrote Sylvius, was formed of three bones, or sometimes "[Galen] writes that the sacrum is formed of four bones, that is three of its own with the coccyx as the fourth." [62] The sternum was variously formed of from two to six pieces, but a sternum of seven "is very rare." Nevertheless, the fact that "the sterna of the skeletons seen by Galen" were formed of seven pieces is readily explained by the different structure of man in Galen's day. [63] It is true that Galen's statement that the humerus was larger than the tibia presented a problem. However, it might well have been that the facts were once as Galen stated them, that is, that this relationship did exist in the skeletons he had observed. It is obvious that Sylvius was uneasy over any suspicions of simian anatomy and in consequence he suggested the possibility of a defective text. "The skeletons seen by Galen had a larger humerus than tibia, or here he excepted the tibia with the femur [as the largest bones], but that part of the text disappeared due to the carelessness of editors." [64]

Sylvius's commentary to *On the bones*, resting upon nothing but dubious assertions of Galen's use of human bones and his somewhat specious observations upon his own skeletal materials, must be termed merely a feeble defense of Galenic anatomy. The work ought to have provided its target with further assurance of the correctness of his own anti-Galenic assertions.

The year 1550 was one for which we have more documented knowledge of Vesalius's activities. A catalogue of the imperial household gives us the names of the medical staff, drawn entirely from the emperor's personally held territories. The physicians and surgeons were: Cornelius Baersdorp, Andreas Vesalius, Petrus Lopez, Jacobus Olivarius, Gregorius Lopez, Gonzales Muñoz, Simon Guadalupe, and Stephanus of Burgundy. [65] The pharmacists were Sebastian Reinbant, Johannes Corbehem, Johannes Ledesma, and Baptista of Antwerp; [66] attached to the family of the King of the Romans were "Petrus Canitzerus, Spanish physician, and two others." [67] Baersdorp, as indicated, was still the premier physician at court, [68] although now surpassed in fame by Vesalius. The latter was mentioned by Paul Eber in his historical calendar for the year as a "distinguished physician and illustrious anatomist," [69] and it was possibly in this year that Vesalius was rewarded by a salary increase of 300 Rhenish florins. This we learn from a letter dated merely 15 May that he wrote from Brussels to his old friend Jean Sturm and that also reflects considerable cynicism on methods of flattery necessary to preferment. [70]

This year also witnessed the death of Granvelle. In June his ankle joints were so swollen and inflamed that Vesalius, seeing they could not be healed, took strenuous measures to provide the chancellor with temporary relief. In a letter to Louis of Flanders, Seigneur de Praet, the physician described his treatment:

> For many years Granvelle had swellings at the ankles, particularly in the summer. In June severe pain with reddening occurred above the exterior malleolus, not unlike ulcerated erysipelas, and it was more severe in the evening. Because it could not be cured in any way, he permitted both legs to be cauterized in that region. [71]

It was probably during this period that Vesalius wrote several other letters to the Seigneur de Praet concerning the general treatment of ulcers. [72]

In August, a month after the opening of the new Diet in Augsburg, Granvelle died in that city, an event that particularly depressed the emperor. It was said that he seemed "to have lost his own soul." [73] Granvelle was succeeded as chancellor by his son, the Bishop of Arras, but this nominal succession may have been preceded by unofficial control of the office as a result of his father's incapacity. Such a situation might have been the explanation for the increase of Vesalius's salary in the spring, as a gesture of good will on the part of his old friend of student days in Louvain.

Although there had been much fluctuation in the state of the emperor's health, generally speaking it became steadily worse after the middle of the century. His incapacitating afflictions recurred with greater and greater frequency, but within limits he bore them courageously. He now began to seek solace in reading and, more particularly, in being read to. Yet from time to time the restraints that bodily weakness placed upon Charles's athletic and martial inclinations led to outbursts of wrath and impatience.

Despite his complaints, Charles remained unable to control his appetite for any long period of time, and despite the conscientious efforts of his physicians he was ever prone to give ear to the suggestions of the newest quack. Under these conditions, the lot of the emperor's personal staff was a far from happy one, and perhaps no one bore a greater burden than the personal physician whose fortunes at this time were portrayed in the letters of Guillaume van Male. This aide-de-chambre, companion, secretary, reader-to-the-emperor, and general factotum, shared with Baersdorp an enslavement to the imperial presence. Esteemed by Charles, yet treated with a kind of thoughtless cruelty and never rewarded for his loyal endurance, van Male has left us a series of letters written to Louis of Flanders, chief of finances for the Netherlands, in which he portrays the daily life and vexations of the imperial household between the years 1550 and 1555. Van Male and Baersdorp were close friends in fact as well as in misery, and the letters frequently describe the lot of the personal physician.

Baersdorp, possibly as a result of his distinguished lineage, had numerous acquaintances in high places. He was on terms of friendship with Louis of Flanders, the correspondent of van Male. He enjoyed the greatest esteem in the imperial family and became titular physician to the Queens Eleanor and Mary, sisters of the emperor. But all this was of no avail in the struggle to retain the confidence of the emperor in his medical ability and to defend his imperial patient against quacks.

The scene of these frustrations is first laid in Augsburg, whither Charles had arrived on 31 August 1550 for a meeting of the imperial Diet. Matters had gone badly for the emperor. His plan for the succession of his son Philip to the imperial throne had been thwarted. The German princes were not favorably disposed toward his plans for the liquidation of the Schmalkalden war and, worst of all, Granvelle had died on 27 August. It was against this doleful background that Baersdorp, although personal physician, was compelled to compete for guardianship of Charles's ever worsening health with a certain Caballus, a physician of no merit but possessed of the knack of gaining and holding the emperor's confidence. Vesalius occasionally appeared on the scene, but the contest was really between Baersdorp and Caballus. Perhaps Vesalius, ever discreet, had decided that at this particular time the personal physician might well be left with full charge of the emperor's health and all the woes pertaining to that charge.

The first description of the imperial patient in Augsburg is in a letter of van Male's of 30 September 1550:

The emperor's health has been sufficiently sound, although a little earlier he was afflicted somewhat with haemorrhoids and a lack of appetite. He forewent public affairs and amused himself with hunting, reading, and the pleasant conversation of his household; sometimes a large part of the day and night was set apart for the determination of very grave affairs, when he called the king and queen into secret councils; he was well, I say, in accordance with his usual and wholly athletic ways and the almost effete weakness of his body. However, behold that thereafter by the bite of a nocturnal gnat at the joint of the hand physicians call the carpus, a slight amount of skin became swollen and provoked an itching; when the emperor was unable to endure it he gently scraped and scratched the surface with his nail. Who would believe it, I ask? Both his hand and his forearm became so inflamed you might think a *carcinoma* had arisen. I laughed to myself at the old proverb about the elephant and the gnat when I saw what the sting of the most insignificant of insects could do to a monarch.[74]

But van Male had overlooked the fact that there are further proverbs that refer to those finding pleasure in the woes of others, and in a letter of 25 November he was compelled to write: "A nephritis is now so tormenting me that as a result of the pain I am unable either to lie down or to stand up. . . . [On the other hand] the emperor is in good health, as you are well aware from Baersdorp's letter." [75] The continuance of his complaint caused van Male to look somewhat askance at the abilities of the emperor's medical staff. On 13 January 1551 he wrote:

For these last two months I have heard nothing except bilious and melancholic humors, phlebotomy, potions, pills, and that kind of thing, usually the very dirge of mortals. Meanwhile, from so great a throng of physicians, thus far no one has gained a true knowledge of my ailment. First Caballus with great assurance announced it to be nephritis; Vesalius, an abscess in the kidneys; Cornelius [van Baersdorp], that this collection of symptoms had flowed into the cloaca of my slight body and produced a wasting away. I asked them that they not number my cooks among this great variety of diseases, as Seneca wrote to Lucilius. . . . Baersdorp usually looked at me with a jaundiced eye whenever Seneca was in my hands, and he would take his departure in formal terms as if he had been insulted. But thereafter I would charm him with the sweetness of my lyre, which he had permitted me to enjoy freely so that its joyous notes would drive away the sadness of the melancholic humor.[76]

However, both the illness of van Male and the good health of the emperor represented only a brief interlude in the normal state of affairs. On 18 January the Venetian ambassador wrote that "the emperor is again ill with the gout," [77] and later that year another Venetian ambassador wrote of the emperor:

The emperor is fifty-one years old and of poor bodily constitution because of the gout from which he has suffered horribly all through the winter, as well as at other times. The physicians say it has begun to ascend to his head and are fearful that it will thereupon cause his death. He suffers frequently from asthma, and it is said that he displays some slight indication of the French disease. . . . All prophesy a short life for him.[78]

Van Male's next letter, 20 January 1551, supports this more doleful description:

Today the emperor for the first time left the bed to which he had hitherto been firmly fixed. Yesterday he took some sort of drug whereby a great contention arose between Caballus and Baersdorp in the presence of the emperor . . . it was a notable conflict and worthy of description. O great ass! that Pantalabus [i.e., Caballus] pronounced a Hippocratic aphorism so ineptly that I have never heard anything so badly distorted; yet he is consulted regarding the health of the emperor. I should despair if schoolboys did not explain Hippocrates more correctly . . . Baersdorp, with his very noteworthy training, was astonished at this false and tyrannical opinion, and came to discuss it with me. I urged him to patience and dissimulation for nothing good could arise from the dispute; and what was most to be desired in this matter finally happened, for the medicament [prescribed by Caballus] was of value only as an emetic and cathartic.[79]

Yet whatever the momentary ascendancy of the ill-trained Caballus, the emperor was compelled to fall back upon some of the time-honored therapy of more reputable physicians. This becomes apparent from a letter of the English ambassador who, however, like one of his predecessors, suspected that Charles feigned illness, at least in part, as a political device. Sir Richard Morison was then the English ambassador, with Roger Ascham as his secretary. There was at this time much talk of reopening the Council of Trent, which had last met nearly four years previously. On 14 April 1551 Morison wrote to the Privy Council from Augsburg that, so far as he was concerned, the more show the emperor made of calling the council, the less it meant; and that the emperor's taking the guaiac cure and writing new letters were but to make men imagine that he thought of nothing but the council.[80]

The council did reopen on 1 May, but Charles remained in Augsburg until October. Meanwhile, France, now ruled by Henry II, was resuming its old hostility toward the emperor. On 30 June, Morison reported to the Privy Council a conversation between the emperor and the French ambassador:

Monsieur, the Emperor said, in France and in Germany I am dead once in a fortnight or once in three weeks. True it is, I am oft sick, and could many times, in my pains, be content if it were God's will to take me from this painful life. But when my pains do cease, and I hear that in France it hath been noised I was dead, or could not live, I pluck a good heart to me again, and think I find no physic that doth me more good than this my mind and desire to disappoint others that so fain would have me gone. Monsieur Ambassador, I am, as you see, alive; and see that you tell your master, if he will not let me alone, I am like enough to live to put him farther trouble than ever I did his father.[81]

The continued vitality of the emperor was owed in part, at least, to his medical attendants, of whom Vesalius was now the most celebrated.

"Tell Henry Ailand," wrote Roger Ascham, "that I am well acquainted with Andreas Vesalius, that noble physician; and yet he was Vahan's physician, and as Vahan saith, the best physician in the world, because he gave him pitcher-meat [i.e., drink] enough." [82]

The next several letters of van Male indicate that the emperor was enjoying better health; however, it is unlikely that the quack had succeeded where the trained physicians had failed. Much more likely, since Charles was so frequently his own worst enemy, the period of diet and rest that accompanied the guaiac treatment had produced some natural recuperation. Nevertheless, personal calamity was never very far from the emperor. In a letter of 9 June we learn that as his health improved, so did his desire for activity. Since as yet he could not walk or ride comfortably, he had a carriage built for excursions and hunting, or warfare if necessary. However, wrote van Male, "because, I believe, Diana is not in sympathy with Vulcan and Mars," the first time Charles attempted to use his carriage he fell and "almost knocked out the few teeth nature had left him." [83] The letter of 20 July relates what had almost become the normal course of events:

> The emperor, so it please the gods, is now afflicted with dysentery, but, as I shall say frankly, since he is responsible for his ailment he can't complain of it. Also those old tormenting haemorrhoids have contributed a new torture . . . and this morning he complained to me that insomnia has now been added to the list of all his ailments.[84]

In view of the fluctuating state of the emperor's health it is not astonishing that a letter of 28 July announces that "the emperor is now in better health and considering his departure." [85] A second letter of 9 August reaffirms this: "The emperor is now in very good health and little by little prepares for his journey." [86] However, Charles was not given to hasty action, and partly as a result of political indecision, partly as a result of the return of poor health, he was still in Augsburg on 4 November. According to van Male:

> The emperor's ailment has sufficiently displayed its cause, but because the care of writing about this matter rests more with Master Baersdorp than with me, I do not wish officiously to interfere with his duty, especially since the emperor's health is so uncertain and doubtful that nothing seems to promise a sure recovery. He has recovered from a recent gout but dubiously and uncertainly. Doctor Caballus says that the emperor's health is in his own hands and that he will remain well or ill according to his own determination. I marvel that he scolds since in all things medical and otherwise he has displayed such great obsequiousness to the emperor.[87]

A recently published letter of Vesalius to his father-in-law indicates not only his own continued association with the emperor during this period but also that his wife shared his long sojourn.[88] But, if we may judge from the letters of van Male, he was not especially involved in the harrowing problem of ministering to the imperial health and perhaps had time to enjoy the admiration expressed for his achievements by

Leonhart Fuchs—although certainly he felt some irritation at the accompanying plagiarism. Early in 1551 this Tübingen professor had published the first volume of a work entitled *De humani corporis fabrica ex Galeni & Andreae Vesalii libris concinnatae epitome,* followed by a second volume sometime after June of the same year.[89] Fuchs's title indicates a borrowing from the *Fabrica,* and Vesalius is praised throughout and quoted *in extenso* to the detriment of Galen, who is treated with respect but little enthusiasm. The work can be readily described by some passages taken from the long preface to the first volume:

Everyone knows that hitherto there have been very few public schools in Germany in which anatomical instruction was offered, although it ought to have held a special place. I believe that there was no reason for this except that there were very few or almost no professors in those schools who gave consideration to that subject or who were able to discuss the parts of the human body because, frankly, they had no knowledge of them, or lacked any suitable text that could be proposed to their auditors for exposition. It is a fact that until recently no text of this sort existed except that one Mondino composed, and this, even though at first its contents were applauded by everyone and judged worthy of being used in all the schools, yet a little later, when it became clearly recognized by some that it contained many errors and had no account of the bones, muscles, and nerves, gradually lost its esteem and was scorned as a guide. . . . Later certain ones came to the belief that dissection ought to be learned from Galen as the best and, in everyone's judgment, the leader of all those professing anatomy. Since he presented his views on dissection not in one book but spread out at length in many . . . several attempts were made to reduce his teachings into an epitome . . . but, as it seems to me, none of them was suited for the teaching of anatomy.

Therefore, if I may express myself frankly, with the exception of the commentaries of our Vesalius on the structure of the human body, clearly learned and produced with remarkable industry, I have discovered no writing that has satisfied me entirely and that I could use suitably for discussion of the human body and its dissection, and I gave great and extended consideration to what I ought to do so that this part of the art, wholly neglected in the schools of Germany, might be returned home and publicly taught in all our schools. I saw that the books of Vesalius on the structure of the human body were too extended and detailed to be understood by everyone and, especially in that poverty of professors skilled in anatomy, to be presented in our schools. Moreover, the *Epitome* he composed is too brief to be grasped by those who do not properly understand those books of his already mentioned. And so, lest I continue to deprive our schools of the advantage of correctly learning the arrangement and dissection of the human body, I began to put together an epitome of the writings of Galen and Vesalius, which for several years thereafter I dictated to my auditors so that in this way they might obtain at least some slight knowledge of anatomy. But since the task of writing and listening was burdensome to many, they objected to it strenuously, and asked that I arrange for publication of what I had put together. Unable to ignore their frequent requests, for their sake I handed over to the printer for publication what I had myself prepared for my auditors, not everything but at first only the first two books, of which one gives an account of the bones, the other of the muscles.

I put my epitome together solely to prepare a pathway for the reader for an easier understanding of the commentaries of Vesalius; indeed, so far am I from desiring to condemn his anatomy that I prefer him to all others, including Galen, for I have no doubt that he was divinely inspired to recall into the light and to make known this part of medicine that was almost extinct and contaminated with infinite errors.

Although Galen provided no little help to anatomy, yet it is clear that he composed his account from apes and dogs rather than from men, as anyone will understand if he uses his eyes as witnesses and is willing to use his hands in dissection. Among those who in our age wrote about the structure of man, Vesalius is the only one to write with exquisite care and to describe in a suitable manner, and had his commentaries not been published we should have been deprived of the true account of many parts of the human body. Hence I am unable to be sufficiently astonished at the insolence of certain ones who dare to clamor so immoderately against the efforts of that man and do not hesitate to defame and to attack him with many lies and insults for no other reason than that he demonstrated that the anatomy of Galen does not conform to the human body. Nay, rather he ought to be praised for his zeal in searching out the truth and he ought to be thanked that he was willing to make such a great effort to restore this part of the art.

The work was distinctly a plagiarism, but it did not make use of the illustrations from the *Fabrica* like the earlier plagiarism of Geminus that had so outraged Vesalius. Fuchs, moreover, supported some of Galen's doctrines even though they had been demolished in the *Fabrica*, but he did lean in general far more toward Vesalius's position than toward Galen's.

If Vesalius viewed Fuchs's efforts with mixed feelings, there was certainly no pleasure at all to be derived from a second book that appeared that same year and that was fanatically critical of all he had done. This was a work entitled *Vaesani cuiusdam calumniarum in Hippocratis Galenique rem anatomicam depulsio* (A refutation of the slanders of a madman against the anatomy of Hippocrates and Galen),[90] Sylvius's continued attack on Vesalius and somewhat hysterical defense of Galen, published in Paris in June 1551. Perhaps because of the lack of success of his earlier edition of *On the bones*, in which the commentary was mainly defensive, and certainly because of the growing influence of the *Fabrica* to which allusion is made in the *Vaesanus*, Sylvius had determined upon stronger measures clearly demonstrating the malice with which he now viewed Vesalius.

Renatus Henerus, who was to write a defense of Vesalius several years later, was sudying in Paris at this time.[91] In his later defense he remarked that he and the other students had expected Sylvius to write a definitive treatise on anatomy [92] but that Sylvius had considered himself forestalled by the success of the *Fabrica*, and "he was completely upset by observing that the prestige he had sought had gone to Vesalius, and it became his earnest desire to make everyone thoroughly despise the great and useful labors of [Vesalius]." Sylvius did complete his treatise, according to Henerus, but himself realized its imperfections by contrast to the *Fabrica* and so withheld publication. This treatise was presumably *In Hippocratis et Galeni physiologiae partem anatomicam isagoge*, declared to have been written as early as 1542 but not published until 1555, a work of more merit than Henerus concedes although far briefer than the *Fabrica* and, as its title indicates, still observing an allegiance to Galen. However, if we give even partial credence to Henerus's description of the situation, it is not difficult to picture the elderly, irascible Sylvius consumed by hatred of his "ungrateful" anti-Galenist student and further enraged by Fuchs's praise of the *Fabrica*. "While Sylvius was in labor with [the *Vaesanus*], as I now realize, we were forced to endure a constant stream of abuse and virtually incessant and furious invective against Vesalius. It wearied our ears and aroused the indignation of many of us." [93]

All Sylvius's restraint was now cast aside, and although the defense of Galenic anatomy was still his fundamental purpose it was essayed by offensive measures that sought to destroy Vesalius's position in the medical world and thereby nullify his importance as a critic of Galen. Undoubtedly the admiration for the *Fabrica* expressed by Fuchs must have contributed to the degree of frenzy apparent in the *Vaesanus*, and in this regard the concluding words of Sylvius's preface have some significance:

> After I had completed this work, behold, Fuchs published an anatomical epitome containing misrepresentations selected from that vast and worthless farrago of the slanderer. In my little book the refutations of those slanders are clearly set forth, and Fuchs will finally realize that Galen, after Hippocrates, is the sole parent of anatomy as well as of the rest of medicine. He will realize this much more clearly if he selects the rest of his epitome—for thus far he has considered only the bones and muscles—from nature's account and not from the slanderer's error-laden filth, and if he relies upon his own senses and judgment as I do when I write. If he applies himself to this study without reliance upon the words of anyone, I am certain he will at once denounce and cast to the furies that insolent and ignorant slanderer who has treasonably attacked his teachers with violent mendacity and time and again distorted the truth of nature.

Without commenting upon Sylvius's statement that he himself placed reliance upon the word of no one—presumably scorning even that of Galen—but based his work solely upon independent research, we note that he declares his own work, published in June, to have been completed before the first volume of Fuchs's *Epitome*, of which the preface is dated 10 January 1551. It seems possible that Sylvius may have stretched the truth slightly and that in fact he previously had had in mind some sort of attack on Vesalius that he felt compelled to compose and rush into print as a result of the praise Fuchs had granted to Sylvius's then-mortal enemy. It is interesting to note that according to the text of the *Vaesanus* Vesalius was guilty of treason because of his remarks critical of Galen who, together with Hippocrates, was declared the teacher of the medical profession. Elsewhere, too, there is the suggestion that this special quality of commanding loyalty was handed down by these ancient teachers and that Sylvius felt, as certainly the most vocal adherent of Galen, that Vesalius had been disloyal to him, too.

As Henerus remarks, in view of the degree of praise of Vesalius and criticism of Galen in Fuchs's *Epitome*, it is astonishing that Sylvius did not also attack Fuchs directly instead of subjecting him merely to indirect censure, but it may be that such attack would have diminished the force of the verbal blows against Vesalius. In consequence, Sylvius took the attitude that Fuchs had been deluded but would eventually realize the error of his ways. In fact, however, over the years anatomy was gradually becoming Vesalian, and not only did Sylvius realize this but examination of his *Isagogae*, already written but not published until 1555, indicates his own acceptance of some of the new anatomy so long as it did not require him to make a clear-cut denial of Galen. No doubt the result for him was spiritual turmoil and further bitterness toward his former student whom he considered responsible for this upsetting state of affairs. As far as the less sensitive world of medicine was concerned, Fuchs's *Epitome* is demonstrable evidence of the ever growing respect for Vesalius's achievement.

The author of the *Fabrica* was probably not especially disturbed by Sylvius's attempts to reëstablish the anatomy that had been demolished by Vesalius's research, but he could not fail to have been shocked by the violent, even hysterical attack upon himself personally. The nature of this unrestrained invective can best be seen in Sylvius's own words. The preface explains the purpose of the author in terms that are certainly extravagant but as yet not so heated as some of the later statements:

Although I have the fullest confidence in the divine Hippocrates and his wholly admirable expositor Galen, the greatest medical divinities after Apollo and Aesculapius, who never wrote anything that was not true about physiology [94] and the rest of medicine, I have heard that a certain mad deserter, wholly arrogant and wholly ignorant, was most iniquitously uttering the vainest slanders against their physiology. Hence, as befitted a loyal disciple, I left no stone unturned to free them from every possible suspicion of error. I believe that I have succeeded in this through my refutation of those slanders and through my annotations on the books *Use of parts*.[95] Hence the loyal reader will now clearly realize that this slanderer wickedly renounced his oath of allegiance to his master Hippocrates, in which he had promised the greatest gratitude to his teachers and to their adopted children, and, furthermore, that he sought in every way to criticize them falsely, since he hoped that by competing with such teachers for the leadership in anatomy he might some day acquire renown.

Having given this preliminary warning against the slanderer, Sylvius continues by noting with some satisfaction the success of his own countermeasures:

In this book I have refuted those slanders, not as they came to my mind and pen, but in the order in which I wrote my *Isagogae anatomicae*. On another occasion, in my annotations on the books *Use of parts*, I refuted them according to the order of [Vesalius's] books, but I did not pollute that sacred discourse with any mention of the slanderer. In both these works I have touched on merely some of the slanderer's more notable and shocking errors, because it would be an endless task to name them all and of little importance for the instruction of the loyal reader.

The introductory preface is followed by Sylvius's refutations of the slanderer's various attacks on Galen's veracity, usually those places where Vesalius had clearly pointed out Galenic error, citing Galen by name and referring to the errant text. The refutations are hardly convincing, although Sylvius appears to have thought them devastating. Shrillness of objection, assertion of Vesalius's inability to comprehend Galen's language, faulty editing of texts, and postclassical alteration in the human structure, are major defenses of Galenic anatomy. *On the bones* is declared "in exact accordance with the bones of man and was written solely about them, as is very clear to anyone who compares them to the human skeleton." [96] Contrary to Vesalius's denial, the cribriform plate was declared to have a number of minute foramina in it to permit the cerebral pituita to drain through and thence finally into the palate and nostrils. "Yet the slanderer utterly denies that we can observe these foramina so correctly described by Galen and even denies that they exist." Sylvius appears to have felt especially confident of his ability to prove the correctness of his opinion on this matter and scolds Vesalius at some length:

Hereafter, my good man, bow to the veracity of your teachers and of nature, of whose structure you are ignorant, and the use of whose works you iniquitously deny. Permit me to recommend that you investigate these matters in a fresh cadaver; then you yourself will recognize your arrogance, disloyalty, ignorance, and ingratitude, and you will not say that the ethmoid bone merely appears to be cribriform but that such is not really its nature. That was your reply to our learned physician Sanctangelus when he showed you the very fresh skeleton of a child that, with some other bones that confute your slanders, I sent by him to Cornelius van Baersdorp, the distinguished imperial archiater.[97]

Vesalius was declared wrong in his criticism of Galen's assertion that the carotid artery entered the skull through the foramen ovale,[98] his denial of Galen's explanation of the movements of the head,[99] and his ascription to man of a premaxillary bone and suture [100] that, as Vesalius had pointed out, are found only in the dog. Also, despite Vesalius's criticism, Galen, according to Sylvius, was correct in composing the lower jaw or mandible of two bones.[101] It was true, he wrote, that the sternum was no longer formed of seven bones,[102] but Galen's description of such a sternum was correct for his own times even though the human race had in a sense betrayed Galen by changing its structure, just as it had allowed the formerly solid bones of the fingers, as he described them, to lose that solidity.[103]

There are in all twenty-eight such refutations, concerned also with the veins, arteries, abdominal viscera, and organs of generation. Despite these refutations Sylvius must have been aware that his cause was hopeless and that Vesalian anatomy was winning over the former disciples of Galen, but he chose to look upon this movement as the result of disloyalty and misrepresentation. The supporters of Vesalius were poor deluded persons and obviously ignorant. "There is today a very large group of such physicians in France, Italy, and Germany, who, despite their total lack of anatomical skill, give their approval to all the writings of the slanderer and support them strenuously." [104] The mere thought of this sort of thing spreading still farther filled Sylvius with a kind of frenzy to which he gave unrestrained voice in his concluding words:

After I had wholly refuted several slanders impiously spread by that madman against the names of Hippocrates and Galen, I explained seven successive lines from chapter 43 of the second book of the slanderer regarding the parts of the hand, which are very clear to anyone; or, more correctly, I expunged almost as many errors as there are lines. I gathered them into a commentary I had intended to add to those aforesaid, but when I realized that not only in that chapter but also in others everything was so filled with grammatical and other errors, as well as an ignorance of physiology, that it would have been easier to cleanse the Augean stables than to remove even the worst lies from this hodgepodge made up of thefts and bloated with slanders, I changed my mind and decided that it must be suppressed. As you see, loyal and honest readers, no solid erudition is to be hoped for from this verbose farrago of the slanderer. To seek errors in it is to look for water in the sea. Let that disloyal slanderer now go where he belongs, let him call the gods into combat, let him slander his teachers, let him sound his little glories and loudly proclaim his own book. After my present work brings about his downfall, let him contend for the title of prince of anatomy among the ignorant. Behold, Nemesis reviles the head of him who has an evil conscience; she demands punishment of those who belittle and slander their teachers.

I implore his imperial Majesty to punish severely, as he deserves, this monster born and bred in his own house, this worst example of ignorance, ingratitude, arrogance, and impiety, to suppress him so that he may not poison the rest of Europe with his pestilential breath. He has already infected certain Frenchmen, Germans, and Italians with his deadly exhalation, but only those ignorant of anatomy and the rest of medicine. If they had acquired even a cursory knowledge of these subjects by reading Galen's books, or, even better, by undertaking or at least observing many anatomies, they would never have been so foolish as to leave their own excellent leaders so hastily for the camp of ignorance. These men deserve pity and pardon if they are willing to learn justice and nature's skill as expressed in us, and provided they do not condemn their divine teachers. They must also abandon the false doctrines of this deserter, for they can acquire perfection only by returning to the liberal, humane, and comprehensive standards of their teachers.

I hear that they now earnestly desire a reconciliation with their teachers and a new oath of allegiance to their forces. I am sure this is highly pleasing to all physicians and all students of medicine. Therefore, you who have been reborn, loyal sons of Aesculapius, Frenchmen, Germans, and Italians, I beseech you to come to me as recruits and to assist me in whatever further defense of your teachers may be needed, since I am wearied by my years and my labors. If this hydra rears some new head, destroy it immediately; tear and tred on this Chimera of monstrous size, this crude and confused farrago of filth and sewage, this work wholly unworthy of your perusal, and consign it to Vulcan. Although it contains a great many of Galen's plumes, they have, so to speak, been defiled by foul barbarity, and have lost their author's splendor. If you remove these plumes, nothing remains except a sea of slanders, insignificant discoveries either utterly false or utterly trivial, and worthless paper. But if, in that verbose farrago of the slanderer, something is found fit to be read—for no writer is wholly vile—it is so slight that it could be limited to a single sheet of paper, provided that you disregard the illustrations, which are covered with shadows, and their indices of letters. It [the illustrations] is a superstitious, obscure, and wholly useless procedure, the illustrations and their lettering more of a hindrance than a help. This is especially so for physicians for whom the art is long but life short and who ought rather to investigate the nature of the parts of the human body by sight and touch in many anatomies than in illustrations and books alone. Neither shipmaster nor military leader nor any sort of artisan is permitted to prepare for his trade by this sort of contemplative exercise; indeed, Galen allowed not even plants to be depicted, *De facultate simplicium medicamentorum,* VI, *initio.*[105]

Distressing as this unseemly attack was, it completely missed its mark. According to Henerus it caused many to turn away from Sylvius in disgust,[106] and it certainly had no influence upon Fuchs, who proceeded to publish the second volume of his *Epitome,* in which he called Vesalius "my very great friend" and borrowed from the *Fabrica* as heavily as he had for his first volume.

Such consolation, if Vesalius considered it so, was no doubt further increased by the appearance of another work dedicated to the harassed anatomist in extremely laudatory terms by its French editor, Jean Canappe,[107] although a Spanish plagiarism which appeared in December probably did not come to his attention until some time later. This latter was the work of Bernardino Montaña de Monserrate[108] who produced a brief anatomical treatise of medieval character containing crude copies of some of the illustrations from the *Fabrica* as well as from the *Commentaria* of Berengario da Carpi.[109] The plagiarisms have the faults that so irritated Vesalius, crudeness and severe reduction in size. He never mentions the work, of which he may not have learned until considerably later, and possibly he was beginning to realize the inevitability of such plagiarisms.[110]

Whatever may have been Vesalius's reaction to these various publications, and despite the frustrations and even irritations arising out of his care of the imperial ailments, we do know that during the long sojourn in Augsburg, which lasted until mid-October 1551, he found great pleasure in his association with the Augsburg physicians, of whom he makes mention of Achilles Pirmin Gasser, Adolph Occo, and Luke Stenglin.[111] As a result of this association he was able also to observe some of their more interesting cases and participate in some of their autopsies. These friendly relationships were certainly a welcome and soothing contrast to the shrill hatred exhibited by Sylvius in the *Vaesanus.* In the second and revised edition of the *Fabrica,* Vesalius recalled a case he had seen in Augsburg of a woman of fifty who had suffered for a year from what may have been, according to the description, an ovarian cyst:

In Augsburg I, together with several other physicians, found in a female weaver after her death more than sixty Augsburg measures of serous water, in her uterus, which alone weighed three pounds. Nowhere, however, was water present around the intestines, nor was there a loose tumor in the hands or feet, or even in the viscera, nor was there otherwise damage of any other organs. In addition to the size of that uterus, its mouth had remarkably thickened and had attached to the peritoneum on the whole right side. The glands of the right ovary had increased astonishingly as if nine or ten goose eggs, or rather an ostrich egg, were therein, and filled with a single humor not dissimilar from the white of egg, but perhaps a little thicker.[112]

A second case in which Vesalius was involved in Augsburg was that of the distinguished and learned Herr von Imersel. Although Vesalius does not appear to have taken part in the case prior to the death of the patient, he did participate in the autopsy examination to which he refers in the revised *Fabrica*. His account of the findings, given below, has permitted a distinguished medical historian to diagnose heart-block and to declare the "fleshy mass" to have been "an intracardiac parietal or lateral thrombus, possibly embedded in a partial aneurysm of the heart."

The heart of a noble and learned man caused us no little astonishment, as in its left ventricle we found almost two pounds of glandulous—but darkish—flesh with the heart distended around that fleshy mass like a uterus. . . . Before death the man was of a somewhat melancholy temperament and very wakeful, with a remarkably uneven and varying pulse that clearly displayed the contraction of the artery. For many months before his death—although otherwise he walked about as if in good health—the pulse, or rather the artery, seemed to contract and remain contracted for an interval of three or four pulses or beats, as if it were attempting expulsion. Indeed, in the final weeks of his life, during an interval of nine beats three or only two dilations of the artery were apparent to the touch. He retained the animal faculty and functions of the animal spirit up to his death, which resulted not so much from the defect of his heart as from gangrene of the left leg, which took its rise from the impeded pulse of the artery as if those pulses, interrupted by the heart's defect, did not properly revive the native heat of the leg; especially since several years earlier that artery extending to the lower leg had been damaged by a gunshot wound.[113]

The case made sufficient impression upon Vesalius for him to refer to it a second time in his later *Examen*.[114] In the same year he was involved in a case of multiple embolism in a servant of Herr von Mol:

So also in the same year the heart of a servant of Herr von Mol was observed, likewise because of a gangrene. First we amputated a leg below the knee, and then a hand, about the middle of the forearm, several days before his death—even though our hopes were slight.[115]

A final observation relates to a two-year-old girl who had developed such a large collection of fluid in her head that in the course of seven months her head had grown to far greater size than a man's. Vesalius's description includes what is certainly one of the earliest observations of brain-stem signs:

In Augsburg I observed a little girl of two years whose head had so enlarged in about seven months that I have seen no man's head as large in mass. It was that ailment the ancients called hydrocephalus, the result of the water that is gradually collected and retained in the head. In this girl's case it had not collected between the skull and the exterior membrane girdling it, or the skin —where otherwise the books of physicians teach that the water is retained— but in the cavity of the brain itself, and in its right and left ventricles. Their capacity had so increased and the brain itself had so extended that almost nine pounds of water or, incredible as it may seem, three Augsburg measures of wine, were contained. In addition, as the brain in the vertex of the head was thin like a membrane, or like a body continuous with its thin membrane, so also the skull was wholly membranous and osseous only in the area representing the girl's skull before her head increased abnormally. It was almost as in recently born children where we observe the frontal bone and bones of the vertex to form where they are otherwise coterminus, and in many children are seen to be membranous over a notable area. Meanwhile, the cerebellum and the whole base of the brain were normal as also the extensions of the nerves. I found water only in the ventricles of the brain, which were augmented, as I have mentioned, and up to the time of her death the girl had all her senses. However, when I observed her a few days before her death, as often as her head was moved by those attending, and however slightly it was somewhat raised, immediately she was disturbed by a severe cough, with difficulty in breathing, suffusion of blood, flushing of the whole face, and a flowing of tears. The rest of her body was weak, but although lax and infirm there was no paralysis of the limbs nor even any notable appearance of emaciation or serous tumor in the limbs or epilepsy. The liver, when it was examined a little after death, was pale and otherwise somewhat more contracted and harder than a normal liver; the spleen appeared very large and soft as if it had functioned for some time in place of the liver; so that, together with the physicians present, I marveled at nothing more than that such amount of water had for so long collected in the ventricles of the brain without greater symptoms.[116]

Throughout this time the emperor was yet in Augsburg but apparently growing weary of it and preparing to move to Innsbruck, since he wrote to his sister Mary on 4 October that "Innsbruck is healthy, and although it may be bad for my chest I need not go out when it is cold." [117] However, the emperor's health was to remain much the same even after his removal to the latter city, where he arrived on 2 November. Here, too, the attendant physician was Baersdorp, although Vesalius was present and may well have been in attendance from time to time or at least consulted by Baersdorp.

A letter to his father-in-law, dated from Innsbruck on 16 October, indicates that Vesalius had preceded the emperor and was still accompanied by his wife who, although she would have preferred to be home in Brussels, had yet enjoyed the natural beauty of the country from Augsburg to Innsbruck. Furthermore, as Vesalius continues, although lodging had been found in Innsbruck, everything was dearer than in Augsburg.[118] The lodging, as we learn from another document, had been no problem since the imperial entourage had been quartered upon the local inhabitants, "le docteur Vesalius b. Kirchpeuler." [119]

The first letter written by the long-suffering van Male from Innsbruck is dated 9 December 1551 and, as may be supposed, was concerned with his imperial charge:

Yesterday the emperor said that his health is astonishing since at this time of year and in this place he is free of arthritis and any kind of ailment, as I believe you are aware from Baersdorp's letter. Two weeks ago we suspected that his bowel and intestines were more or less upset, and Cornelius sent a letter about it to the Queen, which he showed me secretly, not without fear of the emperor's weak constitution. However, he says now that he has changed his opinion since he has observed that everything internal is healthy. The emperor has become an insatiable reader and listens to me reading each night, and when he has prepared for bed he orders the book to be repeated if sleep evades him. Such is my rest.[120]

Several days later, however, on 13 December, the news from Innsbruck was less reassuring. Perhaps as a result of his sense of well-being the emperor had returned to his pleasures, "whereupon a slight fever became his companion, as if of the arthritis but usually germane to his pleasure. That fever ran through almost every joint of his body, and now as if in a final scene it has seized them all."[121] The next letter, a few days later, continued to develop this same doleful theme as well as to portray vividly the manner in which the emperor abused his health, or rather discouraged health by his undisciplined dietary practices:

In these last several days the emperor has not been very well, and Baersdorp has written to the queen about it at length. . . . Baersdorp is my friend and patron; I like and respect him, and advise him of those things I hear that are of some importance to the worthiness of his name and reputation. I am not a physician, but often it is the gardener who speaks words of wisdom. Baersdorp has not been allowed to get at the root of the emperor's many ailments; [the main trouble lies in] his belly and his ruinous gluttony, which is hateful to us, and which is such that even during the strongest attacks and torments of ill health he does not limit his eating and drinking of harmful things. Then the court is enraged, it cries out and rants against both the emperor's gluttony and fickleness and the indulgence and willingness of his accommodating physician. The story is now commonly told that when the emperor dislikes meat it is removed; if he wishes fish it is placed before him; if he thirsts for beer it is not denied him; if he develops a loathing for wine it is withdrawn. His physician— as gossip has it—has become a parasite. What the emperor says, he says; what the emperor denies, he denies. Recently the emperor suffered torments at the termination of his intestines from a very troublesome flux of the bowel. He had contracted the complaint from cold drinks—he is displeased unless they are ice-cold. I do not wish to play the role of Podalirius, but I realized that it was not desirable for him to suffer the calamity of ice-cold beer before dawn, which had been exposed to the open air the whole night. This was prepared for him by a servant many days before, I say, according to those directions and at the temperature he favored so that he did not refuse it even in danger of imminent dysentery. Since I was his before-dawn supplier of drink, for he drank at that hour daily, I heard groans and sighs issuing from him, witnesses of his pains; I asked what was wrong, and he complained of the movement of his intestines, nephritis, haemorrhoids, innumerable ills. I replied that it seemed necessary to alter his harmful drinks, that there is no one of all of us who is Milonian enough in strength and health to endure iced beer at that time without harm, before dawn and in the winter, especially one suffering from age, his years, his state of health, sicknesses, travels, and labor. He recognized the fact, was overcome by these truths, and to repair the damage he had received, to please his sensible counselor, he forbade beer to be exposed to the open air. Also Cornelius interdicted very cold wine at his morning meal and late snack. I don't know how long he will be obeyed. Here we often beseech the Queen to stop sending fish. Who would believe it? Recently in such peril he continued a fish diet for two days, calling for raw, roasted, and boiled oysters, sole, and all the products of the sea.[122]

One may well imagine that Vesalius, since he was not the immediate physician to the emperor, would seek to avoid the thankless task of attempting to handle such an intractable case. Nevertheless, at the end of January Baersdorp was ordered to hasten to the sickbed of the King of Bohemia, and for a week it appears that Vesalius became directly responsible for the emperor's health.[123] Happily, just at this time van Male was able to write that "the emperor is almost miraculously well," [124] and he seems to have remained so throughout the absence of Baersdorp:

> Baersdorp will return tomorrow, as Hubermontius, who returned to us yesterday, has promised. . . . Although Baersdorp has been absent, nevertheless the emperor happily continues in his former health; yesterday he prescribed some pills for himself—there were no unfortunate results.[125]

Even a week after his return, Baersdorp was able to write to Charles's sister, the Queen of Hungary, that "the emperor is well in every respect, God be praised . . . he eats and drinks with a good apetite." [126] But Baersdorp, if not plagued by the emperor, was now bothered by a personal problem. The Neapolitan protomedicus, to whom Vesalius had long ago dedicated his *Tabulae anatomicae*, had just died, and Baersdorp aspired to the position. The emperor, with an indecent lack of gratitude, awarded the title to another, and thereby incensed not only van Male but the entire court at Innsbruck. It was a particularly flagrant case which caused much gossiping as van Male's next letter indicates:

> It is a great consolation to us that in such an adverse state of affairs, one almost to be despaired of, the emperor has displayed such courage, strength of spirit, knowledge of a blameless life, and, what is of great value in such danger, excellent health. During public dangers there is no room for private inconveniences. However, because it is, as I may say, the very law of friendship [that is involved here], the greatness of the wrong compels me to an explanation of the grievance. I wish to explain in a few words to your illustrious lordship the emperor's injustice to Baersdorp, a man deserving much, both by reason of fairness and justice.
>
> Several months ago a protomedicus had to be chosen in place of Narcissus, the Neapolitan physician who had died. By continuity and precedent Baersdorp ought to have been selected, and from the attitude of the court our Cornelius [Baersdorp] believed that what former physicians had attained, in accordance with a kind of fixed order of succession, would not be denied him; nor did the emperor reject Cornelius's request when the latter sought the position from

him last summer in Augsburg; what is more, a number of persons sought to buy the office from Cornelius, even though he had not yet been granted it. I saw a letter in which the Neapolitans bid 4000 crowns. Finally, however, it turned out that Cornelius was denied both the fruit and the honor, and a certain Neapolitan proposed by the viceroy has gained it from the emperor.

Everyone talks of the great wrong inflicted on Cornelius, which he feels as no slight insult, especially since he considers that the successful candidate is unworthy of the favor. I would not bother your illustrious lordship with the matter except that Cornelius sought this service from me; he says that his affairs can be more frankly presented in this way, for otherwise he would be prevented by embarrassment.[127]

Vesalius, as the greatest medical personage at the court, was possibly the only one who had no interest in acquring the meaningless title and was content to allow his abilities to underwrite his fame, and this attitude was probably strengthened at this time by the dedication to him of another work, notable because it had nothing to do with medicine.[128] The year 1552 was also to see further plagiarism through the publication by Jean de Tournes in Lyons of the entire text of the *Fabrica*, although curiously enough illustrated solely by four much-reduced illustrations of the skull.[129]

As a result of the emperor's long sojourn in Innsbruck, the German princes, no doubt encouraged by his debilitated health, were left free to plot amongst themselves as well as with the King of France. Despite his knowledge of such plotting and the characters of the plotters, the emperor, ever more lethargic, was slow to take alarm for his safety—although his bodyguard was slim and his sister Mary had been regularly sending him alarming news and admonitions from the Netherlands. The major danger was Maurice of Saxony, and, as early as 5 October 1551, Mary had sent her brother definite information of that prince's intrigues within Germany and with France. Vexed by her failure to arouse Charles, on 5 March 1552 she sent him a final warning in which she remarked with some asperity that "this incredulity, this refusal to place faith in our warnings, may cost you very dear."[130] But by this time certain intercepted letters had at last fully awakened the emperor from his lethargic complacency, which had no doubt been induced in part by his ill health.

By May, Maurice was threatening Innsbruck, and on the 6th of that month Charles set off secretly with six attendants and plans for making his way to the Netherlands. Legend has it that the Groom of the Chamber took to the imperial bed to impersonate his master where, undetected, he heard the usual morning mass.[131] However, the small imperial party found the way blocked everywhere by the troops of Maurice so that it was necessary to return to Innsbruck, albeit so secretly that few were aware that Charles had ever left.

During the 18–19 May, Maurice's forces moved on Innsbruck, and on the evening of the 19th the emperor, accompanied by his small entourage, including Vesalius, fled. The only route available was over the Brenner pass and was made all the more difficult by the driving rain, the con-

sequent frequent extinction of the torches, and the need to carry the
feeble and gouty emperor in a litter. Two of the baggage mules were lost,
but the little party pushed on without pause until it reached Bruneck.
There, however, food was so short that the emperor ordered the journey
onward to Villach in Carinthia, safely distant from the most immediate
dangers.[132] Some years later Vesalius referred to this episode, recalling
that he had participated in the flight from Innsbruck and that he had
made use of his enforced sojourn in those distant parts to continue his
studies of comparative anatomy:

> We set forth from Innsbruck in the greatest haste for Villach, where I was
> astonished to see how different from my previous observations were the skulls in
> the cemeteries of Styria and Carinthia—which produce different and strange
> types of men both in mind and in body, thereby demonstrating nature's many
> whims as regards shape.[133]

As the emperor's physicians had noted in the past, Charles's health
seemed to improve with danger and the need for exertion. The flight from
Innsbruck and the need therefore to prepare punishment for his rebellious
vassals and to undertake war against France seemed as good a prescription for his recovery as any his physicians had to offer. Yet, as it turned
out, although his spirit had revived his health was too far gone for recovery, and at this time, according to contemporary descriptions, he remained thin and white; his eyes were sunken and his beard snow-white;
he could not walk without the aid of a stick and a friendly arm.[134]

The first problem that now faced the emperor was that of meeting the
French danger. With the Spanish and Italian regiments, which had been
gathered in northern Italy, Charles left Villach on 13 July, traveling by
way of Linz, Brixen, Sterzing, and so back to Innsbruck on 1 August.
Presumably Vesalius was with the imperial party which after a week in
Innsbruck, moved on first to Munich and thence to Augsburg where it
again delayed from 20 to 31 August. Thus Vesalius had an opportunity
to renew his acquaintance with his old friend Wolfgang Herwart, whose
eyesight was troubling him more and more. The matter may have been
discussed between them as well as with the Augsburg physicians, Gasser,
Occo, and Stenglin, with whom Vesalius was now well acquainted.

The imperialists left Augsburg on 1 September, reached Ulm the following day, traveled thence to Strasburg on the 15th, and to Landau on
the 24th. Here once again the emperor was violently attacked by gout,[135]
causing a delay of more than two weeks and providing the French defenders of Metz with sufficient time to render their position impregnable
against the forthcoming siege. It was at Landau that Charles received information from his sister Mary that there was a real desire for peace in
France, fostered in part by a great lack of money; hence immediate action might hasten negotiations. Such information, coupled with the realization that he could not pay his own troops throughout the winter, led
the emperor to determine upon the siege of Metz, the key to Lorraine and
Champagne,[136] but although this objective was the correct one, time had

run out. Already seventeen days had been lost through the emperor's most recent attack of gout, and it was not until 13 October that his forces made contact with those of the Duke of Alba, already in the neighborhood of the fortress.

Moreover, no sooner had the emperor arrived than the ardors of the march proved too much for his enfeebled constitution, and he was compelled to remain in Boulay on 20 and 21 October, moving on the following day to Thionville, his headquarters during the campaign. He was not able to take the field personally for more than two weeks, and during this period of illness and convalescence important decisions were left to subordinates, not to mention the evils of a divided command. Two letters of Baersdorp to the emperor's sister Mary reflect the condition of Charles's health at this time. The first, written on 21 October, recounts that both arms and knees were affected,[137] and the second, of 26 October, indicates not a cure but rather, as time was to prove, a temporary recession of the malady: "His Majesty's gout, which has been strongest in the right arm and hand, although also afflicting both knees and the left shoulder, has begun to recede. There has been the usual fever, but less severe. . . . He sleeps well now and has recovered some appetite, although he eats little." [138] It is likely that at this time Baersdorp was completely in charge of the case since Vesalius had probably been requisitioned for service as a military surgeon.

As a result of the emperor's illness the siege did not begin until 31 October, by which time the Duke of Guise, in command of the French, had had some two and a half months to prepare the defenses and to victual the garrison, while a force had been collected in the field to harry imperial communications.[139] Now that his illness had held up the siege sufficiently to make it a foregone failure, Charles enjoyed an illusory and transitory period of better health, sustained in part perhaps by military demands and a sparser field diet. Thus on 5 November it was possible for Baersdorp to write again to the Queen of Hungary that the "emperor's condition constantly improves"; on the 8 November he was compelled to note a "slight catarrh and a twinge of the gout," both of which had been circumvented.[140] On 10 November, van Male could write that "the emperor is daily in better health" and follow this with a second letter in which he remarked that "the emperor is so well that he could scarcely be better," a remark echoed by Baersdorp on 14 November with the additional statement that Charles had no great desire for food, a fact which may have played some part in his recovery. On 19 November, Baersdorp wrote that the emperor's recovery had reached the point where once again he could sit his horse and visit the troops in the field.[141]

As suggested, Vesalius was very likely acting as military surgeon during this period, a role in which he had by then had much practice, and it was in the course of the siege of Metz that he found himself unwittingly placed opposite his great French counterpart, Ambroise Paré. There seems not to have been any opportunity for a meeting. In his account of his travels, Paré informs us that a belief that the drugs with which the wounded defenders of Metz were treated had been poisoned led the king to send him to the besieged town with such new supplies as a single horse could carry. Managing to evade the imperial forces, he made his way into the town at midnight and, after a week spent in assuring the noble defenders of their king's good will and faith in their courage, finally was able to tend the wounded with his fresh supplies. Furthermore, according to Paré, the winter, which had set in early, was extremely severe. The ground was covered with two feet of snow, and the lot of the imperialists was wretched indeed.[142] Whether or not Vesalius was stationed with the troops in such uncomfortable conditions, ultimately the combination of weather and strong defenses led to the abandonment of the siege on New Year's day.

The six weeks that Charles had spent camped in the field had found him in fairly good shape, bothered by neither his stomach and intestinal complaints nor his gout. Thus wrote Baersdorp to the Queen of Hungary, on 30 December 1552.[143] But once the siege had been given up and the emperor returned to Thionville and thence back to the Netherlands, he fell victim to his old maladies. It was at this time that the English ambassador was joined by Sir Andrew Dudley with instructions for avoiding England's treaty obligations and mediating between Charles and Henry II. At Luxemburg, after having been put off for a week because of Charles's gout, they were granted an audience of which they reported:

The emperor addressing Morison in Italian, as his Majesty was not able to speak loud, and Dudley, by reason of an extreme cold and murre, not being able to hear him; but yet, though hoarse at the beginning, when he [the emperor] came to name his enemy, he spake so loud that Dudley might easily hear what he said . . . In all the time of Morison's being in Germany [1550–1553] he had never seen the Emperor so nigh gone, never so dead in the face, his hand never so lean, pale and wan; his eyes that were wont to be full of life when all the rest had yielded to sickness, were then heavy and dull, and as nigh death in their look as ever he saw any.[144]

The imperial party reached Brussels on 6 February 1553, and the account of the entry into the city, as described by Marcantonio Damula, the Venetian ambassador, indicates how dire Charles's situation had become. "His Majesty returned here in an open litter disclosed to the view, gazing upward, stirring himself very little. . . . All the people ran to see him . . . because it was the common belief that he had died." [145] On the 28th the English ambassador wrote to the Privy Council that "the Emperor is not likely to stir hence a good while; he is said these three or four days to have been shrewdly handled with his gout." Another dispatch of 18 March declared that "I heard it from good place, that upon Saturday was seven days he did take his rites; howbeit, he that did tell it said he did so because he useth to be houseled twice in the Lent. Others deny it plainly, and say it was for that he had before that fallen into a swoon and was for a season like a dead man." [146] On the 24th still further information was forthcoming to the effect that:

The Emperor is somewhat amended, as his poticary saith. A two days since his physician, Vesalius, was with me; unto whom I said "The Emperor will make the world to set less by physic than you physicians would have it; that the Emperor ready to spend millions, can by all your recipes come by no health that is able to tarry with him two months together; I ween his sisters will prove his best physicians." His answer was, "It is rather he that may teach all men to honor physic, which hath so oft plucked him from his grave." He told me that his Majesty taketh guaiacum, and is far better now than he was a twelve days since.[147]

The continued delicate condition of the emperor's health naturally led to its further discussion in later ambassadorial reports, and inevitably mention was made from time to time of the attending physicians. Thus on 14 April a joint dispatch of Morison, the English ambassador to the emperor, and Sir Thomas Chamberlain, resident ambassador to the emperor's sister Mary, regent of the Low Countries, provided the following information:

While all these stirs are growing great in Germany, and while the French King is plying both the sides with his secret aides and unseen practices, the Emperor keepeth his bed, as unfit to hear of the mischiefs that grow round about him as unable to devise how to remedy them if they were still told him. The Emperor's stomach was this last week very much swollen and he in great feebleness. The Queen perceiving that pills made of Soldonella, an herb that cometh out of Italy, had done Mons. du Ruell good, purging his stomach of an incredible deal of water and other raw and gross matter, willed Doctor Cornelius [Baersdorp] to break the matter to the Emperor, and to see whether his mind would serve him to take the same purgation. The Emperor agreed to it, and at four of the clock the next morning took it; which did so work his stomach, so purge him, that (saving your Honors) he that did carry out that that came from him did faint by the way, and had much ado to keep himself on his feet, so much did the savor turn his stomach. It wrought on him nine times, besides twice upwards.

We had not known of this, but I, Morison, having mine uvula fallen, have had need of Vesalius these five or six days, who, amongst other things, told me the Queen and Cornelius did utterly despair of his life. The Emperor, as he saith, is now as glad that he took it as the Queen and Cornelius were sorry that ever they consented to give it unto him. The physician doubteth much the Emperor's recovery; but he hath a body so able to deceive physicians, and so able to live upon small strength that till he be gone indeed we will think he hath still to tarry a little while; for, seeing the purgation did him no more harm, it must needs be that it did him much good.[148]

Still further dispatches, although they made no mention of Vesalius, nevertheless suggested the continued medical problem of the emperor, with which he must have been concerned. On 23 April a further dispatch by Morison, Thomas Thirlby and Sir Philip Hoby, successor to Chamberlain, continued the saga of the imperial health and illness. They had been informed by the imperial ambassador to Rome "that two days agone the Emperor did feel his stomach very good, and did eat a good deal more goat's milk than his physician Cornelius would he should have done; who, perceiving that he had taken more in than he could after well digest, said his Majesty must no more do so. The emperor's answer was, they then must not serve him with too much." On 7 May, Morison wrote that Cardinal Granvelle had remarked that the emperor could not yet sign letters since the gout had seized upon his right hand. "Everybody is bold with the Emperor, and give him what disease they will, and in what place they list." On 13 May, Morison, Thirlby, and Hoby wrote that they had heard from the emperor's majordomo that he had been and still was very sick, but they could obtain no precise particulars "because he is kept so close that no man comes abroad able directly to say the Emperor is in this or that case." On 31 May the three wrote:

> . . . [we were] informed on good authority that the Emperor undoubtedly
> is alive, but he is so weak and pale as he seems a very unlikely man to continue.
> He covets to sit up and to walk and is sometimes led between two, with a staff
> also in his hand; but like as he desires to be thus afoot, so immediately after he
> has been a little up, he must be laid down again, and feels himself so cold,
> as by no means he can attain any heat.[149]

If Brantôme is to be believed, Vesalius had frequently informed the emperor that he had not much longer to live,[150] a statement certainly not conducive to the promotion of convalescence. However, it seems more likely that Vesalius's remark, if made, would have been in the form of a warning of the dire consequences that would result from a continuance of the emperor's excesses.

Meanwhile, the war against France continued. Térouenne was attacked in April 1553 and taken in June. In the following month, the young Prince of Savoy, Emmanuel Philibert, captured Hesdin. Whether Vesalius was at the siege of Térouenne is unknown although it seems unlikely, and although there is no certainty that he accompanied the forces of the Savoyard prince to Hesdin, the words of Paré, who was among the captured forces in the latter town, could refer to him.

Paré had been sent as a military surgeon to the defenders of Hesdin, and upon the surrender of the city he was brought forth with one of the defenders, a Monsieur de Martigues, whose lung had been pierced by the ball of an arquebus. Accosted by a group of gentlemen accompanied by "a physician and surgeon of the emperor," who might well have been Vesalius, "the emperor's physician bade me declare the essential nature of the wound and how I had treated it." Paré thereupon described the wounding of his patient, his examination of the wound, method of treatment, and prognosis of death, and completed his discourse by displaying his patient's wound as he applied a fresh dressing. Upon the death of Martigues, the Duke of Savoy sent some physicians and surgeons with an apothecary and a quantity of drugs to embalm the dead nobleman. They were accompanied by the emperor's surgeon once again, to whom Paré deferred as to a person of renown:

> The emperor's surgeon approached me and very courteously requested me to
> make the incision, but I refused, saying that I was not worthy to carry his in-

strument case for him. He asked me again to do it for the love of him, saying that it would please him greatly. I would have refused again . . . He replied once more that he wanted me to do it, and that if I did not I might have cause to regret. Assured of his desire, and for fear lest he do me some ill service, I took the razor, which I first offered to each individually, telling them that I was not experienced in such an operation; they all refused it.

When Paré had performed the autopsy and the body had been embalmed:

> The emperor's surgeon drew me apart and declared that if I would remain with him I should be well treated. . . . I thanked him very much for the honor he did me, but said that I had no desire to serve the enemies of my country. Then he told me that I was a fool, and that if he were a prisoner like me he would serve the devil to regain his liberty. Finally I told him flatly that I did not wish to remain with him.[151]

Ultimately Paré achieved his liberty without entering imperial service and returned to France. If it was not Vesalius whom he then met, that meeting would occur in Paris in 1559, as we shall see later.

It seems probable that from 1553 until the abdication of the emperor in 1556 Vesalius was able to spend much of his time in Brussels with his family. For a number of reasons we may assume that he had become a man of considerable substance. To begin with, his ancestors were people of means and his own parents did not find it necessary to place financial restraints upon his education. It seems likely, therefore, that some of this wealth passed on to the anatomist, and something also may have come from his wife's family, which was in comfortable circumstances. Then, too, Vesalius's years of service to the emperor were not without rewards, and, quite likely with him as with Baersdorp, there were various perquisites of office in addition to the salary. Finally, throughout the 1550's Vesalius's reputation as a physician had been constantly growing, and during those years of more or less settled existence in Brussels he appears to have developed a flourishing private practice—referring to it on one occasion as "my very great activities" [152]—as well as a widespread reputation as a consultant. Although there is no direct evidence for much of what has just been said, there is evidence of wealth at the end of his life, but those final years, spent in Spain, were not likely to have added greatly to it.

Hence the evidence presented in two letters to Cardinal Granvelle, one mentioning the possession of 30,000 *livres* and an annual income of 5,000 *livres*,[153] the second mentioning 10,000 florins with an income of some 3,000 florins,[154] suggests that an amount somewhere between these two figures must have made Vesalius a comfortably wealthy citizen of Brussels.

As a result of his wealth and newly settled existence, Vesalius undertook to have a home constructed, commensurate with his position.[155] Before that, whenever he was in Brussels with his wife and daughter he must have lived in the house that had belonged to his parents, from whom he had inherited it.[156] His only reference to his new home is in the reply, which he wrote in Spain, to Fallopio's *Observationes anatomicae*, where he compares the ginglymus to certain door hinges that he had learned about during the course of construction of his home:

> When [previously in lectures] I explained the shape of a ginglymus and called attention to those hinges in which mutual ingress [of the parts] resulted in one joint, that [hinge] with which my countrymen expertly hang their very large doors was unknown to me. With the aid of Galen I learned about it some years later in the course of building.[157]

It was about the time that Vesalius was writing this account in Spain, and presumably with little thought of returning to Brussels, that, on 6 November 1561, he transferred title of his home to his daughter Anne as a dowry. Still later, by a testament dated 4 June 1577, this daughter bequeathed the house to her husband Jean de Mol from whom it was purchased by the city of Brussels in 1587 and presented as a gift to the Count of Mansfeld.[158] It was in conjunction with this last transaction that a description of the property was drawn up:

> 1, a large and handsome estate, with houses, galleries, stables, and other buildings, a garden surrounded by walls and other outbuildings, commonly called the House of Vesalius, situated above the Bovendael, on the street called Hellestraete, adjoining on two sides the property of the Count of Mansfeld, on the third side a passage by which the count has access to the street, and on the fourth side to the properties on the street named above; and 2, an orchard planted with many beautiful trees, situated vis-à-vis the house and surrounded on three sides by the public way.[159]

There is also an old view of Brussels, engraved in 1639, showing the house, at that time in the possession of the Minimes of the Order of St. François de Paul, as a building of some magnificence.

Curiously enough it was precisely at this period, *c.* 1553, when Vesalius had returned to an active and prominent civilian life, that a rumor of his death spread, although probably not very widely. It is attested by an epigram written by Bruno Seidel and entitled, "The fame of the dead Vesalius." [160] The rumor probably had its origin in a confusion of Andreas with his brother Franciscus, a public health official in Vienna, who died there during a pestilence in 1552.[161]

The rumor of Vesalius's death must have been quickly dispelled, and in its place came recognition that not only was he very much alive but also a prominent and influential person. It was most likely in 1555 that the recognition of his influence in court circles and his closeness to the emperor led to Vesalius's receipt of an appeal from Johann Herwagen, a Basel publisher and friend.[162] Herwagen, who began his appeal with a flattering address to the "Second Aesculapius," first sought an imperial privilege so that he might publish books "without the irritation of censors." Second, his nephew, son of a deceased brother who had been a priest, was, obviously, illegitimate and needed to have his birth legalized, "if this can be done without too great expense"; then, if this could be accomplished, Herwagen hoped that Vesalius could arrange to have the

263

young man, a law student, appointed an imperial notary. The letter was brief but carried a burden sufficiently great to place a strain on any friendship, and whether or not the requests were granted appears unknown.

It was sometime during this period from 1552 to 1555 that Vesalius's mother, the former Elisabeth Crabbe, died. By her will, dated 2 August 1552, she left the sum of one *sou* per week each to five poor children to be chosen by her heirs and friends. This was to be paid after the mass she had established at the altar of Sainte Viven in the church of Sablon, at which the five children had to assist under pain of losing their weekly *sou*. Later, on 4 May 1555, this foundation was rearranged so that its annual income of fourteen florins was placed under the charge of the city and paid out to five children designated by Vesalius, his sister, and her husband.[163]

Very little is known of Vesalius's local medical activities at this time. However, it is possible that the following letter of 20 June 1553, written by Sir Philip Hoby to Sir William Cecil, Elizabeth's secretary of state, in which Hoby proposed a vacation for himself, had some relation to Vesalius's practice:

> Forasmuch as I am informed that there is, two days journey from hence, two bains, whereunto physicians here, unto whom I have opened the condition of my diseases have counseled me to go out for a fortnight or three weeks together, there to remain and to drink of the water of the same bains, saying that the doing thereof is undoubtedly very wholesome for the helping of my disease.[164]

Although our knowledge of Vesalius's local activities is scanty and conjectural, some of the opinions he wrote in response to requests from abroad have survived. The first of these opinions or consilia, dispatched from Brussels, is dated 6 November 1553 and concerns an Augsburg patrician, Marcus Pfister, the father-in-law of Vesalius's old friend Wolfgang Herwart. Thus it may be assumed that the request was sent to Vesalius through the influence of Herwart or perhaps of the group of Augsburg physicians with whom Vesalius was already friendly. Pfister, who was an old man and who died in 1561,[165] suffered from a skin irritation for which Vesalius prescribed some of the standard remedies of the day. It was not a consilium of particular importance, nor a case that should have had any special interest for Vesalius, and probably represents a favor to a friend or colleagues.

About 1555 Vesalius was called to Augsburg for the case of another patrician of that city, Leonard Welser, a member of the famous banking family of that name, attended by Achilles Gasser and the younger Occo. Ever since a ride on horseback Welser had suffered severe and constant pain. Upon investigation, Vesalius discovered a pulsating tumor in the region of the vertebrae and immediately diagnosed a fatal aneurysm of the aorta. However, after more than two years of suffering, the patient resorted to a quack with, of course, no result except the inevitable death. An autopsy performed on 25 June 1557 by both Occos, Ambrosius Jung, and Luke Stenglin, and the report of it, which Achilles Gasser sent to

Vesalius, revealed the correctness of Vesalius's diagnosis.[166] The aorta had expanded to the size of a palm and become firmly attached to the ribs and vertebrae. Within the aorta there was some thin blood and externally the artery had acquired a fleshy substance of about the thickness of a finger. The neighboring ribs had become carious, and one was completely broken. The vertebrae above the diaphragm, where connected with the aneurysm, had become spongy and so eroded that the tip of the little finger could be inserted into them, but there was no particular foetor. There was no lesion of the lungs, although before death the patient had spewed forth blood so that it might have appeared that he had suffocated. The skin of the back, where the pulsation of the tumor was noticeable, was livid and suffused with blood.

Vesalius replied on 18 July, thanking Gasser for his information and also mentioning that he had received a letter from a member of the family of the deceased Welser. The patient's ailment, wrote Vesalius, had to be deduced from various conjectures. This sort of arterial enlargement differed remarkably from other ailments in respect to its closely packed, contained matter. Some fat that Gasser observed in the autopsy and to which he referred in his letter had been observed by Vesalius to be somewhat similar to the vitreous humor of the eye, while the fleshy substance on the surface of the artery was similar to the fleshy substance on the internal surface of the ventricles of the heart. Moreover, Vesalius declared, he had had some previous experience with such cases, and mentioned that of Granvelle's sister. But, "may I perish if, after Master Leonard [Welser] had been seen by me, I did not meet with at least six other cases of this sort, although [the aneurysm] was located in different regions" of the body.[167]

Vesalius was the first, or certainly among the first, in postclassical times to understand the structure of a spontaneous aneurysm and also to be able to recognize and describe an internal aneurysm in the living.[168] From his remarks to Gasser it appears that the case of Granvelle's sister, regarding which we do possess Vesalius's opinion, was possibly somewhat earlier than that of Welser, although it may have been one of the half-dozen cases that came to his attention after returning from Augsburg. The patient's mother had written to Vesalius to say that she had observed the beginning of the aneurysm during her daughter's childhood but had thought it a pulse. This aneurysm, below the stomach in the anterior abdominal region, "is so loose that you might consider it a ball, now driven to the right side, now to the left, according as she lies on one side or the other." [169]

The year 1555 witnessed both the publication of Sylvius's *In Hippocratis et Galeni physiologiae partem anatomicam isagoge* and the death of its author. Thus Vesalius's most implacable enemy passed from the scene appropriately in the year of the publication of the revised edition of the *Fabrica*. By this time it was apparent that Vesalian anatomy was not only to survive the attacks of the conservatives but to become predominant. As an indication of the victory of the new, more scientific study of the human structure, the same year also witnessed the publication of a direct defense of Vesalius against Sylvius's *Vaesanus*. This was the work of Renatus Henerus of Lindau, mentioned previously in conjunction with Sylvius's attack.[170]

After expressing his displeasure with Sylvian fanaticism and the cult of Galen, Henerus very sensibly remarked that Galen would have been one of the first to cry out against the authority his own name had acquired to the detriment of scientific advancement. Furthermore, it was foolish, he stated, to deny Galen's very words indicating that he had been restricted to research in nonhuman materials; Sylvius had created a false condition of conservative obstruction at Paris [171] which contrasted unfavorably with the attitude of Rondelet at Montpellier where the new Vesalian anatomy had been accepted. Recognizing the fallibility of Galen as a matter of fact, Henerus proceeded point by point to refute Sylvius's arguments against the *Fabrica* as they had been presented in the *Vaesanus*. The defense was a clear-cut expression of the Vesalian victory that would henceforth permit a fairly consistent development of a scientific anatomy and physiology.

In the following year Vesalius was no doubt much occupied as a result of a pestilence that visited Brussels in June 1556. The presence of the emperor and his son Philip, who was once again in the Netherlands, this time for his father's forthcoming abdication of that area in his favor, led to extraordinary precautions in quarantine of infected houses and their inhabitants, and in prohibition of any persons being abroad except physicians, priests, and their assistants. Charles and Philip remained untouched but eventually at the end of June chose the course of discretion and retired from the city to the château of Sterrebeke.[172]

Several letters written by Baersdorp at this period describe the state of the emperor's health and also suggest that Vesalius was no longer sharing, at least to any considerable degree, in the care of the imperial patient. This was not likely to have caused Vesalius any regret since the incorrigible royal patient, already eating himself to death, had now imported a new cook from Portugal, Anna Andrade, capable, so it was said, of spicing dishes to the Emperor's liking and so enticing his lethal appetite. Of course, Vesalius had never officially been the personal imperial physician, and he may well have been occupied with others at court and with his private practice. That he was still in the good graces of the emperor, however, is indicated by a list of the imperial household drawn up in June 1556. Although the court had shrunk greatly in size preparatory to the emperor's abdication, the medical staff, reduced to two physicians, was composed of Baersdorp and Vesalius and, as an interesting sidelight, an Anne Vesalius was listed in the household as laundress.[173]

In the latter part of June 1556 a young student at Louvain, Augustine Teyling, son of the treasurer of the Duke of Egmont, was afflicted with severe fever and nosebleed which he survived, although as he recovered it was found that his legs had been seriously weakened.[174] Probably at the suggestion of the eminent Dutch physician Pieter van Foreest, a relative of the patient, Vesalius's opinion was sought on this case—which, on the basis of statements in his consilium,[175] remotely suggests bacterial meningitis. This was a problem beyond the therapeutic skill of that age, yet astonishingly the patient did recuperate sufficiently to continue his studies in France and Italy although he never regained full use of his legs.[176]

Previously, in April 1556, Vesalius had been created a Count Palatine,[177] one month after a similar title had been bestowed upon Cornelius van Baersdorp.[178] It was a reward for long and faithful service which cost the emperor nothing and was recognized by Vesalius as being a meaningless title, if only because Charles had been overgenerous in his distribution of it.[179] Titles, however, then as now, were looked upon by some as desirable, and it is a further indication of Vesalius's influential position at court that he found himself importuned by the Basel publisher Heinrich Petri for a similar title. In his reply to Petri, Vesalius announced that his petition to the Imperial Council had been unavailing, but that, by presenting the matter personally to the emperor, he had been successful, and that although the required fee was large the printer would receive the title. But, added Vesalius, "what you write of the privileges of a palatine is ridiculous," and the powers theoretically granted were meaningless. However, the register of such grants does not contain the name of Heinrich Petri,[180] and it may be that Vesalius was too sanguine in his assurances to his friend.

Since Vesalius was listed in June 1556 not as physician to the emperor but rather to the household, it was inevitable that in the final reduction of the household to the size the emperor planned to take with him to Spain, Vesalius's position would be done away with. A reflection of this is found in a letter of Simon Sulzer, Bishop of Basel, in which, quoting from a letter of the Zürich reformer, Heinrich Bullinger, he wrote: "Vesalius wrote from Brussels that the emperor has stripped his household, and already has stated privately that he will employ no more than twelve aides." [181] However, Vesalius, if at all disappointed, which seems unlikely, had the consolation, as he wrote on 28 August to Heinrich Petri, that "[although] the emperor has dismissed me from his service" he "[has] given me a desirable pension for life." In the same letter he indicated that he had already taken service with Philip II, "our king whose court I shall hereafter follow," [182] and for such service was to receive "300 florins annually and in addition 30 *sous* daily for subsistence." [183]

A final incident of 1556 was the appearance of another plagiarism of the Vesalian illustrations, one which irritated Vesalius intensely, as he was to indicate later in his *Examen.* The culprit in this instance was Juan Valverde de Hamusco, a native of Spain who associated his anatomical studies with those of Colombo in Rome, and no doubt for this reason acquired even greater Vesalian hostility.[184] Despite an apparently limited experience of anatomy, Valverde produced his *Historia de la composicion del cuerpo humano* (Rome, 1556), with the first edition in Spanish but the several later editions in Italian, Latin, or Dutch.[185] A notable part of the work is comprised of the illustrations of Gaspar Becerra, copper engravings plagiarized from the *Fabrica,* much reduced in size from the originals, and decidedly lacking the artistic quality of the Vesalian figures. Vesalius was still finding it difficult to realize that plagiarism of the *Fabrica,* even inferior examples of that craft, were in fact proof of the greatness of his achievement.

Chapter XI

THE REVISED *FABRICA*

 ESALIUS, as we learn from the *Letter on the china root*, because of the hostility with which the *Fabrica* and its author had been received at the imperial court in 1543 by the conservative and Galenic physicians, had determined to forego further anatomical research.[1] This decision, however, even though it led him to destroy the manuscripts of several studies, was wholly contrary to his intellectual character, and despite his declared intention, even as late as 1546, to undertake no further research, he was in fact already carrying on anatomical studies as his imperial duties permitted. In the *Letter on the china root* itself we are informed that Vesalius had taken advantage of the opportunity offered during the embalming of the Prince of Orange and the Lord of Hallweyn to study the internal organs, and, as we learn later, he was never loathe to participate in autopsies or, as during the flight of Charles V from Innsbruck, to make comparative studies of the skulls in the cemeteries of Styria and Carinthia.[2] There must have been considerable, if intermittent, investigation, partly the result of a compelling urge toward such activities, and partly a response to criticisms of the *Fabrica* and to such writings as supplemented that work. Furthermore, although the story of Vesalius's visit to Fuchs in Tübingen is most likely apochryphal,[3] it is probably representative of visits he did make to various medical schools as opportunity permitted.

As a consequence of such activities, at some unknown time Vesalius and Oporinus came to agreement upon the need for a revised edition of the *Fabrica*. Vesalius had recognized some shortcomings of the first edition even during the original composition, such as, for example, the faulty discussion of human embryology that came partly from a limited supply of proper dissection material, and he was aware that, given the opportunity, he might advantageously revise that section of his work. Also, the first edition, because of its all-embracing character, had not permitted concentration upon certain perplexing problems that had caused the young author to accept the erroneous doctrines of his predecessors or to make hasty and not-always-correct judgments. Revision of detail, extension of certain remarks, minor rearrangements, and more elegant and decorous exposition befitting an imperial physician would vastly enhance a new edition.

From what is known of Oporinus there seems little doubt that he too favored a revised edition of the *Fabrica*. Although not so aware of the faults in the substance of the text, he did realize that the design of the first edition was not entirely above reproach. As printer and publisher, however, he was compelled to heed economic realities. We know that the *Fabrica* was still available from Oporinus in 1547,[4] and it is not likely that he would have been willing to undertake a new edition before the old one had sold out or at least given prospects of being sold out. It may be recalled that in the same year Vesalius paid a brief visit to Basel,[5] and it is tempting to believe that at that time there was discussion of a future edition of the work and that a tentative agreement was reached that it would be undertaken as soon as the stock of the first edition showed signs of being exhausted.

In any event, it seems most likely that Vesalius prepared a revised manuscript of the *Fabrica* during the long sojourn in Augsburg between the close of August 1550 and October 1551, as the first five books of a revised edition of the *Fabrica* were offered for sale in a catalogue issued by Oporinus in May 1552.[6] However, no copy of these five books bearing an imprint of that year is known to exist, and perhaps Oporinus concluded that it would be better to await the printing of the two remaining books and sell only the complete work, or perhaps Vesalius objected to the sale of merely part of the *Fabrica*. To mention but one objection, the elaborate system of cross references would have been gravely injured by the appearance of even so large a fragment of the entire work.

A possible explanation of Oporinus's proposal to sell the first five books separately is found in a letter he wrote in 1555 to Conrad Hubertus of Strasburg.[7] From this we learn that the types used had been cast in moulds borrowed from the Spanish scholar and theologian Francisco de Enzinas—latinized as Dryander but not to be confused with Dryander of Marburg.[8] By the time the first five books had been printed the types had become too worn for further use, at least according to the high standards Oporinus maintained. Meanwhile, Enzinas had died and there was difficulty in borrowing the moulds a second time. It appears to have been this dilemma that for the moment tempted Oporinus to sell the partly printed work, probably to recover some of the capital he had invested in it, but when he abandoned this plan he sought instead, by letter, to buy the moulds—apparently with success—to complete "the work begun three years ago." Since the letter was written on 4 May it was at some time after that date that he succeeded in obtaining the type-moulds and was enabled to print the final two books of which the appended colophon carries the date August 1555. The revised edition of the *Fabrica* thus became available for purchase at or after this time.[9]

As in the examination of the first edition of the *Fabrica*, so in that of 1555 one turns at once to the title page. The printed title has been left as in the first edition except that the author has ceased to call himself "professor of the medical school of Padua" and instead declares that he is "physician of the emperor Charles V," and where in the first edition there was no mention of the publisher but only of Basel as the place of publication, in this edition the name of Joannes Oporinus was deservedly displayed at the foot of the page.[10] The privileges to print—imperial, French, and Venetian—remain the same, even though, as Vesalius had discovered, they had little significance; nevertheless, the length of time for which they had been granted had not yet expired. However, where earlier the privileges were placed upon a curved, decorated panel supported upon a small lion's head, in the new edition they are presented on the surface of a vivisection table along the edges of which remain the ropes and chains used to secure the animals.

Turning to the dissection scene, it is immediately apparent that a new version has been substituted, most likely the result of damage to the original wood block. This second is markedly inferior to its predecessor, but we know no more about the artist and block cutter of the second title page than we do of those of the first—in short, we are totally ignorant of their identities. Nevertheless, there are some indications that the drawing was not made under the supervision of Vesalius. If one inspects the title page of the first edition it is apparent that the anatomist's head, if at all large, is yet within normal limits, but in the new title page his head is grotesquely large and can only be explained as taken from that curious portrait in the first edition and repeated in the second. Apparently the artist of the new title page, without seeing Vesalius, assumed that the portrait displayed the authentic proportion of head to body and so produced a figure of this sort for the dissection scene. A second indication of the lack of direct communication between author and artist is the treatment of the unidentifiable object lying on the dissection table in the first title page. Obviously it meant nothing to the artist, who was nevertheless under orders to reproduce the illustration to the best of his ability. Consequently, in the second title page it has become a piece of paper, so indicated by the writing on it. Furthermore, the artist was apparently puzzled by the series of rings on Vesalius's index finger and thought to rectify this by reducing these multiple rings to a single one.

Whenever it was that Vesalius first saw the new title page, presumably after the block was cut and a proof taken, and too late for any alteration, or even after the new edition was published, he must have been disappointed. Although in other respects the edition of 1555 is superior to that of 1543, the artistry of the title page is decidedly inferior. There is a stiffness that can in part be ascribed to the restrictions of copying, but also a flatness and inferior perspective that must be attributed to the lesser skill of the artist, readily apparent, for example, in the presentation of the cadaver. Moreover, the figures were produced with heavier and coarser lines, in some instances almost caricatures of their more graceful counterparts in the earlier scene. The artist of the first edition was able to demonstrate the interest and emotions of the figures through their physical attitudes, whereas the one of the second edition, lacking this ability, sought to portray these things by facial expression. However, the smallness of the faces, the inability of the artist, or possibly a lack of delicacy on the part of the block cutter, made this effort a failure, and either the artist or the blockcutter had particular difficulty with the eyes.

Also, certain details are lacking from this second version of the dissection scene, such as the foliage growing out of the masonry, and some of the folds and wrinkles of costume. The interlaced I and O have disappeared from the upper wall of the building. Finally, and again for reasons unknown, some definite liberties were taken. Thus the nude figure clinging to a pillar has been clothed, the footgear of the lower-right figure has been altered, and one of the dogs has been changed into a goat.

It is astonishing that Oporinus, in all other respects so meticulous, was willing to accept this inferior work when otherwise the new edition of the *Fabrica* was much improved. It is possible that whatever damage occurred to the original wood block of the title page was the consequence of accident during the course of printing and that the inferior quality of the new block was the result of immediate need for a substitute.

Turning from the title page to the general appearance of the second edition, we note that the text was set in larger type with more space between the lines. The length of the line in the second edition is 18 centimetres, about a half-centimetre shorter than in the first edition, and due to larger type there are from one to three fewer words to the line. Moreover, owing to the larger type and the greater space between lines, the second edition has 49 lines of text to the page, whereas the first edition has 57. The second edition is therefore much easier to read. It may well be that there had been complaints about the difficulty of reading the earlier text since its smaller type, greater length, and closeness of lines frequently cause the reader to lose his place. This mishap is assisted by the fact that Vesalius did not use a particularly large vocabulary and there is frequent repetition of anatomical terms so that it is not unusual to find two successive lines beginning with the same word. Under these conditions there is always the danger that the eye may skip a line of text. On the other hand, the text of the first edition was occasionally broken up into paragraphs while in the second edition there are no such breaks; and although personal names were given in capital letters in the first edition, they are not in the second.

The second edition has been altered stylistically throughout. So important were these alterations to Vesalius that in certain instances he changed the initial word of a book or chapter even though this required the design and cutting of a new initial letter. The initial letters of the books and chapters have been given considerable study [11] so that it is not necessary at present to dwell on that subject. Very briefly, however, attention may be called to the fact that in some instances the larger initial

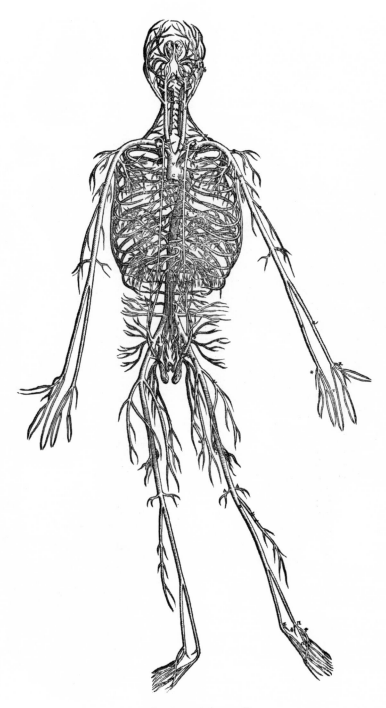

The "arterial man."

PLATE 33

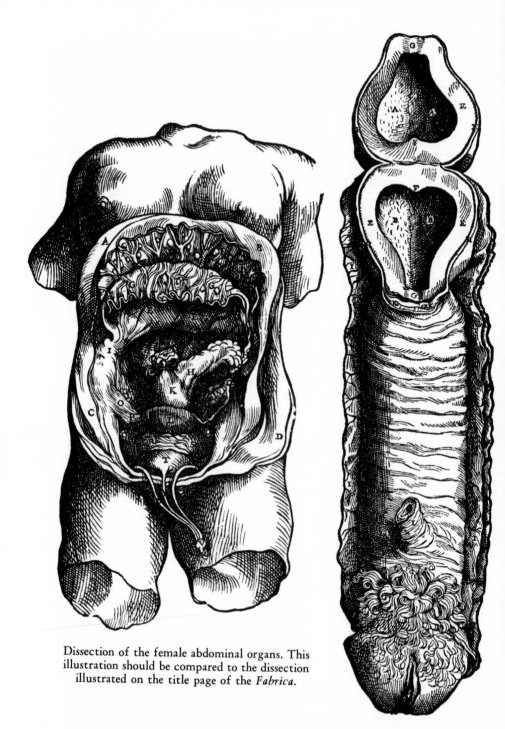

Dissection of the female abdominal organs. This illustration should be compared to the dissection illustrated on the title page of the *Fabrica*.

Dissection of the uterus of a body stolen by Vesalius's students. The uterus, vagina with part of the urethra, and vulva are represented.

PLATE 34

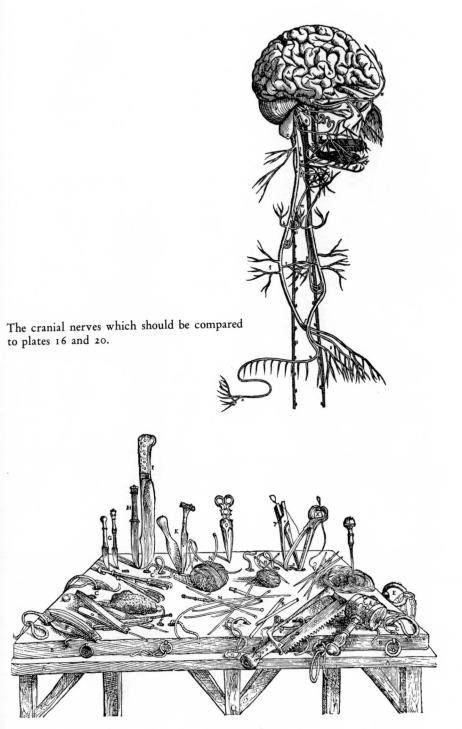

The cranial nerves which should be compared
to plates 16 and 20.

The instruments for dissection.

PLATE 35

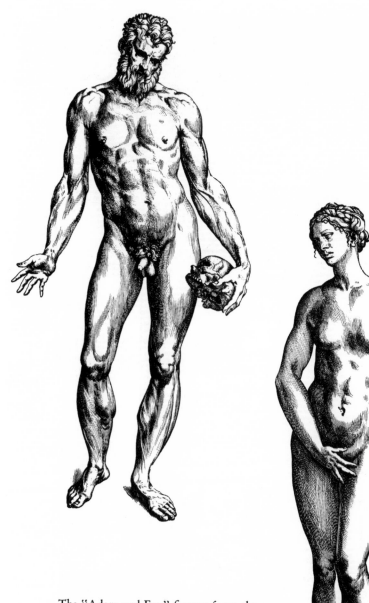

The "Adam and Eve" figures from the
Epitome.

PLATE 36

Dem gütwilligen läser.

Dise kurtze anzeygung der Anatomey / ist inn zwen theyl vnderscheyden / auß welchen der ein in sechs Capittel begriffen / hal-
tet auff das aller kurtzest aller glyder history. Der ander / die schönen contrafeyturen solcher glyder / sampt den Büchstaben / mit welchen sy bezeychnet / bedeütet
werden. Es mag ein jeder nach seinem wolgefallen vnsere ordnung wie er wil achten / vnd eintweders der glyder beschreibung / oder bedeütung / vñ der Büchstaben anzeygung angreyffen / welches man von den nackenden bildtnussen die man vnd des weybs sol anheben / da die namen der aussern glyderen erfunden werden . Die figur zu truck des maß / zeygt die vollkummen zůsamenfügung der beynen. Wiewol die figuren die nach der proport des manns entworffen / vnnd der meüßlin tafel genant / auch nach der ordnung der auffschneidung / die beyn für augen stellend / besunder die viert / vnd die fünfft. Der meüßlin vnnd der banden contrafeytur / soll man
auß der ersten / der dritten vierten vnd fünfften figur der meüßlin genant / begeren vnd nemmen. Die instrumenta der fürung / die durch speys vnd tranck geschicht / dem
nach das hertz / vnd was ihm zu seinem ampt dient / sampt den senen / findt man in den figuren nach der nackenden frowen / da man auch der weyplichen geburt werckge-
schirr sihet. Gleich wie der mannen instrument in der figur / die der fünfften taffel der meüßlin angeleimpt ist. Was aber in der houpeschüdel begriffen / findstu heiter
vnnd volkummen / von der sennader tafel / in den figuren der meüßlin entworffen / vnnd erstlich in dem kopff der ersten figur / demnach der anderen / bald auch der vierten /
sampt der bildtnussen / die in den beyden der selbigen figur begriffen seind. Nach denen kumpt die so in der lincken hand der fünfften fig ur gesehen wirt. vnd
ein andere die eben daselbst (über der außglyderen bildtnus) an der erden ligt. Seind aber weyter an vil orten mehr figuren / welche inn im Latein
nitt begriffen / har in das Teütsch Compendium / dem gmeinen mann zu gut / gesetzt worden.

Title page of the German translation of the *Epitome*. Historical Library, Yale
Medical Library.

PLATE 37

The youthful Charles V, revealing
the "Hapsburg jaw."

Cornelius van Baersdorp.

PLATE 38

Dionisio Daza Chacon. Wellcome
Historical Medical Library, London.

S E G V N D A
PARTE
De la practica y theorica de Cirugia en ro-
mance y en latin, que trata de todas las heridas en gene-
ral y en particular.
+COMPVESTO POR EL LICENCIA
do Dionyſio Daça Chacon Medico y Cirujano de la Mageſtad del Rey
Don Philippe nueſtro Señor ſegundo deſte
nombre.
Dirigida a ſu Mageſtad Catholica.

Año 1595

+CON PRIVILEGIO.
Impreſſo en Valladolid, por los herederos
de Betnardino de Sanctodomingo Impreſſor del Rey
nueſtro Señor.
Eſta taſſado a tres maravedis cada pliego en papel.

Title page of Dionisio Daza Chacon's
Cirugia (1595).

PLATE 39

First declared location of Vesalius's Pisan anatomical demonstrations, as indicated on the engraved tablet. Via della Sapienza, Pisa.

IN QUESTO EDIFICIO
FU L' ANFITEATRO ANATOMICO
DELLO STUDIO PISANO
DOVE PER PRIMO INSEGNÒ
ANDREA VESALIO
NEGLI ANNI 1543-1545
OTTOBRE 1901

PLATE 40

Charles V in 1548, Alte Pinakothek,
Munich.

ANDREAE VE
SALII BRVXELLENSIS, ME
DICI CAESAREI EPISTOLA, RATIO'
nem modumᵉ propinandi radicis Chynæ decocti,
quo nuper inuictiſſimus CAROLVS V. Imperator
uſus eſt, pertractans : & præter alia quædam, epiſto,
læ cuiuſdam ad Iacobum Syluium ſententiam recen'
ſens, ueritatis ac potiſſimum humanæ fabricæ ſtudi.
oſis perutilem:quum quî hactenus in illa ni-
mium Galeno creditum ſit, facile
commonſtret.

Acceſſit quoᵠ locuples rerum & uerborum in
hac ipſa epiſtola memorabili-
um, Index.

Cum gratia & priuilegio Imperiali
ad quinquennium.

B A S I L E AE.

Title page of the *Letter on the
china root* (1546).

PLATE 41

Janus Cornarius.

Joannes Dryander.

PLATE 42

Anthony Perrenot de Granvelle, Bishop of Arras. Nelson Gallery—Atkins Museum (Nelson Fund), Kansas City, Missouri.

PLATE 43

Portrait of Leonhart Fuchs.

LEONHARTI
FVCHSII
DE

Humani Corporis fabrica
Epitomes Pars
Prima,

*Duos, unum de oßibus, alterum de muſcue
lis, libros complectens.*

Title page of the first volume of
Fuch's *Epitome* (1551). Historical
Library, Yale Medical Library.

LVGDVNI,
Apud Antonium Vincentium.
1551.

PLATE 44

GALENVS DE
ofsibus ad Tyrones,
VERSVS QVIDEM A' FER-
dinando Balamio Siculo : erroribus verò
quàm plurimis, tũ Græcis tum Latinis
purgatus, & commentariis illu-
ſtratus, à rei medicæ apud
Parrhiſios profeſſore re-
gio, Iacobo
Syluio.

οὕτως ἡδονῶν ἀπέχȣ τῶν ὀλεθρίων.

Sic perniciofis uoluptatibus abstine.

PARISIIS
Cum priuilegio Regis ad quinquennium.

Apud viduam Iacobi Gazelli, è regione
collegij Cameracenſis.
1549.

Title page of Sylvius's edition of Galen's *On the bones* (1549).

VAESANI CVIVS-
DAM CALVMNIARVM IN HIPPO-
cratis Galenique rem anatomicam depulſio, per Iacobum Syluium, medicæ rei apud Parrhiſios in-
terpretem Regium.

οὕτως ἡδονῶν ἀπέχȣ τῶν ὀλεθρίων.
Sic perniciofis voluptatibus abſtine.

PARRHISIIS

Apud Catharinam Barbé, viduam Iacobi Gazelli, è regione collegij Cameracenſis.

1551.

CVM PRIVILEGIO REGIS.

Title page of Sylvius's *Vaesanus* (1551). Historical Library, Yale Medical Library.

PLATE 45

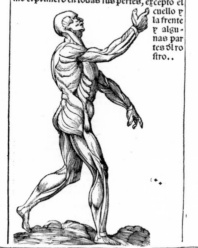

De la Anothomia. Fo.cxxx.

¶Por esta figura se muestrā los musculos primeros q̄ está en el lado de todo el cuerpo y en los lados exteriores y interiores d̄ las piernas y braços, d̄ manera q̄ en la vna pierna y vn braço estan señalados los musculos interiores, y en la otra pierna y otro braço, los musculos exteriores.

¶Entiēde se que esta el cuerpo dessollado como el primero en todas sus partes, excepto el cuello y la frente y algunas partes d̄l rostro..

Plagiarized "muscle-man" from Montaña de Monserrate, *Anathomia del hombre*, Valladolid, 1551.

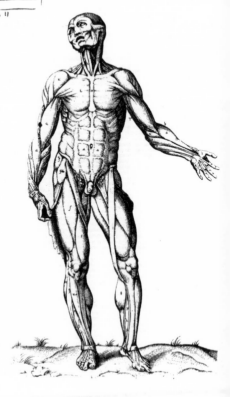

Plagiarized "muscle-man" from Valverde, *Composicion del cuerpo humano*, Rome, 1556.

PLATE 46

Achilles Gasser. Wellcome Historical Medical Library, London.

Adolf Occo *senior* in 1565. Wellcome Historical Medical Library, London.

PLATE 47

ANDREAE VESALII
BRVXELLENSIS, INVI-
ſtiſsimi CAROLI V. Imperatoris
medici, de Humani corporis
fabrica Libri ſeptem.

CVM CAESAREAE
Maieſt. Galliarum Regu, ac Senatus Veneti gratia &
priuilegio, ut in diplomatu eorundem continetur.

BASILEAE, PER IOANNEM OPORINVM.

Title page of the revised edition of the *Fabrica* (1555).

PLATE 48

letters—I, O, Q, T—used to introduce the books of the *Fabrica* could be interchanged to suit verbal alterations. Thus Book II, which in the first edition begins with the word *In*, in the second edition begins with *Tabulae*, and therefore an interchange of letters was possible. On the other hand, a new initial letter V had to be prepared for the beginning of the preface to Charles V and for the beginning of the fifth book. It is slightly larger than the other initial letters and, since the scene within it is that of Apollo flaying Marsyas, it has sometimes been said that this new letter represented a direct attack on Vesalius's critics.

The initial letters of the various chapters within the books were similarly altered. However, with these smaller initial letters the situation was somewhat different, since, with the exception of the letter L, all were redesigned whether or not the initial word of the chapter was altered. The L is found in two forms, one in which the design was changed, for instance in Chapter XIX of Book II, and the other in which the design of the first edition was retained, as in Chapter LI of the same book.

In respect to diagrams and illustrations, two general alterations are apparent in the revised edition. First, an effort was made to place the illustrations so as to improve the appearance of the work. This meant that in some instances where, in the first edition, several illustrations were crowded together, in the second they were spaced, sometimes further removed from one another by rearrangement of the text relative to the illustrations, sometimes even placed on different pages. Second, the letters on the figures were made to stand out more clearly. This was accomplished by reworking the blocks to remove shadows that, in the first edition, frequently made it difficult to read the letters. This improvement was the result of criticism, in particular that of Jacobus Sylvius.[12]

Examination of the individual illustrations indicates that some were removed, others reworked, and still others replaced by completely new figures. Thus the delineation of two umbilical veins [13] disappeared from the revised *Fabrica* and the full-page illustration of the "venous man" [14] was so thoroughly reworked that it seems almost a new figure.[15] An illustration of a bone drill is an example of a wholly new figure [16] not found in the first edition. Of particular interest is the new illustration Vesalius added to depict that form of a joint called a ginglymus. He retained his former illustration of the hinge which he had used for this purpose in the first edition,[17] but added to the revised *Fabrica* a second kind of hinge [18] that was, as with the clearer lettering of the illustrations, the result of criticism. In this instance the critic was John Caius, that erstwhile companion and fellow lodger with Vesalius in Padua. In his *Galeni libri aliquot* (1544) Caius criticized Vesalius's illustration and provided his own type of hinge he thought more suitable.[19] It was this illustration that Vesalius borrowed, without mention of Caius but thereby tacitly acknowledging the correctness of the criticism. Further alterations are mentioned in the notes.[20]

It is amazing how little the wood blocks suffered in the approximate decade or more between the first and second editions. A few had the more delicate tips broken off,[21] but on the whole it appears that either Vesalius or Oporinus had from the beginning thought of a second edition and had looked to the careful storage of the blocks.

The first alterations in text content are in the preface addressed to Charles V. Since this preface retains the subscription of the first edition —Padua, 1542—one would assume that it was left unaltered. But this is not true, since in addition to stylistic alterations the following examples of changes and deletions may be noted.

Referring to the postclassical decline of medicine, in the first edition Vesalius stated that after "the reign of Mansor, king of Persia . . . medicine began to be maimed," but by 1555 Vesalius had increased his knowledge to the point that he was able to write of "Mansor of Bokhara in Persia." A second decline, this time in the art of prescribing drugs, led him originally to refer to "the prescription of drugs [which] the Romans once proscribed from the state considering the practice delusive and destructive of mankind." In the revised edition of the *Fabrica*, however, it is no longer "the Romans" but the more general "many" that had once proscribed this practice, apparently referring to the post-Roman period as well.

Another alteration related to the abdication of the emperor in 1556. In the first edition Vesalius wrote: "However, most august Emperor Charles, I certainly do not propose to give preference to one instrument of medicine over the others." The "most august Emperor Charles" was deleted from the second edition, because, although the *Fabrica* was published in August 1555 and Charles did not abdicate until the following year, his decision had already been made, and we may presume that Vesalius was aware of it. This is further supported by the fact that, in reference to Charles's son Philip, who succeeded to many of his possessions, the phrase "from whom are fully expected whatever things ought to be desired in the best ruler of the whole world" has been removed from the second edition, so indicating that expectation was now considered to have become reality.

Another revision reflecting personal recollection is found in the emendation of the following statement:

[Students] ought to be urged the more strongly to [the use of the hands]. Nevertheless we see that learned physicians abstain from the use of the hands as from a plague, lest the rabbins of medicine decry them before the ignorant mass as barbers and they acquire less wealth and honor than those scarcely half-physicians and stand in less estimation before the uncomprehending mass of the people.

In the revised edition, possibly because of some remembered injury he had suffered in court service, Vesalius added the phrase "as well as of princes."

Thereafter there are several notable deletions of names from the text. These resulted sometimes from personal animosity, sometimes from political or religious discretion, and sometimes from death—as a general practice the names of persons who had died in the interim between publications were deleted. The first name deleted was that of the distinguished imperial servant who had been referred to by Vesalius as late as the *Letter on the china root* in 1546. The following passage was completely removed from the revised *Fabrica*: "Of so many celebrated men engaged in this matter, Gerard van Veltwyck, secretary to your Majesty and a rare example of the age, provides proof; endowed with wide erudition in many disciplines and tongues he is the most skilled of our people in the knowledge of plants." Veltwyck had died in January 1555, which explains the absence of his name. A comparison of this date with that of the publication of the *Fabrica* indicates that Vesalius continued up to the last moment to make alterations in his text.

The name of Jacobus Sylvius was deleted, but this deletion is easily explained and justified by the hostility that was already apparent in 1546 in the *Letter on the china root* and that was compounded by Sylvius's *Vaesanus* of 1551. There is no reference to Vesalius's training under Sylvius or, indeed, any mention of the latter at all, unless it can be discerned in a reference to the "calumnies and utterly false disparagement of certain malicious old men consumed by ill will." [22] In the first edition, in a second reference to the Paris period, Vesalius had written: "When I conducted [the dissection] a second time—the barbers having been waved aside—I attempted to display the muscles of the arm," and so forth. In the revised edition, possibly because of the gradual disuse of barbers, the phrase "the barbers having been waved aside" was omitted.

A reference to the period of Vesalius's anatomical activities in Italy is interesting for an addition rather than a deletion. Thus in speaking of these activities in the first edition of the *Fabrica* he noted: "I have already conducted anatomy very often here [Padua] and in Bologna." Despite the fact that the 1555 dedicatory preface still carried the date 1542, we find that Vesalius extended his remark to include the anatomical demonstration he had given at Pisa early in 1544: "here, Bologna, and Pisa."

Still another revision relates to the illustrations of the *Fabrica* for which Vesalius had gained both praise and criticism:

> Nevertheless, no student of geometry and other mathematical disciplines can fail to understand how greatly pictures assist the comprehension of these matters and place them more exactly before the eyes than even the most precise language. Furthermore, the illustrations of the human parts will greatly delight those for whom there is not always a supply of human bodies for dissection; or if there is, those who have such a fastidious nature, little worthy a physician, that even if they are enthusiastic about the most pleasant knowledge of man attesting the wisdom of the Creator—if anything does—yet they cannot bring themselves even occasionally to be present at dissection.

All that part of the text after the semicolon was deleted from the second edition. However, the following comment, derogatory to Galenic physicians, was allowed to remain:

> I recollect how the physicians—far otherwise than the followers of Aristotle—are usually upset when, in the conduct of a single anatomy nowadays, they see Galen's description of the relations of the human parts and their uses and functions to be incorrect in well over two hundred instances, and how examining the dissected parts they seek fiercely and with the greatest zeal to defend him.

In the second edition Vesalius added to this statement, which then read in part: ". . . in the conduct of a single dissection as I now demonstrate in the schools." Here is some indication that he continued to demonstrate and lecture on anatomy whenever the opportunity presented itself, and such intermittent academic activity certainly helps to explain the revisions of and additions to the second and improved text of the *Fabrica*. Related to Vesalius's scorn of the Galenic physician is the fact that elsewhere in the preface the "divine Galen" of the first edition lost that divinity in the second.

Finally, it is interesting to note that Vesalius spoke in the first edition simply of "my ancestors," but in 1555, possibly as a result of his genealogical research in Wesel in 1546 as recounted in the *Letter on the china root*, or possibly as a reflection of his own improved position, these ancestors were further described as "certainly not obscure physicians."

The letter to Oporinus was not materially changed in the revised *Fabrica*. There are certain stylistic revisions and the name of Narcissus Vertunus has been deleted because of his death and that of Fuchs because of ill will.

In the main body of the text, we notice first some rearrangement of the chapters. The arrangement of Chapters XXXIX and XL of Book I was reversed in the new edition, and a new Chapter XLI, on the instruments of dissection, added. This, to be found as Chapter VII of Book II in the first edition, accompanied by an illustration of the instruments, was moved together with the illustration in the second edition. As a result of this shift the chapter numbers of Book II had to be changed so that VII of the second edition corresponds to VIII of the first, and so on. A new chapter, "Musculorum palpebras moventium administratio," was added as Chapter X and so restored the relationship of chapters between the two editions.

Also the titles of certain chapters were altered for stylistic reasons. Generally speaking Vesalius tried to remove what he considered the older or more barbarous terms so that, to give one example, Chapter XLVII of Book II in the first edition, "De manus ligamentis," was altered in the revised edition to "De ligamentis ab humeri cum scapulae articulo ad extremam usque digitorum aciem consistentibus." In short, Vesalius considered the older meaning of *manus*, that is, the entire arm, indicative of the earlier barbarous school which he opposed. Throughout the text this older usage of *manus* was omitted. As might be expected, the anatomical terminology was restricted to what Vesalius considered genuinely classical terms and all such words of medieval origin, as *zirbus, clypeus*, and the like, were removed. In addition, the subtitles of chapters were frequently shortened, often to half their former length.

The marginalia were considerably increased from the first to the second edition and more precise references were added there to the citations of works.

Revisions of the text fall into several categories. Readily—and already —explained are the deletions of names, indicating either death of the individual or animosity. Thus the very flattering reference to Giambattista da Monte, "physician second to none," and to his work on the Giunta edition of Galen [23] was deleted by reason of his death, but animosity prompted deletion of the name of Dryander.[24] A second form of deletion relates to events in which Vesalius had participated but which for a variety of reasons he decided should no longer have attention directed to them. He also appears to have deleted material occasionally for the sake of greater brevity and sometimes, too, to make the text conform to the typographical design. Additions to the text were to clarify some point or to introduce new material. These revisions can best be explained by a sampling.

One of the first notable deletions is in Book I in the discussion of the various shapes of skulls and the reference to those found in Alpine cemeteries. This and a reference to Christopher Pfluegel do not appear in the revised *Fabrica*.[25] But in the latter edition of this same chapter, there are two new accounts, of a little girl suffering from hydrocephalus, which has already been mentioned,[26] and of a boy with the same ailment.[27]

A few pages later we find that the account of the many bones brought to Vesalius by the students during his anatomical lectures in Bologna [28] has disappeared, presumably because it referred to the pilfering of tombs encouraged by the anatomist. The strongly worded complaint of the withholding by Ferdinando Balamio and Cardinal Rodolfo of a manuscript of Galen's book *On the bones*[29] has been deleted; Balamio was dead but the cardinal was still alive, hence the suppression of his name was perhaps discretionary. Curiously, Vesalius's mention of his toothache—"as I write, my thirty-second tooth is erupting in my twenty-sixth year"[30]—although an incident that had occurred over a decade earlier, has been retained.[31] It is no cause for astonishment that any mention of Realdo Colombo[32] has disappeared; the account of Johannes Centurius of Genoa, the "double-jointed" youth,[33] is likewise missing, probably the result of the young man's early death. Further deletions from Book I are those concerned with the account of the pilfering of bones from tombs in Italy, as well as from the Cemetery of the Innocents at Paris in company with Vesalius's fellow student Matthaeus Terminus, the theft of the remains from the gibbet outside Louvain with the assistance of Gemma Phrysius, the later encouragement given anatomy in that city by the burgomaster, and the mention of Gisbertus Carbo, physician of Louvain, in whose home remained the skeleton Vesalius had articulated.[34] Although the name of Lazarus de Frigeis remains,[35] he is no longer a "distinguished Jewish physician."[36]

Turning to Book II, one notes immediately in the text that accompanies the first "muscle-man" that the reference to the artists' portrayal of the muscles has been considerably compressed. The last seven lines of Chapter I[37] were omitted from the revised edition, possibly to suit the new design of the work, and at the end of Chapter V of the revised edition a short section was added on "The use of fat."[38] On the other hand, the last thirteen lines of Chapter XVI[39] disappeared, and the text of Chapter XVIII was reduced. Those persons capable of wiggling their ears[40] lost that possible immortality achieved by inclusion in the first edition of the *Fabrica*, and to the account of the Turk capable of manipulating great weights with his teeth and jaw muscles[41] was added the further attraction of a Mantuan similarly gifted.[42] At the end of Chapter XIX there are eleven additional lines dealing with "The ligament binding the tongue,"[43] removed from Chapter XX of the first edition presumably for better arrangement of the material. The interesting account of how the cadaver ought to be suspended for anatomical study and how it was suspended for the delineation of the "muscle-men"[44] was deleted as well as Vesalius's remarks on lack of enterprise among students.[45]

Although Books III and IV were not radically altered, nevertheless attention ought to be called to the new material added to Book III on the venous valves. It was possibly as an aftermath of his meeting with Canano in Augsburg in 1546, and the latter's description of the venous valves[46] he had discovered, that Vesalius was led to search for them, too, as opportunity permitted. That he was successful in his search is indicated by the account he added to the revised *Fabrica*, although it is apparent that he, like those of his contemporaries who learned of the valves, had no true understanding of their use. Vesalius's account, furthermore, provides additional evidence that despite his primary duty as an imperial physician he was still able from time to time to carry on anatomical research:

Not only is there provision for the support of the veins in their distribution, but also their walls appear to be thicker and stronger wherever a branch is given off from a vessel or wherever a trunk is divided into branches. There is a projection in the orifice of the branches that, as you will learn, resembles that thicker substance of the stomach, ingeniously constructed like a ring in both [the stomach's] orifices for the sake of strength. When the veins, emptied of blood and flaccid, are incised along their length, this thicker substance is seen to hang down within the vessel and to close the lumen. In consequence some of those present at my dissection have occasionally declared that this substance resembles the membranous body that prevents a reflux of urine into that passage which carries it from the kidneys into the bladder, or they compare the projecting substance of the venous wall to the membranes seen at the orifices of the aorta and pulmonary vein where they issue from the heart. Such, however, would mean that in the course of venesection, in the different movements of the spirit and things of that sort, that the blood could not return to the vena cava from the azygos vein or the veins extending into the arms, head, kidneys, legs, and elsewhere, and this I do not believe. When in the course of dissection in the [medical] schools I have met with this thicker substance of the venous walls, I have maintained that it was created . . . for strength, although I am not unaware of that error of certain ones who do not hesitate to declare that not even air can pass from the azygos vein into the trunk of the vena cava.[47]

In Book V, we note the inclusion of an account of the autopsy examination of that weaver seen in Augsburg in 1550 or 1555.[48] However, the criticism of the belief in a seven-celled uterus, the views of Albertus Magnus and Michael Scot, as well as those of Mondino and Nicolo Gentile, and Vesalius's reference to his conversation with his relative Martin Stern,[49] were all deleted from the revised *Fabrica*. Shortly thereafter we find that the reference to his friends Roelants and Vitus Tritonius in the first edition [50] was altered in the second so that although the name of the former remains, and as not only an ornament "of Brabant" but "of Belgium," [51] the absence of the latter probably indicates his death. The account of the monk's mistress whose body was stolen for dissection has been retained, but whereas in the first edition the hue and cry were raised by the monk and her relatives,[52] in the second it was raised by the monk and her mother.[53] Vesalius also removed reference to his own mother,[54] no doubt because of her death, probably in 1552.

The chapter dealing with the foetal coverings, so subject to criticism in the first edition,[55] was greatly revised and improved in the light of the experience Vesalius gained in later years in dissection of embryological material. In the new edition he was able to state: "I believe that the whole mass of these coverings was called *secunda* or *secundina* by those speaking Latin, just as if there were a second birth or that it were to follow the foetus emerging into the light, and by the Greeks CHŌRION and sometimes CHŌRĒMA," and the terms allantois and amnion were coined to distinguish between the foetal membranes:

> Since those ancients who taught boys in their homes observed not one but several coverings for the foetus, not content with that common name CHŌRION, they believed that a separate name ought to be given to each covering. Hence it is that we possess the two names, ALLANTOEIDĒS and AMNION or AMNEIOS. Those ancients applied the first name to the outer covering of the foetus because of the likeness to a sausage, and the second, derived from lamb, to the inner covering because of its softness and whiteness.

The term "outermost covering" is no longer used to refer to the placenta, although Vesalius never used the word "placenta," and he declares that the foetuses of man, dog, and buffalo have only two covering membranes, with the placenta varying in shape from one animal to another. In man the placenta was a circular mass and hence distinguished from the annular placenta of the dog.[56] "Thus Vesalius has differentiated clearly for the first time in the literature the discoidal placenta of man, the annular placenta of the dog and the cotyledonary placenta of ruminants." The illustrations of the first edition were replaced by "moderately successful illustrations of the discoidal, zonary and cotyledonary placentae of man, the dog and the buffalo, which are of interest as the first illustrations of the comparative anatomy of the placenta." [57]

Even so, as we might expect since investigation could be carried on only as a part-time and somewhat inconsistent occupation, errors still remain or in some instances are compounded, yet distinct advances are apparent. Nowhere else in the *Fabrica* is there such a strong demonstration of the significance of the Vesalian principle of seeking information at the source. At first compelled to rely on past authority and the dissection of animals, his description of the foetal coverings was wholly inadequate, but, provided with human material, even with only intermittent investigation, the new presentation displays a remarkable contrast to earlier ignorance and error. A further contribution is found in the chapter dealing with the "acetabula," that is, cotyledons, in which Vesalius declares that true cotyledons are found only in ruminants.[58]

Book VI contains both additions and deletions. In the first edition Vesalius referred to his investigation of the heart in two subjects who had just been killed and spoke somewhat indiscreetly of the still-pulsating heart.[59] In the revised *Fabrica*, to avoid any possible charge of human vivisection, he adds that one had died in an accident and the other by execution.[60] His reference to the pericardium, which also contained a verbal indiscretion respecting theological opinion on the issue of blood and water from Christ's lance wound,[61] was likewise removed. One of the most important additions to the text of the revised *Fabrica* is that expressing Vesalius's dissatisfaction with the then-current beliefs regarding cardiovascular physiology. As will be recalled, he had already announced himself somewhat dubious over the Galenic pores of the interventricular septum,[62] and now he expressed himself even more strongly:

However much the pits may be apparent, yet none, as far as can be comprehended by the senses, passes through the septum of the heart from the right ventricle into the left. I have not seen even the most obscure passages by which the septum of the ventricles is pervious, although they are mentioned by professors of anatomy since they are convinced that blood is carried from the right ventricle into the left. As a result—as I shall declare more openly elsewhere—I am in no little doubt regarding the function of the heart in this part.[63]

This last statement was amplified at the end of Chapter XV of the revised edition and deserves to be quoted in *extenso:*

In presenting reasons for the construction of the heart and the use of the parts I have in large degree fitted my discourse to the teachings of Galen, not because I believe them to be in entire agreement with the truth but because I am yet hesitant to present a completely new use and function for those parts. Hitherto I did not dare to depart so much as a finger's breadth in this matter from the opinion of Galen, prince of physicians. However, the student ought to consider very carefully the division or septum of the ventricles of the heart as well as the right side of the left ventricle, which is just as thick, compact, and dense as the rest of the heart composing the left ventricle; for—whatever else I may think of the pits in this region, and I am not unmindful of [the example of] the portal vein's absorption from the stomach and intestines—I have no knowledge that even the smallest amount of blood can be taken through the substance of that septum from the right ventricle into the left, especially when the vessels gape by such great orifices into the amplitude of their ventricles; so also I am now silent on the true course of the vena cava from the heart.

While these matters are being considered, there are many things regarding the courses of the arteries that also ought to be questioned. For example, almost no vein seeks the stomach, intestines, and spleen without a companion artery, and the portal vein takes a companion artery for itself in almost the whole of its course. Furthermore, such large arteries are communicated to the kidneys that we may assert that they have not been extended there solely for tempering the heat of the kidneys, just as we may assert that still less have such large arteries been inserted into the stomach, intestines, and spleen solely [to temper] their native heat. In addition, although there is a mutual flux and reflux of materials through the veins and arteries, it can be asserted with much evidence that none of the material in the veins and arteries causes any heaviness or weight. Even if the little membranes [valves] of the heart serve the use previously mentioned, nevertheless they do not prevent all reflux of materials, because during vivisection when the heart has been dissected transversely and its action is wholly at rest, the auricles are still moved and palpitate; and since the valves are so large in foetuses and those newly born it is clear to anyone that they are formed for the sake of some more important service than the strength of the vessels. Moreover, not to mention the relative amplitudes of the orifices of the pulmonary vein and aorta, the reason for the difference in thickness of the parts constituting the right ventricle and the left must be otherwise than for the materials contained in the ventricles. Many things present themselves here that call into doubt the ordinary conclusions of anatomists, but it would take too long to consider them, and I have decided not to alter my account piecemeal— although at the same time I am far from satisfied.[64]

Book VII was not greatly changed although the reference to Marcantonio Contarini,[65] who died in 1546, was deleted, as well as reference to the medieval character of that teaching about the brain to which Vesalius had been subjected at Louvain, and no doubt discretion dictated that references to theologians and theology, notably the concern with the soul,[66] be modified. There are some minor alterations in the chapter on vivisection, an entirely new index with new initial letters, and a greatly enlarged body of errata. Indeed, the errata are so extensive that the printer has, perhaps in desperation, concluded with the statement: "The diligent reader will readily note the remainder." Such numerous typographical faults may have been due to the fact that Vesalius was not in Basel during production of the new edition as he had been for the first.

As the *Fabrica* was republished in revised form in 1555, so it appears that the *Epitome* was also reissued, although not revised, in the same year. The evidence for this rests upon a single known copy of this second issue, once in the possession of Antonio Scarpa, more recently in that of the late Erik Waller, and now permanently housed in the library of the University of Uppsala as part of the Waller collection.

According to Dr. Waller's account of this bibliographical curiosity,[67] with the exception of the final leaf all the others are identical to those of the edition of 1543 and contain the same watermark. The final leaf, however, has been reset, bears the colophon, *Basileae, ex officina Joannis Oporini, MDLV, mense Aprilis*, and contains the same watermark as the paper used for the *Fabrica* of 1555. On the basis of this last fact it seems very unlikely that the leaf could be a later substitution made to perpetrate the forgery of a bibliographical rarity. Far more likely a stock of sheets of the *Epitome* of 1543 was still on hand and Oporinus determined to dispose of them to recoup part of his large investment in the new edition of the *Fabrica*. Possibly this "remainder" was sold with the *Fabrica*, as had happened in 1543, but, for whatever reason, the reissue of the *Epitome* had to be brought up to date if the sale were to be successful. This was easily achieved by resetting and reprinting the final leaf with the new date. The number of copies available may have been small and it is possibly for this reason that a single surviving copy is known today. This is certainly not beyond reason if one considers how few copies remain from the sale of 1543, or the even more extreme case of the *Tabulae anatomicae*, of which only two copies are known to have survived.[68]

Chapter XII

THE FINAL YEARS, 1559–1564

HARLES abdicated his throne in 1556; Vesalius was granted a pension and for a short time was seemingly without any royal duties. It may be assumed that the private demands for his services kept him occupied in and about Brussels, although there appears to be no further information regarding his practice until 1558 when he employed his skill to no avail on behalf of the Princess of Orange, wife of the later "William the Silent." All that is known of this case, which occupied Vesalius during the early part of 1558, is contained in a brief letter he wrote to the prince from Breda. Dated 15 March, it refers to the princess as being without a continuous fever but attacked by a great melancholy which might be dispelled by the prince's return. However, such hope as the physician offered was shattered by the death of his patient on 24 March.[1]

Despite the great renown Vesalius had achieved as a physician there were always those who were skeptical of his ability. Such a one was the Count of Renneberg, George de Lalaing, who appears to have consulted Vesalius on problems of health but been displeased at the unpleasant diagnosis. In a letter dated 20 October 1559, Granvelle notes that Lalaing "is well, as I have heard, and does not very much fear Vesalius's opinion of his maladies, because [Vesalius] always declares them to be mortal so that if [his patients] die, he is not at fault, and if they live, he has wrought a miracle."[2] However, Vesalius's ability was not questioned by his old schoolfellow of Louvain days, Andreas Masius. Writing from Brussels, 28 May 1559, he acknowledged his recovery from a fever as due to "the mercy of God and the efforts of Vesalius."[3]

International recognition of Vesalius's supreme position in the medical world was emphasized by his commanding role in the case of the fatal injury of Henry II of France. To understand how this came about it is necessary to give brief consideration to the international political scene at the time. In February 1556, and prior to the abdication of Charles V, the truce of Vaucelles had been concluded between the emperor and the King of France. It was a bitter disappointment to the recently elected

Pope Paul IV, who held the strongest hatred of Spain, especially as he had concluded a defensive alliance with France in the preceding year. Yet all was not lost since an incident directed by papal representatives against the Spanish embassy in Rome resulted in Spanish retaliation sufficient to bring the Franco-Papal alliance into force. In short, the long-standing Valois-Hapsburg conflict was renewed. The most serious fighting occurred in the Netherlands which, since the abdication of Charles V, were part of the Spanish Empire of his son Philip II. Commanded by the young Duke of Savoy, Emmanuel Philibert, the Spanish had the better of the fighting, and after the capture of St. Quentin might well have threatened Paris itself had not Philip been more concerned with the reëstablishment of peace. There is no known information to indicate whether or not Vesalius served as a military surgeon during this conflict.

The Spanish desire for peace together with various alterations in the international scene led to a peace conference at Cateau-Cambrésis in February 1559, and among the terms, signed on 2 April, was an agreement that King Philip would marry Elizabeth, daughter of Henry II, and Emmanuel Philibert would marry Marguerite, sister of the French king. With the signing of the treaty, Henry returned to Paris to the Hôtel des Tournelles which, on the following day, he ordered cleared in preparation for the forthcoming marriage celebrations, and on 15 June the Duke of Alba, with a retinue of nobles, reached Paris to serve as proxy for Philip, who remained in the Netherlands. On 21 June, Philip, through his proxy, was betrothed to Elizabeth in the great hall of the Louvre, and this occasion was followed by a banquet of pomp and magnificence, somewhat marred by the failure of François de Montmorency, in the role of Grand Master, to reserve places for several of the dignitaries who had been invited. The Duke of Savoy had arrived in Paris in time for the first betrothal, and on 28 June the formalities of his marriage to the French king's sister were completed. Then, in honor of these two events, a three-day tournament began which was to have an unforeseen and fatal result and so make it the last event of this sort ever to be held by the French court.[4]

On Friday, 30 June, the third day of the tourney, Henry, wearing the black and white colors of his mistress Diane de Poitiers, entered the lists. The honor of equipping the king for his course had been granted to Marshal Vieilleville, who took advantage of the occasion to warn Henry of portents of disaster being circulated, but, impatient and heedless of such rumors, the king ran several courses—first with the Duke of Savoy, next with the Duke of Guise, and finally with the Count of Mongonmery, a captain of the Scottish guard, all without harm. It appears, however, that Henry was somewhat dubious of the showing he had made against Mongonmery and, despite the pleas of those about him to forego any further test, since he seemed tired and overheated, he nevertheless determined upon one more encounter. The result was described by several eyewitnesses but, as is usual in such cases, with some discrepancy in detail. However, by weighing these accounts against each other it appears that in the second course Mongonmery's lance struck the king's gorget a little below his visor, which unwisely was raised, or perhaps the stump of the lance that had shattered drove the visor upward and so permitted a splinter to enter and penetrate above the king's right eye. At any rate, thereafter all was confusion, and the accounts vary as to whether the king was unhorsed or retained his saddle, was carried or made his own way into the palace.

Naturally the court physicians and surgeons were speedily assembled and, after extracting several small splinters of wood, dressed the wound. Then the king was purged with a potion of rhubarb and mummy and bled of twelve ounces of blood. After a further purge and the application of cooling remedies, the patient was fed barley-gruel, a medicine frequently employed against fever; thereafter he sank into a stupor, watched over by some of the great nobles, including the Duke of Savoy, the Cardinal of Lorraine, the Duke of Guise, and the Constable Mont-morency. The following morning, after a night declared to have been good or bad according to which report is read, the wound was dressed, and when the king had been given nourishment he fell into a deep sleep broken at intervals only by his thirst. The slight fever that had previously been apparent seemed to have lessened and the pulse rate was only slightly accelerated.

As may well be imagined, the importance of the patient required that the best possible medical opinion be obtained, and despite the presence of Ambroise Paré, the noted French surgeon, "as soon as his Majesty was struck, the Duke of Savoy sent a messenger to Flanders for Vesalius, the great surgeon." News of the accident reached Philip in Brussels on 2 July, and that monarch immediately dispatched Vesalius to the aid of his new father-in-law. Meanwhile, in Paris optimism was fading, since the king's condition was showing no improvement, and the surgeons had begun to fear that the blow had torn the covering of the brain. A consultation was held in which all possible methods of treatment were explored. The stump of Mongonmery's lance was used for experimental thrusts at the heads of four criminals decapitated on the previous day, after which the skulls were dissected, but this grisly empirical investigation failed to re-veal the secret of the wound. On the fourth day the patient developed a violent fever but, as Vesalius was to remark later in his account of the case, it was thwarted by purgative medicines. Nevertheless, a delirium followed, and little by little indications of damage to the brain began to make their appearance.

Vesalius reached Paris on 3 July, immediately made a preliminary examination of the king's injury, and "made trial with a clean white cloth which he put in the king's mouth [to bite] and then pulled it out with some force; whereupon the king threw his hand to his head and cried out in pain. By the depth of the pain Vesalius was able to judge that he would not recover. *Chironium vulnus*, he remarked, a wound that will not heal." Such is the account of Vesalius's friend, Heinrich Petri of Basel, who may have had it directly from the physician.

Although this incident suggests inevitable tragedy, another story of Vesalius's arrival in Paris by the Spanish surgeon Daza Chacon, whose presence was the result of accompanying the party of the Duke of Alba, provides some comic relief. When Vesalius set out hastily from Brussels, he was accompanied by a court favorite who gained a place in the carriage through importunity rather than any particular medical ability, yet his presence with Vesalius led the French protomedicus Jean Chapelain to assume that he must be a person of no ordinary skill. So it was that, upon conclusion of Vesalius's examination of the wounded king, a consultation was held, and "there were many very distinguished physicians and surgeons, all very learned in Latin and Greek, and skilled in surgery." The French gave their opinions first:

. . . and to honor Doctor Vesalius and his companion they were left to speak last. . . . So Vesalius gave his opinion with that Latin and that facility I have seen in many consultations I have had with him, and he treated of the essence of the wound, the signs and prognoses, and the treatment a good surgeon would be obliged to observe, all with such wisdom that it was no wonder that everyone was satisfied and filled with admiration.

It was then the turn of Vesalius's companion, believed by the French to be a surgeon of great consequence and so accorded the honor of giving the final opinion. The attendant physicians and nobles awaited "like the Carthaginians when Aeneas wished to speak from the throne" for the profound and wise discussion anticipated from such a distinguished master. However, the unfortunate surgeon, knowing little Latin and no French, proceeded to give his opinion in a mixture of Spanish and barbarous Latin, saying things better left unsaid, and "the French were so confused that they did not know if they were actually seeing it or whether they were dreaming, because although they saw it they could not believe it."

Nevertheless, this comic interlude was only a momentary thing. Vesalius, now in charge of the case, was in a very unenviable position despite the indication of the esteem in which he was held, especially when we consider that Paré was among the attending French surgeons. The greatness of the issue at stake, the fact that Vesalius was a foreigner and therefore a ready scapegoat, and his own recognition that the case could only terminate fatally, all must have produced a severe nervous strain. The difficulties were further increased by the meddling of nobles, especially those of the house of Montmorency, since the death of the king could well affect them adversely. So it was that the Constable Montmorency "is so curious about the king's accident that he caused the body of an unfortunate man who was assassinated yesterday to be preserved until the arrival of Vesalius, and he wished the latter to show him in the dead man's head the anatomy of the king's injury."

All too obviously the king's condition was becoming worse and his fate became apparent to all. Vieilleville recounts that on 8 July Henry had an interval of consciousness during which he sent for the queen and ordered her to hurry on the marriage of his sister, and that he then made her sign Vieilleville's brevet as marshal, which he had intended to sign himself, and commended to the queen his kingdom and his children. No mention of this scene occurs in the other contemporary accounts, however, and it seems likely that by this time the king must have been unable to talk to anyone. Nevertheless, whether by Henry's direction or another's, the marriage was celebrated at midnight in the little church of Saint Paul adjoining the Hôtel des Tournelles. The ceremony was particularly melancholy, and those in attendance seemed more like mourners at a funeral, which no doubt was more in their thoughts than the marriage.

Since all hope had now been abandoned, Paris became a city of mourning. Queen Catherine ordered public prayer for Henry and forbade the ringing of bells. On 9 July the parochial clergy of Paris organized a general procession for the king's recovery, and on the same day the sacrament was administered. Later, the Bishop of Toulon, Jerome de la Rovère, stated in his funeral sermon that after receiving the sacrament the king summoned the dauphin and "recommended to him his church and his people and declared that he persisted and remained firm in the faith in which he was dying." However, this pious story must be suspect since it is doubtful if Henry was then capable of lucid thought or speech. Desperate measures were in order and, during the evening, the physicians once again discussed the possibility of trephining, but, as the night drew on, the king, ever more enfeebled, broke out in a profuse sweat, "the sweat of death," which was to last throughout the night and which convinced the attending physicians that all remedies would now be in vain. Prior to his death Henry's left side suffered from paralysis while the right was shaken by violent convulsions. Respiration became more difficult, and finally death appeared—hastened, according to Vesalius, by a draught of wine that had been concocted with sage and other irritating substances. Henry, just forty years old and in the twelfth year of his reign, died at one o'clock in the afternoon.

The fact that Vesalius had been placed in charge of the case is indication that his position in the medical world was now supreme, but even his ability was not sufficient to bring about the recovery of the royal patient, an accomplishment beyond the medical skill of that age. Yet, despite his failure, if it can with justice be termed a failure, the presence of this greatest of sixteenth-century anatomists at the autopsy meant that his account would be as searching as knowledge of that day permitted. Thus it is that from Vesalius's report of the post-mortem examination, as well as from other contemporary accounts, we obtain a clear picture of cerebral compression supervening upon concussion following a contrecoup injury to the brain, and subdural haemorrhage. The initial vomiting and restlessness, the gradual loss of consciousness, the slow pulse, stertorous breathing and rising temperature, and finally the signs of contralateral paralysis and ipsilateral convulsions presaged a fatal issue that could not be long delayed. The test with cloth used by

Vesalius, described by Heinrich Petri, appears to have been an original but somewhat severe method of eliciting the head-flexion sign used in the diagnosis of meningitis and was, apparently, the first test of this nature to be described. In the sixteenth century the question of whether or not the brain could be injured without a frank fracture of the skull was a matter of some dispute, and possibly the reason why trephination was not employed in this particular instance. It is of some interest, therefore, that in his report [5] not only does Vesalius emphasize that the autopsy proved cerebral injury had occurred without fracture, but Ambroise Paré later mentioned this case among others in support of the original and similar Hippocratic doctrine.[6] There are minor discrepancies between the versions of Paré and Vesalius, but these may be explained in the former as a lapse of memory during the passage of several years, and in the latter from the very obvious hastiness of the composition of his report.

Since Henry II died on 10 July, we may assume that Vesalius remained several days longer in Paris to participate in the autopsy on the royal body, to write his report of the case, and possibly to join in the obsequies. However, he must have returned to Brussels by the middle of the month since, accompanied by his wife Anne and his daughter of like name,[7] he was required to depart for Spain very shortly in Philip's retinue. Yet if Vesalius hastened his preparations in the belief that departure was imminent, he was to be sorely disappointed. The Spanish king, after designating the Duchess of Parma as regent of the Netherlands with Cardinal Granvelle as principal adviser, gave instructions that he would sail for Spain on 8 August. Nevertheless, when all had been prepared, a counterorder was given, which was, according to the English ambassador Chaloner, the result of neither politics nor religious scruples, but "the foolish Nostradamus with his threats of tempests and shipwrecks this month did put these sailors in a great fear." [8] What must Vesalius, who had already indicated his lack of sympathy with the superstitions of that age, have thought of such an excuse for delay?

Finally, on 23 August, King Philip sailed from Flanders and arrived at Laredo on 8 October. Vesalius, in the retinue, and despite his own realistic appraisal of his title of Count Palatine,[9] seems at least to have gained from it the right to consideration as a gentleman as well as a physician. However, he went to Spain not as a physician to Philip, who was to employ his services upon occasion, but as physician to the Netherlanders at the court of Madrid. Such was the conjecture put forth by Roth,[10] and it appears to be borne out in some degree by a manuscript in the National Library in Madrid that, although listing the names of the physicians to the king and to the members of his family, does not include that of Vesalius.[11]

In addition to his official duties and such personal demands as the king may have made upon his services from time to time, Vesalius appears to have been much sought after as a medical attendant for the foreign embassies. The first record we have of his activities in Spain is in this last category; it is a recommendation that the French ambassador Sébastien de l'Aubespine, Bishop of Limoges, by reason of ill health, be granted permission to eat meat during Lent. This was dated 18 February 1561.[12]

In the same year Vesalius received a copy of Fallopio's *Observationes anatomicae*, just published in Venice and brought to him by Aegidius Dux, or, in the vernacular form, Gilles de Hertogh,[13] a Netherlandisch physician and visitor to Spain who had been a student of Fallopio at Padua. It is likely therefore that his journey was made after the close of the Paduan academic year, and consequently his teacher's gift, which he had brought from Padua, must have come into Vesalius's hands sometime during late summer.

Gabriele Fallopio, 1523?–1562, of Modena, after flirting briefly with the possibility of an ecclesiastical career, directed his attention to anatomy and medicine, first in his native Modena and later in Ferrara where he enjoyed the instruction of Antonio Musa Brasavola and the friendship of Giambattista Canano, likewise the friend of Vesalius. Fallopio may possibly have studied for a time in Padua, although there is no proof of this. A document of 1554 mentions him as a doctor of medicine, although where he obtained the degree is unknown, but it must have been many years earlier since, after teaching for some years in Ferrara, he accepted the chair of anatomy at Pisa in 1548 and that of Padua in 1551. Although Fallopio and Vesalius were never to meet, the younger man was the spiritual disciple of his great predecessor at Padua and had made the *Fabrica* the basic guide for his own studies. Therefore it is not inappropriate that it should have been Fallopio who restored to the Paduan anatomical chair that lustre which had been dimmed by inferior appointments after Vesalius's departure.[14]

Immediately upon opening Fallopio's small volumes, Vesalius must have realized that this was no ordinary work. Assuming that the book came into his hands possibly in August 1561, he must have devoted much of his leisure during the remainder of the year to its study and to the composition of an extended reply inscribed, upon conclusion, as "from the royal court in Madrid, 17 December 1561." The *Observationes* displayed plentiful evidence of originality and careful investigation. Moreover, the evident restraint with which it was written, the willingness to give credit wherever due, in short those elements of the book that were so unlike the usual savage controversy and shameless plagiarism of that age, caused more ready acceptance of such criticisms as the author made. The work was chiefly devoted to praise and criticism of Vesalius and, although the former was always palatable, in this instance the latter also was accepted by its target without offense. It seems likely that Vesalius saw in Fallopio a kindred spirit, and very likely, too, the *Observationes* was of no little importance in arousing a desire for a return to the academic life of Padua. Vesalius's reply to Fallopio, the *Examen,* was written in restrained and cordial terms:

Three days ago, my dear Fallopio, I received your *Observationes anatomicae* through the kindness of Gilles de Hertogh, physician of Brussels. I was greatly pleased, not only because it was produced by you, who are considered highly skilled in the dissection of bodies, as well as in the other parts of medicine, but also because it is the product of the Paduan school, the most worthy in the whole world, where for almost six years I held the same chair you now occupy. . . . I sincerely hope that you may long pursue your studies in that delightful leisure of letters and among those learned men who are so intent upon their studies, and with whom you can constantly compare your thoughts. I feel that the elaboration of our art has come from that arena from which as a young man I was diverted to the mechanical practice of medicine, to numerous wars, and constant travel . . . therefore may our common school, whose memory has always remained so dear to me, be further honored by the results of your talent and industry.[15]

At the time this passage was composed the life of both men was drawing to a close, and it was perhaps fitting that, although they were never to meet, these two greatest anatomists of the sixteenth century should, before death, cross swords or, as their conceit would have had it, scalpels, albeit in friendly fashion, Fallopio through his *Observationes* and Vesalius through his *Examen* of that work. In fact, however, Vesalius's defense against the *Observationes* is not particularly vigorous. He had no facilities for research and consequently whenever criticized for lapse or error in the *Fabrica* was limited to acceptance of correction or recollection that his past observations were not in accord with those of his critic. Occasionally, through misreading of the Vesalian text, Fallopio was unjustly critical, but such instances elicited little irritation from the subject of these remarks, possibly because of the frequent allusion in them to the "divine Vesalius."

The *Examen*, because of the circumstances under which it was written, and because it is therefore illustrative of both the lower level of medicine in Spain and the result of Vesalius's subjection to that stultifying influence, is of no particular merit as a work of scientific anatomy. On the other hand, because of his lack of facilities, Vesalius was constrained to reminisce, and so his reply to Fallopio contains a certain amount of biographical information.

Since the *Observationes* is a critical commentary on the *Fabrica* it closely follows the pattern of that work, and in the *Examen* Vesalius replied in the same sequence. A few excerpts will indicate the nature of the works. In reply to Fallopio's statement of a somewhat different conception of that form of articulation called ginglymus,[16] Vesalius, ever quick to find a comparison among common objects of which everyone ought to be aware, was reminded, as previously noted, of the kind of hinges used for the doors of the home he had built in Brussels prior to taking service in Spain. Also, more and more conscious that he was in an alien country, he added that "here the Spaniards are accustomed to suspend almost all their doors without the use of iron." [17]

Continuing his criticisms, this time of Vesalius's account of the shape of the head and its sutures, Fallopio remarked: "Very often I have been led to wonder how it was that the relationship between the sutures and prominences of the head as described by the great Hippocrates could be so approved by all the anatomists whom I hold in great respect." [18] Again Vesalius was in no position to argue or to discuss the point in any detail. He did indicate that he had been led astray by Hippocrates, but he was also concerned to recall his own study of skulls. In consequence he hearked back to that episode already mentioned,[19] when, together with the small imperial entourage, he had fled over the Brenner pass and into Carinthia, where he investigated skulls found in cemeteries.[20]

In the *Observationes* considerable attention is given to the ear and to those structures with which Vesalius's name has long been associated. Fallopio called attention to a third ossicle of the ear overlooked by Vesalius, who had described only the malleus and incus, and, with his characteristic honesty, giving credit where due, Fallopio declared that despite his description of this ossicle it had actually been discovered by the Sicilian anatomist and correspondent of Vesalius, Ingrassia.[21] Apparently, however, Vesalius had already heard of the discovery and had sought and found the ossicle before reading the *Observationes*. This must have been between 1555, as the revised edition of the *Fabrica* makes no mention of the ossicle, and 1559, when Vesalius went to Spain where, as he wrote later in the *Examen*, it was difficult to acquire even a skull for research purposes. Possibly he became acquainted with the third ossicle from the reference to it—an unacknowledged borrowing from Ingrassia—by Valverde in 1556: [22]

In your *Observationes* you mention an ossicle of [the ear] overlooked by me. When I was cleaning a skull for preparation of a skeleton, an ossicle chanced to fall out of the ear; I opened the auditory organ in a fresh skull, and with that ossicle I found a second. I have described the incident [in the *Fabrica*] exactly as it occurred. Later I heard that a third ossicle had also been discovered, and I soon found that one that is so slight that I felt compelled to praise the carefulness of Ingrassia, the distinguished Sicilian physician who had observed it. I was happy, too, to accept its comparison with the stirrup . . . for it seems to me that it has a very close resemblance to the stirrup as well as to that instrument used for the minting of gold and silver coins that takes its name from the stirrup.[23]

The Fallopian account of the teeth,[24] although brief, was a remarkable contribution to that subject. Vesalius, whose own previous remarks in the *Fabrica* were much inferior, readily comprehended the value of Fallopio's words and voiced his approval with the statement, "What you say about the teeth pleases me very much." [25]

In the *Fabrica* Vesalius had described and illustrated a sacrum composed of six pieces,[26] and although Fallopio did not directly criticize him for this, nevertheless he remarked that five are normal.[27] In his *Examen* Vesalius explained the reasons for his choice; the specimen then available to him had given him the opportunity of harmonizing his description in some degree with that of Galen:

In regard to the number of bones in the sacrum of the adult, I stated in my description that the sacrum is composed of six bones although I asserted that frequently and in many cases it is composed of five. When in the university I had available the sacrum of a middle-aged man, beautifully constructed of six bones, I was able to adapt this more easily to Galen's doctrine than one formed of five. It seemed to many that the three superior bones were the sacrum of Galen and they decided that the three lower bones were the coccyx; at that time the coccyx of man, composed of either three or four ossicles, was considered as a kind of cartilage. But this opinion did not jibe with various other arguments until, after a complete enumeration had been made of the bones of man, of a dog, and of a caudate ape, I declared that then we might more reasonably understand Galen's opinion, found particularly in the book *On the bones* where, in this fuller account, he certainly did not describe any particular number, as far as this matter is concerned. Thus Galen's description of the sacrum is suitable for dogs and caudate and noncaudate apes; and if we take only three of the bones subjoined to the sacrum in a long series, so to speak like vertebrae, in a dog and in a caudate ape, and if we imagine that the third bone ends in a cartilage—although this is different from what actually is found—it agrees somewhat with Galen's account of the coccyx, without that distortion of his book Sylvius wrongfully introduced.[28]

Despite his lack of research facilities in Spain, Vesalius, relying upon his recollections of his studies of former years, considered that his own explorations of the human body had been sufficiently thorough to permit him occasionally to doubt some of Fallopio's asserted discoveries. Thus in the case of Fallopio's announcement of his discovery of a muscle that raised the eyelid,[29] Vesalius's response appears to be only conditional acceptance, and gives an honest picture of the manner in which he had attacked this particular anatomical puzzle:

After I had heard that at Rome a muscle had been discovered that raised the eyelid and I learned that this existed in the bony orbit, I recalled that section I had pondered in Galen's book *The sites of diseases* when I was in great doubt about the motion of the eyelids—that book is preferable for conjecture to your reference to Oribasius, indeed, the latter's description may be from Galen. Galen teaches that a muscle extending from the frontal bone causes the elevation of the eyelid, and because of this statement from time to time I sought a muscle of that sort around the frontal bone. Although I demonstrated that wide, rounded, glandular flesh located at the superior region of the external side of the eye, yet I was very doubtful and did not dare describe it as the muscle raising the eyelid. Likewise, when occasionally I observed a kind of spotted part like a muscle stretched to the muscle drawing the eye upward, I did not consider that as a separate muscle by which the eyelid might be raised but as an adjunct to the muscle moving the eye upward. When, provoked by Roman diligence, by more careful dissection I investigated that whole fleshy portion formed of membrane that goes around the eyelids and is found in their whole amplitude, I became acquainted with the contraction of the eyelids, and by this the eyelids —as the skin of the forehead by its fleshy substance—are moved and wrinkled. Thus I noticed that no part of this circular fleshy mass is suitable for lifting the eyelids. Then in place of muscle I began to consider that wide, rounded, and fleshy part in the orbit of the eye, which I described as glandular, by which we might raise the eyelid; and here I was astonished at its middle composition between the flesh of muscle, glandular substance, and that humor or mucus of the joints found abundantly between the frontal bone and the fleshy substance of that glandular muscle, for the sake of the motion of the brain. Thus I considered a gland in place of a muscle for raising the eyelids, and I shall now add that one you propose.[30]

The instance of the psoas muscles is representative of those few occasions when Vesalius refused to accept Fallopio's correction. The dispute, however, was not over anatomy but rather over anatomical terminology, made more complex by the fact that Vesalius had not been especially precise in his own identification of the muscles in the *Fabrica*. In fact, as Fallopio indicated, what Vesalius appears to have called the psoas muscles were rather the quadratus lumborum.[31] Vesalius's reply rests upon the words of Hippocrates and Galen, which is not what we should expect from this proponent of independent research, yet such research was denied him at the time.[32] His words, furthermore, inform us that his emendated text of Galen's *Anatomical procedures*, which he had prepared for the Giunta edition of Galen's works,[33] had been altered or, as he declared, mutilated in a later edition:

In that place [in the *Anatomical procedures*, Bk. V, chap. 9] where Galen considers the muscles moving the back, and so mentions the PSOA or internal fleshes of the loins and then the external, in the beginning of his account he discusses those muscles that bend the lower part of the back. Among them he places not only those that form my fifth pair moving man's back [Quadratus lumborum] but, in addition, those muscles that are more numerous in the ape than in man. In addition to these there are also found in the loins on each side those that are inserted into the lesser trochanter of the femur. Thus Galen refers to almost three kinds as the PSOAI or internal fleshes of the loins so that I am quite unable to understand why, after my careful effort to emendate Galen's book—which now certain persons have mutilated by forming only one muscle of the loins on each side—and after my exact account of the internal and external muscles of the loins, and your reading of the genuine book of Hippocrates *On luxations*, and Galen's commentaries on it, you are so disturbed that you openly assert that merely the sixth muscle of those moving the leg [Psoas major] is called PSOA.[34]

Fallopio's description of the palmaris brevis muscle [35] was an old story to Vesalius. He had heard of it previously and had searched for it without success. So thorough had been his search that he was sure that Fallopio in this instance was guilty of self-deception as well as—at least in the eyes of Vesalius—giving praise, even though limited, to Valverde. This was all the more offensive since Valverde was not in fact the first to describe that nonexistent muscle, because it had been described by Canano *c.* 1541, and Vesalius had seen that description and the illustration to accompany it: [36]

Before the publication of my books *De humani corporis fabrica*—in which there is a special chapter on the fleshy substance of the finger extended over the palm—I saw an illustration of those muscles called the "mountain of the moon" which you describe as moving the skin of that region. I was not able to find them in the dissection of men or of apes, even with the bones of the hand completely immobile in any position and the skin either extended smooth, or wrinkled. I did not observe that that fleshy substance moved in any way, and I passed over the muscle in silence seeing that it was established without purpose and, furthermore, that Galen did not mention it. Consider, then, whether perhaps while nodding and observing some of the flesh previously mentioned by me, your eyes deceived you, as did those of our mutual friend Giambattista Canano, and, although the skin was completely immobile, through the authority of your eyes you have ascribed some sort of motion to it.[37]

There are one or two flashes of irritation, not against the criticisms of Fallopio but against enemies Fallopio was so indiscreet as to praise. Vesalius had long displayed anger against those who plagiarized his illustrations, one of the most recent of whom had been that Spanish anatomist Valverde who made no secret of the fact that he had employed Vesalius's illustrations for the anatomical textbook he published in Rome in 1556.[38] Vesalius had been further angered by the fact that his illustrations had not only been reduced in size but were also of inferior artistic quality. Finally, Valverde had made common cause with Realdo Colombo, that other enemy from earlier Paduan times, already referred to with contempt in the *Letter on the china root,* and whose name had been deleted from the *Fabrica* of 1555.[39] It was thus too much when Vesalius read that "Valverde ought to be held in no small favor because he wrote his anatomical book with such facile brevity and illustrated it with such very attractive illustrations that it should greatly assist all who understand the Spanish language." [40] It is seldom that Vesalius made unjust criticisms of his contemporaries, usually preferring silence, but he was now led to distinctly unjust ones, perhaps partly explicable, too, as the result of irritation arisen from his Spanish captivity:

Valverde, who never put his hand to a dissection and is ignorant of medicine as well as of the primary disciplines, undertook to expound our art in the Spanish language only for the sake of shameful profit. I would that you grant nothing to his authority which, since you are so far above the common school, you ought to realize that you have surpassed.[41]

A little later he remarked that "there are innumerable things in the Spanish compendium of Valverde from which it can be readily seen that neither he nor his teacher Colombo was even superficially versed in the writings of Galen and others." [42] If Valverde's plagiarism was partly the motive for these remarks, then Vesalius ought to have been much irritated by the *Anatomie universelle du corps humain* (Paris, 1561), of Ambroise Paré, which contained a large number of woodcut illustrations from the *Fabrica,* greatly reduced in size and far below the quality of the originals. However, he made no reference to this plagiarism by the celebrated French surgeon, his associate in the case of Henry II, but it is unlikely that the book would have come to his attention immediately in Spain.

Among the curious errors, survivals of the past, to which Vesalius had long continued to give allegiance was the belief that the veins contained three kinds of fibres which controlled the flow of blood.[43] Even the revised *Fabrica* contained not only a verbal account of these nonexistent fibres but also an illustration of them. Nevertheless, in the succeeding years he came to have doubts of their existence, and in reply to Fallopio's criticism [44] he did not hesitate to admit his former view was erroneous.[45]

An account of the venous valves discovered by Giambattista Canano and the Portuguese physician Amatus was published by the latter in 1551. Fallopio, however, had never been able to find the valves and as a consequence considered that Canano had deluded Amatus into the belief in something nonexistent.[46] Such, replied Vesalius, was not true, and he proceeded to tell how Canano had informed him of the existence of the valves as early as 1546.[47] Indeed, Vesalius had later sought and found them although they appeared to him as merely projections in the veins, supplied for strength:

I am not so sure, as you seem to be convinced, that Canano spoke to me in jest and likewise amused himself at the expense of Amatus and several others. When I visited the ailing Francesco d'Este with him at Ratisbon, the latter told me that at the commencement of the azygos vein, as well as in the orifices of the veins entering the kidneys and the veins near the upper region of the sacrum, he had observed membranes similar to those at the origins of the pulmonary artery and aorta, and he asserted that they prevented the reflux of the blood. Hence when I had an opportunity I undertook a dissection to investigate the matter, and when in addition I learned that Amatus was of Canano's opinion and read that he supported his judgment, at the end of that chapter in which I describe how nature provides for the strength of the veins in their distribution I added very clearly what I thought. I did not find those membranes, but I observed in the veins a notable thickness of the vein's body at the orifice, and I wrote that the projection is for the sake of strength—as we observe at the orifices of the stomach.[48]

In the course of his description of the penis Fallopio made certain somewhat ambiguous statements, or so at least they seemed to Vesalius who thought his critic had erroneously stated him not to have discussed the nerves of that organ in the *Fabrica*. As Fallopio continued with a description of the "nonpainful ganglia" of the penis—that is, various kinds of benign tumors or swellings [49]—Vesalius saw an opportunity for revenge, and in a somewhat oblique and mildly malicious reference to a patient who seems to have consulted Fallopio in Padua, he noted by implication that the patient, presumably dissatisfied with his physician, turned to Vesalius. This was most likely before his removal to Spain:

A certain distinguished man who consulted you at Padua because of those nodules, as well as because of a pain around the spleen and hips, had some nodules which twisted his penis rather remarkably. When he finally died from an abscess of the spleen, he was eviscerated by me so that he might be carried back to his family in Italy.[50]

Vesalius's concluding remarks indicate without question that he had accepted Fallopio's criticisms as those of a student like himself, one removed from the common controversial stage of the period and concerned solely with the truth of his study. That Vesalius would enjoy a return to academic life is also readily apparent as is likewise the stultifying situation in Spain which led to or assisted in leading him to such desire.

It is not without pleasure that I have read through your *Observationes* to the end, and with delightful recollections of the very happy life I enjoyed while teaching anatomy in Italy, true nurse of talents. I would that I might readily reply to those things you have communicated to me with so much profit so that, when you succeed in exposing further mysteries of nature, you will inform me of such new things as arise. I meanwhile can foresee no possible opportunity for performing dissection—here I cannot easily obtain even a skull. Nevertheless I hope that some opportunity will yet be granted me to give attention to our true book of the human body, that is, to man himself . . . because of all that he has to offer and the singular artifice of his maker, he reveals himself worthy of observation, an exact complement to you in the art.[51]

Fallopio's *Observationes anatomicae* had been critical of the *Fabrica* for its scientific lapses—that is, for those instances in which Vesalius had observed structures incorrectly or had failed to observe them at all. The following year there appeared a work of criticism that may be described as an anachronism since it was critical of Vesalius in terms only less virulent than those of Sylvius and was, like Sylvius's attack, because Vesalius had dared oppose the authority of Galen.[52] The author of this last stand of the conservatives was Francesco dal Pozzo, or latinized Puteus, a Galenist physician who practised throughout his career in the environs of Vercelli and had never had any contact with the target of his charges.[53] His polemic is of little significance since it merely reiterated the Galenic position in anatomy and declared that the more distinguished physicians supported his anti-Vesalian position. The author, for reasons best known to himself, mentioned these physicans by name, although many of them, such as Fallopio, were actually staunch supporters of Vesalius. In consequence of this ill-considered manoeuvre, one of them, Gabriele Cuneo, was sufficiently irritated to write against Dal Pozzo and on behalf of Vesalius,[54] although his book was not published until 1564, the year of his opponent's as well as Vesalius's death. It is unlikely that this attack caused Vesalius any concern, if it ever came to his attention at all. Moreover, he was now concerned in a medical case of such importance as to put any trifling irritants like Dal Pozzo's book completely out of his mind.

In the spring of 1562 Vesalius became involved in the most important case of his career, that resulting from the sudden and dramatic injury suffered by Don Carlos, eldest son of Philip II and heir to the Spanish throne. The strange story of Don Carlos may be said to have had its inception with his birth in 1545, since from his earliest days the prince had been a problem. Born with teeth, he chewed the breasts of his wet nurses, causing at least three of them painful injuries and so rendering this profession, at least on the royal level, subject to a rather curious occupational hazard. Left in the charge of an aunt, since his mother had died four days after his birth, the young prince was later handed over to a tutor, and although at first he seemed to demonstrate both application to his studies and ability, unfortunately this promise was not sustained. At the age of twelve he was described by the Venetian ambassador in the following terms:

[He has] a head disproportionate to the rest of his body. His hair is dark. The paleness of his complexion suggests a cruel character. . . . When rabbits are taken in the hunt, or other animals are brought to him, his pleasure is to see them roasted alive . . . he appears to be very bold and extremely attracted to women . . . he has a pride without parallel . . . he is angry more often than a young man should be, and very obstinate.[55]

At the age of seventeen, in 1562, the year of his injury, he was declared so small and slight as to seem more physically immature than his age would suggest. For two years he had been suffering from a quartan fever, and it was during this period that the French ambassador wrote that "the poor prince is so short and thin . . . he moves about so feebly that . . . there is very little hope held out for him at court." [56] The medical profession could do little for such a complaint except to suggest to Philip that he send his son to a healthier region than malarious Madrid of the sixteenth century, and Don Carlos was packed off to the university town of Alcalá de Henares some twenty miles from the capital. There he seemed quickly to improve.[57] Nearly two months passed without any signs of fever, and the joy of Philip, the royal family, and the court, not to speak of the physicians whose reputations were at stake, continued to mount until a disastrous accident occurred which not only destroyed all the hopes which had been raised but, as well, placed the life of the prince in the utmost peril.

The caretaker of the royal quarters in Alcalá had several daughters, one of whom appears to have taken the fancy of Don Carlos. It was a matter that had not escaped the observation of the prince's attendants who were not loathe to indulge the prince since they seemed of a mind that it would occupy his time and presumably keep him out of worse mischief. At any rate, on 19 April, a Sunday, Don Carlos caught sight of the girl walking in the garden outside the palace, and in his haste to pursue her he ran down a flight of steps, missed his footing, turned a complete somersault, and struck his head against the door at the bottom of the staircase. Chaloner, the somewhat unsympathetic English ambassador, in his report to Queen Elizabeth told the story very succinctly: The prince, "in hasty following of a wench, daughter to the keeper of the house, fell down a pair of stairs, [and] broke his head." [58] Ironically, it may be added, Don Carlos's haste was all in vain anyway since, as it turned out, the door at the foot of the staircase was locked. Whatever the purpose of the prince, the girl who would otherwise have been lost in the anonymity of the past is known to us as Mariana de Garcetas.

One may well imagine the excitement produced by this accident and its following injury, particularly so soon after the young prince had seemed finally to have overcome his fever. Indeed, the injury appeared so perilous and the outcome so doubtful that when finally Don Carlos did recover one of the physicians was requested by a member of the royal family to write out a full account of the case, and this record, by Daza Chacon, is not only our major source of information [59] respecting this princely episode, but is also one of the fullest pictures we have of the medical procedure of that age.

Upon examination of the prince he was found to have a wound, as Daza Chacon informs us, "about the size of a thumbnail, the edges well contused and the pericranium laid bare and also appearing to be somewhat contused." Shortly afterward, when the prince recovered consciousness, he complained of the pain from his injury and thereafter still more bitterly of the pain from the dressing of the wound. It was at this time that one of the grandees in attendance suggested to the physicians that they pay no attention to princely whims but treat the patient as an ordinary person. With fine professional independence, somewhat divorced from realism, the reply was given that such was the custom. Then, after the wound had been dressed and the prince properly bedded down, he was, according to the therapeutic notions of the time, bled of eight ounces of blood and coincidentally developed a slight fever.

King Philip, then in Madrid, had, of course, been immediately notified of the accident, whereupon he had dispatched the royal surgeon, as well as a Doctor Portugués, to Alcalá. With the arrival of these two the medical staff, originally composed of Don Carlos's three personal attendants, was augmented to five.

On the morning following the fall, the five physicians held their first consultation, and, since as yet they were unaware of the precise nature of the injury and its seriousness, they were constrained to fall back upon tried and true measures of therapy. In short, taking into account the past medical history of the prince and the fact that he had seldom been purged, and in some manner or other had succeeded in escaping frequent bleeding, it was decided that he could stand the loss of eight more ounces of blood. This made sixteen ounces in two days.

On the fourth day after the injury the prince's fever had increased slightly, and the glands on the left side of his neck had become painful. However, this was thought to be a matter of no great significance since at the time of his fall Don Carlos had been suffering from a cold. In agreement with this argument, the fever appeared to have abated by the seventh day, although the assembled physicians chose to attribute this to their administration of a two-ounce purge of manna.

For the time being, therefore, the prospects of quick recovery appeared favorable, but several days later certain disquieting signs became apparent. The wound began to fester and then the prince was discovered to be feverish; furthermore, according to medical precepts of the time, fever on the eleventh day in cases of head wounds was a bad sign, and the eleventh day was at hand. Obviously another consultation was required, and this time it was decided that the painful glands in the neck could mean only one of two things: an internal lesion; or, due to damage to the pericranium, some remaining shut-in matter. On the basis of these possibilities it was felt that the scalp should be incised, and this task was entrusted to Pedro de Torres, the royal surgeon. However, when the incision was made there was so much haemorrhage that the physicians were still unable to determine whether or not the skull had been injured, and under these circumstances they were unwilling to take further responsibility upon themselves—despite their earlier assertion of professional independence. As a result, a courier was sent off to the king bearing the unfortunate news.

Now Philip wasted no time in going to his son, and he took Vesalius with him. As had been mentioned, Vesalius was physician to the Netherlanders at the royal court rather than physician to the king, since, despite the incompetence of the Spanish medical profession—as a Tuscan ambassador wrote, "Who hasn't seen it can't believe it" [60]—Spanish pride and Spanish dislike of the Netherlanders required the king to avoid direct employment of Vesalius. Nevertheless, given a crisis such as the peril of the royal heir, the king did not hesitate to use the most competent advice available, and so Philip and Vesalius left Madrid before dawn and reached Alcalá in time to observe the morning dressing of the prince's wound. The situation was somewhat parallel to that incident in 1559 when Henry II of France had received a brain injury during a joust. On that occasion also Vesalius was in company with Daza Chacon, the same surgeon who has left us the record of the case of Don Carlos.[61]

During the morning dressing of the wound, with Philip and Vesalius in attendance, an opportunity presented itself for a minute examination of the bone, but except for a small reddish spot neither fracture nor crack could be discovered. The wound was then dressed with one of the complex dressings commonly in use at the time: powdered iris and birthwort, possibly to promote exfoliation. Then an unguent of turpentine and egg yolk was applied to the edges of the wound to assist suppuration. On top of all this and as a cleansing agent was placed honey of roses, and finally a plaster of betony over the whole of this amazing and variegated concoction.

Despite such elaborate precautions, the unfortunate prince made no progress. In the words of one of the attending physicians, there now occurred "a swelling of the head and a considerable erysipelas together with thick blood; the swelling extended first through the left side, the ear and eye, and then the right, so that the abscess covered the whole face and extended to the neck, chest, and arms." [62]

Curiously, in view of the important place held by bloodletting in the therapy of the time and the usual disregard of the patient's ability to withstand it, the physicians now determined not to bleed the prince since it was felt that he had not the strength to bear it. On the other hand, he was cupped, purged, and given potions with no result but delirium.

For the first time strong dissension appears to have occurred among the physicians. Vesalius, who seems to have excited considerable jealousy among the Spanish physicians because, although an alien, he held so favored a position with the king, proposed trephining the skull since he felt there was an internal lesion. Eventually a compromise was reached whereby it was decided to ruginate. This procedure was undertaken on 9 May and led to the conclusion "that there was no damage in the skull nor in the internal part." However, this was of no immediate assistance, and with the prince's condition going from bad to worse the physicians, catching at straws, were induced to allow a Moorish quack named Pinterete to try one of his nostrums. The remedy merely burned the wound, however, and the Moor was dismissed and, as the report of Daza Chacon tells us, "went to Madrid to take care of Hernando de Vego whom he sent to heaven with the help of his ointment."

Three weeks had passed and little hope was held for the recovery of Don Carlos. It was then that the people of Alcalá, who had kept posted on the condition of their prince and who appear to have had a very poor opinion of medical science, arrived at the palace bearing the mummified remains of the Blessed Diego, a Franciscan friar dead for some hundred years but who, during the course of his lifetime, had been celebrated as a performer of miracles. It is almost incredible, if not unthinkable, that the remains of the friar were brought to the prince's bed and placed as close to him as possible, although Don Carlos, and perhaps it was just as well, was in such condition as to be unaware of this religious intercession on his behalf—an action characteristic, although usually not in such degree, of Spanish piety in that age of credulity and superstition.[63]

Despite mundane and supernatural application, the prince appeared moribund, and on the evening of that day King Philip was told to expect the worst. Sorely distressed over the presumed fate of his eldest son and heir to his throne, Philip left during the night for the monastery of San Jeronimo where he gave himself up to prayer and awaited the outcome.[64] Because of this, some presumed the prince already dead and wrote away for mourning costume. Meanwhile, the physicians were left in considerable danger of mob violence as the people of Alcalá learned the worst and, in their superstitious way, appeared to believe it was the fault of the attending physicians.

However, the medical staff remained steadfast and continued the cupping, the fomentations, the application of various restoratives, and finally was rewarded with improvement in the patient's condition, although it would be difficult to determine whether the reason for that improvement was medical, spiritual, or despite both. Philip became convinced that the intercession of the friar Diego was responsible and some years later was instrumental in bringing about his canonization.[65] Naturally this opinion was opposed by the physicians who understandably felt that their contribution to the prince's recovery was being overlooked, while elsewhere appeals had been made to a variety of saints, each of whom had his partisans.[66] In addition, some three thousand of the inhabitants of

Toledo had paraded through the narrow streets of that city, naked to the waist and vigorously scourging each other. Naturally, these flagellants felt that their contribution must have had no little influence on the outcome.

It is rather difficult to assess any particular credit in the treatment of the prince from the evidence at hand, most of it Spanish and naturally favoring the Spanish physicians or acts of Spanish piety. Clearly the medical treatment of the patient was not reviewed with much sympathy by the English ambassador at that time who wrote to his government: "I believe that God's minister, nature, hath in despite of the surgeons' inconsiderate dealing, done more for the Prince than they were aware of." Vesalius, it must be admitted, was wrong in his diagnosis of an internal lesion, although his friend and chronicler of the case, Daza Chacon, generously conceded that "[Vesalius] had a number of good reasons in support of his opinion." What they were is not stated, and we are not informed why the other physicians refused to accept Vesalius's diagnosis, although either view was beyond any real scientific determination at that time. Later, on 16 May, the physicians came to agreement that pressure applied to the prince's left eyeball produced indication of an accumulation of pus behind it, and, according to one account, although not that of Daza Chacon, it was Vesalius who first advised incision and drainage of the left orbit, and a little later the right.[67] This operation was repeated at intervals in the course of which a sequestrum was discharged, and the prince began to show definite signs of improvement. On 22 May his fever vanished completely, and on 1 June the English ambassador was able to write home that "the prince of Spain is well recovered and now the former sorrow turns into feasts." On 5 July Don Carlos was sufficiently recovered to visit and pay his respects to the Blessed Diego, who was to become Saint Diego in 1588,[68] and to attend a bullfight, all on the same day.

Throughout the prince's illness Philip had displayed strong paternal solicitude, making repeated journeys to be at his son's bedside, attending the long medical consultations, and watching the dressings being applied to the wound. Of the grandees, the Duke of Alba, Spain's great soldier, was in constant attendance and spent his nights fully dressed in a chair by the prince's bed.

In all, the attending physicians held some fifty consultations, fourteen of which occurred in the presence of the king. Such consultations lasted from two to four hours and followed a formal and elaborate pattern. The procedure was for the king to be seated and flanked on either side by the Duke of Alba and Don Garcia of Toledo, the majordomo. To the rear stood the remaining grandees. The physicians and surgeons sat before the king in a semicircle. Each in turn was called upon to state his opinion of the case along with the reasons and authorities, such as Hippocrates and Galen, upon which it was founded, and the king would ask each consultant to explain such technical terms as were unknown to him. On one occasion when Daza Chacon was about to speak, he was addressed with these words: "Speak . . . and it is his Majesty's wish that you do not quote so many texts." "This," Daza observed proudly in his report of the case, "was a rare distinction." However, when one considers the hours that Philip spent listening to long-winded physicians quoting innumerable authorities, classical and medieval, the command may not have been so complimentary as the Spanish physician thought.

The purpose of the consultations appears to have been not only to determine the treatment of the prince but also to discuss possible complications that might arise so that proper preparation might be made to meet them. This second procedure was very necessary so that couriers might be dispatched for the various drugs and herbs that were so important a part of the therapeutics of that age.

Such was the bizarre picture of the illness of Don Carlos and the personages and events surrounding him: his solicitous father; the austere and usually terrifying Duke of Alba, later to be called the "bloody duke" but now occupying the role of sick nurse; a Moorish quack and, vis-à-vis, Vesalius, the true man of science; religious processions, flagellants, and the grisly remains of a long-dead friar; ceremonious consultations and the threat of mob violence.

Very little more is known about Vesalius's life and activities in Spain. Between the summer and the end of the year 1562 he was concerned with four cases of empyema for which he employed surgery to produce drainage, a procedure he had used in 1547, although at that time unsuccessfully. No doubt through the years he had developed his technique on unrecorded cases, and in three of the four that came to his attention in Madrid the outcome was successful. In December he treated the French ambassador Saint Sulpice for some unknown complaint, and it is likely that it was to Vesalius that the ambassador also made a payment of "4 *pistolets*" for treatment in November 1563.[69]

During the spring of 1562 Giovanni of Arragona, Sicily, Marquis of Terranova, an acquaintance and former patron of Vesalius at the imperial court but now resident in Palermo, had received a penetrating wound of the left chest and fracture of the fifth rib during a tournament. The marquis was under the care of the distinguished Sicilian physician Gian Filippo Ingrassia who, it will be recalled, was the original discoverer of the third ossicle of the ear. Ingrassia was much disturbed by his patient's failure to respond to treatment and in consequence consulted Italian colleagues, notably Bartolomeo Eustachi, who replied from Rome on 3 August with suggestions for treatment which, however, Ingrassia found unacceptable. For the time being, therefore, nothing seemed to give promise of a cure, although almost eight months had passed since the injury, and Ingrassia proceeded to write out an account of the case, dated 9 December, which, together with various consilia or opinions he had received, he sent to Giuseppe of Arragona, brother of the marquis. In turn Giuseppe sent Ingrassia's reports to the marquis's sons who transmitted them to Vesalius, hitherto not consulted, for his opinion, and he quickly composed and dispatched to Ingrassia a reply dated "Christmas 1562."[70]

Vesalius had learned much about the treatment of empyema and his successes induced him to write "so candidly and familiarly because I desire the complete, prosperous, and lasting health of the very illustrious marquis, my lord and old patron, to whom I was very much obliged when he lived in our court." It was Vesalius's opinion that in wounds of the upper thorax with extravenate blood producing pus and accompanied by dyspnoea and pain in the region of the diaphragm, the proper treatment was surgically produced drainage from the thorax.

As mentioned earlier, Vesalius appears to have been the first in modern times—at least as early as 1547—to have employed surgery for this condition, although still earlier he had referred in the *Fabrica* to its experimental use on animals,[71] a kind of prelude to the more refined procedure he advocated for humans. His practice was to make an incision at the tenth rib at that point where "it runs extended very obliquely to the posterior." This incision had to be sufficiently large to receive the tip of the left index finger which then acted as a guide to prevent penetration into the lung and also, by the finger's pressure, to maintain an opening for exit of the blood. As he understood the case of the marquis it seemed logical that the blow of the lance that had penetrated the thorax and fractured a rib must likewise have ruptured blood vessels which as a result emptied into the thorax. Vesalius was aware of Ingrassia's hesitation to employ surgery, but his own cases, for the most part successful, led him to recommend the procedure, since in recent months in Madrid he had successfully operated on a Biscayne soldier—who had died but not from the operation—a Fleming at the royal court, a Gascon in the French embassy, and the Marquis of Velena.

This advice, although solicited by the injured marquis's sons rather than by Ingrassia himself, was graciously acknowledged by the latter on Christmas day precisely one year later.[72] By this time, as Ingrassia wrote, he was pleased to state that the marquis had for some months been completely free of his fistula, but the consilium of the "mighty Vesalius" ought nonetheless to be considered for the sake of succeeding generations, and Ingrassia was undertaking to have it published:

. . . so that by the authority of such a great man as yourself, and supported by your persuasive reasons and very well-grounded experiences, if ever in a similar case anyone is urged to perform that surgery so much praised by you as suitable and effective, he will be able to undertake it boldly and intrepidly and to complete it according to the method you teach.

Ingrassia further agreed that the operation might well be desirable in some of the cases cited by Vesalius, but he was dubious about its employment in that of the Marquis of Terranova, especially since Vesalius had admitted that from time to time there were fatal consequences.

From October 1563 through January 1564 the Cortes of Aragon was in session at Monzón, some three hundred miles from Madrid, and Vesalius accompanied Philip's court thither. Chaloner, the English ambassador, who was also present, wrote to Queen Elizabeth, on 17 October 1563, that he was much troubled by kidney stones, a condition aggravated "with drinking these Spanish wines" during his long sojourn in Madrid. "Doctor Vesalius" had told him that his kidneys were "exulcerated with the fretting of the stone this journey" from Madrid to Monzón, and that "rest and abstinence from all wine, and to drink only the decoction of liquorice and barley, must be a ground of his cure." [73] Leaving his interpreter William Phayre at Monzón, Chaloner retired to Barbastro some dozen miles to the north to nurse his failing health. There Vesalius visited him from time to time, as is learned from some letters that passed between Phayre and Chaloner in January 1564. On 11 January Phayre wrote that he had called at Vesalius's house in Monzón but found him away. On 13 January Chaloner wrote that he would send for Vesalius within a day or two, and on the following day he wrote that he wished "Doctor Vesalius would dine with him at Barbastro on Sunday or Monday." [74]

Although the Cortes ended its sessions in January 1564, Philip did not return to Madrid until May, but at some time prior to this he had granted Vesalius permission to leave Spain. This departure and his following journey to Jerusalem gave rise to numerous contradictory accounts. The most dramatic, although wholly unacceptable, is that which occurs in a letter allegedly written by Hubert Languet, 1518–1581, the distinguished publicist and diplomat, to Caspar Peucer, physician and son-in-law of Philip Melanchthon. Dated from Paris, 1 January 1565, it is brief enough so that it can be given in its entirety.

> The story is that Vesalius is dead. Undoubtedly you have heard that he set out for Jerusalem, and the reason for that pilgrimage was a remarkable one as it has been written to me from Spain. A Spanish nobleman had been entrusted to his care, but when Vesalius believed him to have died, and because he was not satisfied as to the cause of his death, he sought permission from the relatives of the dead man to open the body; having obtained such permission, when he opened the chest he found the heart still beating. The relatives, not content to accuse Vesalius of murder, also denounced him before the Inquisition as impious, thus seeking to gain an even greater revenge. When the cause of death was explained, it was not easy to excuse such error on the part of so skilled a physician, and the Inquisition fully determined upon his execution. It was only with the greatest difficulty that the king by his authority, or rather his supplication, was able to save him. The prayers of king and court were finally heeded on condition that Vesalius expiate his crime by a journey to Jerusalem and Mount Sinai.

The difficulties in the way of acceptance of this story are many. Not only has no supporting evidence ever been uncovered in Spain, but other accounts of Vesalius's departure are explained by completely different motives. Moreover, Languet's letter is not in the published edition of his collected correspondence but appeared only in 1620 imbedded in the brief life of Vesalius written by Melchior Adam. [75] In consequence doubt must be cast not only upon the early date of the letter but also its authorship, and it is entirely possible that it represents a fabrication based upon the same rumor as that presented by Ambroise Paré who referred, without mention of the name of the culprit, to the instance of a Spanish

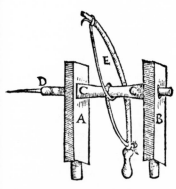

The bone drill; a new illustration added to the *Fabrica* (1555).

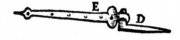

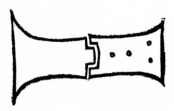

The hinge used to illustrate the form of a
ginglymus or hinged joint: At the top is the
illustration used in the *Fabrica* (1543); next is
the illustration proposed as more nearly correct
and used by John Caius in 1544; at the bottom
is a new illustration used in the *Fabrica* (1555).

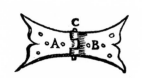

PLATE 49

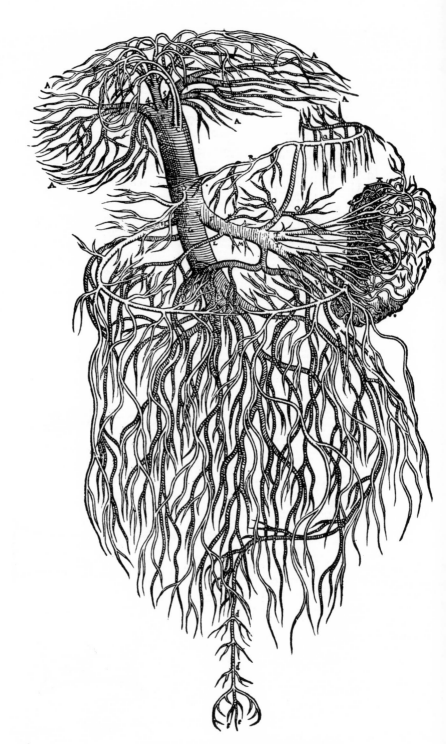

The portal system of veins showing five branches going to the liver. The illustration remains unchanged in the *Fabrica* (1555), although reference to the five branches was deleted from the text. This illustration should be compared with Vesalius's less sophisticated drawing of 1538, plate 17.

PLATE 50

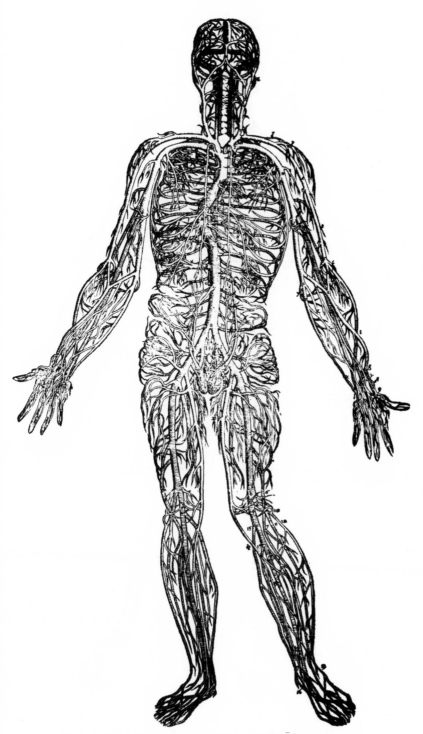

Revised illustration of the "venous man," *Fabrica* (1555).

PLATE 51

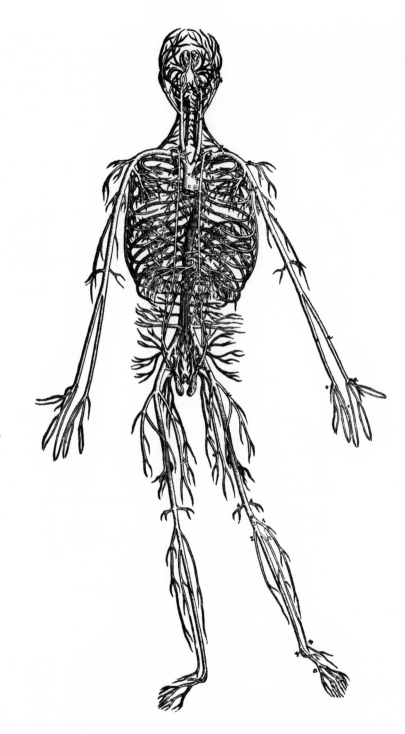

Revised illustration of the "arterial man," *Fabrica* (1555).

PLATE 52

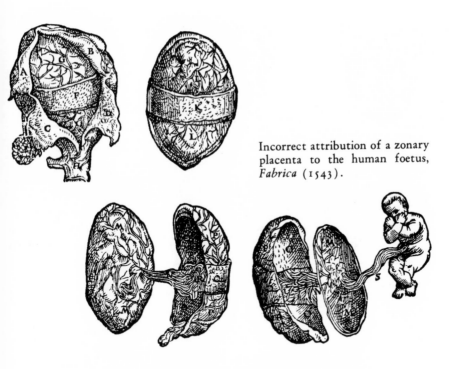

Incorrect attribution of a zonary placenta to the human foetus, *Fabrica* (1543).

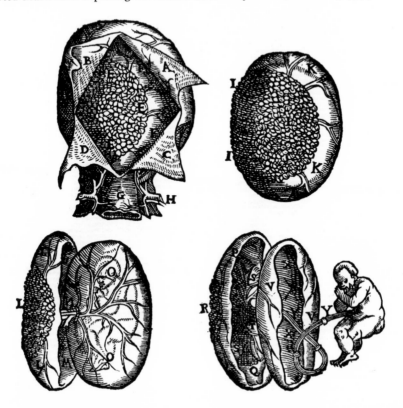

Corrected illustration depicting the human discoidal placenta, *Fabrica* (1555).

PLATE 53

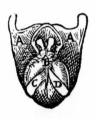

*Præsens figura fexta huius Capitis fronti præpositæ omni
ex parte correspodet: nisi quòd hæc priuatim musculos spe-
ctandos exhibet, quos à secundæ cartilaginis spinâ, ad infe-
riores primæ cartilaginis processus aliquando deductos uidi.
A itaq̃, & A prima laryngis notatur cartilago, B uerò
spina secundæ cartilaginis. C autem, & D duo musculi, à
secundæ cartilaginis spinâ principium sumetes, ac in primam
cartilaginem inserti.*

Left above, an illustration of the thyroid cartilage, *Fabrica* (1543). At the right,
a new, relatively unaltered illustration, suggesting loss of the small, original
block.

Left below, detail of auditory organ, *Fabrica* (1543), and at right, the revised
and more elaborate illustration, *Fabrica* (1555).

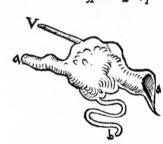

*Hanc rudem figuram in hoc apposui, ut forami-
num ductus in conspectu effet, quæ V, & a, & b*

*Lib. 1. Histor.
animal.cap.11.*

*notamus. Si
gnificet igi
tur rudi Mi
nerua, u-
trunq̃ a au
ditoriũ me
atum. V fo
ramen, su-
periùs V no
tatum. b autem, id quod mox sub litera b ex-
plicabitur.*

PLATE 54

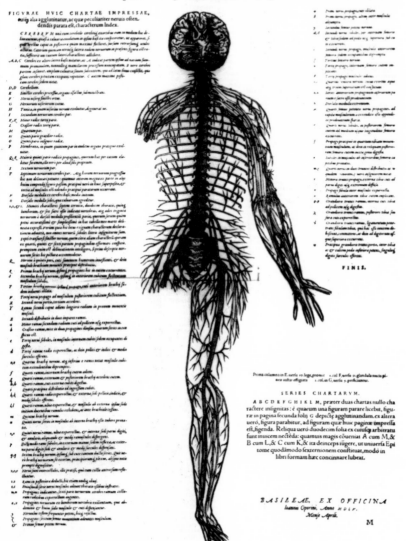

PLATE 55

Title page of Valverde's *Composicion del cuerpo humano*, Rome, 1556.

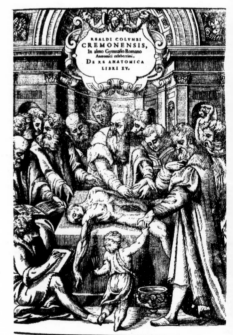

Title page of Realdo Colombo's *De re anatomica*, Venice, 1559, with portrait of the author.

PLATE 56

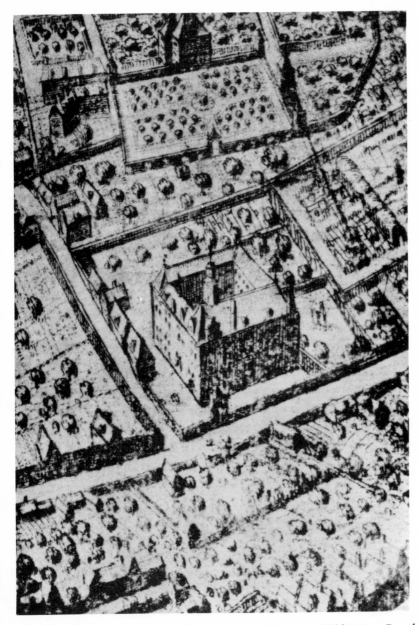

View of Vesalius's home in Brussels as it appeared in 1639. Bibliotèque Royale de Belgique.

PLATE 57

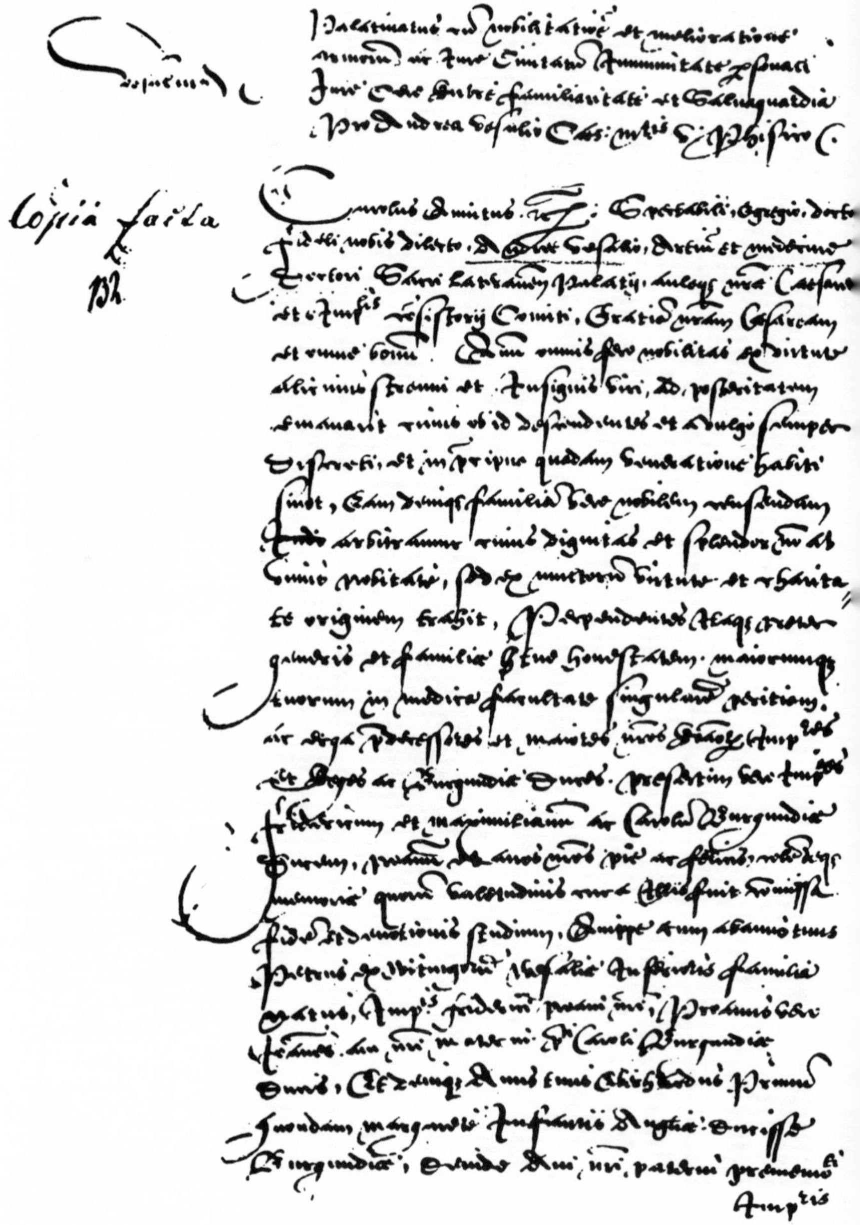

First leaf of the charter by which Vesalius was made a Count Palatine in 1556.

PLATE 58

Henry II's fatal joust with the Count of Mongonmery, or Lorges.

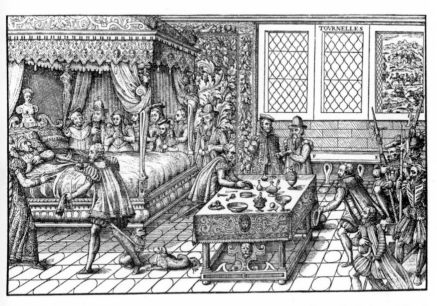

The deathbed scene. Vesalius stands at the head of the table at the left and Paré on the right.

PLATE 59

GABRIELIS FALLOPPII
MEDICI MVTINENSIS
OBSERVATIONES
Anatomicæ.

AD PETRVM MANNAM
medicum Cremonenfem.

Cum Priuilegio Summi Pontificis,
Regis Philippi, Senatusque
Veneti.

Title page of Fallopio's *Observationes anatomicae* (1561).

VENETIIS
Apud Marcum Antonium Vlmum

M D LXI

ANDREAE
VESALII,
ANATOMICARVM
GABRIELIS FALLOPPII
OBSERVATIONVM
EXAMEN.

CVM PRIVILEGIO.

VENETIIS,
Apud Francifcum de Francifcis, Senenfem.

M D LXIIII.

Title page of Vesalius's *Examen* (1564).
Historical Library, Yale Medical Library.

PLATE 60

Philip II of Spain. Cincinnati Art Museum.

Prince Don Carlos.

PLATE 61

Portrait of Vesalius entitled "Vesalius making his pilgrimage to Jerusalem." From the original in the Uppsala University Library, Waller Collection.

PLATE 62

CAROLVS. CLVSIVS.

N. de Larmessin sculp.

Charles de l'Ecluse. Wellcome Historical Medical Library, London.

PLATE 63

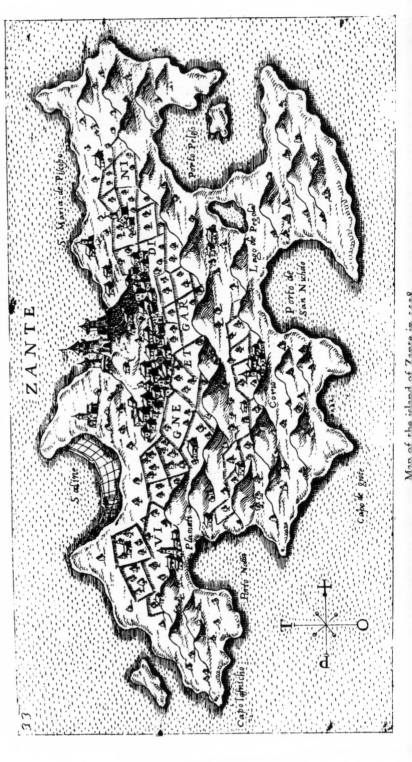

Map of the island of Zante in 1618

VIAGGIO DA VENETIA

ZANTE

PLATE 64

woman who was presumed dead but who, when her body was opened for post-mortem examination, showed evidence of life. This is in Paré's *De la generatione*, 1571,[76] and it is apparent that the later report of the English physician Edward Jorden,[77] in which Vesalius is openly mentioned as the unhappy physician, was based upon Paré's account.

As mentioned above, no evidence has ever been found to support such a tale. The story might also have been based in part upon the same sort of rumor that led to the accusation of human vivisection placed earlier against Berengario da Carpi and later against Gabriele Fallopio. Certainly the ever present danger of such charges seems to have been recognized by Vesalius who, it will be recalled, took pains to revise the account of one of his investigations in the second edition of the *Fabrica*,[78] presumably in order to avoid any such risk. Mention of the share of the Inquisition in the incident is found only in the letter allegedly written by Languet and seems likely to reflect a Protestant bias in what was probably a late forgery built upon Paré's statement, which was itself presumably founded upon idle rumor.[79]

Other explanations of Vesalius's departure from Spain stressed his desire to make a trip to Jerusalem, although there is lack of agreement as to his motivation. Two of the accounts, which seem to contain an element of truth, are that of Giovanni Argenterio,[80] which declared Vesalius to have been beset by the conservative medical element and virtually driven out of Spain, and that of the Belgian botanist Charles de l'Ecluse, which will be considered below at greater length. First, in regard to the assertion of Argenterio, it seems very likely that Vesalius was not popular with much of the Spanish medical fraternity, although it is to be doubted, as Argenterio would have it, that he was denied attendance upon the royal family as a result of his anti-Galenism. Vesalius was not, of course, a physician to the royal family, but he certainly had the confidence of Philip, as events have indicated. It seems rather that the Galenism of Spanish medicine was one of several factors that caused Vesalius to leave the country, although it did not force him to leave against his will, and before turning to the account of L'Ecluse these possibilities must be given some consideration.

Vesalius's determination to leave Spain seems most likely to have had several causes, some of them possibly dating from a few years earlier, even from the period of his retirement from the service of the late emperor Charles. We cannot be absolutely certain that he had entered the service of Philip without some reluctance, since it may well have been that he could not refuse such service to the king of Spain, now lord of Vesalius's native land, nor could he overlook his family's tradition of medical service to the Hapsburgs, a tradition, as we know, extending back at least a century and probably further. Moreover, Philip might have recognized and desired the services of Vesalius personally as royal physician yet been thwarted by Spanish pride and nationalism, as well as by the ever-growing hostility to the Flemings, and so been able to keep him at court only in a different capacity which Vesalius considered of lower status.

Vesalius, also, may have foreseen the not-too-distant death of Fallopio and been already planning a return to his old chair of anatomy at Padua. However, if it was his intention to leave Spain when the opportunity of return to Padua presented itself, he was to find that it was easier to enter Spanish service than to leave it, and whatever his plan he found himself trapped in an unpleasant situation.

First, there was the hostility of the Spanish physicians which arose partly from nationalism and partly from a particular dislike of the Flemings, whose previous popularity with Charles V was especially resented while, in addition, there were now rumblings of the revolt brewing in the Netherlands which was leading to open hostility between Spaniard and Netherlander. The asserted incompetence of Spanish physicians at this time has already been mentioned, and no doubt there was professional jealousy of the ability of Vesalius with all the unpleasantness this could produce.

Vesalius's recognition of his own ability, bolstered by the appreciation of those at liberty to call upon him, must, when contrasted with the jealous restraints placed upon him by his lesser Spanish colleagues, have made his position extremely galling and frustrating. It was a situation somewhat delineated in the Don Carlos case and its aftermath when the cure of the prince was attributed to various saints, sanctuaries, and religious formulae. In short, the general atmosphere of Spain was hardly scientific. Vesalius's memories of Padua must have contrasted sharply with the Spanish situation, and the fact that he had, at just this time, written his reply to Fallopio, no doubt made his recollections even more vivid.

With this situation in mind let us now turn to the account of L'Ecluse who had been prompted to write it by reading what Jacques de Thou had published in his *Historia sui temporis*. L'Ecluse wrote to the author in January 1607 to declare that his account of Vesalius was erroneous and that as leisure was found he would transmit a correct statement. Eventually this statement reached De Thou and was incorporated in later editions of his work.[81]

According to L'Ecluse, he had arrived in Madrid shortly after Vesalius had left Spain, but his information regarding that departure had been acquired from Charles de Tisnacq, councillor to the Netherlanders in Madrid, who was acquainted with Vesalius and was a reliable source. L'Ecluse's account declares that Vesalius had suffered a serious illness from which recovery had been slow and difficult. On this point, however, we must be skeptical, since we have record of Vesalius actively pursuing his medical practice at Monzón as late as mid-January, returning to Madrid at some time thereafter, and leaving the latter city in March, hence not allowing much time for serious illness and protracted recovery. Nevertheless, according to L'Ecluse the pilgrimage to Jerusalem was undertaken in gratitude for recovery, and in that event it might be permissible to wonder if such illness, if it did occur, was not a device, perhaps deliberately magnified, to gain permission to leave Spain.

As the story continues, Vesalius was well supplied with funds for his journey, so much so that he was even able to make loans, repayable to him in the Netherlands, to several impecunious but noble Flemings.[82] Finally, taking leave of the king, who had provided him with a letter granting a kind of diplomatic immunity at the several customs posts within the kingdom and with a sum of money for travel expenses, Vesalius, his wife, and his daughter set out by coach. All went well until the then-frontier town of Perpignan was reached and the king's letter was ignored by the customs officials. However, rather than pay the bribe demanded, Vesalius is declared to have spent several weeks and a considerable sum of money opposing this impertinence in the local courts. Finally, with this obstacle overcome, the party passed into France. At Cette Vesalius separated from his family and, according to Reiner Solenander, an old friend of Paduan days and so possibly a source of truth, the parting was accompanied by an angry quarrel. Whatever the truth may be, to return to L'Ecluse, wife and daughter continued in the coach toward Brussels, while Vesalius journeyed onward to Marseilles, presumably to take ship to Genoa whence he would continue overland across north Italy to Venice. From Cette it is no great distance to Montpellier, but there is no indication that Vesalius paid a visit to the famous medical school there, presumably because his plans required that he reach Venice as quickly as possible.

If it was Vesalius's plan to seek his old chair of anatomy at Padua, as seems likely, this was quite possibly in fulfillment of a desire he had long had, one that may have led to despondency and perhaps feigned illness as a means of gaining permission to leave Spain. It is quite possible that even before he entered the service of Philip II he had had reports that led him to foresee the early death of Fallopio, so removing the incumbent and making the chair once again available. There is evidence that Fallopio suffered from what was called "a chill" all through the course of his lectures in 1556–57, and thereafter there were successive indications of declining health. The anatomical course was omitted in 1559–60, that of 1560–61 was abortive, and no course was given in 1561–62. On 3 October 1562 Fallopio died, reputedly from pleurisy but more likely from the terminal complications of pulmonary tuberculosis.[83] Hence there may well have been more meaning to the sentiment Vesalius expressed in his *Examen* than is immediately apparent when he remarked: "I sincerely hope that you may long pursue your studies in that delightful leisure of letters which is yours," and the genuine nature of Vesalius's expressed regrets at having left Padua and his desire to return there, mentioned earlier, seem beyond question. If it were true that Vesalius had been planning to return, one may well understand his distress when, having ascertained the death of Fallopio, he found that Philip would not permit him to leave Spain, and his resulting anxiety lest the chair of anatomy go to another by default. He must have been relieved upon reaching Venice to find the chair still vacant.

Although there are no official documents extant that indicate Vesalius was reappointed as professor of anatomy, there is little reason to doubt the statement to this effect by Pietro Bizarri which will be given later in another context. Nor is there evidence that Vesalius paid a visit to Padua at this time, but there was no reason for him to do so. The appointments to the university were made by the Venetian senate, and it was more important that he renew his acquaintance with the proper people in Venice. It may well have been that he reëstablished contact with the Contarini and Navagero families whom he had known well in earlier days, and there is indication that he was in touch with Paolo Tiepolo, that former Venetian ambassador to Spain who had brought back the manuscript of the *Examen* for presentation to Fallopio. One further bit of information shows us why Fallopio had not received it before his death and as well indicates a meeting of Vesalius with several friends and the background to the publication of the *Examen* in 1564.

At some time during Vesalius's visit in Venice he entered the shop of Francesco dei Francesci, a publisher and bookseller, who records the visit as a preface to the reader in the edition of the *Examen* he was shortly to publish:

When not long ago Andreas Vesalius was about to set forth from here for Jerusalem he was greeted in my bookshop by Agostino Gadaldino, Andrea Marino, and some other distinguished physicians who had met together by chance, and they asked him what had happened to his *Examen* of the *Observationes anatomicae* of Gabriele Fallopio, which Marino declared he had learned from Alessandro Baranzono had been given to a Venetian ambassador to carry to Padua. Vesalius replied that his *Examen* had indeed been given to Paolo Tiepolo, distinguished representative of the Venetian Senate, when he was departing from the court of King Philip. However, because of the civil war in France and lack of a trireme he had been compelled to remain for many months in Catalonia and had returned to Venice very tardily. Fallopio, as they knew, had died and for that reason Tiepolo had kept the *Examen,* which could be readily obtained from him. Whereupon some of those who were present desired that a copy be made of it, but finally everyone agreed that when it had been obtained from Tiepolo it be given to me and that I make it available to all in print. . . .

Sometime in March, hence prior to the publication of the *Examen* with this preface, which is dated 24 May, Vesalius embarked for his journey to Jerusalem, accompanied by "Signor Malatesta da Rimini, a *capitano* of the Venetian Signoria." This condottiere Giacomo Malatesta, 1530–1600, in Venetian service, was going only as far as Cyprus, which was on the regular itinerary of those pilgrims setting out for the Holy Land from Venice. It appears likely that Vesalius had no intention of returning to Spain, yet perhaps discretion required that he fulfill his obligation of a pilgrimage, and there seemed to be ample time for it before the opening of the new academic year at Padua. Moreover, in the past he had frequently used his leisure for travel, which apparently he enjoyed, and although it is true that this trip was longer than any previous ones, yet the necessary leisure was available and he would be farther removed from the clutches of the King of Spain, if that was a factor of any significance, until such time as he might formally enter the protection of Venetian employment.

About three-quarters of a century earlier one veteran of a pilgrimage had remarked that there were three things that could be neither recommended nor discouraged: marriage, war, and the voyage to the Holy Sepulchre; "they may begin very well and end very badly." Vesalius had already experienced the first two and was about to essay the third. As we may assume that his marriage had begun well but, as at the recent parting from his wife, displayed signs of wear and tear, so his outward trip from Venice seems to have been wholly endurable although the return was to be pure catastrophe.

It may be assumed that the ship followed the usual course along the Dalmatian coast of the Adriatic past Zante, thence along the east coast of Crete, putting in at Candia, continuing onward to Rhodes, thence to Cyprus where Vesalius's companion disembarked, finally terminating at the port of Jaffa where the pilgrims undertook an overland route to Jerusalem. Exactly what Vesalius's itinerary was is not known, except for one brief glimpse of him in the Holy Land. This is found in the book of Bonifacio Stefano da Ragusa, a Franciscan living there at the time, *Liber de perenni cultu terrae sanctae et de fructuosa eius peregrinatione* (Venice, 1573), in which he referred to Vesalius "who traveled with me" on the plain of Jericho.[84]

The return from the Holy Land and the death of Vesalius were several times described by his contemporaries in reports which conflict at various points. The one which seems most reliable and to which reference has already been made is that written by Pietro Bizzari, first published in Italian in 1568:

But what shall I say of the great Vesalius, so excellent and unusual for our times? Has he not again clearly demonstrated to us by his death that great misery and strange accidents hover over the life of man? Although not without great sorrow and unhappiness for everyone who knew him or read his works, through which despite the cruel fortune of his death, he will live in glorious eternity. He was a very great philosopher and physician, but in matters of anatomy so rare and singular that it can deservedly be said that he was almost the founder, and marvelously illustrated and brought that very noble science to perfection. He was very dear and pleasing to the Emperor and to King Philip his son, and finally to all the learned men of our age. Now news has reached me that about the month of April 1564 Vesalius set out for Cyprus with Signor Malatesta da Rimini, a *capitano* of the Venetian Signoria, but not many days passed before the illustrious Senate called Vesalius to the famous university of Padua, with a very honorable stipend, in place of the learned Fallopio who a little earlier had passed to a better life.

Therefore while he was traveling to Italy, driven by fortune and contrary winds, he went ashore on the island of Zante where he was assailed by a sudden and grave illness, and within a short time he miserably closed and terminated the course of his life in a vile and impoverished inn in a solitary place, without any human assistance. A little before his death some Venetian ships had put in, and a Venetian goldsmith who was wandering about the island learned by chance where the unfortunate Vesalius lay ill. Moved by compassion he immediately asked the islanders to aid Vesalius, but they, very suspicious because there had lately been an epidemic, and also perhaps because they lacked humanity and kindliness, left him to die without any assistance. The worthy goldsmith did not fail to do for Vesalius after his death what he had been unable to do for him alive. With great difficulty he gained permission of the islanders to bury him, and with his own hands prepared the grave and buried the body so that it might not remain as food and nourishment for wild beasts.[85]

This was republished in abbreviated form in Latin in 1573.[86]

What happened to Vesalius seems to have been what had happened to many pilgrims before him. He had embarked on a pilgrim ship at Jaffa for the return journey, relying on the captain's promise to provide sufficiently for the necessities and comforts of the passengers, but either the captain had not lived up to the terms of the agreement or had not adequately provided for the possibility of an extended voyage. The Venetian archives contain accounts of many such cases as well as the records of prosecutions directed against the rascally promoters of such pilgrims' tours.

Another of the contemporary accounts written from Cologne and displaying no knowledge of the conditions under which pilgrimages were made does, however, stress the matter of delay at sea as a result of stormy weather. Moreover, it takes Vesalius to task for avarice causing him to sail on a pilgrims' ship rather than waiting for the "Venetian fleet," little understanding the extent of delay that this might have entailed, especially with the new academic year at Padua soon to open. It is this account that has been the source of frequent assertions of Vesalius's avarice, although the charge seems an irresponsible one. With this reservation, the letter from Johann Metellus to Arnold Birckmann is a second document which deserves to be presented:

A certain man of Nuremberg [Georg Boucher] relates that in October of last year Andreas Vesalius died while returning from Jerusalem. It happened as follows. Vesalius, inflamed by greed for wealth, had provided too little money [for his trip], although upon his return he was to receive much from many persons with whom he had entered into an agreement that he would undertake the journey. Through too-great avarice he entrusted himself to a pilgrims' ship, not to the Venetian fleet to which he had a letter of recommendation from Philip and might have received money on credit; also through avarice he provided too slightly for himself in regard to shipboard fare. On the return he fell in with this man of Nuremberg who was considering his return from Egypt to Venice, whom Vesalius induced to leave his ship and join him as a companion, and the man of Nuremberg willingly did it because of their common language. Again Vesalius provided too poorly for himself. [The ship] driven for full forty days by storms was unable to reach land. Several [of the passengers] became sick, partly through lack of biscuit and partly through lack of water, and Vesalius's mind was so disturbed by the casting of the dead into the sea that he fell ill, first through anxiety and then through fear, and asked that if he should die he might not, like the others, become food for the fish. Finally after being tumbled about in the sea the ship reached Zante, and as soon as possible Vesalius lept down from it and made his way to the gate of the city where he fell to the earth dead. That companion from Nuremberg placed a stone for him as a monument, and that same person told these things in the presence of Echt [87] and myself. Therefore consider how the death of that very famous man will serve you and me and will be an example for many.

Cologne, 17 April 1565.[88]

The main points of agreement in the accounts are that on the return voyage the ship ran into stormy weather and was delayed. In consequence the passengers suffered from exposure, supplies of food and water became deficient, and, according to Metellus, some of the passengers died before the ship reached land. Once arrived at the island of Zante, Vesalius went ashore where he died. The cause of his death, and whether or not it was at the city of Zante or elsewhere, has not been determined. To elucidate although not to solve these problems a few words must be devoted to a description of the island.

The island of Zante, *Fior di Levante,* came under Venetian control in 1484. At that time it was seriously depopulated owing to a number of causes, but thanks to the efforts of the Venetians new settlers were established, the incursions of the Turks were successfully resisted, and in 1564 there was a population of between fifteen and twenty thousand, much of it in the city of Zante. There is an inaccurately drawn map of the island in 1598 which, nevertheless, presents the essential conditions as they were at the time of Vesalius's arrival.[89] There was only one city, Zante, established on the eastern side at the only decent harborage of the island. Elsewhere a few small villages existed, but mostly inland. Southeast of Zante is the Lagano Gulf, in the sixteenth century called Porto Peloso. It is exposed to numerous and often stormy south and southeast winds, except for an inlet on the west side of the gulf called Porto Kerf; the hinterland to this inlet was uninhabited because of its marshiness. The west coast of Zante was, and still is, avoided except in good summer weather, and then it is safe only for very small local craft. The third side of the island from northwest to northeast as far as the salt beds of Katastari provided no better harborage.[90] If one takes into account the course from Jerusalem, the possible harbors—recalling that the accounts of Vesalius's trips do not mention shipwreck—it appears that the only likely places for the ship to touch land were the Lagano Gulf or the harbor of Zante. In short, we are thrown back upon the conflicting, contemporary accounts of the voyage.

One would assume that had Vesalius died before the city gate he would have been given burial in the church of the citadel, the only one then on the island that celebrated the Roman rite, and that thereby some memory of the event would have survived. There is, indeed, a story more or less to this effect, possibly based on the account of Metellus, if not on actual fact.[91] According to this account Vesalius was buried in the church of Santa Maria delle Grazie, originally built in 1488, destroyed by earthquake in the nineteenth century, rebuilt, then completely demolished in the great earthquake of 1893.[92] Together with the account there are two versions of the wording supposedly carved on Vesalius's tombstone: *Andreae Vesalii Bruxellensis tumulus / Qui obiit idib. Octobr. Anno MDLXIV aetatis / vero suae LVIII. Quum Hierosolymis*, and *Andreae Vesalii Bruxellensis tumulus / qui obiit idib. Octobr. MDLXIV aetatis suae / LVIII. Quum Jerosolymis rediisset.* The faulty date given for Vesalius's age is obvious in view of the year of his birth.

It has been pointed out by another writer, however, that churches dedicated to the Virgin are numerous, and that if one accepts Bizarri's account that Vesalius's death occurred in some lonely area, assuming a landing in the Lagano Gulf, his remains might have been transported to the village of Melinado, where the church employing the Greek rite was dedicated to the Virgin.[93]

One further matter may or may not concern Vesalius's death on Zante. In a description of the public library of Zante by L. X. Zōē there is mention of an anatomical manuscript described as "seventeenth century." [94] Is it possible that the dating of this manuscript, still extant in 1899, was erroneous and that by the merest chance it may be the single remaining piece of evidence of Vesalius's death on the island?

At some time during the period of Vesalius's absence on his pilgrimage, his *Examen*, which has already been considered and of which the printer's foreword is dated 24 May, was published.[95] The same licence by which the Venetian state permitted this publication, on 6 May, also granted permission to the printer Francesco dei Francesci to publish Gabriele Cuneo's *Apologiae Francisci Putei pro Galeno in anatome examen*, that somewhat delayed defense of Vesalius against the attack made upon him in 1562 by Francesco dal Pozzo.[96] We need not linger over this defense which has been thoroughly studied and, moreover, makes no contribution of any significance except as a further instance of the ever growing support of Vesalian anatomy.

To speculate about Vesalius's possible achievements at Padua, had he survived his pilgrimage, is of course idle, although tempting. His lasting fame rests upon a single book, the *Fabrica* of 1543. It is true that the revised version of 1555 is superior in detail, but nevertheless it remains a revision and not a second original contribution. Had Vesalius survived to return to Padua, could he have made further important contributions or was he at the age of fifty, and long removed from the academic world, too old for such achievements? Obviously there can be no answer to such a question. We know from his own remarks in the revised *Fabrica* that he was, for example, far from satisfied with Galenic cardiovascular physiology although for the time being he accepted it rather than make alterations piecemeal. Had he survived it is possible, although far from certain, that he might have made a real contribution in this area; or he might have turned his attention to the nervous system and done some of that work for which Eustachi was later to gain credit. On the other hand, a new generation of anatomists had grown up since 1543, building its work upon the *Fabrica* and now possibly able to make contributions as great as or even greater than the older Vesalius.

In short, it may well be that Vesalius had already made his full contribution, a great and fundamental one which is most clearly shown by its long-lasting influence. Harvey Cushing demonstrated in detail the influence of the *Fabrica*'s illustrations although he by no means exhausted the subject. The influence of the text was even greater although more subject to concealment since it was a frequent practice to appropriate without acknowledgment what was correct and to point out with righteous self-acclaim what was not. Yet all were henceforth constrained to guide and to control their studies by the Vesalian principle of investigation, and this was the great contribution. There is a tendency to derogate the work of Vesalius by comparing it to that of, for example, Fallopio and Eustachi without taking into account the important fact that the latter published their works about a generation after the appearance of the *Fabrica*. That at this later date these men were able to emendate and to contribute to Vesalian anatomy is in the final analysis a compliment to the earlier fundamental work which provided the foundation for their later achievements, a foundation established only after the bitterest of struggles yet to become a scientific commonplace in later times.

If there is any truth in the story of the unpleasantness that accompanied the separation of husband and wife at Cette, it seems possible, too, that Vesalius's death did not produce any extended period of mourning. Both wife and daughter, safely returned to Brussels, found themselves well provided for. Although there is no record of the disposition of Vesalius's papers and correspondence there is mention of his wealth in two contemporary letters, to which reference has already been made, one speaking of an income of 5,000 *livres* and 30,000 *livres* of capital, the other computing the figures more modestly as 3,000 florins and 10,000 florins.[97] Nevertheless, the women, who are mentioned at the time as particularly concerned to find husbands, were in easy circumstances. This, however, did not prevent the widow from addressing a petition to Philip II for a pension for herself and funds that might be used in aid of her daughter's marriage. On 16 March 1565, Philip wrote to Marguerite of Parma, his regent in the Netherlands, asking for advice on the matter. Although the regent's reply opposed the request,[98] two months later, with a kindliness and appreciation which belies the usual characterization of the king, Philip informed her that, "as the widow of the late Vesalius, and having regard to the long and continual services of her late husband to the Emperor . . . and to me in diverse travels at home and abroad," he proposed to provide her with "an annual pension of 200 florins." [99]

With all their financial attractions it is not astonishing that both women had no difficulty in discovering husbands. The widow married Henri van der Meeren, son of Walter van der Meeren, seigneur of Saventhem. Nothing further is known of this match except that husband and wife were still alive in 1599.[100] Somewhat more is known of the marriage of the daughter Anne to Jean de Mol. We may presume that they lived for a time comfortably in the *Huys van Vesalius* which, in 1571, for purposes of tax computation, was valued at 10,000 florins,[101] a considerable sum for that period. There is also record, however, that during that year, a troubled period in which Brussels was under the iron rule of the Duke of Alba, the property was occupied by Scipio Vitelli, a military engineer with the Spanish forces. Some years later Anne, possibly near death, bequeathed the property to her husband.[102] In 1578 Jean de Mol began to play an active part in civic and national affairs. Elected *échevin* of Brussels, he almost immediately ranged himself with the partisans of Don John of Austria, the new Spanish representative to the Netherlands. When, after the battle of Gemblous, Don John seized and confiscated the towns of Diest and Sichem, Jean de Mol was named *drossart* and lieutenant of the fiefs, on 20 September 1579, although Diest was soon lost again. However, with the appearance of the Prince of Parma, the redoubtable leader of the Spanish forces, Diest was retaken and Jean de Mol returned to assume his titles on 7 January 1584. He held them until, following the death of his wife in 1588, he entered the Capuchin order.[103]

Meanwhile, during the final years of his secular existence, Jean de Mol sold the Vesalian property to the city of Brussels, on 3 April 1587, which in turn presented it to the Count of Mansfeld, leader of the Spanish forces in Brussels and governor of the Duchy of Luxemburg, in gratitude for services rendered the city.[104] This was further confirmed by Jean de Mol, on 2 August 1588, acting in the name of his mother-in-law, now Anna van der Meeren, and her second husband, and the five children of Anne and Jean de Mol.[105] Finally, on the death of the Count of Mansfeld, the *Huys van Vesalius* passed to his widow and in 1616 was purchased from her by the friars minor of the Order of Saint François de Paul,[106] and any identification of the property with its original owner was lost.

Although Andreas Vesalius had been born in Brussels and maintained a home there, yet he spent little of his active life in that city. His life, unlike that of his immediate family and his successors, complacent members of the local bourgeoisie, was lived in the midst of the international scene, his acclaim was international, and it is fitting that he be remembered for a book representing studies in Belgium, France, and Italy, written in Latin, the universal language, published in Switzerland, and dedicated to a monarch of German and Spanish blood. A like international recognition of Vesalius's achievement has become ever wider with the passing centuries.

APPENDIX: TRANSLATIONS

CONTENTS OF APPENDIX

TRANSLATIONS FROM THE *Fabrica* (*1543*)

1. Preface to Charles V
2. Letter to Oporinus

VESALIAN DISSECTION PROCEDURE

3. How the bones and cartilages of the human body may be prepared for inspection
4. Instruments which may be prepared for the conduct of dissections
5. Dissection of the muscles moving the arm
6. The best method for conducting the anatomy, as well as for undertaking privately everything that has been presented in this [fifth] book
7. How to dissect the heart, lungs, and the rest of the organs serving respiration
8. Dissection procedure for the brain

TRANSLATIONS OF VESALIUS'S MEDICAL OPINIONS

9. Consilium for Wolfgang Herwart
10. Consilia on epilepsy and on tinnitus of the ears
11. Consilium for Balthasar von Stubenberg
12. Consilia for Louis de Praet
13. Consilium for Marcus Pfister
14. Consilium regarding Augustine Teyling
15. Letter to A. P. Gasser
16. Report on the death of Henry II
17. Medical dispensation for the Bishop of Limoges
18. Letter to Ingrassia

TRANSLATIONS OF VESALIUS'S NONMEDICAL CORRESPONDENCE

19. Letter to Jean Sturm
20. Letter to Heinrich Petri

TRANSLATIONS OF LETTERS TO OR CONCERNING VESALIUS

21. Letter of Georg Agricola to Wolfgang Meurer
22. Letter of Johann Herwagen to Vesalius
23. Letter of Joannes Oporinus to Conrad Hubertus
24. Letter of Achilles Gasser to Vesalius
25. True account of the head injury of the most serene prince Don Carlos
26. Letter of Gian Filippo Ingrassia to Vesalius

TRANSLATIONS FROM THE *Fabrica* (1 5 4 3)

In the translations from the *Fabrica* the foliation or pagination has been inserted within brackets, and where subheadings of chapters occur as marginalia these have been placed separately within the text.

1. THE PREFACE OF ANDREAS VESALIUS TO HIS BOOKS *De humani corporis fabrica* ADDRESSED TO THE DIVINE CHARLES, GREAT AND INVINCIBLE EMPEROR.[1]

Various things, most gracious Emperor Charles, very seriously hinder those investigating the scientific arts so that they are not accurately or fully learned, and I believe furthermore that no little loss occurs through the too-great separation that has taken place between those disciplines that complement one another for the fullest comprehension of a single art; even much more the very capricious division by practitioners of an art into separate specialties so that those who set the limits of the art for themselves tenaciously grasp one part of it while other things which are in fact very closely related are cast aside. Consequently they never demonstrate excellence and never attain their proposed end but constantly fall away from the true foundation of that art.

Passing over the other arts in silence, I shall speak briefly of that which concerns the health of mankind; indeed, of all the arts the genius of man has discovered it is by far the most beneficial and of prime necessity, although difficult and laborious. Nothing was able to plague it more than when at one time, and especially after the Gothic invasions and the reign of Mansor, King of Persia— under whom the Arabs lived, as was proper, on terms of familiarity with the Greeks—medicine began to be maimed by the neglect of that primary instrument, the hand, so that [the manual aspects of medicine] were relegated to ordinary persons wholly untrained in the disciplines subserving the art of medicine. Once there were three medical sects, that is, Dogmatic, Empirical, and Methodical, but their members consulted the whole art as the means of preserving health and driving away sicknesses. All the thoughts of each sect were directed toward this goal and three methods were employed: The first was a regimen of diet, the second the use of drugs, and the third the use of the hands. Except for this last, the other methods clearly indicate that medicine is the addition of things lacking and the withdrawal of superfluities; as often as we resort to medicine it displays its usefulness in the treatment of sickness, as time and experience teach, and its great benefit to mankind. This triple method of treatment was equally familiar to the physicians of each sect, and those using their own hands according to the nature of the sickness used no less effort in training them than in establishing a theory of diet or in understanding and compounding drugs.

In addition to the other books so perfectly composed by the divine Hippocrates, this is very clearly demonstrated in those *On the function of the physician, On fractures of bones,* and *On dislocations of joints and similar ailments.* Furthermore, Galen, after Hippocrates the prince of medicine, in addition to his occasional boast that the care of the gladiators of Pergamum was entrusted solely to

317

him, and that although age was already weighing him down it did not please him that the monkeys he was to dissect should be skinned by slaves, frequently assures us of his pleasure in the employment of his hands, and how zealously, like other Asiatic physicians, he used them. Indeed, none of the other ancients was so concerned that the treatment made with the hands, as well as that performed by diet and drugs, be handed down to posterity.

Especially after the devastation of the Goths when all the sciences, formerly so flourishing and fittingly practised, had decayed, the more fashionable physicians, first in Italy in imitation of the old Romans, despising the use of the hands, began to relegate to their slaves those things which had to be done manually for their patients and to stand over them like architects. Then when, by degrees, others who practised true medicine also declined those unpleasant duties—not, however, reducing their fees or dignity—they promptly degenerated from the earlier physicians, leaving the method of cooking and all the preparation of the patients' diet to nurses, the composition of drugs to apothecaries, and the use of the hands to barbers. And so in the course of time the art of treatment has been so miserably distorted that certain doctors assuming the name of physicians have arrogated to themselves the prescription of drugs and diet for obscure diseases, and have relegated the rest of medicine to those whom they call surgeons [fol. *2v] but consider scarcely as slaves. They have shamefully rid themselves of what is the chief and most venerable branch of medicine, that which based itself principally upon the investigation of nature—as if there were any other; even today [this branch of medicine] is exercised among the Indians, especially by the kings, and in Persia by law of inheritance it is handed down to the children as once the whole art was by the Asclepiads. The Thracians, with many other nations, cultivate and honor it very highly almost to the neglect of that other part of the art, the prescription of drugs. This the Romans once proscribed from the state considering it delusive and destructive of mankind, and of no benefit to nature since, although seeking to aid nature while it is wholly concerned in an attempt the throw off the sickness, drugs frequently make matters worse and distract nature from its proper function.

Hence it is that so many jibes are frequently cast at physicians and this very holy art is mocked, although part of it, which those trained in the liberal arts shamefully permit to be torn away from them, could readily adorn it forever with special lustre. When Homer, that source of genius, declared that a physician is more distinguished than a host of other men, and, with all the poets of Greece, celebrated Podalirius and Machaon, those divine sons of Aesculapius were praised not so much because they dispelled a little fever or something else of slight consequences, which nature alone could cure more readily without the aid of a physician than with it, nor because they yielded to the summons of men in obscure and desperate affections, but because they devoted themselves especially to the treatment of luxations, fractures, wounds, and other solutions of continuity and fluxions of blood, and because they freed Agamemnon's noble warriors of javelins, darts, and other evils of that sort which are the peculiar accompaniment of wars, and which always require the careful attention of the physician.

However, most august Emperor Charles, I certainly do not propose to give preference to one instrument of medicine over the others, since the aforesaid triple method of treatment can in no way be disunited and the whole of it belongs to the one practitioner; and that he may employ it properly all parts of medicine have been equally established so that the successful use of a single part depends upon the degree to which they are all combined, for how rare is the sickness that does not immediately require the three instruments of treatment. Hence a proper scheme of diet must be determined, and something must be done with drugs, and finally with the hands, so that the tyros of this art ought—if it please the gods—to be urged in every way, like the Greeks, to scorn the whisperings of those physicians and, as nature teaches, to employ their hands in treatment, lest they convert the mangled rationale of treatment into a calamity for the life of mankind. They ought to be urged the more strongly to this since we see learned physicians abstain from the use of the hands as from a plague lest the rabbins of medicine decry them before the ignorant mass as barbers and they acquire less wealth and honor than those [who are] scarcely half-physicians, and stand in less estimation before the uncomprehending mass of the people. Indeed, it is especially this detestable, vulgar opinion that prevents us, even in our age, from taking up the art of treatment as a whole, limiting us to the treatment of only internal diseases, to the great harm of mankind, and—if I may speak frankly—we strive to be physicians only in part.

When first the whole composition of drugs was relegated to the apothecaries, then the physicians promptly lost the necessary knowledge of simple medicines, and they were responsible for the apothecaries' shops becoming filled with barbarous names, and even false remedies, and for so many admirable compositions of the ancients being lost to us, several of which are still missing. Furthermore, they prepared an unending labor for learned men not only of our age but also for those who preceded it by some years, who have devoted themselves untiringly to the study of simple medicines and are seen to have contributed much through their effort to restore that knowledge to its former brilliance; Gerard van Veltwyck, secretary to your Majesty and rare example of this age, is representative of the many celebrated men engaged in this matter. Endowed with wide erudition in many disciplines and tongues he is the most skilled of our people in the knowledge of plants.

Furthermore, this very perverse distribution of the instruments of treatment among a variety of practitioners caused a very baleful disaster and a far more cruel blow to that chief branch of natural philosophy which, since it includes the description of man, ought rightfully to be considered the very beginning and solid foundation of the whole art of medicine. Hippocrates and Plato attributed so much to it that they did not hesitate to award it first place among the parts of medicine, and although at first it was especially cultivated by physicians, who strained every nerve to acquire it, finally it began miserably to collapse when they, resigning manual operations to others, destroyed anatomy. For when the physicians assumed that only the treatment of internal complaints concerned them, believing furthermore that knowledge of only the viscera was sufficient, they neglected the structure of the bones, muscles, nerves, and of the veins and arteries which creep through those bones and muscles, as of no concern to them. In addition, when the use of the hands was wholly entrusted to the barbers, not only was true knowledge of the viscera lost to the physicians, but also the practice of dissection [fol. *3r] soon died away, because they did not undertake it, and those to whom the manual skills had been entrusted were so unlearned that they did not understand the writings of the professors of dissection.

Thus it was impossible that so very difficult and abstruse an art, acquired mechanically by this latter type of men, could be preserved for us, for the deplorable division of the art of treatment introduced into the schools that detestable procedure by which usually some conduct the dissection of the human body and others present the account of its parts, the latter like jackdaws aloft in their high chair, with egregious arrogance croaking things they have never investigated but merely committed to memory from the books of others, or reading what has already been described. The former are so ignorant of languages that they are unable to explain their dissections to the spectators and muddle what ought to be displayed according to the instructions of the physician who, since he has never applied his hand to the dissection of the body, haughtily governs the ship from a manual. Thus everything is wrongly taught in the schools, and days are wasted in ridiculous questions so that in such confusion less is presented to the spectators than a butcher in his stall could teach a physician. I omit mention of several schools where scarcely ever is even consideration given to the presentation of human anatomy, so far has ancient medicine declined from its former glory.

In the great felicity of this age—which the gods desire to be controlled by your sagacious Majesty—with all studies greatly revitalized, anatomy has begun to raise its head from profound gloom, so that it may be said without contradiction that it seems almost to have recovered its ancient brilliance in some universities; and with nothing more urgently desired than that knowledge of the parts of the human body be recovered, I, aroused by the example of so many distinguished men, decided to give what assistance I could and by those means at my command. And lest all others should successfully accomplish something for the sake of our common studies while I alone remain idle, and lest I achieve less than my ancestors, I decided that this branch of natural philosophy ought to be recalled from the region of the dead. If it does not attain a fuller development among us than ever before or elsewhere among the early professors of dissection, at least it may reach such a point that one can assert without shame that the presence science of anatomy is comparable to that of the ancients and that in our age nothing has been so degraded and then wholly restored as anatomy.

My intention could by no means have been fulfilled if, when I was studying medicine in Paris, I had not put my own hand to the matter but had accepted without question the several casual and superficial demonstrations of a few organs presented to me and to my fellow students in one or two public dissections by unskilled barbers. So perfunctory was the presentation of anatomy there where we first saw medicine reborn that I, experienced by several dissections of brutes under the direction of the never-to-be-sufficiently-praised Jacobus Sylvius, at the third dissection at which I was ever present and at the urging of my fellow students and the teachers, conducted it publicly and more completely than was usually the case. When I conducted it a second time—the barbers having been waved aside—I attempted to display the muscles of the arms as well as to make a more-accurate dissection of the viscera, for, except for eight abdominal muscles shamefully mangled and in the wrong order, no other muscle or any bone, and much less an accurate series of nerves, veins, or arteries was ever demonstrated to me by anyone. Later at Louvain, whither I had to return because of the outbreak of war, and where for eighteen years the physicians had not even dreamed of anatomy, in order to assist the students of that university and to acquire greater skill in a subject still obscure but of the first importance for medicine, I dissected with somewhat greater accuracy than at Paris and lectured on the entire structure of the human body. As a result, the younger professors of that university now seem to be seriously engaged in gaining a knowledge of the parts of man, fully appreciating what valuable philosophical material is to be acquired from this knowledge. At Padua, in that most famous university of the whole world, in order not to dissociate myself from the rest of medicine and induced by the salary offered by the very illustrious Venetian Senate, by far the most liberal to professional studies, I gave the lectures on surgical medicine, and because anatomy is related to this, I devoted myself to the investigation of man's structure. Thus I have already conducted anatomy very often here and in Bologna, and, discarding the ridiculous fashion of the schools, I demonstrated and taught in such a way that there was nothing in my procedure that varied from the tradition of the ancients, and the construction of no part met with remained unstudied.

However, the slothfulness of physicians has prevented the preservation for us of the writings of Eudemus, Herophilus, Marinus, Andreas, Lycus, and other distinguished anatomists, since not even a fragment of any page remains of those illustrious authors, more than twenty in number, whom Galen mentions in his second commentary on Hippocrates's book *The nature of man,* and indeed of Galen's anatomical books scarcely a half have been saved from destruction. But if any of those who followed him, among whom I mention Oribasius, Theophilus, and the Arabs, and if our own writers whom I have thus far read—and I ask their pardon—[fol. *3v] handed on anything worthy of being read, they borrowed it from Galen; and, by Jove, to one earnestly concerned with dissection there is nothing in which they seem to have had less interest than in the dissection of the human body. They are so firmly dependent upon I-know-not-what-quality in the writing of their leader that, coupled with the failure of others to dissect, they have shamefully reduced Galen into brief compendia and never depart from him—if ever they understood his meaning—by the breadth of a nail. Indeed, in the prefaces of their books they announce that their writings are wholly pieced together from Galen's conclusions and that all that is theirs is his, adding that if anyone by chance were to criticize their writings they would consider that Galen also had been criticized. So completely have all yielded to him that there is no physician who would declare that even the slightest error had ever been found, much less can now be found, in Galen's anatomical books, although—except that Galen often corrects himself, frequently alluding to his negligence in earlier books and often teaching the opposite in later ones after he became more experienced—it is now clear to me from the reborn art of dissection, from diligent reading of Galen's books and their restoration in several places—for which we need feel no shame—that he never dissected a human body; but deceived by his monkeys—although he did have access to two dried human cadavers—he frequently and improperly opposed the ancient physicians trained in human dissection. Nay, more, how many incorrect observations you will find in Galen, even regarding his monkeys, not to mention that it is very astonishing that Galen noticed none of the many and infinite differences between the organs of the human body and of the monkey except in the fingers and the bend of the knee, which undoubtedly he would have overlooked with the others except that they were obvious to him without human dissection.

However, at present I do not intend to criticize the false teachings of Galen, easily prince of professors of dissection; much less do I wish to be considered as disloyal from the start to the author of all good things and as paying no heed to his authority. For I recollect how the physicians—far otherwise than the followers of Aristotle—are usually upset when in the conduct of a single anatomy nowadays they see Galen's description to have been incorrect in well over two hundred instances relating to the human structure and its use and function, and how examining the dissected parts they seek fiercely and with the greatest zeal to defend him. Nevertheless, even they, influenced by love of truth, have little by little subsided and put more faith in their not-ineffectual eyes and reason than in Galen's writings. They eagerly dispatched these paradoxes, gained not from other authors nor supported merely by masses of authorities, hither and yon to their friends, exhorting them in such earnest and friendly fashion to their own investigation and thereby to knowledge of true anatomy, that there is hope that it will soon be cultivated in all our schools as it once was conducted in Alexandria in the age of Herophilus, Andreas, Marinus, and other outstanding and distinguished anatomists.

That this may occur under the happy auspices of the muses, in addition to those things I have published elsewhere on this matter—and which certain plagiarists, believing me in distant Germany, published as their own—to the best of my ability I have organized my fullest knowledge of the parts of the human body in these seven books, just as I should normally discuss it before a group of learned men in this city or in Bologna. Thus those who were present at those dissections will have a record of the demonstrations and they can expound anatomy to others with less difficulty. Also these things will not be without use for those who are denied any opportunity for inspection of the parts, since the books present in sufficient detail the number, site, shape, size, substance, connection to other parts, use and function of each part of the human body, and many other related matters I have been accustomed to explain during dissection regarding the nature of the parts and the technique for dissection of the dead and living. Furthermore, the books contain illustrations of all the parts, inserted in the text of the discourse in such a way that they place the dissected body before the eyes of the students of nature's works.

In the first book I have discussed the nature of all the bones and cartilages which, because the rest of the parts are supported and made firm by them and are described relative to them, must first be made known to the students of anatomy. The second book treats of the ligaments by which the bones and cartilages are connected to one another, and then the muscles, performers of motion dependent upon our will. The third comprises the very numerous arrangements of veins which carry blood provided for the nourishment of the muscles, bones, and other parts, and then of the arteries controlling the mixture of innate heat and vital spirit. The fourth explains not only the distribution of the nerves that go to the muscles, but also of the others and the branches of all. The fifth presents the construction of the organs serving nutrition, that is, food and drink; and, because of their proximity, the book also describes the organs constructed by the Creator for the propagation of the species. The sixth is given over to the heart, source of the vital faculty, and to the parts serving it. The seventh considers the relationship of the brain and the organs of sensation, but so that the series of nerves taking origin from the brain and described in the fourth book is not repeated. In arranging the order of these books [fol. *4r] I have followed the opinion of Galen who believed that, after the description of the muscles, the anatomy of the veins, arteries, nerves, and then of the viscera ought to be considered. Nevertheless it may be contended with some justice, and especially for the tyro of this science, that knowledge of the viscera ought to be considered along with the distribution of the vessels, as I have done in the *Epitome* which I prepared as a pathway through these books and as an index of matters presented in them. The *Epitome* is honored by the splendor and fortified by the authority of the serene prince Philip, son of your Majesty and a living example of the paternal virtues, from whom are fully expected whatever things can be desired in the best ruler of the whole world.

Now I must recall the judgment of certain men who strongly condemn the presentation of anatomy to students, not merely by words but also, no matter how exquisitely executed, by pictorial delineation of the parts of the human body, maintaining that it is necessary for these things to be learned by careful dissection and observation of the parts themselves, as if I had inserted illustrations—very correct ones, and would that the illustrations of the parts were never spoiled by the printers—in the text so that the student relying on them might refrain from dissection of cadavers; whereas, on the contrary, I, with Galen, have encouraged the candidates of medicine in every way to undertake dissection with their own hands. If the practice of the ancients had lasted down to our times, the practice by which they trained the boys at home in the conduct of dissection just as in writing and reading, I, like the ancients, would readily agree to discard not only illustrations but also all commentaries. However, when for the sake of renown they decided to write about the practice of dissection, they communicated the art not only to the boys but also to foreigners out of respect for their virtues; but as soon as the boys were no longer given the usual training in dissection, as it was no longer accustomed to begin in boyhood, naturally they learned anatomy less well, so much so that the art deserted the family of the Asclepiads, and, by reason of its decline through many centuries, books became necessary to preserve a complete account of it.

Nevertheless, how greatly pictures assist the understanding of these matters and place them more exactly before the eyes than even the most precise language, no student of geometry and other mathematical disciplines can fail to understand. Furthermore, the illustrations of the human parts will greatly delight those for whom there is not always a supply of human bodies for dissection; or, if there is, those who have such a fastidious nature, little worthy of a physician, that, even if they are enthusiastic about that most pleasant knowledge of man attesting the wisdom of the Great Creator—if anything does—yet they cannot bring themselves even occasionally to be present at dissection. Whatever the case may be, I have done my best to this single end, to aid as many as possible in a very recondite as well as laborious matter, and truly and completely to describe the structure of the human body which is formed not of ten or twelve parts—as it may seem to the spectator—but of some thousands of different parts, and, among other monuments to that divine man Galen, to bring to posterity an understanding of those books of his requiring the help of a teacher. I bear to the candidates of medicine fruit not to be scorned.

I am aware that by reason of my age—I am at present twenty-eight years old— my efforts will have little authority, and that, because of my frequent indication of the falsity of Galen's teachings, they will find little shelter from the attacks of those who were not present at my anatomical demonstrations or have not themselves studied the subject sedulously; various schemes in defense of Galen will be boldly invented unless these books appear with the auspicious commendation and great patronage of some divine power. Because they cannot be more safely sheltered or more splendidly adorned than by the imperishable name of the great and invincible emperor, the divine Charles, I beseech your imperial Majesty with all reverence again and again, to permit this youthful work of mine to come into the hands of men—to whom for many reasons it is obnoxious—for a short time, under your splendid patronage, until through the experience, judgment, and erudition that come with age I may render it more worthy of so great a prince or I may offer another acceptable gift on some other subject taken from our art.

It is my opinion that out of the whole Apolline discipline, and so the whole of natural philosophy, nothing could be produced more pleasing or acceptable to your Majesty than an account from which we may learn about the body and mind and, furthermore, about a certain divine power arising from a harmony of both—indeed, about ourselves, that which in truth is the study of man. I came to this conclusion for many reasons, but I first conjectured it because among the large number of books dedicated to your grandfather of happy memory, the great Emperor of the Romans Maximilian, none was ever more pleasing than a little book on the present subject. Nor shall I ever forget with what pleasure you examined my *Tabulae anatomicae*, once presented for your inspection by my father Andreas, chief and most faithful apothecary of your Majesty, and how carefully you inquired about each thing. I shall not mention your incredible love for all disciplines but chiefly for mathematics, and especially for that part of it that deals with the science of the universe and the stars and of the remarkable comprehension of it by so great and heroic a man. So great, that by no means can it be [fol. *4v] that you are interested solely in the science of the universe, but also perhaps you sometimes delight in consideration of the most perfectly constructed of all creatures, and take delight in considering the temporary lodging and instrument of the immortal soul, a dwelling that in many respects corresponds admirably to the universe and for that reason was called the little universe by the ancients.

Nevertheless I decided that your notable knowledge of the structure of man's body ought not be extolled here, that knowledge in itself by far the most commendable of things to which even in Rome men of the greatest attainments and especially those of philosophical learning applied themselves, since, keeping in mind that desire of Alexander the Great to be painted by none except Apelles, cast in bronze only by Lysippus, and sculpt only by Pyrgateles, I considered that it would not be fitting for me to recount your glories lest by a base and unskilled discourse I cover them with shadow instead of light. Furthermore, too great formalism of prefaces ought to be condemned, such as that in which, like some stereotyped formula and for the sake of some cheap reward, learning, singular prudence, astonishing clemency, keen judgment, unending liberality, wonderful love for men of letters and for learning, the greatest celerity in the management of affairs, and the whole chorus of virtues are customarily ascribed without discrimination and almost beyond merit. Nonetheless, your Majesty surpasses all mortals in these virtues as well as in dignity, felicity, and success in your affairs. Such is clear to everyone, even though not mentioned here by me, and even while living you are venerated like some high divinity. I pray that the gods may not grudge this to the learned and to the whole world, but long preserve you unharmed for mankind and maintain and guard you in continued felicity.

Padua, 1 August 1542

2. TO MY VERY DEAR FRIEND JOANNES OPORINUS, PROFESSOR OF GREEK AT BASEL.[2]

Greetings. Through the agency of the Milanese merchants, the Danoni, you will shortly receive, with this letter, the wood blocks for my books *De humani corporis fabrica* and their *Epitome*. I trust that they will reach Basel intact and undamaged since, lest they be disfigured or suffer any damage during transit, I carefully packed them with the help of the engraver and Nicolaus Stopius, the reliable manager of the firm of Bomberg, a youth well versed in the humanities. Separately with each wood block I placed its proof as well as the text for each illustration, and on each I have written where it is to be placed so that the arrangement may present no difficulty for you and your workmen and hence prevent the illustrations being published in the wrong order.

You will readily observe from the proofs where the type characters must be varied, since I have ruled off that part of the main text presented as a continuous account, chapter by chapter, from that explaining the characters engraved on the blocks. For this reason the latter is called the Index of the illustrations and their characters.

In the main text, nowhere interrupted by references to figures, employ the small type that printers call superlinear, which refers to those references I have put in the inner margin—not so much through industry as through tedious labor—in order that they may serve as indication for the reader as to which illustration displays the part under discussion; on the other hand, the annotation in the outer margin to some extent provides a summary of the discussion. To avoid prolixity, when an annotated illustration has been prefixed to a chapter I have observed the practice of providing no chapter number in the inner margin, although I have included it if the figure is to be found in another chapter. Furthermore, if the figure is found in the book in which the reference occurs, I have not added the number of the book to the reference.

In the titles of the books and in the indices of the characters you will find a clear explanation of why I decided that the illustrations ought to be located in this or that place. I have had signs carved on the blocks with which to designate the parts in every illustration, characters of the sort usually employed in printing shops. First upper-case Latin letters were used and then lower-case; thereafter, lower-case Greek and then some upper-case which are not identical with the Latin; since all these did not suffice, I also used numerals even though other indicative signs are to be found in ordinary types. In reference to these indices, observe that a character indicating and having one single explanation is placed in the margin of the book. But if it does not have a special explanation and may be explained as well by another character, add a period to it in the margin so that the distinction will be clear to the reader. Elsewhere I wrote to you at length of this procedure and why in particular I believe that the index of characters ought not be associated with the description of the parts.

Now I urge and exhort you very earnestly to print everything as handsomely and swiftly as possible so that in my books you will satisfy the expectations all have of your printing shop, now for the first time under the happy auspices of the muses, completely devoted to the greater benefit of students. Special care ought to be taken on the impression of the blocks which are not to be printed like ordinary woodcuts in common textbooks; nowhere ought the significance of the illustrations be neglected unless perhaps where the delineation is [verbally] complemented. Although here your judgment is such that I rely wholly upon your careful workmanship, I desire above all that in the printing you copy as closely as possible the proof struck off by the engraver as a specimen, which you will find enclosed in its place together with the wood block, for thus no character, even one concealed in the shading, will lie hidden from the careful and observant reader. Likewise, take care that the thickness of the lines producing gradation in the shadows, which I find artistically pleasing, is nicely reproduced. In the final analysis everything depends on the smoothness and solidity of the paper and especially on the carefulness of your supervision, so that each illustration that issues from your printing shop may be of the same quality as the proofs I am now sending you.

I hope to visit you soon and to remain in Basel, if not for the whole period of printing, at least for some time. I shall bring with me a copy of the decree of the Venetian Senate warning everyone not [fol. *5v] to print the illustrations without my consent. Inasmuch as you generally have an imperial license in all the books you publish for the first time, my mother will send you one from Brussels. It was obtained for me some time ago, but thus far I have not attempted to acquire a more recent one valid for additional years. The Bishop of Montpellier, ambassador to Venice, has undertaken to obtain a license from the French king. I have no concern on this score so long as I am not compelled to fill a page with copies of official decrees, for what effect the decrees of princes have upon booksellers and printers, who have now become ubiquitous, can be learned from the fate of my *Tabulae anatomicae,* originally published over three years ago in Venice and thereafter reprinted everywhere, wretchedly distorted despite grandiose titles.

In an edition published in Augsburg, my letter to Narcissus Vertunus, primary physician to the emperor and to the King of Naples and one of the outstanding physicians of our time, was replaced by a preface by some German babbler who wrongly denigrated Avicenna and the other Arabic authorities and included me among the concise Galenists. Furthermore, in order to deceive the buyer he falsely declared that I had compressed into the six *Tabulae* what Galen had written at length in more than thirty books. Then he declared that he had included the Greek and Arabic words in his translation of the Latin text into German, although in fact not only did he delete them but he left out everything he was unable to translate and whatever had originally given value to the *Tabulae.* In addition, he produced wretched imitations of those woodcuts prepared in Venice.

The engraver of Cologne who put his hand to those same *Tabulae* was far more inept and unskilled than the one at Augsburg even though someone in Cologne praised the printer, declaring that it was possible to grasp the structure of man better from my *Tabulae* than from actual dissection of the human body and that the printer had made my elegant illustrations even more pleasing. The fact is that he spoiled the illustrations and added a delineation of the nerves poorly copied from a rough sketch I had drawn, and to which an index was added at the request of several friends during the course of the work.

At Paris the first three *tabulae* were produced expertly, although the others were omitted, I suspect because of difficulties of engraving; yet if consideration had been given to the students it would have been better to omit the first three.

That one at Strasburg whom Fuchs has denounced so strongly because of his plagiarisms, and whom for my part I can call a plagiarist, ought to be cursed by the students since he has abominably reduced the size of the *Tabulae,* which could never be large enough for them, shamefully colored and irrelevantly surrounded them with the Augsburg text, and published them as his own. Now another one seems envious of this dubious distinction and without any discrimination has stolen illustrations from the books of others and is still publishing works of this sort in Marburg and Frankfurt.

I gladly tolerate, indeed greatly admire, the divine and very-felicitous talents of the Italians, in contrast to my judgment of the German physicians, because the latter seek the services of unscrupulous printers who, for the sake of any sordid profit that can be squeezed out, dare to issue whatever works the physicians abridge, alter or simply copy and publish them under their own names as if new, while the decrees of princes remain silent.

I write these things that you may understand how little I believe that you would do that sort of printing, but nevertheless I feel compelled to state that I shall gladly send the wood blocks to any careful printer and give whatever literary help I can. Likewise, I shall attempt in every way in my power to hinder any inept person from reproducing the illustrations which were made with so much labor for the general use of students, so that regardless of whatever inflated title may be prefixed to them they will not come into human hands as if they had been published carelessly by me. This is the particular reason why I prepared the wood

Appendix

blocks at my own expense, and now once again may I urge that they be employed by you as correctly and elegantly as possible.

Farewell.

Your Andreas Vesalius

Venice, 24 August

3. BOOK I. HOW THE BONES AND CARTILAGES OF THE HUMAN BODY MAY BE PREPARED FOR INSPECTION.

CHAPTER XXXIX [3]

The method of macerating in lime and the cleaning
of the bones in running water.

Those physicians who were not born to prescribe syrups and impose upon mankind, but who are worthy devotees of the Hippocratic art, have been accustomed, although with no little effort, to collect bones for instruction, sometimes joined together, sometimes separated. Usually they have freed the cadaver, whether one dead from hanging or from some other cause, from most of its flesh and cut out the viscera without destruction of any of the joints. Then the body so dissected was placed in a long box filled up with lime and sprinkled with water. After the box had been kept in this way for a week, many small holes were drilled into it, and it was placed in a rapidly flowing stream of water so that in the course of time the lime with the macerated remains of the flesh might flow away and so be removed from the bones. Several days later, after the cadaver had been removed, it was cleaned all over with knives, but carefully so that none of the connections of the bones was destroyed, that the ligaments by which the bones are connected were preserved, and finally that everything except the joints of the bones glistened. The cleansed cadaver was then exposed to the sun so that the ligaments, dried by the heat of the sun, might hold the joints of the bones in that position in which it was desired that it be seen, posed sitting or standing.

This method of preparation, in addition to being troublesome, dirty, and difficult, displays almost none of the bony processes, epiphyses, heads, sinuses, and other things of that sort that ought especially to be seen, because all of them are covered by very dark ligaments. Hence this method of cleaning the bones is wholly unsuited to instruction, just as similarly the ridiculous method of observing the muscles, tendons, ligaments, nerves, veins, and arteries—which the professors of our art have hitherto imposed upon the students of medicine—has no value but merely blunts the minds of the students so that they will not seek from those Rabbins a demonstration of the organs I have now mentioned. These last assert that those things must be learned from bodies wasted away in streams of water—if it please the Gods—but not from the recently dead. However, nothing of value can be learned from bodies prepared, or rather corrupted, in this way, and all these things can be demonstrated to us much better in a recently dead body than by their usual and superficial method of demonstrating the liver, intestines, or heart to the students, in fact demonstrating these very ineptly and not dealing with the other parts of the body.

Appendix

The method of preparing the bones by boiling. Although
frequently elsewhere, especially in Bk. 3 [of Galen's]
Anatomical procedures.

Elsewhere I shall consider how the other parts of the body must be dealt with; but now I shall consider the bones, and if you have a genuine interest, which was Galen's prime requirement for the student of dissection, and are very industrious, you will learn to handle the bones readily. When a cadaver has been acquired from some source, and whatever sort it may be—although one emaciated from disease is the most suitable—have a vessel ready for the flesh, viscera, and blood and place over a fire a large cauldron such as women use for the preparation of lye. This is very well suited for boiling the bones which will be thrown into it. In addition, stretch out a wide piece of paper on a board so that the cartilages, which are not to be boiled, can be arranged in order on it.

[156] With a sharp knife make a circular incision through the frontal, temporal, and occipital regions, penetrating as far as the skull. Saw through the skull at this circular incision without concern as to whether or not you damage the brain or separate the skull a little lower or higher than you had planned, since now the intention is merely to preserve the bones and cartilages.

Divide it as in the seventh figure, Ch. VI, as if seen
freed from the sixth figure. Since you are now concerned
with the bones and cartilages, there is nothing else in
that chapter to interest you.

When the skull has been divided, pull the brain out with your hands and throw it into the vessel, and that part of the skull now removed from the rest of the head must first be freed of the skin of its vertex and then placed in the cauldron. Now cut off each ear very close to the temporal bone and place them separately on that board on which the cartilages are arranged along with the eyelids and tip of the nose, which is formed of cartilage; these things must be cut very close to the skin from those bones to which they are joined. Next free the lower jaw from its connection with the bones of the head, and with a small knife dissect from the ligaments holding the joint those cartilages which previously we said exist in the jaw's articulation with the head, arranging them in order on that paper to which they will readily adhere.

Then separate the lower jaw, incidentally freeing it from both the skin and the tongue—if you desire, from the rest of the attachments of the muscles—and when finally you throw it into the cauldron, be careful not to injure the hyoid bone and the larynx, but lift away from the fauces the intact larynx with that bone, the tongue, and a portion of the oesophagus and trachea, and place it not otherwise cleaned on the board with the ears.

Now attempt an incision from the tip of the pectoral bone [sternum] as far as the pubes, penetrating as far as the omentum, and add to this another incision extending traversely from the right ilium to the left, and like a butcher drawing forth without discrimination everything contained by the peritoneum, throw it into the vessel. Dissect the skin of the abdomen and its muscles from the bones, and, soaking up the blood with sponges, squeeze it out into the vessel. Now make an incision from the root of the neck to the tip of the sternum, penetrating as far as the sternum so that you can lift away the thoracic muscles as well as the skin from the ribs and their cartilages, and so that at the same time the clavicles may appear denuded of flesh. These must be freed from the sternum with a sharp little knife, and you must carefully separate the cartilages of these articulations

328

in the same way you dealt with the cartilages of the lower jaw and then arrange them in order on the paper.

With a thin, sharp knife carefully separate the sternum and costal cartilages from the ribs after you have cut through the cartilages into which the bone of the ribs degenerates. You will do this readily if you remember that the cartilage of the first rib is carried from the middle of the sternum more to the side than is the cartilage of the second rib. Separate from the ribs not only the cartilages attached to the sternum but also the cartilages of the false ribs which are attached to the upper cartilages through the intervention of the intercostal muscles. When the cartilages have been separated in this way, raise the sternum from the root of the neck and free it from the veins and arteries passing through it to the throat as well as from the membranes enclosing the thoracic cavity. Then free the cartilages from the diaphragm and without further cleaning place them on the paper with the sternum and proceed to the dissection of the scapulae and clavicles from the thorax.

Make a long incision in one arm from the acromion through the upper arm and forearm to the thumb, and lay bare the scapula, humerus, forearm, and hand of skin and flesh; but do not be greatly disturbed if some portion of tendons and flesh remains attached to the bones. So, too, it will be enough to make several incisions here and there in the skin remaining on the hand so that afterward the hand may be more easily boiled. Now sever the clavicle from the acromion, noting whether or not there is a third bone there in addition to the process of the scapula we call acromion and the clavicle. When you have done this and have placed the special cartilage of that joint on the paper, throw the clavicle into the cauldron and separate the scapula from the humerus and the humerus from the bones of the forearm. Place the forearm, as yet connected to the hand, into the cauldron, but before the scapula is placed in the cauldron it is well to separate from it that cartilage that somewhat increases the scapular sinus into which the head of the humerus is received, and to place it on the paper with the rest of the cartilages.

After you have carried out the same procedure for the other arm, turn your attention to the thorax and excise from it the lungs with the heart and diaphragm. Before throwing the heart into the vessel, however, separate its base traversely from the rest of its body and remove the base from the vessels that emerge there so that you may secure uninjured the orifices of the pulmonary artery and the aorta; if you so desire you may preserve them along with the cartilages attached to the paper.

When the remaining organs of the thorax have been thrown into the vessel, turn the cadaver into the prone position and as far as possible clean the flesh from the rest of the neck, back, and whole thorax, but take care not to break any of the ribs, which are fragile, nor to damage any of the processes by dissecting too closely. You must be even more careful when you proceed shortly to free the individual ribs from the thoracic vertebrae.

[157] Now return the cadaver to the supine position and proceed to separate the capitulum of the rib from its vertebral sinus with a sharp scalpel; then, having by degree separated the ligaments, free the ribs from the transverse processes of the vertebrae and, after cleaning them, place them in the cauldron.

Treat the legs in the same way you did the arms, cleaning the flesh from the whole femur, then the tibia and the foot. When you have laid bare the knee, cut out the patella from the tendons lying on its anterior aspect and throw it into the cauldron as you did with the femur when you separated it from the hip bone and the tibia. Dissect out the cartilages that increase the sinuses of the

Appendix

tibia receiving the heads of the femur and place them on the paper. Then put the tibia as well as the fibula and foot into the cauldron.

When this has been done for each leg and the bones attached to the sides of the sacrum have been somewhat cleaned, carefully excise the cartilaginous ligaments lying between the vertebral bodies and arrange them in order on the paper. When the ligaments that cover the surface of the vertebral bodies have been severed with a very sharp knife, make an incision between the highest cartilaginous ligament of the sacrum and the lowest lumbar vertebra; that is the ligament or cartilage that appeared to Galen to divide the vertebra from the sacrum. Then make an incision between the body of the lowest lumbar vertebra and the upper part of the aforesaid cartilage, and in this way lift out the entire cartilage. After you have placed it on the paper, excise the successive cartilages until you reach the second cervical vertebra. When thus you have placed the twenty-three cartilages or cartilaginous ligaments on the paper, proceed to disjoint the back into three or four parts, but carefully and gently lest you accidentally break away any of the vertebral processes. For this reason be careful not to separate the first vertebra from the head since you may place it in the cauldron attached to the head, as may also be done with the thoracic vertebrae attached to the lumbar once you have separated them from the sacrum. If you wish, however, you may place the sacrum with those bones attached to it, the ilium, coxendix, and pubic bones, in the cauldron, since the bones of the ilium are difficult to separate from the sacrum while still raw, and if you throw the pubic bones separately into the cauldron at this time, their cartilage, which should be preserved intact, may be damaged.

When you have placed the bones in the cauldron in this way, fill it completely with water so that they may settle deeply and be wholly covered, and during the whole time of boiling no bone must appear above the water, among other reasons so that it may not be discolored by smoke. Hence the cauldron must be large. No special method is required for this boiling process except that in the normal way the scum must be carefully skimmed off to keep the liquid clear and to ensure that the boiled bones not be removed dirty. In the same way all fat, which usually floats on the surface, must be skimmed off and placed in a container since it tends to obliterate the markings and attachments of sinews and tendons.

There is no standard time for the boiling since it will vary greatly acccording to age. Two or three hours may be more than ample for boiling the bones of children since, while cleaning them, you must seek to prevent the epiphyses falling off. In older persons the coalitions are hardly ever dissolved no matter how long the boiling. The purpose of the boiling is to clean the bones thoroughly as you do with a knife when eating, and, to do this more advantageously, from time to time remove the bones from the boiling water with a pair of tongs and clean them individually. If you have a studious colleague he may do this for you, but great caution must be used lest one without skill damage the ridges, processes, heads, and sinuses of the bones while scraping them, or heedlessly throw away any of the smooth cartilages encrusting them; you must especially save these when you remove the flesh, ligaments, tendons, and membranes surrounding the bones. Furthermore I should be loathe to entrust this task to any inept person or one not genuinely interested in anatomy, not only for the reason given but also because if you yourself clean the individual bones you will clearly see their sinuses and heads and especially the nature of the ligaments, the insertion of the tendons, and the origin of the muscles. This will greatly assist you in identification of the parts.

When you have drawn the bones separately from the boiling water, place the

cleaned ones on the ground or in a small basket—without any immediate concern for order. However, upon withdrawing the hand with the bones of the
forearm, be careful not to wrench the wrist from the bones of the forearm but
carefully and by degrees divide the ligaments of the joint with a knife. Then,
using care, free the wrist from the bones of the forearm, and thereafter with like
care separate the metacarpals from the wrist. Do not divide the wrist bones
from one another but disjoint them in their entirety from the forearm and from
the first bone of the thumb and the metacarpals; otherwise merely remove the
covering tendons and ligaments and avoid cleaning the internal and external
surface of the ligaments which hold the bones of the wrist together. Thus, when
the wrist has been exposed to the fire [158] and its ligaments gradually dried,
the bones will be held firmly together and the wrist bones may be connected
to the forearm and metacarpal bones without difficulty—[therefore, do it this
way] unless you are very skilled in the articulation of the bones and wish
to separate the wrist bones from one another to clean off the ligaments and
thereafter unite them with copper wire; or you may wish to keep them separat-
ate.

When in this way one wrist has been placed before the fire, place the thoroughly cleaned metacarpal and digital bones, as well as the sesamoid ossicles, on
a paper in which they should be wrapped so that they will not be confused with
the bones of the other hand and so make articulation difficult. Thus it will be
advantageous to wrap the bones of the hands and feet in four separate papers,
but be sure before you wrap the bones of a hand or foot that none has remained
uncleaned in the cauldron to be thrown out carelessly with the watery waste.
If you care to preserve one of the nails, avulse it while cleaning the digital bones
of the hand or foot, for I have observed that human nails like those of the feet
of birds and quadrupeds disappear when placed in boiling water.

When you clean the ulna and radius do not neglect that cartilage that extends from the radius and in considerable degree separates the ulna from the
wrist. Free this so that it is yet attached to the radius and will intervene between the ulna and wrist when the bones are articulated. In addition, when you
clean the head and are tearing away the membrane surrounding the auditory
foramen, be very careful not to lose the ossicles that are part of the auditory
organ, but introduce a stylus into the foramen by which they may be carefully
loosened and then shaken out. Put these ossicles aside somewhere near the rest
of the bones.

Finally, remove the vertebrae as well as the sacrum from the cauldron unless
you wish to free the coccyx from the sacrum by further boiling; because of
the cartilaginous ligaments which unite them, the ossicles, if boiled too long,
tend to separate. However, if you have removed the sacrum to cut off the
coccygeal bones, you must return it again to the cauldron, but place the coccyx
separately on the paper or in the small basket in which you place the smaller
ossicles such as the teeth—if any have accidentally fallen out—or any bits of the
bones which have been carelessly broken off.

To save the cartilage of the pubic bones, lightly clean the pubic bones on
their anterior and posterior aspects and separate them from one another with
your hands before the ilia are freed from the sacrum. In this way the intervening cartilage may be pulled away from the one and remain attached to the
other. Later, when the bones are assembled, one pubic bone may be joined to
the other without difficulty.

Now, with the exception of those bones of the hands and feet which have
been separately wrapped in paper, count up the bones that have been cleaned.

Appendix

Examine carefully the part of the skull freed from the rest of the head and see if the small parts of the temporal bones attached like scales to the vertex, and which are usually loosened by the saw from the rest of the temporals, have fallen out as a result of boiling, and be careful not to throw them out accidentally with the liquid waste material. Usually they readily fall away from the bones of the vertex if the bone is sawed much above the ears. Then see if any of the teeth have fallen out of the upper or lower jaw. Count up the twenty-four vertebrae, the similar number of ribs, two clavicles, two scapulae, two humeri, two ulnae, and two radii, the sacrum from which the coccyx has been previously removed, two large bones connected to the sides of the sacrum, two femora, two tibiae, two fibulae, and two patellae.

When you have accounted for all of them, it is advisable to put the bones once more into clean, boiling water and, as soon as they are withdrawn, to wipe each with a rough, harsh cloth so that the remnants of the ligaments and membranes, or of the insertion or origin of the muscles, may be rubbed off, but at the same time be careful not to remove the slippery cartilage attached to the bones like a crust. While these bones are being lightly dried before the fire, clean the skin from the cartilages of the ears and attach them to the paper with the rest of the cartilages. Do this also with the cartilages of the eyelids and nose, and while the hyoid bone is still raw clean it as thoroughly as possible of the muscles attached to it. When it has been cleaned, in the same way carefully free the raw cartilages of the trachea of flesh and membranes, as well as the cartilages resembling the shape of the letter C.

Then thoroughly clean the sternum and the cartilages connected to it. This is not easily done since the sternum is covered with several membranes and is fatty, yet it must not be boiled or even splashed with hot water. Indeed, when you strip the cartilages from the flesh, be careful not to remove the membrane intimately covering them and corresponding to that which the Greeks call PERIOSTEON because it goes around the bones. If this membrane has been removed from the cartilages they are less strongly united to the sternum and become contracted and distorted. To avoid shrinkage of the cartilages the sternum must not be dried before the fire but, until you are ready to fasten the bones together, must be placed in some not-too-damp place; otherwise the cartilages would become somewhat flaccid and produce a deformation of the bony thorax, [159] and there is nothing that will so destroy the elegant structure of the skeleton as careless preparation of the sternum and its cartilages which allows them to dry out before and not after the articulation of the bones. However, the rest of the cartilages attached to the paper may be moved a little closer to the fire, provided they do not shrink too much, since it is better that they dry out after articulation.

The bones which are very useful for instruction.

Now the bones are ready for mounting in that way to be described or, if you wish them unmounted, for preservation in the loose state which may also be of great value. Unmounted bones placed in order in a long box can be inspected separately at any time and will provide all necessary knowledge, for when the bones have been articulated they do not display the sinuses and heads so exactly and, to be truthful, contribute more to display than to instruction.

Bones stolen from the Italian tombs, which are almost all constructed like warehouses and so exposed to every rain, or at least to the air, so that in the course of time the bones are subjected to the rain water, are very suitable for instruction. Not only are such tombs damp, allowing the entrance of water

Appendix

which in time macerates everything attached to the bones so that they are stripped and washed, but the bones are left quite intact and no different from other disarticulated bones in a box. They are utterly useless, however, for articulation because of their extreme hardness and because of the loss of the cartilages of the ribs and of the entire body; even if the cartilages are found they are friable and because of their rottenness separate everywhere from the bones. Those bones that, in some countries, are disinterred and preserved in heaps in cemeteries are also useless for this purpose because not only are they decayed from the dryness of the earth but you will never find all the bones of any one body, as is the case in the aforementioned Italian tombs or in the Cemetery of the Innocents at Paris, even though you were to dig up as many piles of bones as those that afforded us such an abundant supply when I first studied the bones with Matthaeus Terminus, distinguished physician in all branches of medicine and lifelong friend and companion of my studies. . . .

How the cleaned bones must be articulated.

But to return to the articulation and erection of the boiled bones, lest they become too hard they must be joined together soon after they have been cleaned. Immediately after they have been boiled the bones can be readily perforated with that special awl with which the soles of shoes are sewn, and then tied together with copper wire, and each one may do this according to the skill of his efforts and the instructions we have thus far described in the whole of this book.

Instruments of this sort are displayed almost seriatim in the Illustration, Chapter VII, Book II, at the characters S, T, V, X, Y.

First make ready several awls and some thick and some thin copper wire which may be placed in the fire to render it more ductile and capable of being twisted without breaking. Add two tenaculae or pincers, one for twisting the wire and the other for cutting it after it has been twisted. Begin by wiring together the bones of the feet. Join the talus to the calcaneum, then the cubelike bone to the calcaneum, the bone resembling a skiff [navicular] to the talus, and the three inner bones of the tarsus [cuneiforms] to that resembling a skiff. Then join the metatarsals to the navicular, and to these in order the digital bones with those ossicles resembling sesame seeds which, because of their solidity and hardness, must be perforated carefully with a finer awl lest they be split.

When you have finished the articulation of each foot, with a long curved knife perforate that tuber of the tibia that separates the sinuses receiving the femoral heads for the reception of the stiff rod which must be thrust into the femur like a peg, and so the tibia is joined to the femur as beams are joined without glue. Then make another hole in the lower part of the femur in line with that made in the tibia so that the same rod can be inserted into both femur and tibia, and in this way the knee joint remains unbent. In addition to the rod, the femur should be united to the tibia on either side with the thicker wire, keeping in mind the cartilages which increase the size of the tibial sinuses. When the bones have been united, these cartilages preserved in the knee joint will strengthen that union. Then wire the fibula to the tibia above and below and also secure the patella to the femur and tibia. After this has been done for each leg, attach the iliac bones to the sides of the sacrum by the thicker wire and unite the pubic bones by their intervening cartilage.

Now prepare a circular board on which the bones are to be mounted, preferably of such circumference that the feet can be suitably supported on it in what-

333

ever pose you decide upon. Make a hole in the center so that it will receive an axle permitting the board to be turned if you should put away the articulated skeleton in an upright box. Also make a second hole near the circumference of the circular board in which can be fitted a wooden lance, spear or scythe—or whatever you like—which will support the skeleton's hand.

[160] Place the feet on this board and then with the aid of an assistant mount the remaining bones of the legs upon the feet. Place the femoral heads in the acetabula of the hipbones and with a wire or rod measure the distance from the board to the lowest point of the foramen carved in the sacrum for the spinal marrow. This will indicate the necessary length of the iron rod which, for support of the bones, must be fastened to the board and inserted into the foramina of the sacrum and vertebrae transmitting the spinal marrow.

This iron rod must be made so that it can be strongly secured in the hole in the middle of the board. Above the sacrum the rod should be somewhat flattened so that it may be bent to correspond to the curve of the back and so adapted to the vertebrae that they will be held in position. Moreover, the rod must be thicker below the sacrum so that this will not slip downward, for if it were not supported the rest of the vertebrae would gradually sink downward and the legs of the skeleton be forced into an undesirable angle; hence the need for accurate measurement of the distance from the circular board to the deepest point of the foramen of the sacrum. It is not necessary to take such care with the upper length of the iron rod, for if it should happen to be too long it can easily be cut off after the bones have been mounted. If you wish to keep the bones in a box it is helpful to make the rod about two palms' lengths longer than the skeleton so that the upper end of the rod can be inserted into a hole in the top of the box and revolved in it.

When the iron rod has been fastened upright in the circular board, with a sharp knife carve out the foramen for the dorsal marrow in the sacrum so that the rod can be easily inserted into it. Since this foramen is by nature considerably curved and oblique it will not otherwise fit on the rod and slide down to that level where it is planned that it be supported by the rod's greater circumference. If it should happen that the sacrum tends to slip below this level, roughen the rod with a file at this point and wrap it with copper wire to ensure proper support.

When the sacrum has been fixed in this way, connect the femoral heads to the acetabula of the hipbones with the thick wire, observing the proper degree of inward or outward rotation so that the legs will not be joined undesirably or the patellae face the interior rather than the exterior of the legs, which could happen unless the heads were fitted precisely to their sinuses. However it is done, do not finally fasten the wire of this connection before you have joined the feet to the circular board and to the tibiae in whatever position seems most desirable to you, and seek especially to obtain this desired pose from the wooden staff which will support the position of the arm, be it a reaper's scythe, lance, spear, Neptune's trident, or whatever is considered appropriate.

Next, arrange all the vertebrae in order so that there will be no difficulty about their proper sequence as indicated by the shape of the vertebrae and the manner of their articulation. When you have placed them in order on a table, join the five lumbar vertebrae by two connections that have been made at the sides of the bodies and that hold the cartilaginous ligaments previously said to lie between the vertebral bodies. These ligaments must be taken in order from the paper on which they were placed—disregarding for the time being those that separate the vertebrae, not yet to be wired together, as well as the ligament or cartilage intervening between the sacrum and the lowest lumbar vertebra and that which lies between the uppermost lumbar vertebra and the lowest thoracic.

When the lumbar vertebrae have been joined, connect the six lower thoracic vertebrae and then join the six upper with the lowest cervical. It is not necessary to wire the rest of the cervical vertebrae, and the intervening cartilage is merely glued to the lower surface of the vertebral body because the cervical vertebrae are not bound together but are held in position by the iron rod thrust through them; hence they are not immobilized like the thoracic vertebrae, which must support the ribs.

As soon as you have united the vertebrae in this way, but before pushing the iron rod through them, lay the connected lumbar vertebrae alongside the rod and carefully bend it to their curve; then join the lowest vertebra to the sacrum as you have already connected the lumbar vertebrae to one another. Now join the thoracic vertebrae to them, bending the rod as required, and then wire the lowest thoracic to the highest lumbar vertebra.

In the same way add the upper thoracic vertebrae to these, and when the lowest of them has been wired to the highest already on the iron rod, prepare a long, flat, black pole fastened to the rear of the iron rod or, if you desire, pushed down between the rod and the vertebrae so that the vertebrae may be more firmly supported, immobilized by the rod, and thus the thorax not be twisted to one side or the other in an unsightly manner.

Perforate the vertex of the skull by a hole corresponding exactly in size to the iron rod and, to prevent any turning of the skull, once you have decided whether the face should look forward or to the side, carve out that hole with a knife transversely or obliquely. [161] Furthermore, make a perforation at that level at which the skull was originally sawed so that the skullcap may be joined by small attachments but remain readily removable upon removal of the skull from the iron rod, for it is important to inspect the cavity of the skull which contains the brain. To do this, make three corresponding holes in each part of the skull with a hot iron or the point of a knife. It is recommended that these be made in each temple and at the occiput.

Join the lower jaw to the upper with copper wire by connecting the sinuses of the upper jaw to the heads of the lower. If this does not bring the teeth into correct apposition and the lower jaw hangs open, make a hole through the sharp processes of the lower jaw and then, by passing a cord through them, under the zygomatic arches and over the vertex, and pulling it toward the forehead or the occiput, the jaw may be opened or closed and the teeth properly apposed with greater elegance.

The greatest care must be taken to see that the iron rod is not bent too much backward or forward but supports the body properly, and this calls for correct understanding of the alignment of the back. Now wire the ribs to the vertebrae and to their cartilages, and in order that this be done accurately, first separate all the right ribs from the left; these can be distinguished by the sinus through which the vein, nerve, and artery are extended to the rib and the fact that the upper part of the ribs is thicker than the lower. Then place the ribs in this order ((())) on the table so that the right corresponds in sequence to the left, and if you recall those distinguishing features I have just mentioned, the arrangement will present no difficulty. From this arrangement of the ribs connect the first of either side by its cartilage to the sternum and then lift up the sternum with its cartilages, holding it in position with its mate, and wire the first ribs to the transverse processes of the first thoracic vertebra. Then join the second ribs to their vertebra and then to their cartilages, and so with the others, but so that they flare outward with exactly the same interval by which they were separated from those cartilages before disarticulation.

Now join the humeri to the scapulae with the thick wire and the clavicles to the acromia with the thin, and then the scapulae to the ribs and the clavicles to the pectoral bone. When you join the humeri to the scapulae, pay close heed to the position in which you place the attachment of the arms. The way in which the head of the humerus is joined to the sinus of the scapula is of great importance, for in this connection the cartilage that increases the scapular sinus must not be overlooked, as also those special cartilages that must be fastened to the mandibular and clavicular joints.

The bones of the forearm must not be joined to the humerus until the hand has been joined to them, and so the radius must be fastened to the ulna above and below. If the wrist bones have been separated and freed from their ligaments they must be reunited although otherwise they are adequately held together by their ligaments. Connect the first bone of the thumb and the four metacarpals to the lower part of the wrist and then the finger bones and sesamoid ossicles. Finally, join the wrist to the radius and then the ulna to the humerus. When this has been done for each arm, fasten the hands to that staff I said was to be made in the form of a scythe or something else, firmly implanted in the circular base.

After the bones have been articulated you may make a necklace from the hyoid bone, the auditory ossicles and the cartilages of the trachea, ears, eyelids, nails, and heart, attached to a chain or to a dried nerve from the leg or arm. . . .

4. BOOK II. INSTRUMENTS WHICH MAY BE PREPARED FOR THE CONDUCT OF DISSECTIONS.

CHAPTER VII [4]

I have frequently mentioned the razor and hook, and since there will be further mention of these and similar instruments of dissection, it will not be amiss to describe those which you may employ in the conduct of dissections, even though they could have been considered at the end of the first book. The instruments are few and easily prepared, although I shall describe more elaborate and numerous ones than I myself now use in public dissection.

Razors.

First collect many knives such as those barbers use for shaving beards and which we usually call razors. It is desirable that some of these be sharp, others more dull, but always have a larger supply than you need. Although it is desirable to have several of the larger ones, purchase many of the smaller and lighter ones from the barbers. Since they are made of very fragile steel they readily snap, especially if you use new ones not yet worn down by sharpening; hence they are easily broken on the scattered membranes, tendons, and ligaments. It will be well to remove, and especially from the smaller ones, that iron knob which prevents the razor from being extended beyond the straight line of the handle. This must be done since [in Italy] no razors are found constructed with a slanted handle of that sort our barbers and those of the French use, for the awkward Italian razors have large, vertical handles, usually unsuitable for oblique incisions since they prevent the twisting of the hand to one's liking.

Appendix

The small knife which may be fitted to a reed.

You ought to have very sharp as well as duller knives which may be fitted to reeds, and of these knives some may have rounded ends, others long and pointed. Of the remainder, those are preferable that are wholly of steel, for when we attempt to cut a transverse ligament with the other sort of knife, the handle can easily be broken after the resin in it has been weakened by frequent washing in hot water, and the steel itself weakened. In dissection, use a sword edge almost entirely; that sort which is curved inward like a sickle is not to be employed and little knives with an inward curve can be used on transverse ligaments only with difficulty.

Ordinary knives.

Two table knives can be used with profit, although one of them ought to be much longer but duller than the other and of iron rather than of steel, or at least not very brittle.

Boxwood knives.

If you desire, you may add two knives made of boxwood or the "wood of India" such as we employ in the treatment of the sick. Cut one slender with a longish point, and the other wider, with a rounded end; however, I use these very rarely since very dull razors are always available.

Hooks.

You may also make two hooks, such as we have illustrated at the beginning of the chapter. I usually make them from common table forks, and if you will file both tines of a fork and bend the points into a semicircle, you will have made yourself a nice hook. If you file the tines you may have one very sharp hook and the other very dull. Nevertheless, you will more frequently use your fingers for lifting structures unless the incision is obscured by the shadow of the left hand.

Styluses.

In addition, see to it that long, short, and very thick styluses are cut for you from silver or copper wire, and that some very soft and flexible lead be drawn out by a goldsmith in the form of wire. These may be conveniently used for various purposes, especially for probing to discover the nature of oblique ducts.

Pipettes.

It is advisable to have a pipette which you may wish to insert into the bladder as you become more expert in manual operations. I make a handle for the pipette; it is desirable to do this also for some of the styluses, of which some ought to be curved like the pipette. It is very useful to have several hollow styluses so that an incision can be made through their hollow by which a stone may be removed from the bladder, or formed like that instrument by which weavers of silk stuffs cut the silk into threads. These instruments resemble the styluses with which we carefully divide a membrane by a long incision when we desire not to injure any of the underlying parts or any of those enfolding the membrane.

Needles.

It is desirable to have a bent rather than straight needle which you can easily make if first you heat and then bend an ordinary needle into the form of the

337

Appendix

letter C or (. Have a supply of large and small; those to carry thread and slender cords, those which are bent, and those to sew up wounds. Hence at any time you will be immediately able to sew the skin if you fear that in your absence inquisitive spectators may harm anything.

Thread.

Silk thread or whatever special kind is used to sew up wounds ought to be available for your needles if you fear that what has been sewn up may be undone or disturbed in your absence; in addition, for binding the vessels of the uterus, [p. 237] you should have that ordinary thread with which we sew the parts of books, especially that imported from Germany into Italy, for that of other nations is very weak and thick, less twisted and smooth.

Saws.

I recommend that saw we use to cut off limbs affected by gangrene or other things of that sort, not rounded as certain mathematicians illustrate in their books of anatomy, deciding in some fashion that I can't comprehend that a rounded head must be sawed with a saw curved like a sickle. If you do not have a saw you can get one from the combmakers.

Scissors.

Scissors are to be used only to cut the cords after ligation. This may also be done with a knife.

Hammers.

A hammer is sometimes needed for driving a very large knife when you are breaking the skulls of animals. Use whatever kind you desire.

Tubes.

It is also desirable to have longish tubes made from reeds with which your assistant can inflate this or that body. Planks on which to perform vivisections are also easily prepared and I shall describe them when we consider vivisection, just as at the end of the first book I described the instruments to be used in articulating the bones properly.

5. BOOK II. DISSECTION OF THE MUSCLES MOVING THE ARM.

CHAPTER XXIIII [5]

Now in whatever manner may seem proper to you, either with the cadaver suspended according to that method I have mentioned, or lying on the table, remove the skin with the fat from the entire thorax and abdomen, but without any injury to the fleshy membrane. Unless you are industrious and desire to learn you will perform this only with great difficulty, since the skin must be freed with many incisions quite differently than if you were to separate the fleshy membrane along with the skin. When the skin has been removed, make one incision in the fleshy membrane from the middle of the chest to the pubic bone, then a second transversely from the pubic bone to the hip joint and to the spine of the sacral bone, and a third from the acromion along the middle of the arm. [269] When these incisions have been made, grasp the fleshy membrane with a hook or with the fingers and lift it away from the whole thorax and abdomen as far as the spine, but as yet preserving its connection to the glands in the axilla.

When the membrane has been torn away, up to the cavity of the axilla, it must be held up to the light and inspected carefully to see if, under the axilla, it may have altered into a fleshy muscle originating from the loins and false ribs. If perhaps—because I do not know what the case may be—you observe it increased by fleshy fibres, separate it from the axilla with that diligence of which you are capable, noting whether it is inserted by a tendon into the humerus, or whether, as is usual in the rest of the thorax, it is connected only to those fibrous parts. Pay close heed lest through inexperience you mistake the fat in the sides of the thorax and the whole back for flesh; I have seen some so unskilled and so negligently versed in recognition of these parts that at first glance they considered the fat of the back to be flesh because due to its compression they observed it to be much redder there than elsewhere. When a cadaver rests on its back for a day or two, the entire compressed region becomes reddish relative to the amount of fat as if it had been affected by an inflammation. In your dissection observe whether or not this membrane is formed of muscle and whether this is for the sake of moving the skin or the arm, although it seems that this membrane is not muscular in man, nor is it inserted by a tendon into the humerus or even touches it.

Dissection of the first muscle of those moving the arm [*Pectoralis major m.*].

When you have freed the whole membrane from the trunk of the body and the middle of the arm, attack the muscle drawing the arm to the chest, above all observing whether that slender muscle possessed by caudate apes and carried obliquely upward from the region of the breast is anywhere prominent. Since, however, you will not find it in man, with a razor or small knife scrape the head of the muscle adducting the arm to the chest from the clavicle, the entire region of the chest, and the cartilages inserted into it, and finally, grasping it with little hooks or the fingers, separate it by means of your fingers or a little boxwood knife from the underlying bodies as far as the humerus. When you free the head of this muscle with a razor, be careful not to remove anything else with it. In dogs and apes the muscle is covered over by the cartilages of the true ribs.

[Galen's] *Anatomical procedures*, Bk. 6.

This muscle is, so to speak, almost part of the rectus abdominis muscle, and Galen said that it was created for the sake of respiration and may be considered in place of a special thoracic muscle, distinct from the rectus. I shall discuss this at greater length when dealing with the muscles moving the thorax. I warn you, however, that even if I do not find this in man, nevertheless the studious will attempt to observe it, and while your colleagues are dissecting they will recall that according to Galen a muscle of this sort lies hidden here; therefore they must free the muscle adducting the arm to the chest from its origin with great care or, if freed without care, it must be cast aside. In addition, attention must be paid to that muscle that in apes is hidden under the muscle moving the arm to the chest, extended differently than in man to the ligament of the joint. Hence it should be no cause for amazement that when I display the structure of man in public dissection I always employ also either the ape or the dog.

Appendix

Dissection of the second muscle of those moving the scapula [Trapezius m.] so that you may undertake the rest skillfully.

Leaving this great muscle that moves the arm to the chest for the present still appended to the humerus, observe the remaining muscles of the arm which you cannot properly dissect unless first you have removed the muscle that is extended from the occipital bone through the entire neck and is inserted into the whole spine of the scapula and the acromion, as well as into the nearest part of the clavicle, then extended downward through the gibbosity and base of the scapula until it is joined at its point to the spine of the eighth thoracic vertebra. This muscle is connected to the apices of the spines and takes origin from them and from the occiput all the way to the eighth thoracic vertebra. We shall consider it later with the others moving the scapula; mention is now made incidentally because the posterior muscles moving the arm cannot be seen readily unless this one has been dissected from the spine and the occiput as far as its insertion. Dissect it with a razor or little knife by making an incision along the length of the spine; this may injure the muscle but not the underlying parts; then make another incision in the occipital part to free the origin of the muscle from the occipital bone. However, if you fear to harm some underlying muscles by these incisions, place one boxwood knife under the external side of the muscle—that is, on the side carried from the occipital region to the clavicle—and then another where it descends from the acromion or clavicle to the spine of the eighth thoracic vertebra. This little knife placed at the side and moved upward and downward will force the separation of that muscle from those underlying it and then you will more easily understand the thickness of its sinewy origin; you can easily follow that muscle, now freed from the underlying bodies, to its insertion.

As we shall say in the special account of this muscle, you must be careful lest, along with this one you have now dissected, you lift away that muscle underneath proceeding from the occiput into the scapula, which Galen asserts also draws the scapula upward. I do not say this as if man had this in common with the ape, [270] but that you may notice carefully whether man does indeed have it; and, when you dissect the ape at the same time, compare my remarks with those of Galen—if you are a diligent admirer of nature—and do not trust even to dogs, which, like horses, oxen, and other animals which lack clavicles, differ very much from apes in respect to the muscles moving the arm and scapula. These have in addition another muscle arisen from the external region of the transverse processes of the first four cervical vertebrae and inserted into the spine of the scapula; this is also lacking in man, although it might be present and, if found, must be dissected.

Dissection of the second muscle of those moving the arm [Deltoid m.].

Therefore, when those three muscles have been dissected out in the ape, but in man merely the first, separate the muscle by which the arm is raised and, with a razor or knife, always cutting very close to the bone and dissecting out from its origin, separate its head from the spine of the scapula, from the acromion, and from the middle of the clavicle until you observe its transverse insertion into the humerus. Observe the muscle raising the arm, its triangular shape, and especially the blunt vertex of the angle of that head that has been dissected; not only must it be observed on each surface, but you must consider with the

340

greatest care whether that whole mass covering the joint exteriorly is one muscle or several muscles lying upon one another, as Galen seems to believe in the fifth book of his *Anatomical procedures* and elsewhere, often charging the ancient professors of dissection—who employed human cadavers—with negligence. Examine the whole origin of the muscle and the manner in which it increases in thickness, and observe how by degrees it becomes fleshy; when you have examined the tendon, divide it transversely. I must confess that sometimes it is duplicated and does not resemble that kind found in the first three muscles arisen from the hipbone which serve the motions of the leg, although at the same time resting on one another so that they may be considered as one muscle.

Dissection of the fourth [*Latissimus dorsi m.*].

When the two first muscles moving the arm have been cut away, free the muscle that moves the arm downward from its underlying parts as far as the insertion. This can be done very easily if you will draw a line along the length of the spine from which the muscle takes origin, the line running through merely the muscle's membranous origin. And so when you have freed the origin, seize it with a hook or the fingers, separating the whole muscle from the underlying muscles with a little boxwood knife or even a somewhat dull razor. In this dissection, observe how this muscle transcends the lower angle of the base of the scapula and adheres to the scapula; if you extend its origin in various ways to the place of origin you will clearly learn how this muscle draws down the arm and also may move the scapula. When you reach that line that separates the origin of the muscle from the apices of the spine, beware lest at the same time you also dissect the origin of the obliquely ascending abdominal muscle and also of that one arisen transversely from the spines of the vertebrae and inserted into the tenth and eleventh thoracic ribs. Therefore, if you trust a little to your hands, you will do the same for this muscle as I advised for that numbered by me as the second of those moving the scapula [Trapezius m.]. Place the extended hand or a little boxwood knife under the external side of the muscle and move it transversely up and down until you think that the muscle, as far as the apices of the spines, has been separated from the underlying structures. In this way you will learn the thickness of its membranous origin and will fully understand how deeply the little knife or razor must be thrust to separate it. But you will do well to extend a long stylus with a rounded knob directly under the origin of the muscle, and by degrees push a knife under the muscle at the side of the stylus and free the origin; then, with the cutting edge of the knife kept outward and slightly oblique, move it forward with the stylus in almost the same way in which we cut paper. Otherwise, employ that procedure by which we evert calculi from the bladder when we place a channeled stylus in the neck of the bladder so that an incision may be made in its channel, in the same way in which the weavers of silk stuff cut the silk into threads; in this way all things that must be cut lengthwise will be nicely divided as you will hear later.

Dissection of the third [*Teres major m.*].

When you trace to the shoulder that muscle by which the arm is moved downward, free the tendon from the shoulder; then, examining the muscle, cut away its origin from the lower rib of the scapula, and consider carefully whether Galen attributed the circular motion of the arm more correctly to this muscle than to that muscle occupying the gibbous seat of the scapula, which I mentioned in the number of those performing this movement.

Appendix

Of the seventh [Supraspinatus m.].

Leave this appended to the arm until you have scraped that one that fills the gibbosity of the scapula from the scapula up to the ligament of the joint, so that you are able to consider each more correctly.

Of the fifth [Subscapularis m.].

Scrape away from the scapula in two lines the muscle that lies in that cavity of the scapula observed between the spine and its superior rib, [271] one led through the superior side of the spine of the scapula, the other following its higher rib; here the muscle is joined to the ligament of the joint of the humerus, which has been considered.

The sixth [Infraspinatus m.].

The muscle moving the arm in circular motion and holding the internal site of the scapula—unless first you set loose the scapula from the clavicle by a series of incisions—does not display itself suitably for observation. Since the muscles moving the scapula are as yet intact it would be wrong to separate the scapula from the clavicle or to remove it with the clavicle from the thorax. Therefore, when you see the scapula freed from the clavicle by a series of dissections, or the scapula in its entirety has been lifted away from the thorax, the dissection of that muscle I have numbered sixth in order of the movers of the arm will be very easy, since then it may be wholly scraped from the cavity of the scapula, and at the same time you may examine the function of this and of the others as you please and without difficulty. I believe also that the dissection of the muscle numbered fifth by me must be reserved until you have freed the scapula from the clavicle, since it is hidden in the hollow of the scapula very near the thorax.

In the following chapter, Vesalius's references to the origins and terminations of veins and arteries must be reversed for comprehension today.

6. BOOK V. THE BEST METHOD FOR CONDUCTING THE ANATOMY, AS WELL AS FOR UNDERTAKING PRIVATELY EVERYTHING THAT HAS BEEN PRESENTED IN THIS BOOK.

CHAPTER XIX [6]

I prefer to arrange this chapter, and then the final one of the sixth book and thereafter the penultimate of the seventh, so that in them consideration may be given in proper sequence to the method for dissection of the organs considered in those books, as if it had been decided to observe only those matters and to demonstrate them to others on some cadaver. Then I wish these chapters to be as descriptive as if there were an immediate connection between them, as if they were in the form of a [connected] book comprising the whole method of dissection which any one properly trained in anatomy might use in a public dissection before students.

Although a dissection presented privately among a few is undoubtedly to be preferred to a public one, since the supply of cadavers is not sufficient for all purposes, I strive that public dissection be carried on as much as possible by the students so that even those with little instruction—there is always some unskilled person who is willing and eager to undertake dissection at the slightest suggestion—if called upon to dissect a cadaver before a throng of spectators, can conduct the anatomy correctly with their own hands; and comparing their studies with one another the students can grasp properly this part of medicine and natural philosophy. This is particularly important in this favored age when anatomy, together with other disciplines, is greatly fostered and promoted, so much so that everything to which I have given consideration in this work I performed several times in the same winter in Padua and Bologna before a large gathering of spectators and in the same arrangement I now present in these seven books.

The order to be observed in the teaching of anatomy.

First, while my students and I displayed the bones of various men and women, old and young, joined together and separated, as well as those of apes, dogs, and several other animals, I read Galen's book *On the bones* to those who were being initiated, and at that time I completed their recognition of the bones and cartilages, or of those things that sustain and support the human structure, as well as the other things I have already described; next I gave attention to the structure of the muscles and ligaments and everything that is considered in the second book. In my prior lectures I had advised the students of Galen's text, which describes those muscles it was my intention to display in the following lecture, but whenever I was compelled to pass over Galen's text, I always gave a digest of his opinion before the dissection. I dissected the man and the dog in the presence of all and, when required, the ape, carefully displaying all those things that were described by me.

With the account of the muscles completed, I briefly displayed the viscera in the same body, those things we ordinarily say are contained in the three venters, preparing the minds of the spectators for instruction on the veins, arteries, and nerves in that way in which I had related the bones to the teaching on the muscles, so that afterward I might more suitably treat the veins, arteries, and nerves in another [548] body. Similarly, before the display of the dissected parts, on the same body I carefully completed the description of those things that relate to the interior, always teaching their structure in that way in which I have sought to remark on it in these books. In the first and second books I have explained how one should approach all these matters, and I shall explain them partly in this chapter and partly at the end of the subsequent books.

In the first book I considered the method of preparing the bones, in the second the method of dissecting the muscles in one body. Here I shall concern myself with the matters so that you may conduct the anatomy of all these things on a single body if that should become necessary because of scarcity; or, if you wish, you may privately perform these investigations separately on different cadavers. It is most desirable of all that the arrangement of the related organs or parts not be upset and that you not be required to explain the veins when the muscles are under consideration or when you are dealing with the nerves.

What sort of body ought to be employed for dissection.

It is desirable that the body employed for public dissection be as normal as possible according to its sex and of medium age, so that you may compare other bodies to it as if to the statue of Policletus. In private dissections, which are undertaken very frequently, any body can be profitably employed because you will also be able to examine whatever its variations and consider the differences of bodies and the true nature of many diseases.

Appendix

At Bologna and Padua we prepared an [anatomical] amphitheatre
such as is presented [on the title page] at the beginning of this book.

Let a theatre and table, on which the cadaver is to be placed, be made in that way in which you determine the cadaver will be most suitably placed for your purpose, and the theatre most suitable for the reception of spectators. In the second book I have described the instruments that must be used for this work. When it is necessary to perform everything on one body, and not seriatim as we teach in these books, things may be considered one by one. As a prelude, and if it appears desirable, briefly indicate on the skeleton, which ought to be available, the value and use of the knowledge of the skeleton of the human body, for today there is scarcely any school that does not have one or more skeletons which can be profitably employed during dissection.

The presentation must be introduced with a
display of all the parts in one body.

After you have distinguished man from other animals, divide the cadaver itself into the head, trunk of the body, and the arms and legs; or establish its regions or capacities which, according to the precept of Plato, are said to be individually for the separate souls; later add to these regions the organs of generation and the arms and legs. Then it will be possible to describe the body and to recount the names of the external parts more accurately than from the various texts of Galen and Aristotle. Seek them summarily from the author of the *Introduction to medicine*, Julius Pollux and Giorgio Valla among others; although throughout the first book I have referred to the names given in *On the bones*, I concluded that those names ought not be neglected now, for the names used for bones may also be given to the superficial regions. Therefore I have sometimes delineated the site of the bones on the skin of the cadaver, so that I might more aptly indicate that the same name is suited to the bone and to the part in which the bone is located. Add to these things the differences in the nomenclature of the parts, subdividing them into similars and into instrumental parts; and here it will be useful to recall whatever parts are placed in the former or latter category, not neglecting the common description of each part my efforts have sufficiently indicated, if you are not presently compelled to require the individual descriptions in their places.

I favor the presentation of the parts from their descriptions, as has been my custom in dissection when I consider everything seriatim. As I teach the part I attempt to show it exposed in some animal; indeed, it is useful to display it to the spectators in a dog or a lamb or whatever animal is available and easy to prepare. It is desirable that in these animals you teach what bone, cartilage, fibre, ligament, fat, flesh, and glandular body are; then what muscle, sinew or tendon, and other parts of muscle are; vein, artery, and nerve; and then that you display the composition of the instrumental parts, for generally, as I said, they can be usefully displayed in any animal whatsoever—thus avoiding injury to the human body during the discussion of the instruments of each member —because otherwise the spectator's ignorance of those parts might compel you to interrupt the sequence of the discussion. I do not propose at present to mention the differences that arise in the discussion regarding the use of the parts, as certain ones make for life, others for the continuance of the species, others for well-being, and others for things too numerous to mention here, because I shall teach them fully throughout the chapters on individual parts. Here I must explain my method of dissection as opposed to that [characteristic

344

of] the high chair (*cathedra*)—that is, ignorance of the parts and mere phi-losophizing from the books of others. And so I shall undertake the former method, aided in the dissection by companions in study rather than assistants.

How to deal with the skin, epidermis, fat, and fleshy membrane in the abdomen.

With a very sharp razor make a circular incision around the umbilicus, deep enough to penetrate the skin, then from the middle of the pectoral bone [sternum] make a straight, lengthwise incision to the umbilicus, and from the lower region of the umbilicus proceed toward the pubes as far as the middle of the root of the virile member—if you are now employing a male cadaver; or, if you are dissecting a female body, as far as the region of the pubic bone be-tween the little mounds of the vulva, so that there is required, as it were, one incision from the chest to the pubes. Next, on each side make an incision from the side of the umbilicus transversely to the loins but penetrating only the skin, which is easily done in man, especially in a very fat one since the thickness of the fat readily prevents you from harming the fleshy membrane. When these incisions have been made in this way, and when the upper right angle [549] of the four right angles of the skin facing the umbilicus has been lifted with a hook or with the tips of the fingers of the left hand, then, putting aside the hook, little by little separate the skin from the fat at the breast and as far as the back by transverse incisions made very close to the skin. When this part of the abdomen and thorax has been laid bare of skin, the three remaining parts must be uncovered in a like manner. Next, investigate the nature of the skin and the epidermis, which latter is called EPIDERMIS in Greek and appears to have no function in the skin. This you can do only by the aid of a candle, for by burning the skin you force the epidermis to separate from it like a blister.

The veins running through the region of the abdomen between the skin and the fleshy membrane.

When you have examined the skin and the veins under it which run upward around the region of the abdomen and downward from the chest, as well as the fat, if the body is plentifully supplied with this last substance—as are almost all who have not died from a wasting disease—just as you have already freed that skin from the fat, so separate the fat from the fleshy membrane; this you will do properly only with a very sharp razor. But if you have obtained a very lean body, permit the fat to adhere to the fleshy membrane, for in that case the fat has no thickness and the nature of the fleshy membrane is observable. What-ever you do, whether you scrape off the fat or leave it attached to the fleshy membrane, when that same incision, which I said must be made in the skin from the chest to the pubic bone and from the umbilicus to the ilia, has been made through the fleshy membrane, the corners of those incisions must be lifted one after another with a hook. If you desire, the fleshy membrane may be separated by a blunt razor, or with the fingers, from the underlying bodies, so that the whole abdomen with a large part of the thorax may be laid bare of the skin, fat and fleshy membrane at one time. I conduct the dissection in this way in the university, although, if one desires, it is also worthwhile to ex-amine the skin, fat, and fleshy membrane as butchers do without any concerted method.

The eight muscles of the abdomen.

I dealt at length in the second book with the nature of these parts and their dissection, and in that same book I taught the method by which you may best approach the muscles of the abdomen, which are four on each side, and so lay bare the peritoneum. At that time I said that the muscles of the abdomen may be dissected in two ways. First, by incision from the middle of the abdomen toward the origins of the muscles. In this way the obliquely descending muscle of the abdomen is first lifted away from the obliquely ascending, then the latter from the rectus and transverse muscles of the abdomen, and then the rectus from the transverse; meanwhile, the insertion of the rectus muscle has been freed from the cartilages of the ribs. The second method is by an incision from the sides to the middle of the abdomen, which also lifts away the obliquely descending muscle from the obliquely ascending; then free this ascending muscle from the transverse and rectus, and in addition the rectus from the transverse; finally free the transverse from the peritoneum by a series of incisions drawn to the middle of the abdomen. If it is your intention to display things individually and seriatim in one body, the method for the muscles of the abdomen can be sought in the second book, which precedent I shall now follow.

The veins, arteries, and nerves creeping through the muscles of the abdomen.

Also the arrangement of veins, arteries, and nerves must be separately examined at this time: of the veins and arteries, those that run from the pubic region upward following the posterior region of the recti muscles toward the region of the umbilicus, and those that advance hither from the chest and give off branches into the nearest regions on both sides; of the nerves, those which are given off from the intervals of the false ribs and are variously distributed from the lumbar vertebrae to the muscles of the abdomen—as has been considered elsewhere.

Separation of the peritoneum from the extrinsic parts joined to it.

When the transverse muscles have been freed everywhere from the peritoneum, the whole of its exterior surface is exposed to view, for it can be seen everywhere except where it is attached to the diaphragm and where it takes origin from the vertebrae and the os sacrum. Furthermore, the peritoneum of man is too weak by nature to be easily torn away intact from the diaphragm, although sometimes when the peritoneum is as yet intact it may be freed from the underlying muscles as far as the spine, and sometimes also from the region of the fleshy diaphragm; it resembles a longish sphere. If the peritoneum seems able to be easily avulsed from the diaphragm—as can be done very readily in swine —then, in man, if you can separate the transverse muscles of the abdomen from the peritoneum with the fingers instead of a knife, seek to remove it little by little from the fleshy part of the diaphragm; and if you are successful, separate the peritoneum from the whole body of the stomach as far as the membranes of the omentum, and then from the gibbous part of the liver; thus you will learn how it provides tunics and coverings for those organs.

The opening of the peritoneum and the dissection of the umbilical vessels.

After you have carefully considered the exterior peritoneum with its foramina, veins, arteries, and nerves, with a razor or little knife carefully make an incision in it from the left side of the umbilicus, for if the knife be driven too deeply you may injure some of the underlying parts. From the umbilicus the same incision, inclining somewhat to the left, must be carried as far as the pubic bone, [550] but so that it deviates to the left side by some interval from the middle of the bone. Furthermore, in this left side of the peritoneum make an incision from the umbilicus to the left ilium, and fold the upper part of the peritoneum toward the ribs, and the lower part toward the ischium. Now, with the left side folded partially upward, and with the right side of the peritoneum folded downward, observe that vein that has more resemblance to a cord covered with much fat than to a vein and which extends from the umbilicus into the liver. Grasp this vein with the left hand where it is very close to the liver and, thrusting a very sharp knife between it and the peritoneum where it leaves the peritoneum approaching the umbilicus, separate it gradually from the peritoneum by transverse incisions. When you have reached that point, with the vein intact make an incision in the peritoneum from the right side of the umbilicus to the ilium, folding back that part of the peritoneum now freed upon the ribs of the right side. As yet one part of the peritoneum, which is lower on the right side, remains attached to the umbilicus and does not hang free; therefore free this, but without damaging anything, and, with the umbilicus grasped in the left hand, make an incision on its right side as far as the pubic bone in that part of the peritoneum that extends on the right by the width of several fingers from the commissure of the pubic bones.

When that part of the peritoneum that as yet extends as a triangle from the umbilicus to the public bone and the fundus of the bladder has been turned downward, three cords are observed to be attached internally to that part but separated from one another. They must be cut from it with a very sharp knife and distinguished from one another, but carefully, lest making an incision too freely toward the pubic bone you injure the fundus of the bladder. Because the human bladder, attached to the peritoneum in the whole anterior region, is covered with much fat, it may deceive the unskilled seeking it in man as it occurs in cattle and dogs and unaware that it reposes here.

When you have carefully considered this, observe that the middle cord of the bladder [lig. umbilicale med.] is attached to the middle of the fundus and is nowhere separated from the peritoneum. Also observe that the two remaining cords [ligg. umbilicalia lat.] running down the sides of the bladder descend through the foramina of the pubic bones into the legs and are extended deeply to the arteries; do not hesitate to free those [cords] from the peritoneum with a very sharp knife as far as their insertion. The middle cord was a passage [urachus] by which—since we are to be concerned with the uterus—urine was excreted into the middle covering of the foetus which takes its name from a kind of sausage. The other two were [umbilical] arteries by which the natural heat of the foetus was refreshed. But none of these three bodies nor that inserted into the liver will be seen to have any cavity, but will clearly appear as lifeless, meagre, and nourished by much fat. Hence they have lain hidden from leading anatomists who assert that, as usually happens in dogs, they are completely destroyed in man when he is born.

Dissection of the vessels of the umbilicus.

Furthermore, after you have carefully inspected the implantation of the vein inserted from the umbilicus into the liver, it is desirable that you dissect the vein along with the umbilicus you have hitherto preserved, and then the three other cords, observing the connection of the peritoneum to the fundus of the bladder and carrying the incision to the omentum.

Appendix

Observation of the site of the omentum.

You will be unable to observe the parts that remain to be seen in the peritoneum unless little by little you lift away the organs from it. But before you move anything from its place, whether in dogs or pigs, and much more in apes, the site of the omentum must be observed as it is extended under the posterior region of the bladder to the pubes; and whether—as is very frequently observed—it extends turned toward the left side and also drawn upward above the middle region of the intestines. If you find the latter, with both hands raise the lower extremity of the omentum slightly, and drawing it by degrees downward in the same way spread it over all the intestines as far as the pubic bone; for thus you will learn how large it is and that it can be rolled down to the inguinal region and scotum and between the bladder and the neck of the uterus [vagina].

So that you may observe the connection of the omentum to the colon intestine where it is extended to the stomach, again with both hands raise the lower end of the omentum to the sternum, and before you dissect the lower part of the membrane of the omentum anywhere, dissect that which arises from the colon as if from a third covering of the colon intestine; stretch out the omentum as far as possible toward the chest, and using only the hands investigate the site of the intestines with as much diligence as possible.

Examination of the site of the intestines.

First, before you disturb the position of any intestine, as the omentum has now been raised, observe them [the intestines] exactly as they offer themselves for inspection; thus when you have learned the course of each intestine and to which region of the peritoneum each is neighboring, you will have knowledge for diagnosing ailments and employing medicaments. Carefully observe the appearance of the rectum intestine and, applying the right hand to it where it rests on the origin of the os sacrum, with the left depress the slender intestines on the right, not all, but that part of them that, as you approach from the right, is nearer to the right hand. In this way, with the left hand serving the right, by degrees move the right hand along from the rectum intestine to the colon, following its course and turnings to the region of the left kidney and thence to the spleen and the fundus of the stomach. When you reach this point, you must reverse your hands; the colon must be seized with the left, and with the right the slender intestine must be pushed somewhat to the left until you have reached the region of the fundus of the stomach and the liver and have traced the colon under the region of the right [551] kidney where it ends.

When you reach that point, raise the termination of the colon somewhat with the left hand, and when the site and shape of the caecum intestine has been observed, grasp it with both the right and left hands, keeping both hands close together, which is easily done until the right hand reaches the origin of the jejunum; then place the left between the liver and the right side of the stomach and seek the origin of the duodenum; when you have found this, move your hand downward along its course and note the origin of the jejunum, still grasping with the right hand that part closest to it.

Examination of the site of the stomach, liver, and spleen.

If it is now your desire—and I strongly advise that this be done—you can examine the site of the intestines from the jejunum to the ileum, thence to the caecum and colon, and from the colon by an opposite course to the rectum, without tearing or damaging anything. When the site of the intestines has been considered and they have been replaced in their site, the omentum must again be laid over the intestines, and the position of the stomach, liver, and spleen examined.

Insert the hand between the diaphragm and the gibbosity of the liver so that that gibbosity and the ligaments come into view, and moving the hand about here and there observe how the thin covering of the liver arises from a particular ligament. Then place the left hand between the hollow of the liver and the right side of the stomach, and the right hand between the diaphragm and the left side of the stomach, drawing the hands together little by little and approaching the superior orifice of the stomach; this will come into view if with the left hand you now shove the liver somewhat upward, and with the right you press the body of the stomach downward; with one and the same effort you will briefly observe the whole region of the hollow of the liver. In addition, do not hesitate to move the hands here and there, now thrusting the liver upward, now depressing the stomach; this action will also accurately indicate the region of the stomach.

Now, if you insert the left hand between the left side of the stomach and the diaphragm, and draw the stomach with the colon to the right side, you will discover the region of the spleen; if the upper part and half the cavity of the spleen reveal themselves, and if you place the right hand between the spleen and the diaphragm and push the slightly raised spleen toward the stomach, its gibbosity will also appear.

Here the liver, stomach, and spleen, considered as if in
the cavity of the thorax, can be extended downward.

When, with little effort, you have done all these things, it will be useful to make a narrow incision in some interval of the ribs as far as the cavity of the thorax. When you have penetrated the thorax, immediately the diaphragm, falling downward, becomes noticeably flaccid, no matter how tense it was before; and, having been drawn upward, it draws the liver and stomach into the cavity of the thorax and thereby makes inspection of them difficult.

Here the omentum must be separated and its origin
investigated, as well as the vessels carried by it.

Now the membranes of the omentum must be separated from one another. This may be done by placing the right hand under the omentum and drawing away the inferior membrane while the superior is grasped with the left hand, for these membranes are readily separated from one another and reveal a kind of pouch or little sac. When this has been done, pull away the membranes from each other so that you may comfortably insert your hand into their amplitude, and separate the upper membrane from the lower on each side and at the lower end of the omentum. Now you may extend the lower membrane over the intestines and stretch the upper to the chest so that it raises the stomach higher than its normal site; but if this cannot be accomplished [alone], it must be done with the help of a colleague so that the origin of the lower membrane of the omentum, and whatever organs are borne by it, come into sight.

You may likewise learn how in man it [the lower membrane] replaces the mesentery for the colon intestine in that region where the colon is extended to the fundus of the stomach, for it will appear that the lesser trunk of the portal vein is carried by and gives forth those branches into which it is divided in this membrance where it is spread under the stomach. Then, in addition to this trunk, an artery [coeliac] is observed which gives off branches to the spleen, stomach, liver, gall bladder, and finally to the omentum, as well as the root of that artery that is disseminated into the upper region of the mesentery; next, you will ob-

Appendix

serve two nerves [gastric and coeliac branches of vagus(?)], of which the right is extended to the sac of the gall bladder and the right side of the fundus of the stomach where it is also extended to the omentum, and the left is distributed to the spleen, to the left side of the fundus of the stomach, and to the right side of the omentum; but in particular observe the glandular body [pancreas] shielding the series of vessels and nerves. At present these things must be protected and no knife employed, but the upper part of the omentum must be carefully determined with the finger tips. When you have observed this, if, with the aid of an assistant, you have kept the stomach elevated and thrust upward, reach from its fundus downward toward the hollow of the liver where the omentum binds together many bodies, and thence through the back where the aorta passes through the diaphragm, following the hollow of the spleen as far as the fundus of the stomach. This is the upper circle of the omentum, even if we said that that sac or pouch is the orifice. A little later I shall explain how you ought to approach its origin.

Here the organs placed in the hollow part of the liver must be observed.

Now, with the stomach as yet in its place, [552] draw it to the left side with the intestines and pull the liver to the right and upward so that you may clearly see its hollow. After you have observed the gall bladder, undertake the very troublesome and difficult dissection of the whole organ, for the biliary passage and the branches of the nerves, arteries, and veins—all of which are attached to the lower membrane of the omentum at the hollow of the liver—must now be investigated, but with a very blunt knife lest you penetrate some vein with the point of a sharp knife and so smear everything with blood. From the [gastric] branches of the sixth pair of cerebral nerves [vagus n.] going to the upper orifice of the stomach, there arises a nervule which is carried from the lower region of the stomach to the hollow orifice of the liver. After you have separated this from the neighboring organs, you must separate from its attachment to the membranes another nerve that sends one branch to the hollow of the liver and another to the gall bladder. Then free the artery extended to this nerve and distributed with it. After you have found the origin of the artery, as well as of the nerve, it is enough for now to separate them one from the other at the hollow of the liver and to learn their arrangement.

Under the artery are the ducts of the gall bladder, now to be freed from the portal vein; first [free] those two that, extended from the hollow of the liver, are bound together from many branches and joined there into [two ducts]: one carried as a single vessel into the gall bladder, the other into the duodenum intestine. When you have separated these from the portal vein going to the intestines and gall bladder, so compress them with your thumb that the ducts, swollen with bile, appear more clearly, and you will notice whether this duct extends from the [gall] bladder into the stomach; if you do not find this duct, lightly incise the duct going into the intestines so that the flowing bile may be proof of your careful examination of that duct.

Now the branches of the portal vein with the arteries and nerves extended to them must be examined.

Now the portal vein must be examined and then its circumscription, where you will observe it to come forth from the liver; its branches must be investigated with a very blunt knife, always with careful consideration for the arrangement of the artery, nerve, and vein extended through the whole of its course.

Appendix

Give attention to the branches of the portal vein that are extended to the gall bladder; then that [branch] that, almost without an accompanying artery [pyloric], goes into the right side of the stomach and is divided into a small number of branches near the posterior region of the lower orifice. Next is that one [left gastric v.] that creeps through the right side of the fundus of the stomach and the middle of the upper membrane of the omentum. Then observe that [superior mesenteric v.] that goes to the duodenum intestine, descending along the length of the intestine into a glandular and fleshy body; but— as I have already warned—use only a very blunt knife in your attempt to lay bare the vein, nerve, and artery existing there.

Now expose the great distribution of the portal vein, and only incidentally observe the trunk that approaches the mesentery. Then, leaving this for the present, give your attention especially to the trunk that is extended to the spleen. In order that you may see this conveniently, you must arrange the stomach and intestines in that way in which they were arranged when you observed the lower membrane of the omentum, when the stomach was lifted by an associate and you took care to press the intestines downward. Now, with the upper part of the lower membrane of the omentum visible, examine with great care all the branches of the lesser trunk of the portal vein, all of which in man you will find extended to the stomach, spleen, omentum, and the colon intestine. As you investigate those branches, free them from the glandular body supporting them and you will observe an artery to be extended to all and a nerve to many parts.

The root of the arteries displays itself in the highest part of the lower membrane of the omentum, where the aorta leading into the mesentery takes origin; then one nerve appears on each side, issuing at the sides of the aorta descending here, shoots of branches of the sixth pair of cerebral nerves which are extended to the roots of the ribs; when you lay bare the veins the branches always come into view with the arteries.

Now the nature of the mesentery must be investigated.

Now it is time to investigate the arrangement of the larger trunk of the portal vein, the artery mentioned a little earlier, and the nerve going through the mesentery, which at their divisions therein rest upon glandules. Using only the hands, move the intestines now this way, now that, twisting them now to the right, now to the left, so that you may observe briefly the nature of the mesentery beyond the incision; then with your nails separate one membrane of the mesentery from the other so you may observe the whole arrangement of the vessels interrupted by divarications and glandules. Do not attempt this through the whole mesentery, for at present it is enough for you to follow several branches of the vessels from the center to the intestines, and then to approach another artery [inferior mesenteric a.] of the mesentery that issues from the aorta to the rear of the origin of the spermatic arteries. You will find this readily if you twist the mesentery with the intestines to the right side, and with your nails or a blunt knife seek to separate the membranes where the artery is attached by a neck under the region of the left kidney. At this point, where the root of the arteries is revealed, the branches of that artery appear joined to the veins. When you find this, follow its divarication so that you may learn here that this, with the vein supported by the mesentery, extends branches to the rectum intestine. Do not be concerned if you do not see its extremity inserted into the rectum intestine, [553] for this will be seen more readily a little later. The sites of the intestines, stomach, liver, spleen, and mesentery must be examined using the same procedure

351

as for the omentum, and, in addition, the branches of the veins, arteries, and nerves extended to them must also be examined.

Here the intestines must be dissected from
the mesentery and removed from the body.

Now I shall consider the procedure by which you may conveniently observe what must as yet be perceived in those organs so that you may demonstrate it to others. When a large semicircular needle has been threaded with that kind of thread used for sewing the signatures of books, draw it through the mesentery under the rectum intestine where it lies upon the sacrum, and, with the faeces in that intestine thrust upward to the amplitude of the colon, bind the intestine. When the superfluous thread has been cut off, force the faeces above the ligature upward further from the rectum intestine, and, after an interval of about three fingers, draw the needle again under the rectum intestine above the former ligature, with the rectum intestine so tied that none of the excrement remains between the two bindings. Then, with a razor divide the rectum intestine between the two bindings, and, with a dull razor—lest through carelessness you injure the intestines—little by little dissect the upper part from the mesentery, and then free the colon, ileum, and jejunum toward the mesentery as far as the beginning of the jejunum, and place the intestines in a jar. In this action, observe the connection of the colon intestine above the fatty coverings of the kidneys as well as the numerous series of vessels enfolding the intestines. When you have reached the origin of the jejunum cut it off by two ligatures, as in the case of the rectum intestine, so that the higher binding is very near the insertion of the passage of the gall bladder, but not higher.

The coverings of the intestines must be examined here.

Remove the intestines from the venter with some menial helper such as we employ here in our dissection, and prepare them for inspection by washing, so that if it seems desirable you may now examine the coverings and length of those that have been washed. At Padua and Bologna after they had been washed I sometimes had them inflated like a bladder and displayed to the students as bolsters, for thus we readily learn not only the length, which is not exactly the same in all— although it is almost fourteen ells—but also the shape and capacity.

When the intestines have been presented in this way it is very easy to investigate their coverings, for the greater part of the mesentery, which appears close to the intestines, is formed of two membranes, an upper and a lower. If you separate these from the intestines with your nails, you will observe a third covering of the intestines provided by the peritoneum. As you will shortly see that the membranes of the mesentery arise from the peritoneum, so here you will learn that the former enclose the intestines. When this covering has been removed from the intestines, make an incision with a blunt razor along the length of the intestine carefully, avoiding injury to it. Then separate the lips of this incision with your fingers, and you will readily free the second covering of the intestines, especially if you do this at the rectum intestine; the coverings of the slender intestines do not come into view so easily. Now invert the intestines, and examine the orifice of that intestine we consider to be blind (*caecum*). Meanwhile, you may incise the coverings of the intestines that yet remain in the venter, although I prefer that that be done when they have been removed. Before you consider the vessels appearing in the hollow of the liver, supported by the lower membrane of the omentum, it will be necessary to remove the intestines in the manner I have mentioned, and that in particular when you undertake a public dissection in which the intestines may perhaps be kept longer than is usual.

> *Now the stomach, spleen, omentum, and mesentery must*
> *be removed at the same time, and what must be observed*
> *in that operation.*

Now you must consider the stomach which, after the nerves inserted into its orifice have been carefully examined, I am accustomed to remove at the same time as the spleen; otherwise I have usually left the stomach until all the parts of the thorax have been dissected so that its orifice and nerves might be examined more conveniently. Since I shall explain how to remove it properly when I consider the gullet, at present I shall explain the proper procedure for the rest. Insofar as it is possible in man, attempt to tear away the peritoneum from the diaphragm as far as the upper orifice of the stomach so that you may see the beginning of the third covering of the stomach. When little by little you have freed this from the orifice of the stomach, seek as much as possible to draw it away, avulsed at the fundus of the stomach, so that you may learn that the upper membrane of the omentum is formed and arises from the third covering of the stomach. Then, when you have drawn a needle under the upper orifice of the stomach, carefully make a binding, and, attached to it, a little above, a binding separating the oesophagus transversely from the stomach. When the stomach has been raised from the venter with the hands—not, however, completely removed lest the veins be ruptured—you will learn the origin of the lower membrane of the omentum and of the mesentery from the peritoneum, using only the fingers for drawing the peritoneum by degrees from the back but cutting off many things by bindings; first, cut off everything at once in the hollow of the liver—portal vein, artery, and bile passage—or, if you prefer, bind them one at a time and separately; after these, cut off those things that are first spread out by the roots of the arteries to the mesentery and lower membrane of the omentum, certainly not omitting that artery [inferior mesenteric] that is carried into the mesentery below the origins of the spermatic arteries. It is sufficient that only one binding be added to all these, although—as I advised in the case of the intestines—there is nothing to prevent two; and especially several bindings are required at the upper orifice of the stomach.

> *Now the coverings of the spleen must be observed*
> *as well as its connections to the stomach and the intestines.*

After ligatures have been employed in this way and the portal vein and other things have been thus cut and tied off, when the stomach [554] mesentery, omentum, and spleen have been removed swiftly and solely with the hands from the venter, place them on the table; and, immediately after the spleen has been withdrawn with a part of the omentum, that part of the omentum attached to the spleen must be removed with the fingers so you may discover which covering of the spleen takes origin from the omentum. Even if I remain silent, I judge that no one doubts the necessity of observing very attentively and carefully whether or not some passage extends from the spleen into the orifice of the stomach and the arrangement of the vessels here. Furthermore, make several incisions in the spleen to observe its substance, and if it has been compressed between two blocks of wood, you may separate its substance from the vessels inserted into it in several places; in this way you may observe the vessels alone stripped of the flesh of the spleen.

Appendix

Examination of the capacity of the stomach and its coverings.

After the stomach has been washed, inflate it like a bladder so that you may observe its greatest capacity; examine its coverings as we taught must be done with the intestines; thereafter invert them, and you will see the insertion of the bile passage into the intestine which is as yet attached to the stomach. When you have removed all these things, if blood should flow forth anywhere and obliterate those that as yet remain in the venter, it must be sponged out several times with plenty of water but no vinegar; if you wipe it with a cloth you will only color it the more, for usually the slender courses of the vessels are blocked with much fat and little membranes and are somewhat difficult to find in man, the more so if covered with blood.

When the blood has been washed away, and those things that as yet remain undissected in the venter have been inspected, and the liver has been injured in no part but preserved in the body for the sake of the vena cava, then attempt to remove, as far as the sacrum, the little membranes that constitute a kind of second covering for the vena cava; but be careful not to remove the right spermatic artery which passes across the body of the vena cava with the membranes. That spermatic artery is slender and shiny like a membrane and is obstructed by much fat in man; hence you will be well advised to seek the spermatic arteries and then ensure that they not be injured before you give your attention to anything else remaining in the venter.

The spermatic arteries must be observed here.

To do this very precisely, give your attention to the right spermatic vein where it arises from the vena cava, then to the origin of the artery that approaches the lower region of the mesentery. Between these two structures, partly ascending and partly descending, with a blunt knife try to separate the vena cava on the left side from the aorta by incising the membranous fibres joining these vessels. In this operation, the roots of the two spermatic arteries come readily into view, and if you now free these arteries from the little membranes to which they are joined all the way from their origin, being careful that no violence is used in pulling them away, you will see whither they are extended.

Now the arrangement of the vena cava and aorta must be observed in the amplitude of the peritoneum.

When you have done these things, so that with the removal of the little membranes the vena cava and the aorta come more clearly into view, examine the branches they give forth in their course through the venter; first the veins of the kidneys enfolded in fatty membranes, and then the branches of the aorta and vena cava carrying down serous blood to the kidneys. Before any dissection inspect the origin of the renal veins and remove those little membranes from the branch of the vena cava adapted to the right kidney; then, by scratching the fatty membrane of the kidney with your nails, carefully examine how it is enveloped.

Examination of the whole nature of the coverings of the kidneys.

When the kidneys have been bared, with a knife investigate the urinary passage [ureter] where it extends from the kidney; then investigate the branch [renal a.]

354

Appendix

of the aorta approaching the right kidney where the vein, artery, and origin
of the urinary passage of the kidneys are seen at one time. Now you will be able
either to examine the nature of the kidney or to leave the kidney until you have
dissected certain other things. But whether you do it now or afterward, the
branches of the vena cava and the aorta must be tied off near the hollow of the
kidney, and then with a sharp razor a straight incision must be made along the
length of the kidney in its convexity and toward its hollow. Thus the kidney
must be opened in two places, and if there is any blood it must be removed with
a dampened sponge. In this way the nature of the sinuses of the kidney, and then
the origin of the urinary passage, may be observed—unless the cadaver is very
fat, for usually fat collected in the second sinus [pelvis] of the human kidney
prevents the nature of the sinuses from appearing to the dissector. Therefore it
is desirable first to examine the kidney of the dog carefully, and then to study the
human.

When the kidney has been divided along the convex or exterior side, with your
finger seek the sides of the second sinus in which the urine is strained, and the
foramen that appears in its middle; or you may introduce a stylus into the external side of the first [renal] sinus of the membranous body of the kidney and
easily extend it into the urinary passage toward the bladder. Then, when you have
observed the connection of this membranous body of the anterior of the first
sinus of the kidney to the posterior, which occurs not far from the external side
of the kidney, to discover the course of those branches and the rest of the body of
the first sinus, as well as the shape and nature of the second sinus, close and bring
together that incised kidney where the mutual connection of those branches
appears more clearly. Then place a stylus in the second sinus, and, when you have
investigated its shape, cut away that substance of the kidney that is attached
to the anterior branches of the first sinus in the posterior region; remove from
the posterior branches that which is continued to their anterior region, and
then the whole [555] first sinus will appear. Now you can insert a stylus into it
so that you may more exactly understand it, and you will be astonished how
ridiculous were the assertions hitherto made by professors of anatomy regarding
kidney function.

Furthermore, if you observe the lips of the incision made in the gibbosity of
the kidney, you will easily discover the covering which, in addition to the fatty
membrane, invests the kidney; for there that covering is usually somewhat
separated from the kidney substance and is readily removed with the fingers as far
as the hollow of the kidney; and you will see how this is extended from the
membrane of the vein and artery into the kidney. After you have observed this
in the right kidney, also free the left from its fatty membrane and investigate
the branch of the vena cava and the artery running toward its hollow.

*Examination of the origin of the vessels seeking
the left testis.*

Before you remove anything, give your attention to the left spermatic vein which
without any dissection you will see to arise from the middle course of the [renal]
vein. So that you may properly observe whether a spermatic vessel also takes
origin from the artery of the left kidney, detach the little membrane from the
vein of the kidney with a somewhat blunt knife—unless you are a very skilled
dissector—and also free the vein carefully from the little membranes as far as the
origin of the spermatic vein; then twist the renal vein somewhat downward from
the artery, and investigate whether or not the branch extended to the left sper-

355

matic vein takes its origin from the course of the renal vein. When you have discovered this—it is not necessary to dissect the left kidney, which is like the right—examine the construction of the spermatic vessels. Now you have investigated the origin of the arteries and of the left vein, and it is apparent without dissection that the right vein originates from the vena cava. Therefore, when you have learned the origin and by degrees have followed and freed the veins from the membranes as far as the arteries, if the cadaver is male, remove the skin of the penis and of the scrotum from the testes.

Stripping the covering from the testes and penis.

First make a straight incision in the skin from the pubic bone through the penis and, when the lips of the incision have been raised with a hook or with the fingers, remove the skin with the fleshy membrane from the penis and note exactly its juncture in the lowest surface of the skin with the fleshy membrane, and [note also] the separation of the fleshy membrane from the body of the penis below the glans. In addition, give attention to the ligament at the root of the glans, then the veins approaching that skin, and finally note that no fat or adipose material is found here between the skin and the fleshy membrane, as it is in the eyelid, so that the [veins] may readily disturb the skin of the penis by hydatid swelling. When the penis has been stripped, and also the legs, make an incision from the pubic bone between the groin and the left testis to the anus, and then free the scrotum with the skin of the penis from the testes and interfemoral region. The incision must always be made to the right side.

Examination of the site of the testes.

When you denude the testes of skin and fleshy membrane [dartos], be careful lest you move or invert the testes from their site. For when they have first been stripped of skin, it is especially necessary to investigate into what part the spermatic vessels are implanted, so that you may learn the providence of nature which placed the testes so that they safeguard their vessels like a rampart. Now with the fingers or a knife separate the right testis with its vessels and coverings from the left and, with the legs of the cadaver pushed together, place the right testis on the upper leg, and with a knife strip the spermatic vein and artery of the right side as far as the peritoneum, where they lie upon the neighboring little membranes, here first in the internal seat and afterward in the external seat of the peritoneum, and discover with the hands alone how the vein and artery cross over. Then forcefully thrust a stylus into the foramen whence they go forth, as far as the lowest part of the testis, and incise the peritoneum as far as the foramen by which the vessels are transmitted.

Opening of the exterior tunic of the testes and display of the seminal vessels.

In addition, when you have inserted a little knife into the foramen along the length of the stylus, incise the first special tunic [tunica vaginalis] as far as the lowest region of the testis. Then, putting the little knife aside, and having distended the tunic, examine its origin from the peritoneum and its strong attachment to the lowest part of the testis as well as to the [cremaster] muscle of the testis, for in this tunic its nature, course, and shape come into view together with slender branches running in numerous series from the vein and artery. Dispensing with the tunic, and carefully lifting and turning the testis and vessels this way and that, distinguish the vein and artery from such things as the coterminus vessel [epididymus] carrying semen to the higher part of the testis.

Appendix

Examination of the spermatic vessels near the testis and of the testis itself.

In order that you may learn exactly the insertion of the vein and artery, free the vessel carrying the semen from the tunic closest to the body of the testis [tunica albuginea], not entirely but as far as that part nearest the terminations of the vein and artery. The vessel itself will be freed easily if you make a transverse incision between the testis and that vessel at its origin, using a very sharp razor. By this procedure you will clearly observe the twisted nature of this vessel and its origin at the attachment of the testis. However, no hollow will be observable in it nor [any way for] it to receive semen from the testis, for with no apparent passage extending into it from the testis there is no ready explanation unless there is some porosity where it is attached to the testis. When the vessel carrying the semen has been freed in this way from the innermost covering of the testis and the little branches of the twisted vein and artery have been removed, the covering closest to the body of the testis will come more clearly into view. In order that they may be completely observed, compress the blood from the twisted vessels toward the testis, then shut off those vessels by a binding so that the blood may not flow back, and dissect the testis along its length; then, from the covering closest to the testis and from the end of the twisted vessels, observe how branches run to the substance of the testis, how that tunic is attached to the testis, [556] and what the substance of the testis is. These things must be examined first in one testis and then in the other. At first they will hardly be apparent to everyone, since hitherto no one has investigated them. Therefore the same procedure must not be constantly employed, but when you have tried that method mentioned for the right testis, it is desirable that you investigate the left according to your own plan. When the testes have been examined in this way and no part of them overlooked, the muscles and body of the penis, the bladder, and the urinary passages, the remainder of the course of the vessels carrying the semen, the insertion with the prostate gland, the veins, arteries, and nerves of all must be dissected.

Examination of the muscles of the penis.

When the legs of the cadaver have been pulled apart and, as I have advised, the skin removed from the interfemoral region, first concern yourself with the two [bulbocavernosi] muscles extending from the orbicular muscle of the rectum intestine into the root of the penis and especially into the common passage for urine and semen; then remove the two others [ischiocavernosi] which take origin from the lower seat of the pubic bones and are inserted into the bodies of the penis; thereafter examine the origin of the bodies of the penis, dividing as closely as possible with a sharp knife the right body from the bone whence it arises.

Origin of the bodies of the penis and examination of the veins, arteries, and nerves extending thither.

When the veins, arteries, and nerves running into the penis have been given a cursory examination, they must be separated from the pubic bones. This can be done readily if the body of the bladder is cut away with a knife from the part of the peritoneum surrounding the pubic bone. Then completely divide the cartilage of the pubic bones by a straight incision with a very blunt knife, for a razor, no matter how dull, is not well suited to that task.

Here the pubic bones must be separated.

Then, with one leg of the cadaver remaining on the table and the other hanging down from it, arrange the cadaver so that its sacrum rests on the side of the table,

357

Appendix

and, with the legs forcibly separated, divide the pubic bones from each other to a width of three or four fingers; you will not do this properly if you remove any portion of the pubic bones, and if it is done improperly and you injure many muscles in addition to other things, the bones will not be of any use to you later for the preparation of a skeleton.

Examination of the urinary passages at the bladder and of the vessels carrying semen to the glandular body of the bladder.

When the cartilage of the pubic bones has been dissected and the bones forcibly separated, first the urinary passages from the kidneys must be freed from the membranes by which they are covered and traced as far as the body of the bladder; then the vessels carrying semen must likewise be laid bare of the very fatty membranes with which they are covered and bent downward from the amplitude of the peritoneum toward the pubic bones as far as the prostate gland. In that task it is necessary that the bladder be grasped now in the right and now in the left hand of a colleague, and this expecially when you seek the arrangement of the vena cava and aorta in this region.

The distribution of the vena cava and aorta under the os sacrum.

These matters must now be considered: first, the branches that the vein and artery extend to the lumbar vertebrae, spine, adominal muscles, and peritoneum are easily found if you bend the vein and artery strongly now to this side, now to that; also, with a blunt knife seek the nerves that are carried under them, and finally follow them to the organs in which they are inserted. After their bipartite division extending above the os sacrum, the branches of the vein and artery will come into view if you will always keep their roots in mind; and with a blunt knife, lest you injure any part of the branches, follow their progress and course, which you may do very easily if you relate our illustrations of the vessels very carefully to your work. When you have observed these things very diligently, separate the left body of the penis from the pubic bone, and as suitably as possible divide the bladder and its neck from the terminus of the rectum intestine to which it adheres by the aid of strong fibres, meanwhile cutting away the veins and arteries running into the bladder and penis. This dissection will not be difficult if first you intercept the vessels by ligatures. Now when the bladder and penis have been removed together, lay the other leg on a small block, and you will finally observe the course of the spermatic vein and artery toward the testis, and of the vessel carrying the semen from the testis to the prostate gland whereby you may note very exactly the relation of the spermatic vessels.

Examination of the muscle of the neck of the bladder and of the fundus and neck of the bladder.

After this, examine the muscle placed at the neck of the bladder [sphincter urethrae]; then insert a long stylus from the glans of the penis to the fundus of the bladder and, with a knife, divide the passage of the bladder along the stylus from the glans to the fundus of the bladder so that at the same time you may observe the cavity of the bladder, its covering, the insertion of the urinary passages, and the common passage for urine and semen extended to the penis. Pierce the urinary passage extending from the kidneys into the bladder and insert a stylus as far as the fundus of the bladder so that in its fundus you may see the little membranes attached to the mouth of that passage; it is also desirable to insert a stylus from the fundus of the bladder into its passages. At your pleasure you may divide the glandular body [prostate] which receives the implantation of the vessels carrying

Appendix

semen and discover in what way those vessels are introduced into the bladder's passage.

The bodies of the penis.

Finally, with a knife separate the neck of the bladder from the two bodies of the penis as far as the glans, and then separate the two bodies from each other and observe their shape and their nature at the glans. In order to learn their substance exactly, make transverse, longitudinal, and lateral sections of the penis.

The muscles of the rectum intestine.

Now, having put aside the bladder and its appendages, examine the three muscles of the rectum intestine, the veins led here from the portal vein, and the branches of the vena cava in this region. [557] When you have done this, put aside the dissected end of the rectum intestine. Then, with a double ligature, cut off the vena cava where it crosses the diaphragm, and especially the branches approaching the leg, so that you may simultaneously lift out the kidneys from the venter, if you have left them in the body, along with all the veins and arteries.

Examination of the origin of the peritoneum.

Thus you will learn the origin of the peritoneum, and also of the muscles and nerves seeking the leg, if, having kept them intact, you decide to deal with them now. Moreover, the liver, as I said before, must be kept thus far uninjured until you deal with the heart and the organs of respiration. This is the system for dealing with the organs of nutrition and generation in man, but in woman it must be as will follow.

The administration of the special parts in woman.
Examination of the breast.

First, the nature of the breasts must be observed, and an incision must be made in the skin from the root of the neck downward—as in man—to the umbilicus; then, from the root of the neck, following the clavicle, another incision [must be made] to the point of the shoulder, and, as in other parts of the body, the skin must be freed from the breasts and separated from the fat. When the skin has been removed and consideration has been given to the branches of the veins extended here from those in the arm, remove the right breast from the muscle adducting the arm to the chest and examine the branches of the veins and arteries rising into the chest from those derived from the muscles resting on the thorax. When the body of the breast has been freed from the thorax and the fat very carefully separated on all sides, the substance of the breast may be learned by making various sections through its body. These things can also be investigated in man, for if he is swarthy in color and somewhat fat by nature he displays the same substance. Then the veins and arteries lying hidden under the recti abdominis muscles are the same in both [man and woman], even though things must be investigated in woman, and the rest of the procedure must also be continued as far as the common origin of the spermatic vessels.

The site of the uterus and bladder must be observed here.

Now you are concerned with the origin of the female spermatic vessels. Before you dissect anything, use your hands to find the uterus and bladder as well as the testes [ovaries] and muscles, and the veins and arteries extended to the fundus and the vagina. When the legs have been drawn apart, make an incision in the skin on both sides from the os pubis along the colliculi of the pudendum as

359

Appendix

far as the fundament, so that the groin may be conveniently stripped of skin; that skin that has been left in the middle of the incision must also be separated from the pubic bones as far as the pudendum, but that of the vulva remains as yet attached.

Examination of the spermatic vessels.

Divide the cartilage of the pubic bones as I taught it ought to be done in man, and having separated them as much as possible with a knife, and as far as the testis [ovary], lay bare the spermatic vein and artery of the right side from the fat which is covered by a membrane, watching lest you injure the extended branches before they turn into the higher part of the fundus of the uterus. After you have followed this turning as far as the testis, just as in the insertion in man, examine the course of the spermatic vessel, its insertion into the uterus, and the substance and form of the testis, freeing that vessel from the fat to which adheres that membrane closely resembling the shape of a bat's wing.

The veins seeking the lower part of the fundus of the uterus and its neck [vagina].

After you have observed these things on one or the other side, give attention to the veins and arteries approaching the lower part of the fundus of the uterus, vagina, and bladder, which are extended from the spermatic vessels into the uterus and all its parts, since in them the veins and arteries swell abnormally.

Examination of the foetus and its coverings.

If the cadaver of a gravid woman has been obtained, and if you desire to observe the uterus with the foetus and its coverings, with a very sharp razor make an incision penetrating the peritoneum from the mucronate cartilage [xiphoid process] of the sternum to the pubic bone; then another on each side from the umbilicus to the ilia. In this way the uterus in this body becomes apparent for inspection; and if you press it down on one side, the veins and arteries inserted into it will appear abnormally swollen, so that neither their arrangement nor origin can lie concealed. Observe these veins and arteries carefully, as well as those ascending under the rectus abdominis muscle, and with a razor make a shallow incision along the length of the uterus, taking care lest you penetrate more deeply than its thickness. [558] After this incision, undertake two others, one on each side and at right angles to the first. Seizing the edges of the incisions with the finger tips, separate them somewhat from one another, and by degrees, with the hands alone, strip the covering of the uterus from the secundine [placenta] and the mouths of the veins and arteries extending from the uterus into the secundine, which you may do very easily in those very close to parturition. Remove the foetus with its coverings from the uterus and place it in a pail of water, washing away the somewhat blackish and greenish liquid which issues from the ruptured mouths of the vessels and covers the secundine. Now, with the finger tips or a little knife, carefully examine the substance of the secundine and whatever things in it ought to be observed, but first notice whether a membrane covers the whole foetus or is only in the form of a wide girdle produced from a substance like that of the spleen. Also observe how the substance of the secundine is attached strongly to the external surface of that covering we compare to a sausage and call the second or middle covering ["allantois"].

When you have carefully examined the nature of the covering, remove the foetus and examine that second covering; observe how it resembles the exterior and note that it goes around the whole foetus, and how by penetrating it here

Appendix

and there with a knife you can cause the foetal urine to flow forth. Unwrap the covering from the foetus and allow it to hang from the vessels of the umbilicus until you learn the relationship of the innermost covering ["amnion"] of the foetus, containing sweat. When this covering has been perforated and evacuated of the sweat, remove it from the foetus and you will be able also to separate it from the umbilicus; by separating the umbilical vessels from one another you will in particular discover that passage [urachus] by which the foetal urine is transmitted into the second covering. You will find this readily if, with a knife, you divide the veins and arteries where they are closest to the umbilicus, and you will find the passage existing in the middle of them.

Examination of the umbilical vessels.

When these umbilical vessels have been cut away with the foetal covering and the foetus has been stretched out on the table, with a knife or razor make an incision from the clavicles through the costal cartilages as far as the pubic bone, somewhat to the left and extending downward to the thoracic and peritoneal cavities. Then you can easily trace the vein from the umbilicus into the liver, the arteries to those branches where they are inserted, and the urinary passage leading to the fundus of the bladder; now you have completed the entire procedure of dissection of the foetus, unless it seems desirable to investigate whether or not there is some special connection in the foetus extending from the vena cava to the pulmonary vein and from the aorta into the pulmonary artery.

Examination of the acetabula [cotyledons].

When the uterus of the sheep or goat has been dissected to whatever degree seems desirable, the acetabula ought to be investigated. And it will be rewarding to examine the cavity of the uterus which in the nonpregnant cow is filled with tubercles not unlike those from which a little later blood will flow forth; or, if a uterus of that sort is dissected shortly after conception, then it is observed to have sinuses which were first given the name of acetabula by the ancient professors of dissection.

In the present chapter we have completed the dissection of the parts presented in this fifth book, and we leave the body in the course of its dissection since it will be useful for the demonstration of the remaining parts which we have not yet discussed.

7. BOOK VI. HOW TO DISSECT THE HEART, LUNGS, AND THE REST OF THE ORGANS SERVING RESPIRATION.

CHAPTER XVI [7]

You may pursue the anatomical investigation in that cadaver you used for the organs described in the previous book, since the cadaver can be suitably employed for this dissection and for that described in the seventh book. Hence you may display the entire human structure to others in the same body with economy of cadavers, although I believe it impossible for you to learn everything exactly for the first time by dissection of only one body. To continue the dissection from the preceding book, place a prop under the neck to stretch it and cause the head to hang rearward. I usually use bricks for this purpose, placing them, with their longer, narrower side resting on the table, under the neck with the head depressed.

Appendix

The dissection of the muscles and vessels.

As I taught in the second book, when the face and whole anterior part of the neck have been bared of skin, on one side I deal with the muscles of the face that move the skin of the forehead and eyelids, then with those of the cheeks, lips, and nasal alae; on the other side, with the branches of veins, arteries, and nerves. When you demonstrate the muscles of the face in that way I have advised, give your attention to those that are special to the hyoid bone and to those carried from the pectoral bone [sternum] to the first laryngeal cartilage which resembles a shield [thyroid]. Then free the muscle adducting the arm to the chest [pectoralis major] from the pectoral bone [sternum] and clavicles, and that [muscle] inserted from the clavicle into the first rib. In addition, separate the muscle adducting the scapula to the chest [pectoralis minor], and, as I remarked in regard to observation of veins, arteries, and nerves, investigate the muscles on merely one side and the veins, arteries, and nerves on the other. If they should escape your memory, refer to the third and fourth books for their arrangement, for if I were again to discuss it here, this section would be greatly increased in size. After this, dissect those muscles that ascend from the sternum and clavicles to the mammillary [mastoid] process of the head, but do so in such a way that they are preserved intact, hanging from the bones into which they are inserted, and so afterward may be related to the remaining number of muscles of the joints demonstrated. In the appropriate place in the second book I have fully discussed how each must be dissected and what must be observed in the course of the dissection.

Freeing the clavicles from the sternum.

Now with a sharp knife free the clavicles from the sternum, dividing the strong ligaments by which they are attached to the sternum, but taking care lest the knife be driven too deeply and injure the vessels lying under this joint. Examine that cartilage that, more than any other articular cartilage, intervenes between the clavicle and the sinus of the sternum; put this aside so that later, if you desire, you may use it for the articulation of the skeleton. Forcibly raise the freed cartilages from the sternum and bend the first rib outward from the sternum, for thus the cartilage of the first thoracic rib, where it is continuous with the bone of the rib, comes into view. This must be freed from the rib with a thin knife, but here you must also be careful lest the knife go too deeply and injure anything in the root of the neck.

Freeing the costal cartilages, with the sternum, from their bones.
Examination of the [pleural] membranes intercepting the thoracic cavity.

When you have dissected the cartilage of the first rib, with a knife or, if you prefer, a razor, separate all the rest in sequence from the ribs, and divide the intercostal muscles with a continuous incision as far as the base of the thorax. Now that the sternum with its cartilages has been freed from the rib bones, it must be bent somewhat upward and then to the right and to the left, and the intercepting [pleural] membranes [600] very close to the sternum must be examined as well as the site of the heart. Then separate the diaphragm by a transverse section from the sternum with its connected cartilages, and by degrees raise it upward by the mucronate cartilage and separate it from the intercepting membranes. When you have done this, bend back the sternum toward the head, and with a blunt knife seek among the little membranes for the vein and artery creeping forward under the thymus gland. When you have secured them separately with threads, remove the sternum with its vessels from the thorax, observing the appearance of the membrane lining the ribs and the nature of the intercostal muscles between the cartilages. If those muscles have not otherwise been examined, after the dissection of the heart replace the sternum for a little time if you desire to display together all the muscles moving the thorax.

In order that those things that remain to be dealt with in the thorax may be demonstrated more readily, with a hook I usually pull away here and there the membrane lining the ribs and separate it with my hands from the lung, if it adheres to any part of that by fibres. Furthermore, by piercing some interval of the ribs to which the lung may be attached, I usually demonstrate in what way man's thorax may be pierced without cessation of respiration or of movement of the lung. Formerly when the intercostal muscles had been divided, I usually broke the ribs almost in their middle, which is easily done if separately they are grasped firmly with the hands and twisted or bent forcibly. However, after I discovered that easy method of preparing the skeleton, I preferred to keep the ribs intact so that they might serve for its construction, and to twist all the ribs at the same time outwardly as much as possible with my hands and then, with the intercostal muscles divided to the greatest extent, gradually to separate the ribs from one another. In this way a sufficiently patent amplitude of the thorax results, especially if you place a stone or something round under the middle of the thorax, by which that rounded part of the back extending outward from the cavity of the thorax is pushed inward and the opening between the ribs of the right and left side is increased.

The nerves of the diaphragm.

With the ribs separated in the one way or broken in the other, the organs of the thorax must be dealt with in order. First, with a little knife, from the [thymus] gland to the region of the diaphragm, separate the nerve on the right from the right membrane dividing the thorax; then if you wish, also separate the left, which you will see to be extended together with the vein advanced from the root of the neck; divide the nerve near the diaphragm, laying it back toward the neck so that afterward you may see its origin. Then with a little knife separate the intercepting membranes from one another along the length of the thorax, and, after freeing them from the pericardium, observe their connection to the diaphragm and the arrangement of veins and arteries in them, and remove them from the thorax.

Examination of the covering of the heart.

Now I must warn you lest some notable vessel be injured, for the branches running through the membranes and woven into the covering of the heart do not produce a large amount of blood even if divided. With the hands, move the heart and its covering back and forth and examine completely the site and shape of the covering. For that inspection it is helpful if the sternum has been somewhat raised, and I wish it to be done with the heart as yet unmoved for the sake of the intercepting membranes. Also, press the lobes of the lung with the hands so that their number, site, and shape may be investigated, and finally that you may know that no part of the lung in man supports the vena cava where it exists between the diaphragm and the heart, but that the vein penetrates the diaphragm and the covering of the heart immediately and without an interval, and that in man where the vein passes the covering the latter is extensively attached to the diaphragm. These things which wholly contradict the conclusions of Galen have been taken from the completely trustworthy book of man, and none of them should be overlooked or you will provide an opportunity for those

Appendix

gossiping pettifoggers who very sharply protect the doctrines of Galen when there is no dissection, but who, with a body present and dissection taking place, are silent as if some one had cut out their tongues. When you have observed the lung briefly, divide the covering of the heart by a long incision and, having taken up its liquid with a sponge, resect the covering from the vessels of the heart, being careful not to damage the origin of the left recurrent nerve.

Examination of the distribution of the vena cava through the thorax and root of the neck.

So that you may examine the transit of the vena cava through the diaphragm and its course through the thorax, make an incision as far as the trunk of the vein, being careful lest you injure the roots of the two branches of the vena cava running together into it; then, ascending a little, without any dissection you will observe where the vena cava is joined to the right auricle of the heart. So also you will find that the azygos vein arises from the right side of the vena cava above the base of the heart, and you will learn its branches and course better if first you raise the right side of the lung toward the left and then twist the left toward the right side; these things become apparent without dissection although with the heart and lungs removed you can observe them still more precisely. Such matters should not be examined cursorily, but you must investigate thoroughly and carefully the artifice of nature in the origin and course of the azygos vein, and determine whether, as in sheep and pigs, [601] a vein is sometimes extended into the left side, arising near the connection of the vena cava to the heart. The distribution of the vena cava in the root of the neck must be investigated with a blunt knife by which the underlying gland [thymus] is separated, and you need employ no other knowledge than that provided in my delineations of the veins which you ought to study with great care so that you do not cut any vein. When you have discovered the arrangement of the vena cava, strongly compress the blood in the jugular and humeraria [cephalic v.] and then in the vena cava where it gives off the azygos vein; tie them off with cords and remove from the body that blood remaining within the ligatures of the veins. Then with the blood cleaned away, you must turn to dissection of the branches of the aorta and the recurrent nerves.

Distribution of the aorta through the thorax, root of neck, and neck, and examination of the recurrent nerves.

Grasping the heart in your hands, observe the roots of the pulmonary artery, pulmonary vein, and aorta where they are closest to the base of the heart; this is most easily done if you consider their colors and locations. The pulmonary artery is close to the right auricle, whitish, seems to issue somewhat toward the left, and is highest among the vessels of the heart. The pulmonary vein is darker and issues lower than the others, lies hidden near the left auricle, and does not display such an extended course. The aorta is seen to be somewhat hidden in the middle of the base of the heart under the pulmonary artery. When first you have observed this, having consulted my delineation of the recurrent nerves with the arteries, examine all the branches of the aorta, of which the higher ones nearer the root of the neck will be apparent without further dissection, unless perhaps there are some remains of the gland there. The trunk, which is reflected to the back, will not be seen unless the left side of the lung is raised toward the right.

To see the recurrent nerves, after you have dissected those common laryngeal muscles originating from the higher part of the sternum and inserting into the

Appendix

shieldlike cartilage [thyroid]—if you did not dissect them with the muscles of
the hyoid bone before you separated the sternum—with a little knife gradually
free the nerve of the sixth pair, first on the right side along the length of the
carotid artery; examine its branch which is extended to the roots of the ribs, as
you approach the thorax, and gives off shoots to the muscles arisen from the top
of the sternum. At the same time trace the nerve near the artery extending to the
right axilla, which reflects three shoots to it—although sometimes two or even
one—so that you may carefully free the nearby membranes with a sharp little
knife; with a blunt knife, by pulling the membrances while cutting them, you
may injure the nerves, although with a sharp one you can incautiously cut the
shoots with the membranes. When you have found the origins of the shoots, with
a sharp knife free that nerve extended along the side of the trachea from the
membrane attached to it and from the trachea itself by a long incision between
the nerve and the trachea. When the nerve has been freed in this way, grasp it
with the fingertips of your left hand and raise it slightly from the trachea; with
your right hand raise the trunk of the sixth pair where it is extended to the
carotid artery, and then, moving your hands in turn now upward now
downward, examine the reflection and nature of the recurrent nerve. In the same
way it is desirable to separate the left trunk of the sixth pair from the carotid
artery of the left side, and to investigate the branches it extends to the muscles
originating from the higher part of the sternum and to the roots of the ribs.

When those branches it extends to the covering of the lung have been observed, and that provided along the left side of the trunk of the pulmonary artery
to the base of the heart has been carefully considered as far as the trunk of the
aorta, and then reflected to the back, the nerve of the sixth pair of that side must
be traced and the branches forming the recurrent nerve must be identified with
a sharp knife. When you have seen these things, extend a blunt stylus under the
trunk of the artery toward the left side of the trachea and, with a somewhat
smaller stylus, slightly separate the trunk of the artery from the back to which
it is very firmly connected. Then free the nerve from the trachea as far as the
trunk of the aorta and display it, turned back with both hands, as on the right
side. The rest of the arrangement of the nerves of the sixth pair to the stomach
will not be seen unless the lung has been removed.

Inflation of the lung.

Now, if you desire, make an opening in the cartilages of the trachea and place a
reed in it; then, with the trachea compressed above the opening, attempt to inflate the lung; if inflated, it displays its shape more clearly and the heart is wholly
enclosed.

Examination of the right ventricle of the heart
and the membranes [valves] of its orifice.

Now, putting aside the lung, with a razor make an incision in the heart from the
root of the right auricle as far as its tip, penetrating into its right ventricle. Then,
while the ventricle is distended with your fingers, wipe away the blood with a
sponge. The vena cava and the pulmonary artery must be compressed so that the
blood flows into the ventricle, and afterward is sponged out. With the blood removed, examine the cavity of the right ventricle; then the three membranes
placed at the orifice of the vena cava must be investigated with a stylus. In order
that they may come fully into view, introduce a little knife from the right
ventricle into the vena cava and make an incision from the ventricle through the

Appendix

body of the auricle as far as the vein; with the ventricle distended, the membranes will be clearly seen, and by this procedure you will readily understand the cavity and nature of the auricle if you invert it.

When you have observed the orifice of the vena cava, [602] the origin of the coronary vein will also appear; if you insert a stylus of soft lead into it you will observe how it girdles the base and provides branches for the surface of the body of the heart. Here I also desire that you introduce a stylus from the cavity of the vena cava into the azygos vein and study its origin from the vena cava; and [then consider] the ridiculous reasoning of our Aesculapians who declare that in an inflammation of the eight lower ribs of each side Hippocrates asserts that blood must not be withdrawn because the heart would seize the blood from the azygos vein, hence nothing could be withdrawn by emission of blood from the vein. As if it were not extremely clear to you, dissecting, that the heart opposes no obstacle to the emission of blood in an inflammation of the eight lower intervals of the ribs, and therefore that blood is emitted; and that Hippocrates was not so stupid as to believe that the eight lower ribs are under the diaphragm or was unaware that inflammation of this region produces tension as far as the clavicle. But, lest this account extend further, I shall call a halt to my conclusion respecting the vein that must be cut in *morbus lateralis*, although, by Hercules, I believe this matter ought never be considered except with investigation of the present veins, nor can it be opposed except through ignorance of the veins and the distorted opinions of authors.

Examination of the origin of the vena cava.

As soon as you have inserted a stylus into the azygos vein, a long and thick rod must be placed in the vena cava, which you may drive without difficulty directly through the vena cava as far as the lowest venter, and you will learn how beautifully Galen and other professors of dissection were deceived when they considered the vena cava to arise from the gibbosity of the liver by one trunk and then, like the aorta, to be divided into two, of which the one extends to the lower parts and the other to the upper. But when you deal with the liver you will see these things more clearly, although there is no reason why you may not now resect the diaphragm as much as possible from the body, and twist the liver to the left so that its posterior region comes into view. Keep the rod inserted in the vena cava from where it faces the heart as far as the region where veins are offered to the kidneys, and notice that the substance of the liver does not cover the vena cava wholly in the posterior part; with a little knife divide the vena cava along the length of the rod, and investigate the orifices of the veins extending from the vena cava to the liver. Then recall those leading professors of anatomy who relied too much on the words of Galen and, reviewing one by one their arguments regarding the origin of the veins, urge your students not to navigate out of commentaries, and commend truth alone to them, not authority or assertions *ex cathedra*.

Examination of the orifice and the membranes
[valves] of the pulmonary artery.

Turning again to dissection of the heart, with a finger or a stylus seek the orifice of the pulmonary artery in the higher part of the right ventricle, and with that little knife that has been inserted, make an incision in the right ventricle as far as the pulmonary artery. When this has been done, and whatever blood there may be has been wiped away, the orifice of the pulmonary artery with its membranes comes into view. Lift the membranes with a stylus so that you may

366

consider them more precisely, and examine the course of the pulmonary artery into the lungs. The coverings forming the artery will easily be seen if you examine the edges or lips of the incision.

Examination of the left ventricle of the heart and its vessels and membranes.

Open the left ventricle of the heart by a similarly long incision made from the root of the left auricle to the point of the heart, and wipe away the blood as in the right ventricle. First observe the amplitude, next the thickness of the substance of the heart in this region, and afterward with a stylus you will easily find the two membranes placed at the orifice of the pulmonary vein, and here you will observe that they press together upon the constriction of the heart. In order that they may appear more clearly, insert a little knife into the orifice of the pulmonary vein, make an incision as far as its cavity, then, with the orifice open and distended, examine the membranes and with a lead stylus seek the first distributions of the pulmonary vein into the lungs. You will find the orifice of the aorta and the membranes attached to it if you insert your finger into the highest part of the left ventricle behind the membrane of the pulmonary artery which is very close to the septum of the ventricle, for it goes under the aorta. Then, with a little knife introduced along the finger into the orifice of the artery, make an incision from the ventricle into the amplitude of the artery. When you do this, and inspect the membranes of the aorta in their site where they rest upon the body of the vessels, you will see the origin of the coronary artery. Now nothing remains for observation in the heart unless, perhaps by dissection of its substance here and there and with the roots of the aorta and pulmonary artery dissected, you decide to seek that bone which professors of anatomy have ascribed to the heart.

Examination of the cartilaginous substance of the heart.

If you find no bone except the aforesaid cartilaginous roots of the vessels, resect them from the remainder of the heart's substance so that they may be stored away with the cartilaginous articulations of the clavicles special to the composition of the bones.

The trachea. The lung.

Now, the heart having been put aside, examine the trachea—preserving the larynx—its cartilages, and the membranes by which they are attached to one another and then its first arrangement in the lungs. When this has been discovered, dissect a lobe wholly from the rest of the lung and insert a stylus into the root of the pulmonary artery and the roots of the pulmonary vein and trachea and, with the membrane of the lung avulsed, investigate the shoots of those branches [603] and the nature of the distribution. This is greatly assisted by rupture of the membrane of that lobe, and by compression of the lobe between two blocks of wood so that the substance of the lung separates from the vessels to which it is attached.

The oesophagus.

Now separate the trachea from its head, and draw it downward from the oesophagus; remove the lung entirely from the thorax, and investigate the course of the oesophagus which comes into view without dissection, with the nerves of the sixth pair enfolding it when the lung has been removed. That you may see the arrangement of the nerves of the mouth of the stomach, the diaphragm must

Appendix

be freed from the oesophagus of which the insertion, if the stomach has as yet been preserved in the body, must be investigated. In addition make a hole somewhere in the oesophagus where it creeps through the neck, insert a reed, and attempt as much as possible to inflate the stomach. Then, with the oesophagus divided near the root of the larynx, draw it with the stomach, or alone if you have already removed the stomach, from the body, at the same time examining those glands that are almost in the middle of its course.

The liver.

Now it is time—unless you have done it already—to separate the liver from the diaphragm and then to remove it from the body. When you do this carefully consider its shape and, thrusting a little knife into the now-flaccid vena cava, open it by a long incision so that it exactly reveals its substance in its transit of the liver and the orifices of its branches into the liver. When you see those two special orifices, thrust the stylus as deeply as possible into one and, having removed the binding by which hitherto you have closed off the portal vein, insert another stylus into its branch, following the passage of the stylus of the vena cava into the liver; then with a blunt knife seek to scrape the substance of the liver from those branches that contain styluses so you may learn the arrangement of the veins through the substance of the body of the liver. Observe the little passages of the gall bladder between the two branches distended by the styluses, and then invert the gall bladder, scraped from the body of the liver, and consider it carefully by itself. Observe the entrance and insertion of the vein led from the umbilicus into the liver, also giving attention to the bodies of the thoracic vertebrae so that with a little knife you may open the large artery along their length and see the orifices of the branches it provides on both sides for the ribs. When those branches have been dissected, separate the artery from the body, and consider the branches of the azygos vein, also freeing it from the bodies of the vertebrae.

Examination of those structures which are extended to the bodies of the vertebrae.

Now there is exposed a branch of the sixth pair of cerebral nerves, which extends along the roots of the ribs to the organs enfolded by the peritoneum. So that you may observe the nervules by which that branch is augmented, draw away from the thoracic vertebrae the tunic lining the ribs so that all the ribs may be seen bare. Where you have removed from the ribs the tunic lining the thoracic cavity, by driving the point of a little knife into the bone of a rib you will observe the tunic which separately enwraps the ribs, that, I say, which some skilled in dissection call the second tunic lining the ribs.

Examination of the muscles moving the arm, scapula, thorax, head, and back.

When in this way you have attended to all these things enwrapped by the peritoneum and the tunic lining the ribs, if it seems desirable attempt as much as possible to replace the ribs in their positions, and, having replaced the sternum with the cartilages attached to it as well as the clavicles, very carefully attempt to place in their sites the muscles that earlier hung from their insertions, the first of those moving the thorax, the first of those moving the arm, the first of those moving the scapula, and that which is carried from the sternum and clavicle into the mammillary [mastoid] process of the head.

Appendix

The temporal and masseter muscles.

When you have done this according to that arrangement I explained in the second book, on the one side deal with all the muscles moving the arm and scapula; then all that control the movements of the thorax and those that serve the motions of the head and back, and finally the temporal and masseter. After the anatomy of the brain you may dissect the muscles moving the forearm, hand, and fingers. I shall not recall those muscles at length, seriatim, and individaully, since you are aware that they were dealt with fully in the second book. On the other side of the cadaver you may carefully investigate the arrangement of the nerves, since that is done very easily if you are acquainted with their description and are skilled in dissection; although afterward I also consider the procedure for a number of vessels and nerves that are thought to be a little more difficult.

The opening of the mouth and examination of the organs placed in the throat.

Now you must examine the mouth, and since you have considered everything external to the face it is necessary that the mouth be opened. You can do this no way better than with a knife inserted by degrees into the lower part of the lower jaw, struck with a hammer, and splitting the bone. In that way, because of the fracture, you will spoil the lower jaw so far as concerns its use in the preparation of the skeleton, but if with the jaw intact you loosen the bone at the temporal joint on one side, and bend it to the other, you will have clearly available for dissection those things you propose to deal with in the mouth. Therefore, with the bone separated in this way, with the back of a strong knife placed in the division and then twisted, you will somewhat separate the bones from one another; then, grasping each with a hand, forcefully twist outwardly and downward and you will open the mouth. Now insert an obliquely angled stylus from the nostrils into the amplitude of the mouth and examine the nature of the uvula. With a little knife make an incision from the root of the uvula into the lining of the mouth as far as the incisor teeth, freeing it somewhat like skin from the organs resting on it. In this operation you will discover the third pair of cerebral nerves joined to the sixth, with the carotid artery and the internal jugular vein, and, if you ascend a little, also the fourth pair of cerebral nerves and some branches of the third and fifth pairs extended to the temporal muscles, providing you gradually separate one organ from another. In addition, the muscles of the tongue will be discovered, as I taught in the second book, and the branches of the nerves running into the tongue, as well as the veins and arteries, will come into view. Here you will also readily find the muscles placed in the lower jaw, that is, that one that, hidden in the mouth with the temporal and masseter, raises the jaw, and that one that originates from the process resembling a stylus and is inserted into the tip of the chin. Furthermore the tonsils and other glands placed in the throat for the distribution of the vessels are clearly apparent to you in this procedure. The laryngeal muscles, as I advised in the second book, have to be considered fully and must be carefully studied while their nerves are dissected.

And so, with the tongue, hyoid bone, larynx, and beginning of the oesophagus removed, completely free the lower jaw from the upper, not overlooking those special cartilages that, like the cartilages between the joints of the clavicles with the sternum, may be saved for construction of the skeleton. In the same way put aside the cartilages of the hyoid bone, larynx, and nasal alae for the same use. Now carefully scrape from the bone the lining of the palate and of the nostrils so that you may learn the connection of those tunics to one another. If, when dealing with the muscles moving the head and back, you do not especially observe the first pair of those moving the back, it will be very easy to do with the removal of those muscles that occupy the throat, so that by a series of dissections you may preserve intact the muscles causing motions of the head and back as far as the lower jaw and those structures contained in the throat. Although all these things ought to be apparent to anyone from the second book, as well as from what was said at the end of the first book, here the ribs must be removed as well as the sternum and the cartilages joined to it, and saved for preparation of the skeleton. You may free the skull or head from the first vertebra of the cadaver in order to learn those things that the following book will discuss, and to that end I shall describe all that must as yet be seen in the cadaver.

8. BOOK VII. DISSECTION PROCEDURE FOR THE BRAIN.

CHAPTER XVIII [8]

How the head ought to be prepared for inspection of the brain.

After you have investigated the muscles of the neck, the nerves issuing from the dorsal marrow of the neck, and the organs of the body dealing with nutrition and vital spirit, I suggest that the head be removed from the body, as I mentioned at the end of the previous book, for one that has been removed can be handled with less difficulty. Heads of decapitated men are much more suitable for this purpose, especially if through the coöperation of friendly judges and prefects you can obtain them immediately after the execution and so scarcely dead. Such a judge is Marcantonio Contarini who, by Hercules, must be looked upon as a Maecenas of students. [651] A distinguished ornament of the illustrious Venetian Senate, famous everywhere for his remarkable knowledge of philosophy and languages and his many very successful diplomatic feats, and now the very vigilant podestà of Padua, he has generously supplied me with dissection material. He himself is a studious and indefatigable spectator of the structure of the human body, like another Boëthus or Sergius of Rome.

How the skull ought to be opened for dissection of the brain.

Whatever sort the head may be, its bone must be sawed. First cut the skin to the bone with a razor or knife, preferably beginning a thumb's breadth above the eyebrows and continuing back from the temples to the most prominent part of the occiput. After this incision has been made, divide the skull along this line with a fine saw such as we use for amputation of a gangrenous limb or such as is used in the manufacture of ivory combs, but using great care lest the saw go deeper than the bone. It is advisable that the hair be not yet shaved from the head nor the ears removed so that, using both hands, your colleague may hold the head steady while it is being sawed. When you have sawed around the skull, draw the point of a blunt knife along the saw-cut to see whether any part of the bone still needs to be cut and, if so, saw that also. This operation is much easier with the help of another, but if you must work alone and fear lest the sawed edge may not be even, encircle the bare skull with a dyed cord such as those employed in the cutting of beams into lengths, and it will make a colored line around the skull to guide the saw. It is best to place the cord around the bone after you have cut the skin; the incision in the skin would not guide your hand because its margins tend to gape here and there when the head is held firmly.

When the skull has been divided in this way, and if it is without the neck and lower jaw, put it on its base on the table and, if it appears likely to fall over, place a stone or something similar on each side. If by reason of the kind of dissection the head is still attached to the body, place bricks or a block of wood under the neck and occiput so the head, bent and raised forward, may rise up to you as if resting on a base. Then place the rear edge of a strong knife into the division of the skull at the forehead, and, when this has been moved up and down for a time, separate the division a little. The same must also be done at the occiput until you consider the skull freed from the dural membrane, and then if the hair is grasped and pulled the bone will follow.

*Examination of the skin, fat, fleshy membrane, lining of the skull,
and the membrane beneath it. Here the extent
of the dural membrane must be examined.*

When the bone has been removed, with your hands you can readily remove the skin with the fat and the fleshy membrane—although here and there first freed with a knife—and then with the point of a knife investigate what is called the PERIKRANION and PERIOSTEON by the Greeks, and the little veins extended from the skin of the vertex into the skull and dural membrane of the brain, or in the reverse order. Now the dural membrane of the brain must be perforated in some part with a knife, and a reed, or a pipe or syphon such as we use for withdrawing urine, placed in the perforation, and the sides of the incision pressed together with the fingers. When the dural membrane has been inflated through the syphon you will learn how much greater its extent is than that of the mass of the brain. You need perforate only one side for, with enough air blown in, the dural membrane will be fully inflated and extended. But if you carelessly cut the dural membrane anywhere when you sawed the skull, that cut must be pressed together when the membrane is inflated lest the air escape. When another incision has been made in the membrane, insert the point of a very sharp knife into the third [superior sagittal] sinus of the dural membrane, which extends through the whole length of the head in the highest part of the membrane, and by a long incision divide it as completely as you can either from the occiput to the forehead or from the forehead to the occiput. If death of the body resulted from hanging or otherwise than by decapitation, this sinus will be observed to be filled with blood which ought to be sponged out so that you may see the shape of the extended sinus and the orifices of the branches that arise from its sides and from its lower part.

Uncovering the thin membrane [pia-arachnoid].

To lay bare the brain of its dural membrane, perforate it at the sides of the third sinus near the frontal bone and then, having inserted a stylus into that opening, with a knife guided by the stylus make an incision at the side of the sinus as far as the occipital bone. When this has been done on each side of the sinus, again perforate the dural membrane with the point of a knife near the ear and very close to the bone, and hence incise directly upward to the first incision along the length of the head. Finally, with your fingernails, raise the adjacent corners of the incisions at the vertex of the head and, pulling them downward, fold them back from the brain, observing the branches that extend from the sides of the third sinus of the dural membrane into the thin membrane of the brain, and

Appendix

from those vessels by which the sides of the dural membrane are enveloped.

When, with your hands, you have slightly separated the right side of the brain from the left, raise as high as possible from the dural membrane that septum [falx cerebri] constructed between the two sides of the cerebrum, as well as the branches ramified on either side from the third sinus of the dural membrane into the thin membrane, so that you may observe how they contribute to the life of the brain. [652] Then, with a very sharp knife, free those branches from their sinus and also that part of the dural membrane from the septum of the olfactory organ [crista galli], and when you have raised it from the brain fold it back and examine its sinus [inferior sagittal] which is extended along its whole lower region like a vein. Its origin will be considered later with other things, but now its course into the thin membrane as well as that membrane itself must be inspected.

When you have laid back the part of the dural membrane recently mentioned and have disunited the two parts of the brain, observe the long ducts [great cerebral and internal cerebral vv.] in this membrane which extend through the length of the head from the termination of the fourth [straight] sinus. Do not yet seek their origin too eagerly lest in separating the brain you accidently rupture something. Rather, when the two sides of the brain have been disunited in the posterior as much as possible, I recommend that, with the point of a very sharp knife, you divide the dural membrane where it begins to pass between the parts of cerebrum as finely as possible from that part of the dural membrane that goes between the cerebellum and the cerebrum [tentorium cerebelli], and then the fourth sinus and its offshoots will be apparent. When the cerebrum has been somewhat raised from the dural membrane going between it and the cerebellum, the little branches extended from that part of the dural membrane into the thin membrane will be seen. However, these things will be better seen when a part of the brain has been removed.

Removal of the thin membrane from the convolutions of the brain.

When those vessels that are carried along the length of the head in the thin membrane above the corpus callosum [anterior cerebral aa.] have been examined, nick the thin membrane with your nails or with a knife and then by degrees with your fingers strip it from the brain and its convolutions. The brain, freed of this membrane, displays its convolutions and how it is contained by the thin membrane, since with that stripped off it spreads out and settles downwards.

Examination of the upper surface of the corpus callosum.

Investigate the height and depth of the convolutions of the brain with your fingers or with a stylus, and with only your fingers explore the upper part of the corpus callosum and the fissures [callosal sulci] which it forms here on either side. When you find these, with a large and very sharp razor remove a large part of the brain on either side by making an incision through the right fissure close to the corpus callosum, which separates all that part of the brain above the fissure from the forehead to the occiput on the right side. If you make further incisions, the results will be disgracefully mangled.

Opening up of the right and left ventricles.

Place the part of the brain removed on the table so that the upper part of the right ventricle is exposed, for this procedure, as I have explained, divides the right ventricle, and if it has been done correctly you will have made the incision along the fissure at the right side of the corpus callosum. When the right side of the brain has been removed in this way, the same must be done on the left by an incision made through the left fissure at the corpus callosum and then removed so that the left ventricle also appears, but with the corpus callosum disturbed as little as possible.

Examination of the septum between the right and left ventricles.

After you have inspected the left and right ventricles of the brain, with the tips of the fingers you must raise the corpus callosum slightly and evenly, and, to see the septum [lucidum] or speculum of the ventricles, remove very carefully and gradually the part of the brain continuous to it on each side. If you elevate the corpus callosum in that way and then place a candle on the side opposite to that you are inspecting, unless bright daylight shines on it the septum will be visible. Now, with a knife free the corpus callosum from the brain in the anterior part where it is very close to the space between the olfactory organs, and then when it has been raised in that part draw it upward with your fingers and sever the posterior part and fold it back. Thus you will see the upper part of the septum or speculum attached to the corpus callosum, but lower than that part of the brain we compare to a tortoise or arch.

Examination of the body shaped like a tortoise [fornix].

The vaulted body, of which the upper part is now accessible from all sides, must be explored with a blunt stylus shaped to the angle of a pipette. Pass this from the right ventricle into the left, and when you have examined the body with a knife divide its anterior part [that is] attached to the substance of the brain not far from the septum; then, when it has been raised, fold it back so that its lower part, hollow like a tortoise shell, may be seen. When this vaulted body has been turned back, with a stylus thoroughly investigate its posterior origin and relationship to the right and left ventricles, and then when it has been replaced in its original position divide it by a long incision with a knife, or, better, remove it wholly. However, before you do this I recommend that you thrust a stylus under it as far as that part from which vessels or ducts extend from the fourth sinus of the dural membrane toward the anterior ventricles under the vaulted body, and examine carefully its use and the very handsome arrangement of its construction.

Examination of the right and left ventricles and of their vessels.

When it has been separated or divided by a long incision and then pulled away, give your attention to the plexus called CHOREOIDES by the Greeks, from the shape of the secundines, and to the ducts extended from the end of the fourth sinus of the dural membrane. First seek the posterior part of the ventricle with a stylus, how it extends downward and forward, and how an artery [choroidal] passes upward through it and, creeping forward, joins the other part of that duct [great cerebral v.] that, from the fourth [653] sinus of the dural membrane, goes under the tortoise and into the cerebrum. Observe that this duct advances directly above the common cavity [third ventricle] of the right and left ventricles for a longer distance and then divided extends toward the right and left ventricles of the brain until finally the aforesaid [choroidal] plexus is formed from it and from the artery. Furthermore, when you observe these ducts creeping forward from the fourth sinus of the dural membrane, also inspect those provided by the fourth sinus for the thin membrane and the lower part of the dural membrane which divides the right side of the brain from the left. When you have seen these, with a knife divide the ducts that extend from the fourth sinus under

Appendix

the vaulted structure into the ventricles of the brain, where they form the aforesaid plexuses. Lift them up and fold them gently back to avoid tearing away the little gland that I said is called KONARION by the Greeks.

The little [pineal] gland lying on the testes.

This gland comes into view when those ducts are removed, but I should wish that a sheep's brain be at hand because it displays that gland and the testes and nates [corpora quadrigemina] of the brain more distinctly than does the human. When this gland has been put back into its place, with your fingers distend the sinus common to the right and left ventricles which looks more like a mere fissure to the observer, and then observe the passage by which the pituita is carried down to the pelvis [infundibulum] from the thin membrane, as well as the origin of the passage [aqueductus cerebri] that extends from the third or common ventricle into the fourth.

The third ventricle and its passage.

When you have inspected these things, by a transverse incision in the brain remove the whole part of the cerebrum that lies on the cerebellum, taking care at the same time not to cut the ducts or arteries ascending through the posterior part of the right and left ventricles. Then there appears that part of the dural membrane dividing the cerebellum from the portion of the cerebrum resting on it, and also the part [falx cerebri] that intervenes between the right and left parts of the cerebrum.

The sinuses of the dural membrane.

Now it is time to examine the four sinuses of the dural membrane. Insert a lead stylus into the third sinus of the dural membrane which you have previously incised through its length. You will easily pass it thence into the remaining three sinuses [right, left, and straight] of this membrane if you push it first to the sides near where the higher part of the cerebellum is very close to the bone, for thus you will find the right and left or first and second sinuses. Then, if you thrust the stylus under the root of that part of the dural membrane that intervenes between the right and left parts of the cerebrum, you will discover the fourth sinus. To see these more exactly, you must open them all through their length with the point of a sharp knife.

Disclosing the cerebellum

The whole of the dural membrane above the cerebellum having been now exposed, it must be divided by a rounded incision along the bone, or by a longitudinal incision in both directions. When the cerebellum has been briefly inspected, turn your attention back to the cerebrum dividing the common cavity of the right and left ventricles and inspect the course of the pituita and more exactly with a stylus. To observe the passage of the common cavity or third ventricle of the cerebrum extended into the cavity of the cerebellum, insert a bent stylus into the passage and let it drop gently into the cerebellum. A heavier stylus curved like a pipette, even when not pushed through the course of the passage, will slip down into the cerebellum. While the stylus is yet in the passage, with your fingers separate the cerebellum a little from the testes until you can see the stylus between the cerebellum and the testes themselves, for then, and especially in the sheep's brain, you will learn what resembles the testes and what the nates.

374

Appendix

Examination of the testes and nates [corpora quadrigemina].

When you have observed this, following the stylus with a knife, divide the testes and nates so that that passage extending from the common cavity of the right and left ventricles to the cerebellum comes into view, and that passage that carries down the pituita from the cerebrum to the pelvis is made a little clearer to the sight. Then you can pick up the thin membrane of the cerebellum with a hook and examine the vein [internal cerebral] that extends from its ducts into the posterior and lower part of the anterior ventricles. You will find this vein very easily if you seek it beside the connection of the front part of the cerebellum with the cerebrum, which occurs especially through the interposition of this vein.

Conjunction of the dorsal marrow with the cerebellum.

To recognize the conjunction of the cerebellum with the dorsal marrow, the head must be bent forward almost on its face, then, with your hand placed between the cerebellum and dural membrane of the cerebrum joined to the occipital bone, pull the cerebellum forward and downward until it falls wholly free from the dorsal marrow. In this procedure you will be able to see the venules and ducts extending into the cerebellum from the origins of the first and second sinuses of the dural membrane, and the veins and arteries creeping through the transverse processes of the cervical vertebrae, as well as the origin of the dorsal marrow from the brain itself, its shape and its cavity which, with that of the cerebellum, forms the fourth ventricle.

Examination of the fourth ventricle.

When the head has been put back and the cerebellum turned forward, observe its sinus [fourth ventricle] and the parts by which it is connected to the dorsal marrow, and especially the display of its beautiful convolutions and windings. From these as a guide you will be led to the two apices of the convolution resembling worms and the terminations of the convolutions extended lengthwise through the middle of the cerebellum.

The vermiform processes.

These will appear very clearly if, by a lengthwise incision made on both sides of these convolutions, you free them from the rest of the cerebellar substance and place what has been excised on the table. [654] The remainder will appear to you as a worm similar to those that drop from willow trees in the spring or like silkworms before they enclose themselves in a sheath, and still more so after they have been enclosed for some time but have not yet gnawed through their sheath. If you have not removed all those middle convolutions together but merely cut off the ends, you can demonstrate two vermiform processes of the cerebellum, an anterior and a posterior. However, you must not acquire a picture of the vermiform processes only when cut off in this way, but will also find it very profitable to examine them in the cerebellum itself when it has been removed from the origin of the dorsal marrow.

Examination of the pairs of nerves.

When the parts of the cerebellum have been inspected, the pairs of nerves must be investigated, and to do this rapidly insert your hand between the cerebrum and the frontal bone and gradually raise the brain so that first you see the processes of the brain usually called mammillary [frontal pole], then the processes that serve the olfactory organ and which must be raised from their sinuses with a stylus or a finger and folded back with the brain; in this operation it will be useful to

375

bend back the head toward the occiput, for thus the complex origin of those processes can be well displayed. At the same time the origins of the optic nerves come into sight as well as their conjunction, and under them the pelvis constructed for the pituita of the brain. Then the entry of the arteries into the amplitude of the dural membrane appears, which are taken partly into the thin membrane, and partly extended into the right and left ventricles of the cerebrum. Here also separate the thin membrane from the brain so that you may see the exact arrangement of those arteries and that the terminations of the ventricles end in convolutions, but not in the olfactory organs and optic nerves, and that the pituita is secreted from the ventricles into those organs and carried down by them to the eighth bone of the head [ethmoid bone].

Now separate the optic nerves from the brain and excise all that part visible to you in the amplitude of the calvarium, but carefully so that you do not remove the pelvis at the same time, for by this procedure the whole of it is beautifully displayed together with the passage which extends thither from the third ventricle and how it ends in the gland [hypophysis] that lies under the dural membrane. This will be easily seen if the special foramen here in the dural membrane has been distended. It will be helpful, however, to preserve the membrane uninjured while you are examining the rest of the cerebral nerves.

Therefore, with the head bent back to the left and the remainder of the brain returned as well as possible to its position, reflect the brain to the left and downward and give consideration to the origin of the second pair; then observe the smaller root of the third pair, and upon this being torn away, deflect the brain still more to the left. Next observe the origin of the third and fourth pairs, and then the origin of the fifth pair which should be similarly divided so that you may see the nervule which, originating near the root of the fifth pair, is carried to the muscle of the temple and to that one lying hidden in the mouth for raising the jaw. The sixth and seventh pairs emerge conspicuously if you will pay attention to their different roots from which they take origin.

When you seek these pairs of nerves there also come into view veinlike ducts running from the sinuses of the dural membrane into the thin membrane. When the origins of the nerves have been seen in the same way on the left, remove what remains of the dorsal marrow or of the brain in the head so that you may see the dural membrane still intact under the base of the brain, and observe the sinuses of the olfactory organs perforated by little foramina through which nerves everywhere emerge. When these have been inspected, examine the origin of the first and second sinuses of the dural membrane and the vessels that go under them, opening them with the point of a sharp knife.

Examination of those things in the base of the dural membrane, of the gland receiving the pituita, and of the adjoining arteries.

The ducts that run forth at the sides of the dural membrane and are conspicuous in its base near the forehead are visible without further dissection, but to see the little gland and the reticular plexus that professors of dissection have fabricated, examine closely the foramen in the dural membrane which receive the middle part of the pelvis or infundibulum and as yet holds an attached portion of the pelvis. Do not neglect meanwhile the artery penetrating the dural membrane on either side of the foramen. When you have briefly noted these things, make an incision with the point of a sharp knife from that foramen on either side as far as the passage of the arteries, and when the lips of the incision have been pulled apart the little gland will appear as well as the arteries adjoining it. These are rendered more conspicuous if here you free or open up the dural membrane as much as possible

Appendix

with hooks and the point of a sharp knife and pass a leaden stylus from the [posterior communicating] artery penetrating the dural membrane into the soporalis [internal carotid] artery as yet existing in the neck.

This is readily done in man if only you do not deny your own eyes in the name of Galen, for here you will observe beautifully how it was in the past that everyone described the reticular plexus in man if only you compare the brain of a sheep or an ox to your dissection. In addition, remove the gland from its site and press the latter to test its hardness, considering whatever Galen may have had in mind when he declared that the pituita is strained through the densest part of the cuneiform bone, which he writes is pervious like a sponge, to the palate, and [considering also] whether he did not rather investigate special passages here for the pituita and for inspired air, not the smallest foramina.

9. CONSILIUM OF ANDREAS VESALIUS WRITTEN TO WOLFGANG HERWART REGARD-
ING PARTLY WEAKENED, PARTLY DESTROYED VISION.[9]

A young man is presented as, I believe, about twenty-seven years old, fairly well-
balanced in regard to the four qualities of temperament, neither exceeding nor
greatly lacking in supply of [animal] spirit. Three serious symptoms disturb
the visual faculty and occasionally affect its functions. The sight in one eye has
been completely destroyed—not very long ago, however—and weakened in the
other. He must look at everything with [one] eye, and he no longer observes perfectly. Furthermore, since his vision has been troubled he is also bothered in
the other eye because he says that he sees now midges, now bugs, and other things
of that sort, which we commonly call vision-blockers and fancied images, and
these particularly when he has employed his vision more than usual for writing
or reading. In addition to these symptoms in the eyes, there is another kind which
consists of the affections of the eyes themselves.

That eye in which vision has been completely destroyed has lost its natural
color and the pupil appears tinted by a suffused glaucous and white color. Therefore I consider that the present ailment is instrumental—residing in the damaged
instrument—that is, a thick humor underlies the watery humor, so thickened
that it may perhaps deserve to be called a complete suffusion, and I shall say something about this matter later. Furthermore, he says that from an early age he was
one of those who had to approach very near to whatever he was going to look at,
and then his vision was sufficiently keen but it became weaker with the passage of
time. Moreover, he says, precautions were taken by very learned doctors to
evacuate the body and to increase the supply of spirit, but they were more harmful than helpful. These are the things it has been possible to learn from the household of the patient; I have neither heard from nor seen the patient himself. Therefore, since these things had to be learned otherwise than from the patient himself,
it may perhaps be considered foolish to write a categorical statement in this matter, and the affection [perhaps] ought to be inspected by those who are able to
judge with a full knowledge of the ailment and its cause. However, since the
household of the patient must be satisfied, I shall consider the matter briefly although with reservations.

Because the whole method of treatment depends upon symptoms arisen chiefly
from internal causes, the causes of disease must be investigated; and because I
have not examined this patient, my great difficulty will be immediately apparent
to any skilled physician. I should wish to know whether things far removed [are
seen] better than others that are nearer and of equal size. Then I should wish to
inquire whether he sees more poorly in a bright light, such as sunshine, than in
the shade, and to make a full examination of the eye itself which I suspect suffers

from suffusion; that is, whether that suffusion deserves to be called complete, whether it so adheres to the cornea that, if it were to admit a needle, that needle might hardly be removed; then, whether or not, in addition to the suffusion, any other affection seems to be present, such as a lack of spirit, obstruction of the optic nerve, injured eye, enlarged crystalline humor, dried, wrinkled, and thickened corneal tunic, or other affections that usually harm, weaken, or destroy the vision. If I knew these things fully, I should hope to be able to predict either a permanent destruction of the patient's vision, or—as God determines— that his vision would be restored, if not fully at least to a degree not to be scorned. If lack of animal spirit is the cause of the ailment, I foresee little help in the matter from any physician, that is, by humectification and a good regimen of diet, sexual continence, and all that is usually prescribed by physicians for augmenting the spirit. Moreover, we understand that he sees those things that are placed very near but not those that are remotely distant, and those that are small but not those that are large; furthermore, it will have to be observed whether or not with one eye closed the pupil of the other is dilated. These are two very sure indications of a lack of spirit and argue an obstruction of the optic nerves. If these things are so, since the ailment is of long duration and, as I said, there has been no diagnosis by any highly skilled physician, I expect to accomplish nothing of great significance. He sees weakly with the other eye, and I believe that with the first one afflicted his total vision will be destroyed—which God avert. If it had occurred very recently through lack of spirit it might be possible to prevent this through the proper use of inducing agents, but I fear that, in addition to obstruction and the lack of the visual spirit, some thick humors have flowed together into the eye.

If the matter were otherwise, that is, if he were able to see those things that are placed farther away better than those that are small, if better in daylight than at dusk and at night, and if with one eye closed the pupil of the open eye were to dilate, I should consider that there was a chance of cure within the space of a year. The first eye, as I believe, is covered by a complete suffusion which cannot be dispersed and removed by application of dispelling drugs; we shall leave this to manual skill. I shall not describe here the signs by which it may be determined whether or not the eye is able to admit a needle, and to what end and purpose this might assist the patient, since, if the patient were to agree, someone could easily be found suitable for this service, nor would I be hesitant myself to undertake that operation to the best of my ability. I urge that excellent man to permit the hand to be employed for his eye, since there is little pain in the procedure, and it is completed very swiftly. I urge him strongly to undergo it rather than to lose the eye which is now of no use, for no great harm can be done to a blind eye. Otherwise, if it turns out that it can in no way be cured with a needle, it will be necessary to resort to that part of medicine called cosmetic and ornamental, that is, that that eye attacked by a glaucoma be tinted in its pupil; and if the patient sees nothing, yet it will be thought that his eye is normal. Moreover, it will be done best by the Galenic medicaments mentioned in the fourth book *On the composition of medicaments according to places;* for example: at intervals apply drops of the juice of sweet pomegranate rind; or: triturate the flower of henbane, or henbane with wine. I believe the following is particularly good: the fruit of the acacia and a portion of ground oak-gall to which is added the juice of anemone so that it has the consistency of honey; then squeeze through a cloth just as liquors are recovered, and let it be used as required.

I believe I ought not speak at greater length about the treatment of the one eye, but the other must be considered, which is presumed to suffer from incipient

Appendix

suffusion. It is clear that those nebulous midges and bugs and other imagined
things do not result from affections of the stomach; first, because these symptoms did not equally affect both eyes, but they first blinded one before the
other perceived any harm. Second, the affection is not greatly increased or decreased at regular intervals. Third, the patient has been troubled by these visions
not for one or two days but for several years, as I have already mentioned.
Fourth, the ailment is not much increased because of good or bad concoction
in the stomach. Finally, when he is seized by these affections and symptoms the
patient has no nausea. Furthermore, it would clearly be ridiculous to consider
frenzy or some hot affection of acute diseases to be the cause. Therefore there
remains to be considered as the source of the ailment some thick humor flowing
into the eye which by its quantity, thickness, and nearness induces various and
multiple images. To prepare for the treatment, first to prevent increase of the
ailment, we require that part of our art that is called preservative, just as we
employ the curative treatment for what has already occurred. Moreover, in the
present instance the two parts are so related to one another that the curative
is the larger part of the preservative, for, if we remove what has already occurred, a large part of the preservative will have been employed, that is, the
removal from the eye of matter which, had it become denser, would have
given rise to a full suffusion.

Therefore it occurs to me that the first advice should be the evacuation from
the eye of that matter that, by causing an obstruction to the visual paths, prevents proper use of the eyes. This evacuation cannot be accomplished except
through medicaments endowed with great powers of dispelling, which, if applied to a head that is replete, attract more harmful humor than they dissipate
from the eye. Indeed it can happen accidentally, although seldom, that a diet
suited in all respects may cause slight vapors which, upon rising, harm the head
and consequently the eyes already weakened by a long ailment; my fourth advice will be to use every effort to draw back and derive such vapors.

I have thus considered four or perhaps five kinds of advice that are necessary
for preservation and treatment, and I shall now consider them in order so that
they may be arranged for the first trial. They are found in the last place in a
resolutive progression, namely the evacuation of the whole body, and the diversion of the matter flowing to the eyes. Therefore, beginning with these
things, the magnitude of the affection, and consideration of the significance of
the patient's organ, the plenitude of his body, and the constant optimum strength
of his whole bodily condition, I judge that the internal vein of the elbow, called
the humeraria or cephalic, ought to be opened. A sufficient amount of blood
must be withdrawn, that is, eight or nine ounces. That side must be selected
that is in line with the eye beginning, as I believe, to be affected by a suffusion.
This venesection will serve for evacuation of the whole body and the withdrawal
of the matter flowing to the upper parts. Because the matter has a certain thickness for which purgation may be effective, let him be bled after the following
potion has been taken in the morning for three days.

Three ounces of the true betonica nobilis boiled in one-half pound of the
water of fennel until a third part has been consumed; when it has been strained
and divided into three parts, add one ounce of oxymel to each part; this concoction is to be drunk in the early morning before breakfast. Also recommended
for the purpose, fennel decocted in wine, which that excellent man may employ
as food. Let fresh fennel be soaked in wine an hour before it is drunk. Now
with the matter somewhat weakened through three days, let these pills be swallowed at daybreak.

Appendix

Rx PILLS
    Hiera two scruples
    Cochia one scruple
Mollify them with the juice of the fennel and let the pills be made. In the evening of the same day, let two drachms of this confection be taken: R_x fennel seed, saxifrage, of each one ounce; nutmeg, juice of fennel, five ounces.
    Let an electuary be made of honey of roses. On the second day in the early morning one-half ounce of the same electuary, well concocted, is to be taken with breakfast, which is to be followed by three hours of fasting. Also suited to the same use and more efficacious is the following electuary:

Rx
    Fennel seed, three drachms
    Mountain willow and Teucrium chamaedrys, of each four drachms
    Euphrasia, one ounce
    Celandine, anise seed, rock-parsley, parsley, pennyroyal, flowers of borage, juniper berries, and saxifrage, of each two ounces
Mix and let an electuary be made with a sufficient quantity of skimmed honey, which, if it seems desirable to the patient, may be used in place of that prescribed. Then let the following potion be drunk for three days. Take three drachms of oriental fennel, or, if this is not obtainable, take that common variety obtained in the mountains, boiling it in one-half pound of water until a third part has been consumed, and with the decoction divided into three parts, let one ounce of oxymel be added to each portion.
    When this has been employed for three days, let these pills be taken early in the morning:

Rx
    Hiera, one scruple
    Cochia, two scruples
Mollify them with the juice of verbena and employ in the prescribed manner, and on the following day at dawn, a medium ounce of the first electuary described above, or of the second to which has been added one drachm of powder of trifolium. Also I should prefer that that excellent man use this electuary, as I said, at the evening hour, always lying down; first, in that way which has already been described, but, after this second purgation, one-half ounce of powder of trifolium always added. Then the third order of potions must be considered. These are made from a decoction of the herb celandine, that is, an ounce of squill added to a potion of oxymel, and this potion, as I have said of the others, taken thrice. The following daybreak these pills may be taken: take two scruples of the pills of cochia, or without these let there be mollified with the juice of chelidon a sprinkling of oxymel and a drop of squill, and let pills be made as I advised above. Also, with the same purpose, vomiting will not be without use, if it can be provoked without great violence and motion of the head.
    When these matters have been attended to and proper precautions taken not only for evacuation of the whole body but also that the matter may be withdrawn, it is necessary to hasten on to the other things through which derivation may be completed and the head itself evacuated. If the skin has been cut, this may be accomplished with cupping glasses: first between the shoulders, then moved up to the back of the head. Second, through section of those veins— if they are apparent—near the inner angle of the eye, or of that one in the

Appendix

middle of the forehead. Or if it is not desirable that these be opened, leeches may be employed, first behind the ears and then on the temples. Third, through those things that, infused into the nostrils or kept in the mouth and gargled, cause evacuation of matter; however, they must be administered prudently lest they harm the head, more disturbing than helpful. Therefore let them be as mild as possible in their nature and applied gently. It will be sufficient to mix beet juice with butter and apply it to the alae of the nostrils with a feather, to gargle an infusion of raisins with frankincense, and to chew nutmeg and mastic, and oxycratum, that is, vinegar with slightly acid water in which fennel seeds and rosemary have been boiled.

Although these things may turn away and draw the matter from the eye, yet there cannot be constant benefit from them nor constant use of them. Therefore that must be contrived through which the matter will be continually drawn away, which may best be done if two openings are made in the region between the occiput and back of the neck and a little cord of silk or woven horsehair inserted to keep the mouth of the wound open for a long time; through this the continually distilled humors are drawn away from the eyes. We usually call this operation *setatio,* and perhaps for the same purpose before the beginning of the following summer one might resort to cautery of the neck and vertex. Then, with cupping glasses moved to various places on the intact skin, some slight benefit may result as also from some exercise in which the hands and feet are moved but not the head. For the thick humor of the head use lye boiled with salvia and chamomile, and at intervals one or two scruples of the pills we last described, taken two or three hours before dinner. In these ways I have given consideration to three matters that concern the producing of disease rather than what has already been caused; as a result they relate to prevention rather than cure.

A fourth consideration remains which concerns the disease already caused, which is what was first proposed to me. Although it cannot be considered fully effective after the others, yet there is no reason why it may not be tried in the form of a mild eye medicine upon completion of the first purgation. Let it be very mild, as verbena decocted in water in which pure, heated gold is dipped five times; a little stronger if the decoction is made in wine and, in addition to the heated gold, copper also is dipped in it; the stronger the wine the more efficacious. Its strength will be further increased by the addition of gall of tortoise or of partridge and of fennel and verbena. Manardi believes that upon completion of the second purgation chelidon ought to be employed and continued, and sagapenum added to the third. When derivations and special purgations of the head are required and no further inflammation remains in the eye, a little euphorbium may be added also. But it must be begun with five grains for each ounce and gradually increased, but so that it never passes a twelfth part, that is for each twelve drachms, a drachm of euphorbium. If a severe burning arises from this or another eye medicine, let the eyes be bathed in whey of goat's milk or rose water. Among other efficacious things is the juice of onion with honey, and the juice of cyclamen with the same and red hens's droppings. The following may also be enumerated as effective: take the juice of fennel and bull's gall, equal parts; to these add twice as much honey. Also the head of a swallow burned in a copper vessel and reduced to a fine powder is believed to be remarkably effective, either by itself or smeared with honey.

Many other things may be added with the approval of ancients and moderns, but these are sufficient, provided the effect can be destroyed by the use of discutients. In the fourth book *On the composition of medicaments according to places,* Galen says: all these things promise great and noble results but are not very effective. Nevertheless they will have to be tried on the uninjured eye, and if they produce no improvement, if it becomes completely suffused it will be necessary to resort to the same manual procedures as for the other eye.

Things to be avoided are gross substances producing vapors from harmful juice, very humid foods, intoxication, revelling, venery, smoke, dust, too much meditation, reading or writing without food, labor, running, long daytime sleep, immoderate wakefulness, heat, cold, wind, and especially that from the south; anger, brawling, noise, very turbid and strong beer, legumes, large fish, old meats, frequent use of cabbage and lettuce.

This is the treatment I have decided upon for this eye, employing the opinion of the learned Manardi. In addition, it would seem to me astonishing if the visual spirit were lacking, since the rest of the sense organs perform their duties properly. There are some things approved by very distinguished men which may be employed, particularly local remedies which cause augmentation of the spirit. Nevertheless they ought to be employed for the whole body and the brain purged. Therefore let him drink light and clear wine in which hyssop and rue have been decocted, and let him receive their fumes in the open eyes while fasting.

Let him regularly swallow fresh eggs sprinkled with this powder: of nutmeg one part, garyophyllon one-half part, of savory two parts. Let vinegar of scylliticum be frequently held in the mouth. Let the blood of an old pigeon be distilled in the manner of an eye medicine, but let this be done very correctly. If you hold up the pigeon to divide the vein and artery under the left wing, you can cause the blood to flow warm and even with force into the raised eyelids of the patient. And if it is necessary to use a more powerful eye medicine, first the eye must be bathed with aqueous water-mead. That is called aqueous in which there is so small a portion of honey that its sweetness is scarcely perceptible to the taste. But take care that the bathing is not done with a sponge, but gradually through a very slender glass tube having a small, rostrated opening. Among all eye medicines the following is much to be recommended in this situation: pompholyx six parts, opobalsam one part, honey two parts, wine of Crete or another powerful, matured white one, a sufficient amount. It must be made in this way: first the opobalsam must be added to the pompholyx ground very fine, then the honey, finally the wine. When you have mixed the ingredients, the mixture must be frequently stirred for three days, and at that time precisely placed in a glass vessel. When its use is required the vessel must be shaken so that all is well mixed, and so it is used. But if the opobalsam cannot be found, a very matured oil in which balsam wood has been well steeped may be substituted. This medicament is especially helpful. These are the things that have occurred to me for repairing the vision of that very distinguished man; as this advice has been sought and written by me, may God cause it to be beneficial.

Andreas Vesalius

Padua, 29 April 1542

10. ON EPILEPSY AND THE USE OF GUAIAC WOOD IN THAT AFFECTION. LIKEWISE OF TINNITUS OF THE EARS.[10]

In writing of that use of guaiac wood your illustrious Lordship wished to have explained, I shall not discourse at length about that affection that has already for many years disturbed your body worthy of better health, for it is apparent that this disease is epilepsy or, as it is called in Latin, *morbus comitialis*, or the sacred disease, for there are those symptoms and accidents attending it that are accustomed particularly to accompany that disease as often as it attacks, and that you have fully experienced in such an enduring and extended sickness and have often heard described by very eminent physicians.

As the disease is so plainly apparent, I do not consider that I need to write of its essence, distinctions, or, finally, causes. It is clear that it has arisen from an obstruction in the brain extending to those processes at the origins of the nerves, and this obstruction is very much like that one that causes convulsion in some part of the body. As epilepsy has symptoms resembling that sort of convulsion, it has partly the same causes furnished by the brain, either immediately or from a consensus of the whole body; or some member transmits an injurious quality to the brain by reason of which the whole body is so convulsed that it is resolved into an apoplexy; this varies somewhat from epilepsy in regard to the site of the affection and particularly in regard to the quantity of the humor causing it. In addition to the humor, some concealed quality seems to be separately present in epilepsy, as many things attest. This is also demonstrated by the fact that all religions have always considered that there is something divine present in this disease, and we physicians say that a bad quality is present, the nature of which we express much as we reckon a fourth quality or specific force in medicaments. As something of this sort is mentioned by physicians in regard to epilepsy, so I believe it ought to be considered as present in this epilepsy of your Lordship.

Your disease is of that third type that separately takes origin from some member transmitting a bad and hidden quality to the brain as a kind of vapor. Your left leg indicates this, because that quality is usually present in spontaneous ulcers, and your leg has been accustomed to discharge a kind of ichor before the epilepsy begins to be troublesome to your Lordship; as soon as it begins, the leg is entirely freed of those ulcers. In addition, when the disease is about to attack, a certain aura or vapor is always felt to be carried from the leg through the hip, then the scapula, upward to the head; then the left leg is agitated by the vehemence of the disease and convulsed more than the other parts, so we may decide that the leg itself is the primary author of the present evil. Insofar as its function is concerned the stomach yields to this, not properly concocting the foods it has procured and so preparing a supply of crude and pituitous juices for the muddy liquid and those [other] things which are carried to or settle down in it. The abundance of excrements seems to attest that such thick and pituitous humors abound in your body which, as I said, the weakness and coldness of the stomach appear to have prepared.

Although it is clear that your Lordship's body in its prime constitution [i.e., in early manhood] did not differ very much from the normal temperament, and there was rather the same excess in heat so that the head and stomach together with the liver possessed heat, nevertheless at present the stomach has lost that temperament and the head is now rather cold and weak, suited to the preparation of defluxions. Although the heat of the liver has been maintained, there is present in you an uneven temperament which begins to display itself around the fortieth year, when, that is to say, vapors are sent jointly from the hot stomach and liver into the head, or, attracted from it, little by little flow back into the stomach. They collect in the head so that the temperament of the body may therefore remain unchanged; meanwhile I shall say nothing of the harmful regimen of diet that precipitated this temperament and at the same time increased it. Insofar as I have considered this matter in order to write my opinion, and insofar as the heat of the liver may also be a cause, it is not true that the veins abound in crude juice, since by so much heat the liver draws to itself what has been poorly concocted by the stomach, and that is the chief reason that the bowel is more constricted.

Although a consideration of this sort may perhaps be of some convenience to the examination of the cause and to a consultation [held in] common with other physicians, yet your Lordship does not hold with this because he was unwilling that things of this sort be discussed very carefully by me, but [wished] merely [that] those [be discussed] that concern the use of guaiac which I with many others suggested to your Lordship for your stomach, the weakness of your head, and also for that leg which we decided is in particular the cause of your present epilepsy. And so since we learn daily how this wood is accustomed to be employed for this sort of crudity of humors in bodies, and how it cures ulcers of the aforementioned malignant and worst sort, and introduces a kind of unseen power into bodies, in addition to other not insignificant reasons that ought to commend its use to your Lordship, it is not astonishing that you may hear it recommended and, as is also known to your Lordship, that physicians insist upon it. You hesitate because of the slender diet which may result in somewhat diminishing your strength, since a very restricted and limited diet is usually prescribed for those whom physicians treat with the decoction of guaiac wood for the Gallic disease. But in your Lordship's case and for that purpose for which we suggest this decoction, we have not decided on the definite period of time in which the decoction would have to be employed, for we must take into account tolerance of the treatment and how you are able to sustain a decoction of this sort; you will be continually at liberty, whenever it seems proper, to discontinue its use, although I should like it to be employed for about a month.

I shall now describe the order of each thing. We shall select the wood, as fresh as possible, which we choose for its density, weight, and sappiness, for the heavier and juicier it is during the scraping and cutting the more efficacious it will be. That which is almost all yellowish and of very small diameter must not be employed since it is from near the ends of the branches and is so thin that the strength of the guaiac is dispersed by its long passage. Thus we shall select the middle portion which is as sharp as possible and of burning taste. Six or seven pounds of this wood are grated either with a file such as combmakers use or with a lathe such as we employ in the manufacture of wooden balls, and then the gratings are ground into a light dust. A few pounds at a time are to be reduced to dust in this way since if a larger portion were grated, its strength, which is best conserved in solid wood, might be dispersed, and it is better to grind as much as is needed when it is needed for the preparation of a suitable decoction. One pound of this dust is placed in a lead-lined, soldered, or glass jar; for our purpose let the orifice be very small, fitted with a cover, and the jar capable of holding about sixteen pounds of water.

To this wood twelve pounds of ordinary pure water are added, and the wood is macerated in it for twenty-four hours. Moreover, it is desirable that hot ashes be placed about the jar so that the wood may be better mixed. Then when the infusion has been made, a clear flame will be applied to the jar and the cooking continues until half has been consumed; therefore, as six pounds of the decoction remain, we must take care of what has been made by setting it aside in a flask as the first water, for such we shall properly call this which has first been decocted. The wood that served for this first decoction must again be placed in the same pot in which it was first boiled, and about four ounces of fresh and uncooked wood must be added to it; twelve pounds of ordinary water are

385

poured into this, and as before the infusion will stand for twenty-four hours, after which the necessary cooking on a clear and continuous flame results in the evaporation of about a third part, so that of the decoction, or water, about eight pounds remain which, preserved in a flask, will be saved for the purpose of the second or later water. This is the usual and very ordinary method of preparing the water although there is no reason why on occasion it may not be strengthened or weakened so that a stronger or weaker decoction may be employed.

When the water is first taken, and at the end of the treatment, it may be less strong, but stronger in the middle period. Furthermore, when these waters are administereed, it must be ascertained that they are not deficient in quality and also that they have not been prepared for a long time before use, that is to say, they must be very fresh and not dissipated. Before the use of the waters is begun it is desirable that the whole body be purged, and this is usually and suitably done with roasted larch twigs to the weight of about two scruples so that from five to seven pills, depending upon the need for more or less, may be made. Moreover, that the pituitous and coarse humors may be better suited for evacuation, for three or four days some kind of syrup ought to be taken in the morning, such as that compounded of purified oil of roses and syrup of lavender, of each one ounce, and of the decoction of lavender, bettony, and germander, three ounces. The pills are properly taken after the syrups have been used, and after the first sleep at night.

The time for this purgation will most suitably be in the spring when we more readily undergo all treatments; in addition to this, the air is then more pure and mild, and then, too, although your present disease readily admits that the taking of the decoction differs according to the season, yet there is no reason why we should not also begin the treatment at once, if it seems desirable to your Lordship.

And so on the day after the purgation, about eight ounces of the first water must be drunk as hot as possible. This must be done about the fourth hour before noon. As much must be drunk again the fourth hour after noon, although it may be desirable to take this latter a little earlier than that taken after breakfast. The time of breakfast will be the eighth hour before noon, and dinner the eighth hour after noon, for in this way the twenty-four hours of the day are so divided that eight hours intervene between food and between the taking of the first water and food. However, if these intervals of time are not observed, little harm will result, nor, indeed, is it necessary to observe all things meticulously so that one may on occasion stop taking the first water if, for example, it seems to cause difficulty and tedium. I desire that during this whole period in which the water is taken there be nothing irksome, and I do not wish anything to be taken with reluctance.

When the first water is drunk one must be in bed, and sweat—if any is produced—must be awaited for about two hours. In this respect it is desirable that the body be covered with several blankets, although no [other] special effort must be employed to provoke sweat. If, however, no sweat is produced, it will be no cause for astonishment, but any produced after an hour or so must be wiped off with a cloth.

While the sweat is thus awaited it will be helpful to dip a cloth in the first water and then, while it is still warm, to wrap it around the entire left leg. This is done purposefully since it helps to drive away the harmful quality of the leg, and it is remarkable how much vigor that water usually induces in the limbs, so that I approve the washing of the entire face and particularly of the forehead. Furthermore, the second water will be the only drink accompanying dinner and breakfast.

The food will be white bread, well-cooked and slightly salted, and if your Lordship does not dislike recooked or toasted bread I strongly recommend it. Raisins, and particularly the very small ones, are to be recommended, and to these may be added almonds and pinenuts. It is usually with these that we nourish patients suffering from the Gallic disease, and your Lordship may use them as a confection with the addition of suitable meats, such as most non-marsh fowl like partridge, pheasant, and thrush, both the mountain variety and that living in brush; and the sparrow is to be highly recommended. All these are to be roasted, nor do we exclude chicken and capon, nor also kid, but all of these, too, must be roasted for as long as the water is used. I believe that the quantity to be consumed ought not to be prescribed, but left to your judgment. Have no fear that your Lordship may die of hunger, for although a slender diet may be of use, nevertheless its limits depend upon the strength of the patient; thus the same amount is not always to be taken, but one must eat according to the requiremeents of one's strength.

The bedchamber in which you will remain may be pleasant and light so long as it is not fully open to the outside air. Also it is desirable that there be a fireplace in it so that it may be heated from the hearth, unless this may be done by a stove in the manner of the ancients. It is not necessary that it be always greatly heated nor must one religiously avoid the opening of any window, since there is no reason why the chamber should not be warmed by sunshine and the temperature of the air. The fact that we shut up patients during this treatment is merely because of the porosity of the body during the sweats which result from the use of the [guaiac] wood, [and because] we do not wish to expose [their bodies] to intemperate and, particularly, to cold air.

The rationale in regard to excrement is similar to that observed elsewhere, so that the bowel may act at the proper time, and if, perchance, it becomes clogged and does not respond, it is desirable to use an enema or clyster prepared from a decoction of guaiac wood with common oil and a little salt, or, if you wish, two or three ounces of honey of roses may be added in place of the salt. Then, usually for ten days in succession, a purge must be employed similar to that I mentioned before, unless there is some reason for requiring other pharmacy. Those pills must be swallowed in the middle of the night or after the first sleep, and on the first day of the purgation water must not be taken early nor at breakfast. Even if the body is rendered weaker in any way from the purgation, nothing is to be omitted because of the purgation, unless perchance on that day food may be taken more freely. The urine flows sufficiently copiously with the use of the guaiac; and also there is usually frequent sweating. There should be no change from the healthy state in the discharge from the nostrils and ears. Also the head is usually not washed although, as I shall write later, it may be useful in addition to the employment of the guaiac. Furthermore, no special method is to be observed in sleep and wakefulness, although wakefulness is always to be preferred in the case of your Lordship, and sleep is to be avoided directly after the taking of food. However, after taking the first water sleep is permitted.

No exercise is prescribed during the taking of the guaiac except that of walking around the chamber, and the wiping away of the sweat, like friction, will take the place of some exercise. It may be added that in the case of your Lordship rest is proposed, only this must not be taken soon after food. Brisk walking is more suitable than other kinds of exercise, and above all those exercises which exercise the lower parts of the body. As I wish the state of your mind always to be a pleasant one without any disturbance, so the mind should not be dejected or serious during the use of the guaiac. However, during that time venery is interdicted, although at other times one need not constantly refrain from these things. The time during which the decoction of guaiac wood must be taken is at the discretion of your Lordship and your ability to endure it, although I should wish it to be taken for at least a month. And once the treatment has been undertaken, one must follow that regimen of diet that has now for a long time been determined as suitable by skilled physicians.

Moreover, in regard to my opinion respecting drink, I approve of beer, which is clear and pellucid, but not of sour wine. Then, because the use of wine is for certain reasons usually prohibited in the present circumstances, I give praise to a drink prepared from honey, water, and cinnamon, if only it appeals to you.

There are many [other] things about which your Lordship has also questioned me, such as the matter of evacuation and purgation of the body; that is, when in particular those things must be tried with medicaments. I am persuaded that the body ought to be purged at least once in the spring and likewise in the autumn; I am silent on the matter of venesection which, although it may seem sometimes to suit the constitution of the whole body, yet is governed by age and may readily be avoided. That kind of purgation I said ought to be essayed before the use and during the use of the guaiac is most suitable for the spring. Indeed, it will not be improper to take the decoction of guaiac for some days also in the month of September. I can prescribe various formulae for purgation, but it is enough to make mention of one of those noted above; therefore, syrup of rose honey, syrup of lavender, bettony, sage, decocted lavender, and then pills of oak berries, and the best larch. Meanwhile, however, I would wish that something be administered for at least several days in succession that will gently purge the stomach and, as it were, the primary routes, such as we recently tried when your Lordship early in the morning for three days took two ounces of rose honey and on the third day before dinner one drachm of pills of aloes with larch, from which three pills had been formed. However, one ounce of recently extracted pith of cassia, or ten drachms, may be employed in almost the same way in the form of boluses, unless in place of the concentration it is desired to dissolve the cassia in some liquor so it may be administered in the form of a drink.

Again, if your Lordship does not mind taking terebinthe, I believe that that also would be especially useful in the present case if, that is, four or five drachms were consumed in draughts early in the morning. It is desirable to choose the best terebinthe and to wash it carefully in white and fragrant wine. Nor in this regard should those pills we call "alephanginae" be discarded, for all these things are somewhat beneficial for that purgation of the stomach and intestines that I first mentioned and that must often be repeated.

When the intestines retain more than is proper, it is not desirable to employ the pharmacies that have been mentioned, and I am persuaded that some soft and nonmedicated clyster should be injected, for I do not wish the intestines to be opened through the eating of herbs or many prunes, since in this way there is too much watery excrement. It may be added that it would be easy to write here a great list of those things that, taken internally or applied externally, ameliorate the strength of the stomach; however, a few of the more recommended will suffice, among which are those imported behen nuts such as are brought preserved to Venice, and which I desire to be used very frequently and early in the morning, that is, one or two hours before food; nor do I disapprove of nutmegs preserved in the same way. To these may be added the aromatic electuary of roses which must also be taken from time to time early in the morning.

If an emplaster is to be used for the stomach, I recommend that which has been made from mastic and the oil of iris. Also, these medicaments that have now been named in good part assist the strength of the head. Moreover, in case you hesitate to wash the head, know that I commend this in particular, only let it be done before food, for after that you must remain at home for some time, and let the head be dried carefully with warm cloths but without great friction. Lye is recommended in which lavender, sage, marjoram, or marjoram with roses have been concocted. Then when the head is washed let it not be inclined much, and rubbed with some larch fungus. In this way you will provoke the pituita through the nostrils, and particularly after the evacuation of the body; I [also] favor [using] the rind of the orange. Also you may chew mastic so that the pituita may be drawn through the mouth. I strongly approve cautery or burning of the leg so that an ulcer under the knee may be kept [open] there continuously, just as I said may be accomplished suitably in the anterior region of the leg, where the fibula or smaller bone is joined to the tibia or larger bone. If that is not done, I am persuaded that sometimes cupping glasses may be employed for the leg; sometimes a lotion of strong and sharp lime to which sulphur has been added may be used to massage the leg. In addition to these things I employ that emplaster called oxycroceum in the shops, and to which I sometimes add euphorbea so that it may excite vesicles and pustules in the skin of the leg so that they carry off its bad qualities. In the same way I also sincerely desire that the whole of your Lordship's sickness be carried off and that you may live long in health and happiness, and I desire that insofar as you place favor in me, you consider me ready to do whatever I can for you, if your Lordship will deign to call upon me.

From Vesalius to the same regarding the same case.

It is clear that sometimes epilepsy, by which we know that your Lordship has been attacked, comes particularly from an affection of the leg, as I have fully explained in the account of the causes of that sickness. I approve of cautery or burning, which may be performed in the anterior region of the leg, almost to the width of a palm under the knee where the fibula or smaller bone begins to separate from the larger bone or tibia.

It is inquired how in particular this burning ought to be performed; we usually employ two methods. One is performed by fire, whether by charcoal or by a hot iron, and we call this sort of searing actual cautery because it acts simultaneously by impulse and force. The other method is the use of medicaments which possess the strength of burning and which act therefore by force, and this sort we call potential cautery. This kind suits our affair more than the actual because it is more readily supported. No surgeon, however ordinary, lacks a medicament of this sort, and our books contain several descriptions of them. Some mix unslaked lime with a detergent or soap, some steep the lime in the strongest lye, and others put sal ammoniac in the strongest dyer's water and cook them together to the consistency of honey; when cooled it hardens like stone. All surgeons have cautery of this sort at hand and also know the manner of application common to almost all of them. They spread out a linen cloth, a diachylon emplaster, or that which is called the Apostles' unguent somewhat in this form.

Appendix

In the middle they cut a small hole so that the skin to be burned appears through it and so that the hole may provide a place for the cautery and yet not much may extend beyond the circumference of the hole. The cautery is placed in that hole and then for some time it is covered by a plaster or a fold of linen cloth and is left for two or three hours in accordance with the surgeon's judgment of the strength of the cautery. When the cautery and emplaster have been removed, butter or lard is placed on the burned spot together with a leaf of cabbage or beet until the crust falls off and a hole appears into which a globule of wax must be pressed to render the hole deeper and prevent the flesh growing and closing it. One may put elder pith or gentian root in it until the hole corresponds to what is desired. Some are accustomed to use a gold or silver instrument of about this form.

I favor a globule of wax which may occasionally be covered with a powder so that it compresses or rather eats the excessive flesh. But these things are so well known to all surgeons that I am ashamed to write them, particularly since things of this sort ought by no means to be essayed except by skilled surgeons.

The second proposition is in regard to the reason for tinnitus of the ears. This arises from the abundance of humor in the brain which dissolves into flatus. As to its treatment, everything was fully explained when it was taught that the whole body must be evacuated of its pituitous humors, and the method is at the same time explained in the way in which the head is purged.

The substance of the pills, or magdaleones, are kept soft for no other reason than that in their first composition they must be moist, and because it is not convenient that we order the frequent addition of liquid to render that portion softer that is separated from the mass for the confection of the pills. Thus when the hard mass is available, such a portion may be cut from it as will be sufficient for the weight of pills to be taken, and a drop of wine or water can be added to it when it is ground in a mortar and the pills properly made. The fumes of juniper berries are very desirable in the present affections. One ought to buy the highly praised behen nuts when they are offered for sale in Nuremberg, but I do not know where good ones are sold here.

11. CONSILIUM FOR BALTHASAR VON STUBENBERG (1547).[11]

The more I examine and consider the report sent to me, the less I know what to write, for in order that ailments be properly understood no little description is required, as well as careful and frequent examination together with the use of the correct medicine; these things provide a considerable part of the knowledge of such ailments. One symptom is described that is located in the animal faculty, movement partly *in situ*, partly in degree that is imperiled by the disease. The site has been vitiated since only the external side of the sole of the foot rests on the ground in walking, while the inner side with the middle of the sole is drawn upward and removed from the ground. In regard to the degree of disease, I refer to that slenderness observed in the lower leg which is said to be more slender below the knee than the whole foot. Furthermore, it is asserted that from an early age this noble youth displayed a contraction of the tendons in the right foot. Although I can grasp all this from what has been related or written to me, it ought to be clear to any skilled physician that I shall require much more information.

Among other things, I am dubious about the assertion of those who consider that some of the nine muscles moving the foot in that joint connecting the ankle with the lower leg may be lax and softened or, to speak more plainly, powerless while others perform well; and whether it may be that some of those nine muscles are dried and contracted. For such is what I understand from what has occurred to this youth's leg, for although contraction of the "nerves" is mentioned, I believe that he who mentioned nerves did not mean other than muscles or tendons, and certainly did not mean ligaments, or those structures that take their origin from the brain and have been given the special name of nerves. In addition, the joint by which the ankle is attached to the lower leg ought to be carefully examined as to whether or not it has suffered some luxation, for there may be a defect in the formation as may perhaps have occurred there where a sinus is carved out in the tibia and fibula. The malleoli may have been separated abnormally or moved apart and become so open that, as sometimes happens, they do not hold the foot straight and so permit it to move or be carried to the side. Furthermore, the internal malleolus has perhaps been insufficiently extended by nature and faces downward so that it permits the foot to be forced to the inner side. Finally, I am unaware whether corrective bindings with braces and other apparatus would promote straightness or if, indeed, things of that sort have been tried by the present physicians. These matters ought to be investigated for a complete knowledge of the ailment before an uncertain and difficult treatment is tried; nor do I write in this way otherwise than that it may be realized how little has been provided me to judge and to express my opinion on the case.

I should like to obey the order of the very illustrious gentleman who presented it to me, rather than of necessity to describe something for the patient. I must say the same of that emaciation, whether it is necessary to refer this to impeded exercise of the leg, or whether to some obstruction—for otherwise in that well-constituted youth there is no condition of defect in the blood and no luxation of any sort of the upper joint. It is necessary first to seek here for the complete knowledge of the cause of that emaciation, that which may impede nutrition, whether the special and peculiar temperament of the leg or whether the vessels by which the material of nutrition is carried have been obstructed by contracted muscles. The treatment must be established on the basis of careful observation, on which subject Galen wrote at length in the sixth book, *On Hygiene*, as also other authors who ascribe emaciation of the limbs to slender and impeded nutrition and propose the use of regular massage by which blood is drawn to the suffering part; then they suggest a method to prevent the blood from flowing and moving away, whether this be done by applications of pitch in the form of an unguent or of an incerated webbing. However, I do not prescribe this sort [of treatment] because I am of two minds regarding the affection and present here no more than can be offered in general in regard to dryness and emaciation of the limbs. He who has a true knowledge of the affections of the legs and is not, like me, in doubt regarding everything, may learn these things more fully from those authors than from my writings.

12. TO LOUIS DE PRAET.[12]

For many years Granvelle had swellings of the ankles, particularly in the summer. In June severe pain occurred above the exterior malleolus with reddening but unlike ulcerated erysipelas; pain was more severe in the evening. Because it could not in any way be cured, he permitted both legs to be cauterized in that area. A caustic medicine applied in fairly large quantity—an aid frowned upon by some—produced much less pain than the suppuration which had led to the formation of a crust that had to be removed from the part. This suppuration, resulting from the sharp humors flowing thither, which had been the cause of that continuous and enduring pain, greatly harassed the man for a long time until we made an opening almost in the shape of an O, which we kept continuously filled with soft wax.

From another letter of Vesalius.

Derivation of the humors to the ulcerated part is performed solely because of pain; and, as not its least purpose, the pain aroused in the ulcers indicates to us where a caustic medicine—we prefer glowing iron or gold—may, by its efficacy, alter the affected part and, as it were, induces a malign disorder; but all believe that this adds strength to the parts. In addition, if calculation requires it, burning medicaments can be employed in all regions of the body; yet in your Lordship's case it would seem to be sufficient if it were done on the arm at the internal side of the insertion of the muscle resembling Δ, and it might also be attempted above the external side of the anterior of those muscles bending the elbow. However, since cauteries are performed for the sake of the whole body, they are considered to be performed more correctly on the legs where the fibula first moves apart from the tibia toward the side; that is, exterior to the tibia and three or four fingers under the knee joint, where cauteries are managed with less difficulty than on the arm.

From another letter of Vesalius.

If cauteries are not now advisable, one may cover over the scab with those powders we usually call precipitates, the root of gentian, the marrow of elder wood, or another powder of similar strength, to make the openings deeper and wider. Since, to say no more, some pain may be aroused by uneven and multiangled shapes, I recommend intermittent compression with one's own hands. After cautery Granvelle felt no pain, but it would have been to the detriment of my name if the matter had turned out otherwise; and you would be astonished if you realized the stubborn minds of certain ones who see that there is sober knowledge even in one of fewer years which they had not at first commended or even observed, either through their ignorance or incomplete employment of the art. I beg your Lordship very strongly not to attempt to cure deep ulcers by one treatment, but over the course of time; meanwhile, bear the pain produced in the ulcers whether by the varying pressure of the globules of wax, as I formerly wrote, by some prick during the cleansing of the ulcers, or sometimes by some sprinkled, biting medicament.

Appendix

From another letter of Vesalius.

By all calculations ulcers ought to be more deeply excavated, whether by the use of some powder possessing the faculty of gnawing away and consuming, or by sponges dipped in sharp lye and then dried, or by the root of gentian or something of that sort commonly used by us, or—what also can be recommended —by the Apostles' unguent; I also approve the use of very large globules of wax. By continuous or intermittent compression I prepare the depth and width of the opening so that it is larger than the size of a chickpea swollen from the sappy pus of the ulcer; in several days the ulcer, shaped by that wax globule, will admit a chickpea, and the spongy and useless flesh fills the remaining space not occupied by the chickpea, which prevents scabbing over. In addition, unless the skin is pervious and sinewy, the part of the muscle underlying it will be somewhat eroded and, so to speak, altered in temperament, and little can be hoped for from ulcers there; nor will they ever deserve the name of "little springs" if now we consider carefully the lesser portions of the tendon which is divided into two parts in the poplites, as in the illustrations in my anatomy, Book II, at the letters ζ, η, and θ.

From another letter of Vesalius.

There is no reason why a dry or dessicated chickpea may not always be placed in an ulcer and a fresh leaf of ivy be applied outside, and twice or thrice the chickpea be removed and a new one substituted; let very large chickpeas be selected. I prefer them to plates of silver and gold, as well as to globules of wax which, nevertheless, I have used from time to time when the size of the ulcers required it; I prefer the chickpea because it is rougher than the pea. We do not cut off the cusp of the chickpea because it is of use as often as the cavity of the ulcer is seen to extend beyond the middle of the cautery. Nor is there any reason to prefer white chickpeas to red; again, it does not much matter whether a leaf of ivy or beet or cabbage, or your citrine unguent, or another gentle and humectifying thing such as basilicum, or another made only of fat and butter with a little wax, be applied outwardly; nevertheless, the use of an unguent is very soothing. Even if the leaf of ivy is dry, yet it does not therefore cause dryness like that of cabbage or beet, so that the humidity it provides is preferred to its power of drying; to be brief, ivy is green the whole year, and if it be placed in a box with chickpeas it will remain sappy for a long time. Chickpeas render ulcers wider at their edges under the skin than at the surface. I should desire these ulcers to flow so that they deserve the name of little springs, and so that they might wholly drive away the causes of that ailment.

From another letter of Vesalius.

The root of gentian may be used to render the bottom of an ulcer wider, yet there is a drying and strengthening quality in it which seems to be undesirable for ulcers which we wish to be foul and fluid; therefore something lacking that quality must be sought which does not cleanse ulcers, unless there is another purpose, such as expansion of the ulcer or the need to remove dirty or fungous flesh.

An obstinate humor tends to develop when fluid does not flow freely to the sores; and when they form scabs we apply pressure so that the blood may flow forth and thus the supply of humors nearby may be impelled thither.

Andreas Vesalius

Augsburg

Appendix

13. TO MARCUS PFISTER.[13]

As the ailment and affection of the distinguished gentleman has been presented to me, I believe that the china root may properly be employed, administered in the way it is normally used by the Spanish and the people of the Indies —for it seems dangerous and unwarranted to employ very strong remedies for one of his temperament; used in this way it lessens the sharp and salty taste of the humors and the very sharp, drying, and parched temper of the liver. At the same time that it provokes a gentle sweat it may perhaps moderate the itching of the little scales occurring on the skin, like a bath of soft water which greatly stimulates the skin and lessens and relaxes its tautness. In my opinion either will be very useful with a moderate, soft, and moist diet. Also I suggest the application by sponge of a lotion of whey with which has been mixed roses and some hypocystis, so that by gentle application with actual moisture some invigorating astringency may be induced.

As for the china—if it is not disapproved by the attendant physicians—it may be repeated or interrupted at intervals. I would not desire that such biting decoctions of it be prepared that it may be necessary to omit them, particularly since they are ordered to be drunk tepid at breakfast and supper. It is not necessary for me to write at greater length of the use of that china because an Italian prescription at the end of my *Letter* provides information and explains its use sufficiently clearly. Therefore the attendant physicians may determine the proper procedure and method of use for the patient to mitigate and remove the itching; and in accordance with their judgment they will arrange to do these things for the other symptoms indicated to me. Then I prescribe warm whey with the juice of fumaria early in the morning. These are the things that, in the midst of my very great activities, I desire to suggest for the ailment that has been described to me. May the gentleman benefit from my advice.

And. Vesalius

6 November 1553

14. CONSILIUM OF VESALIUS, THE VERY DISTINGUISHED IMPERIAL PHYSICIAN.[14]

This youth suffered a heavy flow of blood from the nostrils and was attacked by a continuous fever; finally, when he had recovered from that and began to be restored to health, his legs suffered such an ailment that he could move his lower legs and feet only with great pain and was not able to stand on them except with difficulty; in addition, sensation was in large part lost in those regions. I was informed that there was even a certain troublesome sensation of contraction and at times a loss of sensation in them; but the whole medical picture has been explained to me in so little detail that I doubt very much that I can prescribe anything curative for this case.

Insofar as I have been instructed in any detail by his present physician, I believe that the orifices of the veins of the nose were eroded by a supply of bile mixed with the blood; then the blood, which was very bilious, flowed copiously so that fever followed upon that very great discharge of the blood. When this had been overcome, there remained a great weakness of the organs serving nutrition, and I believe that, when the body was renourished, humors accumulated as in those who have become emaciated and before they have properly regained health; Hippocrates asserted that those humors are created when patients who have been exhausted and emaciated by much and long suffering become fatter and walk as if with dislocated legs. It is as if certain mucous humors had been developed in the sinewy joint of the knee, which is of that kind we know induces spontaneous dislocations of the joints in children as well as in adults who are too much nourished after long sicknesses. With that goal in mind, the body ought to be evacuated of that sort of humors and dried out. Hence I approve the use of guaiac wood—and, not to go into too great detail—accompanied by the usual regimen. I should apply fomentations to the legs and feet, millet or fenigreek with bran and much salt heated on an iron plate and applied in wide, folded, linen bandages which can be wound around the legs. I should use these things rather than hot dispersing oils, warming unguents, and ointments, because the latter always provide active moisture and fat from which there is often more danger than from the potential, innate drying force in the former. Therefore I am not enthusiastic about the use of thermal springs which I should otherwise have considered very well suited to the ailment described to me. No rest ought to be given the legs, even if they suffer and are considered weak, so that they ought to be exercised constantly even in bed, whether this be done by the patient or in some other way by those assisting him. If the patient cannot otherwise stand, he must constantly move about with canes, for nothing renders even a healthy vigorous type so infirm and so weakens and enervates as rest, with no recovery of the animal spirit and no dissipation of the torpor of the native heat. All these things will be regulated by the attending physician in accordance with his keen judgment, and from whom I should like to have a more detailed account of the affection of this youth, for then I could advise better and more exactly as now I must advise generally.

15. TO ACHILLES PIRMIN GASSER.[15]

Together with a letter from Master Bartholomew Welser, I have received yours, most eminent and friendly Master Achilles, in which you describe the case of the late Master Leonard as it was carefully observed by you at autopsy. I am very grateful to you for this, since I am well aware how we are compelled to deduce the ailments of our patients from various conjectures. It is truly remarkable how the enlargement of an artery of this sort is chiefly distinguished by the closely packed matter contained in the blood, and that which in our patient resembled lard I have found in others to be somewhat similar to the vitreous humor of the eyes; and I have furthermore found only a fleshy substance that, on its surface, resembles the internal surface of the ventricles of the heart. The sister of the Bishop of Arras has a similar condition below the stomach in the anterior abdominal region; it is so loose that you might consider it to be a ball which, as she lies on this side or that, is driven now to the left, now to the right. She has had this condition for many years, indeed, from youth; her mother writes that she had perceived its beginnings but considered it a pulse. If we frequently discover [an aneurysm] lying concealed in the body of the living, how often may it be hidden from us in the brain, in the thoracic cavity, and around the pelvic region. May I perish if, after Master Leonard was seen by me, I did not meet with at least six ailments of this sort, but located in different regions. The condition was first seen by me, as I also informed you, in the thoracic cavity near the root of the neck, and it shaped the upper ribs of the chest just as you write that the ribs and transverse processes of the vertebrae were gradually shaped in Master Leonard rather than attacked by caries and putrefaction.

Written at Brussels, 18 July 1557

16. THE TRAGIC TERMINATION OF THE ROYAL INJURY.[16]

In a passage of arms held in public on Friday, the most Christian king, Henry of France, received a direct thrust from the lance of a certain young man, a little below the root of the neck and upon the side armor commonly employed in single combat. The lance was broken through its neck by the impact in such a way that, on striking that part of the helmet below the eyes, the end of the splintered lance, still held in the hand of the noble, drove upward as if by a second thrust into the face of the king, as that time unprotected.

It first struck the middle of the eyebrows, the root of the nose, and the inner part of the left eyebrow. From there it continued on through the whole lower part of the right eyebrow to the temple, and by its many splinters so insinuated itself between the body of the right eye and its socket that the greatest impact was sustained by the socket itself. Many splinters were driven into its lateral wall, and there the end of the lance settled, twisting and compressing and so undoubtedly causing a very severe concussion of the brain.

Upon receiving the wound, the king appeared about to fall first from one side and then from the other, but eventually, by his own effort, he managed to keep his saddle. After he had dismounted and was surrounded by spectators running forward from the crowd he showed loss of consciousness, although he later ascended the steps to his chamber with hardly a totter.

After about a half-dozen splinters of the lance, which surrounded the eye, especially on the outer side, had been picked from the wound by hand, he vomited his dinner, and also later a small portion of a mixture of rhubarb and mummy which had been given to him. Thereafter a large quantity of pituitous blood flowed from the wound, and on the same day a significant amount was passed from the anal veins. About twelve ounces were withdrawn by venesection and a slender antifebrile diet was instituted with trial subductions of the bowels and decoctions prepared to cool the blood and lessen its force.

The king became lethargic, and, although gravely wounded in a part of very exquisite sensibility, he almost never mentioned any pain and seemed benumbed in both his animal and especially in his vital strength. However, no fever had as yet appeared. On the following day, when the wound was treated by the physicians, fibres and splinters of wood were extracted from time to time from the region of the eye socket. As a result of the blow, both the bone and its membrane in that region were observed to be bare and rough. A consultation was held by the physicians, since it was suspected that concussion of the brain, and in that case rupture of the veins, as well as the contusion from the blow on the head, were the cause of the previously mentioned vomiting and lethargy. However, some of the physicians and the attendant nobles to the king interpreted matters more optimistically and were unwilling to acknowledge any damage to the brain, an injury they were loathe to admit in so great a king. Nevertheless, the physicians considered carefully whether or not damage to the brain, if it should be present, could be countered in some manner. Hence they discussed the use and the various methods of trephination of the skull, those things which occur

Appendix

therein, fractures of the skull, and the nature of the blood diffused between the skull and dural membrane of the brain. Finally it was unanimously agreed that trephination could promise nothing.

With the fourth day fever appeared which, although to some it seemed to indicate damage to the brain, yet by most it was considered the result of putridity arisen from harmful material [in the venous system] rather than from the wound or from the brain. This reasoning was based upon knowledge of the royal constitution and upon judgment of his urines. Despite purgative remedies which happily thwarted the fever, delirium appeared. And so, little by little, signs occurred which began to indicate more fully damage to the brain and its membranes, and so any slender hope of assistance vanished. There was a daily and unquestionable increase of the delirium, the appearance of obvious signs such as irregular sweats and rigors, both of which were frequent and are indicative of a fatal outcome in wounds of the joints and of the head.

I do not wish to speak here at unnecessary length of how the wound gaped on all sides and was favorable for the shedding of osseous squames [sequestra] and the splinters of wood, and what consideration was given to remedies which are required for serous swellings of the eye and eyebrows. I shall only add those things which were observed after the death of the king.

Despite the fact that the left eye was immensely swollen, it retained full vision, indicating that there had not been a breakdown of the nervous force. The bone of the skull in the frontal region appeared completely uninjured and intact although there was an oedematous swelling of the forehead. The superior part of the nasal bone was not at all bare and had suffered from contusion rather than abrasion. The external side of the socket of the right eye was completely denuded of membrane and was rough. Its innermost and posterior aspect still contained a large number of splinters which, like stakes, had been driven in a kind of circle which chiefly occupied a position between the socket and the lower aspect of the eye. Their tips had penetrated the hard covering of the eye so that small splinters extended into it from as far as the superior part of the socket and the anterior region of the eye, which otherwise seemed uninjured and intact in content and appearance.

The membranes of the brain and the brain itself at the forehead and at the right socket of the eye, which one might believe could have been preserved only by extraordinary chance, appeared quite unharmed, and the dural membrane appeared everywhere uninjured. But the membrane attached to it somewhat posteriorly at the vertex had a yellowish color for the length of one finger, the width of two, and the depth of a thumb. The whole of the left part was observed to be filled with a serous ichor-like fluid which flowed away as if the whole had recently been affected by putrefaction or some sort of gangrene.

In the region where the suppuration occurred, the dural membrane was observed to have vessels more distended and blackish than elsewhere, but between this structure and the skull there was some grumous blood. The skull and the skin that, as may already have been conjectured, had been scraped off, showed nothing abnormal, although at some time, as a scar indicated, the king had been wounded there. Thus the putrid condition gave proof that the brain had collided with the skull and had been concussed and shocked by it, and not that the condition had been caused by an injury to the skull.

It should not be omitted that before death the left leg and arm became paralyzed while a convulsion of long duration was plainly observed on the whole right side. Never again did vomiting occur, and over and over only a rattling in the throat was audible. Toward the end respiration was very difficult, and ob-

Appendix

servation clearly revealed that the left side of the thorax participated only with difficulty.

Death occurred on Monday in the first hour of the afternoon, that is to say, on the eleventh day, and it had been accelerated because, at the persuasion of some of the nobles, the king had been given some wine to which had been added sage and some very strong calefacients, a prescription prepared under the guise of a potion for the wound. This had increased the necessity for strong respiration.

Andreas Vesalius of Brussels

17. DISPENSATION GIVEN TO M. DE L'AUBESPINE, BISHOP OF LIMOGES AND AMBASSADOR OF FRANCE, TO EAT MEAT DURING LENT.[17]

Because the very reverend lord Bishop of Limoges and very distinguished ambassador of the King of France to this kingdom would do grave harm to his already enfeebled constitution were he to follow the Lenten diet, I have prescribed and strongly recommended the use of meats by the aforesaid very reverend lord during the present Lent.

And. Vesalius

Toledo, 18 February 1561

18. REGARDING THE FISTULA OF THE GREAT AND ILLUSTRIOUS MARQUIS OF TERRANOVA, PENETRATED FROM THE LEFT AXILLA INTO THE CAVITY OF THE THORAX, AND REGARDING MANY OTHER SERIOUS AILMENTS ARISEN THEREFROM BECAUSE OF THE COLLECTION OF PUS ABOVE THE DIAPHRAGM AND ITS IMPROPER DISCHARGE THROUGH THE FISTULA.[18]

Andreas Vesalius sends greetings to the distinguished
Giovanni Filippo Ingrassia.

The sons of the illustrious Marquis of Terranova, distinguished ornaments of our court and the great and youthful hope of that family, have presented me with your account, most learned Ingrassia. You have described the case of an unfortunate and calamitous wound very fully, and your great efforts to cure that wound will be praised by all the physicians whom I shall permit to read your account in order to gain their opinions as to how that wound, and those things still resulting from it or producing effects contrary to nature, may be cured.

Although your zeal and care and that of your colleagues in large part counteracted and repulsed the many grave ailments the wound produced, yet in the lower and anterior region of the left axilla there seems to be a fistula extending into the left cavity of the thorax, with frequent issue of a variety of pus into that cavity. Pains and fever and many respiratory symptoms arise from the amount of pus generated and the different regions it occupies, as well as no few adverse results to the organs under the diaphragm. While these matters cause the illustrious marquis discomfort only at intervals, nevertheless they are in great need of medical treatment and cure.

If, after your account was sent hither, the fistula has served for expurgation of the pus from the thorax, so that the amount has not increased and is no longer generated in the cavity of the thorax, thanks ought to be given to a rare and infrequent kindness of nature as well as to your own great efforts by which health has been restored to the distinguished marquis. In that event there will be no need for gathering the suggestions and opinions of distant physicians. But if because of an abnormal and swift increase of pus, confined by nature to the lower parts and the underlying cavities and passages, and if at intervals the marquis is disturbed, now more, now less, by the usual ills, perhaps it would be desirable to consult the physicians who were requested to give their opinions, and from their various recommendations those in charge of the case could choose that which is most sound.

Your reproofs and epithets, such as tyrant and impious man, gravely dishonor that physician who taught that an incision may be made between the ninth and tenth ribs [19] for the emission of pus, and I can only approve his opinion very highly; indeed, if I had been present when the marquis was wounded, it would have been my opinion. From the indications of lacerated and ruptured costal veins and blood flowing into the thoracic cavity and settling above the diaphragm, and from those things to which you refer, I should have strongly insisted that the source of his ills lay there, and with the indulgence of his attendant friends and for the welfare of the marquis that I be granted permission to make that incision. With its help I should have guarded the lung and the internal region of the thorax from that corrosion the pus gradually induces, and I should certainly not have desired that the health of that man, loved by all, be long entrusted to the unreliable and unnatural purgation of materials through the wound of the axilla. I have performed that operation many times, and I have seen many others perform it satisfactorily, and—may God love me—I have never observed it cause anything unsuitable or contrary to the teachings of our art.

Granted that all in whom this operation has been tried did not survive, and that many have died through a defluxion of bloody fluid through the incision made because of a wound of the thorax, nevertheless it is very certain that, with that wound persisting, the cause of the evil is the blood remaining in the lungs, or in some vein or artery of the thorax that pours forth blood, but not in the new incision. Therefore, as often as any have been wounded in the upper part of the thorax, with the diaphragm as the dividing line, they suffer greatly above and below, and, unless resting directly on the neck and on no part of the thorax, are seen to gasp for breath and to attempt to hold the thorax off the bed; then I immediately give consideration to making an outlet for the extravenate blood which is producing pus, and I undertake that operation I have already mentioned.

I do this with a razor, following the course of the tenth thoracic rib in that part of the back where it turns very sharply to the posterior. With the razor directed toward the upper margin of the rib, I make an incision as far as the bone, and of such size that it will comfortably receive the tip of the index finger of my left hand and so that the upper part of the rib may be touched by the finger. Following the touch of my imposed finger I cautiously extend the razor as far as the cavity of the thorax, and then, with the finger pressed against the incision, I make an exit for the blood collected in the thorax; thereafter liniment is placed on the wound to stop the flow of blood so that the weakened strength may not be further diminished. In this brief, reliable, and not very difficult procedure no important structure is injured, and previously the higher wounds of the thorax have permitted the entrance of air. An incision in this region can be recommended since the vessels creeping along the lower part of the ninth rib, as well as the lung and diaphragm, are preserved unharmed. I do not say that in this event the lung, already flaccid by reason of the earlier wound and the loss of the vacuum, hangs down and does not move with the thorax and hence cannot be harmed by the razor. Indeed, I use the tip of my index finger here very carefully lest the razor, driven too deeply and beyond the thickness of the rib bone, might injure one whose lung is attached by fibrous connections to the coverings of the ribs, for I have written elsewhere that I have often observed an attachment of that kind in different parts of the thorax in normal cadavers with no ailment of the thorax and lung. Thus I have learned that the lung is not at rest in all wounds penetrating into the cavity of the thorax with blood diffused through the hollow of the thorax; so in cadavers there may be no appearance of these grave symptoms that commonly occur about the diaphragm. But if at the termination of the incision I observe the membrane investing the ribs to be attached to the lung, I extend my finger deeply downward to the diaphragm in order to make certain.

The more carefully I have considered my experiences and given my attention very precisely to the nature and essence of the matter, the more readily have I resorted to surgery in that condition of the thorax we have been considering. I recommend it now—if I understand the case of the illustrious marquis correctly. I believe that the part of the lance that caused the wound drove into the fifth and fourth ribs, that the skin in the region of the ribs was injured, as well as that muscle I number as the second of those moving the human thorax, and, as I teach in the dissection procedure for that muscle, almost to be counted in the class of those moving the scapula. In that joust, because the horseman moved his right arm with the scapula upward and backward and directed his left arm and left scapula forward and downward, the physicians observed different parts of the skin and of that muscle at variance with the region of the wounded ribs. When, during the examination of the wound, the marquis sat erect and his left arm was raised, the wound in the skin—even in one of medium stature—rose higher than [it was] when the wound had been inflicted, and thus healthy skin, neither lacerated nor contused, covered the injured ribs and intercostal muscles. Hence I am a little astonished that the physicians present did not follow the doctrine of the Arabs and of Avicenna and immediately investigate whether or not the lacerated skin was in the region of the fractured ribs. This could have been done by a safe and prompt incision in the aforesaid muscle to the sequela of the wound, as we do in fractures of the skull, and so [they could have] cleaned and removed the little fractured bits to prevent their perforating the membrane investing the ribs. Furthermore, the physicians ought to have been on guard lest some vessel pour blood into the thoracic cavity, lest fracture produce internal suppuration, or, if the investing membrane has been abraded, it generate pus and send it into the amplitude of the thorax.

It is clear from your account that by chance some vein close to the fractured ribs and traveling along their length was lacerated or ruptured and emitted this blood into the thoracic cavity. This was the cause of the very grave symptoms which arose below and above the seventh rib, and this blood, at first thickened, was later converted into that watery juice you recommended ought to be drained off and taken from the wound on the fifth or sixth day. Then, when an inflammation had occurred in the region of the fractures, one sinus was produced internally and a second externally. From the many signs, I deduce that an inflammation similar to *morbus lateralis* arose between the membrane investing the ribs and the ribs and intercostal muscles, and that it extended into that abscess and suppuration from which, as you write, pus flowed out unexpectedly upon the injection of certain lotions. In addition, it is very clear that a collection of pus also existed between the fractured ribs and the intervening regions of the muscles extended to them. It is not astonishing if from the different regions—not to mention shattered bits of bone, perhaps separating from the abscess because of the collection of pus—different sorts of pus arose from the wound, contrasting to

Appendix

that usually remaining in the original seat of the pus. Furthermore, I have become convinced that it was promoted in the treatment, and that nowhere did any pus collect in the regions of the fractures outside the thorax that might have flowed thence [inward] through the fistula. The pus, which now issues at intervals, differs greatly in quantity, color, and other ways, and I believe gradually develops there in the left thoracic cavity where this was ulcerated in the form of a very wide sinus because of the presence of pus and corrupted blood for which there was no outlet except that produced by the pus in the superior region. Meantime, because some ulcerated venules in this region pour forth blood from time to time, because there is a significant accumulation of pus far from the fistula, and because of its weight, there is a residual fever, and those grave symptoms have arisen around the diaphragm, chest, and back. They will remain unless an unnatural resting position and a variety of coughs and compressions force them through the fistula and so free the marquis from, as it were, the presence of death.

Therefore, since those ulcerated regions did not admit of treatment by evacuation of the harmful matter by the efforts of nature or the many lotions and injections we normally employ for the cure of ulcerations, there is grave fear that the marquis will be unable for long to sustain such frequently recurring accumulations of pus. I believe that pus to be the source of the evil so that an incision made in the lower part of the ulcerated region collecting the pus would immediately and permanently correct this situation. This might be suitably undertaken since the marquis demonstrates those dire symptoms of the settling of much humor above the diaphragm and the filling of the left cavity of the thorax. I have mentioned earlier that this surgery could be performed safely and harmlessly in a brief time and with no great pain to destroy his strength, and in addition to my arguments the results would demonstrate its effectiveness. Lest, however, you continue to fear surgery as much as you do now, I wish to recall the cases of four patients for whom my services have been employed in this city in recent months, as many physicians here know, and because one patient's case bore close resemblance to that of the marquis.

A Biscayne soldier received two narrow but adjoining sword wounds, two inches wide, above the right nipple. When with several other physicians I saw him one day he was suffering from fever, difficulty of breathing, pains around the right side of the diaphragm, sleeplessness, and inability to rest except with the thorax erect. Hence I concluded that he needed an opening in the lower part of the thorax. However, when this had been made, because of a wound I conjectured to exist in the lung, and from the flow of the blood which may have arisen from the aforesaid wounds, the patient was obviously still in grave peril. He, I say, had attracted my attention by his prayers and by the identity of his costume marked with crosses. When nothing issued from his wounds and day by day he was very gravely disturbed by sleeplessness and seemed constantly on the point of expiring, on the fourth day his case was referred to me; since his pulse indicated that some strength still remained and because his condition was desperate, I performed surgery on him and provided an outlet for much thick blood. Soon the patient breathed much better, rested on the injured side, and, after taking food, slept very placidly. The more putrid blood that flowed through the incision, the better and livelier did the patient appear. Indeed, when no more blood, but red and watery sanies and, on the succeeding days, crude pus flowed at the same time from his three wounds, the patient had great hope of recovery. However, as he recovered strength and—as I believe—the blood in his veins increased, the wounds were again rendered abundantly sanguineous and so indicated

401

Appendix

that new blood flowed from the lowest veins, but so copiously that finally the patient succumbed before the end of the second week; meanwhile, he displayed by no indication that he was at all bothered by having undergone surgery.

A royal attendant, a Fleming, was so wounded by a sword thrust in the interval of the second and third ribs and through the posterior part of the axilla that the wound extended by its two openings into the thoracic cavity. Since there were the aforesaid symptoms, I undertook that surgery mentioned here, and everything turned out so well that he recovered in a short time.

A Gascon in the French embassy received a wound from a slender dagger through the scapula into the thoracic cavity, and, although in accordance with my previously mentioned opinion I conjectured that blood had flowed into the cavity, I was unable to reduce the scapula so that the wounds were in juxtaposition and there was no hope that the blood or pus in the thorax could issue through the bone of the scapula. Then I made an incision between the two wounds. Even though this was useful and brought great relief, yet a portion of blood accumulated between the scapula and the ribs and produced an abscess. When an outlet was made for this near the lower angle of the base of the scapula, the patient recovered fully.

A certain noble, the Marquis of Velena, in retirement in his home at Shalona suffered for a long time from *morbus lateralis,* and near the left nipple had what resembled a small tumor. A physician opened this tumor and provided an exit for the pus that had lain concealed in the thorax for some months. But since this region was suited neither for proper evacuation of the pus nor for treatment of the whole area in which the pus was contained, the noble developed a fistula there, and since at intervals he suffered from a high fever and had great pain under the scapula and in the lower part of the back, he had many things in common with the ailments of the [other] very illustrious marquis. I persuaded him to undergo our surgery, and the results were excellent so that, having been mentioned here as a patient, he now, with all his ulcerations healed, lives in complete health in his marquisate.

I shall not make further mention of those in whom surgery has yielded good results, and of others who, through the unnecessary fear of their attending physicians, unfortunately refused surgery. By order of this noble I expressed my opinion in an account for his household and local physicians before I undertook the treatment, and I presented reasons for which I feared, by Hercules, that he suffered in some degree from two fistulas. Since, in any event, it was more than enough to be troubled by several fistulas, continually bothered by successive and severe attacks of fever, so much pus, many pains in the back, and without hope of a very long life, as if, as I may repeat, to die daily, in my opinion I advised surgery so optimistically that many of the physicians were happy to urge the nobleman to submit to me and to undergo so radical a treatment, as it seemed to them, and were happy to stand by while I was operating.

You will understand that I write these things so candidly and familiarly because I desire the complete, prosperous, and lasting health of the very illustrious marquis, my lord and old patron, to whom I was very much obliged when he lived at our court. Meanwhile, to you, who because of your singular erudition and use of the art in which you are so expert are primarily entrusted with the direction of the matter, I extend my devoted regards, and may they be mutual.

Madrid, Christmas 1562

TRANSLATIONS OF VESALIUS'S
NONMEDICAL CORRESPONDENCE

19. GREETINGS TO MY OLD AND ESTEEMED FRIEND, THE DEEPLY LEARNED JEAN STURM OF STRASBURG.[20]

Master Martin has shown me your letter and has very courteously and kindly delivered your good wishes, and I was pleased to learn that I remain so dear to you and that you return my affection in full measure. The day before yesterday I presented my thanks to [the Bishop of] Arras for assisting me to gain an annual 300 Rhenish florins above my regular salary from the emperor. At the same time I told him that in your letter to me you had asked to be remembered to him, and he seemed sincerely pleased with my message. I don't know whether you write to him often, but if there is no need for writing I believe you would do well to write rather infrequently. On the other hand, I am sure he will always be pleased to accept dedications of books; hence I recommend this practice to you, although you must not expect any remarkable reward.

Praise him for his great linguistic ability and write that he is so thoroughly versed in languages that he is capable of addressing virtually all the nations of Europe, that he seems, in fact, to have been educated in each of them; furthermore, that whenever he has to discuss and deal with matters with any of these nations . . . he can adapt himself so well to its ways that it appears he has imbibed its customs as well as its language. When you describe his learning in the various disciplines, particularly in law, mathematics, medicine, and natural philosophy, mention also his interest in manual skills such as painting, sculpture, alchemy, and architecture, and remark how greatly he excels in these skills, how much he enjoys them—whenever he can snatch any time from his own arduous duties—and what astonishing kindness he demonstrates toward those who work with these skills.

Mention, too, the fact that he is the son of a very great man who is to be counted extremely fortunate since his five sons are all so equally adorned with virtues that it is difficult to determine which of them will show the greatest distinction in the fulfillment of his present activities. Express your amazement at a young man possessing judgment that is neither rash nor overhasty, but fully mature and worthy the admiration of all. However, points such as these should come to your mind more readily than I can write them down. Nevertheless, be sure to add that you have no hesitation in writing rhetoric to so eloquent a man and one who in serious affairs reveals his own ability in this skill, a man who, Atlas-like, so sturdily supports his fatherland, etc. To conclude, my very best wishes to you, and please give my heartiest greetings to Master Guinter.

Appendix

Brussels, 15 May

If you will not laugh at me, I shall request that in your preface you make passing reference to your Vesalius from whom, as from others, you have heard the remarkable attainments of Arras; for as boys we spent almost three years under the same teachers, and, however many honors have been heaped upon him, I have found the bishop always very kindly disposed toward me.

Heartiest greetings,
And. Vesalius

20. TO HEINRICH PETRI.[21]

Greetings, distinguished Heinrich Petri. I have received those books together with your letter which you gave to Martin Verhasselt during the spring fair for delivery to me. Furthermore, the letter has also been forwarded to me in which you seek arms and ennoblement. Truly, this is a greater task than perhaps you realize. At first I was able to obtain from the Bishop of Arras and the vice-chancellor Seldius nothing except arms with a closed helmet and a feudal article, for they said it would not be fitting that ennoblement be granted with the arms so arranged. Believe me that on a suitable occasion I addressed the emperor, using a general recommendation of the Swiss who in every way must be brought into friendship. Then I said that you, beyond others, had been sympathetic toward the house of Austria, and that you had always been on guard not to publish any Lutheran book; and that this had been to your no-small disadvantage, because you had gained the ill will of other printers, and especially of Lutherans. As a result he decided that I might, on his authority, press the matter again before the Imperial Council, and so I shall write you at the next opportunity. The fee will be large but not, however, more than customary. What you write of the privileges of a palatine is ridiculous, as if they were able to grant arms and to ennoble, and as if you would seek them from a count palatine, even if it were possible. Believe me that this favor of yours is the last the emperor has granted. And so hereafter enjoy your rights, even though the letter has not yet been sent to you. If it is within my power I shall try to get it off to you during the fair. Give the money which must be paid to Martin Verhasselt, who will give it to my relatives or to my wife in Brussels, if perhaps I am away with our king whose court I shall hereafter follow, because the emperor, after giving me a desirable pension for life, has dismissed me from his service.

Farewell in haste,
And. Vesalius

Ghent, 28 August

TRANSLATION OF LETTERS
TO OR CONCERNING VESALIUS

21. TO MY LEARNED AND DISTINGUISHED FRIEND, THE PHYSICIAN, WOLFGANG MEURER.[22]

On 24 October Georg Fabricius returned home. . . . He brought me your fine letter full of your good wishes for me. Thus I have received two letters from you in Padua, one, as that of a good and dutiful student, containing high praise of your teachers Giambattista da Monte and Andreas Vesalius; in the other you say that you discussed herbs with Francesco Brancaleone in Naples and also metals and other things with Gisbertus Horstius in Rome. . . . I have not yet seen Vesalius's books on the parts of the human body, since few copies of them were sent to Leipzig and [those few were] sold before I was aware of it. I shall see that they are sent to me from Frankfurt. I am astonished that the subject was not fully explained by the Greeks, especially since Galen, after Marinus, Lycus, and others put so much effort and study into it. If a very intelligent young man does not praise alien discoveries to their disadvantage, no good man will frown upon his studious efforts, and he will gain true and genuine praise. But who will not oppose him violently, as failing Galen, if he rashly places his foot into an alien camp? Our Vesalius, as I hear, was attacked, and I hope that with his many great talents he considered everything judiciously and gave careful explanations; I hope this the more because it is my strong wish that there be men in our age capable of adding something to the discoveries of the ancients.

Now I come to Brancaleone. . . .

Georg Agricola

Chemnitz, 1 January 1544

22. TO THE VERY KINDLY AND LEARNED ANDREAS VESALIUS THE SECOND AESCULAPIUS AND CHERISHED FRIEND.[23]

Greetings. Master Charles Harstus will, as I hope, seek a privilege for me and my son so that I may be able to publish books of known orthodoxy without the irritation of the censors. I ask your help in this matter.

Furthermore, I have a nephew—son of my brother, a priest—who is a student of law and who lives in my house—for he possesses nothing except the name of an unfortunate birth—who seeks legalization of his birth if this can be done without too great expense. Therefore I request your friendly action in this matter. If at the same time he could be created an imperial notary he would be very grateful. In regard to nationality, he is from Tengen, a small city of King Ferdinand in Hegau, my native land. Basel, 23 March 1555 [?1553]

Sincerely yours,

Johan. Herwagen

23. JOHANNES OPORINUS TO CONRAD HUBERTUS.[24] 4 MAY 1555.

Recently I wrote to Michael Toxites to obtain for me from the guardians of Dryanders's children the matrices and tools for the large types with which he had had August Friess print certain writings of Plutarch and other things. Previously Dryander had lent me those matrices to make the type necessary for printing Vesalius's anatomy. Now, however, because some of the types have been worn by use, I must see to it that more are cast in order to complete the anatomy begun long ago, but this is impossible without the matrices and tools. I could easily obtain them from Dryander if he were still alive, but if now I cannot obtain them on loan from the guardians, I am willing to buy them, as well as the tools, provided the price is fair and they are sent to me immediately, at my expense. I prefer to throw away two or three florins rather than be without them longer and so further prevented from completing a work started three years ago. I beg you, my dear Conrad, to see that I have them and that I receive them immediately.

24. ACHILLES GASSER TO VESALIUS.[25]

When the abdominal cavity had been opened in the usual manner, the natural members appeared to be fairly normal. There was no damage in the stomach and intestines, the liver was intact and very large; likewise the vena cava was of very large size, larger perhaps than had ever been seen by us before in any dissection. It was ruptured where the aneurysm had come in contact with it. The spleen [was] very short, and externally partly pallid and almost semiputrid. The kidneys [were] unharmed. The large heart which was full of blood was similarly healthy. No little expansion in the aorta [swelled it] to the size of a palm, [and it] was so affixed to the ribs and vertebrae that it could not be separated intact. Hence when it was pulled away a thin red blood flowed out, like normal arterial blood, which had been contained by a kind of concreted blood or carniform matter lacking fibres; this was surrounded by a palish and hard substance the thickness of a finger and not unlike boiled pork lard in color and appearance. The whole connection of the aneurysm with its contents almost equalled the size of the fists of a medium-sized man, or of an ostrich egg. The ribs around the mid-location of the aneurysm were almost carious, one—without doubt from very strong pressure —wholly ruptured and broken, and the vertebrae in that place where they had been connected to the aneurysm above the diaphragm likewise were spongy and so eroded that the tip of the little finger could be inserted into the surface of them, but without notable foetor. [There was] no lesion of the lungs, and since the patient had spewed forth much blood before his death it may have seemed to those present that he was suffocated by that blood. The undersurface of the skin where the tumor and pulsation could be noted during life was in death livid and suffused with blood, as in flagellants. These are the things that were observed as carefully as possible. Other matters have been omitted because of your knowledge of the ailment.

25. TRUE ACCOUNT OF THE HEAD INJURY OF THE MOST SERENE PRINCE DON CARLOS, OUR SIRE OF GLORIOUS MEMORY, WHICH OCCURRED THE END OF JULY [*sic*] 1562.[26]

So great was the favor that the Lord God granted to all the kingdom and domains of your Highness in permitting a happy outcome in your very grave and alarming case that it appears truly the result of heavenly intercession through the prayers, supplications, and shedding of blood which occurred as a natural course throughout Spain as well as outside it; but [it was] also because, as his Majesty and your Highness were fully informed, all possible [medical assistance] was given, as there was reason should be done in the case of a subject, the most exalted on earth, with the King's Majesty, our sire, so frequently present at the treatments and the many consultations. Your Highness ordered me, although others might have done it better, to write the account and the result of this treatment in as much detail as possible, and this for two reasons. One, because I served your Highness and was present from the commencement of your injury. The other, because, as your Highness knows, the day after the accident the most serene princess of Portugal Dona Juana, whom I serve and have served for many years, sent to me by the Marquis of Sarria, her majordomo, a command that I should write to her Highness what occurred each day, leaving nothing out. I did so, requesting her Highness to preserve all my letters, which she did, that they might be returned to me so that I might recall what I had described during the course of events; otherwise it would have been impossible for me to remember in detail what follows.

In the city of Alcalá de Henares, Sunday, 19 April 1562, exactly fifty days after the end of the quartan fever for which he had been treated in the aforesaid city, on this day after the Prince, our Sire, had eaten at half-past twelve, descending by a very dark staircase of very uncertain steps, five steps from the bottom his Highness missed his footing with his right foot, turned completely over, and fell head first, striking his head a severe blow upon a closed door. He injured himself in a posterior part of the head, on the left side near the commissure called lambdoid, which resembles that Greek letter, Λ.

I was called to examine the wound in the presence of Don Garcia de Toledo, governor and first majordomo, Luis Quijada, master of the horse to his Highness, and the doctors Vega and Olivares, physicians of the chamber. I found the wound to be the size of a thumbnail, the edge well contused and the pericranium laid bare and appearing to be somewhat contused. Having prepared what was necessary, I began to dress the wound, and his Highness complained that he felt it too much. Seeing this, Luis Quijada, thinking that, to spare his Highness pain, I might not do all that was fitting, told me to treat his Highness not as a prince but as an ordinary man. The doctors replied that they would do so. When the treatment of his Highness had been completed, he took to his bed. While the question of bleeding him was being considered he commenced to perspire and continued to do so for an hour and a half, and for this reason the bleeding was postponed. When the perspiration had stopped and been wiped away, he received a medicine with which he was somewhat eased, and after a short time he was bled from the right arm, because we believed that there was a great repletion of the veins of the whole body. We withdrew eight ounces of blood, and soon he developed a slight fever.

When the treatment had been completed, Don Garcia de Toledo sent Don Diego de Acutura, gentleman of the chamber of his Highness, to inform his Majesty of what had happened. When his Majesty had been informed, he ordered Doctor Juan Gutierrez, his physician of the chamber and *protomedico general,* to leave at once for Alcalá and to take with him Doctor Portuguès and Pedro de Torres, surgeons of his Majesty. They arrived at Alcalá the following Monday at dawn.

While I was preparing the treatment, his Highness said to me: Licentiate, it would please me to be treated by Doctor Portuguès. Don't take umbrage at this. Receiving this courtesy from such a great prince, I replied that in so doing I was receiving a great favor since it gave pleasure to his Highness. And it might have cost his Highness his life, as will be seen later. Thus his Highness was treated at eight o'clock in the morning in the presence of those mentioned and of those of us who were in Alcalá. When the treatment had been completed, by order of Don Garcia de Toledo we met in a consultation in his presence. In regard to his Highness's fever, we agreed that it was spring, the fall had been severe, age and past regimen offered no obstacle, that his Highness had had a quartan for twenty months and during that time had always eaten well, that he had been bled and purged only once and very slightly. For all these reasons it appeared necessary to bleed him again, and so it was done, and another eight ounces of blood were taken from the vein of the left arm. This day his Highness ate some prunes, a little broth, and a leg of chicken, finishing off with a little marmalade. This meal was permitted him, as customary and because of his age and the time of year. He dined on some prunes, broth, and a little conserve.

This regimen continued until the seventh day had passed. His fever had abated a little up to the fourth day when it increased somewhat, although little, and we saw some glands on the left side of the neck which were somewhat painful. Also he had a swelling in the right leg which his Highness was accustomed to have sometimes during the quartan. For this reason we did not regard it as serious, nor [did we so regard] his dryness, since at the time of the fall his Highness had had a severe cold. After the fourth day his fever ceased to abate and was the same on the fifth and sixth day, but on the seventh the fever ceased. This was aided by his being purged on the sixth with two ounces of manna, and the purge worked well. The wound was improving, with good suppuration, good color on the edges, and very good color of the pericranium. With this improvement of his Highness we decided to make no change in the order of the regular treatment, the food, or meals.

On the tenth day after the fall, at the hour of the treatment, the wound was not so favorable as before, since we observed it to be somewhat festered and not of such good color, and we feared a relapse such as happens in head wounds. On the afternoon of the eleventh [day] he had a good appetite and slept well; on Wednesday around midnight his Highness felt a slight chill, but, thinking it due to the season, because these days are very raw, called no physician. He tried to sleep, but in vain. For this reason at two o'clock in the morning Don Garcia de Toledo called Doctor Olivares, who at once examined his Highness and discovered him to have a high fever. However, in order not to frighten the prince he said it was nothing, only a slight alteration, but he announced [to the others] that his Highness was feverish, and on the eleventh day of wounds of the head that is a bad sign. Then all the physicians and surgeons were called and met Thursday, the last of April. Don Garcia de Toledo joined them to discuss what ought to be done, and in view of the fact that the pain of the neck, where the sequelae had been, returned, and also the swelling of the leg, it appeared to all that this could mean only one of two things: either [there was] an internal lesion, or, through damage and decay of the pericranium, some matter had remained shut in and was unable to escape. We were in agreement in this, the more so since on the day before, which had been the ninth, Doctor Portuguès had not treated the wound in the usual manner, nor had he wished to do so although he had been so requested, but had placed a tent over the mouth of the wound with many dry compresses around it. In this way the orifice had been blocked, and matter accumulated in the cavity of the wound, which, with its bad quality, was enough to cause the aforesaid results.

Regardless of whatever these things might be, it appeared necessary to open the wound and clear the orifice to let the matter out, if it were an internal lesion; or to give an exit and passage for the matter contained in the wound, because that might easily communicate itself through the commissure to the part within, of it might be there was pus in the cranium. This had not been undertaken before because it was not right that his Highness's life should risked without the strongest reasons—and there is no surgeon who does not know that similar accidents have resulted in damage to the pericranium—since such matter is frequently dislodged naturally.

When I had seen these symptoms, I suggested in consultation that, since there was great doubt in the case, we ought to send for the Bachelor Torres, a surgeon of great learning and experience and my teacher, who lived in the city of Valladolid. This was well received by everyone, and Don Garcia de Toledo immediately ordered dispatch of a courier who displayed such diligence that by 6 May the Bachelor Torres was with us. The six of us who were present had agreed to expose the cranial surface, and an incision in the form of a T was made; the pericranium was spread very easily because it had become putrefied from the contusion that had occurred and from the quantity of matter that had infiltrated it without finding an exit, since on the ninth day without the wound healing the orifice had been blocked. However, when the opening had been made, it was impossible to see if there was damage to the cranium because of the great flow of blood; we could do no more than stop it and apply a dressing. Then a courier was dispatched to his Majesty to relate what had occurred and to declare that it appeared to all of us that there would have been danger in delaying the incision until his Majesty could be advised.

When his Majesty heard this news, he left Madrid on Friday, 1 May, before dawn and reached Alcalá before we had treated his Highness, which was done in the presence of his Majesty and Doctor Andreas Vesalius, a very learned man. During this treatment the skull was examined with much care, and no fracture or crack was found in it, although in one place there was a single small spot which led us to suspect a contusion of the skull, which, were it to remain, would require us to ruginate the skull to ascertain its condition. The day following, which was Saturday, 2 May, his Highness was treated at nine in the morning, and we noticed that the spot had disappeared from the skull. The situation was the same on Sunday, whereupon we decided that [the spot] had been superficial and the color had been from some retained matter. On the two days preceding the opening of the skull his Highness was treated as follows: the surface of the skull with iris powder and birthwort, the edges [of the wound] with an unguent of turpentine and egg-yolk, so long as it was necessary to assist suppuration. Then honey of roses to cleanse, and on top an emplaster of betony because of the condition of the prince when he fell, despite purgation and two bloodlettings and the diet prescribed for him.

Appendix

On Friday, which was one day after the disclosure [of the bone], there appeared a swelling of the head and a considerable erysipelas, as well as thick blood; this swelling extended first through the left side, the ear and eye, and then the right, so that the abscess covered the whole face and was extended to the neck, chest, and arms.

So long as this inflammation was on the head and commissures we used no special remedies there, because they would have had to be repellants which could not be employed since they would have forced the erysipelas inward. Bloodletting was not employed because it appeared to us that the prince had not the strength to permit withdrawal of blood from a vein; chiefly, we had to remember that the wound might continue a long time, and it was necessary to conserve the strength as is done in long illnesses, because the strength is completely destroyed by emaciation [i.e., bloodletting]. Therefore, as was said earlier, we massaged his legs frequently, applied embrocations and cupping glasses, and reduced his diet so that he was given only a little broth when we deemed it advisable. As the swelling of the head decreased, we applied particular and suitable remedies, which were repellents mixed with some resolutives, because already the inflammation had passed the first period, and augmentation had begun.

So great was the heat of the erysipelas, and the tertian fever was so intense, that the heat was communicated to the interior, and his Highness became delirious and remained so for five days and nights. This put us in great alarm and led to a division of opinion; especially as at dawn on Monday, 4 May, his Highness, being on the chamber pot and passing choleric and foul matter, and thereafter being in a litter, took a chill and his pulse became weak, although he felt no chill or tremor. Observing this, Doctor Vesalius and Doctor Portugués were of the opinion that the lesion was inside and that there was no other remedy but to penetrate the skull to the membranes. They remained of this opinion so long as the fever lasted, and ridiculed the discussion of other methods. Everyone else considered that because of the symptoms one of two things had happened; either the bone of the skull was suppurating and hence they ought to ruginate—also because on Monday and Tuesday and all the other days after the incision that little spot we have mentioned had reappeared on the skull; or, that the external inflammation had passed through the sutures to the cerebral membranes. We favored the latter opinion, that is, if there were internal damage it had occurred in this way and no other. I do not deny that Vesalius had many good reasons for his opinions, as can be gathered from what I say, and there was no lack of professional men who said that this case could not be foreseen by our art and that we had gained success merely by chance.

Although it is unnecessary to discuss here anything more than what concerned his Highness's wound, nevertheless, so that physicians who read this may understand our reasons, I shall give them, just as we all gave our opinions in the presence of his Majesty. We held it for certain that the signs did not indicate internal damage, since the fever his Highness had on the eleventh day was without chills and was caused, as I said, from the putrefaction and separation of the pericranium which, as I mentioned earlier, detached from the skull very easily and without any vomiting or convulsions. The swollen glands on the left side of the neck and the pain in that region were [the result of] a catarrhal flux, since, as I said, his Highness had had a cold at the time of his fall. I also said that the numbness of his leg was something he often felt during the time of his quartan fever. The delirium, which began on Tuesday, 5 May, was the result of the fever and erysipelas, and when the latter was over the commissure the fever increased and the Prince was delirious; with the lessening of the erysipelas the delirium of fever was less.

Appendix

As I mentioned, there were no chills, vomiting, or nausea, so that these very apparent causes of the delirium were the same ones that caused lack of sleep and increased the fever, and the erysipelas of the head which had communicated the inflammation through the commissure to the membrane was the real cause of the delirium. Since there were no sure signs of an internal lesion, because these do not usually lie hidden but often are apparent although irregular, we considered our opinion as correct. Also we did not agree that there was damage in the skull because it had been white for two days, hence the spot that had appeared on Friday was considered superficial; if it returned it would be due to the medicaments. If anyone asks why there was a spot on the skull at that place and not over all the exposed area, I say it was because that part was much altered by the air to which it had been exposed for some time and therefore took the color of the medicaments, but not the rest which was cleaner, more polished, and less altered.

I do not wish to say that those who declared the lesion to be internal did not have many and very good arguments; but it is not right that those who had the wisdom to understand what was afterward apparent should be said to have guessed without reasons or sound arguments, although we might have been called guessers since we prognosticated that which was as yet unknown. I have dwelt on this matter because it was one of the most important of all those in doubt, and it was discussed in diverse ways. Therefore his Highness was treated, but without our touching the skull.

On Wednesday, 6 May, the Bachelor Torres arrived, and he advised ruginating the skull although he said it ought to be done at a later time. As the erysipelas was increasing, the Prince's fever was high, and despite the fact that his Highness each day had three, four, and five bowel movements without the application of anything, it seemed that we ought to aid nature; but because we feared that he might vomit the purge, which would have caused great damage because of the incision of the head and the great swelling, we did not attempt to give him other than three ounces of syrup of the nine brewing herbs, which his Highness took willingly and then even asked for the little left in the vessel. There was no trouble in the stomach, and the bowels were so opened that he had more than twenty movements. This purge was given Thursday, 7 May, at four o'clock in the morning, two hours after the consultation, and this was one of the wisest decisions made during the whole course of the illness, although there was no lack of critics to whom things appeared otherwise.

On Saturday at four o'clock in the morning, which was the end of the twentieth day, while we were still in doubt about the lesion of the skull, it was suggested that we ruginate. There was no reason for not undertaking this, since his Highness was so disturbed [in mind] that he could not understand what was being done and therefore would feel no sort of pain. Also, since most of us were of this opinion, and his Majesty and the grandees who were present inclined to it, and since his Highness was in great danger and the signs that were observable gave us little hope of saving him, we agreed to ruginate. This was Saturday, at nine o'clock in the morning, three hours before entering the twenty-first day. Doctor Portuguès began to use the rugine, and a few moments later the Duke of Alba ordered me to take it, and I continued to ruginate and soon reached the skull which was white and solid; a little very red blood began to spurt from the porous part of the bone, and with this I stopped the rugine. It was then seen by all that there was no damage in the skull nor in the internal part corresponding to that place.

Thus all doubts were dispelled, except for Vesalius and Doctor Portuguès, who never changed their opinion, but we understood that the damage had been communicated as an accident of the fever and erysipelas. All this time there was little matter in the wound, and the margins were of poor color, dull, and very widespread. Also the eyes were swollen in such manner that we foresaw that they would suppurate. The wound was doing very badly, although it was clear that the medicaments that were applied were appropriate and there was no fault in them but rather in the prince's lack of strength and in the great force of the fever, since with the strength weakened not only can good results not be obtained in the parts that have no lesion, but much less can they be accomplished in weakened and damaged parts; and the extraneous heat, such as there was from such a great fever, had the effect of consuming or altering the matter.

It had been proposed many times that we treat his Highness with the unguents of Pinterete, a Moor from the Kingdom of Valencia. One of them is white and repercussive; the other is black and hot so that it is necessary to temper it with the white one. Most of us were opposed since we had not used these unguents and did not know their composition, and there was no reason to use such remedies on so great a prince and in so grave a case without an understanding of their effect. Furthermore, it did not seem reasonable to us to use one and the same medicament at all times and for all ages and complexions. But seeing the faith that many had in these unguents and the general opinion of the public, which blamed us for not using them, and also because some of the physicians and surgeons who were present had employed them in some grave cases, we therefore agreed to use them according to the method of the Moor, who was hourly expected to arrive. The unguents were applied Friday and Saturday before he came. The Moor arrived Saturday, the night of 9 May. On Sunday he watched the treatment of his Highness with the unguents. On Monday he applied them himself. On Tuesday in turn Doctor Portuguès applied them. During this period, although all the symptoms of his Highness's accident improved, the wound went from bad to worse because the black unguent had burned it so that the skull became as black as ink, and we recognized that, although the prince's strength had increased and the fever diminished, the unguents were at fault since they did not suit the flesh of his Highness which was very delicate. We agreed to dismiss the Moor along with his unguents, and he went to Madrid to treat Hernando de Vega, whom he sent to heaven with the aid of his unguents.

We returned to our method of treating his Highness, as will be mentioned later. Saturday, the twenty-first day after the fall and 9 May, all his Highness's symptoms were fatal. There was only our confidence in the mercy of God and in his Highness's age, which was not more than seventeen years. Also, we knew that his natural pulse was not very fast. This Saturday afternoon the town came to the palace in a procession and brought the body of the Blessed Diego, whose life and miracles are so well known; it was brought into the presence of the prince and placed as close as possible to him, although on that day his Highness was so beside himself and his eyes so swollen and shut that he could not understand what was happening. Seeing this, his Majesty, who had been informed by Doctor Mena, physician of the chamber, that undoubtedly his Highness was dying, left Alcalá between ten and eleven at night in the darkness and a wild storm and went to San Geronimo in Madrid in great sorrow, as we could all understand.

We were left in great anxiety and with a tremendous responsibility since, despite our position as servants and subjects, we held such a grave matter within our hands. Each one of us realized this to his dismay, and especially I, because the public contention was that I had not done the proper thing since the first treatment. Since delay in such cases is very dangerous, we applied six cupping glasses to his Highness on Friday evening, and two of them scarified; on the same Friday we placed fomentations on the legs for derivation, and others on the head to humectify and produce sleep. We also placed steam under his nostrils, and on Saturday we repeated the same fomentations; that same Saturday we placed six more dry cupping glasses on his shoulders, and in the evening we bled his nostrils with a lancet; at ten o'clock that night we again applied five cupping glasses, and thanks to God with these aids his Highness slept five hours that night, at intervals. In the morning his pulse was stronger and the delirium lessened.

With this appearance of improvement, on Sunday the Duke of Alba sent the constable Malaguilla to his Majesty. The constable reached Madrid at the moment when our Lady of Atocha was being carried in a procession in which followed her Majesty the Queen, our Lady, and the most serene Princess Dona Juana; there he told them the good news, and it can be imagined how their Majesties received it. Sunday night [the prince] slept, as well as on Monday and Tuesday. The wound, as was said, despite all these improvements went from bad to worse after the unguents of the Moor, so that to relieve the great heat of the black unguent, which appeared to us to be a mild caustic, on Wednesday, 13 May, his Highness was treated with dry sharpie close to the skull, and in the lips of the wound was place a little fresh butter washed with rose water, and on top an emplaster of betony. That day his Majesty returned to Alcalá.

His Highness had now recovered his senses and part of his sleep, although with the increase of his tertian this was disturbed. The eyes, despite fomentations and emplasters by which they had been moderately resolved, were yet so full of gross matter that they could not be wholly resolved; the matter matured first in the left eye in which the erysipelas had begun to run and to extend. The urine always held crudity which indicated the need of moderating and tempering, and syrup was taken for nine or ten days. In the evening of Thursday, 14 May, the wound was treated in the same way as the day before, and the matter was found to be better. On Friday, at half-past two, the wound was filled with a quantity of matter, the lips moderately red, consistent, and closer together. From this day on his Highness was treated with iris powder close to the skull, the lips of the wound with a digestive, and on top an emplaster of betony. His Highness ate at four o'clock because we expected a new attack at ten in the evening, but it was anticipated by three hours since it took place at seven; the prince went sleepless. At three in the morning he drank three ounces of water with a wafer of manuchristi, and then he slept until six, which was 16 May. This night he slept about eight hours.

That day, after all of us had felt the left eye, it appeared to us that there was matter in it; only Doctor Portuguès did not find it, although he sought it with much care, and it was agreed that it must be opened with a lancet. Doctor Pedro de Torres opened it, and thick and white matter came forth; if it had been delayed, a fistula might have developed in the eye. The right eye did not appear then to contain matter, and so it was not opened. That day his Highness ate as usual and slept an hour after eating; he woke up feeling better and with little fever. His head was dressed around four, and in general the wound was better; supper at five, and at eight in the evening the right eye was opened up and much matter came forth; it had to be lanced to open it like the left. This Saturday, from the time his Highness awakened until he was treated, on Sunday, 17 May, in the morning, the fever decreased considerably; at five o'clock in the morning the fever was much further decreased. He took some syrup and went back to sleep until eight, and at that hour both eyes were dressed; the matter that escaped from the left eye was thick and lumpy; that from the right was better. That day he ate at nine and felt well all afternoon, although he did not sleep at noon, and at three o'clock his head was dressed and was in better shape than the day before. He dined at five and went to sleep at ten. That day there was some increase [in fever], wherefore he slept less than the night before. We gave him the syrup at half-past five, and at eight we treated his eyes. The right was in good shape, but not the left, since it contained a large quantity of matter because the wound was on that side. He ate fairly well at nine.

Monday, 18 May, he had very little fever all day. The wound was dressed at three and showed continual improvement; he dined between four and five. At eight his eyes were treated, the left eye being much swollen but discharging no matter. Therefore Doctor Torres introduced a probe into the opening that had been made and a quantity of thin matter came out; this resulted in a decrease in the swelling, and his Highness opened his eye much better than before and with less difficulty. The right eye was doing well. That night his Highness slept about ten hours. Tuesday morning the eyes were treated, the right being now well and without any matter; the left, when the opening was enlarged, gave forth a quantity of matter, enough to fill a pigeon's egg. With this the swelling decreased so that the eye could be completely opened. The matter was so deep that the eye had to be lanced twice because of the danger of injury to the eye if the lancet were used without discretion. Therefore those who criticised Doctor Torres because he performed this operation twice were wrong, because he acted according to the principles of the art. This day the prince ate at eight o'clock in the morning, slept an hour at midday, and at three in the afternoon his head was treated in the following manner: iris powder was placed close to the bone of the skull; on that were placed small compresses soaked in turpentine diluted with water, and powder of myrrh; over all this a soft salve.

This night we expected an increase [of fever], but thanks to God there was none, and he slept more than eight hours. Wednesday, 20 May, his eyes were treated at eight o'clock; no tent was placed on the right because it was cured; the left was much better, and on it was placed a small tent, and on top an emplaster of diachylon; he ate between eight and nine; the fever was decreasing little by little so that there was definite improvement. At noon he slept a little. At this time began the thiry-second day after the fall and the twenty-first of fever which had appeared on the eleventh day. At three o'clock the prince's head and eyes were dressed, and everything showed improvement, as was said. From this day it was agreed to treat the head in the morning, prescribe supper at five, and nine hours of sleep during the night. Thursday, 21 May, we treated the head and eyes at eight in the morning; there was more improvement, and the right eye was well, the left eye less swollen, although the eyelids were very red. There was very little fever that day, so that to some it appeared he had none. He ate as usual at nine and at noon slept for an hour; at three the left eye was treated. After the dressing, his Majesty left for Madrid, much pleased, and ordered Don Garcia de Toledo to send him information twice each day on the progress. Supper [was] at the usual hour, sleep at ten. That night also there was no access [of fever], and he slept nine hours. He took the syrup at four in the morning.

Friday, 22 May, at seven, it appeared to all of us that his Highness had no fever. (From this day on, to avoid repetition, I shall not give all the particulars as hitherto, since the same method was constantly employed.) From that day there was no return of fever. Whenever some light remedy was needed, as some medicament or lotion for the eyes, or some change of emplaster, we did whatever was necessary. The head, as was said, constantly improved; also the eyes, although the left was more stubborn and slower in healing. Saturday, 30 May, his Majesty returned to Alcalá, and left on the following Sunday after dinner for Aranjuez. During these days, since his Highness was without fever, he slept ten or eleven hours at night, and therefore not at midday. Tuesday, 2 June, between eight and nine in the morning, which was the end of the forty-fourth day since the fall and began the thirty-third after the operation, while Doctor Portuguès was feeling the skull with a small hook, he poked it two or three times and tore off [a piece of] the skull, which appeared to us to be in the shape of a heart. We all wished that there had been several days delay so that the bone would have fallen off of its own accord without any effort. Thus for a few days it was necessary to digest and cleanse the wound.

From Sunday, 7 June, his Highness was treated twice daily; from the time that [the bone of] the skull had been detached we ceased using iris powder; we used the same mixture, but in place of sweet unguent we applied a double emplaster. As the erysipelas had extended to the whole head, the scalp remained bare in many places, and there were many scabs which caused his Highness itchiness. Also the head was so dirty, especially around the wound, from the unguents and emplasters that had been placed there, that it gave him much discomfort and was not good for the wound. Therefore it appeared to us that it was desirable to shave his head, using a razor, or, where that was impossible, the point of the shears, and to apply to the pustules an ointment of pork fat cooked in white wine. Ruy Diaz de Quintanilla, barber to his Highness, wielded the razor skillfully the three or four times required. Little by little the pustules were dried up with the ointment.

Sunday, 14 June, his Highness arose for the first time, and he did this each day thereafter and after a short time he felt strength in his body and legs. Upon rising he heard mass and received the Holy Sacrament. This day his head was treated with a powder of the bark of the pomegranate tree on the flesh, dry lint, and, on top, an emplaster of diapalm. In the afternoon during treatment we saw that the powder had caused a little scab, and so we used only dry lint, on that a little white unguent and on top the diapalm. Next day at the hour of treatment it was found that the scab formed by the powder was detached, and because the flesh had become spongy and the scar would not form over it, it was agreed to place on it a powder of burned alum. Over the powder was placed the dry lint, and on top of all the emplaster of diapalm. Tuesday, 16 June, around midnight, his Majesty returned to Alcalá. The following Wednesday at eight o'clock in the morning the prince arose and went into his father's chamber, who received him and embraced him with great joy. Then they returned together to the prince's chamber where his head was treated as on the previous evening. The eyes required no treatment. Thereafter his Highness ate as usual, [partaking of] a pie made of the white meat of chicken. Then, at four in the afternoon, the same [head] treatment was applied in the presence of his Majesty, who [thereafter] left at once for Madrid and said that he would send directions for moving from Alcalá, because the heat, which is usually bad at that time of year, was so extreme, and his Highness was very sensitive to cold and heat and therefore wished to leave Alcalá. As the scar was so slow to heal it did not appear proper to undertake the journey while the wound was mending.

From this day on he was treated according to need, either once after using the alum powder or twice when it was not employed, and whenever it was necessary to cleanse the moisture from the wound. This arrangement was followed in the treatment of the scar while the alum powder ate away the superfluous flesh. Sometimes we used dry lint and placed a gemini plaster on top; at others, we washed the wound with alum water. As a result nature was forming the scar, and it is not astonishing that so large a wound, from which so large a portion of the skull had detached, should take so many days.

On Monday, St. Peter's day, the prince went to mass at San Francisco, in the chapel of the Blessed Diego; there he was shown the holy body which had been left outside its sepulchre from the day it had been carried to the palace until the end of the month of June. Then each afternoon his Highness took a walk in the fields after sundown. Sunday, 5 July, he went to hear mass at San Bernardo, the mass being celebrated by his preceptor Honorato Juan, and his godfather, Don Pedro, Ponce de Leon, bishop of Placencia. His Highness ate as usual in that convent. From there, a little before five in the afternoon, he went to the town square to see a bullfight and a performance of the game of spears. He ate dinner at the usual hour in the chamber from which he had watched, and then returned at night to the palace. That night between ten and eleven o'clock news arrived that the most serene Princess of Portugal had had a fever since the previous Friday. On Monday his Majesty sent permission for the withdrawal of the physicians and surgeons who had come to treat his Highness. On Tuesday, before presenting four pesos of gold and seven of silver, as he had promised, to certain religious houses, the prince was weighed. In his shoes and doublet and his coat of damask he weighed ninety-seven pounds.

All this time the scar was forming and, in order to assist it, a powder of white lead was placed on it, then dry lint, and on top the gemini emplaster. Thursday, 9 July, the physicians and surgeons left, and there remained two physicians of the chamber, Vega and Olivares, and I. Friday, 17 July, the wound was very fleshy. His Highness left Alcalá and slept at Barajas, where he remained until Saturday evening, when he left and entered Madrid around ten o'clock at night. The plaster was kept on the wound until 21 July. That day it was removed before he dined, and we made no more applications. Thus from the hour of the fall until the end of the treatment, which was when the emplaster was removed, was ninety-three days minus three hours. In that illness the prince, our Lord, showed great Christian devotion, because not only did the most Christian prince confess, but he received the Holy Sacrament on all occasions when his soul was in peril. As to the honor and service of God, such was his concern that neither this illness nor anything else could deter him from his obligation. Most of the time during the day he attempted to pray to God and to Our Lady and to adore the relics his Majesty ordered brought there, and he promised, provided Our Lord would give him health, to pay personal visits to those many places where the Divine Majesty and the Sacred Queen of Heaven were accustomed to display their miracles, such as at Our Lady of Monserrate, Guadalupe, and the Crucifix of Burgos, and to give, as I said, an offering of four pesos of gold and seven of silver to certain houses of devotion.

The first thing that his Highness saw on opening his eyes was an image of Our Lady which stood on an altar at the front of his chamber, to which he said his prayers with great devotion. So concerned was he with the things of God that, speaking one day with his confessor of those matters that troubled him most, he asked him for the Holy Sacrament; to which the confessor replied that his Highness had received it; saying: You had it a week ago, and that was enough. Indeed, he never failed in matters that concerned his soul; such was his devotion that, according to his Highness's story, on Saturday night, 9 May, the Blessed Fra Diego appeared to him in his Franciscan habit, a cross in his hands, and attired with a true girdle. The prince thought that it was Saint Francis and said: Why don't you have the stigmata? He does not recall the reply except that he was comforted and told that he would not die from his illness. Thereafter his Highness always showed the greatest devotion to the holy Fra Diego and promised several times publicly to work for his canonization.

His Highness also showed great obedience and respect for his Majesty, because he never refused to do those things the Duke of Alba or Don Garcia de Toledo ordered in the latter's name, even in the days of delirium. He likewise obeyed all orders pertaining to his health, being so obedient to the physicians that so long as he was in his senses he readily took all the remedies, regardless how distasteful they might be; he even asked for them, and they were of great aid in restoring his health.

The diligence and care all his servants provided was such as was never seen before; they took their example from his Majesty, the king, our Lord, who displayed his royal soul to be filled with great humanity and devotion. The Duke of Alba, who was there by order of his Majesty, at no hour or moment of time failed in what was necessary, looking after what was to be done as a man accustomed to great bodily and mental toil; and as he had so many times commanded great armies, he did with ease what would have been immense labor for others; he spent all his nights fully dressed in a chair. Don Garcia de Toledo, governor of his Highness, from the day of the fall until the end of the case, worked so hard that there were few nights when he disrobed, and most days, calling the physicians and surgeons into his presence, he gave orders for all things. Luis Quijada, the Prince's master of the horse, worked so hard that he became ill of an erysipelas and fever so that he endangered his own life. The prince's preceptor, Honorato Juan, despite sickness at various times throughout the [previous] winter, and his invalidism, never failed to be present at the treatments, meals, and consultations. It would be difficult to tell the tasks that all performed, especially the gentlemen of the chamber and the majordomos of his Highness, and would require too long an account since none of them ever rested, day or night. All the officials and servants did everything humanly possible in this task. I do not know if they could have done more for their own lives, because they conducted themselves in such a way as to prove that they were ready to die for their lord.

With regard to those who took care of his Highness, I do not care to say anything since I was of that group, and it might appear that I am speaking for myself. But two things must be mentioned. First, there were doubts, as in all cases wherever there is conjecture; but since we all had the prince's health at heart, we finally agreed, always adopting the most reasonable and certain course, so that there was never a greater harmony between so many physicians and surgeons. I ought not fail to mention their great danger because of the hostile sentiments of the ignorant public. The same fate befell Don Francisco de Castilla, alcalde of the house and court of his Majesty, whose zeal was put to a severe test during the illness. As far as we were concerned, we did everything that could be done; we had many consultations, during the day as well as during the night, to discuss what should be done not only for the present situation of the prince, our Lord, but for what might result. Everything was foreseen so that medicaments were always ready for use and no possibility overlooked. These preventive measures will be appreciated by men of experience in matters pertaining to the art and by all men of sound understanding. As for others, they must do without compliments, because being far away they wanted to criticize those who were present and taking care of his Highness. May they be punished by their own shame, and may they be satisfied to have given proof of their ignorance.

The public manifestations that took place upon the occasion of the prince's illness, as well as everyone's sorrow, are too well known to need further mention. These things belong to the province of those whose mission it is to write the history of these times, and I am sure that they will not forget what is one of their most noteworthy events. Not only did the faithful subjects of his

Majesty give proofs of their affection, but many strangers prayed to God for the prince's health and gave thanks when he recovered. For all this his Highness should render thanks to God who accorded him the privilege of making himself dear to everyone and saved him from such peril.

During that illness and convalescence the number of grandees, dukes, counts, marquesses, and other illustrious lords, knights, prelates, and noblemen who came to call was so considerable that it would take too long to give a detailed account of them. Let it suffice to say that not one person of importance, unless prevented by a major circumstance, failed to pay a visit to his Highness. Some offered their services during his illness, others during his convalescence, showing great proof of affliction during the period of distress and happiness and joy during his recovery of health. The physicians and surgeons who took part in the treatment of the prince are the following: from the beginning to the end, Doctor Vega, Doctor Olivares, and the Licentiate Dionisio Daza; from the second day, in addition to the above mentioned, Doctor Juan Gutierrez de Santander, physician of the chamber to his Majesty and his protomedico, Doctor Portugués and Doctor Pedro de Torres, surgeons of his Majesty; after the incision that bared [the bone of] the skull, Doctor Mena, physician of the chamber of his Majesty, and Doctor Vesalius, a rare and superior man; from 6 May, the Bachelor Torres, surgeon from Valladolid, who, as a reward from his Majesty, as for all the other surgeons, was received as a surgeon of the house and of the court, with ordinary establishment and with license for three years to reside at the court, a reward quite in keeping with his knowledge and skill. I shall not give any further praise to those who treated his Highness, since they are well known by their knowledge and skill; each gave proof of his knowledge during the consultations as well as during his long practice.

We held more than fifty consultations during the illness of the prince, our Lord, fourteen of them in the presence of his Majesty. The latter were the longest, some lasting at least two hours and others more than four. His Majesty attended these and with notable humanity and interest asked each consultant to explain to him such terms of the art as he did not understand. This is the manner in which the consultations took place: His Majesty was seated on a chair, most of the time without cover, with the grandees and noblemen behind him and the Duke of Alba and Don Garcia de Toledo at his side; the physicians and surgeons were seated in a semicircle in front of him. Don Garcia called by name the one who was to speak, and the physician thus addressed gave his opinion, supporting his statements by authorities and reasons; each was called upon in turn. One day, as it was my turn to speak, Don Garcia said to me: "Speak, Licentiate Daza, and his Majesty orders that you do not quote so many texts." This was a rare distinction, and I understood it. I mention this because there was no way that we could prepare ourselves by study, and it was easy to observe what each knew by memory.

His Highness's fall had been predicted for many years in the following terms: Prince Carlos of Spain will be in danger of a fall from on high, either from a staircase or from a horse. As far as I am concerned, the judicial part of astrology is all trickery; however, it is not all false in regard to births and the revolutions of the year. All things are as pleases God, and since his infinite mercy has favored our kingdoms by giving health to the prince, our master, then may he keep him alive for many years so that he may spend them with his Majesty in peace and justice as to this day, to the honor and glory of God and for the greater development of our holy Catholic faith. Amen.

Appendix

This report was made in this court and in the city of Madrid, on the day of San Diego, 25 July 1562.

Most High and Powerful Prince:
Here is the report your Highness requested me to write of his wound and its results. If it be not written in a manner to please your Highness, please ascribe it to my incapacity. Your Highness may be certain that, in accordance with your wishes, it does not deviate from the truth. May the Lord our God keep you and give you happiness for as many years as he pleases, with increase in your domains, in accordance with the wishes of your Highness's most humble subject.
Highest and Most Powerful Lord:
Your Highness's humblest servant who kisses your royal hands,

Licentiate Dionizio Daza

26. GIOVANNI FILIPPO INGRASSIA TO VESALIUS. TO THE NO-LESS-LEARNED-THAN-CELEBRATED ANDREAS VESALIUS, JUSTLY THE PRINCE OF ANATOMISTS, THE LASTING GOOD WISHES OF GIOVANNI FILIPPO INGRASSIA.[27]

I have received—my mighty Andreas—your learned consilium, which you composed with great care and consideration, and based on your many experiences, for curing the fistulous ulcer of our illustrious marquis. Although his ulcer has now been completely cured for many months, nonetheless, for the use of succeeding generations, I have undertaken to have your consilium published so that by the authority of such a great man as yourself, and supported by your effective reasons and very well-grounded experiences, if ever in a similar case anyone is urged to perform that surgery so much praised by you as proper and effective, he will be able to undertake it boldly and intrepidly and to complete it according to the method you teach. Indeed, I should agree to that new surgery very gladly, perhaps in the case of a Biscayne soldier or a very robust Fleming or Gascon overwhelmed by very severe symptoms and approaching desperation. Very willingly, Vesalius, I would agree with the father of anatomy operating with his own hands, but not with any tyro or common butcher who is ignorant of the simplest anatomy and has never done it himself or professed to have seen it done before by anyone anywhere. However, in the thorax of our illustrious marquis, of whom you especially have long known the nature and complexion, I would not dare to agree to it so boldly no matter who the operating surgeon, and to you and to the others who are absent I shall rather advance the opinion of Pamphilus when he says [If you were here, you too would feel otherwise]. I am the more hesitant in the case of so great a man since, as you also note, "all in whom this operation has been tried did not survive, and many have died through a defluxion of bloody fluid through the incision made because of a wound of the thorax."

Also, in recent times it has become apparent to us that as often as we have allowed that new surgery the patients were called to the feast of Jove before their time, as we also related in our account. Therefore we shall by no means deny that to some, especially to the very robust, the new surgery may be very useful for providing an outlet for retained pus, and where there is no other hope of existence your surgical procedure will have to be employed. In my account

Appendix

I called that surgeon impious and a tyrant, but I used the term not because of this surgery, but particularly because of those very cruel, crossed incisions that must be made even for a very old wound, and the stripping of the skin from the ribs, or, as he said, denuding them as far as the complete disclosure of the lung, and likewise because of the application of eroding and caustic materials or eschars around the lung and the internal parts, which he was determined to do so rashly and contrary to the opposition of all his colleagues. I shall not mention his many unsuitable, dreadful, and calamitous actions, wrongly performed to the great harm of the patient. We have added your new surgical procedure to those, rather than to the two proposed remedies aforesaid, but we add that it is more reasonable by far than his rash propositions. We have determined that in all other men it is of little danger, but, in the case of the very illustrious marquis, extremely dangerous and for many reasons rather lethal. We do not understand what precaution can prevent such an incision from touching and injuring the lung, since it is joined to the membrane lining the ribs, and where the membrane is lacking the substance of the intercostal muscles holds the connection very closely. Furthermore, we are unable to conceive how it is possible to impose the tip of the index finger, or of another, for the safety of the lung during the course of the surgery. We not only believe that the lung is joined by a fibrous connection in such a case to the internal membrane or muscles of the thorax—howevermuch it appeared otherwise to you in healthy cadavers and in others diseased outside the thorax, and was sometimes observed by us—but that it adheres there by a very strong union or coalescence or, as we prefer to say, joined by agglutination. We maintain this as an absolutely certain conjecture; we have seen it very often in those dead from pleurisy and more from peripneumonia as well as in many dead from a wound of the head or of the thorax, and we have indicated and demonstrated it to many physicians and scholars who were present. Hence it was not at all possible to operate, no matter how delicately and dexterously, so as to separate, without tearing, the substance of the lung, much less its own membrane. Nevertheless, our very illustrious marquis has escaped unharmed—to the honor and glory of God—and now, by Hercules, he is enjoying better health and bodily constitution than before he received the wound.

I should like to add one remark, most distinguished gentleman; even absent you grasped many things, such as the shape of the first wound, the different abscesses, and the suppurations or collections of pus which resulted; if it had been possible for you to be present, all these would have seemed very different to you, extraneous from the nature of the matter, and many even impossible. Hence it is unnecessary to dwell on these matters again, except for those we have explained otherwise through a very true account. May you meanwhile be well, and esteem your Filippo as he in return is your constant advocate and herald of your abilities.

Palermo, in like manner Christmas, 1563

NOTES

A selective bibliography to Chapter I

Walter Artelt. *Die ältesten Nachrichten über die Sektion menschlicher Leichen im mittelalterlichen Abendland.* (Abhandlungen zur Geschichte der Medizin und der Naturwissenschaften, Heft 24). Berlin, 1940.

Guy de Chauliac. *La grande chirurgie.* Ed. E. Nicaise. Paris, 1890.

Johann Ludwig Choulant. *History and bibliography of anatomical illustration.* Trans. Mortimer Frank. Chicago, 1920.

George W. Corner. *Anatomical texts of the earlier middle ages.* Washington, D.C., 1927.

A. Corradi. "Dello studio e dell'insegnamento dell'anatomia in Italia nel medio evo ed in parte del cinquecento," *Gazz. Med. Ital. Provincie Venete,* 1873, 16:no. 37; 18:nos. 7–9.

J. F. Dobson. "Herophilus of Alexandria," *Proc. Roy. Soc. Med.* (Section Hist. Med.), 1925, 18:19–32.

————. "Erasistratus," *ibid.,* 1927, 20:21–28.

Ludwig Edelstein. "Die Geschichte der Sektion in der Antike," *Quellen und Studien zur Geschichte der Naturwissenschaften und der Medizin,* III (Berlin, 1932), 100–156.

————. "The development of Greek anatomy," *Bull. Hist. Med.,* 1935, 3:235–248.

The Fasciculo di medicina. Ed. Charles Singer. Florence, 1925.

Galen. *Oeuvres anatomiques, physiologiques, et médicales.* Trad. Ch. Daremberg. Paris, 1854–1856. 2 vols.

————. "Galen's elementary course on bones," trans. Charles Singer, *Proc. Roy. Soc. Med.* (Section Hist. Med.), 1952, 45:25–34.

————. *On anatomical procedures.* Trans. Charles Singer. London, 1956.

————. *On anatomical procedures. The later books.* Trans. W. L. H. Duckworth. Cambridge, 1962.

P. de Koning. *Trois traités d'anatomie arabes.* Leyden, 1903.

Michele Medici. *Compendio storico della scuola anatomica di Bologna.* Bologna, 1857.

Henri de Mondeville. *Chirurgie.* Ed. E. Nicaise. Paris, 1893.

Mondino. *Anatomies de Mondino dei Luzzi et Guido de Vigevano.* Ed. Ernest Wickersheimer. Paris, 1926.

Luigi Nardo. "Dell'anatomia in Venezia. Con note e giunte del Dott. Cesare Musatti," *Ateneo Veneto,* 1897, 20:fasc. 2–3.

Francesco Puccinotti. *Storia della medicina.* Vol. II. Livorno, 1859.

George Sarton. *Galen of Pergamon.* Lawrence, Kansas, 1954.

Charles Singer. "The anothomia of Hieronymo Manfredi (1490)," in *Studies in the history and method of science* (Oxford, 1917), 80 ff.

————. *Evolution of anatomy.* London, 1925.

————. "How medicine became anatomical," *Brit. Med. Jour.,* 1954, 2:1499–1504.

————. The strange histories of some anatomical terms," *Med. Hist.,* 1959, 3:1–7.

Edward C. Streeter. "The rôle of certain Florentines in the history of anatomy, artistic and practical," *Johns Hopkins Hosp. Bull.,* 1916, 27:113–118.

Karl Sudhoff. *Tradition und Naturbeobachtung in den illustrationen medizinischer Handschriften und Frühdrucke.* Leipzig, 1907.

————. *Ein Beitrag zur Geschichte der Anatomie im Mittelalter.* Leipzig, 1908.

Robert von Töply. "Geschichte der Anatomie," in Puschmann. *Handbuch der Geschichte der Medizin.* Vol. II. Jena, 1903.

Pietro Tosoni. *Della anatomia degli antichi e della scuola anatomica padovana.* Padua, 1844.

Ernest Wichersheimer. "Les premières dissections à la Faculté de Médecine de Paris," *Bull. Soc. l'Hist. Paris et l'ile-de-France,* 1910, 37:159–169.

Notes to Chapter II

Abbreviations

Brandi	Karl Brandi. *Kaiser Karl V. Werden und Schicksal einer Persönlichkeit und eines Weltreiches.* Munich, 1941.
Cushing	Harvey Cushing. *A bio-bibliography of Andreas Vesalius.* New York, 1943.
De Vocht	Henri de Vocht. *History of the foundation and the rise of the Collegium Trilingue Lovaniense 1517–1550.* Louvain, 1951–1955. 4 vols.
Ep.Ch.Rt.	Andreas Vesalius. *Epistola, rationem modumque propinandi radicis Chynae decocti . . . & praeter alia quaedam, epistola cuiusdam ad Iacobum Sylvium sententiam recensens, veritatis ac potissimum humanae fabricae studiosis perutilem: quum qui bactenus in illa nimium Galeno creditum sit, facile commonstret.,* Basel, 1546.
Ep.V.S.	Andreas Vesalius. *Epistola, docens venam axillarem dextri cubiti in dolore laterali secandam: & melancholicum succum ex venae portae ramis ad sedem pertinentibus, purgari.* Basel, 1539.
Examen	Andreas Vesalius. *Anatomicarum Gabrielis Falloppii observationum examen.* Venice, 1564.
Fabrica (1543)	Andreas Vesalius. *De humani corporis fabrica libri septem.* Basel, 1543.
Fabrica (1555)	Andreas Vesalius. *De humani corporis fabrica libri septem.* Basel, 1555.
Fisch	Max H. Fisch. "Vesalius in the English state papers," *Bull. Med. Libr. Ass.,* 1945, 33:231–253.
Roth	Moritz Roth. *Andreas Vesalius Bruxellensis.* Berlin, 1892.
Singer & Rabin	Charles Singer and C. Rabin. *A prelude to modern science. Being a discussion of the history, sources and circumstances of the 'Tabulae anatomicae sex' of Vesalius.* Cambridge, 1946.
Vandenesse	Jean de Vandenesse. *Journal des voyages de Charles Quint, de 1514 à 1551,* in *Collection des voyages des souverains des Pays-Bas.* Ed. M. Gachard, II, Brussels, 1874, p. 53 ff.

Notes to Chapter II

[1] *Ep.Ch.Rt.,* pp. 196–197.

[2] The charter in full is to be found in the present writer's paper, "Andreas Vesalius, Count Palatine," *Jour. Hist. Med.,* 1954, 9:196 ff. The original charter is in the Oesterreichisches Staatsarchiv, Vienna, Reichsregister Karl V, vol. 22, fols. 272v–279r.

[3] Emile Spelkens, "Généalogie de la famille d'André Vésale (Wijtinck dictus van Wesele)," *L'Intermédiaire des Généalogistes,* Brussels, 1961, 16:65–67. Spelkens has based his opinions upon research in the Fonds Houwaerts (Bibliothèque Royale, Section des manuscrits).

[4] R. Westermann, "Von der 'Seel' Wesels, einer niederrheinischen Stadt," *Meine Heimat,* 1934, 8:16.

[5] O'Malley, "Andreas Vesalius, Count Palatine," p. 206.

[6] Spelkens, *op. cit.,* p. 67.

[7] *Matricule de l'Université de Louvain,* ed. Reusens, I, Brussels, 1903, p. 98.

[8] E. Reusens, *Documents relatifs à l'histoire de l'Université de Louvain,* II, pt. i, Louvain, 1903, pp. 7–21, 191, 193–196.

[9] *Ibid.,* pp. 28–85. Later d'Oisterwyk became city physician of Brussels, see Alphonse Wauters, "Quelques mots sur André Vésale," *Mém. Acad. Roy. Belge,* 1897, 55:49.

[10] Reusens, *op. cit.,* pp. 27, 235.

[11] *Ibid.,* p. 236. The "mathematical" or, more correctly, astrological ability of Johannes is confirmed by his work *Exhortatio super calendarii correctione,* addressed to Pope Eugene IV and thus composed somewhere within the years of that pontiff's reign, 1431–1437. The manuscript, although preserved for some time in the monastery of Groenendael, had disappeared by the time Molanus composed his history of Louvain, *Historiae lovaniensium libri XV,* ed. P. F. X. Ram, I, Brussels, 1861, p. 560. Attention has been called to a second work, a manuscript of the fifteenth century signed *Per Johannem de Wesalia,* termed "probably autograph," purchased at auction in 1864 and now in the city archives in Brussels. Entitled merely *Antiquiteyten,* it contains observations presented to a "very illustrious prince"—possibly the Duke of Burgundy—regarding the appearance of a comet in the constellation of Pisces, astrological rather than astronomical in character. See Wauters, *op. cit.,* pp. 11–12. The text of the work was recently published by A. Abel and Mina Martens, "Le rôle de Jean de Vésale, médecin de la ville de Bruxelles, dans la propagande de Charles le Témeraire," *Cahiers Bruxellois,* 1956, 1:41–86.

Notes to Chapter III

[12] *Actes ou procès-verbaux des séances tenues par le Conseil de l'Université de Louvain*, ed. Reusens, I, Brussels, 1903, p. 26.

[13] *Ibid.*, p. 115.

[14] *Ibid.*, p. 345.

[15] *Ibid.*, p. 289.

[16] *Ibid.*, p. 457.

[17] This Ludovicus, or Louis de Vettre de Dienst, d. 1460, matriculated at Louvain in 1427, was promoted licentiate in arts in 1431, and thereafter became rector of the faculty of arts and applied himself to the study of medicine. In 1442 he became M.D., and thus qualified to teach in the faculty of medicine. *Ibid.*, p. 319n.

[18] *Actes*, ed. Van Hove, II, Brussels, 1919, p. 19.

[19] *Ibid.*, p. 31.

[20] *Ibid.*, pp. 31–32.

[21] *Ibid.*, pp. 33–34, 35, 53–54, 56, 61.

[22] *Ibid.*, p. 68.

[23] Wauters, *op. cit.*, p. 11.

[24] *Ibid.*, p. 13.

[25] O'Malley, "Andreas Vesalius, Count Palatine," p. 210.

[26] Wauters, *op. cit.*, pp. 12–13.

[27] Molanus, *op. cit.*, I, p. 560. Wauters, *op. cit.*, p. 13, mentions a pension received by Everard from Maximilian which is recorded in the *Livres Noirs* in the Archives Royales in Brussels.

[28] Wauters, *op. cit.*, pp. 8–9.

[29] *Ibid.*, p. 14.

[30] *Ep.Ch.Rt.*, p. 197.

[31] Wauters, *op. cit.*, p. 14.

[32] *Matricule de l'Université de Louvain*, ed. Jos. Wils, II, Brussels, 1946, p. 221.

[33] Wauters, *op. cit.*, p. 14.

[34] *Matricule*, II, p. 155.

[35] Wauters, *op. cit.*, pp. 14–15.

[36] *Ibid.*, p. 15.

[37] Alexandre Henne and Alphonse Wauters, *Histoire de la ville de Bruxelles*, II, Brussels, 1845, pp. 527–529.

[38] Spelkens, *op. cit.*, p. 68.

[39] Henne and Wauters, *op. cit.*, II, pp. 527–529.

[40] *Ibid.*, III, p. 13.

[41] *Ibid.*, III, pp. 422–423.

[42] Wauters, *op. cit.*, pp. 20–21.

[43] *Ibid.*, p. 17.

[44] François, or Franciscus, who wrote the dedicatory preface to the *Letter on the china root*, remarked therein: "Contrary to my natural inclinations I was repeatedly urged by my parents to the study of law—a study which I have as often abandoned . . . now I am determined to devote my fullest attention to the study of medicine," *Ep.Ch.Rt.*, p. 8.

[45] Wauters, *op. cit.*, p. 17.

[46] *Étoile Belge*, Brussels, 20 July 1895.

Notes to Chapter III

[1] *Libelli quinque*, Nuremberg, 1547, fol. 178r.

[2] Indeed, Cardano appears to have had even more information, since he writes additionally that the birth occurred at a quarter to six in the morning. Also see Harry Friedenwald, "Cardanus's horoscope of Vesalius," *Bibliofilia*, 1933, 35:421–430, who claims that his copy of the *Fabrica* contains this horoscope in Cardano's autograph. P. Eber, *Calendarium historicum*, Wittenburg, 1550, p. 50, as well as in later editions, places the time of birth at a quarter to six on the morning of 1 January 1514–1515. See Roth, p. 58, n. 1. As the later work, Eber's may be assumed to represent a borrowing, and an inaccurate one, from Cardano. The year can be explained as that of the Julian calendar which did not change until March.

[3] *Fabrica* (1543), fol. *4r.

[4] *Ibid.*, p. 543; see Thomas R. Forbes, "The social history of the caul," *Yale Jour. Biol.*, 1953, 24:495–508.

[5] Roth, p. 60.

[6] Vandenesse, p. 508.

[7] Wauters, "Quelques mots sur André Vésale," *Mém. Acad. Roy. Belge*, 1897, 55:17:18. In his memoirs Felix Plater declared that in 1553 his father Thomas had leased his printing establishment to Michael Stern for one florin a week, but that Stern had relinquished it after thirty

Notes to Chapter IV

weeks, *Beloved son Felix. The journal of Felix Platter,* trans. Sean Jennett, London, 1961, pp. 108, 121.

[8] Alexandre Henne and Alphonse Wauters, *Histoire de la ville de Bruxelles,* III, Brussels, 1845, p. 169.

[9] Archives Générales du Royaume. Université de Louvain, n. 24, fol. 21.

[10] De Vocht, I, p. 63 ff.

[11] Reusens, *Documents relatifs à l'histoire de l'Université de Louvain,* IV, pp. 1–11.

[12] *Ibid.,* p. 32.

[13] *Statuts almae universitatis lovaniensis,* in Molanus, *op. cit.,* II, pp. 920–921.

[14] *Ibid.,* pp. 924–925.

[15] *Ibid.,* p. 933.

[16] De Vocht, III, pp. 35–55.

[17] *Ibid.,* pp. 355–358.

[18] See above, p. 470, n.88.

[19] De Vocht, III, pp. 258–261.

[20] *Ibid.,* p. 296n.

[21] *Fabrica* (1543), p. 623.

[22] *Ibid.,* p. 531.

[23] John Ferguson, "Bibliographical notes on the works of Michael Scot," *Records Glasgow Bibl. Soc.,* 1931, 9:75 ff.

[24] *Fabrica* (1543), p. 531.

[25] De Vocht, I, pp. 249, 277–279, 294–295.

[26] *Ibid.,* II, pp. 99–101, 316.

[27] *Ibid.,* II, pp. 220–224, III, 179–190.

[28] Wauters, *op. cit.,* pp. 51–53, where the document is given in full.

[29] De Vocht, I, p. 518n.

Notes to Chapter IV

[1] Years later Gabriele Cuneo was to describe Vesalius as a student and auditor of Sylvius for three years. Since we know that Vesalius left Paris in the summer of 1536, he must therefore have arrived in 1533 for the opening of the medical school in the autumn of that year. See *Francisci Putei pro Galeno examen,* Venice, 1564, p. 44.

[2] De Vocht, II, pp. 582–583. Jean Sturm, originally from Schleiden, in the Eifel, had gone to Louvain in 1524 where he became a student in the Pedagogium Trilingue, studying Latin with Goclenius, Greek with Rescius, and, after finding the lectures of Campensis too advanced for him, studying Hebrew with Clenardus. He remained in Louvain until 1530, so there was the possibility of an acquaintance with Vesalius there, and then went to Paris where he attended some of the lectures on medicine given by Guinter of Andernach, who also had previously been in Louvain. However, Sturm did not pursue this discipline, and his ultimate fame was to rest on his mastery of Latin literature. In 1537 he was called to Strasburg, but he had been in Paris through the whole of Vesalius's sojourn in that city; *ibid.,* II, pp. 579–584. Whatever the cause and place of their acquaintance may have been, Vesalius was to refer later to Sturm very definitely in terms of esteem and friendship.

[3] Abel Lefranc. *Histoire du Collège de France depuis ses origines jusqu'à la fin du premier empire,* Paris, 1893, p. 137.

[4] J.-B.-L. Chomel, *Essai historique sur la médecine en France,* Paris, 1762, p. 142 ff.

[5] *Commentaires de la faculté de médecine de l'Université de Paris (1395–1516),* ed. E. Wickersheimer, Paris, 1915.

[6] Preparations are now being made for their publications, but, in the present work, reference to the Commentaries after 1516 is to the manuscript version kindly supplied in photograph by the Bibliothèque de la Faculté de Médecine.

[7] Chomel, *op. cit.,* pp. 148–149.

[8] *Commentaires,* p. 193.

[9] *Ibid.,* p. xviii.

[10] *Ibid.,* p. 247.

[11] *Ibid.,* p. 312.

[12] *Ibid.,* pp. 459–460, 463, 527.

[13] *Ibid.,* pp. 317–318.

[14] *Ibid.,* pp. 518, 524, 535; A. Corlieu, *L'ancienne faculté de médecine de Paris,* Paris, 1877, p. 6; E. Coyecque, *L'Hôtel-Dieu de Paris,* I, Paris, 1891, p. 288.

[15] Hahn, *Bibliothèque de la faculté de médecine de Paris,* Paris, 1929, p. 36.

[16] Chomel, *op. cit.,* pp. 142–143.

[17] *Commentaires,* pp. xlii–xliii.

Notes to Chapter IV

[18] Corlieu, *op. cit.*, pp. 93–94.

[19] *Commentaires*, pp. liii, 100, 131, 142, 154, 177, 194, 211–212, 225, 299.

[20] Corlieu, *op. cit.*, pp 93–94.

[21] *Commentaires*, pp. 226–227.

[22] Jean Vasses of Meaux, Joannes Vassaeus *Meldensis*, 1486–1550, became baccalaureate of medicine in 1518, *Commentaires*, IV, fol. 675r, licenciate in May, 1520, V, fol. 90v, and doctor on 3 December 1520, V, fol. 101v. At the end of 1521 he became a regent doctor. In 1525 he was chosen professor, V, fol. 178r, and finally was elected dean in November 1532, V, fol. 317r. He died in November 1550. Vasses translated a number of Hippocratic and Galenic treatises from 1531 onward, which gained him considerable distinction, as noted in 1546 in the Commentaries by the then-dean Jacques Houillier, VI, fol. 46r: *Joannes Vassaeus vir sexagenarius . . . plurimas authoritatis et doctrinae qui qui editis operibus versis aliquot Hippocratis et Galeni libris toti Europae innotuit.* In 1537 he published anonymously and as a textbook for the students *De judiciis urinarum tractatus ex probatis collectus authoribus et in tabulae formam confectus*, Paris, 1537. See Edouard Turner, "Jean Vasses de Meaux," *Études historiques*, Paris, 1878, pp. 412–417. Vasses quite obviously was of the Galenic school, if not perhaps still somewhat influenced by more medieval thought.

[23] The great seal of the faculty of medicine, engraved in 1274, was five centimetres in diameter and depicted the seated Virgin facing forward and holding a branch in her left hand and an open book in the right, with two students on either side of her. The legend on the seal ran +S[*igillum ma*]*gistrorum Facultatis medicine Pa*[*risiensis*]. The counterseal, twenty-five millimetres in diameter, represented a seated doctor expounding from an open book, and it bore the legend: *Secret. gloriosissim. Ypocratis.* The two seals were kept in a chest guarded by five locks of which the keys were retained by the dean and the oldest regent doctor of each of the four nations; Corlieu, *op. cit.*, pp. 96–97. A third seal pendant from a silver chain represented the insignia of the dean who, upon giving up office, formally handed it over to his successor as a symbol of the transmission of his power; *Commentaires*, p. liv. It was this seal that was most commonly employed by the dean. As yet the faculty of medicine had no heraldic device.

[24] Chomel, *op. cit.* p. 143 ff.

[25] See E. Wickersheimer, *La médecine et les médecins en France à l'époque de la renaissance* Paris, 1906, p. 41.

[26] Chomel, *op. cit.*, p. 144.

[27] Jean Tagault, d. 1545, like Jacobus Sylvius originally from Picardy, received his medical degree at Paris in 1522 and thereafter taught surgery there. As will be indicated later, he was one of the few members of the faculty actively interested in anatomical studies. This is slightly indicated in his surgical text, *De chirurgica institutione libri quinque*, Paris, 1543, which is illustrated with skeletal figures, although much inferior to the Vesalian skeletons of the same year, and by the remarks of Andres Laguna, see above, p. 58.

[28] *Commentaires*, p. lv; Chomel, *op. cit.*, pp. 158–159.

[29] *Commentaires*, pp. lvii, 45, 202.

[30] *Ibid.*, p. 199.

[31] Chomel, *op. cit.*, p. 165.

[32] Corlieu, *op. cit.*, pp. 19–20.

[33] *Commentaires*, pp. xix, 90, 138–139, 148, 155, 157.

[34] Corlieu, *op. cit.*, p. 5.

[35] Chomel, *op. cit.*, p. 157.

[36] Corlieu, *op. cit.*, p. 18.

[37] *Commentaires*, pp. 479–480, 484, 486.

[38] *Ibid.*, IV, fol. 41r, V, fol. 47v.

[39] Corlieu, *op. cit.*, p. 22.

[40] *Ibid.*, p. 24.

[41] *Ibid.*, p. 18.

[42] *Commentaires*, pp. xxi, 247.

[43] *Ibid.*, pp. xxiv, 427, 529; Chomel, *op. cit.*, pp. 123–126, 150, 153–154; Corlieu, *op. cit.*, pp. 21–22.

[44] *Commentaires*, pp. xxxvi–xl.

[45] Alfred Franklin, *Recherches sur la bibliothèque de la faculté de médecine de Paris*, Paris, 1864, p. 30.

[46] Corlieu, *op. cit.*, pp. 36–37.

[47] *Ibid.*, pp. 37–38, 40–41.

[48] *Ibid.*, p. 41.

[49] *Ibid.*, pp. 42–45.

[50] *Ibid.*, p. 45.

[51] *Ibid.*, pp. 46–49.

[52] *Ibid.*, p. 54.

[53] *Ibid.*, pp. 51–52.

[54] *Commentaires*, p. 286.

[55] *Ibid.*, p. 297.

[56] *Ibid.*, p. 304.

[57] *Ibid.*, p. 353.

[58] *Ibid.*, p. 403.

[59] *Ibid.*, pp. 303–304.

[60] *Ibid.*, pp. 310, 312.

[61] *Ibid.*, p. 331.

[62] *Ibid.*, p. 337.

[63] *Ibid.*, p. 347.

[64] *Ibid.*, pp. 349–350.

[65] *Ibid.*, p. 346.

[66] *Ibid.*, p. 358.

[67] *Ibid.*, p. 404.

[68] *Ibid.*, p. 417.

[69] *Ibid.*, p. 469.

[70] *Ibid.*, p. 495.

[71] *Ibid.*, p. 503.

[72] *Ibid.*, p. 512.

[73] *Ibid.*, IV, fol. 79v.

[74] *Ibid.*, pp. 525–527.

[75] *Ibid.*, p. 390.

[76] Singer and Rabin, p. xix.

[77] *Ibid.*, p. xv. *Claudii Galeni Pergameni de anatomicis administrandis libri novem Ioanne Guintero Andernachio interprete*, Paris, Simon Colines, 1531.

[78] *Ep.Ch.Rt.*, p. 42.

[79] *The Endeavour of Jean Fernel*, Cambridge, 1946.

[80] *Commentaires*, IV, fol. 27v–28r, V, fol. 60v. The "certain other," with the exception of Jacobus Sylvius who was not a member of the faculty of medicine, must have been among the following, who were the other regent doctors at that period: Petrus Rorer, the "ancient," Joannes Ruellius, Ludovicus Burgensis, Petrus Collier, Joannes Le Gendre, Nicolas Laffille, Ludovicus Braillon, Joannes Divry, Claudius Roger, Guillelmus Zolin, Joannes le Grain, Franciscus Myron, Michael Du Monceau, Petrus Rogier, Richard du Tartre, Joannes de Hortis, Guillelmus Milet, Joannes Morelli, Michael Amy, Nicolas Guerin, Petrus Allen, Hubertus Coquiel, Petrus Godefroy, Franciscus Belot, Claudius Magistri, Joannes Tagault, Carolus du Feu, Jacobus Froment, Joannes Maillart, Arturus Rioult, Joannes Columbe, Martinus Akakia, Thomas de Cuelly, Joannes Froideval, Antonius le Cocq, Joannes Guido, Philip de Flesselles, Joannes de Barra, Valerandus Eva, Nicolas Baron, Antonius Gentil, Hieronymus Varades, Jacobus Staphet, Jean Guinter, Joannes de Faxino, Pierre Roussel, Nicolas Vigoreux, and Vicentius Mustel. In the year 1535–36 two new names were added: Ludovicus Le Tourneur and Nicolas Cop, the latter already having been the rector of the university in 1533–34 and soon to be forced to flee from France as a result of his support of religious reform.

[81] Sylvius, *Opera omnia*, Geneva, 1634, p. 704.

[82] *Commentaires*, IV, fol. 301r.

[83] *Ibid.*, V, fol. 62r.

[84] *Oeuvres facétieuses de Noël du Fail*, ed. Assezat, II, Paris, 1874, pp. 145–146.

[85] *Fabrica* (1543), fol. *3r.

[86] *Ibid.*

[87] *Ibid.*

[88] *Ep.Ch.Rt.*, pp. 151–152.

[89] *Vaesani cujusdam calumniarum in Hippocratis Galenique rem anatomicam depulsio*, Paris, 1551, fol. 13v. For more information on Antonio Massa, who was not sympathetic to Sylvius's strenuous Galenism, see above, p. 122.

[90] *Isagoge*, Venice, 1556, fol. 89v.

[91] *Ibid.*, fol. 57r.

[92] *Ibid.*, fol. 11v.

[93] *Ibid.*, fol. 7v ff.

[94] *Ibid.*, fols. 46v–47r.

[95] Curt Elze, "Jacobus Sylvius, der Lehrer Vesals, als Begründer der anatomischen Nomenklatur," *Zschr. Anat. Entw.*, 1949, 114:242–250; C. E. Kellett, "Sylvius and the Reform of Anatomy," *Medical History*, 1961, 5:101–116; Singer and Rabin, p. lxxi.

[96] *Commentaires*, IV, fol. 40v.

[97] *Fabrica* (1543), fol. *3r.

[98] *Ibid.*

Notes to Chapter IV

⁹⁹ Basel, 1571, I, p. 91.
¹⁰⁰ *Commentaires,* IV, fol. 206r. For the biography of Guinter see Edouard Turner, "Jean Guinter d'Andernach, 1505–1574," *Gas. Hebd. Méd. Chir.,* 1881, 28:425–434, 441–448, 505–516; J. J. Höveler, "Ioannes Guinterius Andernacus (Johann Günther von Andernach, ein berühmter Arzt und Gelehrter des 16. Jahrhunderts," *Jber. Progymnasium zu Andernach,* Andernach, 1899, pp. 3–21; W. Haberling, "Die Wahrheit über den Namen, das Geburtsjahr und die Jugendzeit des Dr. Winter," *Scritti in onore del Prof. P. Capparoni,* Turin, 1941, pp. 90–95.
¹⁰¹ *Commentaires,* IV, fol. 298r.
¹⁰² *Ibid.,* IV, fol. 298r.
¹⁰³ *Ibid.,* V, fol. 6r.
¹⁰⁴ *Ibid.,* V, fol. 46r.
¹⁰⁵ Although noting a reference to a Paris edition of this work mentioned by De Feyfer and Roth, Cushing, pp. 44–47, was unable to trace a copy and therefore considered the edition of Basel, August 1536, as the first. However, Josiah C. Trent, *Bull. Hist. Med.,* 1945, 18:109–111, called attention to the priority of the Paris edition, citing his own copy of it. Although the month of publication is not indicated, if we take into account the lapse of time necessary for the publication of the Basel edition in August, either from a copy of the Paris edition or the manuscript of that edition, we can see that it is quite possible that the Paris edition had appeared before Vesalius's departure from the French capital.
¹⁰⁶ *Commentaires,* V. fol. 47v. There is considerable reference to this case during the years 1533–1536, and hence during the time Vesalius was studying in Paris. It is noted in the Commentaires under 17 November 1534 that Tagault, the new dean, read to the assembled regent doctors a petition he had written for presentation to the Parlement of Paris "against certain unlearned men who compose and offer for sale in Paris prognostications and so-called almanachs." "The dean and the doctors of the faculty of medicine humbly petition that since many ignorant men, empirics and imposters without any knowledge of the art and science of medicine and astrology every year boldly undertake to compose, cause to be printed, and place on sale almanachs and prognostications filled with foolish superstitions and great vanities, which can and do lead many persons into error and infidelity, which is a great and enormous plague within Christianity in these times of so many schisms and heresies, therefore that it will please you upon consideration to ordain a restraint and prohibition to all printers, booksellers, and other vendors of books against the printing and offering for sale of any almanachs, prognostications, and such manner of books unless first visited by the doctors of the said faculty of medicine to read them carefully and give either their approval or disapproval," *ibid.,* V, fol. 48v. What was especially irritating to the medical faculty was the fact that Thibault, with royal protection, remained untouched.
¹⁰⁷ Singer and Rabin, p. 46.
¹⁰⁸ *Ibid., passim;* Charles Singer, "Some Vesalian Problems," *Bull. Hist. Med.,* 1945, 17:426–428.
¹⁰⁹ Cushing, p. 45.
¹¹⁰ Singer, "Some Vesalian Problems," p. 427.
¹¹¹ *Canon,* Lib. I, fen. i, doct. v.
¹¹² *Fasciculo di medicina,* ed. Singer, Florence, 1925, II, p. 75.
¹¹³ *Commentaria,* Venice, 1521, fol. CLXXXIVV ff.: *Isagogae breves,* Venice, 1522, fol. 18r–v.
¹¹⁴ *Liber introductorius anatomiae,* Venice, 1536, fols. 33r–35r.
¹¹⁵ Guinter, *De medicina veteri et nova,* I, p. 159.
¹¹⁶ Singer, "Some Vesalian Problems," p. 428.
¹¹⁷ *Commentaires,* IV, fol. 40r. On Laguna see the recent work of Teofilo Hernando, *Vida y labor médica del doctor Andrés Laguna,* Segovia, 1960.
¹¹⁸ Laguna, *Anatomica methodus,* Paris, 1535, fol. 12v.
¹¹⁹ *Ibid.,* fol. 17r.
¹²⁰ *Ibid.,* fol. [62r].
¹²¹ *Ibid., fol.* [62r–v].
¹²² *Ibid.,* fols. 16v–17r.
¹²³ *Ibid.,* fol. 24v.
¹²⁴ *Ibid.*
¹²⁵ *Ibid.,* fol. 28r.
¹²⁶ *Ibid.,* fol. 20r–v.
¹²⁷ *Fabrica* (1543), p. 44.
¹²⁸ *Ep.Ch.Rt.,* p. 194.
¹²⁹ *Fabrica* (1543), p. 159. Vesalius may have had a slight acquaintance with the surgeon Estienne de la Rivière who, as C. E. Kellet's studies have indicated, was to a considerable degree responsible for the anatomical content of the *De dissectione partium corporis humani,* Paris, 1545, which has long been primarily attributed to Charles Estienne, "Perino del Vaga et les illustrations pour l'anatomie d'Estienne," *Aesculape,* 1955, 37:74–89, "A note on Rosso and the illustrations to Charles Estienne's *De dissectione,*" *Jour. Hist. Med.,* 1957, 12:325–336, *Two anatomies. An Occasional lecture on the De dissectione of Charles Estienne,* Newcastle, 1958.

Rivière is mentioned in the Commentaries of the medical faculty as a surgeon attending dissections during the years 1533–1536. Estienne did not receive a medical degree until 1540.

[130] *Fabrica* (1543), fol. *3r.

[131] *Ibid.*

[132] *Ibid.*

[133] *Ibid.*

[134] *Ibid.*, p. 538.

[135] Guinter, *De Medicina Veteri et Nova*, Basel, 1571, I, p. 159.

[136] *Ep.V.S.*, p. 60.

[137] Whether or not Chrestien Wechel published his *Osteotome. i. ossium corporis humani divisio, Ex Galeno praecipue collecta* early enough in 1536 for it to have been seen by Vesalius in Paris is not known. The sole copy of these skeletal figures, seen by Choulant, *History and bibliography of anatomic illustration*, trans. Mortimer Frank, Chicago, 1920, p. 156, and by Roth, p. 462, has, at least for the time being, disappeared, and their descriptions are not sufficiently detailed to permit us to determine whether these figures are similar to those of the issue of 1538 of which copies have recently been discovered in the Royal Library, Stockholm, Sten G. Lindberg, "Chrestien Wechel and Vesalius. Twelve unique medical broadsides from the sixteenth century," *Lychnos*, 1953:56 ff. This second issue is comprised of two sheets each displaying a skeleton of somewhat simian character but more detailed than any other such figure prior to the appearance of Vesalius's *Tabulae anatomicae* of 1538. The edition of the *Osteotome* published in 1538 contains not only the skeletal figures but also the osteological nomenclature related to them, and if this was present in the issue of 1536—possibly, as has been suggested, the work of Guinter of Andernach—it may have been influential upon the Vesalian vocabulary as represented in the *Tabulae anatomicae*. These activities of Wechel are also the answer to a question posed by Charles Singer, "A note on the earliest printed anatomical figures," *ABA Annual*, London, 1952, pp. 10–11. Singer calls attention to the fact that, in a note in Wechel's edition (1535) of Balamio's translation of Galen's book *On the bones*, see above, p. 129, Wechel declares that, since the format of the book was too small for proper illustrations, "we thought that large ones must be used whereby all the bones of the human body might be presented in clear view." "What had Wechel in mind," asks Singer, "in writing of these large pictures of the bones which would be more suitable. . . . In fact he did not publish them, nor are anatomical figures known in any works published in France before 1535. . . . How did the idea enter Wechel's head?" The answer is that Wechel did publish the *Osteotome* in 1536, but since that single copy seen by Roth has disappeared, there was no knowledge of its nature and size. Now that a copy of Wechel's edition of 1538 has been found, it is apparent that this is what Wechel had in mind as illustrations to supplement his publication of Galen's treatise.

[138] *De medicina veteri et nova*, I, p. 261.

[139] This collection, published by Froben in Basel, is now in the Wellcome Historical Medical Library. Michael Securis was the brother of John Securis, or Hatchet, who practised in Salisbury and wrote *A detection or querimonie of the daily enormities and abuses committed in physicke*, 1566. Michael has written at the end of several of the treatises that he read them in 1540 and 1541, which suggests that another had them at the time of Vesalius's departure in 1536 and that they had come into Michael's hands only at a later date, possibly from some student who, between 1536 and 1540, would have had time to obtain the bachelor's degree in medicine and had used these works towards that end.

Notes to Chapter V

[1] Brandi, pp. 322–327.

[2] *Ibid.*, p. 334.

[3] *Fabrica* (1543), p. 161; also "Preface," fol. *r.

[4] The basquine, or vasquine, fashionable toward the end of the fifteenth century, was a corset reinforced in front with wood or metal, see *Breif van Andreas Vesalius . . . behelzende de aanwending van het decoct van chynawortel*, trans. and ed. H. Pinkhof and E. C. van Leersum, Amsterdam, 1915, p. 125n., citing Ernest Leoty, *Le corset à travers les ages*, Paris, 1893.

[5] *Ep.Ch.Rt.*, pp. 141–142. Rhazes's prescription is to be found in his *Ad Almansorem*, IX, 87; that is, in the book edited by Vesalius in 1537, in which the chapter is entitled "De vulvae strangulatu." The prescription includes among other things the use of friction, poultices and sweet-smelling unguents.

[6] *Fabrica* (1555), p. 658. Vesalius no longer speaks of the presence of an unskilled barber or says that he himself took over the dissection; moreover, he mentions the presence of several physicians.

[7] Gemma, son of Reynier, Frisius; that is, a native of Dokkum, Friesland, 1508–1555, mathematician, cosmographer, and physician. He studied at Louvain where he was a student of the Lily pedagogium. After a hiatus Gemma returned to Louvain in 1532 to pursue the study of

mathematics, and also took up the study of medicine in 1534 as a means to a livelihood, hence his acquaintance with Vesalius, *Nieuw nederlandsch biografisch woordenboeck*, VI, Leyden, 1924, pp. 556–557; De Vocht, III, pp. 542–565.

[8] *Fabrica* (1543), pp. 161–162. A lithograph representing the scene is to be found in *Les belges illustres*, Brussels, 1845, III, p. 47.

[9] Petrus Divaeus, *Rerum lovaniensium*, Louvain, 1757, p. 10.

[10] De Vocht, II, p. 517n.

[11] *Ibid.*, p. 520n.

[12] *Ibid.*, p. 523.

[13] Reusens, *Documents relatifs à l'histoire de l'Université de Louvain*, I, pp. 264–266, IV, p. 178.

[14] De Vocht, II, p. 517n.

[15] *Ibid.*, III, p. 333n.

[16] *Ibid.*, p. 532 ff.

[17] Pierre Brissot, *Apologetica disceptatio*, ed. nova Renato Moreau, Paris, 1622, pp. 1–145.

[18] For further details on the controversy, see Saunders and O'Malley, *Andreas Vesalius Bruxellensis: The bloodletting letter of 1539*, New York, 1946, pp. 6–19.

[19] *Epistolae medicinales*, Ferrara, 1521, and later editions; see bk. 12, ep. 5, bk. 14, ep. 1.

[20] *Errata recentiorum medicorum*, Hagenau, 1530, *Apologia contra Hieremiam Thriverium Brachelium*, Hagenau, 1534, *Paradoxorum medicinae libri tres*, Basel, 1535.

[21] *De venae sectione in pleuritide*, Lyons, 1532.

[22] This apparently refers to a personal letter to his old preceptor Florenas.

[23] *Ep.V.S.*, p. 5.

[24] I.e., Noots and Willemaers.

[25] Thus it appears that Guinter had shown the *Velitatio* to Vesalius in Paris.

[26] *Ep.V.S.*, p. 7. It was indeed unjust for Drivère to deride Barlandus's treatise since it had been the opening round in the criticisms of Noots and Willemaers as medievalists, those two professors whose positions Drivère was to acquire in 1542. Now that the tide had turned so strongly in favor of Galen, especially in Paris, any work attacking the older school of medicine would presumably be popular and therefore, in the eyes of the Parisian publishers, desirable.

[27] It is interesting to note that Vesalius's phraseology indicates that he had come to realize the youthful, over-strenuous nature of his defense of the new school of venesection. As to the later career of Drivère, although he used the title *artium & medicinae professor* in his reply to Fuchs, he was not officially so in our sense of the term, since the two ordinary chairs were still held by Arnold Noots and Leonard Willemaers, and the two professorships supported by the canonry of St. Peter could only be held by celibates, whereas Drivère was married. It was not until the dismissal of Noots and Willemaers in 1542, already mentioned, that Drivère became a professor and filled the double vacancy; De Vocht, III, p. 532 ff.

[28] *Libri IIII difficilium aliquot quaestionum*, Basel, 1540, pp. 173, 207, 209.

[29] Pantin later published *Aurelii Cornelii Celsi de arte medica libri octo, multis in locis iam emendatiores longè quam unquam antea, editi Gulielmi Pantini Tiletani medici brugensis*, Basel, Oporinus, 1552. On fol. a2r–v he refers to his teachers Drivère and Goossins and to his friend Vesalius to whom he had shown the manuscript of the work for the sake of his criticism. One may wonder if Vesalius recommended Oporinus to Pantin as a publisher. Pantin eventually, as a licentiate in medicine, became pensionary-physician to the town of Bruges and a friend of Cornelius van Baersdorp, later the colleague of Vesalius as an imperial physician. Vesalius never mentions Pantin, and it may be that the physician of Bruges had presumed upon an acquaintance of schooldays. He died 2 October 1583, De Vocht, III, pp. 333–334.

[30] *Ibid.*, III, pp. 334–335.

[31] *Ibid.*, III, pp. 337–338.

[32] *Fabrica* (1543), fol. *3r.

[33] Cushing, pp. 7–9.

[34] Reusens, *op. cit.*, I, p. 695.

[35] Previously a press had been operated in Louvain by Thierry Martens, or Martini, of Alost, c. 1450–1534. Martens had been a far superior printer who had learned the art in Italy. From 1511 to 1529 he had published more than two hundred books in Louvain, many of them of great significance, but in the latter year he retired and returned to Alost. Rescius had had some experience as corrector to Martens's press, and filled the void created by Martens's retirement by opening his own establishment in 1529 in partnership with Jean Sturm. However, things did not go smoothly, and in 1530 Sturm parted company with Rescius and went to Paris; henceforth Rescius conducted the press under his single proprietorship. Although he had originally announced his intention of printing only to supply the needs of the Pedagogium Trilingue for Greek, Latin, and Hebrew texts, the temptation of gain was too strong for him to withstand, and he proceeded to issue a variety of books of which Vesalius's little treatise is one; see De Vocht, II, pp. 317–318, 621–628, and *passim*.

[36] *Paraphrasis*, fol. 12r.

Notes to Chapter VI

[37] *Ibid.*, fol. 19*r*.
[38] *Ibid.*, fol. 54*v*.
[39] *Ibid.*, fol. 73*r*.
[40] *Ibid.*, fols. 51*v*–53*r*.
[41] Why Vesalius chose a Basel printer is unknown, unless it was on the recommendation of his cousin Martin Stern or because he chanced to pass through the city on his way to Padua. Despite the publication of his book under Winter's sole imprint, the latter was in fact one of four partners, the most famous of them later to be Oporinus, printer of the *Fabrica*. This whole matter will be considered in conjunction with the question of the printing of that work. Robert Winter became a printer only after attempting several other occupations, first that of spice merchant, and then of locksmith. It was under the influence of his wife that he became associated in the printing business with Lazius, Thomas Plater, and Johannes Oporinus, his brother-in-law. The partnership was soon dissolved, however, and Winter seems to have been partly at fault. According to Plater he had no business sense and was pretty much a wastrel, a luxury his means permitted for at least a time. He died between 1550 and 1556. See Paul Heitz, *Basler Büchermarken bis zum Anfang des 16. Jahrhunderts*, Strasburg, 1895, p. xxxii.
[42] Cushing, pp. 7–9.

Notes to Chapter VI

[1] *Commentaires*, V, fol. 75*v*.
[2] Hastings Rashdall, *The universities of Europe in the middle ages*, ed. Powicke and Emden, Oxford, 1936, II, pp. 10–21.
[3] Antonio Favaro, *L'università di Padova*, Venice, 1922, p. 24 ff.
[4] J. Facciolati, *Fasti gymnasii patavini*, Padua, 1757, III, p. 207.
[5] *Statuta almae universitatis D. artistarum et medicorum patavini gymnasii, denuo correcta & emendata*, Venice, 1589, fol. 5*v*. The last major revision of the statutes had been made in 1465 and succeeding printed editions of them had been revised or had added details, usually in the direction of removal of fundamental authority to the government or its agents, that is, the *Riformatori*.
[6] *Ibid.*, fols. 36*v*–37*r*.
[7] *Ibid.*, fols. 46*v*–47*r*.
[8] *Ibid.*, fol. 44*v*.
[9] *Ep.Ch.Rt.*, p. 12. Vesalius also refers briefly in his *Ep.V.S.*, p. 56, to his visits, presumably in Venice, to patients ill with "pleurisy" (*morbus lateralis*) whom "I visited only with my teachers."
[10] Giambattista da Monte, or Montanus, after studies at Padua, practised for a short time in Brescia whence he journeyed to Sicily and then back to Naples where he continued his studies. Thereafter he taught at Naples, Ferrara, and at Padua where he gained renown and gave great impetus to the study and teaching of clinical medicine. He wrote extensively on Galen and Hippocrates as well as on what may be termed general medicine, although most of these works were published posthumously. See Scipione Maffei, *Verona illustrata*, III, pte. IIa, Milan, 1825, p. 318; Giuseppe Cervetto, *Di Giambatista da Monte e della medicina italiana nel secolo XVI*, Verona, 1839; Pier Andrea Saccardo, "La botanica in Italia," *Mem. R. Ist. Veneto di Sci. Lett. Art.*, 1895, 1901, XXV, n. 4, XXVI, n. 6; Francesco Pellegrini, *La clinica medica padovana attraverso i secoli*, Verona, 1939, p. 67 ff. Another testimonial to Paduan clinical teaching is provided by Reiner Solenander, 1524–1601, for many years ducal physician of Cleves, who had studied with Da Monte at Padua. In the preface to his *Consilia medicinalia*, 1596, he remarks: "Those matters in the first part of the second volume are not simply medical *consilia*, but discussions about the sick such as take place between the physician and his students during their visits to them. Those who have been to Italy are acquainted with this very commendable practice."
[11] *Statuta, op. cit.*, fols. 44*v*–45*r*.
[12] Roth, p. 425.
[13] *Ibid.*, p. 426.
[14] *Ibid.*, p. 427. Vesalius had five sponsors: Francesco Frigimeliga, 1491–1558, of Padua, M.D., 1518, who taught the theory and practice of medicine at Padua, 1525–1546, whence he went into papal service, but was enticed by an increased stipend to return to Padua, Vedova, *Biografia degli scrittori padovani*, I, Padua, 1832, pp. 426–430; Oddo degli Oddi, 1478–1558, of Padua, who taught medicine there until his death, except for a brief time in Venice. He was renowned for his exposition of Galen and was referred to as "the spirit of Galen," Vedova, *op. cit.*, II, 1836, pp. 8–11; Giunio Paolo Crasso, *c.* 1500–1575, of Padua, M.D., 1529, where he taught until his death. Although he never rose to the first chair of medicine, he is said to have merited such honor. Crasso published a Latin translation of the anatomical treatise of Protospatharius as well as Latin versions of Areteus, Rufus of Ephesus, and Galen, Vedova, *op. cit.*, I, pp. 300–303. The other two sponsors were Girolamo Tolentino and Girolamo Coradino, also Paduans, but of no special distinction and virtually nothing is known about them.

Notes to Chapter VI

[15] Roth, p. 428, "11 October 1539. The excellent Master Andreas Vesalius, Imperialist, who has lectured on surgery these past years in our University of Padua, has demonstrated such skill in anatomy and the art of dissecting human bodies that his ability in those things is considered admirable and incomparable. He has aroused such favor among all the students that he is strongly requested by them, and such great insistence has been made of it that we ought to retain him with some increase of salary. . . . Therefore let . . . Andreas Vesalius, Imperialist, be rehired . . . at an annual salary of 40 florins, which he has at present, to which let 30 florins be added . . . which his industry and rare ability deserve."

[16] Klaus G. König, "Die Stellung der Anatomen unter den medizinischen Lehren in Padua im 16. Jahrhundert," *Centaurus*, 1960, 7:1–5.

[17] V. Bougiel, *Un célèbre médecin polonais au XVI siècle Joseph Struthius 1516–1568*, Paris, 1901; Lodovico Owikliński, "Clemente Janicius a Padova (1538–1540)," *Omaggio dell'accademia polacca de scienze e lettere all'Università di Padova nel settimo centenario della sua fondazione*, Cracow, 1922, p. 123.

[18] *Statuta, op. cit.,* fol. 37r.

[19] *Ibid.,* fol. 39v.

[20] *Ibid.,* fol. 37v.

[21] *Ibid.,* fol. 67r.

[22] *Ibid.,* fol. 38r.

[23] *Ibid.,* fol. 38v.

[24] Riccoboni, *De gymnasio patavino*, Padua, 1598, p. 27. Although the official university records for this period no longer exist, the account of Antonio Riccoboni, 1541–1599, onetime professor of eloquence of Padua, has the merit of being the one most nearly contemporary with the Vesalian period, and in addition the author states that he has inscribed the names and dates as "they were read by me" in the university records.

[25] Michele Savonarola, *De magnificis ornamentis regie civitatis Padue*, ed. Segarizzi, Città di Castello, 1902, p. 50.

[26] *Fasti gymnasii padovani*, Padua, 1757, I, p. 83.

[27] *Ibid.,* III, p. 207.

[28] *De antiquitate cantabrigiensis academiae*, p. 147, in *Works*, ed. Venn, Cambridge, 1912.

[29] Roth, p. 454.

[30] *Fabrica* (1543), p. 538.

[31] Roth, pp. 454–455.

[32] *Statuta, op. cit.,* fol. 42r–v.

[33] Fol. 184v, in Roth, p. 455.

[34] Fol. 186r–v, in Roth, p. 456.

[35] Fols. 189v–190r, in Roth, p. 456.

[36] *Ep.V.S.,* pp. 60–61.

[37] *Ibid.,* p. 61.

[38] Fols. 192v–193v, in Roth, p. 457.

[39] *Ep.V.S.,* p. 30.

[40] Fol. 203v, in Roth, p. 457.

[41] Fol. 204r, in Roth, p. 457.

[42] *Fabrica* (1543), V, fig. 13.

[43] See above, p. 90.

[44] *Fabrica* (1543), p. 319 [419]. Vesalius wrote that his drawing of the nerves was a "rough sketch I had drawn, with an index added, for one or two friends." Yet as we learn from Vitus Tritonius, some sort of sketch of the nerves was employed during the dissection of December 1537, and, since Vesalius adds that it was this sketch that was published as a plagiarism in Cologne—see above, p. 90—we are aware that it was a relatively finished drawing.

[45] See the query of Max H. Fisch, in the *Jour. Hist. Med.*, 1946, 1:173, and the reply by Fausto Nicolini, *ibid.*, 1946, 1:335–337. Narcissus Parthenopeus, or Narciso Verdú or Verdum, was born in Naples in 1491, descendant of an old noble family of Aragon. Educated in medicine, he was in the imperial service in the Kingdom of Naples, a Spanish dependency, before 1520, and in 1524 Charles V named him protomedicus. Narcissus served in Spain in 1525, and in 1532 was in Brussels where he served Giovan Paolo Coraggio, Neapolitan ambassador to the imperial court. Contemporary opinion did not give him any particular praise as a physician, and mistakes in the treatment of a childhood illness of the emperor's son, the later Philip II, seem to have lost him imperial favor. At any rate, he was back in Naples in 1534, where he died on 20 June 1551, still in possession of his title which appears to have been given false significance by Vesalius.

[46] Singer and Rabin.

[47] First mentioned briefly, however, by Nicolo Massa, *Liber introductorius anatomiae*, Venice, 1536, fol. 34r.

[48] *Fabrica* (1543), p. 642.

[49] Singer and Rabin, pp. lxv–lxxxvi; also Mordecai Etziony, "The Hebrew-Aramaic element

Notes to Chapter VI

in Vesalius' *Tabulae anatomicae sex.* A critical analysis," *Bull. Hist. Med.* 1945, 18:413–424, 1946, 20:36–57.

⁵⁰ On several occasions it has been said that Vesalius owed a debt to Sylvius in regard to anatomical terminology, and perhaps he did acquire something from Sylvius's lectures, although we have no proof of this or even that Sylvius himself had developed such terminology by 1536. However, the reference is made to the *Isagogae* of Sylvius as the source of the debt, but it ought to be noted that that work was not published until 1555, and was written at the earliest in 1542 long after the publication of the *Tabulae* and at the time when Vesalius was completing the composition of the *Fabrica.*

⁵¹ The colophon reads in part: *Imprimebat Venetijs B[ernardinus]. Vitalis Venetus sumptibus Ioannes Stephani Calcarensis.* See Cushing, pp. 12–14, for the bibliographical details.

⁵² In his *Ep.V.S.*, p. 3, Vesalius refers to a letter from Nicolas Florenas in which the latter wrote that the *Tabulae* "were highly commended by his imperial Majesty." Later, in the preface to the *Fabrica* (1543), fol. *4r, dedicated to the emperor, Vesalius declared, "Nor shall I ever forget with what pleasure you examined my *Tabulae anatomicae*, once presented for your inspection by my father Andreas, chief and most faithful apothecary of your Majesty, and how carefully you inquired about everything."

⁵³ The reply to Vesalius's request to the Venetian government for permission to publish is in the Archivio di Stato, Venice, and has been reprinted by Roth, p. 428. It is dated 3 May 1538. "Let the authority of this council be granted to the above-mentioned petitioner Andreas Vesalius, to cause the anatomical illustrations described in his petition to be printed, and as is contained therein for the next ten years, and let him be obliged to observe everything in accordance with our laws regarding printing and distribution."

⁵⁴ See above, pp. 133–134.

⁵⁵ *Fabrica* (1543), fol. *5v. See above, p. 324, for an English version.

⁵⁶ "Chrestien Wechel and Vesalius. Twelve unique medical broadsides from the sixteenth century," *Lychnos*, 1953:50–74. The present author wishes to express his appreciation of Dr. Lindberg's kindness in making photocopies of some of these plagiarisms available.

⁵⁷ Ludwig Choulant, *History and bibliography of anatomic illustrations*, trans. Mortimer Frank, Chicago, 1920, pp. 189–190; Cushing, pp. 17–20.

⁵⁸ Choulant, *op. cit.*, pp. 186, 192; Cushing, pp. 21–28.

⁵⁹ Choulant, *op. cit.*, pp. 148–149; Cushing, pp. 29–32.

⁶⁰ See above, p. 221.

⁶¹ Choulant, *op. cit.*, p. 186; Cushing, pp. 33–43.

⁶² Lindberg, *op. cit.*, p. 54.

⁶³ Choulant, *op. cit.*, p. 156.

⁶⁴ Roth, p. 462.

⁶⁵ Lindberg, *op. cit.*, p. 56 ff., with reproductions, pp. [58–59].

⁶⁶ In this regard Lindberg calls attention to a catalogue of Wechel's publications issued in 1544, in which "at the end of the medical group, *Osteotome picta* and *Tabulae tres de venis & arteriis* are listed consecutively."

⁶⁷ Lindberg, *op. cit.*, pp. 67–68.

⁶⁸ Mortimer Frank in Choulant, *op. cit.*, p. 173n.

⁶⁹ Roth, p. 122.

⁷⁰ Lindberg, *op. cit.*, pp. 54–55.

⁷¹ *Aegidius Macrolios cerebrum animalis facultatis fons et principium, sensum voluntarium per nervos communicans ab se et dorsali medulla enatos universo corpori* [Cologne, 1539]. This is known today only through reference to it in 1852 by Ludwig Choulant, who reproduced both text and illustration; Choulant, *op. cit.*, pp. 186–188; see Cushing, pp. 20–21.

⁷² Choulant, *op. cit.*, p. 187.

⁷³ See above, p. 88.

⁷⁴ *Institutionum anatomicarum . . . libri quatuor, per Ioannem Guinterium Andernachum . . . ab Andrea Vesalio Bruxellensi, auctiores & emendatiores redditi*, Venice, D. Bernardinus, 1538. The full bibliographical description of this as well as of other editions of the work is to be found in Cushing, p. 44 ff.

⁷⁵ *Institutiones*, 1536, p. 14.

⁷⁶ *Ibid.*, 1538, fol. 6v.

⁷⁷ *Ibid.*, 1536, p. 16.

⁷⁸ *Ibid.*, 1538, fol. 8r.

⁷⁹ *Ibid.*, 1536, p. 46.

⁸⁰ *Ibid.*, 1538, fol. 30r.

⁸¹ *Ibid.*, 1536, p. 86.

⁸² *Ibid.*, 1538, fol. 58v.

⁸³ *Ibid.*, 1539, p. 64.

⁸⁴ *Ibid.*, 1536, p. 50.

[85] *Ibid.*, 1538, fol. 32*v*.

[86] *Ibid.*, 1536, pp. 125–126.

[87] *Ibid.*, 1538, fol. 85*v*.

[88] *Ibid.*, 1539, pp. 96–102.

[89] *Ibid.*, p. 119.

[90] *Ibid.*, 1538, fol. 81*v*.

[91] *Ibid.*, 1539, p. 36.

[92] *Ibid.*, 1538, fol. 21*v*.

[93] *Ibid.*, fols. 23*v*–27*v*.

[94] *Ibid.*, 1539, pp. 23–28.

[95] *Ep.V.S.*, p. 7.

[96] *Ibid.* The third edition of Corti's book had been published in 1538. Matteo Corti, or Matthaeus Curtius, 1495–1542, brother of Francesco, a celebrated jurist, was born of a reputedly noble but impoverished family of Pavia. Having become M.D., Corti taught first in his native university and thereafter gained a considerable reputation as professor of the theory of medicine at Padua, 1524–1532. Called thence to become personal physician to Pope Clement VII, upon the pope's death he taught at Bologna and then, upon the invitation of Duke Cosimo de'Medici, at Pisa, where he remained until his death. In the epitaph upon his grave, provided at the expense of Cosimo, he is called "Vindicator of Hippocrates and Galen," Ghilini, *Teatro d'huomini letterati*, II, Venice, 1647, p. 195. While Corti and Vesalius were still friendly, the latter, in his *Venesection letter*, calls him "a man of penetrating judgment." Later, however, after hostility had arisen, Cardano, in mentioning this dispute, indicates a sympathy for Vesalius, remarking upon the restraint he had displayed, *Opera omnia*, Lyons, 1663, I, p. 12. Cardano knew Corti well, having been an auditor as his lectures in Padua, succeeding him at Pisa, and lending him money; *ibid.*, pp. 12, 26.

[97] *Ep.V.S.*, p. 19.

[98] *Ibid.*, p. 19 ff.

[99] Cardano, *Opera omnia*, I, Lyons, 1663, p. 12.

[100] *Fabrica* (1543), pp. 257–259 [357–359].

[101] *Fabrica* (1555), pp. 437–438.

[102] *Examen*, pp. 81–82.

[103] *Andreae Vesalii Bruxellensis, scholae medicorum patavinae professoris publici, epistola, docens venam axillarem dextri cubiti in dolore laterali secandam: & melancholicum succum ex venae portae ramis ad sedem pertinentibus purgari*, Basel, 1539. For bibliographical details, see Cushing, pp. 58–59.

[104] *Ep.V.S.*, p. 7.

[105] In the *Ep.V.S.*, pp. 51–52, Vesalius refers to this prohibition which was later removed after "tedious debates held on the matter at Salamanca." The defeated party then appealed to the Cortes, as Vesalius had learned from Florenas in Spain with the emperor, and declared that the revived classical procedure was no less disastrous for the body than the schisms of the Lutherans for the soul. In 1538 the emperor was at Nice negotiating peace to conclude that war with France which had compelled the young Vesalius to leave Paris in 1536. Vesalius's father, with the emperor at Nice in his capacity of imperial apothecary, wrote to his son that the final decision in the matter of venesection had been left to the emperor but that he, not forgetting the death of "a prince of Piedmont" after undergoing bloodletting according to the medieval procedure, had no intention of prohibiting the use of the newer method.

[106] *Ibid.*, p. 7.

[107] See above, p. 67.

[108] *Ep.V.S.*, p. 56.

[109] *Ibid.*, p. 57.

[110] *Ibid.*, pp. 63–64.

[111] The movements of the head are discussed in the *Fabrica* (1543), pp. 63–68, 276–280, as well as in the *Ep.Ch.Rt.*, pp. 152–153, 159–160.

[112] *Ep.V.S.*, pp. 64–66.

[113] Roth, p. 118.

[114] Cushing, p. xix.

[115] Very little is known about Giovanni Antonio Lonigo, who was also called Plazzi, or Plato, from his habit of referring to that philosopher in his lecture. His family name of Lonigo was also latinized to Leonicus. According to Scardeonius, *Historia de urbis patavii antiquitate*, ed. Graevius, VI, iii, 248, Lonigo had been a student under the surgeon Dominicus Sennus in the year 1531. Realdo Colombo, *De re anatomica*, Venice, 1559, p. 24, declared that he had studied under Lonigo for seven years in Venice, and frequently refers to those years, in one instance with some information on the physical attributes of both teacher and student: "On many occasions I delightedly watched the head of my teacher Joannes Antonius Plato, who was able to move his whole scalp back and forth . . . but now I am the one whose scalp can easily be seen to move

Notes to Chapter VI

since I am very bald, although my skin is without dryness and is soft and lax like the skin of a newly born infant," *ibid.*, p. 122. According to Portal, *Histoire de l'anatomie et de la chirurgie*, I, Paris, 1770, p. 440, Realdo Colombo's father was apothecary to Lonigo, but this seems to be a misunderstanding arisen from the fact that Vesalius's predecessor in the chair of surgery was named Paolo Colombo.

[116] See above, p. 77.

[117] "The very famous professor of Hippocratic medicine received me into his home with great hospitality when I went to Bologna a second time, invited to demonstrate the structure of man," *Fabrica* (1543), p. 78. Giovanni Andrea Bianchi of Parma, doctor of philosophy and of medicine, taught medicine with distinction at Bologna from 1525 until his death in 1565; Giammaria Mazzuchelli, *Gli scrittori d'Italia*, II, pte. 2, Brescia, 1760, p. 1129; Serafino Mazzetti, *Repertorio de tutti i professori antichi della Università di Bologna*, Bologna, 1848, no. 477.

[118] Lodovico Boccadiferro, or Buccaferreus, 1482–2 May 1545, of a once noted and powerful family, studied philosophy and medicine at Bologna with Alessandro Achillini. He first taught logic and then philosophy. Attracted to Rome, he returned to Bologna after the sack of Rome in 1527 and remained there until his death. His writings were almost entirely commentaries on Aristotle, although one very brief treatise is entitled *Oratio de principatu partium corporis* and was published in Francesco dal Pozzo, *Apologia in anatome pro Galeno contra Andream Vesalium*, Venice, 1562. His interest in anatomy was always directed from the Aristotelian point of view; Mazzuchelli, *op. cit.*, 1762, II, pte. 3, pp. 1372–1374; Giovanni Fantuzzi, *Notizie degli scrittori bolognesi*, II, Bologna, 1782, pp. 206–217.

[119] This information is based upon the notebook of a German student who attended these events—Baldasar Heseler, 1508 or 1509–1567, of Liegnitz, Silesia. The manuscript, now in the Royal Library, Stockholm, was discovered and published by Ruben Eriksson, *Andreas Vesalius' first public anatomy at Bologna 1540. An eyewitness report by Baldasar Heseler*. Ed. with intro. trans. into English and notes by Ruben Eriksson, Uppsala, 1959.

[120] See above, p. 223.

[121] Prior to the discovery of Heseler's notebook it was necessary to rely in large part upon the unverified word of the *Fabrica*. It is now possible to evaluate many of Vesalius's statements about his activities and methods by comparison with Heseler's statements. In all such instances Vesalius's remarks appear to be wholly true and unelaborated statements. There are sufficient points of comparison to permit one to give credit to the many similar personal remarks throughout the text of the *Fabrica*.

[122] *Fabrica* (1543), p. 512.

[123] *Ibid.*, p. 27.

[124] *Ibid.*, p. 76.

[125] *Ibid.*, p. 547. It seems that it was most likely to these demonstrations that Susius referred in his account written in 1544, although not published until fifteen years later: "I must admit that that [azygos] vein arises a little above the heart, as I observed when in a former year I watched Vesalius dissecting in Bologna." Jo. Bapt. Susius, *De venis e directo secandis*, Cremona, 1559, fol. 6or.

[126] *Fabrica* (1543), p. 19.

[127] *Ibid.*, p. 584.

[128] *De libris propriis*, pp. 75–76, in the *Works*, ed. Venn, Cambridge, 1912.

[129] Renouard, *Annales de l'imprimerie des Aldes*, Paris, 1834, pp. vi–viii, 73, 91, 124, 141.

[130] Caius, *De libris propriis*, pp. 75–76.

[131] Agnostino Gadaldino, 15 March 1515–1575, of Modena, son of Antonio Gadaldino, a distinguished bookseller and publisher whose long life continued until 6 April 1568, and whose publishing business appears to have been carried on by a second son, Cornelio, until his death, c. 1573. Agostino studied medicine, probably at Ferrara, whence he went to Venice. There is a letter (1543) written to him by Jacopo Bonfadio which speaks of their acquaintance during many years in Ferrara and continues to the effect that Agostino was summoned by Tommaso Giunta, "the richest and most famous book dealer in the world," to take charge of his publishing business, and "in a short time displayed his ability through his editing of the works of Galen." Bonfadio remarks further that Agostino, "being highly esteemed by the very benevolent Senators, was the principal means by which the excellent Fallopio and Sigonia were invited . . . to teach in the flourishing university of Padua and Venice." Agostino also developed a friendship with Pietro Aretino, of which three letters (1545, 1548, 1550) survive, in the last of which Aretino accepts the excuses of Gadaldino for not having been able to attend him during an illness. In another letter of Aretino to Andrea da Perugia (1548), mention is made of the abilities of "the excellent Doctor Agostino da Modena" in the care of the sick, and there are other complimentary expressions regarding him in the writings of Mercuriale, Fallopio, and others. The literary efforts of Gadaldino, although extensive, were largely confined to editing and translating the works of Hippocrates and Galen. His death was possibly due to the plague; Tiraboschi, *Biblioteca modenese*, II, Modena, 1782, pp. 371–376.

Notes to Chapter VI

[182] *Galeni omnia opera nunc primum in unum corpus redacta: quorum alia nunquam antea latinitate donata fuerant, alia aut novis interpretationibus, aut accuratis recognitionibus sunt illustrata: singula summo studio excusa, atque manuscriptis graecorum voluminibus infinitis pene locis restituta. . . . Cum decreta Summi Pont. Senatusque Veneti per annos xv. prout folio viii legitur. Apud haeredes Lucaeantonij Iuntae Florentini.* Venice, 1541. (All the works of Galen now for the first time gathered into one body, some of them never before translated into Latin, while others have been presented in new or more accurate translations. Individually edited with the greatest care and restored in almost innumerable readings from Greek manuscripts . . . With [exclusive] permission of the Pope and of the Venetian Senate for 15 years as may be read on folio viii. By the heirs of Lucantonio Giunta of Florence. Venice, 1541.)

[183] The bibliography of these Vesalian versions has been given by Cushing, p. 63 ff. Curiously, Gadaldino makes no mention of the third contribution of Vesalius to the edition, or rather combines the second and third in an order reversed from that in which they appear. Correctly they are *On dissection of nerves*, and following this immediately, *On dissection of veins and arteries*.

[184] Caius, *De libris propriis*, p. 76.

[185] *Ibid.*, p. 77.

[136] Caius, *Libri aliquot graeci*, Basel, 1544, p. 286.

[137] *Ibid.*, p. 320.

[138] *Ibid.*, p. 287.

[139] *De libris propriis*, p. 82.

[140] There is almost no available information on Simon Arborsellus except that he was the author of a small book of eight leaves entitled merely *Angelo Fortio S.P.D.*, and probably published *c.* 1545, in which he makes the following interesting comment, fol. A4r: "Observe how uncertain is the course of physicians, on the one hand turning their attention to simple and on the other to compound medicaments; and, by the gods, to anyone reading how many and great promises are offered for curing everyone—let it be understood literally . . . However, when I arrived at actual practice, in order to determine whether there were as many results as there had been promises, I discovered the truth of the matter to be that there were few. A good many cases would certainly have been better handled by nature, as Andreas, the learned anatomist and surgeon of Padua, once said to me in the course of an explanation when we were discussing these things and joking with our medical colleagues and proposing to them that our art is of little value if it has nothing more effective for expelling infirmities. In reply to me they went back to the usual argument that they treat those things that are sound but leave solely to prognostics those that are mortal, as was taught by the master of the art himself. I then inquired if it would not be better to leave those matters to nature alone since she, as we see, drives out ailments better if nothing is employed . . . I once propounded this problem for them: Why is it, I asked, that those who receive head injuries in Verona, no matter how slight, cannot be cured and the unfortunate patient, forsaken by the physicians, dies miserably; but, as I have often seen, he is cured in Padua and Venice?"

[141] In this regard, see above, p. 129, regarding a manuscript of Galen's book *On the bones*.

[142] See above, p. 97. Marcantonio Passeri, called Genua or of Genoa, 1491–1563, was the son of Nicolo Passeri. The family, originally from Mantua and Modena, owing to political disturbances had withdrawn to Genoa, and one branch had located ultimately in Padua where Marcantonio was born and received his education. He married Beatrice à Sole, who in due course presented him with five children. In 1528, after having already lectured on philosophy at Padua, he was chosen by the *Riformatori* "to give the ordinary lecture, in the second chair, for two years on philosophy, and for one at option," with an annual salary of eighty florins; Antonio Favaro, "Lo Studio di Padova nei diarii di Marino Sanuto," *Nuovo Arch. Veneto*, 1918, n.s., 36:120. His success is indicated by the fact that in 1531, when the first chair became vacant, it was granted to him for a period of three years and an option of one with an annual salary of 300 florins, *ibid.*, p. 123. As a philosopher Marcantonio was an Aristotelian and published commentaries on *De anima*, *De coelo*, *De generatione*, and the *Metaphysica*. He appears to have had a genuine interest in medicine and there is a reference to him by Pier Valerianus: *Non enim te solis medicinae philosophiaeque terminis cohibuisti*. G. F. Tomasini, *Illustrium virorum elogia*, Padua, 1630, pp. 100–103, with a dubious portrait; G. Vedova, *Biografia degli scrittori padovani*, Padova, 1832, I, p. 457.

[143] Wolfgang, or Wolff, Peter Herwart was born in Augsburg in 1514, the son of Conrad Herwart and Laura Laengin. Presumably he was educated at Padua where Vesalius made his acquaintance. In 1551 Herwart married Anna Pfister, daughter of Marcus Pfister, Burgomaster of Augsburg, by whom he had two daughters, Sabina and Anna. He was elected to the Augsburg council in 1553, in which year he also became partly blind. In October 1563 the Augsburg Council decreed an annual inspection of pharmacies, and Herwart, with four doctors—Adolph Occo, Achilles Gasser, Lucas Stenglin, and Christoph Heyberger—as well as Hieronymus Krayer, were named inspectors. Three of the doctors became friends of Vesalius during and after his sojourn in Augsburg with the emperor. In 1564, as the result of a report of the inspectors,

435

a special tax was levied on pharmacies. Herwart resigned from the council in 1574, requesting that as a result of total blindness he not be reëlected. He died either the 12 or 22 May 1585, and with him also died out that particular branch of the Herwart family that could trace its ancestry back to Heinrich Herwart in the first half of the fourteenth century. Information was supplied from the archives of H. W. v. Herwarth of Heemstede, Netherlands, through the friendly assistance of Dr. R. F. Timken-Zinkann.

[144] See above, p. 378, for an English version.

[145] Klaus König, "Ein bisher unbekanntes Konsilium Vesals über die Behandlung einer Nieren-steinerkrankung," *Sudhoffs Archiv*, 1955, 39:97–112.

[146] See above, p. 383, for an English version.

[147] Roth, p. 429.

[148] *Ibid.*, pp. 429–430.

[149] Prior to taking up his medical studies, however, Colombo had been for a brief time a lecturer in philosophy contemporaneously with John Caius, who refers to him, although the precise term of this activity is unknown; Riccoboni, *op. cit.*, fol. 27v; Caius, *De libris propriis*, p. 86, in his *Works*, ed. Venn, Cambridge, 1912.

[150] *Fabrica* (1543), p. 56.

[151] Roth, pp. 430, 432; in his temporary capacity Colombo received an annual twenty florins, increased to seventy when in October 1544 he received a regular appointment.

[152] Edward D. Coppolo, "The discovery of the pulmonary circulation: a new approach," *Bull. Hist. Med.*, 1957, 31:47–77; R. J. Moes and C. D. O'Malley, "Realdo Colombo: 'On those things rarely found in anatomy,'" *Bull. Hist. Med.*, 1960, 34:508–528.

Notes to Chapter VII

[1] *Ep.Ch.Rt.*, p. 196.

[2] See above, p. 99.

[3] *Ep.Ch.Rt.*, p. 149.

[4] *Ibid.*, p. 194.

[5] "The very conscientious *podestà* of Padua who has supplied me with an abundance of material for dissection, for he is himself a studious and diligent observer of the structure of the human body," *Fabrica* (1543), p. 650. Marcantonio Contarini, of the famous Venetian family whose most distinguished member was Cardinal Gasparo Contarini, was the son of Carlo Contarini. As a young man he engaged in the military defense of Padua, and in 1516 he became a city advocate. In 1523 he was *podestà* of Vicenza and in 1527 became governor of Siena. In 1533 Contarini was sent as ambassador to the imperial court, and in 1536 to Rome. He left this latter post toward the end of 1539 to become *podestà* of Padua. Four years later he was sent on a special mission to the emperor and in 1546 to Candia where he died in the same year. His great interest in philosophy gained him the name of "the philosopher," and he must have been a friend of Marcantonio Genua, the Paduan philosopher and friend of Vesalius who encouraged the composition of the *Fabrica*. During the period of Vesalius's residence in Padua, the *podestà* were Francesco Venier, 16 September 1537 to 14 September 1539, Marcantonio Contarini, 14 September 1539 to 29 May 1541, Andrea Mocenigo, 29 May 1541 to the first half of April 1542, Giann-Andrea Badoer, 1 May 1542 to 16 September 1543; Andrea Gloria, "Serie dei podestà e capitani di Padova dal 1509 al 1797," *Riv. Periodica d. Lavori d. I. R. Accad. Sci. Lett. Arti di Padova*, 1861, 9:172–173.

[6] *Ep.Ch.Rt.*, p. 194.

[7] Although it is impossible to estimate how many human male bodies were available to Vesalius in Padua for dissection, the relatively greater scarcity of female cadavers permits a rough count. In addition to the body of a prostitute who had hanged herself in Paris, which Vesalius had helped Guinter dissect—see above, p. 60—and the young girl at Brussels in the entourage of the Countess of Egmont, in whose post-mortem examination Vesalius had participated—see above, p. 63—at Padua, the youngest female cadaver was that of a girl of six, "stolen from her tomb by one of my students for the preparation of a skeleton," and for inspection of the hymen, since, according to Vesalius, this was one of the few bodies of virgins to which he had had access; see above, p. 201. The dissection was naturally a private one, as was also that of a "woman beat to death by her husband," *Fabrica* (1543), p. 540, and that of a prostitute who had "committed suicide by hanging herself," *ibid.*, p. 538. Four other female cadavers were employed for public dissection. "Last year we obtained . . . a smallish woman of somewhat advanced years and, as I conjectured, dead from starvation," *ibid.*, p. 539. A second body was that of the monk's mistress—see p. 113—and the third was that of a woman who had sought to escape execution by declaring herself pregnant; see above, p. 143. The fourth was that of a woman "whose right eye had become defective in youth although the left was sound," *ibid.*, p. 324 [424]. Vesalius had also twice, albeit hurriedly, dissected the foetus *in*

utero at Padua, *Ep.Ch.Rt.*, p. 143, and in Pisa two more female bodies were available to him in January 1544, that of a nun and of a hunchback girl, see above, p. 201, although these last two were after the publication of the *Fabrica*.

[8] See above, p. 100.

[9] *Fabrica* (1543), p. 538.

[10] A. Corradi, "Dello studio e dell'insegnamento dell'anatomia in Italia," *Gazz. Med. Ital. Provincie Venete*, 1873, 16:305.

[11] *Ep.Ch.Rt.*, p. 194.

[12] *Fabrica* (1543), p. 547.

[13] *Ibid.*, p. 46.

[14] *Ibid.*, p. 292.

[15] *Ibid.*, p. 348 [448].

[16] *Ibid.*, p. 242.

[17] *Ibid.*, p., 510. On this and other instances of anomaly or presumed anomaly, see William L. Straus, Jr., and Owsei Temkin, "Vesalius and the problem of variability," *Bull. Hist. Med.*, 1943, 14:609–633.

[18] Edward A. Boyden, "The problem of the double ductus choledochus," *Anat. Rec.*, 1932, 55:71 ff.

[19] *Ep.Ch.Rt.*, p. 141.

[20] *Fabrica* (1543), p. 124.

[21] *Ibid.*, p. 19.

[22] *Ibid.*, p. 248.

[23] *Ibid.*, p. 221.

[24] *Ibid.*, fol. *3r.

[25] *Ibid.*, p. 269 [369] at H.

[26] *Ibid.*, p. 532.

[27] *Ibid.*, p. 266; also, "when first you have [removed the skin from the foot] in the manner of a butcher," *ibid.*, p. 255 [355], and "the skin must be lifted away with the fleshy membrane . . . in the manner of butchers," *ibid.*, p. 236 [336].

[28] *Ibid.*, p. 383 [483].

[29] *Ibid.*, p. 584. Of another case, which suggests accident rather than judicial execution, he remarks: "That one of Bologna whose heart I observed while he was still alive seemed to contain water, but it was not possible to give suitable attention even though I had been present at the tragedy"; *ibid.*

[30] *Ibid.*, p. 548.

[31] *Ibid.*, p. 162.

[32] *Ibid.*, p. 78. In regard to Vesalius's concern with the comparative study of canine anatomy, see Richard Schmutzer, "Die Anatomie der Haustiere in Vesals Fabrica (1543) und Epistola de radice Chyna (1546)," *Ergeb. Anat. EntwGesch.*, 1938, 32:165–244.

[33] *Fabrica* (1543), p. 263.

[34] *Ibid.*, p. 290.

[35] *Ibid.*, p. 1. Further examples are "the pectoral bone [sternum] which resembles the shape of a sword," "the femur which resembles the outline of Italy," "the coccyx which resembles the beak of the cuckoo." On Vesalian nomenclature see Johannes Steudel, "Vesals Reform der anatomischen Nomenklatur," *Z. Anat. EntwGesch.*, 1943, 112:675–681; Horst Zoske, *Die Osteologie Vesals*, Hanover, 1951.

[36] *Ibid.*, p. 225. Furthermore, "The muscles at the first joint of the thumb are called mice by the people of Brussels and certain other lands, while the anterior of those flexing the forearm is so named by still others. Moreover, the majority of Italians pretend that in certain parts of the body there is some sort of little fish, by that name referring to muscles not unlike the shape of a fish," and the shape of the diaphragm was normally that of the sting ray, "if you will only first imagine its tail to be divided longitudinally"; *ibid.* pp. 224, 225.

[37] *Ibid.*, p. 1.

[38] *Ibid.*, p. 592. Furthermore, the tricuspid valve is similar in structure "to the furrows of spearheads, called in Greek TRIGLŌCHINAI, as if you were to say three-pointed. When the membranous circle is as yet open and round in shape, its three processes come together from the region of the center and form a triangular point not unlike that used today on the weapons of the Turks for penetrating a cuirass; but in order that that long weapon may be effective, the angles are made sharper, and they file away the furrows between two angles so that the spearhead, from the base to the point, displays three angles and a like number of furrows, as you will notice when during dissection you join the three membranous processes together. Furthermore, if you seek to produce a similarity of the whole membranous body with its processes and fibres, you will best take it from the shape of the crown such as was carved for the heads of kings during antiquity and which we see on those statues which are dug up in Rome," *ibid.*, p. 592.

[39] *Ibid.*, p. 154. On the Turkish bowman's ring, see P. E. Klopsteg, *Turkish archery and the*

composite bow, Evanston, Ill., 1947. Also, "The first cartilage of the larynx, outwardly convex and inwardly concave, similar to a kind of shield, not round but longish such as we see older [soldiers] to use in battle, as well as some of the Turks, especially on shipboard," *Fabrica* (1543), p. 153.

[40] *Observationes anatomicae*, Venice, 1561, fol. 43r.

[41] *Fabrica* (1543), p. 498.

[42] *Ibid.*, p. 166. The *Canon* of Avicenna translated into Hebrew by Giuseppe Lorqui and published at Naples in 1491.

[43] "Ricerche su Lazaro Ebreo de Frigeis medico insigne e amico intimo di André Vésal," *La Rassegna Mensile di Israel*, 1949, 15:495–515.

[44] The fact that Lazarus was mentioned in this later edition is fairly good evidence, according to the practice of Vesalius, that he was still alive and that the two men were on amicable terms.

[45] See his remarks above, p. 281, on cardiovascular function in the *Fabrica* of 1555.

[46] *Commentaria*, Venice, 1521, fol. CCCCLXXVIIr.

[47] *Liber introductorius anatomiae*, Venice, 1536, fol. 93r.

[48] *Fabrica* (1543), pp. 34–35; C. D. O'Malley and Edwin Clarke, "The discovery of the auditory ossicles," *Bull. Hist. Med.*, 1961, 35:424–428.

[49] According to Fallopio, *Observationes anatomicae*, Venice, 1561, fol. 4r, Vesalius was "a disciple of Galen, not in the lecture hall as an auditor, but in the library, because he was an insatiable glutton for all of Galen's writings—but he was not deterred by Galen's authority from adding to the art many things that had been overlooked by his preceptor."

[50] See above, p. 17.

[51] For what little information there is on the life of Massa, see Luigi Nardo, "Dell'anatomia in Venezia," with additional notes by Cesare Musatti, *Ateneo Veneto*, 1897, fasc. 2–3; also Singer and Rabin. Since Massa was already over fifty years old when the *Liber introductorius* was published, the vocabulary, as we might expect, does not reflect the alterations in favor of classical terms that the humanists were instituting, nor did he seem to have a true understanding of the great need for clarification of terminology. Nevertheless, Massa was the first to employ the term "panniculus carnosus," although his description of it, while admitting its greater importance in animal than in man, exaggerates both its extent and importance to the latter; fols. 8r–11r. In the course of his account of the abdominal wall he compares the tendinous intersections of the rectus abdominis muscle to that of the digastric muscle, fol. 12r, and he refers very briefly to the inguinal canal, fol. 13r. He describes the intestinal canal fairly accurately, fols. 18v–23r, and includes the appendix, fol. 21r. He also notes the variability in the size of the spleen in those suffering from splenic ailments and declares that he has seen the spleen very large and extending into the lower abdomen, fol. 26v. Massa agrees that the liver is divided into the traditional five lobes, although stating that five are not always found and that he has often seen it divided into only two. However, he declares the portal vein to be divided into five main branches in the liver; fol. 27r. For his study of the liver Massa proposes a maceration technique—but whether as theory or actual practice is not certain—so that "if you macerate the liver for some days and then boil it thoroughly in a pot so that the flesh is completely cooked, it may be readily separated from the vessels, and you will then perceive the substance of the veins to be interwoven into a kind of network," fol. 27v. In his description of the kidneys he proved, by blowing through a reed, that the cavity of the renal veins is not continuous with that of the sinus of the kidney, fol. 31v, a genuine contribution first asserted by Berengario da Carpi, since the kidneys had been regarded as filters straining off the urine from the blood. Like Vesalius, Massa regarded the position of the right kidney as higher than that of the left, although he had twice seen the reverse, fol. 32r, and he briefly notes the difference in levels of origin of the spermatic arteries and veins on the two sides, fol. 33r, a fact, however, that had already been known to Mondino and to Berengario, although unknown in northern Europe until described by Guinter of Andernach in 1536, the same year in which Massa published. There is also a brief reference to the prostate, fol. 34r, the first mention of that particular organ. Massa also denies the existence normally of a third ventricle of the heart and remarks anent this matter that "the wall [of the cardiac septum] is a dense and hard substance without any cavity," fol. 56v, the first denial in the western world of pores in the cardiac septum, but wholly by implication, which Massa may not have realized. On the other hand he declares that in 1534 he saw an extremely large heart which had three ventricles, fol. 56r. He describes the *rete mirabile* in the human, but admits that there were skeptics on this point—indeed, Berengario had tentatively denied its existence—and writes, "some dare to say that this *rete* is a figment of Galen . . . but I myself have often seen the *rete* and I have demonstrated it . . . though sometimes I have found it very small"; fols. 89v–90r. It should be added that Massa's long description of the brain is traditional and unsatisfactory. On the other hand, he was the first writer after Berengario to refer to the malleus and incus, although his brief statement refers to both ossicles under the word *malleolus*, little hammer, fol. 93r-v, and so left to Vesalius the opportunity of providing better and more appropriate names. Massa's reference to and criticism of the *Fabrica* and Vesalius,

438

although not by name, clearly indicate him to have remained in principle a Galenist; *Epistolarum medicinalium*, I, Venice, 1558, "Epistola V."

[52] See above, p. 188.

[53] *Fabrica* (1543), p. 46.

[54] *Observationes anatomicae*, Venice, 1561, fol. 36r.

[55] *Ep.V.S.*, p. 65.

[56] *Ibid.*, p. 66.

[57] *Ep.Ch.Rt.*, p. 194.

[58] On this matter see Erica Tietze-Conrat, "Neglected contemporary sources relating to Michelangelo and Titian," *Art Bull.*, 1943, 35:157–159.

[59] *La vita de'piu eccellenti pittori*, Florence, 1568.

[60] Vasari, *op. cit.*, III, 2, p. 818.

[61] *Ibid.*, III, 2, p. 858.

[62] *Ibid.*, III, 1, p. 319 [309].

[63] *Ecclesiae Londino-Batavae archivum*, ed. J. H. Hessels, I, Cambridge, 1887, p. 390.

[64] *Het schilder-boeck*, Haarlem, 1604; also, *Le livre des peintres*, trans. Henri Hymans, Paris, 1884, 2 vols.

[65] Domenico Bonavera, *Notomie di Titiano* [n. p., *c.* 1670]. On the first illustration is the statement *Ticianus inventor et delineavit* i.e., "Titian composed and drew," and on the succeeding ones the letters *T. I. D.*, although the illustrations are all from the *Fabrica*.

[66] E. Jackschath, "Die Begründung der modernen Anatomie durch Leonardo da Vinci und die Wiederauffindung zweier Schriften desselben," *Medizinische Blatter*, 1902, 15:770–772.

[67] W. M. Ivins, "A propos of the *Fabrica* of Vesalius," *Bull. Hist. Med.*, 1943, 14:576–593; "What about the 'Fabrica' of Vesalius," *Three Vesalian essays*, New York, 1952, pp. 43–128.

[68] *Fabrica* (1543), p. 266 [268].

[69] *Ibid.*, VI, xiv, nerve plexus; V, x, kidney.

[70] *Ibid.*, V, figs. 27–29.

[71] *De libris propriis*, p. 76, in *Works*, ed. Venn, Cambridge, 1912.

[72] *Ep.Ch.Rt.*, p. 198.

[73] *Fabrica* (1543), pp. 262 [362], 268 [368], 295 [395], 305 [405], 311 [411], 312 [412].

[74] E. Jackschath, "Zu den anatomischen Abbildungen des Vesal," *Mitt. z. Gesch. der Med. u. Naturwiss.*, 1903, 2:282–283. He also declared the background to suggest a drawing by Titian without, however, giving more precise information.

[75] "Marginal notes by the printer of the *Icones*," *Three Vesalian essays*, New York, 1952, p. 41.

[76] See, e.g., *Fabrica* (1543), p. 33.

[77] *Ibid.*, p. 331.

[78] *Ibid.*, p. 335, 1, m.

[79] *On the bones* was first translated into Latin by Ferdinando Balamio, here mentioned, and published in Rome, 1535, and in the same year in Paris and Lyons. Vesalius must first have become acquainted with the Paris edition published by Chrestien Wechel, and, whatever his object in desiring to see the Greek manuscript, it is very likely that the one withheld from him was the very one Balamio had used for his translation.

[80] *Fabrica* (1543), p. 42. Ferdinando Balamio, or Balami, said to have been born in Sicily, flourished *c.* 1515 in Rome, where he was physician to Pope Leo X, Mazzuchelli, *Gli scrittori d'Italia*, II, pte. i, Brescia, 1758, p. 76. As a student of the classics, Balamio translated Galen's book *On the bones* into Latin, as mentioned above, presumably from the Greek manuscript Vesalius was unable to borrow. Cardinal Rodolfo Pio, 1499–1564, of the princely house of Carpi, was elevated to the purple in 1536 by Paul III. He is declared to have been generally held in esteem, although we are aware that Vesalius had an opposed, minority opinion; G. B. Migne, *Dictionnaire des cardinaux*, Paris, 1857, coll. 1403–1404.

[81] *Fabrica* (1543), p. 35. See Joshua O. Leibowitz, "Did Vesalius suffer from peptic ulcer?" *Bull. Hist. Med.*, 1958, 32:75–78, for a possible result of the stress and frustration associated with the composition of the *Fabrica* and, according to Leibowitz, a reflection of Vesalius's temperament.

[82] Wiegand, *op. cit.*, pp. 32–34.

[83] This account of Oporinus is based chiefly on Max H. Fisch, "The printer of Vesalius's *Fabrica*," *Bull. Med. Lib. Assoc.*, 1943, 31:240–259, where an extensive bibliography will be found. The question has occasionally been asked why Vesalius chose to have the *Fabrica* printed in Basel rather than Venice. There is little doubt that the Giunta Press could have produced it, especially since the wood blocks were cut in Venice and the proofs taken from them, as we know, pleased Vesalius. It was not the inability of Venetian artists, block cutters, or printers, but that Vesalius had it in mind to seek employment with the emperor, hence in northern Europe, and also had a particular regard for Oporinus. In choosing him as the printer Vesalius was continuing to deal with a printing firm which had already produced two of his books, even though the name of only a single partner, Robert Winter, appeared on them. Now only one partner, Oporinus,

remained, but unquestionably the most competent of the four, and Vesalius was aware that given a free hand Oporinus would produce books far superior to those of the firm in its earlier organization.

[84] Oporinus appears to have had a penchant for widows since two other marriages, in 1564 and 1568, were also to widows.

[85] *Fabrica* (1543), fol. [*5r–v*].

[86] Henry E. Sigerist, "Albanus Torinus and the German edition of the *Epitome* of Vesalius," *Bull. Hist. Med.*, 1943, 14:653, in which Sigerist points out the little likelihood of the route proposed by Cushing, p. 76 f., "by way of Chiavenna and over the Bernina Alps by the Splügen Pass to Chur, the Waldensee, Zürich, and Basel."

[87] C. P. Rollins, "Oporinus and the publication of the *Fabrica*," *The four hundredth anniversary celebration of the De humani corporis fabrica of Andreas Vesalius*, New Haven, Conn., 1943, pp. 32–33.

[88] *De re anatomica*, Venice, 1559, p. 60.

[89] As mentioned above, p. 109, Vesalius's salary had been increased to 200 florins in 1542, "7 August 1542. We have been apprised of the end of the term for which the Excellent Master Andreas Vesalius, Imperialist, was hired to lecture on surgery in our University of Padua. It can be said that during this time he has illustrated the art of anatomy, in which he is truly very excellent, and therefore is much appreciated by the students. . . . let the aforesaid Master Andreas Vesalius be rehired to lecture . . . with an annual salary of 200 florins, beginning with the opening of the university"; Roth, p. 430. Presumably Vesalius had planned to return for the term beginning in October, but meanwhile, as will be indicated, he accepted instead imperial service and returned to Padua only briefly at the close of December 1543. Whether or not it had been the original intention of the authorities to allow him leave with salary, it was nevertheless sought for him in a document signed by university officials on 10 December 1543: "Magnificent and distinguished fathers and worthy restorers of the University of Padua . . . it is requested that you grant Master Andreas Vesalius his salary, which was wrongly withheld from him during last year when permission had been given him to leave without being penalized"; Roth, p. 431.

[90] See above, p. 110.

[91] Roth, p. 128. G. Wolf-Heidegger, "Andreas Vesalius," *Beiträge zur Geschichte der Naturwissenschaften und der Technik in Basel*, Olten, 1959, p. 92, reproduces that part of the matriculation register of the medical faculty in Basel indicating that Vesalius was enrolled between 1 and 16 January 1543 "ob merita," that is, without fee as befitting a distinguished visitor. The rector at the time was Albanus Torinus who was later to translate and produce a German version of Vesalius's *Epitome*.

[92] E. C. Streeter, "Giambattista Canano" in Canano, *Musculorum humani corporis picturata dissectio*, facsimile ed., Cushing & Streeter, Florence, 1925, pp. 25–26. Also R. Manfredini, "L'abitazione di Giambattista Canani," *Mem. Accad. Stor. Arte Sanit.*, 1957, 23:124; R. F. Dondi, "Francesco Vesalio frequentò la casa di G. B. Canani?" *ibid.*, 1958, 24:36–38.

[93] *De miraculis occultis naturae*, Frankfurt, 1598, p. 160.

[94] Roth, p. 127.

[95] *Examen*, p. 71.

[96] Streeter, *loc. cit.*

[97] Giambattista Canano of Ferrara, 1515–1579, studied medicine at Ferrara and in 1541 gained the chair of anatomy in that university, which, as we shall see later, made him one of the teachers of Gabriele Fallopio. Soon after Canano's appointment he began the preparation of an illustrated anatomical work to be issued in parts, of which the first part, devoted to the bones and muscles of the forearm, appeared in 1541 or 1542. Although brief and incomplete the work was a worthy forerunner to the *Fabrica*. The illustrations by Girolamo da Carpi are artistically and accurately reproduced and the text has the merit of containing the first description of the palmaris brevis muscle. In the dedication to Bartolomeo Nigrisoli of Ferrara, Canano attributes his accomplishment to that Ferrarese nobleman: "You have never ceased urging me to produce this illustrated work on the parts of the human body since you thought that it could be so contrived that physicians unable to study the parts of the body by dissection might gain some knowledge from illustrations. . . . Therefore I have decided to publish these illustrations elegantly drawn by Girolamo da Carpi. . . . They have been issued and published under your auspices, most excellent sir, the muscles of the human joints which we have dissected as diligently as possible with the help of Dr. Antonio Maria Canano of Ferrara, my close relative, as demonstrator." In the preface to the reader Canano remarks that, "I have published this first book on the dissection of the muscles and I shall speedily publish the others which are already in the hands of the copperplate engraver." A suggestion has already been offered as to why the work was not continued. Indeed, Canano did not long continue his anatomical studies or his career as an anatomist, but about 1545 became physician to a series of dignitaries, lay and ecclesiastic. Nevertheless he made one further and final contribution, the discovery of the venous valves, in particular those at the orifice of the azygos vein, although he left it to his student Amatus Lusitanus to publish

this important discovery which, as we shall see later, Canano did announce orally to Vesalius in 1546. On Canano, see Streeter & Cushing, *op. cit.*; Luigi Casotti, "Contributo alla Iconografia di Giambattista Canano (1515–1579)," *Boll. Ist. Stor. It. Arte Sanit.*, 1931, 11:43–48.

[98] *Fabrica* (1543), p. 274 [374], 7.

[99] *Ibid.*, p. 335 [435], 1, m. The faulty illustration is on p. 232 [432].

[100] *Ibid.*, p. 181.

[101] *Ibid.*, p. 93.

[102] Gast's account, the basis of later reports, is to be found in Gerhard Wolf-Heidegger, "Vesals Basler Skeletpräparat aus dem Jahre 1543," *Verhandlungen des Naturforschenden Gesellschaft in Basel*, 1944, 55:210–234, where all the details, literature, and ramifications of this incident are presented fully. Some details regarding the skeleton are also in E. Hintzsche, "Andreas Vesal und sein Werk," *Ciba Zeitschrift*, 1946, 9:3686.

Notes to Chapter VIII

[1] Walter Artelt, "Bermekungen zum Stil der anatomischen Abbildungen des 16. und 17. Jahrhunderts," *Actas del Congreso Internacional de Historia de la Medicina*, Madrid, 1956, I, p. 394, considers the scene as under the influence of mannerism.

[2] Walter Artelt, "Das Titelbild zur 'Fabrica' Vesals und seine kunstgeschichtlichen Voraussetzungen," *Centaurus*, 1950–1951, 1:66 ff., suggests the massing of the spectators as influenced by Donatello's relief in the church of San Antonio, Padua, depicting the legend of the heart of the miser.

[3] *Fabrica* (1555), p. 681. This statement is not in the first edition of the *Fabrica*, but we know that Vesalius had a theatre at Bologna in 1540, although the number of spectators was somewhat under two hundred; see above, p. 99. Possibly in the following years such theatres had become more common and larger. The first to mention the construction of an anatomical theatre was Alessandro Benedetti, who may have had one built for his dissections at Padua. At the beginning of the fifth book of his *Anatomice sive de historia corporis humani*, Venice, 1502, he mentions *theatrum nostrum*. If this represents more than a product of his somewhat strong imagination, it was probably a temporary wooden structure, since the few anatomies then performed annually would have made a permanent theatre uneconomical. The design may have been influenced by extant Roman theatres, and Benedetti might have recalled the theatre of Verona. Whether or not Benedetti did have such a structure available to him, the mention of an anatomical theatre in his book that was widely known throughout Italy, in several editions, could have well led others to such construction. That both Pisa and Pavia had theatres in the third decade of the century is indicated by a decree of the University of Pavia, 21 November 1522, which records: "For construction of an anatomical theatre in the shape of the theatre of Pisa and according to the plan provided by Master Cuneo who has knowledge of that theatre"; G. Cervetto, *Di alcuni illustri anatomici italiani del decimoquinto secolo*, Verona, 1842, p. 141, n. 1. There is no reason why the temporary wooden theatre could not quickly have become so commonplace that it was not considered worthy of mention. The standard work on this general subject is Gottfried Richter, *Das anatomische Theater*, Berlin, 1936. (Abhandl. z. Gesch. Med. u. Naturwis., Heft 16.)

[4] Weigand, "Marginal notes by the printer of the *Icones*," *Three Vesalian essays*, New York, 1952, p. 35.

[5] Whoever was responsible for the title page of the second edition appears to have had no supervision by Vesalius and misunderstood the significance of parts of the scene. It may be that it was such perplexity that led to the deletion of the initials from that edition, or, if they indicate a pious reference to the deity emanating from Catholic Italy, possibly they would have been offensive in Basel.

[6] Such was the fate of the luckless surgeon Carlo Cortesi when Vesalius was dissecting in Pisa in 1544; see above, p. 202.

[7] *Fabrica* (1543), p. 225, and above, p. 118.

[8] *Ibid.*, p. 222 [322].

[9] *Ibid.*, p. 263.

[10] *Ibid.*, p. 548.

[11] "Those three savage Venetian prostitutes who, in order to acquire this ossicle [of the right thumb] and the heart of a male child, recently murdered an infant by tearing out the still living heart, and fittingly paid the fullest penalty for their crime," *ibid.*, p. 126.

[12] *Ibid.*, p. 531.

[13] It has been pointed out that the Vesalian anatomy differs from earlier medieval representations not only through the obvious fact that the professor has descended from his *cathedra* to perform the dissection, but also that the book from which the earlier anatomists read while the barber performed the dissection has disappeared. It has been exchanged for the scalpel. Once a require-

Notes to Chapter VIII

ment for the teacher, the book now became a requirement for the auditor or spectator, and books
are frequently indicated in the hands of several students; Walter Artelt, "Das Buch in Anatomie-
bild und das Anatomiebuch im Bild," *Deutsche Med. Woch.*, 1952, 77:637–640.
14 *Fabrica* (1543), p. 532.
15 *Ibid.*, p. 166, and above, pp. 119–120.
16 "To your . . . great-grandfather John . . . the Emperor Frederick III had granted arms of
black or sable color on which—for obvious reasons—are observed three white or silver weasels
courant," O'Malley, "Andreas Vesalius Count Palatine," p. 210.
17 *Fabrica* (1543), p. 14.
18 *Ibid.*, p. 548.
19 *Ibid.*, p. 160.
20 "Seek especially to obtain this desired pose from the wooden staff which will support the
position of the arm, be it a reaper's scythe, lance, spear, or Neptune's trident," *ibid.*
21 Actually this statement is to be found in the *Fabrica* (1555), p. 681.
22 *Fabrica* (1543), p. 376 [476].
23 *Ibid.*, p. 539.
24 On Contarini, see above, pp. 112–113.
25 *Fabrica* (1543), p. 549, also pp. 232, 234.
26 *Fabrica* (1555), p. 681.
27 *Fabrica* (1543), p. 547.
28 See above, p. 79.
29 *Fabrica* (1543), p. 538.
30 See above, p. 108.
31 *Fabrica* (1543), fols. *2r–4v*. See above, p. 317, for an English version.
32 *Ibid.*, fol. [*5r–v*], see above, p. 324, for an English version. The letter is preceded by the
following statement: "The Printer to the Reader. Since the letter we received, sent from Italy by
Andreas Vesalius with the wood blocks for these books, De humani corporis fabrica and their
Epitome, seemed to us to contain many things about which we decided the reader ought to be
advised at the start, and, moreover, it seemed desirable to publicize those decrees of princes, [al-
though they are] of such little value against plagiarizing printers born to disfigure such books as
are published for the use of the learned, therefore, honest reader, we concluded it worthwhile in
this way to impart these matters sent to us." However, the content of the letter is such in part
that it is likely that Vesalius intended or at least hoped that it would be published.
33 The portrait is the source of most of the later portraits of Vesalius, some of them ultimately
bearing only a faint relationship to this original; see M. H. Spielmann, *The iconography of
Andreas Vesalius*, London, 1925.
34 "To Vesalius on the fourth centenary of his De humani corporis fabrica," *Jour. Anatomy*,
1943, 77:264–265.
35 Several have suggested that the head was purposely exaggerated, and reference has been made
to the Droeshout portrait of Shakespeare, Spielmann, *op. cit.*, p. 5n., and to the portrait of
Paracelsus attributed to Hirschvogel, Joshua O. Leibowitz, "The portrait of Vesalius from the
Fabrica," *Jour. Hist. Med.*, 1957, 12:394; but artistic ineptitude remains an excellent reason.
36 *Fabrica* (1555), p. 663.
37 Leibowitz, *op. cit.*, p. 393.
38 AN[NO] AET[ATIS] XXVIII. M.D. XLII.
39 *De re medicina*, III, 4.
40 *De musculis digitos moventibus. Ca. 30 Quü superiori libro quinqz digitorum ossium cõstruc-
tionem prosequerer . . . a aliam quã. . . .*
41 *Ossium quinque digitorum constructionem superiori libro prosequentes longè aliam. . . .*
Fabrica (1543), p. 304, "Investigating the construction of the bones of the five fingers in the
previous book," and continues "by far another sort of joint than at the first joint of the five
fingers." In the Boerhaave and Albinus edition of the *Fabrica* (1725) the text of the scroll was
made to conform with the text of the *Fabrica* and *Ca. 30* was changed to *Ca. 43*, a forced and
not satisfying solution to the problem.
42 Singer, *op. cit.*, p. 265.
43 Spielmann, *op. cit.*, p. 2; p. 3n. is a detailed description of this particular dissection by the
later Professor William Wright.
44 Cushing, p. 85.
45 In his *Vaesanus*, fol. 28r, Sylvius was later to write: "After completely refuting several
calumnies that a madman has circulated against the names of Hippocrates and Galen, I explained seven successive lines from chapter 43 of the calumniator's second book on parts of the
hand that are perfectly apparent to anyone." However, what his criticism was and of what
Vesalian statements is not clear. Nevertheless it could not have been of the first several lines of the
chapter but must have been of some later portion where Vesalius has much to say about Galen's
errors, arisen from his attribution of the anatomy of the monkey's paw to the human.

Notes to Chapter VIII

[46] Charles Metzger, "Les lettrines de l'anatomie d'André Vésale. Scènes de la vie des anatomistes et des chirurgiens au XVIe siècles," *Hippocrate*, 1935, Dec., p. 825; Klaus Rosenkranz, "Die Initialen in Vesals Anatomie. Ein Beitrag zur Geschichte der anatomischen Abbildung," *Arch. Gesch. Med.*, 1937–1938, 30:35–46; Richard Schmutzer, "Die Initialen in Vesals Anatomie," *ibid.*, 1938, 31:328–330; Henry S. Francis, "The woodcut initials of the *Fabrica*," *Bull. Med. Libr. Ass.*, 1943, 31:228–239; Hernâni Monteiro, "As letras capitulares do tratado de anatomia de Vesálio 'De humani corporis fabrica' (Basileia, 1543)," *Arch. Anat. Anthrop. Lisboa*, 1943, 22:433–476; Barry J. Anson, "Anatomical tabulae and initials in Vesalius' Fabrica and in imitative works," *Surg. Gyn. Obst.*, 1949, 89:97–120; Robert Herrlinger, "Die Initialen in Vesals anatomischen Lehrbuch," *Arzt. Prax.* (Bad Wörishofer), 1 July 1950, 2:nr.26; Samuel W. Lambert, "The initial letters of the anatomical treatise De humani corporis fabrica, of Vesalius," *Three Vesalian essays*, New York, 1952, pp. 1–24; Hernani Monteiro, "L'ancienne technique de préparation des os, à propos des lettrines de la 'Fabrica' de Vésale," *Acta Anat.*, 1952, 14:358–364; Robert Ollerenshaw, "The decorated woodcut initials of Vesalius' 'Fabrica,'" *Med. Biol. Ill.*, 1952, 2:160–166; Robert Herrlinger, "Die Initialen in Vesals 'Fabrica.' Eine ergänzende medizin-geschichtliche Studie," *Index Gesch. Med.*, 1953, 1:1–11; A Driessche, "Bij de initialen in Vesalius' werk," *Verh. Vlaam. Acad. Geneesk. Belg.*, 1954, 16:255–271; L. H. Wells, "Note on a historiated initial letter in the *Fabrica* of Vesalius," *Medical History*, 1962, 6:287:288.

[47] Indeed, Galen advised his own arrangement as the best method for the study of anatomy. "I therefore maintain that the bones must be learnt . . . before dissecting the muscles, for these two [namely bones and muscles] form the ground work of the other parts, the foundation, as it were, of a building. And next, study the arteries, veins and nerves. Familiarity with dissection of these will bring you to the inward parts and so to a knowledge of the viscera, the fat, and the glands, which also you should examine separately, in detail. Such should be the order of your training," *Galen on anatomical procedures*, trans. Charles Singer, London, 1956, p. 5.

[48] *Fabrica* (1543), p. 1.
[49] See above, p. 249.
[50] *Fabrica* (1543), pp. 2–3.
[51] *Ibid.*, p. 3.
[52] *Ibid.*, pp. 163–165.
[53] *Ibid.*, p. 18.
[54] *Ibid.*, p. 19, illustrations, pp. 18–20.
[55] See above, p. 116.
[56] *Fabrica* (1543), p. 42.
[57] *Ibid.*, p. 36.
[58] *Ibid.*, p. 47.
[59] *Ibid.*, pp. 43–44. In the *Epitome* of the same year Vesalius adds the qualification that in very young children the jaw is formed "from two bones fusing at the point of the chin." Also see Walter Artelt, *Der zwiegeteilte Unterkiefer. Ein Stück Medizingeschichte am Beispiel einer Irrlehre*, Munich, 1943.
[60] See above, p. 116, in regard to this matter.
[61] Lilian Lindsay, "Dental Anatomy from Aristotle to Leeuwenhoek," *Science, medicine and history. Essays in honour of Charles Singer*, London, 1953, II, p. 126.
[62] *Fabrica* (1543), p. 46.
[63] *Ibid.*, p. 32. Vesalius is actually referring to what he calls the eighth bone of the head, by which he means principally the cribriform plate of the ethmoid.
[64] *Ibid.*, pp. 49–51, "the larger opening [nasolachrymal duct] extends straight downward from the larger internal angle of the orbit into the nasal cavity . . . to transmit to the nostrils some of the pituita which flows from the brain. . . . another rather large aperture [pterygopalatine fossa] is also provided for the pituita which flows from the orbit into the nasal cavity." "The [inferior orbital fissure] . . . provides a passage for the pituita." "This large opening [superior orbital fissure] is hollowed out . . . for the pituita which passes from the brain into the orbit and thence to the nasal cavity."
[65] See above, p. 249.
[66] *Fabrica* (1543), p. 55.
[67] *Ibid.*, pp. 57–58.
[68] *Ibid.*, p. 57.
[69] *Ibid.*, pp. 66, 279, text of discussion, pp. 63–68.
[70] See above, p. 249.
[71] *Fabrica* (1543), p. 77.
[72] See above, p. 100.
[73] *Fabrica* (1543), p. 81.
[74] *Ibid.*, p. 83.
[75] *Ibid.*, pp. 79–80.
[76] See above, pp. 291–292.

Notes to Chapter VIII

[77] *Fabrica* (1543), p. 87. In his illustration Vesalius indicated the three bones, as he calls them, of the adult sternum as well as the lines of union for the immature human. The three lines drawn through the body of the sternum divide it into four parts which, together with the manubrium and xiphoid process, constitute a sternum of six parts or segments in contrast to the seven segments of the nonhuman example described by Galen.

[78] *Ibid.*, p. 91.

[79] *Ibid.*, pp. 92–93.

[80] *Ibid.*, p. 94.

[81] *Ibid.*, p. 105.

[82] *Ibid.*, p. 121.

[83] *Ibid.*, p. 126.

[84] *Ibid.*, p. 142.

[85] *Ibid.*, pp. 125, 142; Chr. I. Baastrup. "Os Vesalianum tarsi and fracture of the tuberositas ossis metatarsi V," *Acta Radiol.*, 1922, 1:334–348; Straus and Temkin, *op. cit.*, pp. 627–630; D. Kerner, "Andreas Vesalius und das os Vesalianum," *Zbl. Chir.*, 1957, pt. i:217–221.

[86] See above, pp. 118–119.

[87] See above, p. 327, for an English version.

[88] See above, p. 64.

[89] *Fabrica* (1543), p. 215.

[90] *Ibid.*, pp. 215–216, illustration, p. 215.

[91] *Ibid.*, pp. 220–221.

[92] *Ibid.*, p. 218.

[93] *Ibid.*, p. 222; E. Bastholm, *The history of muscle physiology*, Copenhagen, 1950, pp. 118–122.

[94] *Fabrica* (1543), p. 223.

[95] *Ibid.*, p. 224.

[96] *Ibid.*, p. 224; also see above, pp. 118–119.

[97] *Fabrica* (1543), pp. 225–229.

[98] *Ibid.*, pp. 229–230. Also, "It is ridiculous to be disturbed about the number of muscles, although in public dissections when I display the muscles of this or that joint so they may be fully recognized, few of the students bother to note anything other than that in this lecture forty muscles have been displayed, considering it sufficient if they can discourage their fellow students by that number and blame the difficulty of the subject on me for undertaking too much in a single demonstration. However, those of them who desire to appear more diligent carefully note where I differ from Galen and often accept what I say without understanding it"; *ibid.*, p. 222 [322].

[99] *Ibid.*, p. 231.

[100] *Ibid.*, pp. 232–233.

[101] *Ibid.*, p. 236. For a detailed discussion, see Adolf Faller, *Die Entwicklung der makroskopisch-anatomischen Präparierkunst von Galen bis zur Neuzeit*, Basel, 1948. (Acta Anatomica, Supplementum VII.)

[102] *Fabrica* (1543), pp. 237–238.

[103] *Ibid.*, pp. 238–239.

[104] *Ibid.*, p. 240.

[105] *Ibid.*, p. 239, fig. 2.

[106] *Ibid.*, pp. 240–241. Vesalius might well have been amazed since here he was guilty of that fault he so strongly criticized in others, the resort to animal anatomy.

[107] *Ibid.*, pp. 242–244.

[108] See above, p. 115.

[109] *Fabrica* (1543), p. 246.

[110] See above, pp. 116–117.

[111] *Fabrica* (1543), p. 276.

[112] *Ibid.*, p. 184.

[113] *Ibid.*, p. 185. Both the line of demarcation and Vesalius's verbal explanation of it have usually been overlooked. It was with the same pedagogical desire for clear understanding that he advised the reader, *ibid.*, p. 299, to dissect the loins of the dog where he would find a muscle also possessed by man, and stated: "You will see the differences between those muscles and wonder what Galen had in mind when he overthrew the teachings of other anatomists who taught the parts of the human body otherwise than he observed them in his apes." The reference is to the Alexandrine anatomists such as Herophilus and Erasistratus who, as Vesalius knew, had dissected human bodies.

[114] *Ibid.*, p. 282. "The recti muscles, arising from two separate origins in the pubic bone, are mutually contiguous and extend straight upward until they reach the umbilicus; there, becoming somewhat wider and separated, they continue to the chest where they are inserted, wide and fleshy, into the cartilage connected to the pectoral bone, at the sides of the xiphoid process."

Notes to Chapter VIII

[115] So too in the same fifth "muscle-man," *ibid.*, p. 184, X, Vesalius notes the introduction of further Galenic or nonhuman anatomy in regard to a muscle he declares he has introduced in accordance with Galen's description of the "third muscle moving the thorax."

[116] *Ibid.*, pp. 274–275.

[117] *Ibid.*, p. 293 f. It is also in this chapter that Vesalius provides a correct account of the caval, oesophageal, and aortic openings in the diaphragm in contrast to Galen's error, *ibid.*, p. 291, "According to Galen's opinion, taken from Hippocrates, there are two [foramina], one that provides a way for the vertebrae, aorta, and the oesophagus descending to the orifice of the stomach; a second by which the vena cava is transmitted to the thorax. I, however, have observed that there are three. . . ." There is an illustration pertaining to this description, *ibid.*, p. 190.

[118] See above, p. 338, for an English version of such a chapter.

[119] Vesalius was especially concerned to demonstrate the correctness of his views by contrast to the errors of Galen in regard to the movements of the head. The subject had long interested him and he refers to it in the *Venesection letter*, see above, p. 97. As he had previously discussed the matter as it related to the first and second cervical vertebrae, so in Book II he continued the subject with a discussion of "The muscles moving the head which Galen has discussed incorrectly in Book IV of his *Anatomical procedures*," *Fabrica* (1543), pp. 276–279, and "The ligaments of the vertebrae," *ibid.*, pp. 300–302. The subject was one that infuriated Sylvius, as did also Vesalius's analysis of the thenar and hypothenar muscles, *ibid.*, p. 308, which Galen had treated collectively.

[120] "Another will perhaps believe with good reason that the description of those parts contained by the peritoneum and by the membranes girdling the ribs and the skull ought necessarily to precede not only the description of the veins and arteries, but also that of the nerves. Since without knowledge of those parts all discussion of the veins, arteries, and nerves will be very difficult, I do not at all object to the present book, as well as the fourth which will be devoted to the nerves, following the fifth, sixth, and seventh, and these latter preceding the present one. This is especially the case for one wholly unskilled in dissection and who has not studied my *Epitome* . . . let him turn to those books first. . . . The reader is free, according to his desire, to transpose my book," *Fabrica* (1543), p. 257 [357].

[121] *Ibid.*, p. 258 [358], first figure, demonstrates this belief by a diagram. "Since [Nature] knew that the vein would of necessity admit blood to itself it provided for it the straight fibres by which the vein attracts the blood into itself. Then, because it was necessary for propulsion of the blood like a stream to the subsequent part of the vein, it also gave it transverse fibres. Lest, however, all the blood be immediately removed and propelled into the next part of the vein, it wove oblique fibres into the body of the vein. And so from these three types the body of the vein is formed in the shape of a white and membranous or sinewy covering suitable for distention and again—that it might properly suit the material contained—for contraction."

[122] *Ibid.*, p. 258 [358], second figure.

[123] See above, pp. 294–295.

[124] *Fabrica* (1543), pp. 258–259 [358–359].

[125] *Ibid.*, pp. 259–260 [359–360].

[126] *Ibid.*, p. 260 [360].

[127] "One issues from the hollow of the liver, advancing into the gall bladder, stomach, spleen, intestines, mesentery, and omentum. A second, taking origin from the gibbosity of the liver, or, as it seems to some, from the right ventricle of the heart, is distributed into the rest of the body in an arrangement of innumerable branches, with the sole exception of the lung. The third, arisen also from the right ventricle of the heart, is distributed into the lungs by numerous branches. However, you will hear that this vein achieves this specially for itself, because it has the body of an artery, wherefore it is called the arterial vein (pulmonary artery). The fourth is extended, as I may say, from the umbilicus into the liver, and serves the animal for nutrition of the foetus, nor can it be considered here correctly in the number of the veins and scarcely is given a special circumscription. From these veins all the rest in the body take origin and are continuous to them," *ibid.*, p. 260 [360].

[128] "The arteries may be considered as two in number, one which, taking origin from the left ventricle of the heart, is distributed through the whole body, with the exception of the lung. The second, extended from the same ventricle of the heart, is distributed only into the lung," *ibid.*, p. 260 [360].

[129] *Ibid.*, p. 261 [361].

[130] *Ibid.*, p. 264 [364] and illustration, p. 262 [362].

[131] *Ibid.*, pp. 264–265 [364–365].

[132] *Ibid.*, p. 267 [367] and corrective illustration, p. 263 [363]. T, V: "That one who had suffered for a long time from this defluxion of blood, and whom I dissected, added great strength to this opinion of mine. For his spleen was very small but very hard, and the vein

running under the rectum intestine almost surpassed the thickness of the thumb and was swollen with blood in that way in which we observe the veins of parturient animals enfolding the uterus to be notably broad and distended."

[133] *Ibid.*, p. 590.
[134] *Ibid.*, p. 275 [375].
[135] *Ibid.*, p. 276 [376].
[136] *Ibid.*, p. 268 [368].
[137] *Ibid.*, pp. 279–280 [379–380], 258 [358], second figure.
[138] *Ibid.*, p. 283 [383], 268 [368].
[139] *Ibid.*, p. 295 [395].
[140] *Ibid.*, pp. 305 [405], 307 [407], diagrammatic figures of the cerebral sinuses.
[141] *Ibid.*, p. 315 [415].
[142] *Ibid.*, p. 316 [416].
[143] *Ibid.*, p. 317 [417].
[144] *Ibid.*, p. 322 [422].
[145] *Ibid.*, p. 322 [422]. Charles Singer, *Vesalius on the human brain*, London, 1952, p. 76, presents the Galenic and Vesalian classifications of the nerves:

Modern Term	Galen	Vesalius
I. Olfactory	Not regarded as separate nerves	Not regarded as separate nerves
II. Optic	"The soft nerves of the eyes"	First pair
III. Oculomotor	"The nerves moving both eyes"	Second pair
IV. Trochlear	Not mentioned	Included with optic nerve
V. Trigeminal	"Third pair of nerves" "Fourth pair of nerves"	Third pair which has two roots Fourth pair
VI. Abducens	United with optic nerve	Included with optic nerve
VII. Facial	"Fifth pair of nerves"	Fifth pair
VIII. Auditory		
IX. Glossopharyngeal		
X. Vagus	"Sixth pair of nerves"	Sixth pair; also includes sympathetic trunk with this nerve
XI. Accessory		
XII. Hypoglossal	"Seventh pair of nerves"	Seventh pair

[146] *Fabrica* (1543), p. 322 [422].
[147] *Ibid.*, p. 324 [424].
[148] *Ibid.*
[149] *Ibid.*, pp. 324–325 [424–425].
[150] *Ibid.*, p. 324 [424].
[151] *Ibid.*, pp. 324–330 [424–430] and illustrations, *ibid.*, p. 319 [419].
[152] *Ibid.*, pp. 338–352 [438–452] and illustrations, *ibid.*, pp. 332 [432], 331 [431], 333 [433].
[153] *Ibid.*, pp. 388–389 [488–489].
[154] *Ibid.*, p. 390 [490].
[155] *Ibid.*, pp. 494–497; illustrations, *ibid.*, pp. 357–358 [457–458]. Vesalius appears to have had some reservations regarding Dryander. According to Roth, p. 149, n. 8, Vesalius's ridicule of a curved saw for opening the skull, *Institutiones anatomicae*, 1538, fol. 73r, and *Fabrica* (1543), p. 237, "not round as certain mathematicians illustrate in their books on anatomy," and so forth, see above, p. 338, was directed at Dryander who recommended such a saw, *Anatomiae, hoc est, corporis humani dissectionis pars prior*, Marburg, 1537, d iiv, "The instrument we use in this anatomical procedure [for sawing off the skullcap] . . . a rounded saw"; also, d ivr, an illustration of the skull with the cap removed and various instruments including the rounded saw. For further information on Dryander, see Ch. IX, n. 177. In regard to the pancreas, any comprehension of its function had to await the introductory efforts of Wirsung a century later, see Alfred Schirmer, *Beitrag zur Geschichte und Anatomie des Pankreas*, Basel, 1893, p. 11 ff.
[156] *Fabrica* (1543), pp. 497–503.
[157] *Fabrica* (1543), p. 500; illustrated, *ibid.*, pp. 460, 461; Curt Elze, "Vesals Beurteilung des Processus vermiformis," *Z. Anat. Entwicklungsgeschichte*, 1943, 112:475–478, with translation from *Fabrica* (1543); Samuel W. Lambert, "Description of the vermiform appendix from the 'De Fabrica' of Vesalius," *Ann. Med. Hist.*, 1937, n. s. 9:422–427, with translation from *Fabrica* (1555). The appendix had earlier been delineated by Dryander, *Anatomia Mundini . . . restituta per Ioannem Dryander*, Marburg, 1541, fol. [15r], although one can never be certain whether this was his own effort or appropriated from another.

[158] *Fabrica* (1543), pp. 504–505.
[159] *Ibid.*, p. 507.
[160] *Ibid.*, p. 506.
[161] *Ibid.*, pp. 509–510.
[162] See above, pp. 115–116.
[163] *Fabrica* (1543), p. 512.
[164] *Ibid.*
[165] *Ibid.*
[166] *Ibid.*
[167] *Ibid.*, p. 515, illustrations, *ibid.*, pp. 372–374.
[168] See above, p. 168.
[169] *Fabrica* (1543), pp. 516–517, illustrations, *ibid.*, p. 515.
[170] *Ibid.*, pp. 371, 516; also see E. Desnos, *Histoire de l'urologie*, Paris, 1914, pp. 82–85, and especially John A. Benjamin, "A discussion of the twenty-first illustration of the fifth book of *De humani corporis fabrica* (1543)," *Bull. Hist. Med.*, 1943, 14:634–651. Fallopio, fol. 181v, and Eustachi, *Opuscula anatomica*, Venice, 1564, pp. 37–38, criticize Vesalius, although the latter not by name, for his declaration of the necessity of using the dog's kidney. More recent writers, apparently consulting only the illustrations, have taken the attitude that Vesalius had fraudulently attempted to impose the dog's kidney on his readers as if it were human, e.g., M. Holl, "Vesals Darstellung des Baues der Niere," *Arch. Gesch. Med.*, 1912, 6:129–148. Vesalius, however, clearly stated the source of his illustrations.
[171] *Fabrica* (1543), p. 515.
[172] *Ibid.*, p. 516.
[173] *Ibid.*, pp. 517–519.
[174] *Ibid.*, p. 520.
[175] *Ibid.*, p. 520 f. See especially the illustration, *ibid.*, p. 372 [472], where the seminal vesicles have only the slightest if any portrayal despite their considerable size in man. Fallopio, fol. 189r, suggests that Vesalius had used the dog, in which they are lacking.
[176] *Fabrica* (1543), p. 525, "The glandular body . . . which Herophilus calls PARASTATAI ADENOEIDĒS is located at the lowest part of the bladder, so to speak midway between the body of the bladder and its neck." The early history of the prostate gland is obscured by terminological confusion, and the problem of determining a name for this structure demonstrates one of the difficulties faced by Vesalius and other conscientious anatomists of that age. Galen referred to certain glandular bodies on either side of the neck of the bladder but did not indicate whether this was a reference to the seminal vesicles or the prostate, although he declared that the name PARASTATAE ADENOEIDĒS had earlier been given to these structures by Herophilus. Vesalius believed that the term PARASTATAS (that which stands beside), with the adjective KIRSOEIDĒS (varicose), had been intended by Herophilus to refer to the seminal vesicles, but with the adjective ADENOEIDĒS (glandular), to the prostate. Hence he called the prostate the "attendant" (*assistens*) gland. The term "prostate" was introduced by Caspar Bartholin in 1611. The first depiction of the prostate is found in the *Tabulae anatomicae*. It is illustrated in the *Fabrica* (1543), pp. 225 [325], 372 [472].
[177] *Ibid.*, p. 524, and illustrated *ibid.*, pp. 370 [470], 372 [472]; they had first been depicted in the *Tabulae anatomicae*. Also see p. 438, n.51.
[178] *Fabrica* (1543), pp. 527–529, illustrated *ibid.*, pp. 225 [325], 372 [472].
[179] *Ibid.*, p. 529. "Here in Padua is a young man of the noble family of Symione of Forlì, a friend of mine and a law student, who has two passages at the tip of the glans, one for semen and the other for urine"; an impossibility since there would have been only a single urethra.
[180] *Ibid.*, pp. 531–532. According to Roth, p. 149, Vesalius aimed his remarks at Berengario da Carpi, *Fabrica* (1543), p. 531, that the "dregs of anatomists . . . speak of the seven cells of the uterus. They declare that there are three on the right side for receiving males and three on the left for females; they declare that the seventh is in the middle of the uterus for hermaphrodites." Roth, however, is incorrect since Berengario was well above any such rude medievalism. Curiously, although Massa, *op. cit.*, fol. 43v, denied that male children are produced on the right side of the uterus and female on the left, he nevertheless accepted tradition to the extent of saying that male children produced on the left were effeminate and female on the right displayed certain masculine qualities. Moreover, he proposed, *ibid.*, fols. 44v–45r, that the doctrine of seven cells might be explained as referring not to seven cavities but rather to seven areas, anterior, posterior, left, right, and so forth.
[181] *Fabrica* (1543), p. 532. Introducing his remarks with the marginal statement, "Galen never inspected a human uterus," he continues: "Here I desire that no student of Galen—and all to whom we have given the name of physician must be close students of him—oppose Galen's doctrines to me and seek to liken parts of the uterus to a horn before he has carefully examined the passages in Galen's *Use of parts*, *On semen*, and *On dissection of the uterus* and compared the uterus

of the cow to that of woman, and finally both to Galen's writings. Thus it may be demonstrated that Galen, not even in a dream, had ever examined the uterus of a woman but only of the cow, goat, and sheep."

[182] *Fabrica* (1543), p. 392 [492].

[183] *Ibid.*, p. 381 [481].

[184] See above, p. 113.

[185] *Fabrica* (1543), p. 538, "Undoubtedly women's menses are evacuated from the veins seeking the uterus, but how this occurs and through what veins in particular, that is, whether that flow of blood is from the fundus or the neck of the uterus [vagina], perhaps you, if you are a sedulous investigator of the works of nature and do not swear by the words of any master, are in doubt, like me." The word "vagina" was introduced by Fallopio in 1561.

[186] Fallopio, *op. cit.*, fol. 197r.

[187] *Fabrica* (1543), p. 539.

[188] *Ibid.*, p. 540, "If I learned anything from the dissection of foetuses and pregnant uteri, and I am accustomed to demonstrate these things in the [medical] school, this was only from animals . . . for hitherto I have had very few pregnant women for dissection."

[189] *Ibid.*, p. 541.

[190] *Ibid.*, pp. 541–543.

[191] *Ibid.*, p. 392 [492]. Vesalius's further confusion is indicated by his reference to two umbilical veins, *ibid.*, pp. 294 [394], 303 [403], illustration, p. 293 [393], an error corrected in the revised *Fabrica*.

[192] *Ibid.*, pp. 543–547.

[193] *Ibid.*, pp. 546–547.

[194] See above, p. 342, for an English version.

[195] *Fabrica* (1543), p. 328 [428].

[196] *Ibid.*, p. 579.

[197] *Ibid.*, pp. 561–568.

[198] *Ibid.*, pp. 581–582.

[199] *Ibid.*, p. 583.

[200] *Ibid.*, p. 584.

[201] *Ibid.*, p. 585.

[202] *Commentaria*, Bologna, 1521, fols. CCCXXXVIv–CCCXXXVIIIv.

[203] *Fabrica* (1543), pp. 587–588.

[204] *Ibid.*, p. 589.

[205] *Ibid.*, p. 590.

[206] *Ibid.*, p. 590.

[207] *Ibid.*, p. 592.

[208] *Ibid.*, p. 594.

[209] See above, pp. 31–32.

[210] *Fabrica* (1543), pp. 623–624.

[211] Charles Singer, *Vesalius on the human brain*, London, 1952.

[212] *Commentaria*, 1521, fol. CCCCLIXr, *Isagogae breves*, 1522, fol. 56v.

[213] *Liber introductorius anatomiae*, fols. 89v–90r.

[214] *Fabrica* (1543), p. 642.

[215] *Ibid.*, p. 622.

[216] *Ibid.*, pp. 622–623.

[217] See above in regard to the optic nerve, p. 170. The statement by Singer, *Vesalius on the human brain*, p. 83, n. 90, that Vesalius declared the nerves hollow, *Fabrica* (1543), p. 642, is due to incorrect translation.

[218] *Ibid.*, p. 623.

[219] *Commentaria*, 1521, fol. CCCCXLVIv.

[220] This residue or excrement, called pituita, was supposed to be carried down from the ventricles to the infundibulum, pituitary gland, so named from this supposed function, and thence into the nostrils and throat by a somewhat fanciful route, although, as mentioned earlier, see p. 154, not filtered through the cribriform plate as proposed by Galen.

[221] *Fabrica* (1543), p. 623.

[222] *Ibid.*, p. 636.

[223] See above, p. 370, for an English version.

[224] *De humani corporis fabrica librorum epitome*. See Cushing, pp. 111–113, for bibliographical details. An interesting sidelight which may provide some notion of the actual time of publication of the *Epitome* is to be found in a letter of Oporinus to the Swiss scholar Joachim Vadianus, *Vadianische Briefsammlung*, ed. Arbenz and Wartmann, VI, St. Gall, 1908, p. 247. The letter, dated 9 August 1543, refers to a copy of the *Epitome* which Oporinus had sent by messenger as a gift. The messenger, upon crossing a bridge over a stream only two miles from Basel, had suffered from vertigo and fallen in. Although he managed to escape with his life the book was

lost and Oporinus promised to send another copy. Much of the *Epitome* has been translated into English; *The Epitome of Andreas Vesalius*, trans. L. R. Lind, with anatomical notes by C. W. Asling, New York, 1949. Unfortunately, however, notes accompanying the illustrations, with one exception, have not been translated, and unfortunately, too, the facsimiles of the original edition of 1543 have been so reduced in size as to be virtually illegible.

[225] Actually there are ten illustrations but one has been repeated.

[226] See above, pp. 149–150.

[227] Looking ahead to Geminus's plagiarism of the Vesalian plates in 1545, see above, p. 223, it may be said that the so-called "Epitome" with which he accompanied them includes, after Chapter IV, the explanatory text of the "Adam and Eve" figures, and contains as well a chapter entitled "Brief enumeration of all the bones of the body," a verbatim abridgment of the *Fabrica*, I, Chapter LX [XL] where it is entitled "The number of bones." Providing further substance to Vesalius's hardly complimentary opinion of plagiarists, as late as the middle-seventeenth century they were industriously stealing this text from one another and publishing it as the *Epitome*, some of them at least in the genuine belief that it was the authentic text. For a plagiarist it was of course much easier to borrow from the most recent unauthorized reprinting with its apochryphal content than to search out a copy of Oporinus's original publication of 1543.

[228] m3, p4.

[229] This is the second, contemplative or "Hamlet" skeleton, *Fabrica* (1543), p. 164, which rests its elbow upon a monumental structure on which is engraved the phrase "Genius endures, all else will perish." In the *Epitome* the engraving is more doleful, "All splendor is dissolved by death." The stygian hue pervades the snow-white limbs and grace of form is brought to nothing."

[230] "The compendium of the books *De humani corporis fabrica* which I now present is divided into two parts of which one, comprised of six chapters, contains a very brief account of all the parts and the other through its several illustrations provides delineations of them with indices of the signs by which the parts are designated. After you have considered my arrangement—which I chose from several possibilities as best suited to the form of the text and the purpose of the illustrations—according to your decision begin with the description of the parts or with the illustrations and their indices of notes. The latter commence with the figures offering nude likenesses of a man and a woman where you will find the names of the external parts as an index to those figures."

[231] One immediately recalls the representation of surface anatomy in the title-page scene and in the first "muscle-man" of the *Fabrica*. On the "Adam and Eve" figures, see the long discussion as well as the general description of the *Epitome* by W. G. Spencer, "The 'Epitome' of Vesalius on vellum in the British Museum Library," *Essays on the history of medicine presented to Karl Sudhoff*, Zürich, 1924, pp. 237–244.

[232] See above, p. 165.

[233] See above, p. 189.

[234] Hernani Monteiro, "A copy on vellum of the 'Epitome' of Vesalius in the library of the Escorial," *Festschrift zum 80. Geburtstag Max Neuburgers*, Vienna, 1948, pp. 346–349. Two further copies on vellum are known, one in the library of the British Museum, probably that once owned by Richard Mead, and the other in the Hunterian Library, Glasgow.

[235] See above, p. 187.

[236] See Cushing, pp. 113–115, for bibliographical details.

[237] Henry Sigerist, "Albanus Torinus and the German edition of the *Epitome* of Vesalius," *Bull. Hist. Med.*, 1943, 14:652–666.

[238] See above, p. 224.

[239] In 1544 Torinus published the *opera omnia* of Rhazes, put together from a variety of translations including Vesalius's edition of book nine, *Ad Almansorem*, see Cushing, p. 8, Sigerist, *op. cit.*, pp. 659–660. This was published in Basel, although not by Oporinus, and although Vesalius never referred to this unauthorized publication it is very likely that he was not especially pleased to have his early schooldays' effort resurrected.

Notes to Chapter IX

[1] Gerhard Wolf-Heidegger, "Ueber Vesals Aufenhalt in Basel im Jahre 1547," *Gesnerus*, 1945, 2:207.

[2] Vandenesse, p. 259.

[3] Brandi, pp. 371–373.

[4] *Ibid.*, p. 405.

[5] *Ibid.*, pp. 405, 409–410.

[6] Henri de Vocht, *Monumenta humanistica Lovaniensia*, Louvain, 1934, pp. 626–627.

[7] *Ibid.*, pp. 627–631.

[8] *Fabrica* (1543), p. 19.

[9] Brandi, pp. 431–432.

[10] O'Malley, "Andreas Vesalius, Count Palatine," pp. 207–208.

[11] *Ep.Ch.Rt.*, p. 176.

[12] "Psychological sidelights on Andreas Vesalius," *Bull. Hist. Med.*, 1943, 14:562–593.

[13] See above, p. 223.

[14] See above, pp. 218, 223.

[15] *Correspondence of the Emperor Charles V*, ed. William Bradford, London, 1850, pp. 365–366.

[16] *Relazioni degli ambasciatori veneti*, ed. Albèri, Ser. I, Vol. I, Florence, 1839, p. 342.

[17] *Mémoire de Charles-Quint*, ed. A. Morel-Fatio, Paris, 1913, p. 199.

[18] *Ibid.*, p. 221.

[19] *Ibid.*, p. 231.

[20] *Ibid.*, p. 239.

[21] Bartholomew Sastrow, *Memoirs of a German burgomaster*, trans. A. D. Vandam, London, 1905, pp. 230–231.

[22] See above, p. 84.

[23] De Meyer, "Notice sur Corneille van Baersdorp," *Ann. de la Soc. Méd. Chir. de Bruges*, 1845, 6:35. A brief recent article with additional bibliography is A. De Witte, "Cornelis de Baersdorp, lijfarts van Keizer Karel. Korrespondentie 1548–1561," *Scientiarum Historia*, 1959, 1:177–190.

[24] De Meyer, *op. cit.*, pp. 18–19.

[25] Etienne Daxhelet, *Adrien Barlandus humaniste belge*, Louvain, 1938, p. 24.

[26] De Meyer, *op. cit.*, pp. 20–21.

[27] *Ibid.*, p. 34.

[28] *Ibid.*, p. 21.

[29] Daxhelet, *op. cit.*, p. 329.

[30] De Meyer, *op. cit.*, p. 35.

[31] Armstrong, *The Emperor Charles V*, II, London, 1902, pp. 16–17.

[32] Dionisio Daza Chacon, *c.* 1510–1596?, a native of Valladolid, where he had his preliminary education and began the study of surgery. Thence to Salamanca where he studied both medicine and surgery and began the practice of surgery *c.* 1530. In 1543 he traveled to Flanders and became a military surgeon in the forces of Charles V, first appearing as a colleague of Vesalius at Landrecies. He remained in Germany for many years, returning to Spain only after the abdication of the emperor. However, he returned for a time so that he was with Vesalius in Paris in 1559 for the consultation over the wounded Henry II, as will be indicated later, but thereafter he returned permanently to Spain where he once again appeared as Vesalius's colleague in the case of Don Carlos. His references to Vesalius are to be found in his *Practica y teorica de cirugia en romance y en latin*, Valladolid, 1595. For the present study the edition of Madrid, 1678, has been employed. There are several studies about him, such as Charles Wilson, "Dionisio Daca Chacon," *Edinburgh Med. Jour.*, 1857, 2:865–894, and J. M. Guardia, "Dionisio Daza Chacon," *Gaz. Méd. Paris*, 1863, although in the final analysis most of the biographical information is drawn from the *Cirugia*.

[33] *Practica in arte chirurgica copiosa*, Rome, 1514.

[34] *De partibus ictu sectis citissime sanandis & medicamento aquae nuper invento*, Venice, 1542.

[35] *De vulnerum a bombardarum et sclopetorum globulis illatorum et de eorum symptomatum curatione tractatus*, Bologna, 1552.

[36] *De curandis vulneribus sclopetorum*, Lyons, 1560.

[37] Alfonso Ferri, *c.* 1500–1549, subscribed to the older method of treatment in his *De sclopetorum sive archibusorum vulneribus*, Rome, 1552.

[38] Daza Chacon, *Practica y teorica de cirugia en romance y en latin*, Madrid, 1678, II, p. 260.

[39] *Ibid.*, I, pp. 163–164.

[40] *Ep.Ch.Rt.*, p. 136.

[41] Roth, pp. 431–432; *Ep.Ch.Rt.*, p. 141.

[42] M. Roth, "Vesaliana," *Virchows Arch.*, 1895, 141:475–478, also an English version is given above, p. 405. Meurer, 1513–1585, of Altenberg in the district of Meissen, Saxony, first studied philosophy in Leipzig, and then medicine. In 1539 he went to Italy with the humanist Georg Fabricius, the later rector of the gymnasium in Meissen, and several young students. Meurer studied medicine in Padua under Vesalius and Da Monte and attended the lectures of Marcantonio Genua, also the friend of Vesalius. At the close of 1542 he took a trip to Rome and Naples in company with Fabricius and a student named Wolfgang Werter. Returned to Padua in early summer of 1543, the friends parted from Fabricius who returned home while Meurer must have remained in Padua until at least February 1544. He was thus at Padua during Vesalius's major successes there and quite possibly witnessed his teacher's return, in December 1543, to the discomfiture of Realdo Colombo. From Padua, Meurer returned to teach philosophy at Leipzig, where he became professor of medicine in 1571.

[43] Roth, p. 181.

[44] See above, p. 98.

Notes to Chapter IX

[45] *Ep.Ch.Rt.*, p. 176.

[46] Franciscus Puteus, *Apologia in anatome pro Galeno contra Andream Vesalium*, Venice, 1562, fols. 116v–117r.

[47] *Ibid.*, fol. 117v ff.

[48] Rashdall, *The universities of Europe in the middle ages*, ed. Powicke and Emden, Oxford, 1936, II, pp. 45–46.

[49] Fabroni, *Historia Academiae Pisanae*, Pisa, 1791, I, p. 103 ff.

[50] Andrea Corsini, *Andrea Vesalio nello studio di Pisa*, Siena, 1915, pp. 8–10, prints excerpts from a number of letters concerning the question of appointments to the new faculty, both consideration of qualifications of possible members and requests for positions.

[51] "The inspection of those things hidden in the human body is very useful and necessary for those who want to study the complete art of healing. Otherwise who would know how to give a suitable and proper remedy for the internal weaknesses and ailments which are hidden from man's observation? Therefore, in order to assist the health of mankind, we have decided that each year in the spring, when it will be most suitable, the rector must [if possible] provide two cadavers for anatomy—preferably one male and the other female—but not less than one. In order more easily to accomplish this, we order that the Commissioner of Pisa be required to assign the said cadavers to the rector from executed criminals. But if at the time of the anatomy such criminals' bodies are not to be found in Pisa, then the rector must write to Florence to the eight masters of the guard and to the *Balia*, ordering them to obtain the said cadavers. We declare that an anatomy may not be performed on the body of any citizen of Florence or of Pisa, or of any doctor or scholar, without the permission of their relatives. In order that the said anatomy may not excite any irregularity and may be carried on in orderly fashion, we declare that the rector and the counsellors must elect two suitable scholars who have completed the arts course in some university, as well as not less than four years of medicine, and who, if possible, have seen other anatomies. Anatomists should be invited to preside over the said anatomies, to provide all that is necessary and according to the expenses, to charge as much as each one wishing to observe ought to pay. But nobody should be admitted to observe unless he is a matriculated scholar or doctor of one of our colleges. However, the rector and all the doctors of the faculty of medicine as well as four poor scholars chosen by the rector and the counsellors may observe the anatomy, if they wish, without any charge. All the others who wish to observe it must pay whatever the charge. Let the order of the dissection and the anatomical lectures accord with what seems proper to the rector and the doctors of the faculty of medicine, as well as five counsellors of the faculty of arts." Chap. L of the Statutes, in Fabroni, *op. cit.*, and also Corsini, pp. 17–18.

[52] Corsini, *op. cit.*, pp. 17–19.

[53] The regular faculty of medicine included Matteo Corti who, despite his age and infirmities, agreed to accept appointment at an annual 1200 *scudi* and a house in Florence. He died, however, almost immediately after going to Pisa. Others were Francesco Gallo of Pontremoli, 1543–1547, Nicolo Goldoni of Milan, 1543–1554, Giovanni Argenterio of Piedmont, 1543–1555, Leonardo Jacchino of Empoli, 1543–1547, and Michelangelo Bargaeus, 1543–1572; Fabroni, *op. cit.*, II, pp. 248–259. There was no regular professor of anatomy until the later appointment of Realdo Colombo.

[54] Francesco Campana, who is frequently mentioned by Vesalius, had long been first secretary and a close adviser of the duke. According to Corsini, *op. cit.*, p. 11, he played a leading role in the reorganization of the university and the compilation of its statutes, as well as in such troublesome matters as finding lodgings for faculty and students.

[55] Corsini, *op. cit.*, p. 5.

[56] Antonio Taddei, "La località ove Andrea Vesalio tenne in Pisa la sua lezione di anatomia," *Boll. Ist. Stor. Ital. Arte Sanit.*, 1931, 11:166–170.

[57] G. Del Guerra, "A proposito della località ove Andrea Vesalio tenne in Pisa la sua lezione di anatomia," *ibid.*, pp. 262–263; "Le giornate pisane di Andrea Vesalio," *Scientia Veterum*, 1954, 2, nos. 5–6:7–8.

[58] Cosimo appears to have had a genuine interest in the university and its development, indicated by his frequent attendance and the lively interest he had in following lectures and discussions. The praise given him by Vesalius seems to reflect a genuine admiration which was echoed by John Caius after his visit to Pisa.

[59] Corsini, *op. cit.*, pp. 5–6.

[60] *Ep.Ch.Rt.*, p. 140.

[61] *Ibid.*, pp. 140–141.

[62] Corsini, *op. cit.*, p. 6. This may have been Carlo Cortesi, a surgeon, *ibid.*, p. 16.

[63] A letter from Captain Giovambattista Borghesi to Duke Cosimo, 28 March 1543, states that "I write to ask if you would like to intercede your grace on behalf of messer Marcantonio Bell'armati, doctor of laws, from Siena, for a position in the University of Pisa. He is now in Macerata, and highly appreciates the activities of your Excellency, and were he to receive an in-

vitation he could resign his present post in a comfortable time." A letter of the duke to Campana directed him to handle the matter, and the presence of Belloarmato in Pisa suggests that he had received an invitation. This is supported by a letter written after his death which said in part that "the lectureship left vacant through the death of mess. Antonio Bellarmati" was requested for "mess. Lactantio Bronconi," see Corsini, *op. cit.,* p. 14.

[64] *Ep.Cb.Rt.,* pp. 173–175.

[65] *Ibid.,* pp. 175–176.

[66] *Ibid.,* p. 40.

[67] Andrea Corsini, *Nuovi documenti riguardanti Andrea Vesalio e Realdo Colombo nello Studio Pisano,* Siena, 1918.

[68] Wauters, "Quelques mots sur André Vésale," *Mém. Acad. Roy. Belge,* 1897, 55:26; Léon Frédéricq, "André Vésale," *Mém. Soc. Roy. Sci. Liège,* 1945, 4 ser. 6:339.

[69] Albin Rozet and J. F. Lembey, *L'Invasion de la France et le siège de Saint-Dizier,* Paris, 1910, pp. 37–59; Alexandre Henne, *Histoire du règne de Charles-Quint en Belgique,* Brussels, 1860, VIII, p. 176.

[70] Henne, *op. cit.,* VIII, p. 176.

[71] Rozet and Lembey, *op. cit.,* p. 97 ff.; Henne, *op. cit.,* VIII, p. 177.

[72] Rozet and Lembey, *op. cit.,* p. 259.

[73] Vandenesse, p. 289. It was reported that an Italian necromancer presented himself in the midst of the group surrounding the fallen prince and offered to cure him with charms; however, the wounded man refused, saying that he preferred death to a life owed to diabolic arts, Reiffenberg, *Histoire de l'ordre de la Toison d'Or,* Brussels, 1830, p. 393.

[74] *Oevres de Pierre Bourdeille, Seigneur de Brantôme,* I, Paris, 1864, p. 245.

[75] Dispatch, 16 July. On this period see the unpublished *Lettere scritte da Bernardo Navagero, cavaliere, che fu poi cardinale, alla serenissima repubblica veneziana, nel tempo che fu ambasciatore a Sua Maestà, cioè dal di 17 settembre 1543 sino al 31 maggio 1546.* These dispatches, Ms. 102 ex Brera, once in the Viennese archives, are now in the Archivio di Stato, Venice. They have been printed in a selected and summarized form by Gachard, *Trois années de l'histoire de Charles-Quint (1543–1546) d'après les dépêches de l'ambassadeur vénitien Bernardo Navagero,* Brussels, 1865. Navagero's relation of his embassy is to be found in the *Relazioni,* Ser. I, Vol. I, Florence, 1839, pp. 289–368. There is an English version of this in the *Correspondence of the Emperor Charles V and his ambassadors,* ed. William Bradford, London, 1850, pp. 435–479.

[76] *Ep.Cb.Rt.,* p. 176.

[77] Vandenesse, p. 289.

[78] Daza Chacon, *Cirurgia,* I, p. 261.

[79] *Ibid.,* I, p. 181.

[80] Rozet and Lembey, *op. cit.,* pp. 119–127; Henne, *op. cit.,* VIII, pp. 180–181. Hallewyn, a captain of ordonnance and *gentilhomme de la bouche* to the emperor, had been struck in the neck by the ball of an arquebus.

[81] *Ep.Cb.Rt.,* p. 176.

[82] Henne, *op. cit.,* VIII, pp, 209–210.

[83] Brandi, p. 451.

[84] Henne, *op. cit.,* VIII, pp. 210–214.

[85] The attack, presumably brought on by the round of royal pleasures, is recorded by Charles in his *Mémoires,* p. 255: "[The emperor] left Brussels, where he had been threatened with the gout, to go to Ghent, where the gout attacked him, so that from the beginning of December to Easter he suffered greatly despite his regimen and diet to which he submitted for the first time. This was his eleventh attack of gout."

[86] Navagero, Dispatch, 18 January.

[87] Fisch, p. 232, citing *State Papers King Henry Eighth,* X, pp. 254, 268.

[88] Navagero, Dispatch, 8 February. Guaiac wood, guaiacan, lignum vitae, lignum sanctum, or holy wood, which was brought to Europe from the West Indies, owed its considerable reputation to assertions that it had cured Spanish sufferers from syphilis in the West Indies, assertions strengthened by the belief that nature located the specific for a disease in the neighborhood of the source of the disease, in the case of syphilis considered to be the West Indies. In his *Historia stirpium,* 1540, Valerius Cordus declares that guaiac had been imported for half a century, although there are no present records that support such an early date. There is a legend that it was imported in 1508 by a Spaniard named Gonsalvo, who may or may not be identified with Oviedo. The first documented date is 1517 when the imperial physician Nicolaus Pol wrote a treatise, not published until 1535, *De cura morbi gallici per lignum guayacanum.* The first actual publication on the subject was that of Leonard Schmaus, a physician of Salzburg, *Lucubratiuncula de morbo gallico et cura eius noviter reperta cum ligno indico,* also printed in German as *Ain recept fon ainem holtz zu brauchen für die kranckhait der frantzösen flüssig.* . . . Both were published in Augsburg, 1518; see George Sarton, "The strange fame of Demetrio Canevari," *Jour. Hist. Med.,* 1946, 1:405–414. The use of the wood was greatly popularized by Ulrich von Hutten who, in his *De admiranda*

guaiaci medicina, Mainz, 1519, declared that guaiac had been the source of his cure from syphilis, the disease that ultimately caused his death. In addition to the use of the wood for this disease it came to be used generally, as in the case of Charles V. The wood was shredded and employed for the preparation of a decoction which might then have other ingredients added. The patient usually was required to remain bedridden in a heated room for a period of weeks, subjected to severely limited diet and activity, drinking the decoction at regular intervals. It was the limitation placed upon his diet that particularly irked the emperor. The china root, smilax china, owed its popularity to the fact that it was of more recent introduction into Europe than the guaiac, of which some had already questioned the properties claimed for it. According to Garcia da Orta, physician to the viceroy of Goa, *Coloquios dos simples e drogas da India,* Goa, 1563, the china root had been introduced into India from China shortly after 1535. Thence it was brought to Europe by the Portuguese who claimed it had the qualities of a panacea and was especially valuable in the treatment of syphilis. China root, like guaiac, was used in the form of a decoction, and it had a temporary appeal for the emperor since it was used with a less restricted diet than the guaiac. However, as Vesalius was to indicate in his *Letter on the china root,* see below, p. 216, the period of its vogue was a short one.

[89] Fisch, p. 232, citing *State Papers King Henry Eighth,* X, p. 274 f.

[90] Navagero, dispatch, 22 March.

[91] See above, pp. 216–217.

[92] *Ep.Ch.Rt.,* p. 15.

[93] Fisch, p. 323, citing *State Papers King Henry Eighth,* X, p. 320.

[94] Dispatch, 27 March.

[95] *Nuntiaturberichte aus Deutschland 1553–1559, nebst ergänzenden Aktenstücken, Bd. VIII. Nuntiatur des Verallo 1545–1546 im Auftrage des K. Preussischen Historischen Instituts in Rom. Bearbeitet von Walter Friedensburg,* Gotha, 1898, pp. 105–106.

[96] On 18 April 1545 the nuncio Verallo wrote to Cardinal Farnese from Antwerp: "Since his Majesty has decided to forego affairs in Mechlin, he will remain here tomorrow and depart for Worms Tuesday or Wednesday, where he has long desired to be by the eighth of May," *ibid.,* p. 105. However, Charles was not to reach Worms until the 16th. It was probably to this period up to the departure from Brussels that Laurentius Grylius of Landshut refers in his *Oratio de peregrinatione studii medicinalis ergo suscepta,* Prague, 1566, p. 9, when he writes: "The season for traveling having passed, I was forced to spend the winter in Belgium. I spent the greater part of it at Louvain with Hieronymus Brachelius [Drivère, see above, p. 66] . . . then I went to the imperial court at Brussels to study medical treatment there and passed two months studying the methods of the pharmacists and surgeons of the city and of the imperial physicians, especially of Cornelius [van Baersdorp] and Andreas Vesalius. With the arrival of spring I prepared myself again for the road."

[97] *Practica y teorica de cirugia,* I, p. 69.

[98] Brandi, p. 452.

[99] Vandenesse, p. 308.

[100] *Mémoires de Charles-Quint,* p. 259.

[101] Navagero, Dispatch, 25 May; *Papiers d'état du Cardinal de Granvelle,* ed. Ch. Weiss, Paris, 1841 ff., III, pp. 107, 149.

[102] Brandi, pp. 452–456. "During the Diet of Worms, the emperor received news that the princess of Spain, his daughter-in-law, had been brought to bed of a son who was called the Infante don Carlos; then, four or five days later, the very different news of the death of the princess, which distressed the emperor as may be imagined," *Mémoires de Charles-Quint,* pp. 264–265.

[103] Navagero, Dispatch, 12 August.

[104] *Ep.Ch.Rt.,* p. 177. Eck, a physician from the Netherlands, *fl.* mid-16th century. After studies at Wittenberg and in Italy he practised in Cologne and demonstrated a special interest in botany. C. G. Jöcher, *Allgemeines gelehrten Lexicon,* II, Leipzig, 1750, col. 272.

[105] Navagero, Dispatches, 23, 29 August; Vandenesse, p. 311.

[106] *Mémoires de Charles-Quint,* p. 265.

[107] Navagero, Dispatch, 30 November.

[108] *Ibid.,* 11 December.

[109] *Ibid.,* 18 December; "I have been somewhat troubled by gout which has caused me to remain in this place. Presently I am better and hope to leave tomorrow for Utrecht"; Charles to the Duchess of Lorraine, 17 December, *Correspondenz des Kaiser Karl V,* ed. Lanz, V, Leipzig, 1845, p. 479.

[110] Navagero, Dispatches, 23 December, 1 January 1546; Reiffenberg, *Toison d'Or,* pp. 396–400.

[111] Vandenesse, pp. 314–330.

[112] *Ibid.,* pp. 317–321.

[113] *Ibid.,* p. 328.

[114] Navagero, Dispatch, 8 January.

Notes to Chapter IX

[115] Vandenesse, p. 328.

[116] Navagero, Dispatches, 11, 15 January.

[117] *Mémoires de Charles-Quint*, p. 265.

[118] Vandenesse, p. 330.

[119] *Ep.Ch.Rt.*, p. 197.

[120] *Ibid.*, p. 11.

[121] See above, p. 22.

[122] On the life of Navagero, see *Relazioni degli ambasciatori veneti al senato edite da Eugenio Alberi*, ser. ii, Vol. III, Florence, 1846, pp. 366–368; Agostino Valiero, *Vita di Bernardo Navagero*, Verona, 1602; Scipione Maffei, *Verona illustrata*, III, pt. ii, Milan, 1825, pp. 352–353.

[123] Dispatch, 19 September, 27 October.

[124] Dispatch, undated.

[125] Dispatch, 16 September 1545.

[126] Dispatch, 11 January 1546.

[127] Dispatch, 14 February.

[128] *Venetianische Depeschen vom Kaiserhofe*, I, Vienna, 1889, p. 452.

[129] *Ibid.*, pp. 459–461.

[130] Dispatch, 4 May.

[131] *Venetianische Depeschen vom Kaiserhofe*, I, p. 481.

[132] *Ibid.*

[133] *Ibid.*, p. 489; Dispatch, 14 May.

[134] *Venetianische Depeschen vom Kaiserhofe*, I, p. 505.

[135] *Ibid.*, p. 530.

[136] "De poculo caesareo et vitreo, quod Bruschio dedit Andreas Vesalius medicus imperatorium," in his *Schediasmata quedam encomiastica et fatidica*, Augsburg, 1550, C3r. Vesalius and Brusch were also in Augsburg at the same time in the following year, when the presentation might also have been made. Brusch, 1518–1559, born at Schlackenwald in Bohemia, studied the classics at Tübingen, and possibly also medicine, since he refers on several occasions to Leonhart Fuchs as one of his teachers. There is some suggestion of relationship with Vesalius even earlier than 1546, since in that year, writing to Joachim Camerarius from Lindau, he recommended a certain "Junckher" to "a relative of mine, Joannes Dannmüller, once a student of Vesalius and now physician of the Fuggers."

[137] Vandenesse, pp. 330–332.

[138] *Venetianische Depeschen vom Kaiserhofe*, I, p. 471.

[139] *Ibid.*

[140] *Ibid.*, p. 479.

[141] Brandi, p. 467; W. Stirling-Maxwell, *Don John of Austria*, I, London 1883, pp. 2–5.

[142] Brandi, p. 469.

[143] Francesco d'Este, b. 1516, first seigneur and afterward Marquis of Massa-Lombara, a dashing leader of light horse rather than a great captain. His first campaign was in Provence in 1536, and in 1543 and 1544 he was captain-general of light horse. The campaign at Vitry was the most successful of his career. At the end of the war the emperor offered him 3,000 crowns which he indiscreetly refused and so gained the ill will of Charles. In 1546 he was passed over for election to a vacancy in the Golden Fleece, and in June the emperor passed over him in assigning the commands for the campaign against the Protestants. As a result, Este asked for his retirement and left Ratisbon on 17 June. However, two months later inactivity caused him to write in early August that he would like to make the campaign regardless of his command, but illness kept him in Mantua and he did not rejoin the imperial army until 8 September near Ingolstadt. He passed to French service in 1558 and became lieutenant-general in Tuscany under Henry II. He died in 1578; Rozey and Lembey, *op. cit.*, pp. 209–210.

[144] Nicolo Zaffarini, *Scoperte anatomiche di Gio. Batista Canani*, Ferrara, 1809, p. 12.

[145] *Examen*, p. 83.

[146] Joachim Roelants was born at Mechlin on 2 July 1496 and matriculated at Louvain 31 August 1512, a student in the Pedagogium Porc. After becoming licentiate in medicine he established himself in Mechlin and was also attached as physician to the court of the regent of the Netherlands, Margaret of Austria. Joachim succeeded his father Cornelius as city physician of Mechlin in 1525, and in 1545 was named superintendent of the poor. He gained a considerable reputation, especially for a book on the sweat, *De novo morbo sudoris quam anglicum vocant, anno 1529 grassantis*, Antwerp, 1530. He died 14 August 1558. See Etienne Daxhelet, *Adrien Barlandus humaniste belge*, Louvain, 1938, p. 256, which includes a considerable bibliography on Roelants. Vesalius refers to him in the *Fabrica* (1543), p. 538, as "the very learned Joachim Roelants, primary physician of Mechlin and singular ornament of our common Brabant."

[147] *Ep.Ch.Rt.*, p. 42. In addition to his efforts to assist young Roelants, during this same period Vesalius sought to help Oporinus by employing one of his stepsons as a kind of general factotum. The youth was apparently worthless and after a year Vesalius dismissed him, "Die Briefe

Notes to Chapter IX

Joh. Oporins an den Strassburger Prediger Conrad Hubert," *Beiträge zur vaterländischen Geschichte*, 1893, n.s., 13:421.

[148] *Ep.Ch.Rt.*, pp. 42–43.

[149] *Ibid.*, pp. 3–5. Franciscus Vesalius must have informed his brother Andreas almost at once that he had sent the letter to Oporinus for publication. There is a letter of Andreas Vesalius to his friend in Basel, Johannes Gast, which has some bearing on this matter. Discovered in Zürich by Fr. Rudolf, "Ein Erinnerungsblatt an Andreas Vesalius," *Basler Jahrb.*, 1943:116–117, he misdates it as August 1542, although actually, as indicated by G. Wolf-Heidegger, "Andreas Vesalius," *Beiträge zur Geschichte der Naturwissenschaften und der Technik in Basel*, Olten, 1959, pp. 100 and 175, n. 5, the date is 1546. In that letter, given in German translation by Rudolf, *loc. cit.*, and by Wolf-Heidegger, *op. cit.*, p. 175, and facsimile of the original Latin text, p. 99, Vesalius refers to "trifles from my pen which I am sending to Oporinus for publication." He continues: "I should be happy to have the work published soon and in elegant format. I request you to advise Oporinus to use the best paper and to see that the book has wide margins. I shall bear the extra cost. Thereby the printing is clearer and the work of the typographer made easier. The larger a book is, the greater my pleasure in it. I know you will laugh at my wishes; nevertheless, I wish it. Nothing gives me more pleasure than a splendid edition of my work. . . . impress on Oporinus that he is not, as is his custom, to allow my manuscript to remain for a long time in his drawer." It may have been that upon learning of Franciscus Vesalius's action, Andreas decided to send a revised copy of the *Letter on the china root* to Oporinus, or at least one free from the errors that might creep into copies made by others. Examination of the Cushing copy of the printed text, which managed to escape the worst ravages of binders, indicates that Vesalius's requests to Oporinus were faithfully carried out. Furthermore, Oporinus must have been aware that the book would enjoy a good sale and hence was as anxious as Vesalius to produce it quickly. Its appearance in October 1546 must have required the concentrated efforts of his entire shop.

[150] This Netherlander was one of Vesalius's students in Padua, perhaps attracted there by the presence of a fellow countryman. He is referred to in the *Fabrica* (1543), p. 260, as "Antonius Succha, a very capable young man, the great and rare hope of our common Brussels and so of the whole of Belgium, because of his unusual knowledge of medicine and mathematics, who was sedulous in learning the construction of the larynx from me."

[151] *Ep.Ch.Rt.*, p. 12. On Caballus see above, p. 241.

[152] *Ibid.*, p. 12.

[153] *Ibid.*, p. 13.

[154] *Ibid.*, pp. 14–15.

[155] *Ibid.*, p. 15.

[156] *Ibid.*, p. 18.

[157] *Ibid.*, p. 19.

[158] *Ibid.*, pp. 19–20.

[159] *Ibid.*, p. 20.

[160] *Ibid.*, pp. 21–39.

[161] *Ibid.*, pp. 39–40.

[162] *Ibid.*, p. 41.

[163] *Ibid.*, pp. 41–42.

[164] *Ibid.*, pp. 42–44.

[165] Here Vesalius was no doubt thinking of the edition of Galen's works published by the Giunta Press, see above, p. 101, and the fact that there was as yet a chair at Padua for the study of Avicenna.

[166] *Ep.Ch.Rt.*, pp. 45–46.

[167] *Ibid.*, p. 46.

[168] *Ibid.*, pp. 46–47.

[169] *Ibid.*, pp. 49–54.

[170] *Ibid.*, p. 55.

[171] *Ibid.*, pp. 55–57.

[172] *Ibid.*, pp. 57–58.

[173] *Ibid.*, p. 60.

[174] *Ibid.*, p. 143. Prior to the publication of the *Fabrica*, "when on several occasions there was . . . opportunity for dissecting the foetus *in utero*, I, with the other physicians present, was so ignorant of those matters, and the dissection had to be performed so precipitately, that there was little opportunity to note the difference between the dog and woman."

[175] *Ibid.*, pp. 152–153, 159–160.

[176] See above, p. 210.

[177] It is true that Jean Guinter of Andernach is not mentioned by name in the *Fabrica* for the reason, as Vesalius declared, that his lack of contribution to anatomy made such mention unnecessary. Johann Dryander, or Eichmann, 1500–1560, of Wetter, Oberhessen, studied medi-

cine and mathematics at Erfurt, Bourges, and Paris, in which last place he became a friend of Guinter, and perhaps on that basis voiced the criticism to which Vesalius replies here. Dryander received his M.D. in 1533 at Mainz and for a time was physician to the Elector of Trier. In 1535 he became ordinary professor of medicine at Marburg, where he was rector on seven occasions. Just at this time the Landgrave Philip of Hesse, who had founded the University of Marburg in 1527, permitted the use of executed criminals for dissection at the university, and Dryander performed the first two dissections in June 1534 and March 1536, and soon thereafter delivered an oration in which he urged the necessity of anatomical study. He made drawings of his dissections, at least those of the brain, which were published; *Anatomia capitis humani in Marpurgensi Academia superiori anno publice exhibita*, Marburg, 1536. This was republished as *Anatomiae, hoc est, corporis humani dissectionis pars prior*, Marburg, 1537, with some additional anatomical figures, the Landgrave's decree permitting dissection of criminals, and Dryander's oration. His next ventures in publication were in part plagiarisms from Vesalius's *Tabulae anatomicae*, to which reference has already been made, see above, p. 89. However, from Vesalius's present words, if they are not meant to be ironic, he had not been aware of Dryander's participation in the plagiarisms which he had previously attributed to some unnamed printer of Marburg. He mentions Dryander in the *Fabrica*, an indication that he was not hostile at that time to the Marburg professor, and refers to correspondence with him. However, he does not grant Dryander the superlatives he sometimes accords to others. "Johann Dryander, the diligent professor of medicine and mathematics, in a long and erudite letter asked my opinion of the Hippocratic aphorism in which it is denied that abnormally obese women can conceive, since the mouth of the uterus is compressed by omentum," *Fabrica* (1543), p. 495. On Dryander, see Edouard Turner, "Les planches anatomiques de J. Dryander et de G. H. Ryff," *Gaz. Hebd. Méd. Chir.*, 1876, 33:785–791, 817–823; Edwin Fuhrmeister, *Johannes Dryander Wetteranus*, Diss., Halle, 1920.

[178] Janus Cornarius, or Johann Haynpul or Hagenbut, c. 1500–16 March 1558, of Zwickau, studied at Leipzig and Wittenberg, and received the M.D. in 1523. He next traveled in Northern Europe and Scandinavia, England, the Netherlands, and France, and lived for a time, 1528, in Basel in association with Erasmus. Cornarius was town-physician to Zwickau, 1530, Nordhausen, 1535–1537, Frankfurt am Main, 1538. He became professor of medicine in Marburg, 1543, and so, during that period considered by Vesalius, returned to Zwickau in 1546, and in 1557 became professor of medicine at Jena. Cornarius was primarily a medical philologist who edited a number of classical medical texts including works of Hippocrates, Galen, Aetius, and Paul of Aegina, and belonged to that group of physicians who, because of their strong and constant belief in the validity of classical authority, were naturally unsympathetic to Vesalius's purpose. On Cornarius, see Otto Clemen, "Janus Cornarius," *Neues Arch. f. sachs. Gesch. u. Altertumsk.*, 1912, 33:36–76.

[179] *Ep.Ch.Rt.*, pp. 177–179. The controversy between Fuchs and Cornarius was more involved than Vesalius's words suggest. Leonhart Fuchs, 1501–1566, of Wemding, Bavaria, studied medicine at the University of Ingolstadt and became professor of medicine at Ingolstadt and later at Tübingen. His major work was his herbal *De historia stirpium*, Basel, 1542, with remarkably fine woodcut illustrations, one of the great books in the history of botany. In 1543 Walther Ryff, to be recalled as one of the plagiarists of Vesalius's *Tabulae anatomicae*, produced an herbal, printed in Frankfurt by Egenolph, with illustrations plagiarized from Fuchs's work. In consequence Fuchs published an attack in 1544, *Apologia, qua refellit malitiosas Gualtheri Ryffi veteratoris pessimi reprehensiones* (An apologia which refutes the malicious charges of that consummate liar Walther Ryff). The content of the attack was as strong as the title and, although not directed against Egenolph the printer, nevertheless threatened his reputation by condemning the quality of the plagiarism. In consequence Egenolph sought to buy up and suppress as much of the edition as possible and additionally produced a tract in his own defence. Promptly Fuchs leveled his sights at the unhappy printer and produced a tract against Egenolph's "unworthy mendacities." It was now that Cornarius who, like Dryander, was teaching at Marburg, entered the fray. There had previously been some hostility between Fuchs and Cornarius, and the latter took full advantage of his opponent's name to produce *Vulpes excoriata* (The fox skinned) as well as two other tracts in which he was able to play upon his adversary's name. The latter had to content himself with *Cornarius furens* (The mad Cornarius), 1545. Like other controversies of that time this one was not long-lived, and by the time that Vesalius wrote it had virtually come to an end. The bibliography of the controversy is given in W. L. Schreiber, *Die Kräuterbücher des XV. und XVI. Jahrhunderts*, Munich, 1924, pp. xxxvii–xxxviii; also see Eberhard Stübler, *Leonhart Fuchs*, Munich, 1928, pp. 83–88, 102–110. As will be indicated later, Vesalius was to have direct dealings with Fuchs in years to come.

[180] *Ep.Ch.Rt.*, pp. 193–196.

[181] See above, pp. 88–89.

[182] See *Compendiosa totius Anatomie Delineatio. A facsimile with introduction by C. D. O'Malley*, London, 1959, pp. 8–9.

[183] *Ep.Ch.Rt.*, p. 4.

[184] *Ibid.*, 198.
[185] *Ibid.*, p. 199.

Notes to Chapter X

[1] Brandi, pp. 471–476.
[2] According to Otto Waltz, "Ein Holograph des Andreas Vesalius," *Virchow Arch.*, 1878, 74:553, there is, or was, a letter, dated Augsburg, 11 August 1546, in the National Library, Madrid, written by Vesalius to the younger Granvelle in which reference is made to treatment of the imperial vice-chancellor Naves. It therefore provides a brief glimpse of Vesalius's court practice at this time.
[3] *Venetianische Depeschen vom Kaiserhofe*, II, Vienna, 1892, p. 13.
[4] *Ibid.*, p. 33.
[5] *Ibid.*, p. 57.
[6] Brandi, pp. 477–483.
[7] Vandenesse, pp. 338–339.
[8] Fisch, pp. 233–234, citing *State Papers Henry the Eighth*, XI, pp. 389–391.
[9] Nicolo Zaffarini, *Scoperte anatomiche di Gio. Batista Canani*, Ferrara, 1809, p. 15.
[10] *Venetianische Depeschen vom Kaiserhofe*, II, p. 131.
[11] Zaffarini, *op. cit.*, p. 15.
[12] Vandenesse, p. 339.
[13] *Mémoires de Charles-Quint*, p. 313.
[14] *Venetianische Depeschen vom Kaiserhofe*, II, p. 154.
[15] J. A. R. Stintzing, *Epistolae Joannis Udalrici Zasii ad Bonifacium Amerbachium*, Basel, 1857. Vesalius's visit to Basel has been the subject of exhaustive study by Gerhard Wolf-Heidegger, "Ueber Vesals Aufenthalt in Basel in Jahre 1547," *Gesnerus*, 1945, 2:207–212, and the present account depends very largely upon it.
[16] *Ibid.*, p. 210.
[17] *Ibid.*, p. 208.
[18] *Ibid.*, p. 210.
[19] "Today it is said that the emperor's departure from here will be delayed a few days. . . . The cause of this delay is said to be his Majesty's gout . . . the emperor's physician has said that his Majesty at present suffers so severely from gout that he cannot leave for at least ten days"; Mocenigo, dispatch, 14 March, *Venetianische Depeschen vom Kaiserhofe*, II, pp. 194–196. "It has been said to me by a friend of mine who is an important person that his Majesty is recovering from the gout and perhaps will soon go to Saxony"; Mocenigo, 18 March, *ibid.*, p. 199. "And it is now believed more generally that the emperor will go to Saxony; this has been confirmed by his Majesty's physician [Baersdorp]"; Mocenigo, dispatch 20 March, *ibid.*, p. 201. Later, Mocenigo wrote from Nuremberg, "This morning it was declared certain that his Majesty will remain here for four or five days since he finds himself again somewhat severely distressed by gout"; dispatch 28 March, *ibid.*, p. 210.
[20] Stintzing, *op. cit.*, Letters II, III, V; Wolf-Heidegger, "Vesals Aufenthalt in Basel," pp. 210–211; *Mémoires de Charles-Quint*, p. 315, "Arrived at Nördlingen he felt so ill from certain indispositions produced by the fatigues he had undergone, that he was constrained to remain there for several days. But, understanding the inconvenience that would result from a long delay, although yet indisposed, for better or worse he set out for Nuremberg in a litter . . . There he had a setback which obliged him to remain longer than he desired. However, he took courage and, in whatever way possible, in a litter . . . or otherwise he arrived at Eger."
[21] Crusius, *Annales suevicorum dodecas tertia*, Frankfurt, 1596, p. 728. The authenticity of the story is denied by Melchior Adam, and Roth, p. 218, n. 1, ascertained that the records of the University of Tübingen contain no reference to any such visit.
[22] Thirlby should have written Maximilian, his son, who was married to his cousin Donna Maria at Barcelona, in October 1548.
[23] Fisch, p. 235, citing Patrick Fraser Tytler, *England under the reigns of Edward VI and Mary*, I, p. 88 f.
[24] Fisch, p. 236, citing Tytler, *op. cit.*, I, p. 98 f. The *Interim* or imperial "Declaration how things are to be managed in the Holy Roman Empire, touching the question of religion, until the general council can be held," was a temporary compromise between orthodox Catholic, Erasmian, and moderate Lutheran views, until the Council of Trent, which had adjourned a year before, should reconvene.
[25] *Nuntiaturberichte aus Deutschland, 1552–1559*, I, p. 79.
[26] Charles de Cossé, 1505–1564.
[27] *Venetianische Depeschen vom Kaiserhofe*, II, p. 325.
[28] Daza Chacon, *Cirugia*, II, p. 232.

[29] *Aphorisms*, VI, xxvii, VII, xliv. In his commentaries on these two aphorisms Galen suggests, however, that the ancient physicians were more prone to employ cautery, presumably because of danger of haemorrhage of the intercostal vessels, *Opera omnia*, ed. Kühn, XVIII, pt. i, Leipzig, 1829, pp. 39–40, 149.

[30] Roth, p. 219.

[31] See his consilium regarding the Marquis of Terranova, above, p. 398.

[32] See the letter of Ingrassia, above, p. 419.

[33] Daza Chacon, *op. cit.*, I, pp. 464–468.

[34] Mocenigo, dispatch, 24 October, *Venetianische Depeschen vom Kaiserhofe*, I, p. 365.

[35] *Bartholomew Sastrow, being the memoirs of a German burgomaster*, pp. 229–230. Christoph von Carlowitz, 1507–1578, was secretary to Duke Maurice.

[36] Achilles Pirmin Gasser, son of Ulrich G., surgeon to Maximilian I, was born at Lindau, on 3 November 1505. After studies at Wittenberg, Vienna, and Montpellier, he became M.D. at Avignon in 1528, and later practised in Feldkirchen and Augsburg. He died on 4 December 1577. Gasser wrote numerous works and carried on a considerable correspondence with Conrad Gesner, see *Epistolae medicinalium Conradi Gesneri*, Zürich, 1577. There are articles on Gasser in Jourdan, *Biographie médicale*, in *Biographisches Lexikon der hervorragenden Arzte*, *Allgemeine Deutsche Biographie*, and by J. Brucker in Schelhorn's *Amoenitates litterariae*. Lucas Stengel, or Stenglin, was born in Augsburg in 1523. He received his degree from Padua in 1549, practised in Augsburg, became city physician, and was responsible for the foundation of the College of Physicians in that city. He died in 1587. On him, see *Biographie médicale* and *Biographisches Lexikon*, as above. Adolph Occo was born in Brixen in the Tyrol in 1494, son of an Adolph who was physician to Sigismund, Archduke of Austria. He studied in Italy and became M.D. at Bologna, 1519. Establishing himself in Augsburg he became physician to the city hospital and died 1572. Adolph III was born in Augsburg on 17 October 1524. He received his M.D. at Ferrara in 1549, whence he returned to assist and then succeed his father. He was ennobled by Maximilian II in 1573, and despite feeble health lived on until 1606. H. V. Bühler, "Das Aerztegeschlect der Occo," *Arch. Gesch. Med.*, 1935, 28:14–42, and C. D. O'Malley, "Camille Picqué's Adolphe Occo III. Le médecin numismate d'Ausbourg et sa médaille au squelette vésalien," *Jour. Hist. Med.*, 1959, 14:434–439.

[37] *The book of my life (De vita propria liber)*, trans. Jean Stoner, New York, 1930, p. 16. Cardano refers to the incident a second time with a few additional remarks, *ibid.*, p. 128: "In the following year through Andreas Vesalius and the Danish ambassador came a proposal, with a consideration of three hundred gold crowns yearly in Hungarian money, and six hundred in addition in impost money, derived from the tax on skins of value. The latter revenues differ from the royal currency by an eighth part, and are collected somewhat slowly; they are not even redeemable at par, and are in a measure subject to certain hazards. The consideration included living for myself, five body servants, and three horses."

[38] Cardano, *Opera omnia*, ed. Spon, X (1663), p. 152. Madruzzo was at the diets that met in Augsburg in 1547 and 1550. The incident could have occurred at either diet, although more likely at the earlier one.

[39] I. Schwarz, "Ein Konsilium des Andreas Vesalius," *Arch. Gesch. Med.*, 1910, 3:403–407.

[40] "A noble youth, Balthasar von Stubenberg, is thirteen years old, of good constitution, red and white complexion, and blond hair. The tendons of his right leg have been contracted from childhood, yet so that it was not noticed either when he was walking or was at rest until two years ago. It is questioned whether that part of the foot where it is joined to the lower leg has been adversely affected. Nevertheless he was accustomed to walk so that he did not rest on the sole of his foot, but with the sole twisted to the side he walked with the foot almost behind him. Now the whole sole of his foot has been almost completely twisted to the side so that he walks with difficulty, and part of the leg from the knee to the ankle has withered and has become much smaller than the left leg."

[41] See the English version above, p. 390.

[42] *Nuntiaturberichte aus Deutschland*, 1553–1559, X, p. 299.

[43] Vandenesse, pp. 374–375.

[44] *Ibid.*, p. 375.

[45] Gachard, *Retraite et mort de Charles-Quint*, "Introduction," p. 18, citing letters of Marillac to Henry II, 6 November and 28 December 1548, 9 and 15 January 1549.

[46] *Oeuvres complètes de Pierre de Bourdeille*, I, pp. 313–317.

[47] *Examen*, pp. 108–109.

[48] E.g., Jacques de Thou, *Histoire universelle*, I, London, 1734, p. 364; Sleidan, *De statu religionis*, Strasburg, 1555, p. 653.

[49] Pantaleon, *Heldenbuch*, Basel, 1570, III, p. 273.

[50] Vandenesse, pp. 376–382.

[51] *Papiers d'état du Cardinal de Granvelle*, III, p. 376.

[52] Fisch, p. 236, citing *CSP, Foreign, Edward VI*, p. 43.

Notes to Chapter X

[53] Vandenesse, p. 388.

[54] *Ibid.*, p. 391.

[55] *Alexandri Benedicti Veronensis de re medica.* . . . Basel, Henricipetri, mense augusto, 1549. The dedication begins: "To that very famous and learned man Andreas Vesalius of Brussels, greatly distinguished doctor of medicine and highly skilled imperial physician."

[56] *Galenus de ossibus ad tyrones, versus quidem a Ferdinando Balamio Siculo: erroribus vere quam plurimis, tum Graecis tum Latinis purgatus, & commentariis illustratus, a rei medicae apud parrhisios professore regio, Iacobo Sylvio.* Paris, Vidua Iacobi Gazelli, 1549.

[57] *Ibid.*, p. 3.

[58] *Ibid.*, p. 4.

[59] *Ibid.*, p. 21.

[60] *Ibid.*, p. 26.

[61] *Ibid.*, p. 36.

[62] *Ibid.*, p. 42.

[63] *Ibid.*, p. 47.

[64] *Ibid.*, p. 52.

[65] *Catalogus familiae totius aulae caesareae per expeditionem adversus inobedientes usque Augustam Rheticam per Nicolaum Mameranum collectus,* Cologne, 1550, p. 21.

[66] *Ibid.*, p. 25.

[67] *Ibid.*, p. 52.

[68] Strictly speaking, the archiater or premier physician was still Narcissus Parthenopeus, who appears to have been forgotten although he was still alive, and, as will be indicated later, upon his death there was a scramble for his title.

[69] *Calendarium historicum,* Wittenberg, 1550, p. 50.

[70] "The day before yesterday I presented my thanks to [the Bishop of] Arras for assisting me to gain an annual 300 Rhenish florins above my regular salary from the Emperor." In reply to Sturm's apparent question as to how to write a flattering dedication, Vesalius suggests: "Praise him for his great linguistic ability, and write that he is so thoroughly versed in languages that he is capable of addressing virtually all the nations of Europe, that he seems, in fact, to have been educated in each of them . . . that he has imbibed its customs as well as its language . . . [praise] his learning in the various disciplines, particularly in law, mathematics, medicine, and natural philosophy; mention also his interest in manual skills such as painting, sculpture, alchemy, and architecture, and remark how greatly he excels in these skills, how much he enjoys them—whenever he can snatch any time from his arduous duties—and what astonishing kindness he demonstrates toward those who work with these skills." Still further suggestions of this nature are made in the letter which is given in an English version in the appendix.

[71] *De arthritidis praeservatione et curatione, clarorum doctissimorumque nostrae aetatis medicorum consilia, opera et studio Henrici Garetii,* Frankfurt, 1592, p. 122.

[72] *Ibid.*, pp. 122–125; and given in an English version above, p. 392. Although without date, the final letter is indicated as written from Augsburg.

[73] Brandi, p. 510.

[74] *Lettres sur la vie intérieure de l'Empereur Charles-Quint, écrites par Guillaume van Male,* ed. Reiffenberg, Brussels, 1843, p. 38.

[75] *Ibid.*, p. 2.

[76] *Ibid.*, p. 15.

[77] *Venetianische Depeschen vom Kaiserhofe,* I, Vienna, 1889, p. 495.

[78] "Relazione di Marino Cavalli," *Relazioni,* Ser. I, Vol. II, p. 211.

[79] *Lettres de van Male,* pp. 22–23.

[80] Fisch, p. 237, citing *CSP, Foreign, Edward VI,* p. 88.

[81] Fisch, p. 237, citing *CSP, Foreign, Edward VI,* p. 135.

[82] Augsburg, 18 May 1551, *The whole works of Roger Ascham,* ed. Giles, I, pt. ii, London, 1865, p. 287.

[83] *Lettres de van Male,* p. 20.

[84] *Ibid.*, pp. 25–26.

[85] *Ibid.*, p. 49.

[86] *Ibid.*, p. 20.

[87] *Ibid.*, pp. 57–58.

[88] C. Tihon, "Deux lettres inédites d'André Vésale," *Archives, Bibliothèques et Musées de Belgique,* 1957, 28:212–213.

[89] Cushing, pp. 136–137 for bibliographical detail.

[90] Paris, C. Barbé and the widow of I. Gazellus, 1551. Republished in 1555 to accompany, pp. 71–135, the defence of Vesalius by Renatus Henerus, to be considered later, and, possibly in reply to this defence, published once more in Basel in 1556.

[91] "When I was in Paris three years ago Sylvius published that tragic, very abusive, and virulent attack upon Vesalius. It was unworthy of Sylvius's years and accomplishments and displayed his

Notes to Chapter X

envy of the fame achieved by another," *Adversus Jacobi Sylvii depulsionum anatomicorum calumnias, pro Andrea Vesalio*, Venice, 1555, "Introduction."

[92] "Many of us had great hopes that he would make a survey of the entire field of anatomy, a thing he had long promised his students. We awaited this with great eagerness, never doubting that in due time he would fulfill his promise," *ibid.*

[93] *Ibid.*

[94] On the use of the word "physiology" by Fernel in 1542, earlier than the time assigned by Sherrington, *op. cit.*, p. 91, and hence preceding this usage by Sylvius, see K. E. Rothschuh, "Der Begriff der 'Physiologie' und sein Bedeutungswandel der Geschichte der Wissenschaft," *Arch. Internat. d'Hist. Sci.*, 1957, 10:219.

[95] This must be a reference to *Galeni de usu partium cura ad Graeci exemplari per Jacobum Sylvius*, Paris, 1538, although, if in an edition late enough to contain anything specifically aimed at the *Fabrica*, possibly the edition translated by Giunio Paolo Crasso and published in Paris by Wechel in 1548 containing notes by Sylvius. This edition has been unavailable to the present writer.

[96] *Vaesanus*, fol. 4r.

[97] *Ibid.*, fols. 4r–5r.

[98] *Ibid.*, fol. 5r.

[99] *Ibid.*, fol. 6r.

[100] *Ibid.*, fol. 6v.

[101] *Ibid.*, fol. 7r.

[102] *Ibid.*, fol. 7v.

[103] *Ibid.*, fol. 8v.

[104] *Ibid.*, fol. 9r.

[105] *Ibid.*, fols. 28r–29r.

[106] Henerus, *op. cit.*, "Introduction."

[107] *Matthaei Curtii in Mundini anatomen commentarius elegans et doctus*, Lyons, Paganus, 1551. The fact that the commentary was by his late critic Corti may have diluted the pleasure.

[108] Little is known of the author, who was born in the latter part of the fifteenth century at Monserrate near Barcelona, and was therefore a Catalan. It is unknown where he studied medicine, although possibly at Montpellier; he practised at least for a time in Valladolid and wrote his book toward the end of his life after forty-five years of practice. Saunders and O'Malley, "Bernardino Montaña de Monserrate: author of the first anatomy in the Spanish language," *Jour. Hist. Med.*, 1946, 1:87–107.

[109] *Libro de la anothomia del hombre*, Valladolid, Martinez, 1551.

[110] Geminus's plagiarism of 1545 had been itself plagiarized and published in 1551 in Augsburg by a German surgeon, Jacob Bauman, see Cushing, p. 132.

[111] See above, p. 234.

[112] *Fabrica* (1555), p. 627. There is a further reference to the case by Occo: "I, Adolph Occo, physician of Augsburg, saw her and was present at her dissection, which was conducted by Vesalius, physician to the Emperor Charles V," Joannes Schenck à Grafenberg, *Observationum medicarum rariorum libri VII*, Lyons, 1644, pp. 597–598.

[113] *Fabrica* (1555), p. 23. On this case, see Joshua O. Leibowitz, "Thromboembolic disease or heart-block in Vesalius," *Medical History*, 1963, 7:258–264.

[114] *Examen*, p. 154, "Those ought to be recalled to mind who have for a long time suffered an amazing mass of glandular flesh in the left ventricle of the heart, and certain other affections, and have died from gangrene of the legs or of some other part—since the native heat of the part could not be revived because of the weakness of pulse—before they complained of any sensation of trouble or pain in the heart; except for the matter of the pulse one could be persuaded that some affection lay hidden near the heart, but a heart condition or death would not be considered. Several physicians of Augsburg saw an example of this sort, who had first been called to the noble and learned Lord of Imersel while he was still living because of a gangrenous affection of his legs; I also was present for postmortem consideration of his heart."

[115] *Ibid.*

[116] *Fabrica* (1555), p. 24.

[117] Armstrong, *The Emperor Charles V*, London, 1902, II, pp. 16–17.

[118] Tihon, *op. cit.*, pp. 213–214.

[119] Quartierliste Karls V. 1551–1552, Stadtsarchiv Innsbruck, U 31, Figdorsammlung.

[120] *Lettres de van Male*, pp. 17–18.

[121] *Ibid.*, p. 53.

[122] *Ibid.*, pp. 91–92, 24 January 1552.

[123] "Yesterday evening we were distressed by the disturbing news that the King of Bohemia had relapsed into that ailment from which he had appeared recovered when he left here. Summoning Baersdorp to him, the emperor ordered him to leave at dawn by a vehicle already prepared," *ibid.*, p. 35, 31 January 1552.

Notes to Chapter X

[124] *Ibid.*, p. 36.

[125] *Ibid.*, p. 5, 7 February 1552.

[126] Gachard, *Retraite et mort de Charles-Quint*, "Introduction," p. 22n.

[127] *Lettres de van Male*, pp. 83–84, 20 March 1552.

[128] *Notitia utraque cum orientis tum occidentis ultra Arcadii Honoriique caesarum tempora*, Basel, Froben, 1552, fol. *2r:* "Sig. Gelenius sends greetings to that very famous man Andreas Vesalius, physician of the invincible Emperor Charles. January 1552." The dedication runs in part, "For some time now I have desired to erect a monument to our mutual friendship," and adds that Vesalius has preserved and protected the health of the emperor more truly with divine than Apollonian aid.

[129] Cushing, pp. 89–90, for the bibliographical details.

[130] Armstrong, *op. cit.*, II, p. 233 ff.

[131] *Ibid.*, II, pp. 256–257.

[132] *Ibid.*, II, p. 259.

[133] *Examen*, p. 17.

[134] Armstrong, *op. cit.*, II, p. 271.

[135] Lanz, *op. cit.*, III, p. 379.

[136] Armstrong, *op. cit.*, II, p. 272.

[137] Henne, *op. cit.*, IX, p. 314.

[138] Gachard, *Retraite*, "Introduction," p. 24n.

[139] Armstrong, *op. cit.*, II, p. 272.

[140] Gachard, *Retraite*, "Introduction," p. 24n.

[141] *Lettres de van Male*, pp. 33, 77.

[142] *Oevres complètes d'Ambroise Paré*, ed. J. F. Malgaigne, III, Paris, 1841, p. 700 f.

[143] Gachard, *Retraite*, "Introduction," pp. 24–25, 29–30.

[144] Fisch, pp. 237–238, citing *CSP, Foreign, Edward VI*, pp. 239 f.

[145] *Venetianische Depeschen vom Kaiserhofe*, II, p. 590.

[146] Fisch, pp. 238–239, citing *CSP, Foreign, Edward VI*, pp. 251, 256.

[147] Fisch, p. 239, citing Lodge, *Illustrations of British History*, p. 165.

[148] Fisch, p. 239, citing Lodge, *Illustrations of British History*, p. 168 f.

[149] Fisch, p. 240, citing *CSP, Foreign, Edward VI*, pp. 267, 277, 280, 285.

[150] *Oeuvres de Pierre de Bourdeille*, I, p. 55.

[151] *Oeuvres d'Ambroise Paré*, III, p. 712 ff.

[152] Consilium for Marcus Pfister; see above, p. 394, for an English version.

[153] *Papiers d'état du Cardinal Granvelle*, VIII, p. 525.

[154] *Ibid.*, VIII, p. 583.

[155] Roth, p. 238, n. 3, offers examples of other physicians who, having achieved position and wealth, proceeded to build homes indicative of such achievements: Rembert Dodoens in Mechlin, 1555, and a second in 1556; Achilles Gasser in Augsburg, 1573; Crato von Kraftheim in Breslau; and Sylvius and Paré in Paris.

[156] A document cited in Henne and Wauters, *op. cit.*, III, p. 396, notes that "Elizabeth Craps, widow of André de Wesel, alias Wytines, and Anne Martin obtained authorization of the authorities to extend their house situated in the street running from the ramparts to the Bovendael." After them, "Master André de Wesele, doctor and physician of his Majesty," owned the house. Apparently the house had been occupied by Vesalius's widowed mother, and the mentioned member of the related Martin family, as indicated previously, lived in the family home, but whether at that time the anatomist's family also dwelt there is unknown.

[157] *Examen*, p. 15.

[158] In 1566 Mansfeld had successfully commanded the defenses of Brussels and thereafter was governor, and it was for his services that the city gave him the Hôtel de Vésale on 8 April 1585. It was thus joined to properties which Mansfeld already held on the Rue aux Laines, *Mémoires de Viglius et d'Hopperus*, ed. Alphonse Wauters, Brussels, 1858, p. 189.

[159] Henne and Wauters, *Histoire de la ville de Bruxelles*, III, Brussels, 1845, p. 396; Wauters, "Quelques mots sur André Vésale," *Mém. Acad. Roy. Belge*, 1897, 55:43–44.

[160] *Poematum Libri Septem*, Basel, 1555, p. 310.

[161] The records of the faculty of medicine of the University of Vienna note under the year 1552: "During this winter's disturbance an atrocious epidemic raged in Vienna, and through not only the whole of Austria but also of Germany; it also attacked physicians so that those best of men were carried off, Franciscus Vesalius . . . doctor of medicine and not the least among the members of our association," *Acta facultatis medicae Universitatis Vindobonensis*, ed. Karl Schrauf, III, Vienna, 1904, p. 258.

[162] Roth, p. 434, who publishes the text of this letter, gives it the date 1555, although, p. 240, he reserves the possibility of the year 1553; see above, p. 405, for an English version.

[163] Wauters, *op. cit.*, pp. 18–19.

[164] Fisch, p. 240, citing *A collection of state papers relating to the affairs in the reigns of King*

Notes to Chapter X

Henry VIII, King Edward VI, Queen Mary, and Queen Elizabeth . . . left by Wm. Cecil Lord Burghley, I, p. 151.

[165] See above, p. 394, for an English version. Previously in 1550 Giambattista da Monte had provided a consilium "Regarding weakness of the stomach, for Master Pfister of Augsburg," Consultationes medicae Ioannis Baptistae Montani, Basel, 1572, cols. 483–486. It may be assumed that Herwart, in consequence of his years in Padua and acquaintance there with Da Monte, was responsible for obtaining the consilium.

[166] "Finally, as I recall, Andreas Vesalius was summoned . . . he immediately diagnosed an aneurysm of the aorta. . . . When the body was dissected we found what Vesalius had predicted," Joannes Schenck a Grafenberg, Observationes medicae, Lyons, 1644, p. 687. This report is by Adolph Occo.

[167] See above, p. 395, for an English version.

[168] See Roth, p. 240. There is further reference to an aneurysm in the Examen, p. 97. Vesalius's Spanish colleague, Dionisio Daza Chacon, reported a case of aneurysm he observed in Spain at about the same period: "While I was practising it happened that there was one who had an aneurysm over the bifurcation (caused by dilation of the artery), and many good surgeons were gathered over the case. Thinking it was a suppurating abscess they decided to open it and were about to execute this decision when the licentiate Arias and the licentiate Herrera, surgeon of his Majesty, saw it. Although in agreement, they postponed the operation for a day, and having thought much about the matter that night, at the next day's meeting [they] recognized the aneurysm and the fact that if they had opened it the patient would have been lost." A second but later case was that of a man of Burgos who "had another aneurysm below the bifurcation, and through dilation of the artery, and the sharpness of the blood which had gathered in it, it happened that not only was the substance of the artery corrupted, but finally the skin above it, and such a great flow of arterial blood gushed forth that no remedy was possible and he died within a quarter of an hour," Cirugia, I, p. 184.

[169] See the English version in the Appendix.

[170] See above, p. 246.

[171] However, even at Paris, in the absence of Sylvius's feared and dominating personality, "I recall Antonio Massa [see above, p. 51]—who died shortly before Sylvius's [Vaesanus] was published—performing the dissection of a Parisian woman who had died as the result of a difficult birth. Massa was a thoroughly experienced dissector and, with Sylvius absent as usual, he frequently demonstrated to his spectators, including my friend Jacques Goupyl, a learned physician, that the facts differed from Galen and especially from Sylvius's refutations [of Vesalius]," Henerus, op. cit., pp. 11–12.

[172] Gachard, Retraite, "Introduction," pp. 128–129.

[173] Ibid., II, pp. 78–79.

[174] Observationum et curationum medicinalium libri tres . . . Petro Foresto Alcmariano auctore, Frankfurt, 1602, p. 434, "In regard to atrophy of the legs by which they are observed to have been weakened."

[175] See above, p. 394.

[176] Observationum et curationum medicinalium libri . . . Foresto auctore, pp. 434–435.

[177] O'Malley, "Andreas Vesalius, Count Palatine," p. 196.

[178] De Meyer, "Notice sur Corneille van Baersdorp," p. 17 ff.

[179] See the years 1555–1556 in Lothar Gross, Die Reichsregisterbücher Kaiser Karls V, Vienna, 1930.

[180] Ibid.

[181] Roth, p. 241n.

[182] See above, p. 404, for an English version.

[183] In 1568 the Spanish King was strongly desirous of having at his court a physician, surgeon, and confessor from the Netherlands. The physician would be a replacement for Vesalius, who had left Spain in 1564. "It is the pleasure of his Majesty to summon hither one of our physicians in the place of Vesalius," wrote Joachim Hopper from Madrid, Van Meerbeeck, Recherches historiques et critiques sur R. Dodoens, 1841, p. 39. At one time it appeared as if Rembert Dodoens would accept the position, and although he ultimately was too reluctant to leave his native land, correspondence over details gives some knowledge of the material advantages he would have enjoyed in Spain. As an enticement it was suggested that Dodoens be promised the same salary that Vesalius had received, "300 florins annually and in addition 30 sous daily for subsistence," ibid., p. 44. Some notion of the significance of this salary is indicated by the fact that the surgeon and the confessor were receiving only twelve sous daily for subsistence, ibid., p. 42.

[184] Virtually nothing is known of the life of Valverde, who seems to have come to Italy as physician to a Spanish cardinal—hence his location in Rome. Prior to that he published a medical work, De animi et corporis sanitate tuenda, Pavia, 1552, Venice, 1553.

[185] See Cushing, pp. 147–152, for the bibliographical details.

Notes to Chapter XI

[1] See above, pp. 218, 222.

[2] See above, pp. 205–206, 257.

[3] See above, p. 228.

[4] See above, p. 228.

[5] See above, p. 227.

[6] Roth, p. 224, citing *Joannem Oporinum partim excusorum hactenus, partim in eiusdem officina venalium index . . .* Basel, 1552, p. 6: *Andreae Vesalii Bruxellensis medici caesarei de humani corporis fabrica libri V. summa diligentia ab eodem recogniti et aucti. fol.* At the end of December 1551 Oporinus wrote to the Strasburg preacher Conrad Hubertus that a second edition of the *Fabrica* would soon appear, "Die Briefe Joh. Oporins an den Strassburger Prediger Conrad Hubert," *Beiträge zur vaterländischen Geschichte*, 1893, n.s., 13:398. That Oporinus was in perilous financial condition is indicated by further letters, *ibid.*, p. 417.

[7] See above, p. 406, for an English version.

[8] Francisco de Enzinas, latinized as Dryander, b. 1520 in Burgos, converted to Protestantism while studying at Louvain, and devoted himself to translating and publishing the classics in Spanish. At the period of Oporinus's letter he had, in conjunction with August Fries, a printer of Zürich, prepared a Spanish edition of Plutarch's *Lives*. The types used appear to have been the ones in question and had previously been made available to Oporinus by Dryander during a visit to Basel at the end of 1549 and the beginning of 1550, *ibid.*, p. 398; Max H. Fisch, "The printer of Vesalius's *Fabrica*," *Bull. Med. Libr. Assoc.*, 1943, 31:254; Menendez Pelayo, *Historia de los heterodoxos espanoles*, III, Santander, 1947, p. 280 ff.

[9] Roth, p. 224, calls attention to the appearance of Conrad Gesner's *Appendix bibliothecae*, Zürich, 1555, in which, p. 8, there is reference to the appearance of the revised *Fabrica* in 1554: *Andreae Vesalii de hum. corp. fabr. libri septem . . . 1554 ab auctore recogniti et aucti.* Since Gesner's *Appendix* bears the date March 1555 for completion, that is, before the appearance of the *Fabrica*, Gesner's statement may have been based on some earlier but too-optimistic hope of Oporinus.

[10] For collation and related bibliographical details, see Cushing, p. 91. In several letters of May 1555 Oporinus asked his friend Conrad Hubertus to seek out sixty or seventy sheets of parchment "of the same shape as the anatomy of Vesalius, begun to be printed by me some time ago," or else the work would once again have to be interrupted, "Die Briefe Joh. Oporins," p. 400. If Oporinus had any thought of printing a copy of the *Fabrica* on parchment, there is no further knowledge of any such achievement, and it may be that he planned to print a few presentation copies of the *Epitome* on parchment as had been the case in 1543.

[11] Henry S. Francis, "The woodcut initials of the *Fabrica*," *Bull. Med. Libr. Assoc.*, 1943, 31:228–239; B. J. Anson, "The initial letters of 1555 edition of Vesalius's *Fabrica*," *Quart. Bull. Northwest Univ. Med. Sch.*, 1945, 19:326–335; Adolf Faller, *As iniciais da IIª edicao (1555) da obra "De humani corporis fabrica libri septem" de Andreas Vesalius*, Rio de Janeiro, 1951.

[12] See above, p. 251.

[13] *Fabrica* (1543), p. 293 [393].

[14] *Ibid.*, p. 268 [368].

[15] *Fabrica* (1555), p. 450.

[16] *Ibid.*, p. 196.

[17] *Fabrica* (1543), p. 14.

[18] *Fabrica* (1555), p. 17.

[19] *Galeni libri aliquot*, Basel, 1544, pp. 298–299.

[20] The illustrations of the skull, *Fabrica* (1543), p. 20 ff., as presented in the revised edition of the *Fabrica* (1555), p. 25 ff., are good examples of the effort made to present the illustrations on a better-designed page. The design of the auditory passage of the *Fabrica* (1543), p. 52, was considerably altered in the *Fabrica* (1555), p. 66. A second appearance of the hinge as originally presented in the *Fabrica* (1543), p. 67, was deleted from the second edition. There is an illustration of cartilage in the *Fabrica* (1555), p. 121, that is not in that of 1543. The illustration of the laryngeal cartilages in the *Fabrica* (1543), p. 259, has been replaced by a new one in the *Fabrica* (1555), p. 307, presumably because the small block had been lost or broken. The illustration depicting the five branches of the portal vein going to the liver, *Fabrica* (1543), p. 262 [362], has been retained in the revised *Fabrica* (1555), p. 444, but mention of the five branches has been removed from the text. The full-page figure delineating the aorta, *Fabrica* (1543), p. 295 [395], was replaced by a more elaborate figure, *Fabrica* (1555), p. 483. On the other hand, the nerve figure, of which the omission of certain nerve branches was admitted by Vesalius as being due to his oversight, *Fabrica* (1543), p. 335 [435], l, m, and above, p. 136, remains unchanged in the revised *Fabrica* (1555), p. 530. The folding plate from the *Epitome*,

Fabrica (1543), p. 313 [413], has had its text shortened so that, for the convenience of the reader, it might contain as an inset the figure of the female genital organs, *Fabrica* (1555), p. 505, formerly on the verso of the sheet where its position was inconvenient. Two initial letters illustrating the glossicomion and inset in the *Fabrica* (1543), p. 329 [429], have been deleted from the revised edition. On the other hand there are a few additional diagrams in the *Fabrica* (1555), pp. 674, 712, and the interior view of the skull is repeated from Book I in Book VII, *Fabrica* (1555), p. 755. Finally, among these examples of alterations of illustrations, the embryological figures of the *Fabrica* (1543), p. 382 [482], that are so strongly subject to criticism were radically altered, improved, and rearranged relative to the text, *Fabrica* (1555), pp. 586, 588, 674.

[21] *Ibid.*, p. 527 as an example.

[22] *Ibid.*, p. 107.

[23] *Fabrica* (1543), p. 309.

[24] *Ibid.*, p. 495. The reference to Dryander has been removed since, as Vesalius informs us in the *Letter on the china root*, he had learned of his implication in the plagiarisms of the *Tabulae anatomicae*. There is no mention of that other plagiarist, Leonard Fuchs, although an uncomplimentary reference, perhaps directed at him, refers to those "trained in dissection not even in their dreams," but who seize upon the "labors of others under any pretext" and achieve a "golden mediocrity" by putting "my efforts into an epitome" or "dispendium," i.e., lost effort, and so practise a "harmful deceit" upon students, *Fabrica* (1555), p. 281.

[25] *Fabrica* (1543), p. 19, and above, p. 188.

[26] See above, p. 253.

[27] *Fabrica* (1555), pp. 23–24, "I believe that that boy suffered from the same complaint as the two-year-old girl I saw in Augsburg whose head enlarged in about seven months so that it surpassed in size the head of any man I have ever seen. It was the ailment the ancients called hydrocephalus from the water that is little by little gathered and collected in the head."

[28] *Fabrica* (1543), p. 27.

[29] *Ibid.*, p. 42.

[30] *Ibid.*, p. 46.

[31] *Fabrica* (1555), p. 58.

[32] *Fabrica* (1543), p. 56.

[33] *Ibid.*, p. 124.

[34] *Ibid.*, pp. 159–162.

[35] *Fabrica* (1555), p. 206.

[36] *Fabrica* (1543), p. 166.

[37] *Ibid.*, p. 218.

[38] *Fabrica* (1555), p. 280.

[39] *Fabrica* (1543), p. 250.

[40] *Ibid.*, p. 242.

[41] *Ibid.*, p. 248.

[42] *Fabrica* (1555), p. 295.

[43] *Ibid.*, p. 303.

[44] *Fabrica* (1543), p. 266 [268].

[45] *Ibid.*, p. 222 [322] and above, p. 142.

[46] See above, p. 214.

[47] *Fabrica* (1555), pp. 442–443.

[48] *Ibid.*, pp. 442–443, and above, p. 252.

[49] *Fabrica* (1543), p. 531.

[50] *Ibid.*, p. 538.

[51] *Fabrica* (1555), p. 662.

[52] *Fabrica* (1543), p. 538.

[53] *Fabrica* (1555), p. 663. Attention may also be called to the description of the hymen, *ibid.*, p. 654, to which allusion was first made in the *Letter on the china root*, and recollection of the post-mortem examination of the young girl in Brussels in 1537 when Vesalius first observed a corpus luteum, see above, p. 63.

[54] *Fabrica* (1543), p. 543.

[55] *Ibid.*, p. 540 ff.

[56] *Fabrica* (1555), p. 671 ff.

[57] *Ibid.*, pp. 586, 588. Reference is here made to Howard B. Adelmann, *The embryological treatises of Hieronymus Fabricius of Aquapendente*, Ithaca, New York, 1942, pp. 60–61, who gives an excellent summary of Vesalius's position.

[58] *Fabrica* (1555), pp. 669–670, and figure, p. 588.

[59] *Fabrica* (1543), p. 584.

[60] *Fabrica* (1555), p. 728.

[61] *Fabrica* (1543), p. 585.

Notes to Chapter XII

[62] *Ibid.*, p. 589.

[63] *Fabrica* (1555), p. 734.

[64] *Ibid.*, p. 746.

[65] *Fabrica* (1543), p. 650.

[66] *Ibid.*, pp. 633–634.

[67] Erik Waller, "Eine unbekannte Ausgabe von Vesals Epitome," *Lychnos*, 1936:251–260; Cushing, pp. 115–116.

[68] At this point something must be said of the fate of the wood blocks employed for the celebrated illustrations of the *Fabrica* and *Epitome*. So carefully prepared, transported from Venice to Basel and preserved between editions, they had now performed their final service for Oporinus and Vesalius, and for some time thereafter all trace of them is lost until they come into the possession of Andreas Maschenbauer, an Augsburg publisher who used them in two editions of an anatomical treatise, 1708, 1723. Again lost, rediscovered, and used for another publication, this time in Ingolstadt, 1783, they passed from there to Landshut and finally into the comparative security of the library of the University of Munich.

There they were locked away and forgotten until 1893, after which they were employed once more in 1934, a remarkable instance of longevity and sturdy workmanship. For the details of this fascinating and frequently imperiled existence, see Cushing, pp. 97–109, and Willy Wiegand, *op. cit.*, p. 27 ff. In his account, Cushing remarks, "Time alone can tell what in another four centuries may happen to these historic wood-blocks." The year following the publication of these words, man's increased destructive power succeeded in accomplishing what time's ravages had failed to do. On 13 July 1944 a block of the university was burned, as a result of bombing, but the cellar, behind fireproof doors, preserved its contents, including the wood blocks. Three days later, however, on the 16 July, bombs once again fell on the now-ruined building and set fire to the still-glowing ashes. This time the contents of the cellar could not be saved; Robert Herrlinger, "Das Schicksal der hölzernen Druckstöcke zu Vesals anatomischen Lehrbuch," *Münch. Med. Wschr.*, 1951, 93:614–616.

Notes to Chapter XII

[1] *Unpublished letters from the collection of John Wild*, ed. R. N. Carew Hunt. New York, 1930, pp. 175–176. More recently this letter, the only one known which Vesalius wrote in French, has come into the possession of the Historical Library of the Yale University Medical Library. It has been reproduced in a reduced facsimile with a revised transcription in *Jour. Hist. Med.*, 1953, 8:448.

[2] *Papiers d'état du Cardinal Granvelle*, V, p. 282.

[3] *Briefe von Andreas Masius*, herausgegeben von Max Lossen. Leipzig, 1886, p. 317.

[4] For details and documentation regarding the incident see O'Malley and Saunders, "The 'Relation' of Andreas Vesalius on the death of Henry II of France," *Jour. Hist. Med.*, 1948, 3:197 ff.; F. K. Kessel, "Neurochirurgische Bermerkungen über einige französische Könige," *Munch. Med. Woch.*, 1959, 101:1585 ff.; and very recently Ferdinand Wagenseil, "Vesal beim Tode Heinrichs II. von Frankreich," *Arch. Gesch. Med.*, 1962, 46:333–349. Contemporary delineation by J. Tortorel and J. Perrissin has been reproduced in *Les grandes scènes historiques du XVIᵉ siècle. Reproduction fac-simile du recueil de J. Tortorel et J. Perrissin publié sous la direction de M. Alfred Franklin*. Paris, 1886, with a brief accompanying text by Franklin.

[5] See above, p. 396, for an English version.

[6] "Des playes récentes et sanglantes en particulier," ch. 9, *Oeuvres*, ed. Malgaigne, II, pp. 23–25. Hippocrates, *Aphorisms*, VI, 14, ed. Littré, IV, p. 581; *Épidémics*, V, 50, ed. Littré, V, p. 237.

[7] The daughter, now sixteen years old, was at marriageable age, and her father indicated his recognition of this by giving her his home in Brussels as a dowry, on 6 November 1561, an action that suggests he had no intention of returning, at least permanently, to the Netherlands, Wauters, "Quelques mots sur André Vésale," *Mém. Acad. Roy. Belge*, 1897, 55:44.

[8] H. Forneron, *Histoire de Philippe II*, I, Paris, 1881, p. 128.

[9] See his letter to Heinrich Petri in the Appendix.

[10] Roth, p. 244.

[11] Ms. 6149, fol. 106v.

[12] See above, p. 398, for an English version.

[13] Almost nothing appears to be known about this Brabantine physician except that he was the son of another Gilles de Hertoghe, possibly the physician to Mathias Corvinus, King of Hungary. There is an article on the older Hertoghe by G. Dewaique, *Biographie nationale de Belgique*; also Valerius Andreas, *Bibliotheca belgica*, 1643, p. 26, and Vanderhaeghen, *Bibliotheca belgica*, V, p. 112.

[14] Fallopio published only one book during his lifetime, his *Observationes anatomicae*, Venice, 1561. Although other writings were published posthumously under his name, they seem to be either lecture notes prepared for the press by others or completely spurious writings. He does

refer, however, in his *Observationes,* to an elaborate work on human and comparative anatomy with many illustrations which, owing to his death, was never published. Both manuscript and illustrations have disappeared.

The *Observationes* is not a general anatomical textbook but an unillustrated commentary or series of observations on the *Fabrica* of Vesalius, in which Fallopio seeks to correct errors committed or to present new material overlooked by Vesalius. The criticism is temperate and friendly so that, in his later *Examen* of these *Observationes,* the "divine Vesalius," as Fallopio calls him, indicates he had taken no offense and was amenable to justified correction and instruction. Since the *Observationes* is not an all-inclusive textbook it never received the popular acclaim given to the *De re anatomica* of Colombo, despite a number of editions, but, on the other hand, it is a work of great originality and importance.

Fallopio dissected many foetuses and the bodies of small children which permitted him to make numerous observations upon the primary and secondary centers of ossification; hence he was able to demonstrate that the frontal bone is formed of two elements. He denied the then-current belief that the sagittal suture passed through the occipital bone to the foramen magnum and also disproved the Vesalian assertion that the ethmoid was formed of two separate bones. Fallopio settled the controversy over the nomenclature and construction of the innominate bone as well as that over the ossification of the sternum. He was the first to give a clear description of the primary dentition, the follicle of the tooth bud, and the manner of growth and replacement of the primary by the secondary tooth, and, more remarkable, to recognize the dental lamina and its connections with the surface mucous membrane, as well as its relationship to the development of the secondary tooth.

He made major contributions to the anatomy of the middle and internal ear. Although his name remains associated with the facial canal, he also presented the first clear account of the round and oval windows, the cochlea, the semicircular canals, the scala vestibuli, and the tympani. He likewise described the stapes, although he was sufficiently honest to admit its discovery by Ingrassia.

Although Fallopio made numerous contributions to myology, the most important concerns the arrangement and function of the muscles of the eye. He gave the first description of the levator palpebrae muscle, of the compound action of the oblique muscles, and of the trochlea of the superior oblique, which takes its name from his description. He likewise observed the nictitating membrane of mammals, once known to Aristotle, and, like Colombo, was aware of the nonhuman nature of the choanoid muscle.

Like his contemporaries, Fallopio was more interested in the venous system than the arterial. His chief contribution to the anatomy of the vascular system was his denial that the walls of the veins were formed of fibres in three directions to contain and control the movement of the blood, a belief Vesalius finally rejected after reading this account. However, despite the discovery of the valves in the veins by Canano, and a published announcement of the fact by Amatus Lusitanus, Fallopio declared himself unable to see them and denied their existence. This seems to have been his major blunder.

A further contribution was the description of the uterine or Fallopian tubes, which in fact he described correctly as resembling small trumpets: "[The extremity] resembles the bell of a brass trumpet, wherefore the seminal passage, with or without its windings, resembles a kind of trumpet." Owing, however, to incorrect interpretation of Fallopio's word *tuba,* some of the descriptive meaning has been lost in English. He also contributed to the terminology of other aspects of anatomy, since we owe to him the present usages of the term vagina, clitoris, and cricoid. In the last case Vesalius had already called attention to the ringlike formation of this cartilage, and Fallopio, taking the hint, supplied the Greek form of the word "ring." The only significant biographical study is by Giuseppe Favaro, *Gabrielle Fallopia Modenese,* Modena, 1928.

[15] *Examen,* pp. 1–2.
[16] *Observationes,* fols. 12r, 16r.
[17] *Examen,* p. 15.
[18] *Observationes,* fol. 18v.
[19] See above, p. 257.
[20] *Examen,* p. 17.
[21] *Observationes,* fols. 25v–26v, "Give ear to the manner in which the third ossicle later became known. In the year 1548 when I first began to lecture at Pisa no mention of this bone had been made either by Vesalius, who had conducted anatomy at Pisa long before, or by Colombo. . . . At the time when I was engaged in this work a student of mine . . . related by marriage to Ingrassia, came to me and stated that Gian Filippo had discovered a third ossicle in the tympanum and because of its shape had given it the name of stapes. . . . And since it was the shape of the stirrup or foot-piece of our ancestors he properly called it the stapes, for the stirrups of earlier times were a kind of triangular plate without the distinct hole we added later and through which a strap can be drawn."
[22] *Historia de la composicion del cuerpo humano,* Rome, 1556, fol. 7r.

[23] *Examen*, p. 24.

[24] *Observationes*, fol. 37*v* ff.

[25] *Examen*, p. 33.

[26] See above, p. 157.

[27] *Observationes*, fol. 47*r*, "The very ancient anatomists, because they said that the sacrum is composed of three or four vertebrae, are very bitterly censured by those of the present day since, as the latter assert, the bone consists of six, or sometimes five. However, I have observed that it is more frequently formed of five segments than of six."

[28] *Examen*, pp. 37–38.

[29] *Observationes*, fols. 64*v*–65*r*, "Respecting the muscles of the eyelids which cover and uncover the eyes, I have long been in error with Galen and the divine Vesalius and at the same time with the whole school of anatomists. Since I had always dissected into two parts that external muscle [Orbicularis oculi] arising from the internal angle and encircling the whole eye, I thought that one portion of it opened and the other closed, and so deceived myself and others many times in public and private dissections. Later, when I chanced upon a place in Oribasius in the book *On dissection of muscles according to Galen*, XXV, 29, of the *Collections*, I began to have doubts on the subject, but was unaware of how to extricate myself from the dilemma . . . This passage raised suspicion in my mind and made me so diligent that finally I discovered the truth. . . . the head of a seal was sent to me . . . [and] after . . . I had begun to dissect it . . . I observed that this animal moves each eyelid and uncovers the eye from all sides. The instruments were four very wide muscles lying hidden in the orbit with the rest of the ocular muscles and attached to the origin of those [recti muscles] that cause the straight movements of the eye. . . . I immediately began to look for a similar instrument in the eye of the ox and found the single muscle [Levator palpebrae superioris] that raises the upper lid only. Made more skilled by this example, I discovered a small, very thin muscle in the human eye, which arises in the same place as the origin of the [superior rectus] muscle that draws the eye straight upward. This small muscle, ending in a very wide cord, is inserted into the whole of the tarsus of the upper eyelid and, raising the lid, uncovers the eye."

[30] *Examen*, pp. 47–48.

[31] *Observationes*, fol. 101*v*.

[32] Vesalius also informed Fallopio, *Examen*, p. 70, that he then possessed no copy of the Greek text of Galen's *Dissection of muscles*, and that it was not possible to obtain it in Spain.

[33] See above, p. 104.

[34] *Examen*, p. 70.

[35] *Observationes*, fols. 102*v*–103*v*, "In the part of the palm called the 'mountain of the moon' by Antiochus Tibertius, I find a fleshy mass [Palmaris brevis muscle] in the fatty covering of the hand. This has the shape of a muscle but frequently consists of two and sometimes three very thin and short muscles, the origins of which are fleshy and arise from the hairy or lower part of the mount where the eighth carpal [Pisiform] bone is located. This fleshy mass, arising from the fatty panniculus or from the membrane covering the muscle forming the little 'mountain of the moon,' is dispersed through the fat and, passing transversely into the interior and middle of the palm, reaches the spread-out cord [Palmar aponeurosis], and the whole is implanted completely covered by the fleshy membrane and fat. In my opinion its function is to wrinkle the skin of that part rather than to stretch it. This, indeed, is not my discovery but that of Giambattista Canano. . . . When I practised at Ferrara about thirteen years ago this very celebrated anatomist communicated this discovery to me. . . . However, the first to describe these muscles in a published work was Valverde in his anatomy written in the Spanish language, although not entirely correctly since he says that there is only one muscle, created for tensing the region."

[36] See above, p. 136.

[37] *Examen*, p. 71.

[38] On Valverde, see above, p. 462, n.184. Not only was Vesalius incensed by all aspects of the plagiarism but as well by certain criticisms of the *Fabrica* in Valverde's text.

[39] After the departure of Vesalius from Padua, the discomfited Colombo, see above, p. 197, acquired his former teacher's position which he soon relinquished (1545) for a similar chair at Pisa. He moved to Rome in 1548 and remained there until the end of his life, pursuing anatomical research and teaching in the Sapienza. His single book was published the year after his death, *De re anatomica*, Venice, 1559. Colombo was at once a boastful man, not unwilling to claim the discoveries of others as his own, and also a highly capable anatomist. Although the large number of dissections he declares he performed can be accepted only with considerable reservation, and his claim to have been the discoverer of the third ossicle of the ear and the palmaris brevis muscle must be completely denied, nevertheless he must be applauded for his genuine achievements, not the least of them associated with his researches on the eye. His description of the eye muscles was certainly an improvement on previous accounts, and he was the first to demonstrate that the choanoid or retractor bulbi muscle of ruminants was not present

Notes to Chapter XII

in the human. His criticism of Vesalius in this matter, unlike that of Fallopio, was a source of irritation, as were his various other criticisms or corrections of the *Fabrica*. Colombo's greatest contribution, his description of the pulmonary transit or lesser circulation of the blood, lies outside the present consideration.

[40] *Observationes*, fol. 105r.

[41] *Examen*, p. 73.

[42] *Ibid.*, p. 93.

[43] See above, p. 95.

[44] *Observationes*, fol. 114r ff.

[45] *Examen*, p. 82.

[46] *Observationes*, fols. 118r–119r, "Amatus the Portuguese physician . . . asserts that small membranes, *ostiola* or so-called *opercula*, such as are found in the orifices of the cardiac vessels, are present in the origin of the azygos vein. . . . I wish . . . that you were acquainted as well as I am with the irreproachable character and flawless teaching of Giambattista Canano, since then you would judge the man capable of anything rather than the forging of lies and you would not believe that this dogma had ever been propounded by him—unless for the sake of a laugh he was jesting with some of those present with Amatus. As a matter of fact these valves are found neither in man nor in animals I have dissected."

[47] See above, p. 214.

[48] *Examen*, p. 83.

[49] *Observationes*, fol. 190v, "There are two nerves which ascend through the middle of that bifurcation from which the penis takes origin onto its dorsum, and, running along the dorsum with many branches communicated to the underlying sinew, [they] are at length inserted into the glans and the whole of the distal neck. The nerves are notable and very obvious, such that they could not lie hidden except to the purblind. Nonpainful ganglia or glandules, as they are called by the empirics, occur in them and their coverings, which later on, when the pudendum becomes erect, are the reason why it swells twisted like a ram's horn."

[50] *Examen*, p. 140.

[51] *Examen*, pp. 170–171.

[52] *Apologia in anatome pro Galeno contra Andream Vessalium* [*sic*] *Bruxellensem*, Venice, 1562.

[53] Son of a physician and born in Villanova di Casale on the Po at some unascertained date, he studied medicine with Mateo Corti at Pavia and with Jacobo Pacini and Bartolomeo Maggi at Bologna. Dal Pozzo was present at Vesalius's anatomical demonstration at Bologna in January 1544 and declared that at that time it was in his mind to attack the anatomical doctrines of Vesalius but he was prevented by Vesalius's unannounced departure, see above, p. 198. Dal Pozzo died in Vercelli on 29 November 1564; Giovanni Martinotti, "Francesco dal Pozzo e la sua critica di Vesalio," *Mem. R. Accad. Sci. Ist. Bologna*, 1921–1922, 9:31–43.

[54] *Gabrielis Cunei Mediolanensis apologiae Francisci Putei pro Galeno in anatome examen*, Venice, 1564; Arturo Castiglioni, "The attack of Franciscus Puteus on Andreas Vesalius and the defence by Gabriel Cuneus," *Yale Jour. Biol.*, 1943, 16:135–142.

[55] L. P. Gachard, *Relations des ambassadeurs Vénitiens*, p. 63 ff., citing the account of Federigo Badoero.

[56] H. Forneron, *Histoire de Philippe II*, II, Paris, 1881, p. 10 f.

[57] *Documentos inéditos para la historia de Espana*, XVIII, p. 537.

[58] L. P. Gachard, *Don Carlos et Philippe II*, I, p. 72 ff. Chaloner, the English ambassador, was hardly the most sympathetic witness of events. His letter of 1 May, the first of a series dealing with the incident, notes that Don Carlos's fall "forced his physicians twice to let him blood, and for fear of apostemation to make a larger incision for search, lest the scalp should be crazed. But now he is deemed quit of that danger, like as also of his quartan. Howbeit, the natural imbecility of the Prince (being of such a sprawlish body) and thereto the tokens that he giveth by the manner of his curious questioning and solemnity, causeth the father (as I understand from some wise men) to conceive small hope of him, partly fearing lest hereafter he should somewhat take after the humours of the Emperor's mother," Fisch, pp. 246–247, citing *CSP, Foreign, Elizabeth*, V, p. 27.

[59] The account is given in full in an English version, above, p. 407.

[60] Leonardo da Nobile to Cosimo de'Medici, 14 May 1562, in Gachard, *Don Carlos et Philippe II*, II, p. 637.

[61] "The King brought Dr. Vesalius (not unknown for his excellent skill) from Madrid with him, whose better learning the Spanish [physicians] make not account of according to his worthiness, *quia figulus odit figulum*. So he came *post festum* when the other bunglers not searching the hurt deeply had promised all good hope to the king and made untimely haste to the healing up of the incision, whereby the bone putrefied, as at the second incision in the King's presence appeared (having discovered so much of the scalp as by a pattern thereof here inclosed may appear), but yet the hope all the day and the next was great of recovery," *CSP, Foreign, Elizabeth*, V, 28, cited by Fisch, p. 247.

[62] "Next day [7 May], being Ascension Day, because his face began to swell, his doctor gave him an easy purgation, which wrought upon him fourteen times, overmuch by the half in his constitution to bear it out. The same afternoon the swelling increased, with small fiery pimples called erysipelas, which redoubled the doubts of the doctors and heaviness of the King. On Friday the 8th inst. his state impaired, the wound of his head waxing dry. This Saturday [9 May] the swelling so increased that his eyes were closed up, so that when the King came to visit him he was obliged to lift up his eyelids. The tokens aforesaid, with other notes (as voiding of blood and matter at the ears and nose), signify some apostemation," Chaloner to Elizabeth, *CSP, Foreign, Elizabeth,* V, p. 29, cited by Fisch, p. 248.

[63] San Diego, born 1400 in the vicinity of Seville, joined the order of Franciscans minor and is said to have displayed notable examples of virtue and saintly character during a prolonged sojourn in the Canary Islands. Returned to Spain, he died at Alcalá, 12 November 1463, Lucio Ma Núñez, "Documentos sobre la curación del principe D. Carlos y la canonización de San Diego de Alcalá," *Arch. Ibero-Amer.,* 1914, 1:424–446.

[64] "On Saturday night the King, leaving the Prince for desperate, departed from Alcalá, and has come to the monastery hereby of St. Jeronimo, intending (if the Prince dies) to remove to some other more retired," Chaloner to Elizabeth, *CSP, Foreign, Elizabeth,* V, p. 29, cited by Fisch, p. 248.

[65] S. Diego d'Alcalá, later painted by Murillo, risen from the ground in a state of ecstasy while the angels crowd around his kettle. Known in the Louvre as "Cuisine des Anges." In a letter to Sir William Cecil, Chaloner had shrewdly noted, "If God send the Prince to escape, that friar is not unlike to be canonized for his labor."

[66] Notably Nuestra Senora d'Atocha. The Bishop of Limoges gave all credit to the moor Pinterete, Forneron, *op. cit.,* II, p. 108, which was hardly a proper return to Vesalius for the latter's intercession to gain the bishop permission to eat meat during Lent. On the other hand, Saint-Sulpice, the next ambassador, gave the credit to Vesalius.

[67] Letter of Charles de Tisnacq to the Duchess of Parma, L. P. Gachard, *Don Carlos et Philippe II,* Brussels, 1863, I, p. 89; according to Cardano, *Opera omnia,* 1663, X, p. 153, "Vesalius . . . by his skill preserved Don Carlos from evident death."

[68] The canonization was not achieved by Philip without considerable effort, since he made repeated but unsuccessful entreaties to Pius IV, Pius V, and Gregory XIII. It was not until the pontificate of Sixtus V that the canonization was accomplished, on 12 July 1588. San Diego's feast day was officially determined as 12 November by Innocent XI on 19 July 1681, *Propylaeum ad acta sanctorum, Decembris,* Brussels, 1940, p. 518.

[69] *Ambassade en Espagne de Jean Ebrarde, Seigneur de Saint-Sulpice de 1562 à 1565,* ed. Cabrié, Paris, 1903, pp. 104, 172.

[70] See above, p. 398, for an English version. Ingrassia, 1510–1580, of Recabuto near Palermo, M.D., Padua, 1537, was professor of medicine at Naples, but returned to Palermo in 1560 where he was made archiater of Sicily.

[71] *Fabrica* (1543), p. 658 [662].

[72] Earlier, on 1 February 1563, Ingrassia had sent an account of the successful conclusion of the case to Giuseppe of Arragona along with Vesalius's consilium which, although received too late to play any part in the recovery of the marquis, was nevertheless such as to merit great esteem and perpetual acknowledgment, all the more so by contrast to that consilium, presumably Eustachi's, "carelessly written from Rome."

[73] Fisch, p. 251, citing *CSP, Foreign, Elizabeth,* VI, p. 571.

[74] *Ibid.,* VII, pp. 12, 13, cited by Fisch, p. 251.

[75] *Vitae Germanorum medicorum,* Heidelberg, 1620, p. 133.

[76] *Oeuvres complètes d'Ambroise Paré,* II, pp. 754–755, "So it happened to a great anatomist of this century, great and celebrated, I say, whose books today assist the studies of learned men. He then being resident in Spain was ordered to open the body of a woman of the court who was considered to have died from a suffocation of the uterus. At the second cut of the razor the woman began to move and, to the great astonishment of the assistants, to demonstrate by other indications that she still lived. I leave it to the reader to imagine the perplexity of the good man performing the task and how the hue and cry followed him so that he could do nothing else but leave the country; for those who ought to have pardoned him were those who attacked him; and being exiled he soon after died of sorrow, which was not without great loss to the commonwealth [of medicine]."

[77] *A briefe discourse of a disease called the suffocation of the mother,* London, 1603, fol. 11r, "But the most pitiful example of all other in this kinde, is that which Ambrose Paré reporteth of Vesalius, a worthie Physition, & for anatomicall dissections much renowned, who being called to the opening of a Gentlewoman in Spaine, which was thought to be dead through the violence of one of these fits, began to open here, and at the second cut of the knife she cried out, and stirred her limbes, shewing manifest signes of life to remaine. The beholders were exceedingly amazed at the sight, and blamed the Physition much for it; who though hee tooke

here for dead, yet tooke he great apprehension of sorrow for the accident, that he estranged himselfe. After through griefe and remorse of conscience for his error, pretended (as others say) a pilgraimage for the absenting of himselfe, and therein died."

[78] See above, p. 280.

[79] On all of these points and the whole problem of Vesalius's departure from Spain, see G. Matheson Cullen, "The passing of Vesalius," *Edinburgh Med. Jour.*, 1914, 13:324–339, 388–400.

[80] *Opera omnia*, Hanover, 1610, "To the readers."

[81] J. A. de Thou, *Historiarum sui temporis libri*, London, 1733, VII, pp. 13–14, 16–17.

[82] Curiously, Zilboorg, "Psychological Sidelights on Andreas Vesalius," *Bull. Hist. Med.*, 1943, 14:572, has mistranslated Roth, p. 276, declaring him incorrectly to have borrowed rather than correctly to have lent money, and uses this erroneous rendering as evidence for "the terminal stage of a chronic depressive condition."

[83] Favaro, *Gabrielle Falloppia Modenese*, Modena, 1928, p. 130 ff.

[84] Annie Fraenkel and Enrico Emilio S. Franco, "Postille alla biographia del Vesalio. Andrea Vesalio in terrasanta (1564)," *Physis*, 1962, 4:219–226.

[85] Pietro Bizzari, *Historia della guerra fatta in Ungheria*, Lyons, 1568, pp. 178–180.

[86] Petrus Bizarrus, *De bello Cypriaco et Pannonico*, Basel, 1573, p. 284. In this second account, however, "some Venetian ships" becomes "an Adriatic ship," and the account ends with the statement, "This was told me in good faith by the goldsmith himself in the presence of Giulio Borgaruccio, physician of Urbino."

[87] See above, p. 210.

[88] Cushing, p. 209, n.287b, but correctly the Nicholas Senn copy. Metellus wrote a second and shorter letter to Georg Cassander mentioning the man of Nuremburg by name as Georg Boucher, *Illustrium et clarorum virorum epistolae selectiores*, Leyden, 1617, p. 372; also reprinted in Niceron, *Memoires*, X, pt. 2, Paris, 1731, pp. 153–154, and briefly paraphrased in Wauters, *op. cit.*, p. 33.

[89] Gioseppe Rosaccio, *Viaggio da Venetia a Costantinopoli*, Venice, 1598.

[90] The best geographical account of Zante is that of J. Partsch, "Die Insel Zante," *Dr. A. Petermanns Mitteilungen aus Justus Perthes' Geographischer Anstalt*, 1891, 37:160–174. It is accompanied by an excellent large-scale map.

[91] Ludwig Salvator, *Zante*, Prague, 1904.

[92] Earthquakes appear to be an almost everyday occurrence on Zante. The best work on the subject is by A. Issel and G. Agamennone, "Interno ai fenomeni sismici osservati nell'isola di Zante durante il 1893," *Annali dell' Ufficio Centrale di Meteorologia e Geodinamica*, Rome, 1894, in which pp. 32–91 list the earthquakes recorded on Zante since 464 B.C., and pp. 143–149 describe the destruction of the city of Zante in 1893. Despite their detailed description the authors make no mention of anything related to Vesalius. Pietro Capparoni, "Ricerche sulla morte e sulla tomba di Vesal," *Yperman*, 1923–1924, 1:17–18, was unable to find any record of Vesalius in the church of Santa Maria delle Grazie. According to Nik. A. Barbianis, *Andreas Vesalius and the progress of anatomy* (in Greek), 1952 (not seen), shipwreck and debarkment were at Kalogerata on the border of the Lagano gulf, where Vesalius died and was buried.

[93] Wauters, "Quelques mots sur André Vésale," *Mém. Acad. Roy. Belge*, 1897, 55:36.

[94] Hē dēmosia bibliothēkē Zakynthou, 1899.

[95] See Cushing, p. 195. The *Chirurgia magna*, Venice, 1568, edited and attributed to Vesalius by Prospero Borgarucci, can be readily dismissed as a false attribution, see Cushing, pp. 216–217.

[96] See above, p. 296, and Roth, p. 433.

[97] *Papiers d'état du Cardinal Granvelle*, VIII, pp. 525, 583.

[98] *Ibid.*, p. 525.

[99] *Correspondence française de Marguerite d'Autriche*, I, Utrecht, 1925, p. 27.

[100] Wauters, *op. cit.*, p. 43.

[101] *Ibid.*, p. 44.

[102] *Ibid.*, p. 44, 4 June 1577.

[103] *Ibid.*, pp. 43–44.

[104] Henne and Wauters, *Histoire de la ville de Bruxelles*, III, p. 396.

[105] Wauters, *op. cit.*, pp. 45, 54–56.

[106] *Ibid.*, p. 45. Not much is known about the children of Anne and Jean de Mol—Henri, Louis, Anne, Adrienne, and Elisabeth—except that the last-named child married, on 12 February 1615, Charles van Baussel, who was *drossart* of Diest and died 5 October 1625. Elisabeth died on 7 February 1647. Whatever the composition of the intervening generations, it has been said that the last descendant of the family Vesalius, Jean-François, was born at Brussels on 3 November 1797, served briefly in the imperial guard of Napoleon I, married Reine van Lerberghe, and died at Courtrai without descendants but in the possession of a bedcover declared to have been given to Andreas Vesalius by Charles V. The Van Lerberghe family presented it to the Musée de

Courtrai where it is still preserved, D. "Le couvre-lit de Charles-Quint," *Revue et Bull. Officiel. Touring Club de Belgique*, 1 March 1934, pp. 70–71.

Notes to the Appendix

[1] *Fabrica* (1543), fols. *2r–4v.
[2] *Ibid.*, fol. *5r–v.
[3] *Ibid.*, pp. 155–161.
[4] *Ibid.*, pp. 236–237.
[5] *Ibid.*, pp. 266 [268]–271.
[6] *Ibid.*, pp. 547–558.
[7] *Ibid.*, pp. 599–604.
[8] *Ibid.*, pp. 650–654. There is an earlier translation by Singer, *Vesalius on the human brain*, pp. 61–72.
[9] *Consultationes medicae Ioannis Baptistae Montani. Antea quidem Ioannis Cratonis Vratislaviensis medici Caesarei opera atque studio correctae, emendatae, adauctae: nunc vero et novorum consiliorum appendice & necessarijs additionibus locupletae*, Basel, 1572, coll. 137 [129]–138 of the Appendix. For later editions, see Cushing, p. 178. The consilium is also to be found in Roth, pp. 388–396.
[10] *Consiliorum medicinalium conscriptorum a praestantiss. atque exercitatiss. nostrorum temporum medicis liber singularis. Nunc primum studio & opera Laurentii Scholzii a Rosenaw med. Vratisl. hoc modo in lucem editus*, Frankfurt, 1598, coll. 109–119. For further bibliographical details, see Cushing, p. 181. Also see Roth, pp. 409–419.
[11] Ignaz Schwarz, "Ein Konsilium des Andreas Vesalius," *Arch. Gesch. Med.*, 1910, 3:406–407.
[12] *De arthritidis praeservatione et curatione clarorum doctissimorumque nostrae aetatis medicorum consilia. Opera et studio Henrici Garetii Lovaniensis*, Frankfurt, 1592, pp. 122–125. Also see Roth, pp. 506–509.
[13] Roth, p. 397, transcribed from a manuscript copy in the library of the University of Basel.
[14] *Observationum et curationum medicinalium libri tres: nempe octavus de exterioribus vitiis & morbis cutaneis capitis: nonus de variis capitis doloribus; decimus de universis ac cerebri & meningum eiusdem symptomatis ac morbis . . . D. Petro Foresto Alcmariano auctore*, Leyden, 1590, pp. 694–696. Edition used, Frankfurt, 1602, p. 436. For further bibliographical details and editions see Cushing, pp. 179–180. Also in Roth, pp. 405–406.
[15] *Georgii Hieronymi Velschii sylloge observationum et curationum medicinalium*, Augsburg, 1667, p. 47. Also in Roth, pp. 420–421.
[16] Vesalius's original report has disappeared, but there is a copy of it in the Bibliothèque Nationale, Mss. fr. vol. 10190. This has been published by Ferdinand Wagenseil, "Vesal beim Tode Heinrichs II. von Frankreich," *Arch. Gesch. Med.*, 1962, 46:336–339, and emendates its previous publication in Alphonse de Ruble, *Antoine de Bourbon et Jeanne d'Albret*, I, Paris, 1881, pp. 432–435.
[17] First published in facsimile by A. Burggraeve, *Études sur André Vésale*, Ghent, 1841, from a manuscript then in the Château de Beernem near Bruges. Also printed in *Négociations lettres et pièces diverses relatives au règne de François II*, Paris, 1841 (Collection de documents inédits sur l'histoire de France), pp. 879–880. Also in Roth, p. 420.
[18] *Illustrissimi Ducis Terraenovae casus enarratio et curatio. E quibus tum penetrantis in thorace vulneris, tum fistula curandi methodus elucescit*, pp. 92–98, in *Ioannis Philippi Ingrassiae . . . quaestio de purgatione per medicamentum* . . . Venice, 1568. Also in Roth, pp. 398–405.
[19] Ingrassia's reference is not to a physician but to a surgeon whose name, however, he does not give, *ibid.*, p. 28.
[20] Roth, p. 421, transcribed from the autograph manuscript in Strasburg.
[21] *Beiträge zur Vaterländ. Geschichte*, n.s., 1886, 2:178, transcribed from the autograph manuscript in the library of the University of Basel. Also see Roth, pp. 423–442.
[22] M. Roth, "Vesaliana," *Virchows Arch.*, 1895, 141:477–478.
[23] The original was at one time, and may still be, in the possession of the Börsenverein der Deutschen Buchhändler in Leipzig. It has been reproduced in facsimile in *Bilderheften zur Geschichte des Bücherhandels*, herausg. von Heinrich Lempertz, Leipzig, 1853–1865, tab. 5. Also see Roth, p. 434, where the date is given as 1555 but with a query as to the possibility of the year 1553.
[24] Roth, pp. 438–439, from the original letter in Strasburg. Also an English version in Max H. Fisch, "The printer of Vesalius's *Fabrica*," *Bull. Med. Libr. Assoc.*, 1943, 31:254.
[25] Joannes Udalricus Rumler, *Observationes medicae e bibliotheca Georgii Hieronymi Velschii, cum eiusdem notis*, in Velschius, *Sylloge observationum et curationum medicinalium*, Augsburg, 1667, p. 46; also see Roth, pp. 435–436. Rumler notes with Gasser's letters "When in 1557 that noble gentleman Leonard Welser finally died from an internal aneurism from which he had long

suffered its various symptoms, on 25 June Adolph Occo, father and son, Ambrose Jung, and Lucas Stengel, physicians of Augsburg, dissected the body in order to find the cause of death, and Achilles Gasser, my maternal grandfather, sent their findings to Vesalius."

[26] Daza Chacon, *op. cit.*, II, pp. 190–201. Also in *Colección de documentos inéditos para la historia de España*, XVIII, pp. 537–563. There is an abbreviated account, *ibid.*, XV, pp. 553–573, but given under the name of Doctor Olivares.

[27] *Ducis Terraenovae casus enarratio et curatio,* pp. 99–101; also see Roth, pp. 436–438.

INDEX OF NAMES

Index

Index

Index

Valla, Giorgio, 17, 18, 122, 344
Valois, Elizabeth of, 284
Valois, Marguerite of, 284
Valverde de Hamusco, Juan, 267, 291, 294, 462 n.184, 467 nn.35 and 36
Varades, Hieronymus, 426 n.80
Vasari, Giorgio, 125–126, 127
Vasses, Jean, 37, 41, 46, 47, 214, 425 n.22
Vatable, François, 47
Vega, Cristobal de, 407, 416, 418
Vega, Hernando de, 300, 412
Velena, Marquis of, 303, 402
Veltwyck, Gerard van, 31, 209–210, 217, 275, 319
Venier, Francesco, 436 n.5
Verallo, Girolamo, 230, 453 n.96
Verhasselt, Martin, 403, 404
Vertunus, Narcissus, 84, 194, 255–256, 326, 431 n.45, 459 n.68
Vesalius, Andreas [references to Vesalius in the notes, 421 ff., have not been included in the index]: as founder of modern anatomy, 1, 20; ancestors and relatives of, 21–27 (see also Vesalius, Wesalia, Wesele, Witing, s'Winters); birth of, 28; life and early education of, in Brussels, 29; at University of Louvain, 29–34; as advised on education by Nicolas Herco, 33–34; and matriculation at medical school of University of Paris, 35–38; studies of, 39–42; teachers of, 47 ff.; and anatomical instruction of Jacobus Sylvius, 48–51; and anatomical instruction of Guinter of Andernach, 53–55; and independent study of osteology, 59–60; departure of, from Paris, 62; and participation in autopsy examination in Brussels, 63–64; and theft of body from gibbet, Louvain, 64; his continued medical education at University of Louvain, 65–70; his hostile references to Jeremiah Drivère, 68; and composition and publication of Paraphrasis, 69–72; and completion of medical studies at Padua, 73; matriculation and studies of, at Padua, 75–76; awarded M.D., 76; and acceptance of chair of surgery, 77; first anatomy of, 79–82; Tabulae antomicae of, 83–88; and plagiarisms, 88–90; and revised edition of Guinter's Institutiones anatomicae, 90–94; and first trip to Bologna, 94–95; Venesection letter of, 95–97; success of, as teacher of anatomy, 98; anatomical demonstrations of, in Bologna, 98–100; dwelling of, with John Caius in Padua, 101; and work on Giunta edition of Galen, 101–108; and friendship with Marcantonio Genua and Wolfgang Herwart, 108; first consilia of, 108–109; Realdo Colombo as student of, 109–110; and initiation of composition of Fabrica, 111–113; and pedagogical aspects of the Fabrica, 114–121; and possible literary influences on the Fabrica, 121–123; and problems of Fabrica illustrations, 124–129; and preparation of Fabrica wood blocks, 130; and choice of Oporinus as the printer, 131–135; and

departure from Padua and visit to Ferrara, 135–136; and visit to Basel, 136–137; and dissection and articulation of the skeleton of Jacob Karrer, 137–138; and publication of Fabrica and Epitome, 139; and significance of the title page, 139–144; and preface to Charles V, 145–147; portrait of, 147–149; and initial letters, 149; and arrangement of contents of the Fabrica, 149–151; on osteology, 150–159; on myology, 159–165; on angiology, 166–168; on nerves, 168–171; on gastrointestinal organs, 171–173; on reproductive organs, 173–174; on thoracic organs, 175–178; on the brain, 178–180; general consideration of the Fabrica of, 181–183; Epitome of, 183–186; and presentation of the Fabrica and Epitome to emperor, 189; enrollment of, as imperial physician, 189; first service as military surgeon, 189; and consideration of the imperial patient, 190–194; and continued service as military surgeon and first treatment of gunshot wounds, 196; and return to Padua and hostility toward Realdo Colombo, 197–198; anatomical demonstration of, in Bologna, 198–199; anatomical demonstrations of, in Pisa, 199–202; post-mortem examinations by, 202–203; and renewed service as imperial military surgeon, 203–206; and new treatment of gunshot wounds, 205; first surgical cases of, 206; and care of imperial patient, 207 ff.; and care of Bernardo Navagero, 211–213; and meeting with Giambattista Canano in Ratisbon, 214; and hostility of Jacobus Sylvius and Letter on the china root, 215 ff.; and plagiarism of Thomas Geminus, 223–224; trip of, to Basel in 1547, 227–228; possible visit of, to Tübingen, 228; and surgical treatment of empyema, 230; relations of, with Augsburg physicians and with Cardano, 234; and case of Balthasar Stubenberg, 235; and prediction of death of Maximilian of Egmont, 236; Sylvius's further attack upon, 238–240; and Epitome of Leonhart Fuchs, 244–246; and Sylvius's Vaesanus, 246–251; autopsy reports of, on cases in Augsburg, 251–253; at Innsbruck with emperor, 256; and flight to Villach, return to Augsburg, 257; further service of, as, military surgeon, and possible meeting of, with Paré, 260–262; practice of, in Brussels, 262–263; and cases of Marcus Pfister and Leonard Welser, 264–265; and case of Augustine Teyling, 266–267; created Count Palatine, 267; as pensioned by Charles V, and taking of service with Philip II, 267; and preparation of revised edition of Fabrica, 269–270; and published revision of Fabrica, 270–282; and reissue of Epitome, 282; and injury and death of Henry II, 283–288; voyage of, to Spain, 288; and medical dispensation for the Bishop of Limoges, 289; reply of, to Observationes anatomicae of Fallopio, 289–296; and case of Don Carlos,